Estonia, Latvia & Lithuania

written and researched by

Jonathan Bousfield

www.roughguides.com

Contents

Food and drink
colour section following
p.184

The great outdoors
colour section
following p.312

◀◀ Folk festival, Estonia ◀ Tallinn Old Town

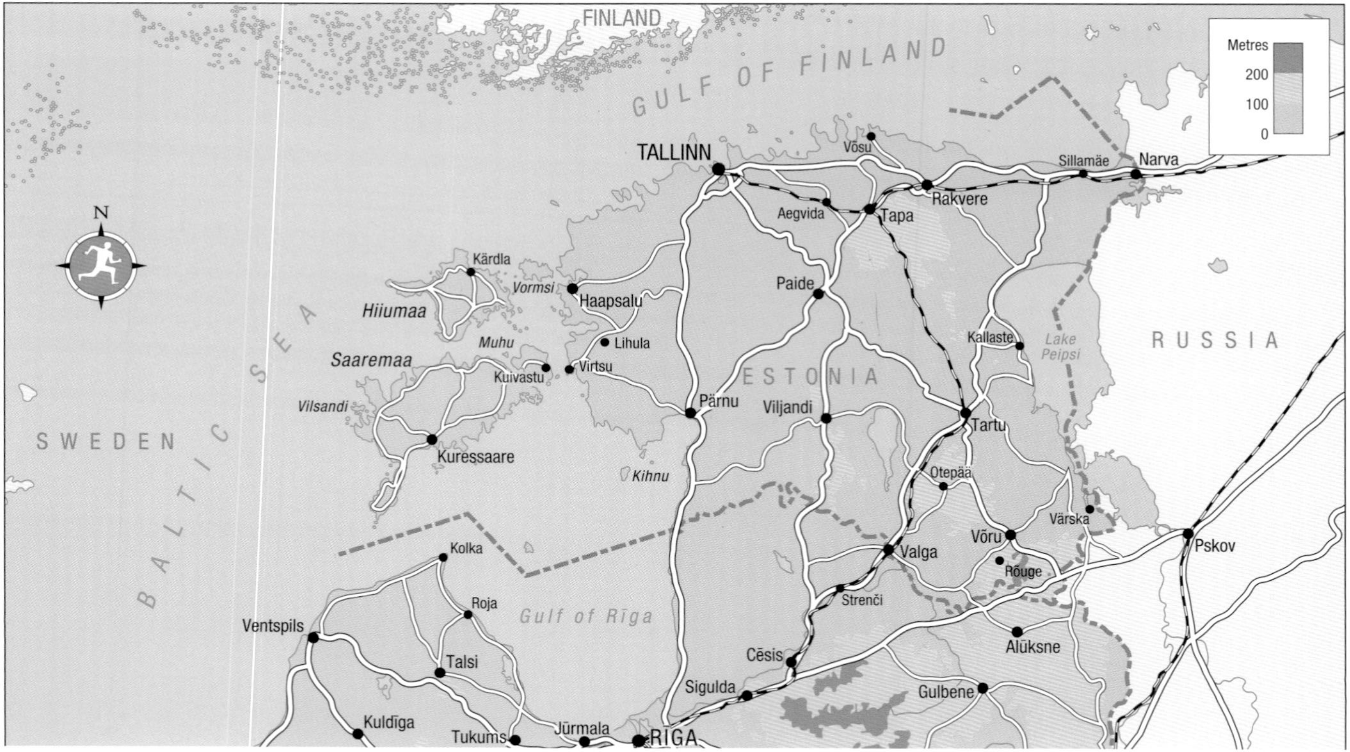
Metres
200
100
0
N
FINLAND
GULF OF FINLAND
RUSSIA
SWEDEN
BALTIC SEA
ESTONIA
Lake Peipsi
Gulf of Rīga
TALLINN
Võsu
Sillamäe
Narva
Rakvere
Aegvida
Tapa
Kärdla
Vormsi
Haapsalu
Paide
Hiiumaa
Muhu
Lihula
Kallaste
Saaremaa
Kuivastu
Virtsu
Pärnu
Viljandi
Tartu
Vilsandi
Kuressaare
Kihnu
Otepää
Värska
Võru
Valga
Rõuge
Pskov
Kolka
Roja
Strenči
Ventspils
Alūksne
Cēsis
Talsi
Sigulda
Gulbene
Kuldīga
Tukums
Jūrmala
RIGA

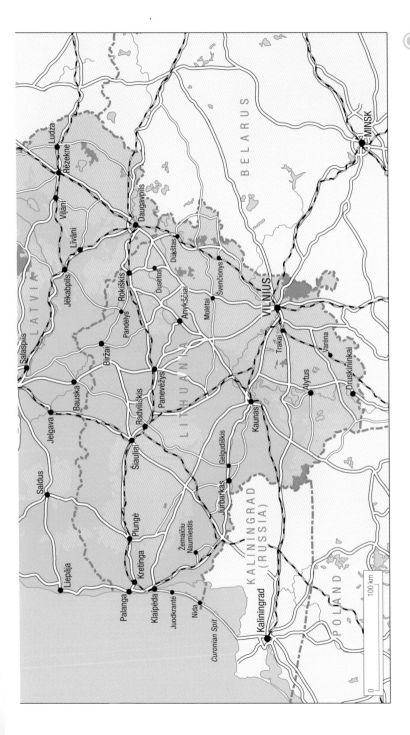

Introduction to

Estonia, Latvia & Lithuania

Lithuania, Latvia and Estonia – the Baltic States – are graced by three of the most enthralling national capitals in Eastern Europe, each highly individual in character and boasting an extraordinary wealth of historic buildings, as well as an expanding and energetic nightlife and cultural scene. Outside the cities lie great swathes of unspoiled countryside, with deep, dark pine forests punctuated by stands of silver birch, calm blue lakes and a wealth of bogs and wetlands, all bordered by literally hundreds of kilometres of silvery beach. Peppering the landscape are villages that look like something out of the paintings of Marc Chagall, their dainty churches and wonky timber houses leaning over narrow, rutted streets. As you'd expect from a region periodically battered by outside invaders, there are dramatic historical remains aplenty, from the grizzled ruins of the fortresses thrown up by land-hungry Teutonic Knights in the thirteenth century, to the crumbling military installations bequeathed by Soviet occupiers some seven hundred years later.

Although the half-century spent under Soviet rule has left Lithuanians, Latvians and Estonians with a great deal in common, they're each fiercely proud of their separate status and tend to regard the "Baltic States" label as a matter of geographical convenience rather than a real indicator of shared culture. The Latvians and Lithuanians do at least have similar **origins**, having emerged from the Indo-European tribes who settled in the area some

two thousand years before Christ, and they still speak closely related languages. The Estonians, on the other hand, have lived here at least three millennia longer and speak a Finno-Ugric tongue that has more in common with Finnish than with the languages of their neighbours. In historical and religious terms, it's the Lithuanians that are a nation apart – having carved out a huge, independent empire in medieval times, they then converted to the Catholic faith in order to cement an alliance with Poland. In contrast, the Latvians and Estonians were conquered by Teutonic Knights in the thirteenth century and subjected to a German-speaking feudal culture that had become solidly Protestant by the mid-1500s. From the eighteenth century onwards, the destinies of the three Baltic peoples began to converge, with most Latvians and Estonians being swallowed up by the **Tsarist Empire** during the reign of Peter the Great, and the Lithuanians following several decades later. Despite their common predicament, no great tradition of Baltic cooperation emerged, and when the three Baltic States became independent democracies in 1918–20 – only to lose their independence to the USSR and Nazi Germany two decades later – they did so as isolated units rather than as allies.

The one occasion on which the Baltic nations truly came together was in the 1988–91 period, when a shared sense of injustice at the effects of Soviet occupation produced an outpouring of **inter-Baltic solidarity**. At no time was this more evident than when an estimated two million people joined hands to form a human chain stretching from Tallinn to Vilnius on 23 August, 1989, the fiftieth anniversary of the 1939 Molotov-Ribbentrop pact – the cynical Soviet–Nazi carve-up that had brought the curtain down on interwar

▲ Vilnius cathedral

Baltic independence. Baltic fellow feeling became less pronounced in the post-Soviet period when each country began to focus on its own problems, and it's now the differences – rather than the similarities – between the Baltic peoples that most locals seem eager to impress upon visitors.

How different they actually are remains open to question, with both locals and outsiders resorting to a convenient collection of clichés whenever the question of **national identity** comes under discussion: the Lithuanians are thought to be warm and spontaneous, the Estonians distant and difficult to get to know, while the Latvians belong somewhere in between. In truth there are plenty of ethnographic similarities linking the three nationalities. A century ago the majority of Lithuanians, Latvians and Estonians lived on isolated farmsteads or small villages, and a **love for the countryside**, coupled with a contemplative, almost mystical feeling for nature, still runs in the blood. Shared historical experiences – especially the years of Soviet occupation and the sudden reimposition of capitalism that followed it – have produced people with broadly similar outlooks and, wherever you are in the Baltic States, you'll come across older people marked by fatalism and lack of initiative and younger generations characterized by ambition, impatience and adaptability to change.

The Baltic peoples today are also united by gnawing concerns about whether such relatively small countries can preserve their distinct identities in a rapidly globalizing world. Integration into NATO and the EU has been broadly welcomed in all three countries, not least because membership of both organizations promises protection against any future resurgence of Russian power. However, locals remain keenly aware that they can only be bit-part players in any future Europe. Lithuania has a **population** of 3.3 million, Latvia 2.2 million and Estonia just over 1.3 million – hardly the stuff of economic or cultural superpowers. Combined with this is a looming fear of population decline in countries that share some of the lowest birth rates in the world. Such anxieties are particularly strong in Estonia and Latvia, where the indigenous

Midsummer's Eve

Given the shortness of the Baltic summer, it's no great surprise that the arrival of the longest day of the year is celebrated with much enthusiasm in all three Baltic States. Although the festival is known by the Christian name of **St John's Day** (*Jaanipäev* in Estonian, *Jāņi* in Latvian, *Joninės* in Lithuanian), it's an unashamedly pagan affair, with families or groups of friends lighting a bonfire on the night of June 23 and staying up to see the sunrise, often fortified by large quantities of alcohol. As well as being the last chance for a booze-up before the hard work of the harvest season began, Midsummer's Eve was traditionally a fertility festival in which the bounty of nature was celebrated in all its forms. Folk wisdom still maintains that herbs, grasses and even morning dew collected early on the 24th can have magical medicinal powers. Above all it was – and still is – a great opportunity for young members of the community to get together and do what comes naturally, with couples setting off into the forest supposedly in search of the mythical fern flower (which, rather like the four-leafed clover, will bring untold good fortune to whoever succeeds in actually finding it).

Storks

If there's one thing that characterizes the countryside in Estonia, Latvia and Lithuania during the spring and early summer it's the sight of large numbers of **white storks**, nesting atop telegraph poles and farmyard buildings, or poking around in recently tilled land looking for tasty insects. Arriving in late March or early April, the birds hatch their young in May, then spend a couple of months filling up on bugs and frogs before returning to their wintering grounds towards the end of August. While the twentieth century saw a dramatic decrease in the stork population in Western Europe, their numbers are actually on the rise in the Baltics – the unspoilt expanses of food-rich wetlands combined with the comparatively low use of pesticides in Baltic agriculture having made the region into something of a haven for the creatures. With folk wisdom maintaining that the presence of a stork's nest promises good fortune and protection from fire and lightning, their presence is much appreciated by the locals.

populations are in many towns and cities outnumbered by other **ethnic groups** – particularly Russians – who were encouraged to move here during the Soviet period. Only 60 percent of Latvia's inhabitants are ethnic Latvians, and the figure in Estonia, at 68 percent, is only marginally higher. Eager to immerse themselves in the new Europe and yet profoundly concerned with the need to preserve their national uniqueness, the Baltic States find themselves at a challenging crossroads.

Travel in the Baltic States presents no real hardships, providing you're prepared to put up with badly surfaced roads or don't mind bumping along in rural buses that look as if they belong in a transport museum. Gloomy,

◀ Cyclists, Lithuania

Soviet-era hotels are everywhere now outnumbered by spanking-new establishments offering high standards of **accommodation** at slightly less than Western-standard prices. Even though the three national capitals are taking off as popular city-break destinations, the volume of visitors remains low by Western European standards, leaving you with the sense that there's still much to be discovered.

When to go

ate spring and summer are the best times to visit the Baltic States, when there's usually enough fine weather to allow you to stroll around the cities and make significant forays into the great outdoors. On the whole though, the only thing that's predictable about the Baltic climate is the deep, dark winters – in all other seasons the weather can be changeable in the extreme.

Summers are relatively short (roughly mid-June to late August), and although you may well experience a string of hot, dry days during this period, showers and chilly nights are equally likely. Remember to pack a waterproof jacket and warm sweater alongside your T-shirts. Temperatures cool down rapidly from mid-September onwards, although **autumn** can be an extraordinarily beautiful season in which to visit, with the golden brown leaves of deciduous trees contrasting with the dark-green pines.

Soviet shadows

The 45-year occupation by the Soviet Union is the one historical experience that all three Baltic States have in common. Commemoration of this period – whether in museums, monuments or memorial ceremonies – is an inevitable feature of the local landscape.

The Occupation Museums in Rīga (see p.173) and Tallinn (p.75) are the best places to get to grips with this tragic period in Baltic history, and will leave you with impressions that prove hard to shake off.

Elsewhere the approach can be more lighthearted: the former naval prison in Karosta, Liepāja (p.212) offers an interactive experience in which visitors are herded around like inmates, while the nuclear command bunker at Līgatne (p.223) offers a startling insight into the absurdly paranoid world of the Soviet top brass. Most famously of all, Grūtas Park in Lithuania (p.322) displays salvaged Soviet-era statues in a theme-park-style ambience. More sobering experiences are on offer at the Genocide Museum in Vilnius (p.271) or the KGB Museum in Tartu (p.135), where the sight of torture-cells and execution rooms brings visitors face to face with the realities of Soviet power.

The first snowfalls might come as early as mid-November, and by early to mid-December **winter** sets in with a vengeance. Average daytime temperatures can remain below zero right through until March, plummeting to minus 15–20°C in particularly cold spells. Winter can of course be a magical time, with lakes, rivers and large expanses of the Baltic Sea freezing over, and crunchy snow cover adding an air of enchantment to medieval city centres. However, rural areas can be difficult to get to without a four-wheel-drive vehicle (only the main highways are snow-ploughed), and you'll have to be well togged up in order to endure anything but the shortest of walks. Wherever you are in winter, some form of hat or head covering is absolutely essential.

Even when the **spring** thaw sets in, the countryside can remain

▼ Traditional Lithuanian house

▲ Beer gardens, Rīga

grey and barren until well into April (or even May in northern Estonia), when a sudden explosion of colour transforms the landscape. The countryside takes on a green lushness, drawing cattle and horses out from their winter barns, while city-dwellers indulge in a frenzied stampede for the pavement cafés.

Average monthly temperatures and rainfall

	Jan	Feb	Mar	Apr	May	Jun	Jul	Aug	Sep	Oct	Nov	Dec
Vilnius												
Max/Min °C	−4/−9	−2/−8	3/−4	11/2	18/18	21/11	22/12	22/12	16/8	10/3	4/−1	−1/−5
Max/Min °F	26/16	29/18	38/25	51/35	65/46	70/51	72/54	71/53	62/46	50/38	38/30	31/23
rainfall mm	41	38	39	46	62	77	78	72	65	53	57	55
Rīga												
Max/Min °C	−2/−8	−2/−8	3/−5	10/1	16/6	20/10	22/12	21/12	16/8	10/4	3/−1	0/−4
Max/Min °F	28/18	29/18	37/24	50/34	61/43	68/50	71/54	70/53	61/46	51/39	39/31	33/24
rainfall mm	34	27	28	41	44	63	85	73	75	60	57	46
Tallinn												
Max/Min °C	−3/−8	−3/−8	1/−6	7/0	14/5	19/10	21/13	20/12	15/8	9/4	3/−1	0/−5
Max/Min °F	27/17	27/18	33/22	45/32	57/41	66/50	69/55	68/54	59/46	48/39	38/30	32/23
rainfall mm	45	29	29	36	37	53	79	84	82	70	68	55

things not to miss

It's not possible to see everything that Estonia, Latvia & Lithuania have to offer in one trip – and we don't suggest you try. What follows, in no particular order, is a selective taste of the countries' highlights – unforgettable cities, outstanding architecture and natural wonders. You can browse through to find the very best things to see, do and experience, arranged in five colour-coded categories. All highlights have a page reference to take you straight into the guide, where you can find out more.

01 **Trakai** Page **286** • This wonderfully restored island fortress recalls the grandeur of Lithuania's medieval empire, which once stretched from the Baltic to the Black Sea.

02 **Estonian Open-air Museum** Page **82** • For an insight into how nineteenth-century Estonians used to live, visit this vast ensemble of timber-built farmhouses gathered from all over the country.

04 **Saaremaa** Page **98** • Enjoy weather-beaten coastal wilderness, castles and windmills on Estonia's most enchanting island.

03 **Kaziukas Fair** Page **256** • Woodwork, ceramics, textiles and Easter palms fill the streets of Vilnius for one of Europe's biggest handicraft fairs.

05 **Rīgas melnais balzams** Page **187** • Many locals swear by the elixir-like qualities of the gloopy, herb-flavoured spirit that is Rīga Black Balsam – just don't be surprised if it turns out to be something of an acquired taste.

06 **Kumu Art Museum** Page **80** • As well as showcasing Estonian past and present, Tallinn's dazzling art museum is an attraction in itself.

07 Potato pancakes Page 240
& *Food and drink* colour section •
Served with lashings of sour cream and bacon bits, these delicious pancakes are the perfect introduction to the Lithuanian love of the potato.

08 Going to jail in Liepāja
Page **212** • The former Soviet naval prison at Karosta is a living museum where you can tour the cells, or even spend a night in them.

09 Vilsandi National Park Page **104** • Pebble-strewn shores, juniper thickets and lonely lighthouses on Saaremaa's northwestern coast.

10 Hill of Crosses Page 325 • Bristling with crosses, statues and wood-carved shrines, this otherworldly pilgrimage site packs a powerful spiritual punch.

11 Piusa sand caves Page 146 • These eerie man-made caverns make for one of the more offbeat attractions of southeast Estonia.

12 Erratic boulders Page 116 • Enigmatic lumps of rock left behind long ago by retreating glaciers lie scattered along the shores of the Lahemaa National Park.

13 **Grūtas park** Page 322 • Rescued from the scrap merchant and replanted in rural parkland, this collection of Soviet-era statues provides a walk-round history lesson you're unlikely to forget.

14 **Tartu** Page 126 • An invitingly easy-going university town with an attractive jumble of historic buildings and plenty of student-filled pubs.

15 **Āraiši Lake Fortress** Page **225** • This quietly impressive replica of a ninth-century log-built settlement evokes the simplicity and harshness of life in ancient Latvia.

17 **Bogs** Page **37** & *Great outdoors colour section* • The Baltic region is especially rich in these bewitchingly barren landscapes of squelchy mosses and stunted trees.

16 **Rīga Art Nouveau** Page **178** • The Baltic States' one true metropolis, Rīga can muster the kind of architectural monuments that any capital city would be proud of – including one of the biggest collections of Art Nouveau buildings in Europe.

18 Vilnius Old Town Page **258** • Every one of Vilnius's cobbled alleys seems to have a magnificent church at the end of it, and the Gothic masterpiece that is St Anne's is no exception.

19 Gauja National Park Page **217** • Dramatic sandstone cliffs and virgin forests combine to make the unspoilt Gauja Latvia's most beautiful valley.

20 **Nida** Page **338** • Silky-smooth beaches and towering dunes add an air of Saharan majesty to Lithuania's popular summer resort.

21 **Aglona basilica, Latgale** Page **229** • The spiritual centre of Latvia's Catholic minority, located amid the rolling hills and tranquil lakes of the far southeast.

22 **Dzūkija Forest** Page **314** • Bordered by meandering rivers and boggy heaths, this sandy-soiled forest of dark pines represents woodland Lithuania at its most unspoilt.

23 Tallinn Old Town Page **66** • Tallinn's Old Town is an addictive warren of maze-like alleys and grand medieval squares.

24 Jewish heritage Page **183** • Both Lithuania and Latvia were home to a flourishing Jewish civilization before World War II. The Holocaust memorial in Rīga's Bikernieki forest is a fitting and eloquent monument to its disappearance.

25 Pärnu beach Page **108** • Estonia's premier bucket-and-spade resort is also a big hit with free-spending, fun-seeking youngsters.

26 Rundāle Palace, western Latvia Page **196** • The Baltic aristocracy certainly knew a thing or two about interiors, as the beautifully restored ballrooms and bedchambers of this Rococo country palace attest.

27 Pape Page **214** • A magnificently unspoilt stretch of coastal heath in southern Latvia, famous for its free-roaming herd of wild horses.

Basics

Basics

Getting there

From the UK and Ireland the most convenient way of getting to the Baltic States is to fly – there's a reasonable choice of direct and non-direct flights taking from three to five hours respectively, whereas the overland journey by car, train or coach can easily run to two or three days. While there are no direct flights to the Baltic capitals from North America or Australasia, plenty of airlines offer one- or two-stop connections. Budget deals from either continent are often hard to find, however – it may work out cheaper to get a bargain flight to a Western European destination and continue your journey by land. It's relatively easy to combine a visit to the Baltic States with a more general trip around northeastern Europe, with Poland to the west and Scandinavia to the north providing plenty in the way of bus and ferry links respectively.

Airfares always depend on the **season**. Peak times for flights to the Baltic States are May to September, and around the Easter and Christmas holidays; at these times be prepared to book well in advance. Fares drop during the "shoulder" seasons (April & Oct); and you'll usually get the best prices during the low season (Nov–March, excluding Easter and Christmas). Some Baltic cities are served by **budget airlines** from other cities in Western Europe (such as Amsterdam, Berlin or Copenhagen), making a variety of approaches possible. The best deals are usually to be found by booking through discount travel websites or the websites of the airlines themselves.

For a full **list** of airlines and tour operators, see pp.31–33.

Flights from the UK and Ireland

The UK and Ireland currently enjoy good connections with the Baltic States, with (largely low-cost) airlines such as Ryanair, easyJet, Wizz Air, Star 1, Air Baltic and Estonian Air operating **direct flights**. Good transport connections between the main Baltic cities ensure that it is perfectly feasible to fly into one Baltic state and continue your journey to another by land.

London enjoys direct services to all three Baltic capitals, and there are direct flights from Dublin to both **Rīga** and **Vilnius**. Travelling from other airports in the UK and Ireland, Rīga and Lithuania's second city

Kaunas are the two best served destinations. **Flight times** from the UK and Ireland hover around the 3 to 3 hour 30 minute mark. **Prices** vary enormously depending on when you travel and how far in advance you book: you can pick up one-way fares for under £50/€60 in the off-season, although costs can rise to £150/€180 one-way if you are booking at peak times or at short notice.

Tours

An increasing number of **tour operators** are including Vilnius, Rīga and Tallinn in their **city-break** brochures. This is an excellent way of getting a flight-plus-accommodation **package** at a reasonable price – the comfortable three- to four-star hotels used by tour operators would probably work out more expensive if you tried to book them independently. A **three-night city break** in one of the Baltic capitals costs in the region of £350–380 in the low season, rising to £420–500 in high season, with additional nights costing £40–60.

In addition, several specialist companies offer **general Baltic tours** taking in all three capitals and a few outlying attractions. Costs vary according to group size and hotel quality, but expect to pay upwards of £900 for a week-long tour taking in a little of all three states, and from £1200 for a two-week trip. **Baltic specialists** (see p.32), such as Regent Holidays and Baltic Holidays, are the best places to enquire about tailor-made itineraries and special-interest tours.

Flights from the US and Canada

Although there are **no direct flights from North America** to the Baltic States, there are plenty of indirect routings to choose from. If you're departing from one of North America's gateway cities you'll probably only have to change planes once – otherwise, a two-stop flight seems more likely. Flying **from Canada**, airlines such as CSA, KLM, LOT and Lufthansa offer one-stop connections with Baltic capitals.

Fares vary widely according to which Baltic capital you're flying to and which city you're setting out from, and it might make sense to fly to whichever Baltic destination offers the cheapest return fares, then continue your trip by land. One money-saving option is to fly to the UK with a low-cost airline, and continue your journey to the Baltics with another budget carrier such as Ryanair or easyJet (see p.31). The best fares tend to be with north European airlines with frequent Baltic connections: flying **from New York** to Vilnius, Rīga or Tallinn with Finnair (via Helsinki) or SAS (via Copenhagen), for example, currently costs around US$1100 in low season, US$1500 high. Return fares **from Chicago** to the Baltic capitals with SAS or LOT (via Warsaw) cost around US$1000 and US$1500 respectively. From elsewhere in North America, the cheapest scheduled fares to the Baltic capitals fluctuate between US$1500 and US$2000 return – although it's always worth looking out for special seasonal fares. A typical peak-season return fare **from Toronto** to Rīga, Tallinn or Vilnius weighs in at Can$1650.

Tours

A small but growing number of companies operate **organized tours** to the Baltic States from North America, ranging from city breaks to two-week cultural tours of the whole

Six steps to a better kind of travel

At Rough Guides we are passionately committed to travel. We feel strongly that only through travelling do we truly come to understand the world we live in and the people we share it with – plus tourism has brought a great deal of **benefit** to developing economies around the world over the last few decades. But the extraordinary growth in tourism has also damaged some places irreparably, and of course **climate change** is exacerbated by most forms of transport, especially flying. This means that now more than ever it's important to **travel thoughtfully** and **responsibly**, with respect for the cultures you're visiting – not only to derive the most benefit from your trip but also to preserve the best bits of the planet for everyone to enjoy. At Rough Guides we feel there are six main areas in which you can make a difference:

- Consider what you're contributing to the **local economy**, and how much the services you use do the same, whether it's through employing local workers and guides or sourcing locally grown produce and local services.
- Consider the **environment** on holiday as well as at home. Water is scarce in many developing destinations, and the biodiversity of local flora and fauna can be adversely affected by tourism. Try to patronize businesses that take account of this.
- Travel with a purpose, not just to tick off experiences. Consider **spending longer** in a place, and getting to know it and its people.
- Give thought to how often you **fly**. Try to avoid short hops by air and more harmful night flights.
- Consider **alternatives to flying**, travelling instead by bus, train, boat and even by bike or on foot where possible.
- Make your trips **"climate neutral"** via a reputable carbon-offset scheme. All Rough Guide flights are offset, and every year we donate money to a variety of charities devoted to combating the effects of climate change.

region. Booking a flights-plus-accommodation deal through a specialist travel agent (see p.32) can often work out cheaper than organizing things yourself. Group tours tend to be more expensive, ranging in price from US$1500 for seven days to US$2200 for a fortnight, not including flights from North America.

Flights from Australia and New Zealand

Flying to the Baltic States from **Australia and New Zealand** with major airlines usually involves two stops en route and can work out quite expensive – fares hover around the Aus$3200 or NZ$4500 mark. It probably makes more sense to aim for a big European city such as London or Berlin and then travel on to the Baltics on a local budget airline. This can work out quite cheaply if booked well in advance online.

A small number of operators offer **package holidays** in the Baltic States from Australia and New Zealand, including accommodation, sightseeing packages and rail passes.

By train

Travelling to the Baltic States **by train from the UK** is more expensive than flying, but it gives you the option of stopping off in other parts of Europe on the way. From Western Europe there's only one route into the Baltics – the line from Warsaw in Poland to Vilnius in Lithuania. Beyond Vilnius, the Baltic rail network itself is pretty limited, and onward travel to Rīga and Tallinn will most likely be by bus.

The main **London–Vilnius** itinerary runs via Brussels, Cologne, Berlin and Warsaw, and takes about 45 hours if you're lucky with connections – somewhat longer if you cross the Channel by ferry rather than taking the Eurostar. Buying a through ticket for this route isn't easy: most major UK train stations can sell tickets as far as Brussels, but are rarely equipped to deal with destinations beyond. The **agents** who specialize in international train journeys (see "Rail Contacts" p.33) may be able to book your passage as far as Warsaw, but are unlikely to sell tickets further east. The **cost** of a London–Warsaw

Useful publications

The *Thomas Cook European Timetables* details schedules of over fifty thousand trains in Europe, as well as timings of over two hundred ferry routes and rail-connecting bus services. It's updated and issued every month; the main changes are in the June edition (published end of May), which has details of the summer European schedules, and the October edition (published end of Sept), which includes winter schedules; some also have advance summer/winter timings. The book can be bought online (which gets you a ten percent discount) at Ⓦ www.thomascooktimetables.com or from branches of Thomas Cook (see Ⓦ www.thomascook.co.uk for your nearest branch) and costs £15.99. Their *Rail Map of Europe* (regular price £8.99) is also useful.

return using Eurostar hovers around £260 – you'll need to add a further £30–40 to cover the Warsaw–Vilnius leg. It will work out slightly cheaper if you cross the Channel by ferry, but as none of the ticket agents sells through tickets on continental journeys not using Eurostar, you'll have to buy tickets as you go.

Rail passes

If you're travelling across Europe by train, it's worth considering one of the many **rail passes** available, covering regions as well as individual countries. None of them actually extends to the Baltic States themselves, but they're a useful way of getting across most of the other countries on the way. For rail ticket **agents**, see p.33.

Inter-Rail passes are only available to European residents, and you'll be asked to provide proof of residency before being allowed to buy one. They come in over-26 and (cheaper) under-26 versions, and cover 31 countries. Lithuania, Latvia and Estonia are not covered, but Belgium, Germany and Poland are. The passes do not include travel between Britain and the Continent, although holders are eligible for discounts on rail travel in the UK and cross-Channel ferries.

A pass for five days' travel in a ten-day period (£228, or £146 for under-26s) will get you to the Baltic States and back but won't give you much time to look around while you're there; better to buy a pass for ten days' travel within a 22-day period (£329/£219) or for one month's continuous travel (£549/£366).

Non-European residents qualify for the **Eurail Global pass**, which must be bought before arrival in Europe (or from Rail Europe in London, see p.33). The pass allows unlimited free first-class train travel in seventeen European countries, including Belgium and Germany but not Poland or the Baltic States – so you'll have to buy a regular ticket to cover the last leg of the journey. The pass is available in increments of fifteen days (US$665), 21 days (US$859) and one month (US$1069). A **Eurail Global Flexi pass** will give you ten days' first-class travel in a two-month period for US$785. If you're under 26, you can save money with a **Eurail Global Youthpass** (US$429 for fifteen days, US$695 for one month, or US$509 for ten days' travel in a two-month period). Further details of these passes and other Eurail permutations can be found on ⓦwww .raileurope.com.

By bus

Given the number of low-cost airlines flying to the Baltic States, attempting the journey by **bus** is unlikely to save you a great deal of money. **Eurolines** (see p.33) operates several weekly services from London to Rīga involving a change in Germany, the whole journey taking around 45 hours. It's not as gruelling as you might think, with refreshment stops at regular intervals, although spending the best part of two days in the same seat will not be to everyone's taste. Tickets to Rīga cost £189 return, with a ten percent reduction for under-26s and seniors.

If you're travelling **from Ireland**, there are Eurolines services to London from Dublin, Cork, Killarney, Limerick, Tralee and Belfast.

By car and ferry

Driving to the Baltic States involves a long haul of 1800km from Calais or Ostend to the Lithuanian border, followed by a further 170km, 360km or 660km to Vilnius, Rīga or Tallinn respectively. Using the motorways of Belgium, Holland and northern Germany, you'll find the first 1000km of the journey are reasonably straightforward and might easily be covered in a couple of days' hard driving. From the Polish border onwards however, roads are mostly single carriageway and are not always in the best state of repair – you'll have to adopt a leisurely approach to the Polish leg of the journey if you want to arrive with your nerves intact.

The most convenient **Channel crossings** are on the P&O Stena services from Dover/ Folkestone to Calais, Norfolkline from Dover to Dunkirk, or Eurotunnel's Le Shuttle Channel Tunnel option from Folkestone to Calais. Once in Calais or Ostend, you can pick up the main motorway route east through Belgium and beyond, bypassing Brussels, Düsseldorf, Hannover and Berlin on the way.

You could also take one of the nightly P&O ferries **from Hull to Rotterdam**, or the DFDS service from Newcastle to Amsterdam.

If you don't fancy driving across Poland, you might consider a handful of **ferries from northern Europe** that would cut the country out of your itinerary. Scandline operates a thrice-weekly service from the German port of Travemünde near Lübeck to Ventspils and Liepāja. There are also thrice-weekly sailings operated by Lisco **from Kiel** to Klaipėda (20hr), and **Sassnitz** (a small port northeast of Rostock) to Klaipėda (21hr). For details of ferries from Sweden to the Baltic States, see opposite.

From Poland

Travelling **overland from Poland** to the Baltics is very cheap, with train and bus tickets from Warsaw to the Lithuanian capital Vilnius rarely exceeding €30/£25/US$36 return.

Vilnius receives daily **buses** from Warsaw's Warszawa Zachodnia terminal (8–10hr) and Gdańsk (12hr; overnight), five weekly from Olsztyn (8hr; overnight), and two a week from Kraków (16hr; overnight). A daily bus from Warsaw travels to **Rīga** via Białystok (18hr).

A direct **train** runs **from Warsaw to Vilnius** daily; otherwise head for the near-border town of Suwalki from where there are two trains a day to Šeštokai on the Lithuanian side of the frontier, each of which is met by a connecting service to Kaunas and Vilnius.

There are **flights** too, though at around €160/£135/US$200, they're not much of a bargain. The Polish national carrier LOT operates daily flights from Warsaw to Vilnius and Rīga.

From Finland

One of the most popular jumping-off points for travel into the Baltic States is the Finnish capital **Helsinki**, with four **ferry** companies – Eckerö Line, Lindaline, Tallink and Viking – offering daily services to the Estonian capital **Tallinn**. The 85km crossing takes 2 to 3 hour on the car ferries operated by Eckerö, Tallink and Viking; 90min on Lindaline's catamarans (which only run when the sea is free of ice – usually April–Nov).

All services depart from Helsinki's South Harbour, an easy ten-minute walk from central train and bus stations.

From Sweden

Sweden enjoys **ferry** links with all three Baltic States and, although crossings involve spending one night on the boat, fares are reasonable enough to make this a good budget alternative to flying.

From Stockholm, Tallink operates overnight ferries to both **Tallinn** and **Rīga**. The port of **Karlshamn**, 350km southwest of Stockholm, is the departure point for both Lisco's thrice-weekly ferry to Liepāja in Latvia and Scandlines' thrice-weekly services to Ventspils in Latvia. Note that Karlshamn ferry terminal is 4km west of town, and there's no public transport – so foot passengers should budget for the cost of a taxi.

Airlines, agents and operators

Airlines

Aer Lingus ⓦ www.aerlingus.com. Direct flights from Dublin and London Gatwick to Vilnius.
Air Baltic ⓦ www.airbaltic.com. Daily flights from London Gatwick to Rīga and Vilnius; also one-stop

flights from Edinburgh, Glasgow and Liverpool with a change in Amsterdam, Copenhagen or Stockholm.
Air Canada ⓦ www.aircanada.com. Flights from Canada to major European hubs, with onward connections to the Baltics handled by a partner airline.
Air New Zealand ⓦ www.airnewzealand.co.nz. Daily flights from Auckland to London via LA, then onward connections to Rīga, Tallinn and Vilnius.
American Airlines ⓦ www.aa.com. Flights from North American cities to major European hubs.
Austrian Airlines ⓦ www.aua.com. Flights from North America to Vilnius with a change of plane in Vienna.
British Airways ⓦ www.ba.com. Daily to London from several North American cities, and from Sydney, Melbourne or Perth with onward connections to the Baltic capitals.
Continental Airlines ⓦ www.continental.com. Daily flights from North American cities to most major European hubs, with onward connections to Baltic capitals.
CSA (Czech Airlines) ⓦ www.czechairlines.com. Flights from North America to Prague with onward connections to Rīga and Vilnius.
Delta Air Lines ⓦ www.delta.com. Flights to Stockholm, London and other European hubs with onward connections to Tallinn, Rīga and Vilnius.
easyJet ⓦ www.easyjet.com. Direct flights from London Stansted to Tallinn.
Estonian Airlines ⓦ www..estonian-air.ee. Direct fights from London Heathrow to Tallinn.
Finnair ⓦ www.finnair.com. Direct flights from Dublin, Heathrow and Manchester to Helsinki, from where there are connecting flights to Vilnius, Rīga and Tallinn. Also flights from New York and Toronto to Tallinn, Rīga and Vilnius, changing at Helsinki; and flights from Australia via Bangkok or Singapore to Helsinki, with onward connections to Tallinn, Rīga and Vilnius.
LOT (Polish Airlines) ⓦ www.lot.com. Direct flights from London, Manchester, New York, Chicago and Toronto to Warsaw, with connecting flights to Vilnius and Rīga.
Lufthansa ⓦ www.lufthansa.com. Flights from North American and Australian airports to Frankfurt or Munich, with onward connections to all three Baltic capitals.
Northwest/KLM ⓦ www.nwa.com. Flights from North American and Australian airports to Amsterdam, followed by connections to Tallinn, Rīga and Vilnius.
Qantas ⓦ www.qantas.com. Flights from Sydney to Frankfurt with connections to Vilnius and Rīga.
Ryanair ⓦ www.ryanair.com. Direct flights to Kaunas from Birmingham, Bristol, Dublin, Liverpool, London Luton and London Stansted; and to Rīga from

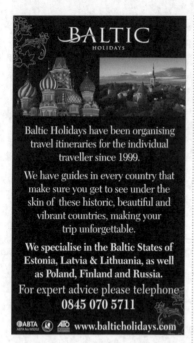
Bristol, Dublin, East Midlands, Glasgow, Liverpool and London Stansted.

SAS Scandinavian Airlines ⓦ www.scandinavian .net. Flights to all three Baltic capitals from UK, Irish, North American and Australian airports, changing at Copenhagen or Stockholm.

Star 1 ⓦ www.star1.aero. Direct flights from London Stansted, Dublin and Edinburgh to Vilnius.

US Airways ⓦ www.usairways.com. Flights from North America to European hubs, with onward connections to the Baltic capitals.

Virgin Atlantic ⓦ www.virgin-atlantic.com. Flights from North America to London.

Wizz Air ⓦ www.wizzair.com. Direct flights from London Luton to Rīga.

Agents and operators

North South Travel UK ☎ 01245/608 291, ⓦ www.northsouthtravel.co.uk. Friendly, competitive travel agency, offering discounted fares worldwide. Profits are used to support projects in the developing world, especially the promotion of sustainable tourism.

STA Travel US ☎ 1-800/781-4040, UK ☎ 0871/230 0040, Australia ☎ 134 782, New Zealand ☎ 0800/474 400, South Africa ☎ 0861/781 781; ⓦ www.statravel.com. Worldwide specialists in independent travel; also student IDs,

travel insurance, car rental, rail passes, and more. Good discounts for students and under-26s.

Trailfinders UK ☎ 0845/058 5858, Ireland ☎ 01/677 7888, Australia ☎ 1300/780 212; ⓦ www.trailfinders.com. One of the best-informed and most efficient agents for independent travellers.

Travel CUTS Canada ☎ 1-866/246-9762, US ☎ 1-800/592-2887; ⓦ www.travelcuts.com. Canadian youth and student travel firm.

USIT Ireland ☎ 01/602 1906, Northern Ireland ☎ 028/9032 7111; ⓦ www.usit.ie. Ireland's main student and youth travel specialists.

Specialist tour operators

Adventure Center US ☎ 1-800/228-8747 or 510/654-1879, ⓦ www.adventurecenter.com. Two-week Baltic tours.

Adventures Abroad US ☎ 1-800/665-3998, ⓦ www.adventures-abroad.com. A range of seven- to twenty-day tours of the Baltic capitals, with optional visits to St Petersburg and Warsaw.

Baltic Holidays UK ☎ 0845/070 5711, ⓦ www .balticholidays.com. City breaks to the Baltic capitals, seven- to fourteen-day tours of Lithuania, Latvia and Estonia (individually or in combination) and tailor-made accommodation-plus-flights packages.

Bentours Australia ☎ 1800/221 712, ⓦ www .bentours.com.au. Tours and tailor-made arrangements in the Baltics and Scandinavia.

Eastern Eurotours Australia ☎ 07/5526 2855 or 1800/242 353, ⓦ www.easterneurotours.com .au. Flights, accommodation and city breaks in the Baltic States.

Explore Worldwide UK ☎ 0845/013 1537, ⓦ www.explore.co.uk. Two-week tours of Baltic cities and national parks.

Gateway Travel Australia ☎ 612/9745 3333, ⓦ www.russian-gateway.com.au. Eastern European and Russian specialists.

Isram World of Travel US ☎ 1-800/223-7460, ⓦ www.isram.com. City breaks in the Baltic capitals and a good variety of Baltic tours.

Martin Randall Travel UK ☎ 020/8742 3355, ⓦ www.martinrandall.com. Two-week cultural tours with expert guides, taking in the main historical sights of all three Baltic states.

Regent Holidays UK ☎ 0845/277 3315, ⓦ www .regent-holidays.co.uk. City breaks to Tallinn, Rīga and Vilnius. Accompanied ten- and fifteen-day tours through the Baltics and tailor-made arrangements for independent tourists.

Scantours US ☎ 1-800/223-7226, ⓦ www .scantours.com. City breaks in Vilnius, Rīga and Tallinn, general Baltic tours, plus bicycle tours in Lithuania. Also agents for European rail passes.

Travel Editions UK ☎020/7251 0045, ⓦwww.traveleditions.co.uk. Three-city tours of the Baltic capitals.

Travellers Cities UK ☎01959/540 700, ⓦwww.travellerscities.com. City breaks to Tallinn, Rīga and Vilnius.

Vytis Tours US ☎1-718/423-6161, ⓦwww.vytistours.com. Baltic specialist offering tailor-made accommodation-plus-flights packages, tours and car rental.

Rail contacts

CIT World Travel Australia ☎1300 361 500, ⓦwww.cittravel.com.au. Eurail passes.

Deutsche Bahn UK ☎0871/880 8066, ⓦwww.bahn.co.uk. Timetable information and through ticketing on European routes.

Europrail International Canada ☎1-888/667-9734, ⓦwww.europrail.net. European rail passes.

Eurostar UK ☎0870/518 6186, ⓦwww.eurostar.com. Passenger train from London St Pancras to Paris (2hr 15min) and Brussels (1hr 51min).

The Man in Seat 61 ⓦwww.seat61.com. Enthusiast-run site packed with information on all aspects of international rail travel. Far more reliable than many official sites.

Rail Europe US ☎1-877/257-2887, Canada ☎1-800/361-RAIL, UK ☎0870/584 8848; ⓦwww.raileurope.com. Agents for Eurail, Inter-Rail and Eurostar.

Rail Plus Australia ☎1300/555 003 or 03/9642 8644, ⓦwww.railplus.com.au. European rail passes.

Trainseurope UK ☎0871/700 7722, ⓦwww.trainseurope.co.uk. Inter-Rail passes and through-tickets on European routes.

Bus contacts

Eurolines UK ☎0871/781 8181, ⓦwww.eurolines.co.uk; Republic of Ireland ☎01/836 6111, ⓦwww.eurolines.ie.

Ferry contacts

DFDS Seaways UK ☎0871/522 9955, ⓦwww.dfdsseaways.co.uk. Newcastle to Amsterdam.

Eckerö Line Finland ☎+358/9 2288 5333, ⓦwww.eckeroline.ee. One daily Helsinki–Tallinn ferry (3hr 30min).

Lindaline Finland ☎+358/600 6668 970, ⓦwww.lindaline.fi. Six daily catamarans from Helsinki to Tallinn (1hr 30min).

Lisco Lithuania ☎8-46/395 051, ⓦwww.dfdslisco.lt. Kiel to Klaipėda; Sassnitz to Klaipėda; Karlshamn to Klaipėda.

Norfolkline UK ☎08715/747 235, ⓦwww.norfolkline-ferries.co.uk. Ferries from Dover to Dunkirk.

P&O UK ☎08716/645 645, ⓦwww.poferries.com. Dover to Calais; Hull to Rotterdam; Hull to Zeebrugge; Dublin to Liverpool.

Scandline ☎+49/1805 116 688, ⓦ www
.scandlines.com. Nynäshamn to Ventspils,
Travemünde to Ventspils, Travemünde to Liepaja.
Tallink ☎+372/640 9808, ⓦ www.tallinksilja
.com. High-speed car ferries (2hr) from Helsinki to

Tallinn. Also overnight ferries from Stockholm to Rīga
and Stockholm to Tallinn.
Viking ⓦ www.vikingline.ee. Daily ferries
(2hr 30min) from Helsinki to Tallinn.

Getting around

Although each of the Baltic States has a small train network, there are no rail
services linking the Baltic capitals themselves. Buses are however plentiful and
reasonably cheap. A one-way bus ticket from Tallinn to Vilnius costs around
€33/£27.50/$40; Rīga to Vilnius or Tallinn is around €16/£13.50/$20.

Flights between the capitals take only 45
minutes, but are ten times more expensive
than buses.

   For further information about public
transport, along with **car rental** and driving,
see each country's "Getting around" section
and the "Travel details" at the end of every
chapter.

Car rental agencies

You may find it more convenient to arrange
rental before setting off; the international
operators have agents throughout the Baltic
States.
Avis ⓦ www.avis.com.
Budget ⓦ www.budget.com.
Europcar ⓦ www.europcar.com.
Hertz ⓦ www.hertz.com.
SIXT ⓦ www.sixt.com.

Festivals and events

There is an increasingly inviting choice of summer festivals and year-round cultural happenings in the Baltic States. Further information can be found under
each individual country's "Festivals" section. The list below uses the following
abbreviations: EST = Estonia; LAT = Latvia; LITH = Lithuania. Events marked with
the 🏃 icon are well worth planning your itinerary around.

January
(EST) Tallinn Light festival (Valgusfestival)
ⓦ www.valgusfestival.ee. Light installations by
contemporary artists at various sites throughout
the city.

February
(LITH) Shrove Tuesday (Uzgavenes) ⓦ www
.etno.lt. Ritualistic burning of the *morė* (a straw
puppet), followed by plenty of music and dancing.

March

(LITH) **Kaziukas Fair** (St Casimir's Fair). Weekend nearest to March 4; Vilnius. Possibly Europe's biggest handicrafts market, with stalls taking over the city's streets.

(LITH) **Cinema Spring** (Kino Pavasaris) ⓦwww.kinopavasaris.lt. Late March-early April; Vilnius. Recent features from Europe and beyond.

(LITH) **Birštonas Jazz Festival** ⓦwww.visitbirstonas.lt. Last weekend in March (even-numbered years only); Birštonas. Long-standing jazz bash with an emphasis on big bands and swing.

April

(LITH) **Young Music** (Jauna Muzika) ⓦwww.lks.lt. Vilnius. New works by young composers.

(LAT) **Bach Chamber Music Festival** ⓦwww.music.lv. Rīga. International ensembles and soloists perform in museums and guildhouses.

(LITH) **Lithuanian Theatre Spring** (Lietuvos Teatrų Pavasaris) ⓦwww.girstutis.lt. Mid-April; Kaunas. Major productions by some of Lithuania's best directors.

(EST) **Jazzkaar** ⓦwww.jazzkaar.ee. Late April; Tallinn. Superb line-up of international jazz.

(LAT) **International Baltic Ballet Festival** ⓦwww.ballet-festival.lv. Mid/late April; Rīga. International dance troupes (not just from the Baltics) perform throughout the city.

(EST) **Haapsalu Horror and Fantasy Film Festival** ⓦwww.hoff.ee. Late April; Haapsalu. Scary stuff in a town famous for its ghosts.

(EST) **University Spring Days** (Ülikooli kevadpäevad). Late April to early May; Tartu. Five days of partying, feasting and fancy dress, straddling May 1.

(LITH) **Kaunas Jazz** ⓦwww.kaunasjazz.lt. Late April/early May; Kaunas. International jazz festival.

May

(LITH) **New Baltic Dance** (Naujasis Baltijos Šokis) ⓦwww.vilniusfestival.lt. Early May; Vilnius. High-quality contemporary dance.

(LITH) **Poetry Spring** (Poezijos Pavasaris) ⓦwww.rasytojai.lt. Late May; Vilnius.

(LITH) **Skamba skamba kankliai** ⓦwww.etno.lt. Late May; Vilnius. Lithuanian folk festival with performances in Old Town squares and courtyards.

(LITH) **Vilnius Festival** ⓦwww.vilniusfestival.lt. Second half of May; Vilnius. International opera, ballet and orchestral music.

(EST) **International Dance Festival** (Rahvusvahelisel tantsufestival). Late May/early June; Tartu. Estonia's premier dance event, with a strong contemporary edge.

(LITH) **Kaunas City Festival** (Kauno dienos) ⓦwww.kaunodienos.lt. Third weekend in May; Kaunas. City-wide party with concerts in parks and squares.

(EST) **Old Town Days** Late May/early June; Tallinn. Medieval parades and jousting tournaments.

(LITH) **Kunigunda Lunaria** ⓦwww.dangus.net. Late May; Vilnius. Dark-metal and Goth music with strong Baltic-pagan undertones.

June

(LITH) **Pažaislis Music Festival** ⓦwww.pazaislis.lt. June–Aug; Kaunas. Opera, orchestral music and solo concerts in the grounds of Pažaislis monastery and other venues around Kaunas.

(LITH) **Klaipėda Jazz Festival** ⓦwww.jazz.lt. Early June; Klaipėda. Broad-ranging jazz fest with international participation.

(LAT) **Rīga Opera Festival** ⓦwww.opera.lv. Mid-/late June; Rīga. Review of the previous season's best operas.

(EST & LAT & LITH) **St John's Eve** June 23/24. Bonfires and all-night carousing.

July

(EST) **Baltoscandal** ⓦwww.baltoscandal.ee. Early July; Rakvere. International festival of cutting-edge theatre.

(EST) **Juu Jääb Future Music Festival** ⓦwww.nordicsounds.ee. July; Muhu. Contemporary jazz from Estonia and abroad in a number of venues around Muhu and the neighbouring island of Saaremaa.

(LAT) **Organ Music Festival** July; Rīga. The Latvian capital's church organs are put through their paces by top musicians.

(LITH) **Christopher Summer Festival** ⓦwww.kristupofestivaliai.lt. Early July to late Aug; Vilnius. Concert season featuring everything from chamber music to pop.

(EST) **Sunset Music at Kõpu Lighthouse** Saturday-evening concerts throughout July; Hiiumaa.

(LITH) **Experimental Archeology Festival** ⓦwww.kernave.org. Early July; Kernavė. Enthusiasts in Iron Age dress demonstrate ancient Lithuanian music, dancing and traditional crafts.

(EST) **Haapsalu Early Music Festival** (Haapsalu Vanamuusikafestival) ⓦwww.concertogrosso.ee. Early/mid-July; Haapsalu. Local and international ensembles perform in the cathedral.

(EST) **Tallinn medieval days** (Keskaja päevad) ⓦwww.folkart.ee. Early/mid-July; Tallinn. Early music, traditional handicrafts and a lot of dressing up.

(LAT) **Early Music Festival** (Senās Mūzikas
Festivāls) ⓦ www.smf.lv. Early/mid-July; Rīga and
Rundāle Palace. Chamber concerts.

(EST) **Võru Folk Festival** ⓦ www.werro.ee. Early/
mid-July; Võru. Estonian and international ensembles.

(EST) **Hansa Days** (Hansapaevad) ⓦ www
.hansapaevad.ee. Mid-July; Tartu. Medieval-style fair
with street musicians, tournaments and craft stalls.

(LAT) **Positivus** ⓦ www.positivus.com. Mid-July;
Salacgriva. Weekend-long arts and rock festival with
big international names, up the coast from Rīga.

(EST) **Hiiumaa Folk Festival** ⓦ www.hiiufolk.ee.
Mid-July; Hiiumaa. Long weekend of folk music with
a handful of foreign guests at Kassari.

(EST) **Viljandi Folk Festival** ⓦ www.folk.ee. Late
July; Viljandi. Estonia's biggest ethno bash.

(LITH) **Tomas Mann Festival** ⓦ www.mann.lt.
Mid-July; Nida. Classical chamber music.

(EST) **Saaremaa Opera Days** (Saaremaa
Ooperipäevad) ⓦ www.concert.ee. Late July;
Kuressaare. Large-scale productions in the grounds
of Kuressaare castle, often with top international
performers.

(LITH) **Klaipéda Sea Festival** Last weekend in July;
Klaipéda. Carnival floats, folk dancing and pop music.

August

(LAT) **International Sacred Music Festival**
(Starptautiskais garīgās mūzikas festivāls) ⓦ www
.koris.lv. Rīga. Outstanding choral works sung by
Latvian and international ensembles.

(EST) **Days of the Setu Kingdom**
(Setokuningriik) ⓦ www.mikitamae.ee
/setokuningriik. Early Aug; Luhamaal, near Obinitsa.
Folk festival celebrating the culture of the Setu people
in Estonia's far southeast.

(LAT) **Sigulda Festival** ⓦ tourism.sigulda.lv.
Sigulda. Opera in the courtyard of a medieval castle.

(EST) **Kuressaare Chamber Music Days**
(Kuressaare Kammeramuusika Päevad) ⓦ www
.kammerfest.ee. Early/mid-Aug; Kuressaare.
Attracting some of best European soloists and
ensembles.

(EST) **Kuressaare Maritime Festival**
(Merepäevad) ⓦ www.merepaevad.ee. Early Aug;
Kuressaare. A long weekend of folklore, seafood,
crafts markets and jazz concerts.

(EST) **White Lady Days** ⓦ www.kultuurimaja
.ee. Mid-Aug; Haapsalu. Drinking and dancing in the
castle courtyard.

(LITH) **Menuo Juodaragis** ⓦ www.mjr.lt. Late
Aug; location may change every year.
Outdoor gathering of folk, post-folk, rock and
electronic bands with a strong Baltic-pagan theme.

September

(EST) **Eclectica** ⓦ www.eclectica.ee.
Early Sept; Tartu. Electronic music and cutting-edge
DJ culture.

(EST) **Draama** ⓦ draama.festival.ee. Early Sept;
Tartu. Contemporary theatre festival featuring the best
new work from Estonia alongside challenging drama
from abroad.

(LAT) **Skaņu Mežs** ("Sound Forest")
ⓦ www.skanumezs.lv. Sept; Rīga.
Experimental music and film.

October

(LITH) **Poetry Autumn** ⓦ www.rasytojai.lt. Early
Oct; Druskininkai. Readings from Lithuanian poets
and international literary guests.

(LITH) **International Festival of Modern Dance**
(Tarptautinis Modernaus Šokio Festivalis) ⓦ www
.aura.lt. Early Oct; Kaunas.

(LITH) **Sirenos** ⓦ www.sirenos.lt. Early Oct; Vilnius.
Contemporary theatre festival with a reputation for
attracting the international big guns.

(LAT) **Arena New Music Festival** ⓦ www
.arenafest.lv. Mid-Oct. Rīga. International festival of
new music from contemporary composers.

(LITH) **Vilnius Jazz** ⓦ www.vilniusjazz.lt. Mid-Oct.
Vilnius.

(LITH) **Gaida** ⓦ www.vilniusfestivals.lt. Late Oct;
Vilnius. Contemporary music festival, frequently
featuring premieres of new works.

November

(LITH) **Mama Jazz** ⓦ www.vilniuscityjazz.lt.
Mid-Nov; Vilnius.

(LITH) **Virus Contemporary Arts Festival**
ⓦ www.menas.siauliai.lt. Mid-/late Nov; Šiauliai.
On-the-edge art, theatre, music, film and fashion
shows in venues throughout the city.

(LITH) **"Iš Arti" International Contemporary
Music Festival** Late Nov; Kaunas. Probing the
boundaries between electronica, classical music
and jazz.

(EST) **Black Nights Film Festival** (Pimedate
Ööde Filmifestival). ⓦ www.poff.ee. Mid-Nov/early
Dec; Tallinn. Contemporary cinema with a strong
showing from the Baltic and Nordic regions.

December

(EST & LAT) **Advent markets** Throughout Dec;
Rīga and Tallinn.

Outdoor activities

For many visitors, the Baltic States' wide range of outdoor pursuits constitutes the region's chief allure. If you like the outdoors it's a truly wonderful place, abounding in dense forests, secluded lakes, long, sandy beaches and large tracts of wilderness rich in wildlife. Best of all, you won't find the countryside overcrowded – there's plenty of space to get away from it all.

Hiking

Despite the absence of anything remotely resembling a mountain, the low-lying Baltic States offer a rich menu of **hiking** possibilities. If you like **forests**, then you'll love the **woodland trails** on offer in Estonia's Lahemaa National Park (see p.116) or the Dzūkija National Park in Lithuania (see p.314), where it's possible to walk for miles without seeing another soul. Latvia's Gauja National Park (see p.217) probably offers the most exciting terrain, with lush woodland, knobbly hills and twisting riverbanks overlooked by ruddy sandstone cliffs. The forests support a variety of **fauna** – you're certain to catch sight of roe deer, beavers abound wherever there are streams, and if you're lucky you might also see wild boar, moose, elk or even bears.

It's easy to combine a forest hike with traditional activities like **berry-picking** in summer and **mushrooming** in autumn – although for the latter you really need to know what you're looking for. You're usually banned from picking the cranberries that cover the region's **peat bogs**, a number of which have become important nature conservation areas. Many of these regions of mosses, stunted conifers and marshy pools can be explored via specially constructed wooden walkways – most notably in the Soomaa National Park in Estonia (see p.111), the Ķemeri National Park in Latvia (see p.200) and the Čepkeliu Nature Reserve in Lithuania (see p.317).

For a short, non-strenuous **nature walk**, there are plenty of well-maintained paths through areas of natural beauty, with signboards detailing the local flora and fauna – good examples are the Slītere Nature Trail near Cape Kolka in Latvia (see p.200), or the Šeirė Nature Trail in western Lithuania (see p.349).

If you do want to climb a hill, consider **Suur-Munamägi** in southern Estonia, which at 318m above sea level is the highest point in the Baltic States; the vicinity offers plenty of other wooded heights to explore.

Finally, the glorious expanses of sand that run almost uninterruptedly along the Baltic coast provide any number of opportunities for **beach walking**. While the Sahara-esque dunescapes around Nida in Lithuania can't be matched in terms of spectacle, the wild beauty of Cape Kolka in Latvia shouldn't be overlooked. Beach walkers can try their luck hunting for **amber**, especially after storms, when tiny nuggets of the stuff are washed up along the coast – especially the stretch between Liepāja and Ventspils in Latvia.

Canoeing

Large stretches of the Baltic landscape are dotted with lakes, and it's relatively easy to rent a variety of watercraft. The number of **navigable waterways** ensures that there's a host of **canoeing and kayaking** itineraries to choose from, often involving overnight stops at campsites en route. The most popular routes involve the Gauja and Abava rivers in Latvia, the lakes of the Aukštaitija National Park in northeastern Lithuania and the Ūla and Merkys rivers in southern Lithuania. In Estonia's Soomaa National Park, you can try your hand at paddling a *haabja*, a traditional canoe hewn from a single trunk of aspen.

Cycling

Although few places in the Baltic States are equipped with cycle paths or cycle lanes, the flat, quiet country roads of many rural areas are ideally suited to exploration by bike. Unfortunately, the business of **bike rental** has yet to be developed in many areas, but it shouldn't be too difficult to pick up a bicycle from agencies in the major national parks and in regions where cycling is beginning to take off – notably the islands of Saaremaa and Hiiumaa in Estonia and the Curonian Spit in Lithuania.

Birdwatching

Occupying a key position on north–south migration routes, the Baltic States are visited by hundreds of **bird species** every year. Most visible of these are white storks, which arrive in their thousands every spring and proceed to set up home on roofs and telegraph poles all over the region – with many birds returning to the same nesting spot year after year. Fish-rich wetland areas bordering the Baltic coast attract many migrating birds that have been all but squeezed out of Western Europe by intensive farming – bitterns, corncrakes, black storks, cranes, mute swans and all manner of geese, among them. Many wetland areas have been declared protected zones, some of which are totally off-limits to visitors, although you'll usually be able to make use of observation towers on the edges of these reserves.

Key areas for birdwatching **in Estonia** include the Lahemaa National Park (p.116), Vilsandi National Park on the island of Saaremaa (p.104) and the Matsalu Nature Reserve (p.94) south of Haapsalu. **In Latvia**, reed-shrouded lakes at Engure and Pape (p.214) are well worth visiting; the website ⓦ www.utni.lv is a useful source of information on other locations. **In Lithuania**, the Curonian Spit National Park and the Nemunas Delta Regional Park are the best places to spot wading birds.

Skiing

Despite the largely flat landscape, the Baltic States boast a handful of **downhill skiing** opportunities, although pistes tend to be short. The Baltic climate does at least ensure that snow cover is guaranteed for a good four months of the year. The most versatile of the winter resorts is **Ötepää** in southern Estonia: it has a wide range of downhill slopes and endless opportunities for **cross-country skiing**, as well as a lively nightlife. If an undemanding day out on the slopes is all you're after, you could do worse than head for the Gauja Valley in Latvia, where resorts like Sigulda (see p.218) are within easy day-trip range of the capital, Rīga. It's pretty easy to rent gear on arrival; a day's use of skis and boots rarely costs over €15/£13/$19.

Travel essentials

Crime and personal safety

Despite an increase in theft, corruption and mafia-style organized crime in the years following the collapse of communism, the Baltic States are relatively unthreatening countries in which to travel, and most tourists will have little or no contact with the local police. Technically, everyone is required to carry ID at all times, so it's a good idea to have your passport (or other form of photo ID) handy in case of random police checks.

The principal crimes to which visitors are likely to be exposed are **petty theft** and **mugging**. Your main defence against these is to exercise common sense and refrain from flaunting luxury items, expensive cameras and snazzy mobile phones. Beware of pickpockets in markets, bus stations and areas popular with tourists – especially the historic quarters of the three capital cities and busy beach resorts like Palanga and Jūrmala.

Take out an **insurance policy** before you leave home (see p.40) and always stow a photocopy of the last page of your passport in a safe place – this will enable your consulate to issue you with new travel documents in the event of your passport being stolen.

Car theft (either its contents, or the whole vehicle) is an ever-present danger. It's worth paying to leave your car in a guarded car park (hotels will either have one of their own or tell you where the nearest is), and avoid leaving your car on the street unless it's equipped with immobilizers. Never leave anything of value in your car if you park it in unguarded car parks, near isolated beaches or in rural beauty spots (especially national parks) – all high-risk areas for theft.

Although younger policemen are likely to understand at least some English, Russian is more common among their older colleagues. **Police** are usually courteous and businesslike in their dealings with foreigners, but may be slow to fill out reports should you be unlucky enough to have anything stolen. A mixture of patience and persistence should be enough to resolve most problems.

Electricity

220 volts. Round, two-pin plugs are used, so it's best to get hold of an adaptor before leaving home.

Entry requirements

Citizens of the US, EU member states, Australia, New Zealand and Canada are allowed **visa-free** entry into Latvia, Estonia and Lithuania. Nationals of other countries should check on visa regulations at the relevant embassy or consulate before setting out.

Visitors are allowed to stay in each Baltic State for a total of ninety days in any given calendar year. If you wish to stay longer you'll need to apply for a residence or work permit – simply crossing the border and re-entering again every ninety days won't work. Up-to-date **information** on entrance regulations and visa costs can be found on the websites of the relevant foreign ministry: ⓦ www.vm.ee for Estonia, www.mfa.gov.lv or www.am.gov.lv for Latvia, and www.urm.lt for Lithuania.

Baltic embassies and consulates

Australia and New Zealand Latvia: ☎ 02/9555 7230, ⓔ birzulis@tpq.com.au; Lithuania: ☎ 02/6253 2062.

Canada Estonia: ☎ 613/789-4222, ⓦ www.estemb.ca; Latvia: ☎ 613/238-6014, ⓦ www.ottawa.am.gov.lv; Lithuania: ☎ 613/567-5458, ⓦ www.lithuanianembassy.ca.

Ireland Estonia: ☎ 01/219 6730, ⓔ embassy.dublin@mfa.ee; Latvia: ☎ 01/428 3320, ⓔ embassy.ireland@mfa.gov.lv; Lithuania: ☎ 01/668 8292, ⓦ ie.mfa.lt.

UK Estonia: ☎ 020/7589 3428, ⓦ www.estonia.gov.uk; Latvia: ☎ 020/7312 0040, ⓔ embassy.uk@mfa.gov.lv; Lithuania: ☎ 020/7486 6401, ⓦ uk.mfa.lt.

US Estonia: ☎ 202/588-0101, ⊛ www.estemb.org; Latvia: ☎ 202/328-2840, ⊛ www.latvia-usa.org; Lithuania: ☎ 202/234-5860, ⊛ www.ltembassyus.org.

Gay and lesbian travellers

Although homosexuality is legal in the Baltic States, social attitudes remain conservative. Generally speaking, young, educated urban-dwellers are increasingly open-minded on questions of sexual preference, but few other sections of society can muster much in the way of tolerance. The Estonian capital **Tallinn** boasts a broad range of openly gay bars and clubs, whereas Lithuania's main city **Vilnius** has just a couple. The Latvian capital **Rīga** is somewhere in between. Outside the capitals, the scene is either non-existent or so far underground that you won't be able to find it without local knowledge. Good general sources of **information** are ⊛ www.gay.ee in Estonia; www.gay.lv in Latvia; and www.gay.lt in Lithuania.

Health

The health risks of travelling in the Baltic States are minimal, and no immunizations are required before you visit. If you plan to do a lot of walking in woodland areas between March and October, it's worth considering getting vaccinated against tick-borne **encephalitis**, though the chance of contracting the disease from a single tick-bite is very low.

The local **tap water** is safe to drink, despite frequently being somewhat less than palatable.

Minor complaints can be treated at a **pharmacy** (*apteek* in Estonia, *aptieka* in Latvia, *vaistinė* in Lithuania), most of which stock a wide range of international drugs. Pharmacy **opening hours** vary widely, but generally they're Mon–Fri 8am–8pm, Sat 8/10am–3pm; some city-centre establishments open on Sundays as well. Big cities will have at least one pharmacy with a night counter; details of where to find the nearest one are posted in the windows of most other pharmacies.

For serious complaints, head for the nearest **hospital** (haigla in Estonia, *slimnīca* in Latvia,

ligoninė in Lithuania) or call an **ambulance** (☎ 112 in all three Baltic States). Emergency treatment is free in all three Baltic States, but in the event of your being admitted to hospital, you'll be charged a small fee for your bed space and for drugs. Although the standard of medical training is high, public hospitals are under-funded and staff are unlikely to speak much English. **Private clinics** with English-speaking doctors exist in the major cities – and are a much better bet if you have a decent travel insurance policy (see "Insurance" below). Always check what the fee covers when booking an appointment with a private practitioner – many of them assume that all Westerners are insured to the hilt and will happily pay through the nose for unnecessary treatment.

Insurance

Even though EU healthcare privileges apply in Estonia, Latvia and Lithuania, you'd do well to take out an **insurance policy** before travelling to cover against theft, loss and illness or injury. Before paying for a new policy, however, it's worth checking whether you are already covered: some all-risks home insurance policies may cover your possessions when overseas, and many private medical schemes include cover when abroad. In Canada, provincial health plans usually provide partial cover for medical mishaps overseas, while holders of official student/teacher/youth cards in Canada and the US are entitled to meagre accident coverage and hospital in-patient benefits. Students will often find that their student health coverage extends during the vacations and for one term beyond the date of last enrolment.

After exhausting the possibilities above, you might want to contact a specialist travel insurance company, or consider the travel insurance deal offered by Rough Guides (see box opposite). A typical travel insurance policy usually provides cover for the loss of baggage, tickets and – up to a certain limit – cash or cheques, as well as cancellation or curtailment of your journey. Most of them exclude so-called dangerous sports unless an extra premium is paid: in the Baltic States dangerous sports can include skiing, though probably not

Rough Guides travel insurance

Rough Guides has teamed up with WorldNomads.com to offer great **travel insurance** deals. Policies are available to residents of over 150 countries, with cover for a wide range of **adventure sports**, 24 hour emergency assistance, high levels of medical and evacuation cover and a stream of **travel safety information**. Roughguides.com users can take advantage of their policies online 24/7, from anywhere in the world – even if you're already travelling. And since plans often change when you're on the road, you can extend your policy and even claim online. Roughguides.com users who buy travel insurance with WorldNomads.com can also leave a positive footprint and donate to a community development project. For more information go to ⓦ**www .roughguides.com/shop**.

kayaking. Many policies can be chopped and changed to exclude coverage you don't need – for example, sickness and accident benefits can often be excluded or included at will. If you do take medical coverage, ascertain whether benefits will be paid as treatment proceeds or only after return home, and whether there is a 24-hour medical emergency number.

When securing baggage cover, make sure that the per-article limit – typically under £500 – will cover your most valuable possession. If you need to make a claim, you should keep receipts for medicines and medical treatment, and in the event you have anything stolen, you must obtain an official statement from the police.

Maps

The **maps** in this book should be adequate for most purposes, but drivers, cyclists and hikers will require something more detailed. The city plans and regional maps stocked by local tourist offices tend towards the rudimentary and are rarely given away free.

Latvian publishers **Jāņa Sēta**, who themselves run a lovely travel bookshop in Rīga, provide the most comprehensive coverage of the Baltics with regularly updated maps. The three countries are available separately at 1:500,000, or combined into a pocket-size atlas at the same scale, with 72 street plans in addition. Jāņa Sēta also produces the best individual fold-out maps of the three Baltic capitals, as well as most other cities and provincial towns in Latvia and Lithuania.

If you intend to do some serious **hiking** you'll need to get hold of more detailed

maps. In **Latvia**, Jāņa Sēta produces indispensable maps of the national parks, while other areas are covered by the 1:50,000 maps in the Latvijas republikas satelitkarte series, though they're hard to get hold of – the Jāņa Sēta bookshop (see p.190) is the most likely outlet.

In **Lithuania**, local firm **Briedis** publishes a series of 1:130,000 regional road maps that cover just about every country lane and farmstead. Lithuania's national park areas are badly served, and you might have to rely on the rough-and-ready maps provided by local tourist offices.

In **Estonia**, the highly detailed 1:50,000 **Eesti kaardikeskus** series are useful for walking, although not all shops stock them. Also handy are the **Regio** 1:100,000 maps of national parks and islands.

The media

Specific information on Estonian, Latvian and Lithuanian newspapers, magazines and TV can be found in the Guide under each country's "Media" section.

A small number of useful **English-language publications** are available Baltic-wide. Prime among these is the *Baltic Times* (ⓦ www .baltictimes.com), a pan-Baltic weekly newspaper based in Rīga. Published every Thursday, it carries a mixture of local news, features and business info, with entertainment listings for the coming weekend. It is sold in newspaper kiosks in all three Baltic capitals and in a few provincial cities like Kaunas in Lithuania and Tartu in Estonia, but is hard to get hold of elsewhere.

Other handy publications are the small-format **city guides** produced by In Your

Pocket (® www.inyourpocket.com). Incorporating information on accommodation, eating, drinking and sightseeing, their separate publications on Tallinn, Rīga and Vilnius (each updated every two months) are lively, opinionated and up-to-date – and an invaluable source of Yellow-Pages-style information. The same company produces guides to Tartu and Pärnu in Estonia and Kaunas and Klaipėda in Lithuania, each of which is updated annually. The guides are on sale in big bookshops in the three Baltic capitals, but can be hard to find in the provinces.

Money

Estonia adopted the **euro** on January 1, 2011, and the national currencies of Latvia and Lithuania are both pegged to the euro, ensuring fairly stable exchange rates for the foreseeable future. The Latvian lats (Ls) works out at about 0.70Ls to €1, 0.85Ls to £1 and 0.55Ls to US$1; and the Lithuanian litas (Lt) at about 3.45Lt to €1, 4Lt to £1, 2.80Lt to $1.

The major **credit and charge cards** – Visa, MasterCard, American Express and Diners Club – are accepted in the bigger hotels, restaurants and shops throughout the Baltic States, although most medium- and small-sized businesses only take cash.

Phones

Phone boxes offering international direct dialling are plentiful; English instructions are often posted inside. **Phone cards** are most commonly available from newspaper and tobacco kiosks, although post offices and supermarket checkouts often sell them as well.

GSM **mobile phone** networks enjoy almost blanket coverage in the Baltic States – and the absence of high mountains helps ensure that there are very few blind spots. Check with your phone provider whether your mobile will work abroad, and what the call charges are; you may need to pay a hefty deposit to get your international access switched on. If you want to retrieve messages while you're away, you'll have to ask your provider for a new access code, as your home one is unlikely to work abroad.

One of the most convenient ways of phoning home is to buy a **telephone charge card** from your phone company back home. Using a PIN number, you can make calls from most hotel, public and private phones and the calls are charged to your account; contact your phone company for information.

For information on pre-paid **SIM cards**, see each individual country's "Basics" section.

Saunas

Most Baltic hotels will have a sauna on site. Usually it costs money to use them, though they're often free to guests at certain times of the day. Many people have saunas built into their homes, and visitors are often invited to share one – it's a sure sign that they value your friendship and the offer should not be refused lightly. In the

---

International dialling codes

To **phone the Baltic States**, dial your country's international access code, then:
Estonia ☎372
Latvia ☎371
Lithuania ☎370

To phone **from the Baltic States**, dial:
Australia ☎0061 + area code minus its initial zero.
Britain ☎0044 + area code minus its initial zero.
Ireland ☎00353 + area code minus its initial zero.
New Zealand ☎0064 + area code minus its initial zero.
US & Canada ☎001.

countryside, look out for old-style, log-fired saunas – smokey, pungent and usually followed by a dip in an ice-cold lake.

Time

Estonia, Latvia and Lithuania are two hours ahead of the UK, and seven hours ahead of New York, with clocks going forwards and backwards in March and October respectively.

Tourist information

Each of the Baltic States has a national **tourist board**, and is in the process of setting up **information centres** in other European capitals. If there is no Lithuanian, Latvian or Estonian tourist information office in your home country, you can contact their central offices (in Vilnius, Rīga and Tallinn respectively).

Almost every major city and resort in the Baltic States has a **tourist office** where you can pick up information; most can also book accommodation on your behalf. Staff usually have a working knowledge of English; German and Russian are the other most frequently spoken languages. You'll find details of individual offices throughout the guide.

National tourist boards

Estonian National Tourist Association ⓦwww .visitestonia.com.
Latvian Tourism Development Agency ⓦwww .latviatourism.lv.
Lithuanian State Department of Tourism ⓦwww.travel.lt.

Tourist offices in the UK
Latvian Tourism Bureau 72 Queensborough Terrace, London W2 3SH ⓣ020/7229 8271, ⓔlondon@latviatourism.lv.
Lithuanian Tourist Information Centre 86 Gloucester Place, London W1U 6HP ⓣ020/7034 1222, ⓦwww.lithuaniatourism.co.uk.

Travellers with disabilities

Many public places in the Baltic States are **wheelchair-accessible**, especially in larger cities, though in general, access to public transport and tourist sites still leaves a lot to be desired.

Spa visits, rest cures and mud baths have been an important aspect of Baltic tourism since the mid-nineteenth century, and it's in the **spa resorts** that you're most likely to find hotels used to receiving guests with disabilities. In Estonia, Haapsalu, Kuressaare and Pärnu have a particularly good range of facilities. Forest-fringed Druskininkai, Lithuania's oldest health resort, also caters well to disabled visitors.

Elsewhere, especially in the capital cities, there's a growing number of **wheelchair-accessible hotels**, though these tend to be in the more expensive price brackets. Tourist offices throughout the Baltics will usually identify suitable accommodation facilities in their region if you ring in advance, but be sure to double-check the information they give you – some hotels advertise disabled facilities, but haven't got round to building them yet.

Work and study

Casual work in the Baltic States is hard to find unless you know one of the local languages, and wages are in any case low – anything above €600/£500/$720 a month is generous. The back pages of the *Baltic Times* (see p.41) occasionally advertise vacancies for English-speaking job-seekers, but opportunities are thin on the ground.

Teaching English is probably your best bet: there's a growing demand for native-language English teachers in the private language schools that have recently sprung up all over the region. However, you'll need a **CELTA** (Certificate in English Language Teaching to Adults) qualification in order to secure a job at any but the most fly-by-night organizations. Vacancies are sometimes advertised in the education supplements of Western newspapers; otherwise it's a question of touting your CV around the language schools and making use of local contacts once you arrive.

There are several **language-learning** opportunities in the Baltic States. In Lithuania, Vilnius University organizes two- and four-week intensive **Lithuanian courses** in summer, as well as a one-year programme spanning two university semesters. Full details are available from the Department of Lithuanian Studies, Vilnius University,

Universiteto 5, 2734 Vilnius (☎+370 5/268 7215, ⓦwww.lsk.flf.vu.lt).

Lithuania is also a good place to learn **Yiddish**: the local Jewish community, in association with Vilnius University, organizes intensive four-week language courses in August, as well as year-long university courses. Full details are available on ⓦwww .judaicvilnius.com. In Latvia, the Valodu Mācību Centrs ("Language Study Centre"), Elizabetes iela 85a, Rīga (☎6735 8032; ⓦwww.vmc.lv), offers tuition in **Latvian**.

In Estonia, Tartu University runs a year-long **Estonian** language course for foreign students and has been known to organize short-term intensive courses – consult ⓦwww.ut.ee/english for details. The same university also organizes a two-semester **Baltic Studies** programme (ⓦwww.baltic .ut.ee), taught in English and featuring a pick-and-mix menu of politics-, history- and culture-related courses. The website ⓦwww .studyinestonia.ee has more information on long-term study possibilities in the country.

Guide

Guide

Estonia

Estonia highlights

✳ **Tallinn Old Town** A tightly packed maze of narrow streets overlooked by proud merchants' houses and medieval church spires. See p.66

✳ **Kadriorg, Tallinn** This leafy park, laid out by Peter the Great for his mistress, is now home to the finest art museum in the Baltics. See p.78

✳ **Saaremaa** This popular holiday island offers the best of Estonia's maritime landscape, its starkly beautiful heathland dotted with windmills, lighthouses and even the odd meteorite crater. See p.98

✳ **Pärnu** A glorious white-sand beach and vibrant, summertime nightlife. See p.105

✳ **Lahemaa National Park** You'll find an unparalleled variety of unspoilt natural environments here, from dense pine forests to bogs and desolate, boulder-strewn shores. See p.116

✳ **Tartu** Handsome historic architecture, quirky museums and a vibrant after-dark drinking scene characterize this easy-going university town. See p.126

✳ **Setumaa** Home to the Setu, a dwindling branch of the Estonian people attached to the Orthodox Church, Setumaa is one of the most rewarding and mysterious corners of the country, with bucolic villages set amid rippling hills. See p.144

△ Kadriorg Palace

Introduction and basics

It's a tribute to the resilience of the Estonians that during the short years since the Declaration of Independence in August 1991 they've transformed their country from a dour outpost of the former Soviet Union into a forward-looking, economically stable nation that boasts the highest rates of computer and mobile-phone ownership in the Baltic region. Estonia weathered the recent storms of financial crisis better than her Baltic-Tiger neighbours, ensuring relatively pain-free admission to the eurozone in January 2011. The creation of a go-ahead, technologically advanced nation-state is even more impressive in light of the fact that Estonians have ruled their own country for barely forty years out of the past eight hundred. A Finno-Ugric people related to the Finns, the Estonians have had the misfortune to be surrounded by powerful, warlike neighbours. The first to conquer Estonia were the Danes, who arrived at the start of the thirteenth century; they were succeeded in turn by German crusading knights, Swedes and then Russians. Following a mid-nineteenth-century cultural revival known as the National Awakening, the collapse of Germany and Tsarist Russia allowed the Estonians to snatch their independence in 1918. Their brief freedom between the two world wars was extinguished by the Soviets in 1940 and Estonia disappeared from view again. When the country re-emerged from the Soviet shadow in 1991, some forty percent of its population were Russians who had been encouraged to settle there during the Soviet era.

Where to go

Estonia's capital, **Tallinn**, is a fascinating combination of quaint medieval town and glitzy, go-ahead metropolis, with a choice of restaurants, bars and clubs wide enough to bring out the hedonist in anyone. By way of complete contrast, the **Lahemaa National Park**, east of Tallinn, possesses one of the most enticing mixtures of forests, fishing villages and manorial estates in the Baltics, its deeply indented coastline pebble-dashed with an enigmatic collection of boulders.

Of the east Estonian cities, the gruff border city of **Narva** is worth visiting for its superb fortress, although it's the historic university town of **Tartu**, full of inviting museums, pubs and parks, that exerts most appeal. Tartu is also a great base from which to visit the unspoilt countryside of the south, with ski-resort **Otepää** and small-town **Võru** providing access to a rolling landscape of pudding-shaped hills – one of which, **Suur-Munamägi**, is the highest point in the Baltics at a cloud-scraping 300m above sea level. In the far southeast, bucolic villages inhabited by the Russian sect of Old Believers and the Orthodox Estonian Setu provide an insight into the country's cultural diversity.

Most beach tourism is located on the west coast, where laid-back, genteel **Haapsalu** and boisterous, party-hard **Pärnu** are the main places to aim for. For a taste of the Estonian coast's desolate beauty, head for islands like **Hiiumaa** and **Saaremaa**, their lighthouse-scattered shores and inland juniper heaths perfect for hiking and cycling. As well as being a popular spa resort, Saaremaa's capital **Kuressaare** boasts one of the finest castles in the Baltics.

Getting around

Given the relative lack of fast, two-lane highways, Estonia can be a slow country to get around. That said, if you're relying on **public transport** you're more likely to use the well-organized and extensive bus network than Estonia's trains, which have been cut back drastically.

Buses

Bus travel is the main form of public transport in Estonia, and there's hardly a town

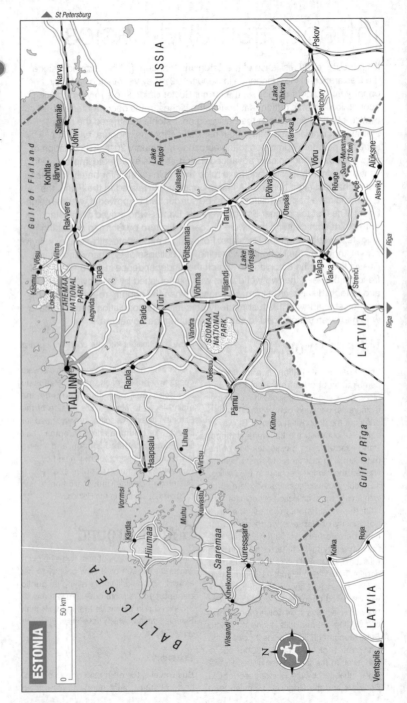

ESTONIA

St Petersburg

RUSSIA

Narva
Sillamäe
Jõhvi
Kohtla-
Järve
Rakvere
V
Gulf of Finland
Käsmu Võsu
Loksa
Viitna
LAHEMAA
NATIONAL
PARK
Aegviidu
Tapa
Turi
Paide
Vändra
SOOMAA
NATIONAL
PARK
Jõesuu
Rapla
Haapsalu
Lihula
Virtsu
Vormsi
Kärdla
Hiiumaa
Kuivastu
Muhu
Saaremaa
Kuressaare
Kihelkonna
Vilsandi

TALLINN

Pöltsamaa
Võhma
Viljandi
Lake
Võrtsjärv

Pärnu
Kihnu

Gulf of Riga

Kolka
Roja

Ventspils

LATVIA

LATVIA

BALTIC SEA

Kallaste
Lake
Peipsi
3

Tartu
Otepää
Põlva
Võru
Rõuge
Suur-Munamägi
(318m)
Aluksne
Alsviki
Apē
Varska
Petchory
Lake
Pihkva
Pskov

Valga
Valka
Strenči

Riga
Riga

N

BALTIC SEA

0   50 km

in the country that isn't served by at least one daily service from Tallinn. Buses linking the main cities are frequent, fast and comfortable, while those on rural routes often look like museum pieces and rarely exceed speeds of 30km/hr. Express buses (marked with a red "E" on timetables) make fewer stops and cost slightly more than regular services.

Tickets (*pilet*) can be bought from the driver or from the bus-station ticket office in advance – wise if you're travelling on a popular inter-city route at a weekend, when buses fill up quickly. Luggage is usually stowed in the luggage compartment. Prices differ according to the operating company, but you should expect to pay around €10 for major inter-city journeys such as Tallinn–Tartu and Tallinn–Pärnu, much less for shorter trips in the provinces. Buses from the mainland to the islands are more expensive, but the price of the ferry crossing is included in your ticket – expect to pay around €15 for the Tallinn–Kuressaare or Tartu–Kuressaare journey.

Estonian bus **timetables** (*sõiduplaan*) are quite complicated at first glance, with lots of specific annotations that are important to get the hang of if you want to be sure that a particular service is travelling on a particular day. Days of the week on which a service runs are usually denoted by a letter (eg "E" for *esmaspäev* or Monday; see p.392 for the days of the week in Estonian). The abbreviation "v.a." before a particular letter means "runs every day except…". *Iga päev* means "every day"; *tööpäev* means "working day" (ie Mon–Sat). The Estonian for "departure" is *väljub*, and "arrival" is *saabub*. Some timetables simply list a departure time and nothing else; others may have four columns of timings, denoting time of departure, time of arrival at destination, time of departure back to original starting point, time of arrival back at original starting point – useful if you're planning a day out.

Although a few bus-station employees speak English (especially in Tallinn), it's best to have a pen and paper handy. The English-speaking **information** line on ☎1182 handles inter-city bus information, while timetables for most of the national network are available at 🌐www.bussireisid.ee.

Trains

Trains are on the whole slower, less frequent and only slightly cheaper than buses, so unless you have a particular preference for rail travel, there's no compelling reason to use them. Tallinn is the only place in the country that has a permanently manned **train station** – all the rest either have sporadically open ticket windows or are simply unstaffed. Destinations you can reach by train are limited: regular commuter trains run from Tallinn to nearby towns, and there are less frequent long-distance services to Rakvere and Viljandi. Moscow (daily) is the only international destination covered.

For international services, **tickets** (*pilet*) should be bought in advance. For domestic services, buy them in advance if you're beginning your journey from Tallinn – otherwise, pay the conductor. Train **timetables** use pretty much the same terminology as those displayed in bus stations (see above).

Driving

Driving in Estonia is not too nervewracking, with main roads in reasonable condition and traffic fairly light outside the towns. Reckless driving is the exception rather than the rule, but watch out for people showing off in BMWs and four-wheel drives. There's no motorway to speak of – just a few stretches of two-lane highway either side of Tallinn and another near Pärnu.

To bring a car into Estonia you need a valid Green Card. **Speed limits** are 50kph in built-up areas and 90kph on the open road – some sections of highway allow speeds of 100kph or 110kph. The wearing of seatbelts is compulsory for the driver and all passengers, and headlights should be switched on at all times. In towns it's forbidden to overtake stationary trams so that passengers can alight in safety, and it's against the law to drive after drinking any alcohol whatsoever. Petrol stations can be a little thin on the ground in rural areas, so it's advisable to carry a spare can.

For information on **car rental**, see Basics, p.34.

Ferries

Roll-on, roll-off **ferries** operated by the state shipping line (🌐www.laevakompanii.ee)

Addresses

In Estonian addresses the name of the street or square comes first, the number second. The following terms or their abbreviations are commonly encountered: *väljak* – square; *tee* or *mantee* (mnt) – road; *puistee* (pst) – avenue; and *tänav* (tn) – street.

connect the Estonian mainland with the main islands, with services from Rohuküla near Haapsalu to **Hiiumaa** (5–7 daily), and sailings from Virtsu serving **Saaremaa** (hourly) and **Vormsi** (2–4 daily). The smaller islands of Vormsi and Kihnu are served by Veeteed (both 2 daily; www.veeteed.com)

Prices are very reasonable: if you're travelling by bus, the cost of the crossing will be included in your ticket; otherwise, expect to pay €3–4 per person one-way for these services, with an additional €5–6 for a car. Although journey times are short (about 90min to Hiiumaa, less than 1hr to Saaremaa and Vormsi), ferries have a well-stocked cafeteria on board.

The island of **Kihnu**, off Estonia's southern coast, is served by a couple of daily, **privately run** ferries from the tiny port of Munalaiu, southwest of Pärnu. Prices are around €4 per person, €10 per car.

Cycling

Estonia, being predominantly flat, makes perfect **cycling** terrain, although there aren't any cycle lanes and – on the mainland at least – you can't expect much consideration from other road users. Things are slightly better on the **islands**, where cyclists are common in summer and there's more in the way of prepared routes and signage. While motor traffic can still be a problem on the roads of the two biggest islands, Saaremaa and Hiiumaa, cyclists will have the country lanes to themselves on Vormsi and Kihnu, where there are far fewer cars.

Flights

Although there are no domestic services linking Estonia's inland cities, **flying** can be a quick way of getting to the islands. Avies (℡ 605 8022; www.avies.ee) operates flights from Tallinn to Kärdla; while Estonian Air (www.estonian-air.ee) handles the Tallinn-Kuressaare route.

Accommodation

Tallinn and other Estonian cities boast a healthy stock of modern, comfortable hotels on a par with those in any Western European city. Most towns also have one or two reasonable budget hotels, and an increasing number of inexpensive guesthouses and B&Bs exist in rural areas and on the islands. Other cheap options include a handful of hostels, a few private rooms (mostly in Tallinn) and a scattering of campsites.

Hotels

Estonian **hotels** (*hotell*) come in all shapes and sizes, from the international-style blocks mushrooming all over Tallinn to the more characterful, mid-size places you're more likely to find in small towns and on the islands. Most hotel stock has been either refurbished or built from scratch in the last ten to twenty years, and swish interior design and gleaming bathrooms tend to be the rule rather than the exception.

A buffet **breakfast** is included in the price in almost all but the cheapest hotels, where you'll probably have to buy your own in a nearby café. **Prices** for plain, but clean, double rooms range from €40 to €60. For this, you're likely to get a basic en-suite shower, WC, and a small TV. If you want plusher furnishings and swanky bathroom fittings you'll be paying more like €60–€80. Anything more than this will buy you international-standard four-star comforts. Rates in the main cities and towns are the same all year round – although many offer weekend discounts and it never hurts to ask. In coastal areas, hotels are often twenty- to thirty percent cheaper in the off-season (Oct–April) – even hotels that don't advertise an off-peak rate will usually be open to bargaining during this period.

Small hotels in rural areas may close from October to April. Even those that claim to stay open during the winter may refuse to take bookings from individuals or groups of less than four or five – it's not worth their while turning the heating on if only one or two rooms are occupied.

Families are better catered for in Estonia than its Baltic neighbours: children under 3 usually stay for free, while those under 14 (sometimes 16) get a thirty- to fifty percent discount if sleeping in the same room as their parents. Many hotels offer two-room suites with a bedroom and a living room with fold-down beds.

All hotels of any size will have one or more **saunas**. They cost from €13 to €20 an hour to use, although guests might be allowed to use them for free during off-peak hours (ie early in the morning). Provision of **non-smoking** rooms is standard, and the vast majority of small and medium-sized hotels are non-smoking throughout.

Guesthouses, B&Bs and private rooms

In Tallinn's suburbs, provincial towns and rural areas a growing number of small, family-run establishments offer homely bed-and-breakfast accommodation for lower prices than those offered by the hotels. If one of these places has five rooms or more, it's classified as a **guesthouse** (*külalistemaja*); otherwise it's a **B&B** (*kodumajutus*). Standards are hard to predict: the snazzier places will have en-suite rooms with TV; others will offer simply furnished, but cosy, rooms with communal WC/shower in the hallway. Guesthouses and B&Bs based on working farms often go under the name of **turismi-talu** or "tourist farmstead", and may offer horseriding and other activities as part of the package. Prices for guesthouses and B&Bs range from €30 to €50 for a double.

Tourist offices provide information on local guesthouses and B&Bs, and will in most cases make reservations on your behalf.

The **Estonian Rural Travel Association**'s website (🌐 www.maaturism.ee) contains locations and contact details for rural B&Bs throughout the country; rural B&Bs can also be booked through Latvian agency Lauku ceļotājs (see p.152).

In Tallinn, Tartu and Pärnu, another cheap alternative to hotels are **private rooms**. These usually involve staying in the spare room of an apartment-block dweller and sharing their WC/bathroom. Although you'll usually be greeted by a spick-and-span room and a friendly host, these standards can't be guaranteed. Prices are around €20 for a single, €35 for a double. The Rasastra agency in Tallinn (see p.61) can fix you up with rooms in all three cities; otherwise contact Tartu's tourist office (p.127).

Hostels and camping

Estonia has a growing number of backpacker-friendly **hostels**. Most are concentrated in Tallinn, although there is a handful in the provinces. Bunk-bed accommodation in dorms is the norm, although most hostels have the odd private double or triple. Prices start at around €10 per person.

The most basic form of **campsite** (*kämping*) in Estonia is a simple patch of ground where you're allowed to pitch a tent for €4–€6. Earth toilets may be provided, but running water usually isn't. These sites are particularly common in the Lahemaa National Park (where camping is actually free, provided you stick to the official, park-run sites) – wardens call every day to collect rubbish and drop off free firewood. Many small hotels and guesthouses in rural Estonia allow camping in the garden for about €5 – in these places you'll be allowed access to a toilet and running water.

Some larger campsites are equipped with toilets and washing facilities and also provide

---

Accommodation price codes

The hotels and guesthouses listed in the Estonian chapters of this guide have been graded according to the following price bands, based on the cost of the least expensive double room in summer.

❶ €30 and under
❷ €31–40
❸ €41–50
❹ €51–70
❺ €71–100
❻ €101–130
❼ €131–200
❽ €201 and over

accommodation in three- to four-bed **cabins** for around €12 per person. Caravans are a novelty in Estonia, although there are at least a couple of sites (at Pärnu and near Võsu in the Lahemaa National Park) that have electricity points for trailers.

Food and drink

For centuries, rye bread, salted herring and beer formed the Estonians' staple **diet**, with roast pork making an appearance on festive occasions. Such staples are still the norm, although there's a great deal else besides.

Eating in towns and cities usually takes place in **restaurants** (*restoran*) with menus and table service, or in **cafés** (*kohvik*) where you order and pay at the counter. Cafés often provide a simpler menu of main courses than restaurants and are usually much cheaper – they're also good places to tuck into snacks and sweets. In rural or well-touristed areas you'll come across traditional **inns** (*kõrts*), which cater for both eaters and drinkers and concentrate on standard Estonian meat-and-potato dishes. In addition, a lot of **pubs** and bars (see "Drinking", opposite) offer a full menu. Restaurants and inns are usually open till 10pm in small towns and rural areas, 11pm or midnight in cities and resorts. Cafés usually close at around 7/8pm, earlier on Sundays. By and large, you should be able to have a decent meal (two courses and a drink) for around €15 in restaurants, €8 in cafés, although **prices** in Tallinn are creeping ever upwards. Look out for restaurants and cafés offering excellent deals on a dish of the day (*päevapraad*).

For self-catering and **picnicking**, basics like bread, cheese, smoked meat and tinned fish can be picked up in supermarkets, while the full range of fruit and vegetables is available at outdoor markets in most towns of any size. Most high streets have a bakery (*pagariän*).

What to eat

As in much of northern Europe, calorific meat dishes and dairy products set the tone, although you can find plenty in the way of salads and ethnic foods – especially in Tallinn

and other cities. You'll find a **glossary** of food and drink terms on p.393.

Snacks, starters and salads

The most characteristic Estonian **starter** is *sült*, a mixture of pork bits set in jelly that is an acquired taste; a family meal or festive occasion would be unthinkable without a big bowl of the stuff on the table. Salted herring (*heeringas* or *räim*), smoked eel (*angerjas*) and sliced sausage (*voorst*) frequently feature as restaurant starters or bar snacks and invariably come with a few slices of delicious dark rye bread (*leib*).

Soup (*supp*) is eaten either as a starter or a lunchtime snack; available pretty much everywhere is *seljanka*, a broth of Russian origin featuring meat, vegetables and pickled gherkin. Other light meals that you'll come across – in cafés more often than in restaurants – include *pelmenid* (ravioli-like parcels of minced meat), *pirukas* (dough stuffed with bacon, cabbage or other fillings) and *pankoogid* (pancakes) which can come with cheese, meat or mushrooms.

Many cafés offer **salads** (*salat*), which can range from a sorry-looking bowl of peas and gherkins drenched in sour cream to a healthy platter of greens and other ingredients, substantial enough to serve as a light meal in its own right – tuna salad (*tuunikasalat*) is one of the most common.

Main courses

The quintessential Estonian **main course** comprises pork (*sia*), potatoes (*kartulid*) and sauerkraut (*mulgikapsad*) – and during the Soviet era this was all that most restaurants ever bothered serving. **Pork** is most commonly served roasted or pan-fried in the form of a *karbonaad* – a chop coated in tasty batter. Cuts usually come with a healthy rind of fat which, when properly cooked, can be quite delicious. Other **meats** that crop up regularly on menus are chicken (*kana*), steak (*biifsteik*) and a locally produced form of blood sausage known as *verevoorst*. Lamb (*lamba*) is much less common unless you're eating in a grill restaurant devoted to Caucasian cooking, in which case it will probably feature in a *šašlõkk* (shish kebab). Freshwater **fish** (*kala*) figures strongly on restaurant menus, with pan-fried trout (*forell*), perch (*ahven*) or pike (*haug*) being the most popular. Main courses are usually served with potatoes and seasonal vegetables and often sour cream (*hapukoor*).

Vegetarians are not well catered for, though a few places make a token effort – especially the growing number of (generally pretty good) ethnic restaurants in Tallinn.

Desserts

Estonian cafés serve up a mouth-watering array of **sweets**, most of which crop up on restaurant menus, too. The satisfyingly smooth *mannapuder* (semolina pudding) rules the roost as far as indigenous desserts are concerned – it often comes garnished with local fruits and berries. Pancakes, usually filled with jam, are also ubiquitous. If you want a daytime nibble to go with your coffee then you can choose between a sticky bun (*sai*) or a slice of cake (*kook*) – the latter is a blanket term covering everything from chocolate cake and cheesecake to fruit flan. One local delicacy you'll see in the best bakeries and delicatessens is *kringel*, a sweet loaf filled with dried fruit.

Drinking

Estonians are enthusiastic drinkers, with **beer** (*õlu*) being the most popular tipple. The principal local brands are Saku and A. Le Coq, both of which are rather tame, lager-style brews, although both companies also produce stronger porters (*tume*). The strongest beers are found on the islands – best known is the deceptively sweet Saaremaa õlu (widely available in supermarkets, less so in bars), which has twice the alcohol content of regular brands. Inland, a number of smaller breweries continue to supply the pubs in their local areas, notably Wiru in the northeast – their Palmse porter is well worth trying. Beer is sold in measures of 0.3 or 0.5 of a litre, although many establishments outside Tallinn only stock 0.5 litre glasses, believing the consumption of lesser quantities to be an affectation.

Most common of the spirits is **vodka** (*viin*) – either the locally made Viru Valge or Russian brands – which is usually drunk with juice or a fizzy-drink mixer. Local alcoholic specialities include *hõõgvein* (mulled wine) and Vana Tallinn, a syrupy, medicinal-looking liqueur, best mixed with blackcurrant juice or black coffee.

Coffee (*kohv*) sometimes comes as espresso or cappuccino in the better cafés, although filter coffee is more common and it's usually served black, unless you specify *koorega* (with cream).

The media

Given a national population of 1,340,000 (of which only 68 percent are native Estonian speakers), the range of newspapers and magazines cluttering up Estonia's street kiosks is staggering, with titles covering every conceivable interest group from computer nerds to dog breeders.

The most prestigious of the **national daily newspapers** is *Eesti Postimees* (Ⓦ www .postimees.ee), founded in Tartu in 1867 and still required reading for the political and business elite – the Friday edition carries good cultural listings, too. Mass-market **tabloids** *Eesti Päevaleht* and *Sõnumileht* make up for lightweight news coverage with racy showbiz gossip. Best of the **weeklies** is *Eesti Ekspress*, which mixes political reporting with extensive cultural coverage.

There's also a huge array of Moscow-published newspapers and magazines in the kiosks, including the seductively stylish Russian-language editions of major international fashion and design monthlies. Locally produced **English-language** publications are thin on the ground, although there's good pickings if you're interested in the visual arts: *kunst.ee* is a superbly designed art monthly with intelligent articles in Estonian and English.

The state-run Eesti TV and the privately owned TV1, Kanal 2 and TV3 offer a varied diet of home-grown and imported **television** programming, although many Estonians (and most Estonian hotels) have cable packages offering a range of English, German, Finnish and Russian channels. All the Estonian stations show imported films and dramas in the original language with Estonian subtitles. For details of pan-Baltic media in the English language, see p.41.

Festivals

Although traditional festivities and folk practices don't fill the Estonian calendar as they do in Latvia and Lithuania, there are several major **seasonal events**, many of which are related to the traditional work-cycle of the agricultural year.

As elsewhere in Europe, **Easter** is both a Christian feast and a more general celebration of the coming spring, with painted eggs and general over-consumption of festive food. Easter is celebrated with more gusto by Estonia's Orthodox minority, who process around churches with lighted candles at midnight on Easter Saturday – Orthodox Easter takes place anything up to five weeks after the Catholic/Protestant event.

Jaanipaev (St John's Day) is celebrated on June 24. Originally the last chance for a knees-up before the hard work of the harvesting season began, St John's Day is still associated with hedonistic abandon – and for working Estonians it's the most important day off of the summer. On June 23 most people head for the countryside with family and friends and spend the night drinking and carousing, staying up long enough to greet the sunrise on the longest day of the year.

Before World War II, late October was marked by the four-day holiday known as **kliistripühad** ("shutting the windows"), when people mended cracked window frames and sealed up draughty cavities in preparation for the coming winter. Early November is traditionally a period of remembrance roughly analogous to All Souls' Day in Catholic Europe, when families visit cemeteries to tidy graves and lay flowers. This period traditionally comes to an end on **Mardipäev** (St Martin's Day) on November 11, when – in some areas – children dressed as beggars do the rounds of neighbourhood houses asking for treats. Christmas (**Jõulud**) is pretty much the same as in the rest of Europe, with children hassling a fat, bearded bloke (Jõuluvana) for gifts while their parents pig out on roast pork (*seapraad*), gingerbread (*piparkoogid*) and mulled wine (*hõõgvein*).

Entertainment

There's a wide range of classical music and theatre on offer in Estonia, especially in Tallinn, which also has many clubs, cinemas and live music venues.

Classical music

Estonia's principal musical institutions – national symphony orchestra, chamber orchestra, opera and ballet – are all based in Tallinn, although they frequently perform in the provinces, most notably at Tartu and Pärnu. The Ⓦ www.concert.ee site carries schedule details.

Contemporary **classical music** occupies an important place in the regular Estonian repertoire, thanks in large part to local-born composer **Arvo Pärt** (b.1935), whose sparsely orchestrated, meditative pieces have earned him a towering international reputation. Having spent the 1960s experimenting with serialism and other modernist techniques, the devoutly religious Pärt began to develop a much more personal style in the 1970s, with works like *Summa* (1977), the *St John Passion* (1982) and *Stabat Mater* (1986) being acclaimed as classics of spiritually inspired minimalism. No stranger to the Estonian choral tradition, Pärt has also used German-language evensong and medieval Latin in his works.

Considerably more rooted in indigenous folk tradition is Pärt's near-contemporary **Veljo Tormis** (b.1930), whose choral works take their inspiration from the mesmeric, chant-like runic songs that form such an important part in Estonian musical heritage. The best known of Tormis's works is *Curse Upon Iron* (1972), which combines sweeping orchestral passages with archaic, shamanistic drum beats. The other big name in Estonian contemporary music is **Erkki-Sven Tüür** (b. 1959), whose edgy pieces are a regular feature of the Estonian concert repertoire and are increasingly heard abroad.

Clubbing and pop music

There's a growing and increasingly sophisticated choice of **club culture** to be sampled in Tallinn, where you'll find everything from heaving discos playing mainstream chart music to ironic retro clubs and all manner of niche DJ styles. There's a lot of activity outside the capital, too, especially in the student town of Tartu and beach resort of Pärnu.

Some clubs in Tallinn and Tartu host live **gigs** by local pop-rock acts and there is a handful of alternative clubs hosting live bands and DJs, both domestic and foreign. The **Jazzkaar** festival (held in Tallinn every spring; see p.85) is arguably the best jazz event in the Baltics, attracting major international names.

Few Estonian pop-rock acts have made an impression internationally, save perhaps for the manufactured duo of Tanel Pader and Dave Benton, who had the dubious honour of winning the Eurovision Song Contest in 2001. Pader has subsequently re-emerged as a reasonably respectable rock-pop solo artist.

Cinema

Cinemas in Estonia show mainstream movies pretty much immediately after their release in Western Europe. They're shown in the original language, with Estonian subtitles.

During the Soviet period, the Tallinn Film Studio churned out several workmanlike films a year, many of which were made in Russian to appeal to a wider Soviet market. As far as the locals are concerned, the outstanding product of this era was the Estonian-language *The Last Relic* (*Viimne Reliikvia*; 1969), a cross between swashbuckler, sex comedy and musical, set amidst the religious struggles of the sixteenth century and intended to demonstrate that Estonian cinema was as capable of producing lavish historical epics as anyone. It's still great to look at, and some of the countryside scenes could almost pass for an advertisement for the Estonian Tourist Board. Internationally, Estonia is known less for its full-length features than for its animated films, thanks largely to the efforts of the Tallinn-based studio **Nukufilm** (🌐www .nukufilm.ee). Established in 1957 by Elbert Tuganov, the studio has garnered a global reputation for its use of superbly fashioned dolls and puppets. Most of its output is intended for children, although some of the studio's more surreal products – especially recent work by Riho Unt and Mait Laas – go down equally well with the European arthouse crowd.

The big, award-winning name in Estonian cartoon animation is **Priit Pärn**, whose darkly comic films (such as 1998's *Night of the Carrots*) have garnered worldwide cult status.

Travel essentials

Internet

Wi-fi access is more widespread in Estonia than in most other European countries and is usually free: you will find it in hostels, hotels, cafés, bars, and public spaces in town centres. Many of the express bus services operating the Tallinn–Tartu route offer free wi-fi on board – ask when booking your ticket. The rise in wi-fi availability has led to a decline in the number of internet cafés (*interneti kohvik*), although hostels and hotels will usually have at least one terminal for guests. Public libraries, too, have at least one internet terminal available for public use free of charge, although they're often busy.

Left luggage

There's usually a left-luggage office (*pakihõid*) in big-town bus stations, charging €1 per item.

Mail

Estonian post offices (*postkontor*) are in the main efficient, easy to use, and often staffed by English-speakers. They are usually open Monday to Friday 9am to 6/7pm and Saturday 9am to 3pm. You can buy stamps (*postmark*) at post offices and at most newspaper kiosks. Sending a letter or postcard costs €0.50 within Estonia, €0.80 to the rest of Europe, €1.30 to North America or Australasia.

Money

Estonia adopted the euro in January 2011, and the previous national currency (kroon) was withdrawn from circulation. Although costs are rising in Estonia's capital, Tallinn, it's still a reasonably inexpensive destination compared with cities in Western Europe.

Emergencies

Police ☏110; ambulance and fire ☏112.

Things are cheaper still outside the capital. Estonia is one Baltic country in which it's worth having a student discount card: ISIC cardholders get ten percent off in many hotels, reduced entry in museums and often up to thirty percent off theatre and concert tickets. For accommodation and transport costs, see p.52 and p.51.

Credit cards can be used in some of the more expensive hotels, restaurants and stores and in some petrol stations in Tallinn; although you will find places that accept cards outside Tallinn, it's best not to count on it. With plenty of ATMs scattered around town centres, you should have no problem drawing instant cash with a valid debit or credit card. Major banks (*pank*) such as Nordea, SEB and Swedbank can change cash for a commission, cash travellers' cheques (Thomas Cook and American Express preferred) and give cash advances on most major credit cards for a commission of around three percent. Banks are usually open Monday to Friday 9am to 4/6pm; major banks in the cities often open on Saturday from 9am to 2 or 3pm. Exchange offices (*Valuuta vahetus*) usually work longer hours and open on Sundays, too, and in many cases offer lower commission rates than the banks for cash transactions.

Opening hours

Most shops are open Monday to Friday 9/10am to 6/7pm and Saturday 10am to 2/3pm. Some food shops stay open until 10pm or later and are also open on Sundays. Opening hours of museums and galleries vary greatly, although they're usually closed on Mondays and frequently on Tuesdays as well. Estonia's Protestant churches generally close outside Mass times unless they're of historical or artistic importance, in which case their opening hours will be similar to those of museums. Orthodox churches frequented by Estonia's Russian minority are much more likely to be open all day for the benefit of devout locals.

For post office and banking hours, see above.

Phones

Estonia has a problem-free telephone system. Direct international calls can be made

For accommodation and transport costs, see p.52 and p.51.

Public holidays

Most shops, banks and museums close on the following public holidays:

Jan 1 New Year's Day
Feb 24 Independence Day
March/April (variable), Good Friday Easter Sunday
May 1 May Day
June 23 Victory Day
June 24 St John's Day
August 20 Day of Restoration of Independence
December 25 and 26 Christmas

from all phones – simply dial ☎00 followed by the country code. Public telephones (*telefoniputka*) use magnetic cards (available in denominations of €5 and €10 from post offices and newspaper kiosks). For English-language directory enquiries dial ☎1182.

For general information on using mobile phones in the Baltic States, see p.42. If you have a GSM mobile phone you can cut the cost of local calls by buying a pre-paid SIM card (available from newspaper kiosks) from Estonian operators like EMT, Elisa or Tele2.

Smoking

Smoking is largely banned from public places including restaurants, cafés and bars; although establishments which have summer terraces allow smoking on some or all of their outdoor tables. Some bars and nightclubs have a designated smoking area inside, although this is frequently no larger than a cupboard.

Tipping

Tipping is only expected in Estonia if you're in a restaurant or smart café with table service, or if you've had a meal and/or big round of drinks in a bar. In these cases, round up your bill by ten to fifteen percent.

Toilets

Public toilets (*tualettid*) can usually be found in bus stations. Gents are marked with a letter "M" or a ▼ symbol; ladies with an "N" or a ▲ symbol.

1.1

Tallinn

One of the best-preserved medieval towns in northern Europe, **TALLINN** never fails to make a positive first impression. The cobblestone alleyways, slender steeples and barrel-shaped bastions of the **Old Town** – a UNESCO World Heritage site – could have jumped straight out of the pages of a medieval illustrated manuscript. However, Tallinn is no historical theme park, but rather the commercial and political heart of a rapidly changing nation, which boasts one of the fastest-growing economies in the European Union. Brand-new business parks, designer stores, stylish lounge bars and the ubiquitous wi-fi access signs provide the backdrop to a work-hard-play-hard culture that imbues the city with a palpable, restless energy.

Despite being the capital of an independent Estonia from 1918 to 1940 and again from 1991, modern-day Tallinn is more of a hybrid creation than many Estonians would care to admit. The city's name, derived from the Estonian *taani linnus*, meaning "Danish Fort", is a reminder of the fact that the city was founded by the Danes at the beginning of the thirteenth century, and since then political control has been for lengthy periods in the hands of foreigners – Swedes and particularly Germans have left lasting influences. Russians, meanwhile, continue to make up around 45 percent of the population, and the Russian language persists as an ever-present shadow culture, heard on the streets and in neighbourhood bars.

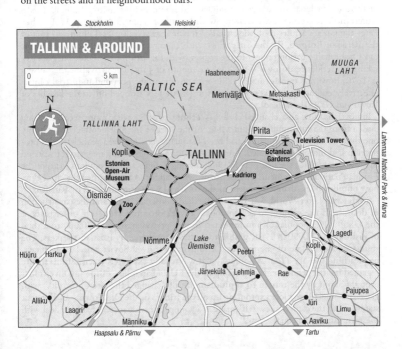

June, July and August are the most popular times to visit Tallinn, but the city's year-round cultural attractions and vibrant nightlife ensure that it's a rewarding weekend destination whatever time of year you choose to visit. Specific seasonal attractions include the Advent period, when there's a **Christmas Market** selling handicrafts, gingerbread and other treats on the town hall square (Raekoja plats); and the **Old Town Days**, which run for a week in mid-June, when there are concerts on the main square.

Some history

Although Tallinn began life as a fortified Estonian trading post, its urban history only really begins in 1219, when it was conquered by empire-building Danish **King Valdemar II**. Valdemar built a castle and a cathedral on the rock now known as Toompea, and a town of merchants and craftsmen soon grew up at its foot. Most of those who chose to settle in Danish-ruled Tallinn were of German or Flemish stock and they called the town Reval – a name that stuck until 1918. Estonians, drawn to the city to work as servants and labourers, were allowed to reside there, but were not given full citizens' rights.

With the **Teutonic Knights** gobbling up more and more of Estonia from the 1220s onwards, the Danes hung on to Tallinn until 1347, when cash-strapped King Valdemar III sold it – along with the rest of his remaining possessions in Estonia – to the Livonian Order for 19,000 silver marks. By this time the town had already become a member of the **Hanseatic League**, a trading alliance that counted many northern European cities as its members – stimulating the emergence of a boisterous mercantile culture. The townsfolk of Tallinn, resentful of the power wielded by the knights and bishops on Toompea, enthusiastically adopted Protestantism in the early 1500s; riots in September 1524 destroyed most of the town's medieval altarpieces and put monks and clergy to flight.

Weakened by the Reformation and squeezed by neighbouring powers, the Livonian Order dissolved itself in 1561, leaving Tallinn to be fought over by Russians and Swedes. The resulting **Livonian Wars** led to a decline in trade, and despite serving the victorious Swedes as an important military and administrative centre, Tallinn's days as a mercantile powerhouse were over. Swedish control came to an end in 1710, when Peter the Great's armies took the city. For the next two centuries Tallinn was part of the **Russian Empire**. By the early nineteenth century it had established itself as the most fashionable bathing resort in the region, with the cream of St Petersburg society taking up residence in town for the whole month of July. The arrival of the railway in 1870, however, transformed Tallinn into an important port and industrial centre, effectively ending its days as a seaside resort (Baltic folk trooped off to the beaches of Pärnu and Haapsalu instead).

Industrialization also changed Tallinn's **ethnic profile**, with more workers being drawn from the surrounding countryside. At the start of the nineteenth century barely one third of Tallinn's population had been Estonian, yet a hundred years later this proportion had more than doubled. Estonian-language parties won a majority of seats on the town council for the first time in 1904, turning Tallinn into the obvious focus of the Estonian national movement. The Germans, who had for so long formed the city's elite, now numbered less than ten percent of the total and were outnumbered by Russians.

Soviet rule after World War II led to further industrialization and the construction of dour, high-rise suburbs to accommodate a workforce imported from other parts of the USSR. The population mushroomed from a prewar figure of 170,000 to a total of just under 420,000 in 1991, with Estonians outnumbered by Russian-speakers. The spire-studded skyline of the medieval Old Town survived Soviet rule largely intact, bequeathing the city a tourist potential that was readily exploited when Estonia finally regained its independence. Membership of the EU and an influx of foreign investment brought about by the **return to capitalism** has also changed the face of the city, with glass-and-steel office blocks sprouting up on the fringes of the Old Town – an eloquent statement of the capital's new self-image as a young, dynamic society ready to deal with Western Europe on equal terms.

Arrival and information

Tallinn's **airport** (Lennujaam), 4km southeast of the city centre, is linked to Viru väljak, just east of the Old Town, by bus #2 (Mon–Sat every 20min; Sun every 30min; 10min; €1.30). A **taxi** to the centre should cost around €9. **Trains** arrive at the **Balti Jaam** (Baltic Station) on Toompuiestee, a five-minute walk northwest of the Old Town. The **long-distance bus station** (Autobussijaam) is 2km southeast at Lastekodu 46 – trams #2 and #4 run from nearby Tartu mnt to Viru väljak, right on the eastern fringes of the Old Town. The passenger **port** (Reisisadam) for most ferries is a fifteen-minute walk northeast of the Old Town at the end of Sadama, although high-speed catamarans dock at Linnahall harbour, fifteen minutes' walk north of the Old Town.

Tallinn's main **tourist office**, a few steps south of Raekoja plats at Nigulste 2/ Kullasseppa 4 (May & June Mon–Fri 9am–7pm, Sat & Sun 10am–5pm; July & Aug Mon– Fri 9am–8pm, Sat & Sun 10am–6pm; Sept Mon–Fri 9am–6pm, Sat & Sun 10am–5pm; Oct–April Mon–Fri 9am–5pm, Sat 10am–3pm; ☎645 7777, ⓦwww.tourism.tallinn.ee), provides advice about the city and a free sightseeing map, and sells a selection of more detailed maps and guides. There is a smaller information booth with longer opening hours in Viru Keskus (daily 9am–9pm; ☎610 1557). In summer, the determinedly unofficial **Traveller Info Tent** (June–Aug daily 10am–9.30pm; ☎555 42111, ⓦwww.traveller.ee) sets up opposite the main official tourist office. Run by local students, it gives the lowdown on Tallinn's more offbeat attractions and its nightlife, as well as running fun, budget tours.

The **Tallinn Card**, sold at the official tourist offices, entitles you to free use of public transport, entrance to all museums and major sights, a city tour, discounted car rental, and savings in some shops and cafés (24hr €24 [€13 for children]; 48hr €28/€15; 72hr €32/€16; ⓦwww.tallinncard.ee) – worth it if you're planning a serious blitz round the museums. The excellent *Tallinn in Your Pocket* city guide (€2.25; ⓦwww.inyourpocket .com) carries informed restaurant and bar **listings**, as well as plenty of info on local services and shopping; it's available from shops and hotels.

City transport

Most of Tallinn's sights can be covered on foot; those slightly further out are served by an extensive **tram, bus and trolleybus** network. Services are frequent and cheap, though usually crowded, with tickets common to all three systems available from kiosks near stops for €1 (a book of ten is €8) or from the driver for €1.30. Tickets need to be validated using the on-board punches. The main focus of the city's bus network is the **municipal bus terminal** on the basement level of the Viru Keskus shopping centre on Viru väljak.

In theory, **taxis** are reasonably cheap – however they are also notorious for over-charging. You're best booking one in advance from a recommended taxi company (see p.88) and fixing a rough price beforehand; there are also taxi ranks at all major entrances to the pedestrianized Old Town. Start-up charges are around €3.50, followed by €0.80 per kilometre (€1 between 8pm–6am).

City Bike Tours, Uus 33 (☎511 1819, ⓦwww.citybike.ee), rents out bikes and runs **bicycle tours**.

Accommodation

Tallinn has plenty of modern, high-standard accommodation, with a lot of establishments that would fit into the international luxury bracket – especially in the Old Town. Several central **hostels** have also sprung up recently, the majority of them pretty good, and there's also a handful of homely **B&Bs**, mostly in outer residential districts.

Private rooms are another good option if you want somewhere cheap and close to the heart of things, although conditions vary widely: in most cases you'll be sleeping in a small, minimally furnished room and sharing your host's bathroom. The **Rasastra** accommodation-finding service at Mere 4 (daily 9.30am–6pm; ☎661 6291,

Moving on from Tallinn

Tallinn is the Baltic Sea's main gateway to **Scandinavia**, with a host of high-speed ferries and catamarans travelling across the Gulf of Finland to **Helsinki**. Catamarans operated by Lindaline are the fastest means of crossing the Gulf (90min), although they only operate in ice-free months (roughly April–Oct). Car ferries take between 2 to 3 hour. There is also a daily Tallink ferry to Stockholm (16hr; overnight). An easy ten-minute walk northeast of the Old Town, the Passenger Port (Reisisadam) is divided into three terminals: A, B and D. A and B are together on the northern side of the port, at the end of Sadama; D is on the south side, an extra ten-minute walk round the dock (bus #2 makes the trip every 20–30min). Terminals A and D have cafés, exchange offices, and luggage lockers.

Most **travel agents** (see below) in the Old Town sell tickets to Helsinki and Stockholm, and the main operators have offices in the harbour-front terminals. The leading **operators** for Helsinki are Lindaline at the Linnahall terminal (☎699 9333, ⓦwww.lindaliini.ee); Eckerö Lines at Terminal A (☎664 6000, ⓦwww.eckeroline.ee); Viking at Terminal A (☎666 3945, ⓦwww.vikingline.ee); and Tallink at Terminal D (☎640 9808, ⓦwww.tallink.ee). Tallink's service to Stockholm is also at Terminal D, though bear in mind that getting an onward connection from Helsinki to Stockholm may be quicker than going direct.

All domestic and international **bus routes** are served by the long-distance bus station (Autobussijaam), 2km southeast of the Old Town at Lastekodu 46 (tram #2 from Mere pst or #4 from Pärnu mnt to the Autobussijaam stop). In summer and on weekends it's worth booking international bus tickets in advance – as there are no agencies in the centre of town handling reservations, you'll have to trek out to the bus station itself to do this. The main international destinations covered are St Petersburg in Russia, Rīga in Latvia and Vilnius in Lithuania.

Train services from the Balti Jaam (Baltic Station), on the west side of the Old Town, are less frequent and take longer than buses. The overnight train to Moscow is the only international service offered. Tickets are sold from windows in the main hall.

Tallinn's **airport** (Lennujaam; flight information ☎605 8888, ⓦwww.tallinn-airport.ee), 4km southeast of the centre, is reached by bus #2 from Gonsiori.

As for **travel agents**, Baltic Tours, Jõe 5 (☎630 0460, ⓦwww.baltictours.ee), deals in international plane tickets and hotel reservations within Estonia, while Estravel, Suur-Karja 15 (☎626 6266, ⓦwww.estravel.ee), sells tickets for all the major ferry lines and is agent for American Express.

ⓦwww.bedbreakfast.ee) offers the widest range of central rooms (singles from €20, doubles from €30, apartments from €55), and can fix up similar accommodation in Tartu, Pärnu, Haapsalu and Viljandi.

Hotels

Old Town and around

The establishments below are shown on the "Central Tallinn" map on p.68.

Baltic Hotel Vana Wiru Viru 11 (entrance round the corner on Müürivahe) ☎669 1500, ⓦwww.baltic hotelgroup.com. A swish four-star with an enticing combination of top-level comfort, a superb Old Town location and competitive prices. Rooms are tastefully decorated in pale yellows, blues or greens, and come with satellite TV and free internet access. ⑥

Braavo Aia 20 ☎699 9777, ⓦwww.braavo.ee. With rooms spread around the parking lot of a fitness club

this looks a bit odd at first sight, but it's actually one of the best bargains in the city. The en-suite rooms are bright, comfortable and quite spacious, and the Old Town is a 2min walk away. ⑤

City Hotel Tallinn Paldiski mnt 1/3 ☎660 0700, ⓦwww.uniquestay.com. A hyper-modern hotel within spitting distance of the Old Town. Standard rooms are stylishly minimalist and feature desktop computers with free internet; more expensive "Zen" rooms add to this whirlpool baths and NASA-designed chairs. ⑥

Domina Inn City Vana-Posti 11/13 ☎681 3900, ⓦwww.dominahotels.com. Stylish rooms in a restored eighteenth-century building, with plenty of classy touches like marble bathroom fittings and computers with internet access in every room. Service is particularly good. **⑦**

Merchant's House Dunkri 4/6 ☎ 697 7500, Ⓦ www.merchantshousehotel.ee. In a three-storey, fourteenth-century building steps from the town square, this boutique hotel is a perfect blend of old and new. Some of the chicest rooms in Tallinn come with exposed bricks and wooden beams; the opulent suites are wonderful. Excellent online deals. **⑥–⑦**

Meriton Grand Hotel Tallinn Toompuiestee 27 ☎ 667 7000, Ⓦ www.meritonhotels.com. Just down the hill from the Old Town, this four-star's functionalist exterior doesn't make a good first impression. Inside, however, you find spacious, recently renovated rooms; those facing east have great views of Toompea. **⑦**

Meriton Old Town Hotel Lai 49 ☎ 614 1300, Ⓦ www.meritonhotels.com. Set in a restored nineteenth-century building that contains part of the old city wall, rooms here, though small, have all modern comforts. **⑥**

Metropol Roseni 13 ☎ 667 4500, Ⓦ www .metropol.ee. A big, mid-range establishment not far from the port, the *Metropol* has decent en-suites with faintly 1970s decor and a casino. A solid if unexciting mid-range choice. **⑥**

OldHouse Guesthouse Uus 22 ☎ 641 1464, Ⓦ www.oldhouse.ee. This friendly, six-room B&B has an intimate feel. Rooms with shared facilities are bright and pristine, while the owners also rent out two- and four-person apartments (€70–105/night) close by. **③**

Scandic Palace Vabaduse väljak 3 ☎ 640 7300, Ⓦ www.scandic-hotels.com. A handsome interwar building overlooking a lively downtown square, offering sizeable, comfortable rooms, with deep-pile carpets and pastel tones. **⑦**

Schlössle Pühavaimu 13/15 ☎ 699 7777, Ⓦ www .schlossle-hotels.com. The five-star luxury of this impeccably restored fifteenth-century building attracts the great and the good – and from the medieval charm of the entrance to the artfully decorated rooms to the intimate atmosphere, it's easy to see why. Doubles start at €190. **⑧**

Sokos Hotel Viru Viru väljak 4 ☎ 630 1390, Ⓦ www.viru.ee. All the big-hotel facilities – beauty centre, several bars and restaurants, three saunas – make this 22-storey place on the edge of the Old Town very popular with tour groups, particularly those from Finland. Modern en-suites come with satellite TV, minibar and subtle blue or cream colour schemes. Great views of the Old Town from the upper floors. **⑦**

St Petersbourg Rataskaevu 7 ☎ 628 6500, Ⓦ www.schlossle-hotels.com. The oldest continually operating hotel in Tallinn has smart, bright rooms (with DVD players) and a few Art Deco touches in the common areas. Only marginally less luxurious than its sister hotel *Schlössle*. **⑧**

Three Sisters Pikk 71 ☎ 630 6300, Ⓦ www .threesistershotel.com. A wonderfully renovated trio of neighbouring medieval merchants' houses, dating back 450 years, the award-winning *Three Sisters* has fantastic rooms. Painted ceilings, exposed brickwork and wooden beams blend seamlessly with tasteful, modern designer furnishings. Unsurprisingly, all the rooms are suites, from €210. **⑧**

Outside the Old Town

The establishments below are shown on the "Tallinn" map on p.64.

Domina Inn Illmarine Põhja pst 23 ☎ 614 0900, Ⓦ www.dominahotels.com. A 150-room affair in a beautifully restored warehouse, midway between the Old Town and the up-and-coming Kalamaja district. Offering four-star comforts for significantly less than four-star prices, this is an exceedingly tempting option. **⑤**

Hotel G9 Gonsiori 9 ☎ 626 7100, Ⓦ www.hotelg9 .ee. A simple place on the third floor of an office block 5min walk from the Old Town, with spotless, airy singles, doubles, triples and quads, all with bathroom and TV. No breakfast, but staff are welcoming and help make *G9* an excellent-value option. Book ahead. **③**

Nepi Nepi 10 ☎ 655 1665 or 655 2254, Ⓦ www .nepihotell.ee. This small and welcoming B&B in the residential suburb of Kristine has plain rooms with en-suite shower and TV. A couple of apartment-style rooms come with more tasteful, if vaguely 1970s-era, furnishings. Bus #17 or #17A to Koolimaja, or bus #23 to Ööbiku. **②–③**

Radisson Blu Olümpia Liivalaia 33 ☎ 669 0690, Ⓦ www.radissonblu.com. Glass-and-steel slab built in 1980 (when Tallinn hosted the Olympic yachting events), with levels of comfort and service that fully justify its four-star status. The top-floor sauna, swimming pool and gym boast stunning views of the city. 500m from the Old Town. **⑦**

Radisson Blu Tallinn Rävala pst 3 ☎ 669 0000, Ⓦ www.tallinn.radissonsas.com. One of the tallest structures in Tallinn, this business hotel is in a sleek modern building a 10min walk from the Old Town. Rooms, which are decorated on Scandinavian, Oriental, Italian or nautical themes, deliver high standards of comfort and quality. **⑦**

Tatari 53 Tatari 53 (entrance behind Pärnu mnt 69) ☎ 640 5150, Ⓦ www.tatari53.ee.

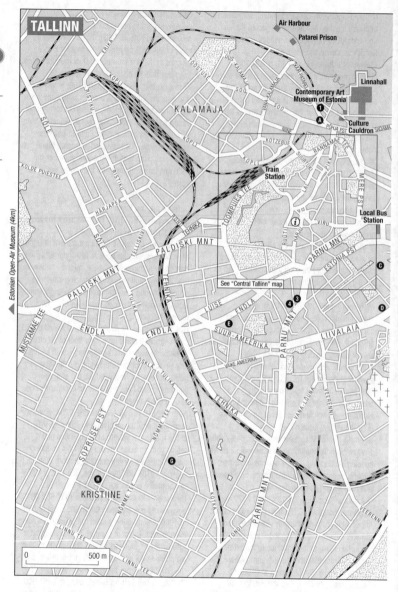

A straightforward, no-frills mid-range choice a 15min walk from the Old Town, *Tatari 53* has comfortable en-suites with TV and smooth service. ④

UniqueStay Mihkli Endla 23 ☎ 666 4800, ⒲ www.uniquestay.com. The sister hotel to *City Hotel Tallinn* has the same state-of-the-art rooms

at slightly lower rates, as a result of its location 450m from the Old Town. ⑤

Valge Villa Kännu 26/2 ☎ 654 2302, ⒲ www .white-villa.com. The "White Villa" is a homely B&B tucked away on a quiet suburban street in residential Kristine. Comfy en-suite rooms have wood-panelled walls and plenty of character, and

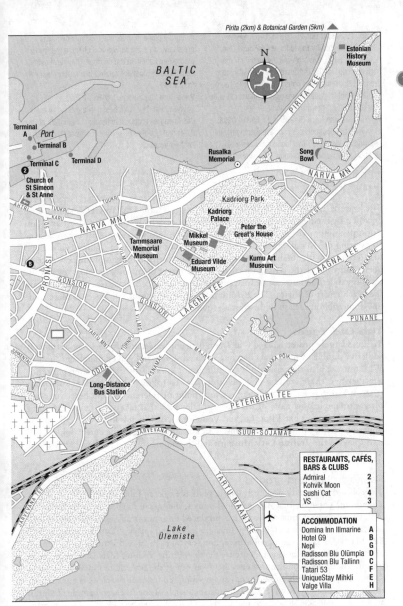

Pirita (2km) & Botanical Garden (5km) ▲

N

BALTIC
SEA

Estonian
History
Museum

PIRITA TEE

Terminal
A
Port

Terminal B

Terminal C   Terminal D

Church of
St Simeon
& St Anne

Rusalka
Memorial

Song
Bowl

NARVA MNT

AHTRI

TUUKRI

KARU

NARVA MNT

TUUKRI

Kadriorg Park

VALGE

Tammsaare
Memorial
Museum

Kadriorg
Palace

Mikkel
Museum

Peter the
Great's House

Kumu Art
Museum

LAAGNA TEE

VÕIDUJOOKSU

PAEKAARE

PRONKSI

J. VILMSI

GONSIORI

Eduard Vilde
Museum

GONSIORI

TARTU MNT

J. VILMSI

TÕRNU

LAAGNA TEE

PALLASTI

PAE

PUNANE

MAJAKA

LUBJA

LASNAMÄE

MAJAKA

MAJAKA PÕIK

PAE

Long-Distance
Bus Station

ODRA

PETERBURI TEE

JÄRVEVANA TEE

SUUR-SÕJAMÄE

JÄRVEVANA TEE

TARTU MAANTEE

Lake
Ülemiste

**RESTAURANTS, CAFÉS,
BARS & CLUBS**

Admiral	2
Kohvik Moon	1
Sushi Cat	4
VS	3

ACCOMMODATION

Domina Inn Ilmarine	A
Hotel G9	B
Nepi	G
Radisson Blu Olümpia	D
Radisson Blu Tallinn	C
Tatari 53	F
UniqueStay Mihkli	E
Valge Villa	H

the family who own and run it provide the warmest of welcomes. Bus #17 or #17A to the Räägu stop, or trolleybus #2, #3 or #4 to the Tedre stop. ②–❸

Hostels

The establishments below are shown on the "Central Tallinn" map on p.68.

Euphoria Roosikrantsi 4 ☎5837 3602. Conveniently placed just off Vabaduse väljak, *Euphoria* offers dorm rooms (from €10) doubles (❶) and self-catering apartments. Indian textiles in the common-room and psychedelic murals in the stairwell provide the necessary colour and character.

OldHouse Hostel Uus 26 ☎ 641 1464, ⓦ www .oldhouse.ee. Run by the folks at *OldHouse Guesthouse* (see p.63), this high-quality hostel on the northern edge of the Old Town has six-bed dorms (from €12), immaculate bathrooms and a TV room. Homely singles, doubles, triples and quads (all with shared facilities) are also available.

Tallinn Backpackers Olevimägi 11 ☎ 644 0298, ⓦ www.tallinnbackpackers.com. Welcoming hostel enjoying an ideal Old Town location, with six- to eight-bed dorms, some en-suite. The common-room

is a great place to relax and meet people: films are shown on a big screen and cheap day-trips to places like Lahemaa are on offer. They have extra beds in other locations around town. Dorm beds from €10.

Vana Tom Väike-Karja 1 ☎ 631 3252, ⓦ www.hostel.ee. This hostel in the heart of the Old Town has a decent collection of smallish dorms (€14) and good-value private rooms (❷), all with kitchen access.

The City

The heart of Tallinn and location of most of its sights is the **Old Town** (Vanalinn), once enclosed by medieval walls, significant stretches of which still exist. Above it looms **Toompea**, hilltop stronghold of the knights and bishops who nominally controlled the city during the Middle Ages. Beyond the medieval core, much of Tallinn is bland and uninteresting, with notable exceptions. The old industrial buildings of the port districts north and west of the centre are currently the target of major redevelopment, while established destinations east of the centre include the park and palace at **Kadriorg** and the beach resort of **Pirita**. The **Estonian Open-Air Museum** in Rocca al Mare is the one unmissable attraction in the western suburbs.

The Old Town

Tallinn's largely pedestrianized Old Town is an enjoyable, atmospheric and ultimately addictive jumble of medieval churches, cobbled streets and gabled merchants' houses. With a street plan that comprises a confusion of curving streets and interconnecting passageways, there are few obvious itineraries to follow, although **Raekoja plats** ("Town Hall Square") provides an obvious point of reference. From here, your best plan is to amble down any of the adjacent alleyways that take your fancy, emerging onto sinuous streets like **Pikk**, **Lai** and **Vene** – each of which is lined with tall, quietly imperious medieval warehouses. Must-visit attractions include the entertaining history displays at the **Tallinn City Museum** and the show-stopping medieval artworks in **St Nicholas's Church**.

Raekoja plats and around

The cobbled and gently sloping **Raekoja plats** is as old as Tallinn itself. Surrounded by a handsome ensemble of pastel-coloured houses, the square has become a trademark of both the city and Estonia as a whole, reproduced on innumerable souvenirs and tourist posters. It is also a popular rallying point and a focus for displays of Estonian patriotic feeling: May 2001 saw a vast open-air reception for Tanel Padar and Dave Benton, winners of that year's Eurovision Song Contest – the then Prime Minister Mart Laar made a since oft-quoted remark about Estonia singing its way out of the Soviet Union and into the EU.

On the square's southern side stands an imposing reminder of the city's Hanseatic past: the fifteenth-century **Town Hall** (Tallinna raekoda), boasting an elegant arcade of Gothic arches and a delicate, slender steeple. Look out for the waterspouts in the shape of green dragons just below the roof. Near the summit of the steeple you'll spy Vana Toomas (Old Thomas), a sixteenth-century weather vane in the form of a stout, spear-wielding sentry. According to legend, the real-life model for the weather vane was a local lad who excelled at the springtime "parrot-shooting" contests (which involved firing crossbow bolts at a painted wooden bird on top of a pole) organized by Tallinn's German-speaking elite. Unable to receive a prize owing to his low-born status, Toomas was instead rewarded with the job of town guard for life. Subsequently immortalized in copper, Toomas continues to watch over Tallinn and its citizens. In summer, the **chambers** (July & Aug:

Mon–Sat 10am–4pm; €4) offer a small history display and a chance to climb up into the attic to admire the building's steeply-angled roof. The highlight, however, is the main council chamber itself, a small but beautifully decorated space featuring a wood-carved frieze of huntsmen and their dogs, and seventeenth-century bible scenes painted into the niches above. Look out for a pair of fourteenth-century magistrates benches, each featuring exquisitely carved end panels.

Of the other old buildings lining the square, the most venerable is the **Town Council Pharmacy** (Raeapteek) in the northeastern corner; its cream-coloured facade dates from the seventeenth century, though the building is known to have existed in 1422 and may be much older. It's still a working pharmacy – which is probably a good job, judging by the rather half-hearted attempt at creating a museum (Mon–Fri 9am–7pm, Sat 9am–5pm; free) in one of its corners. If the Raeapteek leaves you underwhelmed, head for the former jail (Raevangla) behind the Town Hall at Raekoja 4/6, now home to the **Photography Museum** (Fotomuuseum; daily except Wed: March–Oct 10.30am–6pm; Nov–Feb 10.30am–5pm; €1.50), an entertaining little collection with views of Tallinn from the days when it was still known as Reval and portraits of Estonians in traditional costume.

The Church of the Holy Ghost

Next to the Raeapteek, a small passage, Saiakang, leads through to Pühavaimu tänav and one of the city's most appealing churches, the **Church of the Holy Ghost** (Pühavaimu kirik; Jan–April Mon–Sat 9.30am–5.30pm, Sun 10am–4pm; May–Aug Mon–Sat 9.30am–6.30pm, Sun 10am–6.30pm; Sept–Dec daily 10am–5.30pm; €1). A small Gothic building with stepped gables, it served as the Town Hall chapel before becoming the main church of Tallinn's Estonian-speaking population. In 1535, priests from the church compiled an Estonian-language Lutheran catechism, an important affirmation of identity at a time when most Estonians had been reduced to serfdom. The ornate clock set into the wall above the entrance, dating from 1680, is Tallinn's oldest public timepiece. The interior of the church – dark-veneered wood and cream-painted walls – has an intimate beauty and contains one of the city's most significant pieces of religious art, an extraordinary triptych centred on an intricately rendered grouping of painted wooden statuettes representing the *Descent of the Holy Ghost* (1483) by the Lübeck master Berndt Notke (1430–1509).

House of the Great Guild

At the northern end of Raekoja plats sprouts a sequence of small alleyways crammed with cafés and souvenir shops. Most of them emerge onto medieval Tallinn's main thoroughfare, **Pikk tänav** ("Long Street"), cutting northeast to southwest through the town. It would have been an important link between the ecclesiastical and military buildings of Toompea and the port area, traversing the main business district on the way. Along the street's 800-metre length lie some of the city's most important secular buildings from the Hanseatic period, kicking off with the forbidding Gothic facade of the **House of the Great Guild** (Suurgildi hoone) at Pikk 17. Completed in 1430, this provided a home for the most powerful of the city's guilds, uniting the German-speaking mercantile elite into an organization that effectively controlled Tallinn's commerce. The Great Guild's doors were closed to petty merchants and artisans, who were instead organized into lesser institutions, such as the largely Estonian-speaking Guild of Corpus Christi. The Great Guild was the focus of many of medieval Tallinn's social events, notably the traditional springtime tournaments, when the so-called May Count was chosen – a practice recently revived to form the centrepiece of the Old Town Days festival, a tourist-oriented piece of pageantry in late May and early June. The Great Guild houses a branch of the Estonian History Museum (W www.eam.ee), although it is currently closed for long-term renovation.

House of the Blackheads

If the appearance of their headquarters is anything to go by, the guild that occupied the **House of the Blackheads** (Mustpeade maja), Pikk 26, were a more exuberant bunch

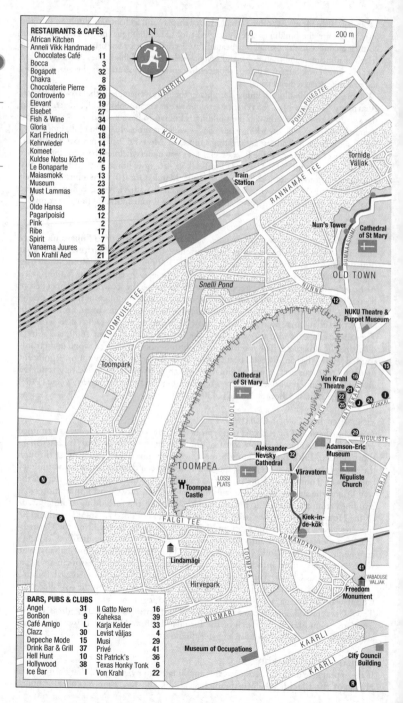

RESTAURANTS & CAFÉS

African Kitchen	1
Anneli Vikk Handmade Chocolates Café	11
Bocca	3
Bogapott	32
Chakra	8
Chocolaterie Pierre	26
Controvento	20
Elevant	19
Elsebet	27
Fish & Wine	34
Gloria	40
Karl Friedrich	18
Kehrwieder	14
Komeet	42
Kuldse Notsu Kõrts	24
Le Bonaparte	5
Maiasmokk	13
Museum	23
Must Lammas	35
Õ	7
Olde Hansa	28
Pagaripoisid	12
Pink	2
Ribe	17
Spirit	7
Vanaema Juures	25
Von Krahli Aed	21

BARS, PUBS & CLUBS

Angel	31	Il Gatto Nero	16
BonBon	9	Kaheksa	39
Café Amigo	L	Karja Kelder	33
Clazz	30	Levist väljas	4
Depeche Mode	15	Musi	29
Drink Bar & Grill	37	Privé	41
Hell Hunt	10	St Patrick's	36
Hollywood	38	Texas Honky Tonk	6
Ice Bar	I	Von Krahl	22

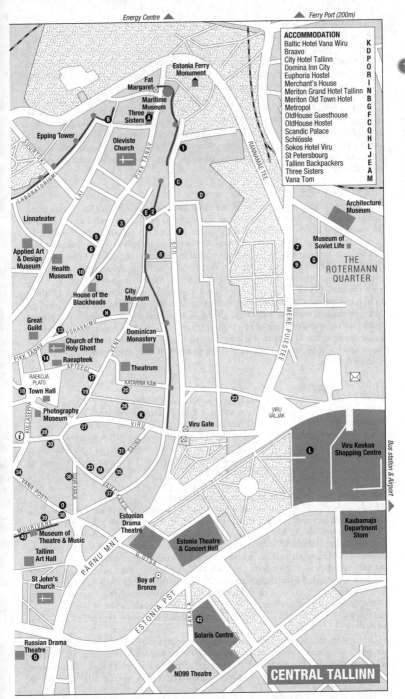

Energy Centre ▲

▲ Ferry Port (200m)

ACCOMMODATION

Baltic Hotel Vana Wiru	K
Braavo	D
City Hotel Tallinn	P
Domina Inn City	O
Euphoria Hostel	R
Merchant's House	I
Meriton Grand Hotel Tallinn	N
Meriton Old Town Hotel	B
Metropol	G
OldHouse Guesthouse	F
OldHouse Hostel	C
Scandic Palace	Q
Schlössle	H
Sokos Hotel Viru	L
St Petersbourg	J
Tallinn Backpackers	E
Three Sisters	A
Vana Tom	M

Estonia Ferry Monument

Fat Margaret

Maritime Museum

Three Sisters

Epping Tower

Oleviste Church

Linnateater

Applied Art & Design Museum

Health Museum

House of the Blackheads

City Museum

Great Guild

Church of the Holy Ghost

Raeapteek

RAEKOJA PLATS

Town Hall

Photography Museum

Dominican Monastery

Theatrum

Viru Gate

VIRU VÄLJAK

Viru Keskus Shopping Centre

Bus station & Airport

Museum of Theatre & Music

Tallinn Art Hall

St John's Church

Estonian Drama Theatre

Estonia Theatre & Concert Hall

Kaubamaja Department Store

Boy of Bronze

Russian Drama Theatre

Solaris Centre

NO99 Theatre

Architecture Museum

Museum of Soviet Life

THE ROTERMANN QUARTER

CENTRAL TALLINN

69

than the merchants of the Great Guild. The Renaissance facade of their building, inset with an elaborate stone portal and richly decorated door, cuts a bit of dash amid the stolidity of Pikk. Like its namesake in Rīga, Tallinn's Brotherhood of the Blackheads was formed to accommodate visiting bachelor merchants and took the North African St Maurice as its patron – hence its name. Unlike in Rīga, however, the Blackheads here also served a military purpose, organizing defence detachments (Blackheads fought off Russian besiegers during the Livonian Wars) and honouring visiting dignitaries with parades. Legend has it that the guild was founded to defend Tallinn during the Estonian uprising of St George's Day in 1343, though in later years it seems to have degenerated into a drinking club. The Brotherhood moved here in 1531 and stayed until 1940, when the Soviets turfed out a dwindling crew of survivors. Nowadays, the house's main hall is the venue for regular chamber concerts – probably your best chance of getting to see the elegant, wood-panelled interior.

The Oleviste Church

Continuing north along Pikk brings you to the **Oleviste Church** (St Olaf's), first mentioned in 1267 and named in honour of King Olaf II of Norway, who was canonized for massacring pagans in Scandinavia. This slab-towered Gothic structure would not be particularly eye-catching were it not for the height of its **spire**, which reaches 124m and used to be even taller. According to local legend, the citizens of Tallinn wanted the church to have the highest spire in the world in order to attract passing ships and bring in trade. Whether Tallinn's prosperity in the Middle Ages had anything to do with the visibility of the church spire is not known, but between 1625 and 1820 the church burnt down eight times after being struck by lightning. Occupying a niche low down on the rear exterior wall of the church is the tombstone of plague victim Johann Ballivi, an outstanding piece of fifteenth-century stone-carving, featuring a deliciously macabre depiction of a decaying body surrounded by delicately rendered mourners. The church's unexceptional interior is the product of extensive renovation between 1829 and 1840.

The Three Sisters

Most striking of the Old Town's gabled merchants' houses are the **Three Sisters** (Kolm õde), just beyond St Olaf's Church at Pikk 71. Among the city's best-preserved Hanseatic buildings, these supremely functional buildings, with loading hatches and winch-arms set into their facades, would have been dwelling places, warehouses and offices all rolled into one. Recently, they have been converted into an upmarket hotel (see p.63) and painted in snazzy citrus colours, giving them the appearance of a monumental trio of ready-to-lick Gothic lollies.

Fat Margaret and the Maritime Museum

At its northern end Pikk is straddled by the **Great Sea Gate** (Suur rannavärav), a sixteenth-century arch flanked by two towers. The larger of these, the barrel-shaped **"Fat Margaret"** (Paks Margareeta), has walls 4m thick. Pressed into use as the city jail, the tower witnessed Tallinn's first outbreak of violence during the Revolution of March 1917, when striking workers joined mutineering soldiers and sailors in an assault on the prison, murdering the warders and setting the tower alight. It now houses the **Estonian Maritime Museum** (Eesti meremuuseum; Wed–Sun 10am–6pm; €3), a diverting collection of model boats and nautical ephemera spread out over several floors. Sounding a poignant note, one of the exhibits is a scale model of the *Estonia*, the car ferry that sank midway between Tallinn and Stockholm on September 28, 1994, with the loss of 852 lives.

The area on the far side of Fat Margaret, now occupied by a road junction and a few scrappy bits of park, used to be known as the Parrot Garden in honour of the "parrot shooting" contests (see p.66) held here every spring in medieval times. Victors were presented with a silver salver and then borne in triumphal procession along Pikk to the Great Guild.

The Applied Art and Design Museum

Southwest of Fat Margaret, **Lai tänav** ("Broad Street") is another of the Old Town's set-piece thoroughfares, with rows of high-gabled merchants' houses haughtily presiding over the cobbled streets below, their cast-iron weather vanes creaking in the wind. Occupying a courtyard behind Lai 17, the **Applied Art and Design Museum** (Tarbekunstimuuseum; Wed–Sun 11am–6pm; €2.50) pays tribute to Estonia's strong design traditions with a well-presented collection of textiles, jewellery and ceramics; highlights include the highly desirable "caveman" tea-set designed in 1937 by Adamson-Eric (see p.72), with spindly human figures chasing mammoths and other beasts around the cups and saucers; and the groovy pop art-influenced furnishings of the 1960s and 70s.

The NUKU Puppet Museum

Inside the NUKU Puppet Theatre at Lai's southern end is the highly enjoyable **NUKU Puppet Museum** (Tues–Sun 10am–7pm; €3.30), a colourful journey through the history of the theatre, featuring a host of marionettes, stage designs and film clips. Characters that every Estonian will recognize (but which others may be meeting for the first time) include Kriimsilm the Wolf, star of a popular children's TV show from 1962 onwards.

The city walls

Running roughly parallel with Lai to the east is one of the longest surviving sections of Tallinn's medieval **city wall**, here featuring nine complete towers and three gates. Passing through any of the gates and crossing the park-like expanse of Tornide väljak on the other side provides a wonderful view back towards the towers, which look like a series of squat crimson crayons. The walls were largely constructed during the fourteenth century, then added to over the years until improvements in artillery rendered them obsolete during the eighteenth century. Citizens of medieval Tallinn were each obliged to do a stint of guard duty – one of the annual exercises required them all to gather on the walls in full armour and shake their weapons as a sign of military readiness. Two of the towers along this stretch are open to visitors: the **Nun's Tower** (Nunnetorn; May–Sept daily 11am–7pm; €2) on Gumnaasiumi provides access to a short section of the parapet and the empty, echoing halls of the nearby Sauna and Golden Foot towers; while the **Epping Tower** (May–Sept daily except Wed 10am–6pm; €4) on Laboratoriumi has a small display of arms, armour and fortification diagrams.

The City Museum

The main street running northeast of Town Hall Square is Vene, where the **Tallinn City Museum** at no. 17 (Tallinna linnamuuseum; daily except Tues: March–Oct 10.30am–6pm; Nov–Feb 10.30am–5pm; €3.50; ⑳www.linnamuuseum.ee), contains a superbly arranged collection brought to life by the inclusion of costumed wax figures, medieval street sounds and English-language texts. A cutaway model of a sixteenth-century merchant's house reveals how these buildings once functioned, with vast cranes jutting from facades hauling merchandise to the upper storeys to be warehoused before being re-exported or sold in the shop space at ground level. Original furnishings and costumes feature in a display of nineteenth-century interiors, while events of the twentieth century unfold through a collection of posters and photographs (including one of an enormous Stalin poster draped incongruously over the facade of the Town Hall), and videos document the growth of the independence movement.

The Dominican Monastery and Katariina käik

Diagonally opposite the museum at Vene 16, the **Dominican Monastery** was one of the most powerful institutions in medieval Tallinn – until it was comprehensively trashed by anti-Catholic rioters in 1525. The site was subsequently used as a school, hospital and arsenal before a new church was built in the mid-nineteenth century; it remains the city's main Catholic place of worship. Some of the former monastery buildings now accommodate the **Dominican Monastery Museum** (Dominiiklaste kloostri muuseum; mid-June to mid-Sept daily 10am–6pm, at other times by appointment; €6; ⓦ www.kloostri.ee), home to an extensive collection of medieval and Renaissance stone-carving, including some intricate fourteenth-century tombstones. Look out for a delightful relief of an angel in a triangular frame courtesy of Arendt Passer – the doyen of sixteenth-century stone masonry who also worked on the portal of the House of the Blackheads (see p.67) and Pontus de la Gardie tomb's in the cathedral (p.74).

Immediately south of the monastery, a narrow alleyway known as **Katariina kaik** ("Catherine's Passage") runs round the surviving wall of the original monastery church, passing a string of craft workshops where you can observe potters, bookbinders and glaziers at work (see "Shopping", p.87).

The Niguliste Church

Heading south from Raekoja plats along Kullaseppa leads to the imposing **Niguliste Church** (St Nicholas's; Wed–Sun 10am–5pm; €3.50). A three-aisled basilica fashioned from huge chunks of limestone, this was initially put up by Westphalian merchants in the thirteenth century, although most of what can be seen today dates from the fifteenth – especially the apse and the sturdy tower, built with defence in mind. Extensively restored following Soviet bombing raids at the end of World War II, it's now a **museum**, gathering together the surviving crop of Tallinn's medieval artworks – most of which perished in the Protestant riots of September 1524. St Nicholas's itself was saved from a thorough ransacking by the quick-thinking of the warden, who – so the story goes – poured lead in the locks to prevent the raiders from gaining access. Standing out among a clutch of Gothic altarpieces is a spectacular double-winged altar by Herman Rode of Lübeck from 1481, in which scenes featuring the life of St Nicholas figure prominently, although St George is also shown effortlessly skewering a dragon on one panel, and getting his head chopped off in another. Standing to the left of the altar is a sixteenth-century Crucifixion scene attributed to Adriaen Isenbrandt of Bruges, in which Jerusalem is embellished with the kind of medieval towers and bastions that wouldn't look out of place in a north European city like Tallinn. Over on the right, the **Altar of the Blackheads** was painted for the Brotherhood by another Bruges master, who depicted robed Blackhead members kneeling in prayer on the inner sides of the wings. The central panel shows a golden-tressed Madonna flanked by saints George and Maurice.

Occupying pride of place at the rear of the church is a largish fragment from a fifteenth-century *Dance of Death* frieze by Berndt Notke. It's an outstanding example of the genre, with skeletal figures swaying gracefully to a bagpipe ditty while cajoling a bishop, king and noblewoman to join in the fun – unsurprisingly, they look less than enthusiastic. On the left side of the canvas, a preacher addresses the viewer on the need to repent – his words relayed, almost comic-book style, in gothic lettering below.

The church's sonorous **organ** is put through its paces every Saturday and Sunday, with **recitals** starting at around 4 or 5pm: details are posted at the entrance.

The Adamson-Eric Museum

A few steps west of the church entrance, Lühike jalg climbs uphill to Toompea (see opposite). The medieval merchant's house at no. 3 houses the **Adamson-Eric Museum** (Wed–Sun 11am–6pm; €2.50), charting the career of Estonian art's most talented all-rounder. Born Erich Carl Hugo Adamson, Adamson-Eric (1902–68) drifted through various art and design schools in Tartu, Berlin and Paris before settling in Tallinn in the 1920s. He quickly garnered a reputation for producing accessible figurative paintings, while simultaneously churning out unabashedly abstract designs for tapestries, book-bindings and ceramics – all showcased here to good effect. The most popular of his paintings on display, *In Summer* (1938), is also one of his most mischievous, subverting traditional Estonian ideas of rural wholesomeness by portraying a female subject clad in national costume – but only from the waist down. Like many nonconformists of his generation, Adamson-Eric supported the Soviet Union in the 1940s (his fawning portrait of Stalin entitled *On the Coast of the Baltic Sea* is sadly not on display), but fell out of favour with the regime in the 1950s and was banned from exhibiting until the 1960s – by which time he'd taught himself to paint with his left hand after a stroke had put paid to his right. Later works – Cubist designs for café murals, and irregularly shaped ceramic tiles bearing primitive animal forms – show that he remained at the peak of his powers to the last.

Along Harju

On the eastern side of St Nicolas's Church, Harju tänav leads past an attractively landscaped park, with terraces of raised beds and benches in the shape of reclining deckchairs. On the opposite side of the street, the snazzy *Fish & Wine* restaurant at Harju 1 (see p.83) is in the erstwhile **Pegasus** building, a hip writers' and artists' café in the early 1960s that still preserves its super-cool, Modernist interior. The building's most famous feature was the spiral staircase topped by Edgar Viies's sleek *Pegasus* – supposedly the first piece of abstract sculpture ever to appear in Soviet Estonia. Notwithstanding its small size, this graceful, three-pronged piece of aluminium is still as eloquent a statement of 1960s optimism as you'll find anywhere. A replica is on display here – the original is in the Kumu Art Museum (see p.80).

The Museum of Theatre and Music

Turning left at the south end of Harju brings you onto Müürivahe, a narrow street running east then north alongside what were once the city walls – chunks of medieval masonry still pepper the walls of many of the buildings. The **Museum of Theatre and Music** at Müürivahe 12 (Teatri-ja muusikamuuseum; Wed–Sat 10am–6pm; €3) boasts publicity stills of stage stars in its stairwell and a motley collection of keyboards, music boxes and folk instruments upstairs – most striking is the *põispill*, a stringed instrument incorporating an animal-skin soundbox which looks like the result of an unnatural union between a cello and a bagpipe. More glamorous by half is the frilly black dress once worn by Meliza Korjus (1909–80), the soprano who made her name singing in the Estonia Concert Hall before emigrating to Hollywood – her appearance in the 1938 film *The Great Waltz* seemed to promise great things, until a car accident brought her movie career to a premature end.

Toompea

Looming over the Old Town to the southwest is the limestone outcrop known as **Toompea**, the site of an Estonian stockade fort until the Danes took it over in 1219 and built a stone castle, later wrested from them by the Livonian Order. As the nerve centre of the Christian effort to convert the pagan Estonians, Toompea (from the German word "Domberg", meaning "Cathedral Hill") often led a separate life from the rest of Tallinn below – which was much more interested in trade than ideology. The seat of several state and religious institutions, it still stands apart from the rest of central Tallinn – a somewhat secretive lair of bureaucrats and ministers rather than the happy-go-lucky habitat of shoppers and drinkers.

The most atmospheric approach to Toompea from the Old Town is through the sturdy gate tower – built by the Livonian Order to contain the Old Town's inhabitants in times of unrest – at the foot of Pikk jalg (Long Leg). This is the cobbled continuation of Pikk, the Old Town's main street, and climbs up to Lossi plats (Castle Square).

Cathedral of Alexander Nevsky

Lossi plats is dominated by the onion-domed Russian Orthodox **Cathedral of Alexander Nevsky** (Aleksander Nevski katedraal; daily 8am–7pm; free). Built in 1900 to remind the local Estonians of their subservient position in the Tsarist scheme of things, this gaudy concoction has always had the slightly inappropriate appearance of an over-iced cake at a funeral feast. Inside, however, an aura of spiritual calm reigns supreme, with incense wafting over a lofty, icon-packed interior.

Toompea Castle

At the western end of Lossi plats is **Toompea Castle (Toompea loss)**, on the site of the original Danish fortification. The castle has been altered by every conqueror who raised his flag above it since then; these days it wears a shocking-pink Baroque facade, the result of an eighteenth-century rebuild under Catherine the Great. The northern and western walls, the oldest part of the castle, include three defensive towers, the most impressive of which is the 50m-high Hermann (Pikk Hermann) at the southwestern corner, dating from 1371.

As the home to the **Riigikogu**, Estonia's Parliament, Toompea witnessed many of the events leading up to the re-establishment of Estonia's independence – most notably on May 15, 1990, when citizens gathered to defend the building against followers of the pro-Soviet Intermovement, who were attempting to storm it.

The Cathedral of St Mary the Virgin

From Lossi plats, Toomkooli leads north to the **Cathedral of St Mary the Virgin** (Toomkirik; Tues–Sun 9am–6pm), a homely, whitewashed structure that, despite numerous rebuildings, doesn't appear to have changed much since the first stone church built by Danes here in 1240. Inside, set apart from the ordinary ranks of pews are glass-enclosed family boxes that would have been reserved for local notables, enabling them to keep their distance from the hoi polloi. Presiding over the pews is an ornate seventeenth-century pulpit by Christian Ackerman, who also carved many of the 107 coats of arms of noble families that adorn the white walls of the vaulted nave and choir. Stealing all the attention on the right-hand side of the main altar is the tomb of Pontus de la Gardie, the French-born mercenary who captured Narva for the Swedes in 1578, before massacring, it is said, six thousand of its inhabitants. The sarcophagus bears tender likenesses of Pontus and his wife, a fine piece of sculpture by local master Arendt Passer. Look out, too, for Giacomo Quarenghi's Neoclassical memorial to Admiral Samuel Greigh (died 1788) halfway down the aisle, ordered by Catherine the Great as a tribute to the Scots-born seadog who led Russian naval campaigns in both the Mediterranean and the Baltic.

Kiek-in-de-Kök and the Bastion Tunnels

South of Lossi plats, a sloping park abuts another impressive stretch of town wall. Among the towers here is a gruff, grey blockhouse that once served as a prison for prostitutes – ironically named the Neitsitorn ("Virgin's Tower"); once home to one of Soviet-era Tallinn's most fashionable café-bars, although its future remains uncertain. Immediately south of the Neitsitorn is the impregnable-looking bastion known as **Kiek-in-de-Kök** (Tues–Sun: March–Oct 10.30am–6pm; Nov–Feb closes 5pm; €3), built in 1475 to provide a home for Toompea's main gun battery. Named in honour of a Low-German expression meaning "look in the kitchen" (the bastion's sentries could see straight into the parlours of downtown Tallinn), it now contains an entertaining, if sparse, collection of artefacts linked to the town's defences. There are suits of armour, rusty-looking weapons and replicas of the cannon once stationed here, variously nick-named Lion, Fat Girl and Bitter Death – this last being engraved with the following cheerful rhyme:

**Bitter Death is my name
Thus I travel everywhere
Killing the rich and the poor
To me, who I slay is all the same.**

Kiek-in-de-Kök is the starting point for atmospheric tours of the **Bastion Tunnels** (Bastionkogid), a recently rediscovered network of seventeenth-century passages beneath Toompea. Originally built by the Swedes in order to supply their hillside gun positions, they were used during World War II as air-raid shelters and subsequently modernized by the Soviets, before slowly falling out of use. English-language **tours**

(€7) run daily throughout the summer; you should ring to check times and reserve a place (☎644 6686).

Lindamägi and Hirvepark

West of Kiek-in-de-Kök, paths climb a wooded knoll known as **Lindamägi** ("Linda's Hill") after the woman in sculptural form who squats pensively at its summit. According to Estonian folk myth, Linda was the loving wife of Kalev and mother of superhuman hero Kalevipoeg. On the death of Kalev, Linda laboured to build a mound of rocks in his honour – Toompea is said to be the result. The statue is the work of August Weizenberg (1837–1921), a cabinet-maker who paid his way through art college in St Petersburg and Munich to become Estonia's first professional sculptor. Below Lindamägi to the south lies the leafy **Hirvepark**, scene of a 2000-strong gathering to mark the fiftieth anniversary of the Molotov-Ribbentrop Pact on August 23, 1987, one of the first big anti-Soviet demonstrations in the Baltics.

The Museum of Occupations

Some 250m south of Kiek-in-de-Kök at Toompea 8 is the **Museum of Occupations** (Okupatsioonide muuseum; Tues–Sun 11am–6pm; €2; Ⓦ www.okupatsioon.ee), which provides a gripping account of the 1940–91 period, when Estonia suffered occupations by both Nazi Germany and the Soviet Union. A modern structure houses a wide range of exhibits from propaganda posters and military uniforms to the surveillance equipment used by Soviet security forces. Particularly poignant are the personal effects of Estonians deported to work camps in the east during the late 1940s, many of whom never returned. Newsreel footage chronicles the whole period, with the anti-Soviet demonstrations of the 1987-91 period proving particularly engrossing.

Vabaduse väljak and around

Just outside the Old Town's southern border is **Vabaduse väljak**, a large open space formerly used for parades on Soviet holidays, and given a thorough revamp in 2009. It's overlooked by the **Freedom Monument**, erected in 2009 to commemorate the Estonian independence struggles of 1918-20. Comprising a large Estonian cross mounted on a 24m-high pillar of dimpled glass, it looks rather like an ice sculpture that's in imminent danger of melting – a deliberate effect designed to symbolize freedom's fragile nature. The monument is a controversial piece of work, however, with many Tallinners regarding it as an overstated patriotic gesture rather than the dignified memorial the square needs.

The Bronze Soldier

Just west of Vabaduse väljak on Tõnismägi near the Estonian National Library, a small park used to be the site of Tallinn's most notorious statue, the so-called **Bronze Soldier** or *Pronksõdur*. Erected in 1947 as a memorial to the Red Army, it was largely forgotten after the restoration of Estonian Independence in 1991 – until those ethnic communities who felt excluded from the Estonian national dream began to gravitate towards the Soldier as a positive symbol of their common Soviet past. It became increasingly popular with Tallinn's Russian-speakers, who would gather here on May 9, the eternally ambiguous "Victory Day" that symbolizes both the defeat of Nazi Germany and the renewed Soviet occupation of Estonia. Fearful that the monument was becoming a focus for ethnic tension, the Estonian government suggested first demolishing the monument, and second moving it to an out-of-city-centre site. Although popular with right-wing Estonian voters, the move was regarded as an attack on their culture by Tallinn's Russian community. Preparations to dismantle the Bronze Soldier led to the **Bronze Night** of April 26–27, 2007, when local youth – predominantly Russian – rioted in the city centre and looted shops. The statue can now be seen at the Military Cemetery, just southeast of the bus station on Filtri tee.

Elsewhere, the square boasts several architectural monuments dating back to the interwar years. Standing on the northern side of the square is the seven-storey modernist cube erected by an Estonian building society in 1934 and clearly intended as a muscular statement of the republic's self-confidence. Also dating from the 1930s – and a major institution ever since – is the **Tallinn Art Hall**, Vabaduse väljak 6 (Tallinna Kunstihoone; Wed–Sun noon–6pm; price depends on exhibition), whose high-profile exhibitions showcase the best in contemporary Estonian art.

In front of the art hall, steps lead down to a pedestrian underpass where the **AHHAA Science Centre** (daily 10am–8pm; €5.20) allows children to play with a variety of machines and gadgets, all with an educational purpose.

The dominant feature of the south side of the square is a vivacious red-brick structure built for the EKA insurance company in 1931 and now serving as the seat of **Tallinn City Council**; its facade is enlivened by chevrons and zany brickwork patterns.

Northeast of Vabaduse väljak

Running northeast from Vabaduse väljak, Pärnu mnt and Estonia pst follow roughly parallel paths round the eastern fringes of the Old Town. Presiding over Pärnu mnt at no. 4, the eye-catching **Estonian Drama Theatre** (Eesti draamateater), built in 1910 as the city's main German-language theatre, mixes Art Nouveau with Nordic folk motifs to produce a wealth of quirky detail: roofs resemble the shingles of village huts, and ancient bards in frieze form preside over the main entrance. Behind the theatre looms the much grander, but less engaging, **Estonia Theatre and Concert Hall**, financed by public contributions and completed in 1913 to provide Tallinn's Estonian-speaking majority with a cultural institution superior to anything that the city's Germans or Russians could muster. With the Estonian Philharmonic Orchestra occupying one wing and the opera and ballet performing in the other, it's still very much the nation's cultural flagship. On the southwestern side of the Concert Hall, just across G. Otsa tänav, a sculpture of a nude youth – the so-called "**Boy of Bronze**" – honours the high-school pupils who fell in the post–World War I struggle for independence. When Tallinn was in danger of falling to the Bolsheviks in the winter of 1918–19, the Estonian Commander-in-Chief General Laidoner was so starved of manpower that he had no choice but to appeal to the patriotic instincts of local schoolboys: equipped with improvised uniforms and obsolete rifles, they somehow managed to save the city.

Viru väljak and the Rotermann Quarter

Exit the Old Town to the east and you'll emerge on **Viru väljak**, a bustling traffic interchange and shopping area overlooked by the huge grey slab of the **Sokos Hotel Viru** (see p.63). Built in the 1970s for holidaying Finns, the *Viru* long enjoyed the reputation of being the only Westernized hotel in the USSR – and was the honeymoon venue of choice for any Soviet couple who could afford it.

Due north of Viru, Mere pst heads north towards the port area, skirting the eastern ramparts of the Old Town on the way. On the eastern side of Mere lies the **Rotermann Quarter**, an area of decaying factories and warehouses established by nineteenth-century industrialist Christian Abraham Rotermann. Neglected during much of the Soviet era, it's now prime inner-city redevelopment territory, with swanky bars, cafés and shopping plazas standing beside shabby buildings whose appointment with the restorer still awaits.

The Museum of Soviet Life

Housed in a former grain elevator on the south side of the Quarter is the privately run **Museum of Soviet Life** (June–Sept Tues–Sun 10am–6pm; €5), an odd jumble of exhibits that doesn't add up to much thematically but is nevertheless quite entertaining. Domestic knick-knacks, bicycles, and dowdy fashions provide an ironic commentary on the limited choice of consumer goods available to Soviet shoppers. Home-made lawnmowers – and even a home-made car – reveal the resourcefulness of citizens starved of affordable industrial products.

The Architecture Museum

The most impressive of the Rotermann Quarter's buildings is the **Estonian Architecture Museum**, which occupies the former Salt Storage Warehouse at Ahtri 2 (mid-May to Sept Wed–Fri noon–8pm, Sat & Sun 11am–6pm; Oct to mid-May Wed–Sun 11am–6pm; €3; ⓦwww.arhitektuurimuuseum.ee). Built by Christian Abraham's grandson, Christian Barthold Rotermann, in 1908, it was renovated in the mid-1990s to serve as an exhibition space. Top-notch exhibitions, many focusing on international architectural themes, are shown to advantage in the minimalist limestone-and-steel interior.

The Church of St Simeon and St Anne

A hundred metres east of the Architecture Museum stands the **Church of SS Simeon and Anne** (Tues–Fri 11am–6pm, Sat noon–4.30pm, Sun noon–3pm), a pretty, pea-green wooden church that serves an Estonian Orthodox congregation. Used as a sports hall during the Soviet era, it was renovated and reconsecrated in 2001. A small museum in the bell tower displays vestments and prayer books.

North of the Old Town

The shoreline **north of the Old Town** is dominated by the sprawling bulk of the **Linnahall concert hall**, a stepped, flat-roofed structure that looks like a ziggurat that has had its top sliced off. Built in 1980 it has not aged well, and discussions about far-reaching renovation work are currently ongoing. The parking lot in front of the Linnahall has been earmarked as the site of a new town hall – a cluster of cube-shaped buildings designed by Danish architect Bjorke Ingels.

West of the Linnahall is the **Culture Cauldron** (kultuurikatel; ⓦwww.kultuurikatel .eu), an arts centre and performance space based in a former power station that once provided much of Tallinn with its central heating. Something of an icon to fans of industrial chic, the red-brick chimney at the entrance to the complex once enjoyed a walk-on part in Soviet cinema history – this was where cult director Andrei Tarkovsky placed the entrance to the mysterious Zone in the 1979 metaphysical classic *Stalker*.

Occupying another former industrial building just across the road, the grandly named **Contemporary Art Museum of Estonia** (Eesti kaasaegse kunsti museum or EKKM; Wed–Sun noon–7pm; donation requested) is in fact an art project that aims to present an informal alternative to contemporary culture institutions like the Kumu (see p.80). The exhibitions here are well worth catching, as are the frequent live gigs and DJ events.

Kalamaja

Northwest of the Old Town the suburb of **Kalamaja** is a peaceful residential area lined with traditional timber houses. The northern, shoreline end, characterized by crumbling factories and unused port facilities, is the subject of major development plans – and already boasts at least two essential tourist attractions in the shape of the **Patarei Prison** and **Air Harbour maritime museum**. Both are walkable from the Old Town in about 15–20 minutes.

Patarei Prison

Occupying a former Tsarist naval fort 1km northwest of the Old Town at the end of Suur-Patarei, **Patarei Prison** (Wed–Sun 10am–6pm; €2) served as Tallinn's

---

Aegna and Naissaar

In summer boats run from the Linnahall harbour to the islands of **Aegna** and **Naissaar** (both around 1hr; check timetable with the Tallinn tourist office, see p.61). Aegna, just three square kilometres in size, is a protected nature area, while the significantly larger Naissaar has numerous military ruins and a nineteenth-century cemetery for soldiers who died in the Crimean War; both islands have appealing sandy beaches.

top-security gaol from 1919 to 2004. Garlanded with wreaths of rusty barbed wire, this crumbling complex of cell blocks has been left pretty much untouched ever since, and with little in the way of labelling the complex is largely left to speak for itself. Visitors can explore three floors of cells, administrative offices and hospital facilities, or take a stroll in one of the tiny, six-metre-square exercise yards. The "hanging room" – a plain chamber with a trap-door in the floor – sends a chill down the spine. Round the front of the building is the seashore, with fine views of Tallinn's port over to the east.

The Air Harbour

West of the prison is the so-called **Air Harbour** (Lennusadam; Wed–Sun 10am–6pm; €3), the site of a huge hangar built in 1916 to hold the Russian Admiralty's squadron of seaplanes. Looking like a conjoined trio of Byzantine cathedrals, the cavernous triple-domed building supported by angled pillars was considered one of the wonders of concrete construction at the time. Inside, a raised walkway guides visitors past various exhibits, most prominently the submarine *Lembit*, built in 1937 by British company Armstrong-Vickers for the Estonian Navy. Several naval vessels are moored outside, notably *Suur Tõll*, the ice-cream-coloured, steam-powered ice breaker built in 1914.

Kadriorg Park and around

Generously planted with oak, chestnut and lime trees and criss-crossed with avenues, **Kadriorg**, 2km east of the Old Town, is Tallinn's favourite **park.** Together with the **palace** at its centre, it was built for Tsar Peter the Great; after his conquest of Estonia in 1711, Peter began planning the park as a gift to his mistress Marta Skavronskaya. A serving girl of Lithuanian origin, Skavronskaya was taken as war booty by General Sheremetiev during one of his campaigns in Livonia and used as human currency at the Russian court – Sheremetiev gave her to Prince Menschikov, who in turn presented her to Peter in 1703. She remained the Tsar's companion thereafter, becoming Empress Catherine in 1724, hence the name of the park – Kadriorg is Estonian for "Catherine's Valley". Peter, who personally supervised the planting of the trees, always intended the park to be open to the public, and a stroll in Kadriorg soon became an essential fixture of the Tallinn social round. In the mid-nineteenth century, when Tallinn was one of the Russian Empire's most popular seaside resorts, Kadriorg was the place all the summer visitors gravitated towards, enjoying a constant stream of what German writer J.G. Kohl called "promenades, balls, illuminations and pleasure parties". The **main entrance** to the park is at the junction of Weizenbergi tänav and J. Poska (tram #1 or #3 from Viru väljak).

Swan Lake and the Kreuzwald Monument

The tree-lined Weizenbergi cuts southeast through the park, passing first of all **Swan Lake**, a rectangle of water bordered by formal flowerbeds and patronized by a fair number of ducks. Presiding over the eastern shore of the lake is a statue of **Friedrich Reinhold Kreuzwald** (see p.142), the Võru doctor who kickstarted the Estonian literary renaissance by publishing *Kalevipoeg* ("The Son of Kalev"), an epic poem composed of original fragments of folk material and Tolkien-esque episodes made up by Kreuzwald himself. Before Kreuzwald's time the Estonian language had been regarded as an uncultured country dialect by the German-speaking Baltic elite, and *Kalevipoeg* was hugely influential in inspiring a new generation of native-born intellectuals to start writing in their own tongue. At the base of the statue, plaques depicting harp-strumming bards and heroic warriors convey the required tone of myth and mystery.

The Kadriorg Palace Art Museum

Beyond the lake, Weizenbergi ascends gently towards **Kadriorg Palace** (Kadrioru loss), a late-Baroque residence designed by the Italian architect Niccolo Michetti to provide Empress Catherine with a comfy Baltic pad and used as an imperial residence right up until 1918. These days the palace's opulent staterooms accommodate the **Kadriorg Art Museum** (Kadrioru kunstimuuseum; Tues–Sun 10am–5pm; €4.50), an impressive

Kadriorg literary museums

The sedate streets south and west of Kadriorg are the setting for memorial museums honouring two of twentieth-century Estonia's literary giants – well worth a detour if you've a passion for Estonian culture or an interest in well-preserved interwar interiors.

The **Eduard Vilde Museum**, south of the Kreuzwald monument at Roheline 3 (Edvard Vilde memoriaalmuuseum; daily except Tues: March–Oct 11am–6pm; Nov–Feb 11am–5pm; €1.50), is in the house presented to him by the government in honour of his life's work. Inspired by the naturalist novels of Emile Zola, Vilde (1865–1933) was the first Estonian novelist to write about recent Estonian history in realist, documentary style. As well as being filled with social analysis and economic statistics, his narratives were also the popular, page-turning blockbusters of their time. His most famous novel *Mahtra sõda* ("The War in Mahtra"; 1902), dealing with peasant rebellions of the 1850s, began life as a serial in the newspaper *Teataja* – readers hungry for the latest instalment would queue outside the editorial offices on the day of publication. An opponent of the Tsarist autocracy as well as Estonia's German-speaking landowning classes, Vilde spent long periods of exile in Western Europe following the failed 1905 Revolution – first-hand experience of cosmopolitan cities like Paris and Berlin lent his writing a modern, urban edge unique in Estonian literature at the time. Not surprisingly, Vilde's battered travelling trunks are given pride of place in this charmingly reverent display of authorial heirlooms and period furnishings.

Heading west from the Vilde Museum along Koidula tänav brings you to the **Anton Hansen Tammsaare Memorial Museum,** Koidula 12A (A.H. Tammsaare memoriaalmuuseum; daily except Tues 10am–5pm; €1.50), occupying the handsome timber house where this dour novelist lived for the last decade of his life. Tammsaare (1878–1940) was born into a farming family in Järvamaa, central Estonia, and went on to study law at Tartu University, although he never graduated because of poor health. His literary reputation rests primarily on the five-volume, semi-autobiographical *Tõde ja Õigus* ("Truth and Justice"), a panorama of Estonian life from the 1870s to the 1930s that still forms the staple fodder of Estonian schoolchildren. It's famous (or infamous) both for its enormously long sentences, some of which last half a page, and for an oft-quoted line from volume 2, said to sum up the mixture of doggedness and resignation that defines the Estonian character: "Work hard, sweat hard, and then love will come". Alongside manuscripts and first editions, the museum displays some charming old postcards of Tallinn (including a mesmerizing 1930s vista of a Zeppelin floating over St Olaf's Church), and a startlingly lifelike dummy of Tammsaare staring out of his study window.

collection of European painting and sculpture over the centuries. The display opens on an exuberant note with Pieter Brueghel the Younger's small-scale *Wedding Feast*, followed by a room of seventeenth-century Dutch still lifes – the glistening, ready-to-eat surface of Hans van Essen's *Still Life with Lobster* being an obvious highlight. The Main Hall of the palace is an artwork in its own right, with chunky fireplaces topped by trumpet-blowing angels and two-headed eagles. A central ceiling painting illustrates the legend of Diana and Actaeon, in which the latter is transformed into a stag for having surprised Diana while bathing, and is hunted and killed by his dogs (Diana here represents the Russian Empire of Peter the Great, Actaeon the impudent and over-ambitious Swedish king, Charles XII). The adjoining lime-green Banqueting Hall is in fact a large conservatory tacked on in the 1930s, packed with soft furnishings and plants. There follows a room full of pictures by followers of Caravaggio and a representative sample of nineteenth-century Russian Realists like Ivan Shishkin and Ilya Repin – although Aleksey Bogolyubov's *Port of Tallinn* (1853) provides most in the way of local interest.

The Mikkel Museum

On the opposite side of Weizenbergi, the palace's former kitchen building houses the **Mikkel Museum** (Wed–Sun 10am–5pm; €3), whose collection, donated by prominent

Estonian collector Johannes Mikkel, features paintings, engravings and sculptures from Estonia, Western Europe, Russia and the Far East dating back to the sixteenth century. Intricate Chinese porcelain from the Qianlong period (1736–95) is one of the highlights.

Peter the Great's House

Between 1714 and 1716, Peter the Great lived in the so-called Dutch House, a small cottage about 200m uphill from Kadriorg Palace. Today this simple building harbours the **Peter the Great House Museum** (Peeter I majamuuseum; May–Aug Tues–Sun 11am–7pm; Sept–April Wed–Sun 11am–4pm; €2), decked out in the kind of utilitarian furnishings that practical-minded Peter favoured. Little in the house is original, save for a pair of slippers beside the bed, said to be the Tsar's own.

Kumu Art Museum

Built into the hillside at the eastern end of the park is the **Kumu Art Museum**, the main gallery of the Art Museum of Estonia (Kumu Kunstimuuseum; Tues–Sun 11am–6pm; €4.50; Ⓦ www.ekm.ee). Designed by Finnish architect Pekka Vaapuori and opened in 2006, this crescent-shaped wedge of Estonian limestone emerges from the grassy ridge like a surfacing submarine. Three floors of exhibits trace Estonian art from its awakenings in the nineteenth century, with the imposing portraits of St Petersburg-educated Johan Köler (Estonia's first academically trained painter) proving the early highlights. However it's in the 1920s and 30s that the collection really takes off, with Konrad Mägi's Expressionist take on the Estonian countryside, and the Cubist-inspired experiments of Arnold Akberg and Jaan Vahtra. Elsewhere, the "Socialist Realism" of the early Soviet period is contrasted with the surrealism, pop art and conceptual work that surfaced in the 1970s and 80s. There are also temporary exhibitions, lectures and film screenings, the latter often in English.

The Song Bowl

Heading north from Kumu leads, after around fifteen minutes, to Narva mnt. On the other side of this busy road is the **Song Bowl** (Lauluväljak), a vast amphitheatre that has been the venue for Estonia's Song Festivals ever since its construction in the 1960s. These biennial gatherings, featuring massed choirs thousands strong, have been an important form of national expression in Estonia since the first all-Estonia Song Festival was held in Tartu in 1869. The structure, which can accommodate 15,000 singers (with room for a further 30,000 or so performers on the platform in front of the stage and countless thousands of spectators on the banked field beyond it), was filled to capacity for the June 1988 festival, when up to 100,000 people a night came here to express their longing for independence from Soviet rule, giving rise to the epithet "Singing Revolution". Since then the Song Bowl has hosted concerts by numerous representatives of Western urban folklore – the Rolling Stones (1998) and Metallica (2006) among them. In winter the grassy spectators' slope is transformed into a winter-sports arena, with scores of kids hurling themselves down the incline on sleds, old tyres or bits of cardboard.

The Rusalka Memorial

A tree-lined avenue runs downhill from the amphitheatre to Pirita tee, which follows the seashore. A left turn here brings you to the **Rusalka Memorial**, built in 1902 in memory of the *Rusalka*, a Russian ship that had gone down nine years earlier. Designed by Amandus Adamson, the leading Estonian sculptor of the day, it comprises a rocky pillar on which an angel stands on tiptoe, waving an Orthodox cross in the direction of the Gulf of Finland.

Maaramäe, Pirita and the Botanical Gardens

Beyond Kadriorg, Pirita tee extends along the Bay of Tallinn, passing the **Estonian History Museum** at Maaramäe Palace before arriving at the haunting ruins of **Pirita Convent**. Uphill from here, the luxuriant **Botanical Gardens** and the **Television**

Tower, with its unbeatable views of the city, are sufficiently distant from central Tallinn to have the feel of a rural excursion.

Buses #1, #1A, #34 and #38 from Viru keskus pass the History Museum and Pirita; #34 and #38 continue all the way to the Botanical Gardens.

The Estonian History Museum

The **Maarjamäe Palace** (Maarjamäe loss), a neo-Gothic residence built for an aide of the Tsar, Count Anatoli Orlov-Davidov, in 1873, was long considered a beauty spot on account of its position overlooking Tallinn Bay. Today it houses the **Estonian History Museum** (Eesti ajaloomuuseum; Wed–Sun: March–Oct 11am–6pm; Nov–Feb 10am–5pm; €3; ⓦ www.eam.ee), which covers the nation's past from the late nineteenth century onwards. The text-heavy display is intended for Estonian visitors, but many of the exhibits speak for themselves – from grainy photographs of the Estonian volunteers who battled Bolsheviks, White Russians and Germans in the aftermath of World War I, to pictures of the "Forest Brothers", Estonian partisans who fought Soviet occupation into the 1950s. One display reveals the kind of underwear worn by Estonians during the Soviet era – the sexiest garments, explains the accompanying caption, were reserved for export, leaving local shops full of frumpy gear.

Ironically, Maarjamäe Palace was earmarked as the site of a "Museum of Soviet Friendship" during the 1980s, a project which never got off the ground owing to the untimely demise of the state it was intended to celebrate. However, Evald Okas's 1987 frescoes, featuring cosmonauts, scientists, gymnasts and other symbols of communist achievement, can still be admired in the main hall.

Just beyond Maarjamäe Palace, a huge concrete needle marks the site of a Soviet-era **war memorial** honouring the dead of World War II – intended to symbolize the Soviet role in "liberating" Estonia in 1944–5, it is nicknamed "Pinocchio's Grave" by locals.

Pirita

Pirita tee enters the suburb of **Pirita** (buses #1, #1A, #34 and #38 from Viru väljak) 2km northeast of Maarjamäe, at the point where the Pirita River flows into the Baltic Sea. The sailing events of the 1980 Moscow Olympics were held here, and a lively marina stretches along the river's western bank. Running east of the river mouth is the forest-backed **Pirita beach**, a 3km-long stretch of fine white sand that offers great views west towards Tallinn's port. Inland from the beach, next to the main road bridge across the river, rowing boats (€10/hr), kayaks (€6.50/hr) and pedaloes (€6.50/hr) provide the ideal means of transport with which to explore the Pirita's reed-fringed inland stretches.

East of the road bridge loom the ruins of **St Bridget's Convent** (Pirita klooster; daily: Jan–March, Nov & Dec noon–4pm; April, May, Sept & Oct 10am–6pm; June–Aug 9am–7pm; €1.30), founded in 1407 when Tallinn merchants invited the Swedish Bridgetine Order to the city. The order was unusual in admitting both male and female novices, who resided in different wings under the strict rule of a single abbess. The convent was destroyed and abandoned during the Livonian Wars and all that survives is the shell of its church, whose hugely impressive facade recalls the gabled merchants' houses of Tallinn's Old Town. Beyond the church lie the traces of old cells, backing onto a tributary of the Pirita River.

The Botanical Gardens and the Television Tower

Just beyond Pirita Convent, buses #34 and #38 turn sharp right into Kloostrimetsa tee and begin climbing into the hilly Kloostrimets ("Convent Wood"), a peaceful area of thick pine forest and suburban cottages that seems a world away from the city. On the north side of the road, tracks lead into the Forest cemetery (Metsakalmistu), Tallinn's most desirable final resting place. On the south side, just beyond the Kloostrimetsa bus stop, paths head to the **Botanical Gardens** (Botaanikaaed; daily: May–Sept 11am–7pm; Oct–April 11am–4pm; €3), a landscaped area of woodland centred on a rather wonderful palm house. Just beyond it are alpine and rose gardens, although you'll have to come in late spring or summer to enjoy them at their best.

Half a kilometre further along Kloostrimetsa tee, beside the Motoklubi bus stop, a side road leads off to the **Television Tower** (Teletorn), whose panoramic revolving-deck café has long been a favourite weekend destination for Tallinners. It's currently closed, awaiting renovation.

The Estonian Open-Air Museum

The one attraction in Tallinn's western outskirts is the **Estonian Open-Air Museum** (Eesti vabaõhumuuseum; daily: May–Sept 10am–8pm; €6.50; Oct–April 10am–5pm; €3.50; ⓦwww.evm.ee), 6km west of town in the upmarket suburb of Rocca al Mare – buses #21 and #21B run here from Balti Jaam (every 20–30min).

Arranged in a spacious wooded park, the museum brings together more than a hundred eighteenth- and nineteenth-century village buildings from different parts of the country. Exhibits illustrate how Estonian dwellings developed from single longhouses in which humans and animals lived cheek by jowl to more sophisticated farmsteads, in which barns and other outbuildings were built to accommodate the beasts. Estonian living rooms were traditionally built around open hearths with no chimneys – the resulting fug facilitated the drying of grain and the curing of meat and fish. Until the twentieth century most Estonian houses were built from spruce or pine – except on Saaremaa, where stone walls were sometimes used – as evidenced by a pair of farmsteads on display here. The museum also includes an appealing wooden church, taken from the village of Sutlepa north of Haapsalu – traditionally an area of Swedish settlement – its roof supported by swelling, cigar-shaped pillars. The *Kolu Kõrts* café serves up traditional bean soup and beer.

Eating

Many of Tallinn's ever-expanding array of **restaurants** serve high-quality food. International cuisines, particularly French, Italian, Russian, Chinese and Indian, are increasingly popular; most other establishments feature the solid meat-and-potatoes common to many north European countries. The Old Town's more expensive restaurants pull this off with panache, usually offering a number of global dishes in addition. In the more modest places, however, the pork chop still rules the roost.

As you'd expect, restaurants are more expensive in Tallinn than elsewhere in the country – you'll rarely pay less than €8 for a main course. However, cafés, bars and pubs often have a quite substantial menu of meals, generally cheaper than in full-blown restaurants, which also often offer good-value lunch specials.

Restaurants are **open** daily from noon until 11pm or midnight unless otherwise stated. Cafés are a law unto themselves, with the more old-fashioned places closing between 6pm and 8pm, the trendier joints working until 11pm or later.

Cafés and snacks

The following places are shown on the "Central Tallinn" map on p.68.

Anneli Viik Handmade Chocolates Café Pikk 30. Dozens of tempting handmade chocolates, as well as Illy coffee, draw in the crowds, who can also watch the chocolatiers at work. Mon–Sat 11am–9pm, Sun 11am–7pm.

Bogapott Pikk jalg 9. This curious, quirky café on Toompea, located in a ceramicists' workshop, has delicious home-made cakes and pastries. Daily 10am–6pm.

Chocolaterie Pierre Vene 6. Quaint café with creaky floorboards, antique-looking furnishings and outdoor tables strewn across the cobbled alleyway of Meistrite hoov. Pierre's handmade chocolates are the stars of the show, although all manner of cakes and quiches are also on offer. Daily 9am–10pm.

Elsebet Viru 2. Attached to the *Peppersack* restaurant, this genteel, old-fashioned café has cakes and snacks on the menu. Daily 8am–8pm.

Kehrwieder Saiakang 1. A relaxing coffee house on the main square, with low ceilings, wooden tables and a succulent range of cakes. The outdoor terrace quickly fills up in summer. Daily 11am–midnight.

Komeet Estonia 9. Chic top-floor café in the Slaris shopping centre (take the lift), complete with fantastic downtown views, sun-loungers, a roof garden and a menu of daytime coffees and night-time cocktails. Mon–Thurs 10am–11pm, Fri & Sat til midnight, Sun til 9pm.

Maiasmokk Pikk 16. The city's most venerable café – founded in 1864 – with a beautiful
wood-panelled interior. You may have to queue for
a seat, however, as it's hugely popular with elderly
ladies and tour groups. Mon–Sat 8am–7pm, Sun
10am–6pm.

Pagaripoisid Nunne. Old Town branch of the
national bakery chain, offering quality pastries,
sandwiches and cakes at a good price. Indoor
seating or take-away. Mon–Fri 8am–7pm, Sat
10am–7pm, Sun 10am–6pm.

🏃 **Pink** Olevimägi. This cute two-table café
bakes its own bread and pies, and also
serves Mediterranean salads. They have an original
range of crafts for sale, too, with block-print bags,
tablecloths and T-shirts. Mon–Sat 10am–6pm, Sun
10am–3pm.

Spirit Mere pst 6e. Ultra-chic café-bar with
design-catalogue interior, a full menu of drinks
and gourmet food. Housed in the same building as
the *Ö* restaurant (see p.84), but note that *Spirit*'s
entrance is in the courtyard at the back. Daily
noon–11pm.

Restaurants

Unless otherwise stated, the following
restaurants are shown on the "Central
Tallinn" map on p.68.

Admiral Lootsi 15 ☎ 662 3777; see Tallinn map,
p.64. Balkan grilled food including *cevapcici*
(minced-meat rissoles) and *vešalice* (skewered
strips of pork) served in a small steamship moored
in a crook of Tallinn's passenger port. With tables
on deck it's a good place to enjoy the evening sun.
Mains from €12. Daily noon–11pm.

African Kitchen Uus 34. Leopard-print cushions,
tribal masks and mini palm trees make this a fun
and atmospheric experience. Tasty, well-priced
African food, including chicken peri-peri and good
vegetarian options, with mains from €9. Colourful
and potent cocktails named after African countries
provide a novel way of working your way across
the continent in the space of an evening. Sun–
Thurs noon–midnight, Fri & Sat noon–2am.

Bocca Olevimägi 9 ☎ 641 2610. This designer
restaurant draws a well-heeled, fashionable crowd
with its excellent, and predictably expensive, Italian
cuisine. Mains from €13. Daily noon–midnight.

Le Bonaparte Pikk 45. *Le Bonaparte* provides
a high-quality French dining experience, with
delicious food (particularly the cheeses) and stylish
decor. Prices, however, are steep – main courses
around €20 – and portions can be on the small
side. Daily noon–midnight.

Chakra Bremeni käik 1. A pleasant and reliable
place to enjoy a well-spiced curry, in an atmospheric

ensemble of brick-lined chambers decorated with
replica erotic sculptures from Indian temples. Mains
are usually in the €12–14 range, although inexpensive lunchtime specials are frequently chalked up
outside. Daily noon–midnight.

Controvento Vene 12 ☎ 644 0470. Located in a
fourteenth-century granary, this tasteful, authentic
Italian restaurant has a good selection of pizzas
and pastas and a decent wine list. Main courses
from around €8. Reservations advised. Daily
noon–11.30pm.

Elevant Vene 5. A chic Indian restaurant with mellow decor and a wide range of authentic dishes,
including plenty for vegetarians, and a few forays
into Estonian-Indian fusion such as curried moose.
Mains from €10. Daily noon–11pm.

Fish & Wine Harju 1 ☎ 662 3013. Fish and seafood with a Mediterranean slant, in a three-storey
temple to 1960s Modernism in the heart of the
Old Town. Mains are around €12, but quick-lunch
soups and salads are significantly cheaper. Mon–
Sat 11am–11pm.

Gloria Müürivahe 2 ☎ 644 6950. *Gloria* has been
producing top-quality French cuisine since 1937,
which, combined with the Art Nouveau decor
and the best wine list in the country, makes for a
memorable dining experience. Frequently voted the
best restaurant in Estonia; mains from €17. Daily
noon–11pm.

Karl Friedrich Raekoja plats 5. This "pepper
restaurant" – pepper being a key flavour in all
dishes – serves fish specialities and succulent
steaks in an elegant, olde-worlde interior. Some of
the starters cost as much as main courses in other
restaurants, but they're probably worth it. Daily
noon–midnight.

🏃 **Kohvik Moon** Võrgu 3 ☎ 631 4575; see
Tallinn map, p.64. Stylish cooking in a
contemporary interior in the up-and-coming
Kalamaja district. Roast beef, duck breast, pike-
perch and other Estonian standards predominate,
each with a modern twist. Mains €11–14. Tues–Sat
noon–11pm.

Kuldse Notsu Kõrts Dunkri 8. The "Little Piggy
Inn" offers Estonian country dishes in rooms
decked out with rustic textiles and wooden benches. Go for the roast pork or try wild boar in juniper
sauce. Mains around €12. Daily noon–midnight.

Museum Vana-Viru 14 ☎ 646 0901. Exposed
brickwork, matt-black surfaces and swivel chairs
set a suitably swanky lounge-bar tone, while sepia
pictures of fire trucks serve as a reminder that this
building was once the city's main fire station. The
modern-European menu covers a handful of meaty
classics, well-prepared risottos and pastas, and a
lot of good sushi. Mains from €12. Daily noon–11pm.

Must Lammas Sauna 2. The "Black Sheep" – a Georgian restaurant – specializes in superbly spicy stews and grills, served in stylish surroundings with a few ethnic touches. Mains from €11. Daily noon–11pm.

Olde Hansa Vanaturg 1. The longest-established and best of Tallinn's medieval-themed restaurants, with wooden benches set out in atmospherically lit rooms in the Town Hall. Meaty dishes based on medieval recipes, appropriately costumed staff and live minstrels. Main courses from €10. Daily 11am–midnight.

Ö Mere pst 6e ⊕ 661 6150. Modern Estonian cuisine with an upmarket twist, with traditionally inspired rabbit, veal and venison dishes exquisitely prepared and served in an environment that comes across as part-stylish lounge, part-contemporary art gallery. Mains €18–24. Daily noon–11pm.

Ribe Vene 7 ⊕ 631 3084. Smart but not over-formal restaurant with soothing decor and jazz soundtrack. The menu goes for Estonian ingredients and modern-European style, with classic pork, duck and Baltic-Sea fish dishes predominating. Mains €13–20. Daily noon–11pm.

Sushi Cat Roosikrantsi 16; see Tallinn map, p.64. Informal sushi bar just steps away from the Old Town, with Manga-inspired decor, swift service, and decent prices. Sushi sets in the €6–12 range. Mon–Thurs noon–10pm, Fri noon–11pm, Sat 1–11pm, Sun 1–10pm.

Vanaema Juures Rataskaevu 10 ⊕ 626 9080. "Grandma's Place", a cosy cellar restaurant decorated with sepia photos and antique candle-holders, has some of the best Estonian food in Tallinn, including mouth-wateringly tender pork, elk, wild boar and salmon; mains around €11. Reservations essential. Mon–Sat noon–midnight, Sun noon–6pm.

Von Krahli Aed Rataskaevu 8 ⊕ 626 9088. Traditional Estonian duck, pork and freshwater fish dishes prepared and presented in modern-European style, with a couple of vegetarian alternatives, in an atmospherically lit farmhouse-kitchen interior. Outdoor seating on the street or in a tiny courtyard. Mains around €10. Mon–Sat noon–midnight, Sun noon–6pm.

Drinking

Most young Tallinn locals are enthusiastic, sociable drinkers, ensuring the Old Town remains lively most nights. At weekends the drinking scene can be particularly raucous, with bars filling up with holidaying Finns and city-break tourists from across Europe – stag parties included – drawn by the comparatively cheap prices.

The **Old Town** could have been made for drinking, its narrow streets lending themselves perfectly to all manner of smoky dens, stylish lounge bars and laid-back pubs. Most places offer meals, making it possible to hunker down for an evening's drinking while also appeasing your hunger pangs. Many bars feature **DJs** and/or live bands at the weekends, making them a good alternative to the pay-to-enter clubs (see p.86). Most places open around 11am and don't close until 1am or 2am at the earliest.

All bars listed below are in the Old Town, and marked on the map on p.68, unless otherwise stated.

Clazz Vana Turg 2. Popular bar, around the corner from the main square, which strikes a winning balance between lively pub and lounge bar. Good cocktails, Mediterranean food and live jazz most days keep the joint jumping, and there's plenty of seating on the wooden deck outside. Daily noon–3am.

Depeche Mode Voorimehe 4. Dedicated to the only famous thing ever to have come out of Basildon, *DM* is not the heavy-handed theme bar you might imagine – the moody black-and-red colour scheme and leatherette couches will appeal to anyone who enjoys mildly alternative cellar bars. The background music, however, may well get on your nerves sooner or later… Daily noon–3am.

Drink Bar & Grill Väike-Karja 8. A living room-sized temple to good beer that offers a great selection of international brews on tap and plenty more in bottled form. Laid back, friendly, and with a predominantly Anglophone clientele. Good food, too. Daily noon–1am.

Hell Hunt Pikk 39. Don't be put off by the name – it means "Gentle Wolf". *Hell Hunt* is a vibrant pub and mainstay of the Tallinn expat scene, offering hearty meals washed down by the pub's own-brand lager and porter brews. Daily noon–2am.

Ice Bar Dunkri 6. The tiny bar at the *Merchant's House* hotel is a similarly chic blend of old and new: space-age bar stools, stained-glass windows and a fourteenth-century painted ceiling. Even the drinks are stylish – cocktails or vodka in a shot glass made of ice – and there's also a quality restaurant and a café with great milkshakes and lunch specials. Sun–Thurs 9am–midnight, Fri & Sat 9am–2am.

Il Gallo Nero Rataskaevu 4. Italian deli that also functions as daytime café and night-time wine bar, with cosy checked-tablecloth interior, tasty panini snacks, and a wide choice of Mediterranean wines. Daily 11am–midnight.

Kaheksa Vana-Posti 8. With dark drapes, settees and a sunken central area edged with potted trees, this is a swanky-but-cool place in which to tuck into salads and pasta dishes during the day, or moodily sip cocktails come the evening. Sun–Thurs noon–1am, Fri & Sat noon–3am.

Karja Kelder Väike-Karja 1. This treasured relic of a cellar bar has preserved its old-fashioned dark-wood fittings and its predominantly local crowd. Competitive prices are an added bonus. Sun & Mon 11am–1am, Tues–Thurs 11am–2am, Fri & Sat 11am–4am.

Levist Väljas Olevimägi 12. A unmarked door opposite the *Tallinn Backpackers* hostel provides access to this legendary underground bar on two floors, with bare stone walls, thrift-shop furnishings, cheap drinks, a predominantly local crowd, and alternative music on the sound system. Daily 5pm–3am or later.

Musi Niguliste 6. With a prim café in the front room and chic pastel-coloured sofas at the back, *Musi* is a nice mix of the cosy and the classy. It's primarily a wine bar, although it does stock other liquids and has a lengthy food menu. Mon–Sat 5pm–midnight.

St Patrick's Suur-Karja 8. The most popular of the four *St Patrick's* pubs is in a wonderful medieval building. Every fourth Saku is free and the substantial Estonian staples on the menu are surprisingly authentic. Sun–Thurs 11am–2am, Fri & Sat 11am–4am.

Texas Honky Tonk Pikk. Part Tex-Mex restaurant, part C&W-themed pub, this is a pleasantly laid-back location in which to work your way through several Estonian or Mexican beers. There's a small outdoor terrace at the back. Sun–Thurs noon–midnight, Fri & Sat noon–2am.

Von Krahl Rataskaevu 12. Mildly arty-alternative bar at the back of the Von Krahl theatre (see p.87), with inexpensive draught beers and a handy menu (till 10pm) of soups, salads and beer snacks. There's a patio in the yard. Frequent DJs, indie bands and jazz musicians, when there's an entrance fee. Sun–Thurs noon–1am, Fri & Sat noon–3am.

VS Pärnu mnt 28; see Tallinn map, p.64. A hip DJ bar some 200m south of the Old Town, featuring industrial decor and restaurant-quality food (including some mouth-watering Indian dishes); mains around €8. Try to bag one of the purple sofas by the window. Mon 10am–midnight, Tues–Thurs 10am–1am, Fri 10am–3am, Sat noon–3am, Sun noon–1am.

Nightlife and entertainment

In addition to the range of **classical music** and **theatre** that you would expect from a capital city, Tallinn, partly due to its increasing popularity as a city-break destination, also has a burgeoning **club scene**, offering a hedonistic menu of entertainment every night of the week – apart from Monday, when everybody takes time off to recharge their batteries.

Major cultural **festivals** include **Jazzkaar** (Ⓦwww.jazzkaar.ee), when big names in world jazz visit Tallinn in April; and the **Dark Nights Film Festival** (see p.87). **Tickets** for many theatre and music events are bookable through Ticketpro either online (Ⓦwww.ticketpro.ee) or through box offices at the Nokia Concert Hall and the Estonia Concert Hall.

Clubs and live music

Mainstream discos churning out top-40 hits, house and techno remain the rule, although an upsurge in the local **DJ culture** ensures that you'll be able to find most genres of dance music most nights of the week. Dedicated clubbers should look out for street posters or pick up flyers in internet cafés and record stores. Expect to pay €5 and up for **admission**, rising to twice that for weekend events with big-name DJs.

Tallinn is never likely to become the rock 'n' roll capital of the universe, although you'll find a motley collection of alternative musicians, middle-of-the-road rockers and cover bands playing in clubs, or in some of the bars listed on above. International touring bands play at the 10,000-capacity **Saku Suurhall**, 5km west of the centre at Paldiski mnt 104B in the suburb of Rocca al Mare (Ⓦwww.sakusuurhall.ee; bus #21 from Balti Jaam); the Nokia Concert Hall (see below) round the back of the Solaris shopping mall; and at the outdoor **Song Bowl** (Lauluväljak; see p.80).

The following clubs are shown on the "Central Tallinn" map on p.68.

Angel Sauna 1. Tallinn's best gay club has a strict "face control" policy; if you get in, however, you're virtually guaranteed a raucous night. The attached café is almost as popular, drawing a mixed gay and straight crowd. Wed–Sat till 5am.

BonBon Mere pst 6E ⓦwww.bonbon.ee. One of the hottest tickets in town, *BonBon* pulls in the fashionable set, who come to dance under the chandeliers and sip expensive cocktails. Wed, Fri & Sat till 6am or later.

Café Amigo beneath the *Viru Hotel*, Viru väljak 4. Locals and (particularly Finnish) tourists flock to this cheesy but likeable disco, which alternates live bands with mainstream dance music. Estonian pop-rock acts make regular appearances. Sun–Thurs 9pm–4am, Fri & Sat 9pm–5am.

Hollywood Vana-Posti 8 ⓦwww.clubhollywood .ee. Housed in a former cinema in the heart of the Old Town, *Hollywood* has become a Tallinn nightlife institution. Tourists and youthful locals tear it up on a huge dancefloor, while DJs play anything from house to hip-hop. Wed & Thurs 10pm–4am, Fri & Sat 10pm–5am.

Privé Harju 6 ⓦwww.clubprive.ee. Trendy club with higher-than-average prices and a fairly strict door policy, attracting well-known, predominantly dance-music DJs from the Baltic and beyond. Wed & Thurs 10pm–4am, Fri & Sat 10pm–5am.

Classical music, opera and ballet

Both the Estonian National Symphony Orchestra and the National Opera have solid reputations and attract their fair share of big-name conductors and soloists from abroad. There's also an impressive choice of chamber music on offer, much of it in Tallinn's suitably atmospheric medieval churches and halls; ⓦwww.concert.ee is useful for finding out what's on in the bigger concert venues. The **box office** at the Estonia Concert Hall, Estonia pst 4 (☏614 7760), sells tickets for some, but not all, of the classical concerts around town.

Estonia Concert Hall (Estonia kontserdisaal) Estonia pst 4 ☏614 7760, ⓦwww.concert.ee. Prestige venue for classical music and choral works, including performances by the Estonian National Symphony Orchestra. Box office Mon–Fri noon–7pm, Sat noon–5pm, Sun 1hr before performance.

Estonia Theatre (Estonia teater) Estonia pst 4. Next door to the Estonia Concert Hall, home of the National Opera (Rahvasooper; ⓦwww.opera.ee), ballet and musicals. Same box office as the Estonia Concert Hall.

Estonian Music Academy (Eesti muusikaaka-deemia) Rävala 16 ☏667 5768, ⓦwww.ema.edu .ee. Chamber music several times a week.

House of the Blackheads (Mustpeademaja) Pikk 26 ☏631 3199, ⓦwww.mustpeademaja .ee. Frequent chamber music and solo recitals. Box office 1hr before performance.

Niguliste Church Niguliste 3 ☏631 4330, ⓦwww.ekm.ee. Organ recitals at weekends; details are usually posted outside.

Nokia Concert Hall Estonia pst 9 ☏615 5111, ⓦwww.tallinnconcerthall.ee. State-of-the-art venue staging big-name concerts in all styles.

Väravatorn Lühike jalg 9 ☏614 7760. The HQ of internationally acclaimed early music ensemble Hortus Musicus – they play here once or twice a month.

Theatre

There's a great deal of top-quality **theatre** in Tallinn, but with most of it performed in Estonian, your best bet is to stick to major productions and concentrate on the stage-craft – or simply treat the whole experience as a social event.

Estonian Drama Theatre (Draamateater) Pärnu mnt 5 ☏680 5555, ⓦwww.draamateater.ee. The country's flagship theatrical institution, offering classical drama in a wonderful building. Box office daily noon–7pm.

Linnateater Lai 23 ☏665 0800, ⓦwww .linnateater.ee. Top-quality contemporary work. Box office Mon–Fri 9am–6pm, Sat 10am–6pm.

NO99 Sakala 3 ☏660 5051, ⓦwww.no99.ee. Challenging contemporary stuff from an internationally recognized company.

Nukuteater Lai 1 ☏667 9555, ⓦwww.nukuteater .ee. Puppet theatre, with most productions kicking off at lunchtime.

Russian Drama Theatre (Vene teater) Vabaduse väljak 5 ☏611 4911, ⓦwww.veneteater.ee. Drama from the classical Russian canon, as well as contemporary international work in Russian translation. **Theatrum** Vene 14 ☏ 644 6889, ⓦ www.theatrum .ee. Youth and student productions.

Von Krahli Teater Rataskaevu 10 ☏ 626 9090, ⓦ www.vonkrahl.ee. Modern, challenging work in a lovely old-fashioned theatre.

Cinemas

The number of **cinemas** in central Tallinn is dwindling as smaller movie theatres are replaced by modern multiscreens. Films are shown in the original language with Estonian subtitles. One event that attracts cineastes from all over the Baltic is the **Dark Nights Film Festival** (Pimedate ööde festivaal; ⓦ www.poff.ee), celebrating contemporary art-house movies.

Artis Solaris Centre, Estonia pst ☏ 663 1380, ⓦ www.kinoartis.ee. Mostly non-Hollywood movies in a modern auditorium in the Solaris shopping mall. **Coca-Cola Plaza** Hobujaama 5 ☏ 1182, ⓦ www .superkinod.ee. State-of-the-art multiplex with

eleven screens and a healthy sprinkling of cafés and restaurants.
Kinomaja Uus 3 ☏ 646 4068, ⓦ www.kinomaja .ee. Art house films and cinema classics in a lovely Old Town building.

Shopping

The streets of the Old Town are perfect for **souvenir shopping**: a string of outlets along Pikk and Dunkri sell linen, patchwork quilts, amber jewellery, woolly jumpers and mittens. The best place to browse for woollens is the open-air **market** on Müürivahe, beneath the stretch of city walls immediately north of the Viru Gate.

Bookshops

Apollo Viru 23. Tallinn's biggest and brightest bookstore, offering plentiful maps, guidebooks and English-language classics in paperback. Mon–Sat 10am–7pm, Sun 11am–5pm.
Rahva Raamat Pärnu mnt 10 and in Viru Keskus. Estonia's oldest bookshop has a solid selection of maps and some English-language novels and magazines. Mon–Fri 9am–7pm, Sat 10am–5pm, Sun 10am–4pm.

Chocolates

Anneli Viik Handmade Chocolates Pikk 30.Devilishly tempting selection of own-brand chocolates and chocolate bars, made on the premises (you can see the chocolatiers working away behind a glass screen). Mon–Sat 11am–9pm, Sun 11am–7pm.
Kalev Roseni 7. In the Rotermanni quarter. A cavity-inducing range of sweet treats from Estonia's famous confectioner. Mon–Sat 10am–8pm, Sun 11am–5pm.

Markets

Kalaturg (Fish market) Kalasadam. Fish and seafood direct from Baltic fisherfolk. A great place to get your hands on a whole smoked eel. Saturday 10am–4pm.
Rotermanni trg Local food including a lot of organic products. Also handicrafts on Sundays. In the main plaza of the Rotermanni quarter. Wed-Sun 10am–4pm.

Shopping centres

Viru Keskus Viru väljak. High-street chains, coffee shops and a well-stocked supermarket in the basement. Daily 9am–9pm.
Solaris Estonia pst. Central shopping mall offering a good choice of shops and cafés. Daily 9am–11pm.

Souvenir and specialist shops

🏃 **Eesti Kasitöö** Pikk 22. If it's hand-knitted, hand-woven or hand-embroidered you'll probably find it here. Mon–Sat 9.30am–6.30pm, Sun 10am–5pm.
Hindrikus Lühike jalg 2. High-quality woollens, felt hats and ethnic-inspired jewellery. Mon–Sat 10am–6pm, Sun 11am–4pm.
🏃 **Katariina Gild** Vene 12/Katariina käik. An ensemble of craft workshops squeezed into Katariina käik (Catherine's Passage), where you can watch applied artists at work and check out their wares. Experts in stained glass, ceramics, patchwork, leatherwork, millinery and jewellery all get a studio each. Mon–Sat noon–6pm.
Loovala Rotermanni 5. A department store with a difference, this is an open studio in which graphic artists and jewellery-, glass- and textile designers have a small workshop space – and items for sale.
Lühikese Jala Galerii Lühike jalg 6. An art gallery selling modern tapestry, textiles, jewellery and sculpture. Daily 10am–5pm.
🏃 **Masters' Courtyard (Meistrite hoov)** Vene 6. Jewellery, ironmongery, quirky

ceramics and tempting handmade chocolates in a medieval courtyard that also hosts art exhibitions. Daily 11am–6pm.

Morš Väike-karja 1 (in the courtyard and up the steps). Vintage clothing, vinyl records, household bric-a-brac and other arty jumble. Mon–Fri noon–7pm, Sat 1–5pm.

Myy Art Müürivahe 36. Quirky-but-cool ceramics, textiles, glasswork and graphic art on sale in this gallery-shop. Daily 11am–5pm.

Nu Nordik Vabaduse väljak 8. Clothes and domestic utensils by Estonia's most promising young designers. Mon–Sat 11am–6pm, Sat 11am–5pm.

Sepa Ari Olevimägi 11. Traditional and contemporary blacksmith work, including accessories for the kitchen and garden.

Veta Pikk 4. Best of a whole line of linen shops on Pikk, selling tablecloths as well as the kind of linen clothes that you won't be ashamed to wear when you get home. Daily 10am–6pm.

Zizi Vene 12. Classy textiles for the home, with a few ethnographic touches. A good place to stock up on pure linen pillowcases, sheets and towels. Mon–Sat 10am–6pm, Sun 11am–4pm.

Listings

Airlines Air Baltic, Estonia pst 1/3 ☎630 6666; Estonian Air, at the airport, ☎640 1160; Finnair, at the airport ☎626 6309.

Bicycle rental City Bike, Uus 33 ☎511 1819, ⓦwww.citybike.ee.

Embassies and consulates Australia, Marja 9 ☎650 9308, ⓔmati@standard.ee; Canada, Toom-Kooli 13 ☎627 3311, ⓔTallinn@canada.ee; Finland, Kohtu 4 ☎610 3200, ⓦwww.finland.ee; Latvia, Tõnismägi 10 ☎627 7850; Lithuania, Uus 15 ☎631 4030; Russia, Pikk 19 ☎646 4175; UK, Wismari 6 ☎667 4700, ⓦwww.britishembassy.ee; US, Kentmanni 20 ☎668 8100, ⓦwww.usemb.ee. Citizens of Ireland, New Zealand and South Africa should contact one of the English-speaking embassies to find out who is currently representing their interests.

Hospital The main hospital is at Ravi 18 ☎620 7070; for an ambulance call ☎112.

Internet Almost all hotels, and many cafés, restaurants, bars and pubs have wi-fi networks, often for free.

Laundry Seebimull, Liivalaia 7.

Left luggage In the ticket hall of the bus station (Mon–Sat 6.30am–10.20pm, Sun 7.30am–10pm; from €0.70); and at the train station (7am–7pm).

Pharmacies Centrally located pharmacies that are open daily include Koduapteek, Aia 7; Ülikooli Apteek, in the Viru Keskus shopping centre; and Tõnismäe Apteek, Tõnismägi 5. The latter has a 24hr emergency counter (ring the buzzer).

Police Pärnu mnt 11 ☎644 5266.

Post office Narva mnt 1, opposite the Sokos Hotel Viru (Mon–Fri 8am–8pm, Sat 8am–6pm).

Taxis Ranks on Vabaduse väljak or just outside the Viru gate. Otherwise call Klubitaxo ☎638 0638 or Linnatakso ☎644 2442.

Travel details

Trains

Tallinn to: Narva (1 daily; 3hr 30min); Tartu (5 daily; 2hr 30min–3hr); Viljandi (3 daily; 2hr 30min).

Buses

Tallinn to: Haanja (2 daily; 5hr); Haapsalu (every 1hr; 1hr 45min); Kärdla (3 daily; 4hr 30min); Kuressaare (every 2hr; 4hr 30min); Narva (hourly; 3hr 40min); Pärnu (hourly; 1hr 45min); Tartu (every 30min; 2hr 20min); Viljandi (hourly; 2hr 15min); Võru (12 daily; 3hr 45min).

International trains

Tallinn to: Moscow (1 daily; 14hr).

International buses

Tallinn to: Berlin (1–2 daily; 30hr); Rīga (7 daily; 5–6hr); St Petersburg (8 daily; 7–8hr); Vilnius (1 daily; 10hr).

International flights

Tallinn to: Copenhagen (up to 3 daily; 1hr 40min); Frankfurt (7 weekly; 2hr 40min); Helsinki (up to 8 daily; 1hr); London (2–3 daily; 3hr); Moscow (3 weekly; 3hr); Paris (1 daily; 3hr 30min); Rīga (up to 3 daily; 1hr); Stockholm (up to 5 daily; 2hr); Vilnius (up to 4 daily; 1hr 30min).

1.2

Western Estonia

With its jutting coastline, archipelago of islands and hinterland of thick forest and heaths, **western Estonia** is a microcosm of the country. Many locals maintain that it's in this region's juniper-covered heaths, quaint country towns and wave-battered shores watched over by solitary lighthouses, that the true soul of the nation ultimately lies. Although many of the coastal towns have been resorts since the nineteenth century, when the cream of the Baltic aristocracy came to bathe their weary limbs in medicinal coastal mud, much of western Estonia was treated as a sensitive border area during the Soviet period and tourism didn't really get going again until the 1990s. Happily, the desire to develop western Estonia has been tempered by the realization that the region's wealth of unspoilt natural landscapes is its

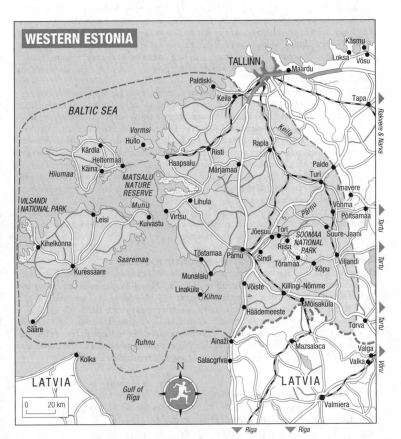

WESTERN ESTONIA

most valuable asset. The area also boasts a rich variety of wildlife, including sizeable communities of deer, moose, elk and beaver, as well as thousands of migrating birds in the spring and autumn.

The main gateway to the northwestern coast is the resort of **Haapsalu**, an endearing mixture of belle époque gentility and contemporary chic, and a convenient staging post en route to the tranquil islands of **Vormsi** and **Hiiumaa**. South of Hiiumaa, **Saaremaa** is the biggest and most popular of Estonia's islands, its enjoyably animated capital Kuressaare providing access to a beautiful hinterland of forest, heath and swamp. The southwestern coast is dominated by **Pärnu**, Estonia's one true beach resort. Inland from Pärnu, the laid-back provincial town of **Viljandi** is one of Estonia's prettiest and provides access to the beautiful, desolate peat bogs of the **Soomaa National Park**.

Western Estonia is easy to access, with frequent **buses** from Tallinn to the coast's principal towns, Haapsalu and Pärnu. The islands are served by regular **ferries** from the mainland. In addition, express buses run from Tallinn to Hiiumaa and Saaremaa, with the ferry crossing included as part of the deal. Local transport on the islands themselves is scarce, and unless you have a car you'll need to adopt a leisurely approach to exploring.

Haapsalu and around

Straddling a three-kilometre-long strip of land pointing out into the Baltic Sea, **HAAPSALU** is an appealing mix of traditional seaside resort and modern spa town. Surrounded on three sides by water, it has been optimistically dubbed by some locals as the "Nordic Venice". This requires a significant degree of imagination, but Haapsalu has an undeniable charm, with narrow, winding streets of haphazard wooden fisherman's cottages, stately neo-Gothic villas gazing proudly out to sea and an imposing thirteenth-century castle.

The town has been popular with holidaymakers since the early nineteenth century, when local doctor Carl Abraham Hunnius (1797–1851) began to publicize the curative properties of the local mud. Haapsalu soon became a magnet for St Petersburg high society – both Tsar Alexander II and son Alexander III were regular visitors. By the mid-twentieth century, it was a mass-market bucket-and-spade resort, although tourism was subsequently wound down by the security-conscious Soviet regime, which turned northwestern Estonia into one vast military installation. Since independence, it has become increasingly popular again, not least for the attractive stretch of sand just west of town at Paralepa. Meanwhile, many of the hotels still offer the mud treatments that first made the town famous.

Haapsalu is 10km from the Rohuküla ferry terminal, which serves the islands of Hiiumaa and Vormsi. The latter is an easy day-trip from town, as is the bird-rich nature reserve of **Matsalu** on the mainland to the south.

Arrival, information and accommodation

Buses arrive in the forecourt of the old train station on the southwestern side of town, ten minutes' walk from the **tourist office** at Karja 13 (mid-May to mid–Sept Mon–Fri 9am–6pm, Sat & Sun 10am–4pm; mid-Sept to mid-May Mon–Fri 9am–5pm; ☎473 3248, ℮haapsalu@visitestonia.com); staff can book you into local **B&Bs** (①–②). Some **hotels** drop their prices from October to April, and even those that don't officially do so may be open to bargaining. There are two **campsites**, one in Paralepa forest (*Paralepa Camping*, ☎515 5666, ⓦwww.paralepacamping.ee) and another south of the centre at Manniku 34 (*Camping Pikseke*, ☎475 5779, ⓦwww.campingpikseke.com).

Hotels

Kongo Kalda 19 ☎472 4800, ⓦwww.kongohotel .ee. Smallish but crisply modern en-suites, all white surfaces and pale wood. Built on the site of a bar that was so notorious for drunken brawling in the early 1970s that it was nicknamed "Congo" after the vicious civil war then taking place in that country. ⑤

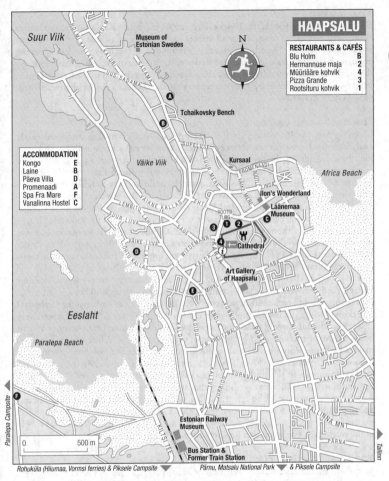

HAAPSALU

RESTAURANTS & CAFÉS	
Blu Holm	B
Hermannuse maja	2
Müüriääre kohvik	4
Pizza Grande	3
Rootsituru kohvik	1

ACCOMMODATION	
Kongo	E
Laine	B
Päeva Villa	D
Promenaadi	A
Spa Fra Mare	F
Vanalinna Hostel	C

Suur Viik

Museum of Estonian Swedes

N

Tchaikovsky Bench

Väike Viik

Kursaal

Africa Beach

Ilon's Wonderland

Läänemaa Museum

ROOTSI TURG

Cathedral

Art Gallery of Haapsalu

Eeslaht

Paralepa Beach

Estonian Railway Museum

Bus Station & Former Train Station

0   500 m

Paralepa Campsite

Tallinn

Rohuküla (Hiiumaa, Vormsi ferries) & Piksele Campsite ▼   Pärnu, Matsalu National Park ▼ & Piksele Campsite

---

Laine Sadama 9/11 ☎472 4400, ⊛www.laine.ee.
A large, Soviet-era sanatorium with plain en-suites
just as comfortable as those in any international,
mid-range hotel. Mud baths and other therapeutic
treatments on site. ⑤

Päeva Villa Lai 7 ☎473 3672, ⊛www.paevavilla
.ee. Each of the en-suites in this comfortable
establishment is decorated in a different style
(as well as photos of old communist leaders, for
example, the "Soviet room" has books by Leonid
Brezhnev for if you have trouble sleeping). There's
a decent restaurant on site too. ⑤–⑥

Promenaadi Sadama 22 ☎473 7250, ⊛www
.promenaadi.ee. A venerable shoreside structure
built as a private holiday villa in 1859 and extended
in the 1990s. Ask for one of the rooms in the

modern wing, which have chic furnishings and
– the real high point – lovely little sea-facing
balconies. Bike rental available to guests. ⑤

Spa Fra Mare Ranna 2 ☎472 4600, ⊛www
.framare.ee. Large, low-rise complex in the woods
behind Paralepa Beach, with smart modern rooms
and small indoor pool. Rooms with wooden furniture and dowdy decor are fine but unexceptional;
there are some spacious suites. Mud baths,
aromatherapy and paraffin treatments, and bike
rental for guests. ⑤–⑥

Vanalinna Hostel Jaani 4 ☎473 4900, ⊛www
.vanalinnabowling.ee. The only hostel in Estonia
with a bowling alley downstairs offers bright and
spotless singles, doubles and triples, some en-
suite, but no dorm beds. ②

The Town

Haapsalu's main thoroughfare, **Posti tänav** and its extension **Karja tänav**, terminates at the northern end of town at a small market square (more of a circle, actually) known as the **Rootsiturg** – "Swedish market" – a reminder of the large Swedish-speaking population that was once concentrated in the villages north of Haapsalu. Although settled in the area since the Middle Ages, the majority of Swedes fled to the motherland in 1944 to avoid persecution by a Soviet regime that saw them as a potentially treacherous pro-Western minority.

The castle and cathedral

Looming over the Rootsiturg are the stark grey walls of Haapsalu's combined **castle and cathedral**, built in the thirteenth century to serve as both military and spiritual headquarters of the bishops of Ösel-Wiek (the German name for Saaremaa and northwestern Estonia). The bishops were given northwestern Estonia following the Teutonic conquest, and they lorded it over Haapsalu and the neighbouring islands until the combined effects of the Livonian Wars and the Reformation sent them packing. Swashbuckling Swedish general Jakob de la Gardie (son of Pontus de la Gardie; see p.74) bought the castle in 1628, but it was largely destroyed by Peter the Great a century later and, although the church was rebuilt in the 1880s, the fortifications never really recovered. You can still see surviving stretches of the 10m-high wall that once enclosed the **Castle Park** (Lossipark; daily 7am–midnight; free). Parts of the semi-ruined keep have been rebuilt to accommodate the **Castle Museum** (daily: May and first half of Sept 10am–4pm; June–Aug 10am–6pm; €2.30), where you can examine rusting medieval weaponry and scramble up a section of the watchtower. More an expression of brute ecclesiastical power than beauty, the adjoining barn-like **Cathedral** is reckoned to be the largest single-nave church in the Baltic and has an impressively cavernous, though largely unadorned, interior. Haapsalu's nineteenth-century tourist boom no doubt encouraged the invention of the legend of the White Lady, a medieval maid who supposedly donned male guise in order to enter the cathedral precinct and canoodle with her priestly lover. Once discovered, she was impaled on the battlements (and/or immured in the walls, depending on which version of the tale you prefer), bequeathing Haapsalu a lovelorn ghost that still appears at a cathedral window every August at full moon – although it might just be an illusion caused by moonbeams pouring through the window onto a wall behind. The apparition provides the perfect excuse for the good-natured ghoul-fest known as the **Days of the White Lady**, held in the castle park every summer (see opposite).

The Läänema Museum

Just north of the castle, at the junction of Lossi plats and Kooli tänav, a pea-green, eighteenth-century Town Hall now houses the **Läänemaa Museum** (Tues–Sat: mid-May to mid-Sept 10am–6pm; mid-Sept to mid-May Wed–Sun 11am–4pm; €2.30), where sepia photographs of crowded beaches reveal what a fun place pre-World War II Haapsalu must have been. A shrine-like corner is devoted to Tsarist-era mayor Gottfried von Krusenstern, who did much to promote the town's tourist profile before being shot on the main square by army deserters in 1917.

Ilon's Wonderland

Just across the road from the museum is **Ilon's Wonderland** (Iloni Imedemaa; May–Aug daily 11am–6pm; Sept–April Tues–Sat 11am–4pm; €5), a museum, gallery and hands-on play centre celebrating the work of Ilon Wikland, the Estonian-born artist who emigrated to Sweden in 1945 and went on to illustrate the children's books of Astrid Lindgren. There's an English-subtitled film about Ilon's life – although born in Tartu and raised in Tallinn, she spent her most formative years with grandparents in Haapsalu. Along with her affectingly charming illustrations the place is full of dolls' houses, games, puppets, and (at weekends) actors dressed as characters from Wikland-illustrated books.

Africa beach and along Promenaadi

Beyond the museum lies one of the most attractive parts of Haapsalu, a web of quiet, cobbled streets lined with low, nineteenth-century houses. Following these eastwards will bring you to **Africa Beach** (Aafrika rand), so named because bathers used to coat their bodies in the medicinal black mud found in the bay. Just behind the beach a bird-watching tower provides sweeping views of nearby reed beds.

From here, Promenaadi winds west then north along the shore, passing the delicately carved eaves of the wooden **Kursaal** before arriving at the *Laine* and *Promenaadi* hotels, in front of which lies the stone seat known as the **Tchaikovsky Bench** (Tšaikovski pink). Placed here in 1940 to commemorate the 26-year-old composer's stay in 1867 (when he is said to have worked on parts of his first major opera, *Voyvod*), the memorial emits a light-activated blast of music whenever anyone approaches it.

The Museum of Estonian Swedes

The **Museum of Estonian Swedes**, Sadama 32 (Rannarootsi muuseum; Tues–Sat: May to mid-Sept 10am–6pm; mid-Sept to April 11am–4pm; €3.50; ℗www.aiboland .ee), celebrates the heritage of this once-thriving community with a colourful display of richly embroidered costumes and household textiles. You can also see Swedish-language newspapers once published in Haapsalu, including copies of the short-lived *Sovjet-Estland*, which appeared for a few months in 1940–41 and was so successful in selling the benefits of Soviet power that almost all of its target audience fled to Sweden when the Red Army returned in 1944. The highlight is the 20m-long tapestry, made in 2002, recalling the history of the Estonian Swedes – from horn-helmeted Vikings onwards – in vivid, comic-strip style. Outside the museum is a replica of a **jaala**, a traditional, three-sailed fishing boat from the island of Ruhnu.

The Estonian Railway Museum and Paralepa Beach

Built in 1904, Haapsalu's train station, in the southwest of town, saw its last passenger service in 1996, but remains an enduring monument to the Tsarist Empire's belle époque – not least because of the elegant 214m-long canopy above the platform, built to shelter aristocratic arrivals from the unpredictable Baltic weather. Ensconced in the former imperial waiting room, the **Estonian Railway Museum** (Wed–Sun 10am–6pm; €2) has a modest collection of tickets, uniforms and travel posters, with a couple of vintage locomotives parked out the back. A ten-minute walk west of the station, the forest-fringed **Paralepa Beach** is the sandiest of Haapsalu's bathing areas.

Eating, drinking and entertainment

Haapsalu's scattering of places to **eat and drink** are concentrated on Posti tänav and Karja tänav. The **Kursaal** (May to mid-Sept; ℗www.kuursaal.ee) hosts easy-listening crooners and (somewhat tame) discos in season, with outdoor concerts of light classics in the adjacent concert bowl in good weather. International ensembles take advantage of the cathedral's excellent acoustics during the **Haapsalu Early Music Festival** in July, while the decidedly more low-brow **Days of the White Lady** festival (℗www.haapsalu.ee) in mid-August involves live music, DJs and late-night partying in the castle park.

Cafes and restaurants

Blu Holm *Hotel Laine* (see p.91). High-quality fish and seafood, served up in classy, starched-table-cloth surroundings. Grab a window table for a good view of the reedy coast. Daily noon–midnight.

Hermannuse maja Karja 1A. A reasonably smart, yet relaxed, pub-restaurant serving a mix of Estonian and international food. There's a small beer garden at the back. Daily noon–11pm.

Müüriääre kohvik Karja 7. With comfy sofas and warm coloured fabrics, eating at Müüriääre is like being invited round to tea at your artistically gifted best friend's house. It's a great place for coffee, leaf teas, quiche, and an eye-goggling array of fresh cakes and tarts. June–Aug Mon–Sat 10am–10pm, Sun 10am–8pm; Sept–May Fri & Sat 10am–10pm, Sun–Thurs 10am–8pm.

Pizza Grande Karja 6. Economical thin-crust pies in rather plain surroundings – although the spacious back yard is a major plus in summer. Sun–Thurs 11am–midnight, Fri & Sat 11am–2am.

Rootsituru kohvik Kaarja 3. Homely café in a wooden house, offering *shashlik*-style skewer-kebabs, Greek salads and other mildly Mediterranean/Middle Eastern dishes. Filling, cheap and friendly. Daily 11am–midnight.

Vormsi

Lying 3km off the mainland, **Vormsi** (Ⓦwww.vormsi.ee) is a lush, green island, covered in forest, juniper heath and occasional patches of grazing land. Although only about 10km by 20km in size, the air of rustic calm and plentiful walking and cycling opportunities make a visit to Vormsi appealing. It was home to well over two thousand Estonian Swedes until 1944, when the vast majority left for the motherland. Although the island was partially repopulated with Estonians during the Soviet period, humans are now outnumbered by elk, roe deer and wild boar.

Ferries from the mainland arrive at the small port of **SVIBY**, within easy walking distance of the main settlement, **HULLO**, 3km west. At the northern end of Hullo, the otherwise undistinguished **St Olav's Church** is worth a look for the thicket of wheel-shaped stone grave crosses in its cemetery. The remotest place on the island and the best spot for a swim is stubby **Rumpo peninsula**, 2km southeast of Hullo, a rock-strewn stretch of shoreline backed by juniper heath and peat bog.

Practicalities

Two daily **ferries** (€2/person, €5 for cars; check timetables at Ⓦwww.veeteed.com) make their way to Sviby from **Rohuküla** (bus #1, which runs roughly hourly from Haapsalu). Tanel Viks rents out **bikes** (€9/day; ☎517 8722, Ⓔtanvx@neti.ee) on Sviby harbourfront, but they disappear fast on summer weekends, so it's best to reserve in advance. Otherwise, rent one in Haapsalu and bring it with you.

Haapsalu tourist office (see p.90) is the best place for information about Vormsi and may have a list of B&Bs on the island. *Mäe Farm*, Rumpo (April–Nov; ☎506 0745, Ⓦwww.hot.ee/streng; ❸), offers charming rooms in two outbuildings (one of which is a traditionally built log cabin), as well as bike rental and camping space. Alternatively, try the *Elle-Malle Guesthouse*, Hullo (☎473 2072, Ⓦwww.vormsi.ee/ellemall; ❷), which has chalet-style accommodation, as well as a cosy double in a small windmill. Nearby, the *Hullo Trahter* is a pleasant pub offering light meals and simple snacks.

Matsalu

Thirty kilometres south of Haapsalu, **Matsalu Bay** is one of the biggest stop-off points for migrating birds in Europe, attracting thousands of ducks, barnacle geese, corncrakes, moorhens and mute swans every spring and autumn, as well as providing a year-round habitat for cormorants and gulls. All three sides of the bay have been under the protection of the **Matsalu National Park** (Matsalu rahvuspark; Ⓦwww.matsalu.ee) since 1957, although it is the southern shore, with its dense reed beds and grassy coastal heaths, which provides the best opportunities for getting up close to the birds.

The gateway to the area is the small provincial town of **LIHULA** (Ⓦwww.lihula .ee), served by Haapsalu–Virtsu and Tallinn–Kuressaare buses. Some 3km north is the **Matsalu Nature Centre** in Penijõe Manor (Wed, Thurs, Sat & Sun 8am–5pm, Fri 8am–3.45pm; ☎472 4236, Ⓦwww.matsalu.ee), where you can pick up maps, information on boat trips and contact details for guides. There's also a small museum (same times; €0.70) devoted to the local flora and fauna. From the centre, follow tracks northwest to the birdwatching tower at **Suitsu**, 4km beyond Penijõe, for good views of coastal wetlands edged by yellowy-gold reeds. Another tower can be found at **Keemu**, 6km west on the road to the village of Matsalu.

Staff at the Nature Centre can put you in touch with the handful of **B&Bs** in the rustic communities near the reserve; otherwise *Luige Villa* in Lihula (Tallinna mnt 23, ☎477 8872, Ⓦwww.luigevilla.ee; ❸), has well-equipped doubles and more frugal, four- and five-person rooms.

Hiiumaa

HIIUMAA is the perfect place for anyone seeking a rural idyll. Estonia's second largest island – 75km east to west, 50km north to south – is also one of its most sparsely populated, and while its natural beauty is on a par with that of its more popular neighbour Saaremaa (see p.98), it has had far less tourist development. Hiiumaa's thin, sandy soil has never supported much in the way of agriculture, so most of the island remains covered by virgin pine forest, peat bogs and shrubby heathland – habitats favoured by elk, roe deer and wild boar. The picturesque coastline meanwhile, dotted with isolated lighthouses, deserted beaches and tranquil coves, encourages gentle exploration.

The main tourist office and most other facilities are in **Kärdla** on the north of the island. For a taste of undiluted natural wilderness, head for the juniper-carpeted island of **Kassari**, linked to southern Hiiumaa by a causeway, or the wind-battered **Kõpu peninsula** at Hiiumaa's western end.

Getting to and from Hiiumaa

Laevakompanii (Ⓦwww.laevakompanii.ee) runs **ferries** (4–6 daily; 90min; €3/person, plus €5/car) from Rohuküla, just west of Haapsalu (see p.90), to the Heltermaa terminal on Hiiumaa's eastern coast, where there's a small **tourist office** (June–Aug daily 7.30am–7pm; ☎463 1001). Four daily Tallinn–Kärdla **buses** (calling at Haapsalu) also make the crossing, with the ferry trip included in the ticket, and Avies (☎605 8022, Ⓦwww.avies.ee) flies small **planes** from Tallinn to Kärdla (2 daily; from €50 one way).

There's a ferry service from Sõru on Hiiumaa's southern tip to Triigi on **Saaremaa**, although it's a small vessel that can take only a limited number of cars (4 daily in summer, 2 in winter; expect queues at weekends; €3/person, plus €5/car) and it's not met by buses. Eomap's 1:50,000 **map** of Hiiumaa (widely available in bookshops) is the best for detailed exploration

Kärdla

Perched on the island's northeastern shoulder some 30km from Heltermaa, **KÄRDLA** is a wonderfully uneventful place with an infectiously laid-back atmosphere. It's Hiiumaa's

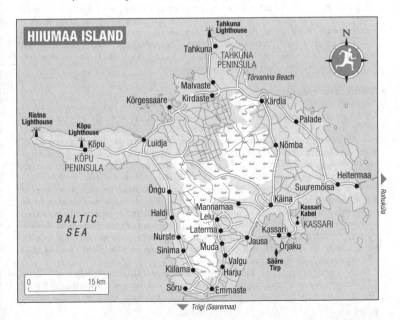

only real service centre and transport hub – if you don't have your own vehicle it's the best place to base yourself. Pretty timber houses surrounded by beautifully well-kept gardens are the main features of this low-rise town. Most households come complete with a mound of earth resembling an air-raid shelter – they are, in fact, traditional potato cellars.

Kärdla was an important textile-producing town in the nineteenth century, and the factory manager's house at the northern end of the town – known as the Pikk Maja or "Long House" – now holds a branch of the **Hiiumaa Museum** (Mon–Fri 10am–5pm, Sat 11am–2pm; €1). The sensitively restored rooms provide the perfect venue for seasonal art and photography displays, alongside a permanent exhibition devoted to Kärdla's mill-town heritage. The disused **power station** (elektrijaam) next door, a fine piece of early twentieth-century industrial heritage in its own right, hosts art exhibitions and concerts in summer. Five minutes northwest is Kärdla's most attractive feature, a grassy, boulder-strewn seaside park that fills up with bathers on summer weekends.

Practicalities

Buses stop on the fringes of the centre at Keskväljak, a few steps south of the **tourist office** at Hiiu 1 (mid-May to mid-Sept Mon–Fri 10am–6pm, Sat & Sun 10am–4pm; mid-Sept to mid-May Mon–Fri 10am–5pm; ☎462 2233, ⓦwww.hiiumaa.ee); staff can arrange B&B accommodation (❶–❷) throughout the island. They also have the *Lighthouse Tour* booklet, a guide to exploring Hiiumaa by car, filled with stories, history and legends.

Hotels include the friendly *Sõnajala*, a fifteen-minute walk southwest of the centre on Leigri väljak (☎463 1220, ⓦwww.sonajala.ee; ❸), offering neat en-suites. For a homely atmosphere, try *Kivijüri Külalistemaja* at Kõrgessaare mnt a little over 1km south of the tourist office (☎469 1002, ⓦwww.hot.ee/kivijuri; ❷), which has four bright, modern en-suites, some with sofas. *Padu*, at the eastern entrance to Kärdla at Heltermaa mnt 22 (☎463 3037, ⓦwww.paduhotell.ee; ❸), is more upmarket. Attractive log-cabin-like en-suites come with satellite TV and small balconies, while stuffed animals and moose heads populate the lounge. The most stylish accommodation, however, is above the *Nordtooder* café at Rookopli 20 (☎509 2054, ⓦwww.nordtooder.ee; ❹), where rooms come with wooden floors, sleek black fittings and elegant bathrooms.

If you're picnicking, head for the *Konsum* **supermarket** (daily 9am–9pm) on the main square. *Gahwa*, just off the square at Pollu 3 (Mon–Sat 10am–6pm, Sun noon–4pm) is a mellow **café**, while the nearby *Nordtooder* (see above) offers passable meat-and-potato dishes in an atmospheric bare-brick interior. The *Rannapargu* **restaurant** (Mon–Sat noon–11pm, Sun noon–7pm), beside the beach at Lubjaahu 3, offers the best shoreside views – and hosts occasional DJ nights at weekends.

Tahkuna peninsula

Arguably the finest sandy beach on the island, **Tõrvanina** lies 6km northwest of Kärdla on the eastern side of the Tahkuna peninsula. It can be reached by car (it's just off the road to Tahkuna lighthouse), although by far the most adventurous approach is to walk, picking up the **Tõrvanina nature path** (matkarada) that begins at the edge of Kärdla at the eastern end of Tiigi tänav. The well-marked path leads through dense forest, becoming a boardwalk trail as the ground becomes increasingly boggy. After about 35 minutes the path emerges to skirt a reedy stretch of coast, where a birdwatching tower allows you to observe goings-on out on the water. After another 20 minutes of forest, the path hits the approach road to Tõrvanina Beach, which lies a minute or two to the right. With about 3km of fine white sand, punctuated by tree stumps smoothed by seawater into strange sculptural forms, it's not the kind of place you can easily drag yourself away from. There are no facilities (so bring your own food and drink), but the beach attracts an ad-hoc windsurfer scene in the summer, and has clearly marked areas where you can light fires or pitch a tent.

At the northern tip of the Tahkuna peninsula is the **Tahkuna lighthouse**, built in 1875 and the site of a fierce battle between German and Russian soldiers during World War II. Close to the lighthouse is a monument to the victims of the ferry *Estonia*, which sank during a storm on September 28, 1994, 48km north of Tahkuna. A cross and bell, which only rings when the wind is the same speed as it was on the night of the disaster, commemorate the 852 people who lost their lives.

Kassari and around

One of the main attractions in the southern part of the island is **KASSARI**, a separate land mass 8km long and 4km across, joined to the main body of Hiiumaa by a causeway. Containing some of the most unspoilt conifer-covered heathland in the region, it is compact enough to be explored on foot or by bike in a day.

The main jumping-off point for exploring Kassari is **KÄINA**, a small town on the Hiiumaa side of the causeway. Built around the sombre ruins of a fifteenth-century church destroyed by World War II bombing, it's otherwise pretty forgettable. The nearby **Käina Bay** is home to a bird reserve, however, with over seventy different species; there's an observation tower close to the port of Orjaku. Käina is one of the few places on Hiiumaa served by regular bus from Kärdla, and has some decent **accommodation**. *Liilia*, a family-run hotel just east of the bus stop at Hiiu mnt 22 (T463 6146, Wwww.liiliahotell.ee; ❸), has cosy en-suites with TV, and a very good restaurant. One kilometre west of town in Lõokese, the *Lõokese Spa Hotel* (T463 6146, Wwww.lookese.ee; ❸–❹) is one of the swankiest places to stay on Hiiumaa, offering rooms with shower and TV, outdoor swimming and paddling pools, spa facilities, and a **campsite** in the grounds.

The road to Kassari leaves the Käina–Heltermaa road 3km east of Käina, crossing the causeway before passing after a further 3km a turn-off to the stocky, medieval **Kassari Kabel**, the only reed-roofed church in Estonia. A couple more kilometres beyond the turn-off is **KASSARI** village itself, an appealing agglomeration of timber houses and tumbledown barns nestling among thickets of juniper. Just north of the village's main street is another branch of the **Hiiumaa Museum** (mid-May to mid-Sept Mon–Fri 10am–5pm; at other times by appointment; €1; T469 7121), offering a small but intriguing display of traditional agricultural implements and embroidered folk costumes. Beside the museum, the *Keldrimäe* **guesthouse** (T518 2210, Wwww.keldrimae .ee; ❸) has several simple rooms, as well as a pyramid-shaped lodge in the garden, the design of which is claimed to "raise levels of sexual energy".

At the western end of Kassari village a signpost points the way to **Sääre Tirp**, a pebbly promontory jutting out into the sea. After 2km, the track along the promontory terminates in a car park, and a path lined by juniper bushes leads to the foot of Sääre Tirp, ending in a desolate, otherworldly shingle spit that peters out into the sea.

East of the Sääre Tirp, the scattered settlement of **ORJAKU** sprawls along a starkly beautiful stretch of reedy coast. Rooms at the *Dagen Haus*, a popular **B&B** in a beautifully restored farmstead at the northeastern end of the village (T518 2555 Wwww .dagen.ee; ❹), are well worth reserving in advance.

The Kõpu peninsula

Up to five buses a day wend their way west from Kärdla to the **Kõpu peninsula**, a rugged, rock-fringed tongue of heathland that juts out into the sea 45km or so west of town. Buses terminate at the village of Kalana, on the tip of the peninsula, although it's worth hopping off at the village of Kõpu, 35km out of Kärdla, to see the **Kõpu lighthouse** (Kõpu tuletorn), one of the oldest continuously operating lighthouses in the world. On the western side of the village, it dates back to 1531 and was built at the request of the Hanseatic League to warn ships away from the Hiiu Madal sandbank and the pirate-infested coastline. Strengthened by a quartet of bulky, angular buttresses at its base, it looks at first sight more like a Maya temple than a piece of maritime architecture. Climb it for a sea view (May to mid-Sept daily 9am–10pm; €1.50). From July to mid-August live classical and folk music is performed at the lighthouse every Friday evening; check with Kärdla tourist office.

Some 12km west of Kõpu lies the equally striking maroon-coloured **Ristna lighthouse**, a rocket of a building that presides over a boulder-strewn stretch of shoreline.

Like many nineteenth-century lighthouses in this part of Estonia, it was built abroad (in this case in France in 1874) and reassembled here on arrival.

Saaremaa

For Estonians, the island of **Saaremaa** epitomizes the nation's natural beauty more than any other place in the country. Cloaked with pine forest, juniper heath and grasslands, its coastline girdled with sandy beaches and tawny reed beds, it has long appealed to nature-loving, well-to-do Tallinners and increasingly attracts Scandinavian and Western European tourists too. Estonia's largest island is also a fertile source of myths and legends, with local folklore centring on the adventures of **Suur Töll**, a friendly but short-tempered giant, and his wife Piret.

There is a scattering of farmstead-based B&Bs across Saaremaa, although most accommodation is concentrated in the island's alluring capital, **Kuressaare**, site of the one must-see historic attraction, the **Bishop's Castle**. North of Kuressaare lie some of Saaremaa's best-known sights, notably the enchanting **Angla windmills** and the mysterious **Kaali meteorite crater**. On the western side of the island is the little-touristed coastal wilderness of the **Vilsandi National Park**, ideal for hiking. Historic churches crop up just about everywhere, with some especially fine examples at **Karja**, **Kaarma** and **Kihelkonna**.

Public transport is limited, with services to most destinations leaving Kuressaare at different times on different days of the week, making scheduling something of a nightmare – the Kuressaare tourist office is your best source of information. Thanks to its largely flat terrain, however, exploring by **bike** is a viable option; these can be rented in Kuressaare.

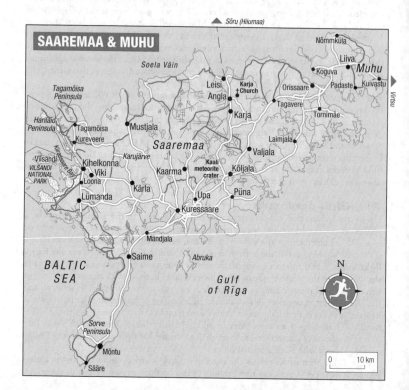

Getting to Saaremaa

Saaremaa is reached by taking the **ferry** (hourly in summer, every 2hr in winter; €3.50/person, plus €6 per car; ⊛www.laevakompanii.ee) from Virtsu on the mainland to Kuivastu on **Muhu**, a small island from which a causeway leads to Saaremaa itself. In addition, numerous daily **buses** run from Tallinn and Pärnu to Kuressaare – the price of the ferry crossing is included in the ticket. Approaching from Haapsalu is more awkward, although in summer there are three daily buses to Virtsu, where you can change onto one of the Tallinn–Kuressaare or Pärnu–Kuressaare services. Ferries from Hiiumaa dock at Triigi near the village of Leisi on the northern coast; Leisi's tourist office (June 4–Aug 31 noon–8pm; ☏457 3073) is on the main street. If travelling by **car**, bear in mind that there are long queues for the ferries on summer weekends – leave it too late in the day and you may end up stranded.

Estonian Air (⊛www.estonian-air.ee) operates daily **flights** from Tallinn to Kuressaare airport (€35; ☏453 3793, ⊛www.eeke.ee). Eomap's 1:300,000 Saaremaa **map**, available from Kuressaare tourist office or bookshops in Tallinn, is useful if you intend to explore the island in any depth.

Muhu

The main launching point for Saaremaa, the island of **Muhu** is also worth visiting in its own right – with pine forests, juniper thickets, windmills and thatched cottages, it's just as attractive as its better-known island neighbour. Among its draws is the village of **LIIVA**, 6km inland from the Kuivastu ferry terminal and site of the thirteenth-century **St Catherine's Church** (Katariina kirik), an angular, whitewashed building, looking fashionably Modernist with its trio of steep-roofed sheds seemingly concertina-ed together.

Three kilometres beyond Liiva, a minor road branches right towards **KOGUVA**, a settlement on Muhu's west coast that has been declared a "museum-village" on account of its rich stock of stone-built, reed-thatched farmhouses. Far from being museum pieces, the majority of these houses are still inhabited by local farmers.

If you want **to stay** in luxury on Muhu, head for ⋇ *Pädaste Mõis,* on the coast, 6km south of Liiva (March–Oct; ☏454 8800, ⊛www.padaste.ee; ❼), one of the best hotels in Estonia, in an old manor house. The decor in the luxurious doubles and split-level suites preserves a reassuringly rustic quality, while the top-class **restaurant** serves innovative – but, by Estonian standards, very expensive – dishes like fillet of hare with parsnip purée.

Kuressaare

Midway along the island's south coast, Saaremaa's "capital", the captivating market town of **KURESSAARE**, is the island's only real town and service centre. Wherever you're aiming for, you're likely to pass through here at least once, and this captivating place will tempt you to linger. The centre remains much as it was before World War II, with traditional houses, shady avenues and a spectacularly well-preserved castle, and just a scattering of Soviet-era buildings on the outskirts. This is not to say that Kuressaare is stuck in the past; it also boasts fashionable cafés, boutique hotels and innovative restaurants. All of this combines to give the town a chic, cosmopolitan air that draws well-to-do Estonians and, increasingly, Western Europeans too. As well as being a beach resort, Kuressaare has a health-tourism pedigree dating back to the 1840s, and many of the hotels do a brisk trade in mud baths and spa treatments.

Arrival and information

Kuressaare's **bus station** is just off Tallinna, the main street, five minutes' walk northeast of the **tourist office**, inside the Town Hall at Tallinna 2 (2nd half of May & 1st half of Sept Mon–Sat 9am–5pm, Sun 10am–3pm; June–Aug Mon–Fri 9am–6pm, Sat 10am–4pm, Sun 10am–3pm; mid-Sept to mid-May Mon–Fri 9am–5pm; ☏453 3120, ⊛www.saaremaa.ee), where you can buy local maps and get info on walking and biking trails. The library at Tallinna 6 has free **internet** access. You can rent a **car** at Hertz, Tallinna 9 (☏453 3660, ⊛www.hertz.ee), or a **bike** from Bivarix Rattapood, Tallinna 26.

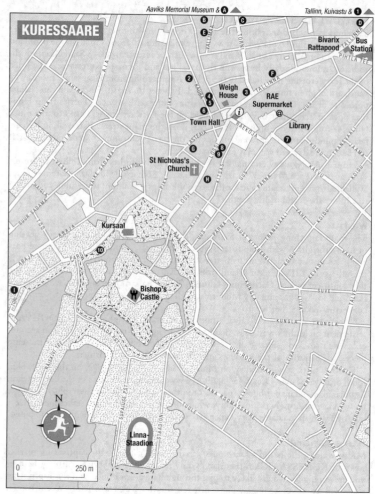

Aaviks Memorial Museum & **A** ▲   Tallinn, Kuivastu & **1** ▲

KURESSAARE

ACCOMMODATION					RESTAURANTS, CAFÉS & BARS			
Arabella	**C**	Linnahotel	**G**		Chameleon	**6**	La Perla	**8**
Arensburg	**H**	Mardi	**B**		John Bull		Rose	**F**
Georg Ots Spa Hotel	**I**	Repo	**E**		Pub	**10**	Sadhu	**9**
Grand Rose		Ruubimajutus	**D**		Kapiteni Körts	**2**	Vana Konn	**5**
Spa Hotel	**F**	SYG	**A**		Lokaal	**3**	Vanalinna	**4**
					Monus Villem	**1**	Veski	**7**

Accommodation

There's a growing range of **hotels** in Kuressaare, with a glut of places pitching three-star comforts and spa treatments to a mid-range market. Although it's a good idea to book in summer and at weekends throughout the year, prices tumble in the off-season (Oct–April) when it's relatively easy to pick up a bargain. The tourist office can book **B&Bs** (**1**–**2**) both in Kuressaare and on farms across the island – the latter are an excellent way of savouring the local countryside, but you'll need your own transport to reach them. *SYG* at Kingu 6, off Hariduse, ten minutes northwest of the centre

(℡ 455 4388, ⓦ www.syg.edu.ee) is a **hostel** for local high-school students, but usually has space for travellers in four-bed dorms (€9–11); simply furnished singles and doubles with shared facilities are also available (①).

The nearest **campsite** is the *Mändjala*, 11km west of town just beyond the village of Nasva (May–Sept; ℡ 454 4193, ⓦ www.mandjala.ee); it also has en-suite cabins (③). Kuressaare–Järve buses pass by.

Arabella Torni 12 ℡ 455 5885, ⓦ www.arabella.ee. A spruced-up, Soviet-era, green and grey residential block, *Arabella* has a fresh feel and good-sized en-suites, all with fridge and Ikea-style furniture. ④

Arensburg Lossi 15 ℡ 452 4700, ⓦ www.sivainvest.ee. Through a castle-like entrance lie compact, elegant and affordable rooms, many with bathtubs rather than showers. The restaurant, complete with cigar room, is equally smart and there's a pleasant garden and children's play area. ④

Georg Ots Spa Hotel Tori 2 ℡ 455 0000, ⓦ www.gospa.ee. Don't let the concrete exterior put you off – the hotel inside is first-class. Chic rooms come with king-sized beds, views of either the sea or the castle, and vivid, striped carpets. There's a bewildering array of spa treatments on offer, as well as one of the best restaurants in town. ⑥

Grand Rose Spa Hotel Tallinna 15 ℡ 666 7012, ⓦ www.grandrose.ee. Kuressaare's top hotel. No two rooms are the same, but all are impeccably decorated, feature swanky bathrooms and ooze class. Some have chandeliers and rich carpets,

others balconies and polished wood floors. There's an indoor pool, a spa and massage centre, and the attached *Rose Restaurant* (see p.102) is a bonus. ⑥

Linnahotel Lasteaia 7 ℡ 453 1888, ⓔ linnahotell@kontaktid.ee. A friendly hotel tucked away in an appealing warren of alleyways. Alongside the usual mid-range facilities, rooms come with tea- and coffee-making facilities and small balconies. ⑤

Mardi Vallimaa 5A ℡ 452 4633, ⓦ www.hotelmardi.eu. Bright twins, triples, suites and family rooms with pale-yellow walls, laminate flooring and big bathrooms. The hotel is spotless, the service is great and there's an excellent self-service daytime café. ④

Repo Vallimaa 1A ℡ 453 3510, ⓦ www.saaremaa.ee/repo. Close to the *Mardi*, *Repo* is a friendly hotel with small, pristine rooms with showers and cable TV. ③

Ruubimajutus Tallinna 31 ℡ 564 77533, ⓦ www.ruubimajutus.com. B&B opposite the bus station offering cute rooms with shared bathrooms and a common kitchen. ②

The Town

Most life in Kuressaare revolves around the elongated central square formed by the junction of Tallinna, Lossi and Raekoja streets. On the eastern side, an agreeable pair of stone lions guard the entrance to the seventeenth-century Town Hall (Raekoda), where an **art gallery** (Tues–Fri 10am–5pm, Sat 10am–3pm; free) hosts seasonally changing contemporary exhibitions. One floor up, the main council chamber harbours an exuberant eighteenth-century ceiling painting in which flesh-flaunting Bacchantes enjoy an alfresco picnic. It was salvaged from a local house, but it's not known who painted it or for whom.

Opposite the Town Hall is one of Kuressaare's oldest surviving buildings, the step-gabled **Weigh House** (Vaekoda), dating from 1633 and now a pub. Just to the west, cobbled alleys lead into an atmospheric quarter of low timber houses, many now occupied by shops and cafés.

Heading southwest along Lossi takes you past a **monument** to the dead of the 1918–20 War of Independence, sculpted by Amandus Adamson, Estonia's leading interwar sculptor and recently restored to pride of place after a lengthy Soviet-era absence. Just beyond, it's impossible to miss the jaunty bell-shaped domes of **St Nicholas's Church** (Nikolai kirik), an eighteenth-century Orthodox foundation serving an Estonian rather than Russian congregation – an estimated twenty percent of Estonia's population joined the Orthodox Church when the country belonged to the Tsarist Empire. A certain Estonian sobriety is retained in the interior decor – noticeably plainer than in Russian Orthodox churches.

Lossi continues south to the magnificent **Bishop's Castle** (Piiskopilinnus), a sturdy, sandy-coloured structure built from locally quarried dolomite. The original castle was built in 1261 by Bishop German of Ösel-Wiek in order to keep the restless Saaremaa natives in check. The castle as it stands today, surrounded by a star-shaped system of earthworks and a deep-gouged moat, dates largely from the fourteenth century and is such a well-preserved quadrangle of smooth stone that – from a distance at least – it looks like a movie set. Surrounding it are bastions and ramparts thrown up by Danes and Swedes in the seventeenth century, now a grassy park. Used as a barracks by the Russians, the castle was restored by the Saaremaa nobility after 1904, to serve both as a symbol of provincial pride and to provide the local authorities with much-needed office space.

The labyrinthine keep now houses the **Saaremaa Regional Museum** (Saaremaa koduloomuuseum; May–Aug daily 10am–6pm; Sept–April Wed–Sun 11am–6pm; €4), a didactic parade of artefacts covering the history of the island from prehistoric times to the present. Chunky chain jewellery worn by Iron Age Estonian chieftains and their molls helps to cheer up the proceedings, as do chalices and silverware once belonging to the Kuressaare bishops. Most absorbing is that part of the display devoted to the post-1940 period, with uniforms, weapons and newsreel clips throwing the Soviet occupation into dramatic relief. The former chapterhouse contains a spectacular fifteenth-century altar with a central scene of *St Mary's Coronation* painted by Henning van der Heide of Lübeck. In the park surrounding the castle moat you'll find the wooden **Kursaal** building, dating from 1889 and now a genteel café.

Eating

Kuressaare has plenty of places to **eat** offering a wide range of decent food at reasonable prices. You can pick up **picnic supplies** from the RAE supermarket on the main square (daily 9am–10pm).

Lokaal Tallinna 11. This subterranean bar-restaurant splices the old and the new: original stone ceiling and walls alongside red seats, black tables and tinted glass. The menu features the usual Estonian standards. Fri & Sat till 6am, Sun–Thurs till 2am.

La Perla Lossi 3 ☏ 453 6910. A smart Italian with good-value, thin-crust pizzas and pastas in the €6.50 range, and Mediterranean-influenced mains from €12. Attentive service, and a good list of Italian wines. Mon–Fri noon–11pm, Sat & Sun 1–11pm.

Rose Tallinna 15 ☏ 666 7000. The *Grand Rose Spa Hotel's* cellar restaurant is the place for a formal dining experience, first-class service, good wines and excellent food (try rack of Saaremaa lamb in redcurrant sauce). Mains €11–16. Booking advised in the summer. Sun–Thurs noon–11pm, Fri & Sat noon–midnight.

Sadhu Lossi 5 ☏ 453 3145. Mediterranean salads, local fish dishes, wild-boar kebabs and English breakfasts served in a groovy, mildly Middle Eastern-inspired interior. Relaxing back-garden terrace with oriental drapes and lanterns. Mon–Fri 8.30am–10pm, Sat 10.30am–midnight, Sun 10.30am–4.30pm.

Vanalinna Kauba 8. A great spot for salads, freshly baked pastries, quiches and cakes – including a divine rhubarb meringue pie. Mon–Sat 8am–7pm, Sun 10am–4pm.

Veski Pärna 19. A café-restaurant in a unique setting: inside a (sadly motionless) windmill, with sails that light up at night. Sit around wooden tables or on vast millstones of polished granite and sample unusual dishes like chicken with pear or pork in beer sauce; mains from €8. Sun–Thurs 11am–10pm, Fri & Sat 11am–2am.

Drinking and entertainment

There's a good range of **bars** in Kuressaare, mostly cosy, convivial places that become enjoyably raucous at weekends. Make sure to try Saaremaa-brewed beer, which packs a bit more of a punch than Saku or A. Le Coq.

Despite the lack of a regular theatre or concert hall, a good deal of quality **culture** comes to town in the summer. A canopy-covered podium next to the Kursaal becomes a bandstand-cum-concert bowl, hosting brass bands, classical performances and the occasional crooner. The castle courtyard is employed to dramatic effect during **Kuressaare Opera Days** (Kuressaare Ooperipäevad; ⊛www.festivals.ee/kuresoop_eng.html), when two major operas are performed over a long weekend at the end of July. The castle is also pressed into service during the **Kuressaare Chamber Music Days** (⊛www.kammerfest.ee) in August, featuring top performers from Estonia and further afield.

Bars and pubs

Chameleon Kauba 2. Smart central café with lounge-bar aspirations, boasting matt-black surfaces, couches strewn with cushions, and a menu that includes sushi. Pleasant colonnaded terrace facing the main square. Mon–Thurs 11am–11pm, Fri & Sat 11am–1am, Sun noon–10pm.

John Bull Pub Pargi 4. A lively, pale-green wooden hut pub, with a great location overlooking the castle ramparts. You can perch at a bar made out of a bus chassis, or lounge around in a Soviet corner overlooked by Lenin portraits. The good food ensures a constant stream of custom. April–Sept daily 11am–2am.

Kapiteni Kõrts Kauba 13. This faux-rustic beer hall comes complete with wooden benches, fishing nets and snug alcoves. Daily 11am–3am.

Monus Villem Tallinna 63B. Something-for-everyone-pub opposite the Maxima supermarket 1.5km northeast of the bus station, with a full menu of food, a kids' play room, big-screen sporting events, and late hours (with the chance of live gigs) at weekends. Sun–Thurs 11am–midnight, Fri & Sat 11am–2am.

Vana Konn Kauba 6. Comfy pub with Czech beers, a full menu of food, and a small beer garden. Mon–Thurs 11am–11pm, Fri & Sat 11am–4am, Sun 11am–9pm.

North of Kuressaare

There are several sights, notably the **Kaali meteorite crater** and the **Angla windmills**, strung out in the villages north of Kuressaare, many of which are on or near the Kuressaare–Leisi road and served by local buses. Just off this route, 10km north of Kuressaare and 5km west of the Leisi road, the village of **KAARMA** is worth a detour for its venerable thirteenth-century **church** (Kaarma kirik), a large, red-roofed building unusual in having twin aisles. Inside is a christening stone from the same period and a pulpit supported by a wooden Joseph figure from 1450. The church's graveyard is littered with ancient stone crosses – the oldest are the so-called "sun crosses", set within a circle carved in stone.

The Kaali meteorite crater

Returning to the Kuressaare–Leisi road and heading north for 6km brings you to the turn-off for the village of **KAALI**, 2.5km further southeast, famous for its 4000-year-old **meteorite crater**. Signs at the entrance to the village direct you up onto the lip of the *kraater*, a 150m-wide pit surrounded by a huge embankment composed of the rubble thrown up on impact and now covered in mossy trees. At the base of the pit lies a murky, green pool. It's an eerily beautiful spot and one of the world's few easily accessible meteorite craters. The **Kaali Visitors' Centre** in the village (daily 9am–8pm; ☎514 4889, ⓦwww.kaali.kylastuskeskus.ee) has a small museum (€1.70) and simple accommodation (❸). On the opposite side of the car park from the crater, the *Kaali Trahter* **café-restaurant** is a good place for a breather, although it can get busy at lunchtimes.

   Getting to Kaali by public transport you can either catch the Kuressaare–Leisi bus (get off at the Liiva putla stop beside the Kaali turn-off and walk 2.5km southeast) or hop aboard a Kuressaare–Kuivaste–Tallinn bus (get off at Kõnnu and walk 3km northwest) – either way, be sure to check return times first.

Angla and Karja

Around 15km north of Kaali is **ANGLA**, a village famed for its five wooden **windmills** (Angla tuulikud) standing in a much-photographed line by the roadside. The windmills aren't open to the public, but they're mesmerizing enough to merit a stop-off, exuding an ageless dignity. Kuressaare–Leisi buses pick up and drop off at the northernmost of the mills.

   A right turn just beyond the windmills leads after 2km to the thirteenth-century **Karja Church** (Karja kirik), a plain white structure with an unusual Crucifixion carving above its side door. Inside are more stone-carvings, depicting religious figures and scenes from village life.

Western Saaremaa

Western Saaremaa is arguably the most attractive part of the island, its rugged, deeply indented coastline backed by a sparsely populated hinterland of grasslands, juniper heath, small lakes and bogs. Many of its more beautiful stretches fall under the aegis of the **Vilsandi National Park**, founded in 1993. Named after Vilsandi island, 3km off Saaremaa's western shore, the park covers much of the island's northwestern corner. Offshore islets and reed-shrouded shores provide a multitude of habitats for migrating birds, with hundreds of species – including mute swans, greylag geese, oystercatchers and Arctic terns – gathering in the area in the spring and autumn.

The main entrance point to the park is the visitors' centre at **Loona**, 2.5km south of the village of **Kihelkonna**, an easy bus ride from Kuressaare. The northwestern extremities of the park on the **Harilaid Peninsula** offer most in the way of desolate beauty, although you'll need your own transport to explore them.

Viki, Kihelkonna and Loona

The road west from Kuressaare forges through a landscape of arable land and forest before arriving after some 25km at the village of **VIKI**, home to the **Mihkli Farm Museum** (mid-April to Oct daily 10am–6pm; April & Sept Wed–Sun 10am–6pm; €1.30), a recreation of a typical nineteenth-century Saaremaa farmstead. With a wind-mill in full working order and a small cluster of thatch-roofed farmhouses smothered in moss, it's as delightful a taste of traditional Saaremaa life as you'll get. From here it's only 5km further to **KIHELKONNA**, a bucolic village draped around a dazzlingly whitewashed **parish church**. Dating from the 1260s, it's one of the oldest on the island, although its dominant feature – a sky-rocketing steeple, for a time also a light-house – was only added in 1897. Crowning a hillock 200m south of the church is a squat, grey building that looks like a cross between a cow shed and a gun emplacement – it's actually the church's seventeenth-century belfry.

Thirty-five minutes' walk south of Kihelkonna on the Lümanda road, a signed right turn leads to Loona manor (Loona mõis), a nineteenth-century gentry farmstead hous-ing the **Vilsandi National Park Visitors' Centre** (Mon–Fri 9am–5pm; ☎454 6880), where you can buy maps and get advice on where to walk. The park comprises over 150 uninhabited offshore islets favoured by local birdlife, as well as a narrow coastal belt criss-crossed by (largely unmarked) dirt roads. The quickest way to get a taste of the area is to follow forest paths due west of Loona, emerging after fifteen minutes onto the reed-fringed Kiirassaare Bay (Kiirassaare laht), which offers fleeting glimpses of rocky offshore islands. From here you can turn northeast back to Kihelkonna (20min), or improvise your own itinerary by following the coast southwest through a tranquil region characterized by pine woods, grassland and swamp.

The best place **to stay** in the Kihelkonna–Loona region is the National Park Visitors' Centre itself, which has a handful of tasteful en-suite rooms (May–Sept; ☎454 6510, ⓦwww.loona.ee; ❸). Somewhat more frugal is the *Kihelkonna Parsonage* (Pastoraadi Oomaja; ☎454 6558, ⓔkihelkonna@eelk.ee; ❶) next to the church, offering four rooms with shared facilities. There's a well-stocked food shop in Kihelkonna across from the bus stop.

Towards the Harilaid peninsula

North of Kihelkonna the national park boundary continues to follow Saaremaa's west coast, ballooning out after some 20km to envelop the **Harilaid peninsula**, a compact thumb of land offering some of the island's most strikingly stark scenery, characterized by stony ground with a sparse covering of waist-high junipers. The easiest way to get here from Kihelkonna is to follow the northbound Tagamõisa road and take a left turn onto a dirt road 5km north of the village of Kureveere. This passes through the once-flourishing settlement of Kõruse, depopulated after World War II when the Soviets turned the area into a military zone and now a virtual ghost village. Carrying on, you arrive at a sandy neck of land that joins the main body of Saaremaa to the Harilaid peninsula – Harilaid was a separate island until the narrow channel between it and Saaremaa silted up in the seventeenth century. This is as far as cars can go; a national park information board bears details of hiking trails around the peninsula – the com-plete circuit is about 12km, but even a short walk will give you an idea of Harilaid's other-worldly beauty. The centre of the peninsula is thick with pines and junipers, ringed by a belt of steppe-like grassland, which in turn gives way to a part-sandy, part-pebbly shoreline supporting a stubborn covering of mosses and heathers. It takes about an hour to walk up the eastern side of the peninsula to the northern tip, just beyond which lies the slender, black-and-white-striped Kiipsaare lighthouse, built in 1933 and no longer in use – with its foundations battered by the sea, it's now listing dramatically.

Pärnu and around

Estonia's premier seaside resort, **PÄRNU** is the country's self-declared "summer capital" – a fair description, considering one in four Estonians visit at least once during the holiday season. The town's biggest asset is its 7km-long sandy beach, which is packed with sunbathers in July and August and a popular place for a walk year-round. While there are plenty of beach-side bars for the party-hard hedonists, Pärnu itself, spread around the estuary of the Pärnu River, preserves a small-town gentility, with shady parks, wide avenues lined with lime trees and an appealing mix of traditional wooden houses and Bauhaus-inspired interwar villas. The town also enjoys a rich cultural life: its prestigious theatre and state-of-the-art concert hall mean that this is one of the few places outside Tallinn and Tartu where you can enjoy top-quality drama and music all year round.

The town itself has few sights. Most visitors come to soak up the summer atmosphere, and with regular bus connections to Tallinn, Tartu and Rīga, it's a convenient place to rest if you're in the middle of a Baltic tour. The rustic charms of **Kihnu Island** (see p.110) and the desolate, boggy beauty of the **Soomaa National Park** (p.111) provide the main targets for day-trips.

Arrival and information

The **bus station** is on Pikk at the northeastern edge of the Old Town (the ticket office is round the corner at Ringi 3). The **tourist office** at Uus 4 (mid-May to mid-Sept Mon–Fri 9am–6pm, Sat 10am–4pm, Sun 10am–3pm; mid-Sept to mid-May Mon–Fri 9am–5pm; ☎447 3000, ⓦwww.visitparnu.com) has helpful advice and plenty of English-language brochures. There's also a small tourist information booth on the beach in July and August (daily 11am–5pm). The booklet-sized *Pärnu in Your Pocket*, available from news kiosks for €1.60, is a useful source of local listings information, updated annually. Log on to the **internet** at the New Art Museum, Esplanaadi 10 (24hr; €2/hr), or Rüütli Internetipunkt, Rüütli 25 (Mon–Fri 9am–9pm, Sat & Sun 9am–6pm; €1.70/hr).

Bikes can be rented from the outdoor Rattarent stand near the beach on the corner of Ranna and Supeluse (€2.70/hr; €6.60 for 6hr).

Accommodation

Most of the town's **hotels** are on the grid of streets between the centre and the beach. They're packed in July and August, so always reserve ahead if possible. The tourist office has accommodation price lists, but won't make bookings on your behalf. Rates drop by around 25–40 percent in the low season (Oct–April).

The central *Lõuna*, Lõuna 2 (☎443 0943, ⓦwww.hot.ee/hostellouna), is the best **hostel** in town, with dorm beds for €14; there are also small, freshly decorated doubles (❷). *Konse Holiday Village* (☎534 35092, ⓦwww.konse.ee), 1.5km northeast of the centre at Suur-Jõe 44A, on the banks of the Pärnu River, has clean, modern facilities, and two- to four-person cabins (€15/person).

Ammende Villa Mere pst 7 ☎447 3888, ⓦwww .ammende.ee. A gorgeously restored Art Nouveau villa built for the Pärnu magnate Herman Ammende in 1905 and opened as a hotel in 1999. Rooms boast exhaustively researched repro decor, service is top-notch and there are opulent sitting rooms. There are also less luxurious but still comfy rooms in an annexe, formerly the gardener's house. Even if not staying here, soak up some of the atmosphere at the lovely – and suitably expensive – restaurant. ❻–❽
Delfine Supeluse 22 ☎442 6900, ⓦwww.delfine .ee. The black marble floors and water feature

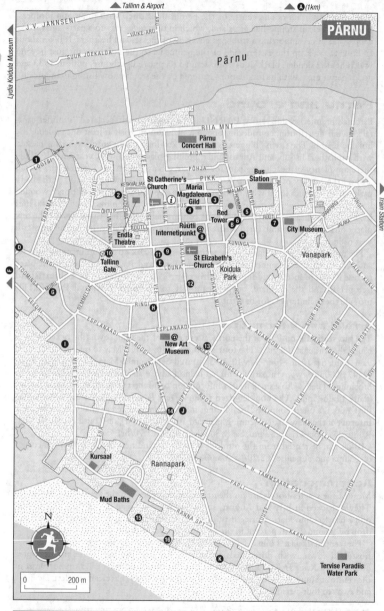

PÄRNU

▲ Tallinn & Airport ▲ **A** (1km)

Pärnu

▶ Train Station

Pärnu Concert Hall

Bus Station

St Catherine's Church

Maria Magdaleena Gild

Red Tower

City Museum

Ruutli Internetipunkt

Endla Theatre

Vanapark

St Elizabeth's Church

Koidula Park

Tallinn Gate

New Art Museum

Kursaal

Rannapark

Mud Baths

Tervise Paradiis Water Park

N

0   200 m

ACCOMMODATION				RESTAURANTS & CAFÉS					
Ammende Villa	**I**	Konse Holiday Village	**A**	Asian Village	**7**	Steffani	**12**	Rannakohvik	**15**
Delfine	**J**	Lõuna	**E**	Kohvik Georg	**6**	Supelisaksad	**13**	Sunset	**16**
Green Villa		Ranna Villa	**D**	Mõnus		Yacht Club	**1**	Tallinna	
B&B	**H**	Rannahotel	**K**	Margarita	**2**			Väravad	**10**
Hommiku Hostel	**B**	Vesiroos		Postipoiss	**11**	BARS, PUBS & CLUBS		Veerev Õlu	**4**
Koidulapark Hotell	**C**	Villa Marleen	**F**	Seegi Maja	**3**	Mirage	**5**	Viies Villem	**9**
				Si-Si	**14**	Picadilly	**8**		

in the lobby set the tone for this excellent mid-sized hotel on the road to the beach. Rooms are compact but immaculate, and come with swanky bathrooms. ⑤

Green Villa B&B Vee 21 ☎443 6040, ⓦwww
.greenvilla.ee. A friendly guesthouse on a leafy street overlooking a park. The spacious, homely rooms have original wood floors; cheaper rooms have shared facilities, and there is a guest kitchen. ③

Hommiku Hostel Hommiku 17 ☎445 1122, ⓦwww.hommikuhostel.ee. A hostel in name and price only, *Hommiku* has a fantastic central location and tastefully decorated, modern en-suites, with big windows or skylights, TVs and mini-kitchens. ③

Koidulapark Hotell Kuninga 38 ☎447 7030, ⓦwww.koidulaparkhotell.ee. Open April–Nov, this lusciously restored wooden villa provides friendly service and swish, modern en-suites with wooden floors. Ask for one overlooking the park. ⑤

Ranna Villa Ringi 52 ☎445 1120, ⓦwww
.rannavilla.ee. No frills but neat-and-tidy hotel offering smart, modern en-suites with TV. Breakfast in the neighbouring pub. ③

Rannahotel Ranna pst 5 ☎443 2950, ⓦwww
.scandichotels.com. A cool, Bauhaus-inspired structure dating from 1937, right on the beach. Cream-coloured, smallish rooms boast neat black furnishings and small balconies, many with sea views. ⑥

Vesiroos Esplanaadi 42A ☎443 0940, ⓦwww
.hotelvesiroos.com. This modernist glass and concrete structure offers no-nonsense en-suites overlooking a small pool. ④–⑤

Villa Marleen Seedri 15 ☎442 9287, ⓦwww
.marleen.ee. Spread over two houses, a couple of minutes' walk from the beach, this welcoming guesthouse has simple but neat and spacious rooms, and a small café. ④

The Town

With most of Pärnu laid out in neat grids, it's a fairly easy place to navigate. The main thoroughfare is **Rüütli**, a pedestrianized shopping street running from east to west and featuring a fair sprinkling of attractive two-storey wooden houses. Occupying a rather more staid brick building near Rüütli's eastern end at no. 53, the **City Museum** (Linnamuuseum; Wed–Sun 10am–6pm; €3; ⓦwww.pernau.ee) houses some of Estonia's oldest archeological finds, many of which originated in an 11,000-year-old Neolithic settlement unearthed near the village of Sindi just inland – among the pottery fragments, look out for a small human form carved from animal horn. After this promising start, the collection deteriorates into a rather colourless and badly labelled trot through local history.

Two blocks west of the museum, just off Rüütli on Hommiku, is the **Red Tower** (Punane torn), a fifteenth-century remnant of the medieval city walls and the town's oldest surviving building. Despite its name, this squat, unassuming cylinder is actually white – only the roof tiles are red. A few steps west of the tower, the **Maria Magdaleena Gild** at Uus 5 (Mon–Fri 11am–5pm, Sat 11am–3pm) houses the workshops of local designers and craftspeople, with a big range of clothing and accessories for sale.

West from **Pühavaimu** along Uus, you come to **St Catherine's Church** (Ekateriina kirik), built during the reign of Catherine the Great. Encrusted with sea-green domes and pinnacles topped by wrought-iron crosses, it's one of the most delicious Baroque buildings in Estonia and has an icon-rich interior. Immediately west of the church lies a flagstoned plaza dominated by the **Endla Theatre**, a functional piece of 1960s architecture built to replace the original theatre building, erected in 1911 and feted throughout northern Europe as an Art Nouveau masterpiece until bombed to smithereens in World War II – you'll see photographs of it in history museums both here and in Tallinn (notably at the Maarjamäe Palace). One of the most talked-about pieces of architecture in today's Estonia is the coquettishly curvy **Pärnu Concert Hall** (Pärnu kontserdi-maja), between greying blocks just northeast of the Endla Theatre at Aida 4. Opened in 2002, this vast, glass-and-steel hatbox of a building accommodates a state-of-the-art thousand-seat auditorium for top-notch music and drama, and also finds room for the **City Art Gallery** (Linnagalerii; Tues–Fri 10am–6pm, Sat 10am–4pm; price varies), where you can catch high-profile exhibitions by contemporary Estonian artists.

From the Tallinn Gate to the New Art Museum

South of the Endla Theatre, Vee runs down to Kuninga, the western end of which is marked by the seventeenth-century **Tallinn Gate** (Tallinna värav), an elegant relic of the Swedish occupation, set into the remains of the city ramparts and now home to a quaint bar (see p.110). The south side of the gate, with its massive gable and decorative pillars, looks more like a Baroque chapel. West of the gate, the former ramparts and a stretch of seventeenth-century moat have been turned into an attractive park.

Heading east from the Gate along Kuninga leads to the eighteenth-century **St Elizabeth's Church** (Eliisabeti kirik; Mon–Sat noon–6pm, Sun 10am–1pm), which boasts a maroon and ochre Baroque exterior and plain, wood-panelled interior. As well as being the principal Protestant place of worship in town, it's also home to a famously sonorous organ, put through its paces at weekend concerts. From here, Nikolai leads south to Esplanaadi, where an office block that was once the headquarters of the Pärnu communist party now serves as the **Pärnu New Art Museum** (Pärnu uue kunsti muuseum; daily 9am–9pm; €3; ⍟www.chaplin.ee). Its collection of twentieth-century Estonian paintings is complemented by contemporary works donated by international artists, including Yoko Ono.

The beach

In the south of town, at the southern end of Supeluse, the colonnaded **Pärnu Mud Baths** (Pärnu mudaravila; closed pending renovation), are a bombastic piece of Neoclassicism that couldn't be more different from their contemporary, the interwar **Rannahotel**, 400m east at Ranna 5, a cream-coloured ocean liner of a building that has become an icon of Estonian Modernism. Both buildings gaze out onto Pärnu's glorious white-sand **beach** and its 500m promenade backed by cafés and ice-cream stalls. At the western end of the beach is a stretch of sand designated for women only – an age-old Pärnu tradition that is strictly observed.

A couple of kiosks rent out kitesurfing and windsurfing gear at the southeastern end of the beach. There's also the Tervise Paradiis **Water Park** at Side 14 (daily: June–Aug 10am–10pm; Sept–May 11am–10pm; ⍟www.terviseparadiis.ee; day ticket €16–20), which has four slides, various swimming pools, a Jacuzzi and a climbing wall.

The Lydia Koidula Museum

The grid of postwar suburban buildings stretching north of the Pärnu River is as unexciting as you would expect, and there's not much point in venturing out here unless you're keen to check out the **museum** honouring nineteenth-century poet **Lydia Koidula** (see opposite), a ten-minute hop over the river from the city centre at J.V. Jannseni 37 (Tues–Sat 10am–6pm; €1.30). Occupying the building where her father ran a primary school from 1857 to 1863, the museum remembers Koidula through a modest collection of family photographs and rooms, including a recreation of the bedroom (in the Russian town of Kronstadt) where Koidula breathed her last in 1886.

Eating and drinking

Pärnu has a respectable spread of cafés, restaurants and bars serving a wide range of food and drink.

Restaurants and cafés

Asian Village Rüütli 51A. This six-table restaurant has a strong local following for its huge range of (pretty authentic) Chinese, Thai and Indian favourites like Singapore noodles, satay and chicken tikka. Daily 11am–11pm.

Kohvik Georg Rüütli 43. A bustling self-service café that's popular with downtown shoppers for its low-priced and tasty meals and snacks. Mon–Fri 7.30am–10.30pm, Sat & Sun 9am–10pm.

Mõnus Margarita Akadeemia 5. A reasonably priced Tex-Mex joint, with Aztec-inspired paintings and decent – if not exactly explosively spicy – food. Lively at the weekend. Sun–Thurs 11am–midnight, Fri & Sat till 1am.

Postipoiss Vee 12. A rustic Russian restaurant with long wooden tables and waiting staff in an amateur dramatist's idea of folk costume. Excellent light meals include *pelmeni* or *blini* with caviar, as well as mainstream northern European meat dishes. Fills up with late-night drinkers at weekends, when you can expect live entertainment in crooner-meets-electronic-keyboard style. Sun–Thurs noon–11pm, Fri & Sat till 2am.

Lydia Koidula 1843–86

Estonia's leading nineteenth-century poet was born **Lydia Emilie Florentine Jannsen** in Vändra, where her father, Johann Voldemar Jannsen, was the village schoolteacher. The family moved to Pärnu in 1850, where Lydia was among the handful of Estonians admitted to the prestigious German-language Pärnu School for Girls.

In 1857, her father launched the first-ever Estonian-language weekly, *Perno Postimees* ("Pärnu Courier"), aiming to spread literacy among the local peasantry. Koidula was roped in to help and ended up writing much of it herself, a role she continued when Jannsen moved to Tartu in 1863 to found the *Eesti Postimees* ("Estonian Courier") – a publication that bound together the nascent Estonian intelligentsia and transformed Jannsen into a pivotal figure in the national movement. A self-taught country boy of limited literary abilities, Jannsen was outshone as a writer and editor by his daughter, but her contribution to the paper had to remain in the background as nineteenth-century Estonia was not the kind of place where well-brought-up young women embarked on literary careers. When Koidula's first collections of lyric poems were published anonymously – *Vainolilled* ("Meadow Flowers") in 1866, *Emajõe Ööbik* ("Emajõgi Nightingale") in 1867 – Jannsen himself published reviews of them without knowing the identity of the author. Regular visitors to the family home were in no doubt about Lydia's literary potential, however. One, Karl Robert Jakobson, gave her the pseudonym "Koidula" ("of the dawn") so that he could include some of her poems in an Estonian-language primer. Koidula's greatest admirer at this time was Friedrich Reinhold Kreuzwald, compiler of the Estonian folk epic *Kalevipoeg* (see p.142), with whom Koidula started to correspond in 1867. The epistolary relationship between the intelligent, witty Koidula and a man forty years her senior quickly became a mutual intellectual obsession. Koidula visited Kreuzwald in Võru in June 1868, but the trip was cut short due to the hostility of Kreuzwald's wife.

Thanks to her father, Koidula remained at the centre of Estonian cultural life, helping him set up the Vanemuine Society (the first Estonian-language drama group), and organize the first All-Estonian Song Festival in Tartu in 1869. Her patriotic poem *Mu Isamaa* ("My Fatherland"), set to music by a Tartu choirmaster for the occasion, has been a prime ingredient of song festivals ever since – during the Soviet period, audiences insisted on closing festivals with a rousing rendition of the song.

In 1873 Koidula married stolid Latvian doctor Eduard Michelson. The couple went to live in Russian-speaking Kronštadt, a Tsarist naval base in the Gulf of Finland, and had four children (two of whom died in infancy). Although Koidula continued to write poems, her contacts with Estonian literary circles were effectively severed, and her early death from cancer prevented her from fully enjoying the acclaim she deserved. Koidula exerted a huge influence over subsequent generations – she demonstrated that the Estonian language was versatile and lyrical enough to challenge the cultural predominance of German – and there's hardly an Estonian alive today who can't recite at least a few of her poems by heart.

Seegi Maja Hospidali 1. An atmospheric, impeccably restored seventeenth-century almshouse, with an inviting fireplace and waiters in traditional costume, *Seegi Maja* serves up expertly prepared meat and fish dishes. Those with adventurous palates can order the baked bear with honey sauce. Mains from €9. Daily noon–midnight.
Si-Si Supeluse 21 ☎ 447 8911. Situated in a stately pre-World War I house with a large garden, *Si-Si* serves decent-quality pizzas, pasta dishes and big salads in relaxing surroundings. With prices rarely exceeding the €6.50 mark it's popular, so go early or reserve. Daily noon–2am.
Steffani Nikolai 24. Buzzing pizzeria offering generous portions of thin-crust pie, alongside pastas, chilli con carne and salads. The big outdoor terrace is one of the most popular dining spots in town. Sun–Thurs 11am–midnight, Fri & Sat till 2am.
Supelsaksad Nikolai 32. Relaxing café serving strong coffee, proper leaf teas, super salads and the cakes and pastries of your dreams. On the ground floor of a former family house, it has the feel of a quirky private flat, with

bare floorboards, lots of pinks and blues and the odd ravishing roll of retro wallpaper. Garden seating in summer. Daily: June–Aug 8am–midnight; Sept–May until 9pm.

Yacht Club Lootsi 6 ℡ 447 1760. Marina-side restaurant with bright white interior and nautically themed design details, serving a predominantly fishy menu with a Mediterranean twist. With a spacious outdoor patio and frequent live music in summer, it's also a popular place for a drink. Daily 9am–midnight.

Bars and pubs

Picadilly Pühavaimu 15. Café by day, wine bar by night, *Picadilly* is an intimate place with orange walls, scores of cushions and subdued lighting. As well as a strong wine list, it has home-made chocolates, light meals and often live jazz in the evenings. Mon–Thurs 11am–11pm, Fri & Sat till midnight, Sun till 6pm.

Rannakohvik Ranna pst 1. This modern glass and steel structure, spread over three floors, right on the beach, is a great drinking spot – the sea views from the terrace and the relaxed ambience make it very difficult to leave. Sun–Thurs noon–midnight, Fri & Sat till 2am.

Tallinna Väravad Vana-Tallinna 1. An atmospheric, if surprisingly staid, bar in the top storey of the Tallinn Gate (see p.107) in a frumpily furnished attic space. The outdoor terrace is more fun. Daily 11am–11pm.

Veerev Õlu Uus 3A. The "Rolling Beer" is an enjoyably unpretentious wooden-bench bar attracting an agreeable mixture of holidaymakers and garrulous locals. Daily noon–midnight.

Viies Villem Kuninga 11. A roomy basement pub that rounds up an enthusiastic cross-section of drinkers most nights. Decent salads and meaty main courses. Sun–Thurs noon–midnight, Fri & Sat till 2am.

Entertainment

The Endla Theatre, Keskväljak 1 (℡ 442 0666, ⓦ www.endla.ee), hosts top-quality **theatre and dance**, while the Pärnu Concert Hall, Aida 4 (Pärnu kontserdimaja; ℡ 445 5800, ⓦ www.concert.ee), provides the perfect venue for chamber **concerts** and major classical music events – the Estonian National Symphony Orchestra plays here a couple of times a month. Regular organ recitals are given at St Elizabeth's Church; ask at the tourist office.

Annual events attracting top-class international participants include the **Pärnu Days of Contemporary Music** (Pärnu Nüüdismuusika Päevad; ⓦ www.schoenberg.ee) in mid-January; the **David Oistrakh Festival** (ⓦ www.oistfest.ee) in the first half of July, featuring star conductors and soloists; and the **Festival of Documentary and Anthropological Film** (ⓦ www.chaplin.ee), also in July.

For clubbers, *Mirage*, Rüütli 40, is a year-round, seven-nights-a-week **disco** as well as a convenient late-night drinking joint, while the beachfront *Sunset*, Ranna pst 3 (ⓦ www.sunsetclub.ee) attracts a trendier, party-animal crowd.

Kihnu

Forty-five kilometres southwest of Pärnu, the mellow island of **KIHNU**, 7km long and 3.5km across, offers an enticing mixture of pine forest, juniper heath and pasture. The island supported a population of 1200 until the end of World War II, when a third fled to the West, and the seafaring activities of those who remained were severely curtailed by the security-conscious Soviet authorities. Nowadays, only around six hundred souls live on Kihnu and many of the older female residents still wear traditional costume, especially the highly distinctive, red-tasseled headscarves and red-, green- and yellow-striped skirts.

The island is compact enough to explore on a day-trip from Pärnu, although you can stay in one of a handful of farmhouse **B&Bs** (booked through Kihnurand; ℡ 446 9924). Kihnu is served by **ferries** from the port of Munalaiu, 40km southwest of Pärnu (May to mid-Sept Mon & Tues 3 daily; Wed, Thurs, Sat & Sun 2 daily; Fri 4 daily; mid-Sept to Dec Wed & Thurs 2 daily, Fri & Sun 1 daily; €3 one-way; ⓦ www.veeteed.com). Pärnu–Tõstamaa **buses** pick up and drop off by the harbour.

Two kilometres west of the ferry harbour, Kihnu's main settlement of **LINAKÜLA** huddles around a plain parish church that began as Lutheran when it was built in the eighteenth century, but became Orthodox in 1858 after the mass conversion of most of the islanders – they switched faiths in order to take up an offer of free land promised by crafty Tsarist bureaucrats. The church graveyard is the final resting place of Kihnu Jõnn, a much-travelled merchant seaman who came to symbolize the sea-roving lifestyle of the average Kihnu male, for whom years of hard graft at sea – punctuated by intermittent bouts of drinking and fighting – was the norm. Jõnn drowned off the coast of Denmark, where he was buried in 1913, only to be reinterred here eight decades later. A small museum opposite the church contains several sprightly canvases by self-taught local painter Jaan Oad (1899–1984), whose pictures of pre-World War II fisherfolk exude a vitality that seems largely absent in the laid-back Kihnu of today.

Soomaa National Park

Extending across the flatlands some 20km due east of Pärnu, the **Soomaa National Park** (Soomaa rahvuspark; ☏435 7164, ⓦwww.soomaa.ee) was established in 1994 to protect a patchwork of grassland, peat bog and riverine forest – home to elk, beavers, flying squirrels, brown bears, lynx and 160 bird species. The area is susceptible to flooding during the spring thaw, when roads in the centre of the park may become impassable – especially around the village of Riisa, where the Raudra, Lemmjõgi and Halliste rivers meet. Soomaa is the traditional home of the *haabja*, a canoe carved from a single trunk of aspen, and propelled by an enormous paddle, rather like a punt. *Haabjas* are still made in the area and a handful of local tour operators organize guided *haabja* excursions along Soomaa's waterways – although canoes and kayaks are more common. If you prefer to stick to dry land there are plenty of marked walking trails.

You'll need your own **transport** to reach the park, accessible by road from either Pärnu or Viljandi. Tourist offices in both can provide **information**; the one in Viljandi is more clued up about accommodation and **canoe trips**. One of the best of the local canoe outfits is Soomaa.com (☏506 1896, ⓦwww.soomaa.com), who offer guided canoe trips (from €25 per person), bog walks, beaver-watching, and sessions in floating raft-based saunas. They can pick you up from Pärnu.

Regio's invaluable 1:100 000 *Soomaa jõed/Rivers of Soomaa* **map** can be obtained from Viljandi's tourist office or from bookshops in Tallinn, Tartu and Pärnu. A day-trip is enough to get a flavour of the park, but there's a smattering of accommodation for those who fancy a longer stay.

Into the park

The best way to reach the park from Pärnu is to head 35km northeast as far as the village of **JÕESUU**, where the River Navesti flows into the broader Pärnu. From here you can choose between the Kaansoo road, which follows the northern bank of the Navesti, or the Tipu road, which heads south through the centre of the park. The latter route provides a good first taste of Soomaa's archetypal bog-scape in the shape of the **Riisa Bog Trail**, signed off the road to the left after 7km. A boardwalk leads across the peaty soil, which supports a carpet of lichens, grasses and heathers punctuated by slender birches and stunted conifers.

Some 4km south of Riisa is **TÕRAMAA** (a road junction rather than a full-blown settlement) and the **National Park Visitors' Centre** (May–Sept Tues–Sun 10am–6pm; Oct–April Tues–Sat 10am–4pm; ☏435 7164, ⓦwww.soomaa.ee), which has leaflets on what to see in the park, a small exhibition devoted to conservation issues and a handful of **rooms** (❷). The centre marks the start of the short **Beaver Trail** (Koprarada), which leads along the banks of the Tõramaa stream, passing enthusiastically gnawed tree trunks and branch-built dams. The minor road running east from the visitors' centre brings you after 3km to the **Lemmjõe Keelemets**, a short, but fascinating, marked trail through the riverine forest on the north side of the road.

South of the visitors' centre, the road runs along the western edge of the Öördi bog before veering east towards Viljandi. Twenty kilometres out, just beyond the village of **IIA**, a dirt road heads north towards Lake Öördi (Öördi järv), where there's a 2km boardwalk path through a serene environment of squelchy mosses, speckled red with cranberries in the autumn. Back in Iia and heading east, it's just 5km to **KÕPU**, where you can pick up the main road to Viljandi.

Viljandi and around

Roughly midway between Pärnu and Tartu, **VILJANDI** is one of Estonia's more pleasant provincial centres – a low-rise jumble of houses draped around the north-western end of 5km-long, boomerang-shaped Lake Viljandi. The grizzled ruins of a once-mighty castle bear witness to the town's erstwhile importance as a staging post on the Rīga–Novgorod trade route, although it's the handsome stock of early twentieth-century red-brick buildings and prim timber cottages that give the modern-day centre its character. The town is at its busiest during July's **Viljandi Folk Festival** (Viljandi pärimuusika festival; Ⓦwww.folk.ee) in the castle grounds.

Arrival, information and accommodation

Viljandi's **bus station** is at the junction of Tallinna and Uus, ten minutes' walk north of the centre. The train station is 2.5km west of town on the Pärnu road. Viljandi's **tourist office**, Vabaduse plats 6 (May–Aug Mon–Fri 9am–6pm, Sat & Sun 10am–3pm; Sept–April Mon–Fri 10am–5pm, Sat 10am–2pm; Ⓣ433 0442, Ⓦwww.viljandi.ee), has free town plans and information about the Viljandi region – notably the Soomaa National Park (see p.111). There's a handful of decent **hotels and B&Bs**, and the tourist office can provide details of rural accommodation in local villages – they're happy to call on your behalf if the owners don't speak English.

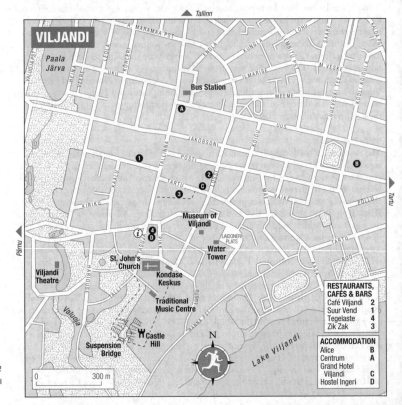

Alice Jakobsoni 55 ☎434 7616, ⊚www.matti
.ee/~alice. A seven-room B&B in a Bauhaus-
influenced suburban building, a 10min walk east
of the bus station. Small but bright en-suites come
with TV and parquet floors. ❸
Centrum Tallinna 24 ☎435 1100, ⊚www
.centrum.ee. Opposite the bus station, the
glass-fronted *Centrum* sits on top of a shopping
centre-cum-office block and has spacious, sunny
en-suites aimed at business travellers. ❸
Grand Hotel Viljandi Tartu 11/Lossi 29 ☎435
5800, ⊚www.ghv.ee. The poshest place to stay in

Viljandi, this Art Deco hotel's stylish and elegant
en-suites come with all the comforts you would
expect from a four-star, but are let down slightly by
an unimaginative grey-brown colour scheme. ❺
Hostel Ingeri Pikk 2C ☎433 4414, ⊚www
.hostelingeri.ee. Across a wooden footbridge from
the tourist office, this small hostel looks out onto
the castle ruins. Spick-and-span rooms with
shared facilities are good value. Doubles ❷; dorms
€20 per person.

The Town

The most obvious place to start exploring Viljandi is the tree-shaded expanse of **Castle Hill** (Lossimäed), at the southern end of Tallinna and its extension Tasuja pst. Built by the Livonian Order in the thirteenth century, the castle was one of the most important strongholds in southern Estonia until the 1620s, when Swedish siege guns blasted it into a state beyond repair. A few jagged sections of wall are all that remain of the keep, but there's a sweeping view of the lake from the grassed-over ramparts. West of the ruins, a stretch of the former moat is spanned by a dainty, pedestrian-only **suspension bridge**, built in 1931 by public-spirited aristocrat Karl von Mensenkampff and nowadays a much-photographed landmark.

At the northern end of the castle park, Viljandi's **Traditional Music Centre** (Pärimusmuusika Ait; Mon–Fri 9am–7pm, Sat & Sun 11am–5pm) hosts history exhibitions – frequently with a strong cultural theme – and also has one of the best-stocked folk-music CD shops in the country.

North of the castle, a tangle of cobbled alleyways behind the whitewashed **St John's Church** provides the setting for one of the country's more in-your-face art museums, the **Kondase Keskus** at Pikk 8 (Wed–Sun 10am–5pm; €1). It's primarily devoted to self-taught local painter Paul Kondas (1900–85), an outwardly conventional primary-school teacher who escaped into a psychedelic dream world whenever he put brush to canvas. Kondas clearly believed that a wild zest for living lay behind the outwardly unexcitable nature of the Estonian national character, and his pictures of St John's Eve celebrations and summer bathing trips are filled with uninhibited dancing, nudity and mischief. Canvases of the German city of Dresden being bombed by UFOs, or US astronauts being greeted by moon-dwelling aliens, display a strange and at times disturbing penchant for the surreal.

A block north, at Laidoneri plats 10, the **Museum of Viljandi** (Wed–Sun 10am–5pm; €1.30) offers a neatly arranged display of peasant interiors, local costumes and an impressive model of the castle as it looked in the thirteenth century. Upstairs a horde of local oddities includes ceremonial horsehair-plumed helmets once worn by the Viljandi fire brigade and unintentionally absurd Soviet-era dioramas showing socialist farming methods.

East of the museum, the well-tended lawns of **Laidoneri plats** bask beneath a 30m-high **Water Tower** (May–Sept daily 11am–6pm; €0.70), built in 1911 when the town was plumbed into the public water supply for the first time. Looking like a huge octagonal treehouse perched atop a factory chimney, it contains photographs of Viljandi past and present.

Heading east from the square along Tartu brings you to tranquil, sandy-shored Lake Viljandi (Viljandi järv), where there's a beachside café and a place to rent pedalos. A round-trip run, known as the **Lake Viljandi Race** (Viljandi järve jooks), held here on May Day every year since 1928, is one of the major events in the Estonian cross-country calendar.

Eating and drinking

There are lots of places to **eat** in and around the town centre. *Café Viljandi*, Lossi 31, is a popular local teahouse with settees and Art-Nouveau light fittings, serving sweet and savoury pastries and cream-filled cakes. For a modern, slinkier feel, head for *Zik Zak*, Arkaadia Aed 5, which has an imaginative menu of soups, healthy salads and mains. *Tegelaste*, near the approach to the castle at Pikk 2B, offers a broad spread of Estonian meat dishes, with plenty of chicken and fish, and outdoor seating on a wooden deck above the former moat. You can also eat at **pubs** like *Suur Vend*, Turu 4, which has a good range of hearty meals and bar snacks.

Travel details

Trains

Pärnu to: Tallinn (2 daily; 3–3hr 20min).

Buses

Haapsalu to: Kärdla (3–4 daily; 2hr); Tallinn (hourly; 1hr 50min); Virtsu (2–3 daily; 1hr 30min).
Kärdla to: Haapsalu (3–4 daily; 2hr); Tallinn (3–4 daily; 4hr 30min).
Kuressaare to: Karujärv (summer: Mon–Fri 1 daily; Sat & Sun 2 daily; winter: 1 daily; 25min); Kihelkonna (5 daily; 50min); Leisi (Mon–Fri 5 daily, Sat & Sun 4 daily; 1hr 10min); Tallinn (8 daily; 4hr 30min); Tartu (2–3 daily; 6hr); Undva (2 daily; 1hr).
Pärnu to: Kuressaare (3 daily; 3hr); Tallinn (hourly; 2hr); Tartu (hourly; 2hr 45min–3hr 45min).
Viljandi to: Kuressaare (2–3 daily; 4hr 45min); Tallinn (13 daily; 2hr 30m–4hr); Tartu (8 daily; 1–1hr 20min).

Ferries

Munalaiu to: Kihnu (summer: 2 daily; winter: 10 weekly; 2hr).
Rohuküla to: Heltermaa (Hiiumaa; 4–6 daily; 1hr 30min); Sviby (2 daily; 50min).
Triigi to: Sõru (2–4 daily).
Virtsu to: Kuivastu (for Muhu and Saaremaa; summer: hourly; winter: every 2hr; 30min).

Flights

Kuressaare to: Rīga (2 weekly; 45min).
Pärnu to: Kihnu (daily; 15min); Ruhnu (2 weekly; 25min).
Tallinn to: Kärdla (1–2 daily; 40min); Kuressaare (1–2 daily; 55min).

International buses

Pärnu to: Rīga (5 daily; 3hr 20min); Vilnius (1 daily; 8hr 45min).

1.3

Eastern Estonia

E astern Estonia may not attract as many visitors as the island-scattered west coast, but it offers just as much variety. Much of the countryside is typically Estonian – birch and pine forests alternating with arable land and patches of bog – but it also possesses landscapes less commonly found in the Baltics, notably the rippling hills of the southeast, the broad freshwater expanse of **Lake Peipsi** and the boulder-strewn beaches of the northeast coast. Long stretches of the last fall within the boundaries of the **Lahemaa National Park**, a vast area of primeval woodland, reed-shrouded coast and beautifully preserved fishing villages; just 50km east of Tallinn, it's one of the most accessible areas of natural wilderness in the country.

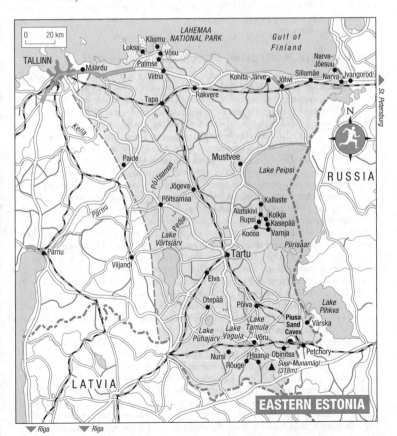

EASTERN ESTONIA

The landscape east of Lahemaa is brutally different, characterized by the dour mining towns and cone-shaped slag heaps of Estonia's oil-shale industry, and there's little of interest until you arrive at **Narva**, a historical fortress town on the border with Russia. Though somewhat blighted by postwar architecture, it's nevertheless an atmospheric base from which to explore the sweeping, sandy beaches at **Narva-Jõesuu** and the Stalinist-era architecture of **Sillamäe**.

The southeast is dominated by **Tartu**, a university town that combines nineteenth-century gentility with raw, student-fuelled energy. The one place outside Tallinn with a sufficient menu of urban sights to keep you going for several days, it's also a good base from which to explore the lakes and rolling hills of the far south, with **Suur-Munamä-gi**, the highest point in the Baltics, and the winter sports resort of **Otepää**, both within easy striking distance. Bearing witness to Estonia's cultural and racial diversity, Russian **Old Believers** continue to inhabit bucolic fishing settlements along the western shores of Lake Peipsi, while surviving communities of **Setu** – an Estonian people with a distinct folk culture – still live in the scattered villages of the extreme southeast.

Getting around is fairly straightforward, with buses from Tallinn and Tartu serving almost all the places mentioned in this chapter. In addition, the market town of **Rakvere** is a useful transport hub for the Lahemaa National Park, while calm, lakeside **Võru** serves many of the smaller places in the far southeast. There's a wide range of **accommodation** in Tartu and Otepää and a flourishing B&B trade in parts of the Lahemaa National Park – elsewhere in this part of the country, however, tourist facilities are less well-developed than in western Estonia, giving it much more of an off-the-beaten-track feel.

Lahemaa National Park and around

Extending over a deeply indented stretch of coastline an hour's drive east of Tallinn, the **LAHEMAA NATIONAL PARK** (Lahemaa rahvuspark; ⓦ www.lahemaa.ee) embraces 725 square kilometres of the most varied and beautiful terrain in the country. Its most distinctive features are the four evenly spaced peninsulas sticking out into the Baltic Sea, each fringed with custard-coloured beaches, tawny reed beds and mossy forests. Five to 10km inland is a limestone plateau covered with juniper heath, peat bog, forests of alder, ash and elm and patches of potato- and rye-growing farmland. Dividing the plain from the plateau is the **North Estonian Glint**, a limestone escarpment that runs from east to west through the middle of the park – although it's so smothered by soil and vegetation that it looks more like a gentle slope than a cliff and in some parts of the park is barely visible. A more conspicuous geological phenomenon is the profusion of so-called **erratic boulders**, isolated lumps of rock strewn all over this part of Estonia by retreating glaciers some 12,000 years ago.

After World War II the coastline became a high-security border area that non-residents needed a permit to enter, which ironically helped to preserve the natural landscape by stifling economic activity. However, the Soviet military remained suspicious of Estonian environmentalists, which makes it all the more surprising that the authorities sanctioned the creation of the Lahemaa National Park – the Soviet Union's first – in 1971. The national park ethos, in which the preservation of nature was given a higher moral value than the furtherance of communism or any other ideology, immediately turned Lahemaa into a cult destination for Estonian intellectuals. Nowadays Lahemaa is one of the most popular destinations in the country, particularly in the summer, when tour groups descend at weekends. It is equally appealing in the winter, with few tourists, and snow and ice to enhance the park's desolate beauty.

Many of the park's most exciting **natural features** can be accessed by marked paths, ranging from deep-forest hikes long enough to satisfy seasoned walkers to well-designed study trails that take just an hour or two to complete. Restored palace complexes at **Palmse** and **Sagadi**, in the southeast, provide an insight into the feudal manor-house culture of the German barons who once held sway over the region, while the charmingly under-commercialized beach resorts of **Võsu** and **Käsmu** are another

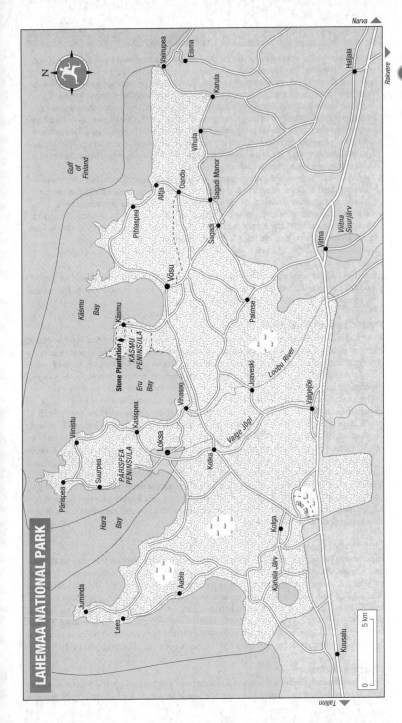

LAHEMAA NATIONAL PARK

N

Gulf
of
Finland

Vainupea
Eisma
Karula
Vihula
Oandu
Altja
Pihlaspea
Sagadi Manor
Sagadi
Võsu
Vitna Suurjärv
Vitna
Käsmu
Bay
Käsmu
KÄSMU
PENINSULA
Palmse
Loobu River
Stone Plantation
Eru
Bay
Joaveski
Vihasoo
Valgejõe
Viinistu
Kasispea
Valge Jõgi
Loksa
Kotka
Suurpea
PÄRISPEA
PENINSULA
Pärispea
Hara
Bay
Kõiga
Juminda
Kahala Järv
Aabla
Lees
Kuusalu

5 Km

0

Fauna in Lahemaa National Park

With its array of unspoilt natural landscapes, **Lahemaa National Park** supports a rich variety of **wildlife**. You're most likely to catch sight of roe deer, large numbers of which roam the forests and occasionally graze on farmland, especially early in the morning. Wild boar and moose are less common and stick to the forests in winter, although you may see them foraging in open countryside in summer. The park's forests are also home to large populations of hares, martens and foxes and a small number (in the tens rather than the hundreds) of badgers, lynxes, wolves and brown bears. Beavers are extremely secretive, but signs of their industry are everywhere: dams beside the Beaver Trail at Oandu (see p.122) and elsewhere, and what look like clumsily felled tree trunks (a sure sign of their nocturnal gnawing activities).

As well as the resident songbirds thronging the forests, Lahemaa hosts several migrating **bird** species in spring and autumn. Eru Bay just west of Võsu is the best place to see migrating waterfowl, while Kahala Lake in the far west is popular with ducks and grebes. White storks and cranes can be seen feeding in agricultural land from May onwards; black storks nest deep in the forest and are rarely sighted. The fields around Käsmu Bay are thick with corncrakes in June.

attraction. If you want to explore the park in depth, it's worth getting hold of Regio's 1:60,000 *Lahemaa Rahvuspark* **map**; you can pick it up from bookshops in Tallinn and at the Park's Visitors' Centre in Palmse (see opposite).

Park practicalities

Most Lahemaa-bound tourist traffic approaches from the west along the Tallinn–Narva highway (which forms the park's southern boundary for a lengthy stretch) before arriving at Viitna, a major crossroads from which the road to Palmse, Võsu and Käsmu branches off to the north. The account below covers this main route first, before fanning out to explore outlying areas of the park – although any number of itineraries are possible.

The main source of **information** is the Visitors' Centre in the inland village of **Palmse** (see opposite), and if you're driving then this should be your first port of call. If you're dependent on public transport it makes more sense to aim for the seaside villages of Võsu and Käsmu, which offer much more in the way of accommodation and bus connections – you can always hike or hitch to Palmse once you get settled in. **Käsmu** is the best base if you want a range of hiking possibilities on your doorstep, with a number of local trails ranging in duration from forty minutes to four hours. Staying in **Võsu** or elsewhere in the park, you'll still be able to see a great deal on foot, providing you don't mind tramping 20–30km a day. Otherwise, you'll need a car or bike to access all the main areas of interest. Võsu is the one settlement in the park that has a decent number of food and drink shops.

Getting to the park

In summer (June–Aug) there are several daily services **from Tallinn bus station** to Võsu and Käsmu. At other times, there is just one early-morning service (currently 6.30am) to Võsu. A good year-round option is to catch one of the many buses to **Rakvere** (see p.122), just outside the park, where you can catch connecting services to Võsu and Käsmu (aim to get to Rakvere before 3pm), or, on four days a week, to Palmse. See "Travel details" on p.146 for more detailed bus information. City Bike in Tallinn (see Tallinn "Listings"; p.88) organize **day-trips** to the park from €50 per person. If you do **drive** to Lahemaa, leave nothing of value inside your car, wherever you park.

Accommodation

Small **hotels and B&Bs** are scattered throughout the park, with the biggest concentration in and around Käsmu. Summer weekends are often booked up several months in advance. Most establishments claim to be open year round, although in reality the smaller B&Bs will turn away individuals or small groups in the October–April period – they can't afford to turn the heating on unless they have a houseful. In summer, **hostel**-style accommodation is available in Võsu, Käsmu, Palmse and Sagadi. There's also a network of free National Park-run **campsites** (May–Sept), in which firewood is provided but little else – although there may be a couple of dry toilets on hand. The sites are nicely spaced out so that hikers can feasibly walk to a new one each day.

Viru Bog

Approaching Lahemaa from the Tallinn direction, the first of the park's set-piece attractions you come across is **Viru Bog** (Viru raba), an area of peat bog, just over 2km square, created over a period of 10,000 years by decaying mosses, about 50km out from the capital. It's just north of the Tallinn–Narva highway – take the Loksa turn-off and look for a sign for the **Viru Bog Nature Trail** (Viru raba õpperada) on your right after about 1km. A 3.5km-long wooden walkway curves northeast across the bog, providing a superb vantage point over this strange landscape of grey-brown lichens and stunted conifers, with pine-covered dunes just visible to the northwest. Late May to early June is the best time to visit, when stretches of the bog are covered in wild flowers.

Viitna

Some 22km beyond the Loksa turn-off, **VIITNA** has served as an important rest-stop on the Tallinn–Narva road since medieval times, and is still the place where most people break for a breather before turning north towards Palmse and the central area of the park. Viitna's enduring popularity is in large part due to the presence of the *Viitna kõrts* **tavern**, built in imitation of an eighteenth-century coaching inn and boasting an atmospheric timbered interior – the perfect place to fill up on pork and freshwater fish dishes. Immediately south of the tavern, a 2.5km-long nature trail skirts **Great Viitna Lake** (Viitna suurjärv or Viitna pikkjärv), a glacier-gouged finger of water formed by retreating ice some 11,500 years ago. Fringed by pine forest, it's a supremely restful spot. Should you wish **to stay**, head for the *Viitna Holiday Centre* (☎329 3651, ✉linajarv2@hot.ee; ❷), down a side road 500m east of the main crossroads, offering somewhat austere en-suite doubles and bunk-bed quads in pleasant wooded surroundings.

Palmse and around

The village of **PALMSE**, home to the park's Visitors' Centre (see below), began life as a Cistercian convent before being bought in 1677 by the von Pahlens, a leading family of Baltic barons who stayed here until they were booted out by the land reform of 1919. Their eighteenth-century complex of manorial buildings subsequently served as a barracks, then a children's holiday camp, before the Lahemaa National Park authorities set up their HQ here in 1972. An impressive ensemble of cream and pale-blue buildings is grouped around a central courtyard, bound by fruit orchards and landscaped parkland. Inside the courtyard, a balustraded staircase sweeps up to the doors of the Neoclassical **Manor House** (daily: May–Sept 10am–7pm; Oct–April 10am–4pm; €5), filled with antique furniture from all over Estonia and sepia photographs of the estate as it was in the Pahlens' time. Outside, an old creamery (July & Aug; same times) contains an exhibition of sleds and coaches, and beyond this lies a conservatory filled with palms and cacti.

You'll find the **Lahemaa Visitors' Centre** (mid-May to mid-Sept daily 9am–7pm; mid-Oct to mid-April Mon–Fri 9am–5pm; other times daily 9am–6pm; ☎329 5555, ⊛www.lahemaa.ee), in a former coach house at the entrance to the manor courtyard. With an exhibit on Estonia's national parks and conservation issues, it's well stocked with maps and English-language leaflets describing various trails. Next door, the *Park-Hotel Palmse* (☎322 3626, ⊛www.phpalmse.ee; ❹) is one of the swishest **hotels** in the park: a converted vodka distillery with bright, airy wood-floored en-suites, some with bathtubs. Only slightly less comfortable is the *Palmse Guesthouse* (☎324 0070, ⊛www.palmse .ee; ❷) in another of the manor's outbuildings, offering a pair of en-suite apartments, three doubles with shared facilities, and a handful of triples and quads. The *Park-Hotel Palmse* has a good **café-restaurant**.

Võsu

Strung out along the southern shores of Käsmu Bay (Käsmu laht), 8km north of Palmse, **VÕSU** has been a holiday resort since the late nineteenth century, when its pine-fringed beach was discovered by the St Petersburg intelligentsia. This uneventful little place is a good base: within striking distance lie wood-shrouded Oandu (see p.122) and the fishing village of Altja (opposite), both reached via a 10km-long forest trail starting at the southern entrance to Võsu, while the Käsmu peninsula, strewn with erratic boulders, is just 8km northwest.

Võsu is over 2km long from east to west, and **accommodation** is scattered: the *Männisalu Hostel*, signed off the main road at Lääne 13 (☎323 8320, ⓦwww.mannisalu .ee; ❷; May–Sept only), has sparsely furnished doubles with wooden floors and doors, more comfortable suites, and dorms (€25), with breakfast included. At the western end of the village, the smart *Rannaliiv*, Aia 5 (☎323 8456, ⓦwww.rannaliiv.ee; ❸), boasts slick en-suites with wooden furnishings and TV; suites come with balconies. *Camping Lepispea*, 2km west of the centre on the Käsmu road (mid-May to mid-Sept; ☎5564 5455, ⓦwww.hot.ee/lepispeale), is one of the best-equipped in the country, with clean toilet blocks, sauna, barbecue area and electricity points for caravans. The *Grillbaar*, a **pub-restaurant** midway through the village on the main street, serves a decent range of pork and chicken dishes. The *Võsu Pagariäri* bakery, near the eastern entrance to the village, is the place for cakes, pastries and pancakes.

Käsmu

People speak in superlatives about **KÄSMU**, an appealing ensemble of pastel-coloured houses and neat gardens that meets expectations of what a traditional Estonian village ought to look like. The place owes its prosperous, white-picket-fence appearance to a brief period in the seafaring limelight just before World War I, when Käsmu Bay – not as prone to thick ice as some of the other spots along the northern coast – became a popular winter anchorage for sailing ships. A maritime school was opened here in 1884, many of whose graduates chose to settle down in the village once their ocean-going days were over, earning Käsmu the nickname of "Captains' Village". The development of deep-hulled steamships put paid to Käsmu's importance, however, and it's now a pleasant summer-holiday village, offering plenty of B&B accommodation and excellent walking opportunities in the forests of the Käsmu peninsula.

Käsmu's maritime heritage is remembered in a private **museum** (open whenever the owner's family is around – usually most days), signed off the main street midway through the village. There's an atmospheric, pre-World War I living room containing the furniture of the owner's grandfather, while elsewhere are displays of bits of old boats, fishing tackle and baskets made from birch-bark. Just inland, the **parish church** is renowned for its charming graveyard, planted with a kaleidoscopic array of flowers every spring.

At the northern end of the village a path leads to the tip of the Käsmu peninsula, where you can gaze at a chain of erratic boulders stretching away towards the uninhabited island of Kuradisaare. From here a path leads along the rock-strewn northern and western coasts of the peninsula, before looping back to Käsmu village through dense forest – a scenic circuit of about 14km. For a shorter woodland walk head west from the village along the track that starts roughly opposite the *Lainela Holiday Village* (see below). This soon lands you in the **Stone Plantation** (Kivikülv), a vast, eerie expanse of moss-covered erratic boulders sheltered by pines.

Accommodation

Käsmu has a string of **B&Bs** on the main street; contact them in advance to check availability and make sure someone is there to meet you when you arrive. Most allow camping in their gardens for around €4–5, although they'll turn campers away if things get too busy. A good fallback is the free national park **campsite** on the shores of Käsmu järv, a forest-shrouded lake about an hour's walk southwest of the village. The simple **café** at the *Holiday Village* (see below), is the only place to eat around these parts.

Lainela Puhkeküla (Lainela Holiday Village) Neeme 70 ☎323 8133, ⓦwww.lainela.ee. A former children's holiday camp now open to everyone, with seven hostel-like halls offering sparsely furnished two- and three-bed rooms, with showers and WC on the corridors. Despite its hundred-bed capacity it's still likely to be packed with groups in the summer. Open May–Sept. ❷

Merekalda Neeme 2 ☎323 8451, ⓦwww.merekalda.ee. A plush B&B at the southern end of the village, right on the shore, with a range of en-suite rooms and apartments in the main family house or in the annexe in the pleasant sea-facing garden. ❸

Rannamännid Neeme 31 ☎323 8329, ⓦwww.rannamannid.ee. On the main street, this smart B&B offers eight sunny rooms, some en-suite; those on the top floor have sloping ceilings and are particularly atmospheric. There's also an attractive terrace, sauna and barbecue area. Half-board is well worth the extra cost. ❸

Uustalu Neeme 78A ☎325 2956, ⓦuustalu.planet.ee. This cosy B&B in a beautiful position near the northern tip of the peninsula has simple, snug en-suites, with wooden floors and furniture and pastel-coloured walls. Campers can pitch a tent in the garden. May–Sept only. ❷

West of Käsmu Bay: the Pärispea peninsula

West of Käsmu Bay, roads from Võsu work their way along the southern shore of Eru Bay (Eru laht) before heading north onto the **Pärispea peninsula**, another inviting area of desolate, boulder-strewn beauty. You need a car to explore this area, as public transport is negligible and settlements are far-flung.

As you head up the east coast you'll pass lots of reed beds, a paradise for migrating birds in late spring, especially mute swans, mallards and barnacle geese. The first village of any interest is **VIINISTU**, on the northeastern corner of the peninsula. During the interwar years Viinistu was known throughout Estonia as the "Village of the Spirit Kings" ("Piiritusekuningate Küla") on account of the huge profits made from smuggling vodka to Finland. After World War II, a sizeable fishing fleet was based here until that industry went into decline, and large parts of the portside canning factory have been transformed into the **Viinistu Art Museum** (Viinistu kunstimuuseum; Wed–Sun 11am–6pm; €2). Based on the private collection of Jan Manitski, a Viinistu native who made it big in Sweden, the gallery provides a definitive overview of Estonian art from the early twentieth century onwards, kicking off with one of the most frequently reproduced paintings in the country, Aleksander Vardi's impressionistic view of Paris's Boulevard Clichy. There are some interwar graphics of North African tribesmen by the much-travelled artist Eduard Wiiralt, and a room devoted to the often unsettling conceptual creations of the post-1991 generation. The gallery also offers **accommodation**, with simple but pristine doubles with shower in an adjacent building (☎608 6422, ⓔhotell@viinistu.ee; ❷). On the landward side of the gallery, *Viinistu Kõrts*, in an old, whitewashed house, is a cheery place for fried fish and a cold beer.

The western side of the peninsula is characterized by a string of former Soviet military settlements, beginning with **PÄRISPEA** in the northwest, built to serve a radar installation on the headland, 2km to the northeast. A track runs past abandoned barracks to reach the headland, where an earthen mound (the erstwhile perch of the biggest of the eight radar dishes once sited here) provides a superb point from which to survey a chain of sea-splashed erratic boulders strung out to the north. The free national park **campsite** just below the mound is very popular on summer weekends.

East of Käsmu Bay

The road east out of Võsu skirts the northern fringes of Oandu forest and leads to **ALTJA**, a charming fishing village with timber buildings, 15km away. For walkers, there's a more direct, 10km path through the forest, starting at the southern end of Võsu and emerging near the Oandu nature trails described below. Altja's main landmark is an enormous **wooden swing** at the eastern end of the village. Before World

War II, every Estonian village would have had one of these: they provided a summer-evening social focus where local youth would gather in the days before bus shelters were invented. Beyond the swing there's a short stretch of sandy beach and a group of fishermen's cottages and net sheds, many sporting restored thatched roofs. Built in the style of a nineteenth-century tavern, *Altja Körts*, near the swing, serves good local fish.

Oandu

Beyond Altja the road climbs uphill to the south, passing after 1.5km the start of the **Oandu Beaver Trail** (Koprarada) on the left side of the road, a 1.7km-long circuit that passes several beaver dams; you'll also see tree trunks bearing fresh gnaw marks. Just under 1km north of the Beaver Trail, **OANDU** itself is no more than a couple of scattered farmsteads in the forest. Signs mark the start of the **Oandu Forest Nature Trail** (Oandu loodusmetsa rada), a circular, 4.7km-long path designed to offer a taste of the park's varied forest landscape: a mixture of evergreen and deciduous trees drawing a dark-green canopy over a woodland floor covered in mosses and ferns. Scarred tree-trunks bear witness to the activities of itchy-scratchy moose and bark-nibbling bears. There's a free national park **campsite** just north of the Oandu Forest Nature Trail, beside the road and overlooking a small lake.

Sagadi

Three kilometres beyond Oandu lies **Sagadi Manor** (Sagadi mõis), a handsome ensemble of cherry-and-cream buildings lying behind a low, brick wall. Built for the von Fock family in the mid-eighteenth century, it is now the regional HQ of the Estonian Forestry Commission. Presiding over a large, oblong courtyard, the **Manor House** (May–Sept daily 10am–6pm; combined ticket including Forestry Museum €3) harbours an attractively arranged collection of period furniture and paintings, beginning in the central hall with a curious canvas by an unknown artist of a dog and cat fighting over a chicken. Occupying outbuildings on one side of the courtyard, the **Forestry Museum** (Metsamuuseum; same times) is mainly intended for schoolchildren, with a didactic display of stuffed woodland animals and a thorough run-down of all the types of tree found in Estonia. Sharing the same building as the Forestry Museum, the *Sagadi Manor* **hotel** (☎676 7888, ⍟www.sagadi.ee; ⑤) offers comfortable en-suites with wi-fi and satellite TV; most also feature attic ceilings. The more expensive "guest rooms" have French windows that open onto an inner courtyard. Occupying the former bailiff's house on the opposite side of the courtyard, the impressively high-ceilinged quarters at *Sagadi Manor* **hostel** (same contact details) are sparsely furnished but comfortable, with beds (€16) in a crowded dorm; breakfast is available in the hotel café for an additional €6.50. Hostel and hotel guests can also rent **bikes**.

Rakvere

The laid-back, unindustrialized town of **RAKVERE** lies some 27km beyond the southeastern border of the park, just off the Tallinn–Narva highway. Its dominant feature is a long, grassy ridge topped by the sombre grey ruins of **Rakvere Castle** (Rakvere linnus; May–Sept daily 11am–7pm; €4.60), built by the Danes in 1220 and expanded by the Livonian Order when they took over in 1346. A restored tower contains a display of archeological oddments, and you can walk a short section of the battlements. Just north is an enormous, golden-horned statue of an aurochs (a now-extinct breed of cattle) placed here in 2002 in honour of the beasts that long ago roamed the plains below.

Downhill from the aurochs, at Tallinna 3, the high-profile temporary exhibitions on Estonian historical themes at the **Rakvere Exhibitions House Museum** (Tues–Fri 10am–5pm, Sat 10am–3pm; €2) are usually worthwhile. Heading from Tallinna along the eastern flanks of the castle hill, **Pikk** is the most atmospheric of Rakvere's streets, with a largely low-rise jumble of pre-World War I buildings. At Pikk 50 the **Rakvere Citizens' House Museum** (Rakvere linnakodaniku majamuuseum; Tues–Sat 11am–5pm; €1.30) preserves a neat nineteenth-century interior, complete with a welcoming samovar on the sideboard, and all sorts of charming period crockery.

Rakvere's **bus station** is ten minutes' walk southeast of the centre on Laada, just beyond a brochure-stocked **tourist office** at Laada 14 (mid-Sept to mid-May Mon–Fri 9am–5pm; mid-May to mid-Sept Mon–Fri 9am–6pm, Sat & Sun 10am–3pm; ☎324 2734, ⓔrakvere@visitestonia.com). The ☆*Katariina* guesthouse at Pikk 3 (☎322 3943, ⓦwww.katariina.ee; ❸) has cosy rooms, the cheaper ones with shared facilities, in a building originally built in the 1840s for a Russian merchant. There's also a **restaurant**, often featuring live music, and a small art gallery. The classy *Art Café*, Lai 13, serving up tasty omelettes, burgers, salads and pancakes, is an excellent spot for an evening **drink**.

Narva and around

"For sheer romantic medievalism, **NARVA** ranks even above Tallinn," wrote author Ronald Seth in 1939, unaware that this atmospheric city of cobbled streets was about to be pummelled into oblivion by German–Soviet artillery battles. On the country's far eastern border, with a population that is over ninety percent Russian-speaking, Narva is closer – geographically, socially and culturally – to St Petersburg than to Tallinn.

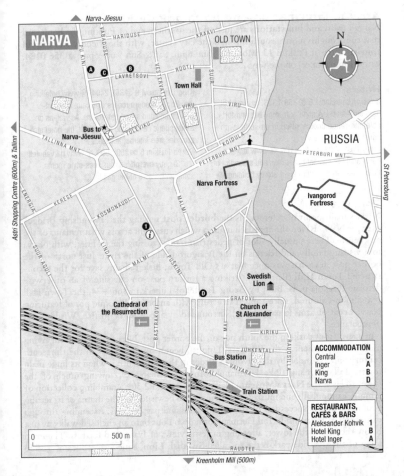

Economic activity has slumped since the collapse of communism, however, and as Estonia as a whole looks to the future, its third-largest city appears trapped in limbo.

It's hardly surprising that this oft-disputed border town has ended up this way. Founded by the Danes in 1229 and bequeathed to the Livonian Order a century later, the city, on the Narva River, marked for centuries the frontier between the Teutonic-ruled western Baltic and the emerging Russian state. The building of Narva Castle on the western side of the river was soon followed by the construction of Ivangorod on the opposite bank; the two strongholds continue to glower across the water at each other to this day. Narva was repeatedly fought over by Russians and Swedes from the mid-sixteenth century onwards, before Peter the Great's successful assault of May 1704 settled the issue. Under Tsarist rule Narva flourished as a port and became a world-famous centre for the textile industry with the founding of the Kreenholm cotton mill in 1857.

Now even its position on the main Tallinn–St Petersburg highway fails to bring much in the way of tourism or prosperity, with most travellers – like the Estonian establishment – generally happy to ignore it. This is a mistake: its truly impressive **castle** and unique, melancholy atmosphere, as well as the nearby Stalin-era model town of **Sillamäe** and the beach resort of **Narva-Jõesuu** – both easily seen on a side trip – more than justify a stay of a day or so.

Arrival, information and accommodation

Narva's **train and bus stations** are just off the southern end of Puškini, the boulevard that runs roughly north–south through the city centre, with the friendly and helpful **tourist office** at Puškini 13 (Mon–Fri 9am–6pm, Sat & Sun 9am–3pm; ☎356 0184, Ⓦtourism.narva.ee) on the way.

Hotels

Central Lavretsovi 5 ☎359 1333, Ⓦwww.hot .ee/centralhotel. A slightly frumpy but comfortable mid-range choice, offering en-suites with small TVs. ❸

Inger Puškini 28 ☎688 1100, Ⓦwww.inger.ee. Functional but pleasant en-suites and a handful of fancy suites in a modern eight-storey building. ❹

King Lavretsovi 9 ☎357 2404, Ⓦwww.hotelking .ee. Bright, modern rooms with faux wrought-iron fittings and smart bathrooms. As well as an atmospheric cellar-style restaurant, the hotel also provides free internet access. ❸

Narva Puškini 6 ☎359 9600, Ⓦwww.narvahotell .ee. Slightly overpriced, business-style rooms, some with views of the castle. ❹

The Town

Narva's main point of reference is the **border post** serving the "Friendship Bridge" over the Narva River, the approach road to which cuts right across what remains of the city centre. There's usually a lot of pedestrian traffic crossing the frontier, with Narva folk visiting family and friends on the Ivangorod side of the river. Just north of the border post lies what was once Narva's Old Town; little remains save for the reconstructed **Town Hall** (Raekoda), striking a forlorn pose on one side of an otherwise desolate Raekoja plats. Built by Georg Teuffel of Lübeck in 1668–74, the Town Hall is a salmon-coloured, spire-topped structure with an ornate Baroque portal featuring Narva's coat of arms (a pair of fish) surrounded by allegories of Justice, Wisdom and Temperance.

In a riverfront park on the south side of the border post, Narva's one great surviving medieval monument is the **Fortress** (Linnus), begun by the Danes in the thirteenth century and expanded by the Livonian Order in the fourteenth – when its huge main tower, Tall Hermann (Pika Hermanni torn), took shape. Occupying much of the tower today is the **Narva Museum** (daily 10am–6pm; €2.30), a rambling collection of armour, cannonballs and muskets that demands to be visited for the drama of its setting – an atmospheric succession of stone-built halls and passageways. Ascending through exhibition galleries inside Tall Hermann brings you out onto an enclosed walkway just below the top of the tower, affording majestic views of Ivangorod fortress. The main focus of the riverside park is the so-called **Swedish Lion**, a modern replica of a 1936 memorial commemorating Charles XII's victory over Narva's Russian besiegers in 1701, when the Swedes audaciously used a driving snowstorm as cover for their attack. As an implicitly anti-Russian monument, the Lion, its tail dismissively turned to the east, is just about tolerated by the locals. Further south lie a handful of architectural oddities, beginning with the Lutheran **Church of St Alexander** (Aleksandrikirik; Tues–Sat 10am–6pm) between Grafovi and Kiriku, a curious rotunda built for Kreenholm cotton-mill workers in 1884 and largely gutted in 1944. Restoration is ongoing, although you can marvel at the huge hexagonal nave and visit a small museum in the first floor of the belfry. About 200m west, the roughly contemporaneous **Orthodox Cathedral of the Resurrection** (Õigeusu Ülestõusmise kirik) is an impressive barrel of red brick bursting with Byzantine domes.

Southeast of here, a footbridge crosses the railway tracks towards the southbound Joala tänav, lined with Stalin-era apartment buildings rich in Neoclassical mouldings. Further down Joala lie some impressive workers' housing projects of the pre-Soviet era, huge slabs of red brick encrusted with neo-Gothic detail, built to house workers at the **Kreenholm Mill**. The mill itself sprawls at the southern end of Joala, the three vast towers of its facade mounting a confident nineteenth-century challenge to the medieval battlements of Narva Castle and Ivangorod just downstream.

Eating, drinking and entertainment

Narva isn't exactly overflowing with decent places to **eat and drink**. One of the best bets is *Aleksander Kohvik*, Puškini 13, a cheap, restful place in which to relax over coffee and cakes or more substantial snacks; try the delicious *pelmeni*, served with sour cream. Otherwise the restaurant of the *Hotel King* is an atmospherically lit brick-lined place with a solid menu of pork chops, *shashliks* and steaks. The bar of the *Inger* hotel is on of the few decent places to drink. The Astri shopping centre, 1km out of town on Tallinna mnt, has a **cinema** and **bowling alley**.

Narva-Jõesuu

The road leading northwest out of Narva runs along the left bank of the Narva River, passing a string of German and Soviet military cemeteries – a reminder of just how fiercely the region was fought over in 1944. After 13km, the road winds up in the beachside settlement of **NARVA-JÕESUU**, a 4km-long line of holiday homes and concrete hotels sheltered by pines. One of the most glamorous watering holes in the Baltic during its pre-World War I heyday, Narva-Jõesuu now has the half-abandoned air of so many post-Soviet resorts. A central spa park, complete with swan-patrolled lake and bandstand, serves as a reminder of past glories, as does the neighbouring *Kursaal* public hall, now falling into ruin, where the cream of St Petersburg high society would congregate for concerts and balls. The sandy **beach** is as good as they come, however, and Narva-Jõesuu is a peaceful, more restful alternative to Narva.

Narva-Jõesuu is easily reached from central Narva on municipal **bus** #31 from outside the post office on Puškini (every 20–30min). Of the high-rise **hotels**, one of the most basic is the beachside *Hostel Mereranna* (☎357 2827, ⓦwww.narvahotel.ee; ❷) which has no-frills rooms; you'll get more creature comforts at the *Liivarand* at the western end of the resort (☎357 7391, ⓦwww.liivarand.ee; ❸), where you can choose between standard en-suite doubles, and plusher "business class" and "de luxe" rooms. Hidden away in the back streets near the *Liivarand*, the more intimate *Pansionaat Valentina* at Aia 19 (☎357 7468, ⓦwww.valentina.ee; ❸) offers cosy B&B.

Sillamäe

Some twenty-five kilometres west of Narva and served by hourly buses, the seaside town of **SILLAMÄE** is a living memorial to the showpiece architecture of the late Stalinist period, its elegantly proportioned apartment blocks combining neo-Egyptian pilasters and scallop-shell lunettes with hammers, sickles and facade-topping, five-pointed stars. The model town's inhabitants were almost all employed in the local uranium mine, built by prison labour in 1948. The mine fed the USSR's nuclear energy programme before being closed down by the Estonian government in 1991. The mine's environmental legacy constitutes a considerable headache for the authorities, with a waste pond just west of town bleeding radioactive material into both sea and soil – an EU-funded clean-up operation is under way. Neat-and-tidy Sillamäe itself is an enchanting urban relic and well worth a trip from Narva.

From the bus station on the edge of town, a tree-lined boulevard takes you past manicured parks to the set-piece **main square**, where a statue of a bare-torsoed miner juggles a confusion of hoops and balls – signifying, presumably, molecules orbiting the nucleus of an atom. The nearby House of Culture, a notable example of Stalinist-era architecture, flaunts the kinds of colonnades and pediments you'd expect to see on a Greco-Roman temple. From the House of Culture, a mauve-and-turquoise staircase leads down to the stately apartment buildings of Mere pst, at the far end of which you'll find a shingle seashore – the brown headland over to the west is where most of the mining took place. The renovated *Krunk* **hotel** on the square (⊕392 9030, ⊛www.krunk.ee; ❸) dates back to 1949 and has comfortable en-suites with satellite TV and a decent **restaurant** specializing in Caucasian grilled-meat cuisine.

Tartu

Set across the banks of the River Emajõgi, the tranquil, leafy city of **TARTU** is the undisputed intellectual centre of the country and home to a 370-year-old university that remains the most prestigious seat of learning in the Baltics. The academic world remains absolutely central to the character of Estonia's second-largest city: one fifth of the population of 100,000 is reckoned to be made up of students and their teachers, while many of the city centre's Neoclassical buildings date back to the university's nineteenth-century heyday.

Tartu has long been considered the home of the nation's educated elite, and ambitious Estonians still tend to choose to study here in preference to the capital. The city's tangible sense of superiority over Tallinn is bolstered by the fact that it's one of the most truly Estonian urban centres in the country – it was spared mass immigration from other parts of the Soviet Union and less than a quarter of today's population count Russian as their first language. While it may be flushed with self-importance, Tartu has an engaging small-town feel – and as a student capital it's naturally also overflowing with cafés suitable for discussing the meaning of life, raucous drinking venues and vibrant nightclubs that stay open till the sun comes up. A couple of days are enough to take in Tartu's sights, although the relaxed atmosphere of its parks and pubs will tempt you to stay longer. It's certainly an excellent base from which to explore the south of the country, with Lake Peipsi, Võrumaa, Setumaa and even Viljandi (see p.112) within easy day-trip range.

Some history

An Estonian hilltop stronghold conquered by the Livonian Order in the thirteenth century, then fought over by Russians, Poles and Swedes in the sixteenth – the history of Tartu (or Dorpat as it was known until 1918) would be much the same as that of any other Estonian provincial city were it not for the decision of the Swedish king, Gustav Adolphus, to found a **university** here in 1632. With government jobs in Swedish Livonia open only to those who had a degree from Tartu, it soon became the only academic institution in the region worth attending. The early history of the university was somewhat chequered, largely owing to Tartu's proximity to a zone of almost constant Swedish–Russian warfare: it was evacuated to Tallinn in 1656, didn't function at all between 1665 and 1690, and spent ten years in Pärnu after 1699.

When Peter the Great captured Tartu in 1708, he deported its leading citizens and had the city walls demolished. The townsfolk were allowed back in 1714, but the university had to wait until 1802 before it could resume its activities. Energized by the prospect of having a prestigious seat of learning in their own backyard, the Baltic nobility poured money into the university's reconstruction. The resulting rash of assembly halls, libraries and lecture theatres lent Tartu a distinguished, neoclassical appearance that still prevails today.

Despite being an almost wholly German-speaking institution, the university became an important centre for research into Estonian culture. The Gelehrte Estnische Gesellschaft (Estonian Learned Society), founded by Tartu professors in 1837, was one of the first organizations to treat the local language as a serious object of study. Those Estonians lucky enough to be admitted to the university still had to Germanize their names in order to be socially accepted, but as the nineteenth century progressed Tartu nevertheless established itself as a major centre of Estonian learning. Cultural activist Johann Voldemar Jannsen chose Tartu as the place to publish *Eesti Postimees* ("Estonian Courier"), the nation's first genuinely influential newspaper, in 1863, founded the Vanemuine cultural society here in 1868 (an institution that is still going strong), and organized the first-ever All-Estonian Song Festival a year later.

This upsurge in Estonian consciousness coincided with a period of creeping **Russification** throughout the empire. Russian became the sole language of instruction at Tartu University in 1889, and the town itself was renamed Yuryev four years later. In other respects the university remained a progressive institution by Tsarist standards: women were allowed to follow courses (but not sit exams) from 1905 and were admitted as full students in 1915. Jews were not discriminated against as they were elsewhere – on the eve of World War I they made up 23 percent of the student body.

After **World War I** the university was largely cleansed of Russian and German influences, and the city strengthened its position as Estonia's intellectual capital. Tartu was at the centre of opposition to Soviet rule after June 1940, with medical students turning the university's Health Care Society into a front for subversive activities. On July 10, 1941, the society's members led a citywide revolt against the Soviets, aiming to establish an independent Estonian administration prior to the arrival of the Germans. The latter were unimpressed, closing the university down and planning its rebirth as an elite academy serving the Nazi province of Estland.

After 1945, a revitalized university preserved its pre-eminence in Estonian academic life, but found it difficult to retain international contacts – the presence of a Soviet bomber squadron at Tartu airport rendered the city virtually off-limits to foreigners. Since the regaining of independence, however, the university has lost no time in rejoining the international academic mainstream. Estonia's entry into the EU has encouraged an influx of foreign students and lecturers, turning Tartu University into one of the most cosmopolitan seats of learning on the continent.

Arrival, information and getting around

Tartu's **bus station** is ten minutes' walk east of the centre at Turu 2. The **tourist office** in the town hall at Raekoja plats 14 (Mon 9am–6pm, Tues–Fri 9am–5pm, Sat & Sun 10am–2pm; ☎744 2111; ⓦwww.visittartu.com) is an efficient source of information on just about everything in Tartu and the region, and also offers free **internet** access. With almost everything of sightseeing interest within walking distance of the centre, you're unlikely to need Tartu's municipal **bus** network unless you're staying in the suburbs. Flat-fare tickets (€0.80 from kiosks, €1 from the driver) must be inserted into the ticket-punch machines on board. **Taxi** ranks can be found at the bus station and at the junction of Raekoja plats and Turu; otherwise call Tartu Taksopark (☎730 0200) or Linna Takso (☎736 6366).

Accommodation

There's lots of good-quality accommodation in the centre, although most of it is geared towards foreign businesspeople, and prices are creeping up. You will find a few mid-range choices in the centre, and a scattering of cheaper **hotels** and family-run **guesthouses** in the suburbs, although you should reserve in advance if you're looking for a bargain.

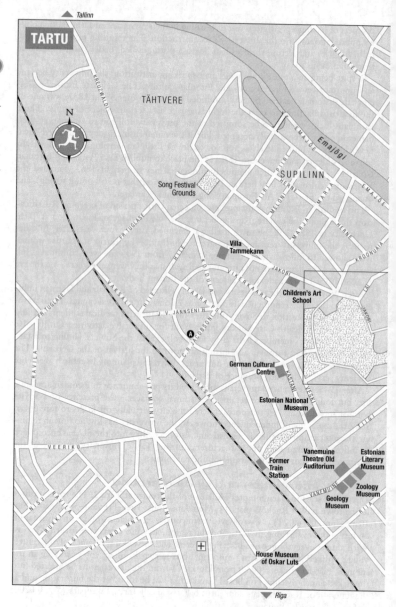

A number of private households in the suburbs offer **B&B** accommodation in the €25–35 range, although few of the hosts speak English: the tourist office will be able to book them for you. To rent short-stay **apartments** on and around the main square, try Carolina (℡742 2070, ⓦwww.carolina.ee), or Domus Dorpatensis (℡5333 3031, ⓦwww.dorpatensis.ee).

Unless otherwise stated, the following hotels and guesthouses are on the "Central Tartu" map on p.131.

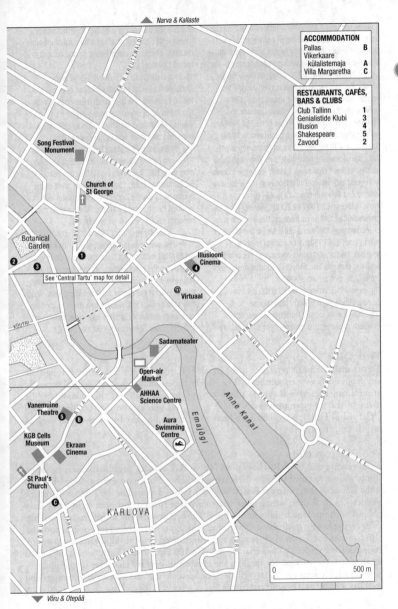

Map labels:

- Narva & Kallaste

ACCOMMODATION

Pallas	B
Vikerkaare külalistemaja	A
Villa Margaretha	C

RESTAURANTS, CAFÉS, BARS & CLUBS

Club Tallinn	1
Genialistide Klubi	3
Illusion	4
Shakespeare	5
Zavood	2

Map labels:
- FR RAEUTZWALD
- Song Festival Monument
- PUIESTEE
- Church of St George
- NARVA MNT
- PIKK
- KIVI
- Botanical Garden
- Illusiooni Cinema
- RAATUSE
- UUS
- See 'Central Tartu' map for detail
- @ Virtuaal
- KÜÜTRI
- PARNA
- ANNE
- LIIS
- PAJU
- SOPUSE PS
- Sadamateater
- Open-air Market
- TURU
- RIIA
- AHHAA Science Centre
- Aura Swimming Centre
- Emajõgi
- Anne Kanal
- PIKK
- Vanemuine Theatre
- KALEV
- KGB Cells Museum
- Ekraan Cinema
- KALDA TEE
- St Paul's Church
- VÕRU
- TÄHE
- KALEV
- KARLOVA
- TOLSTOI
- TURU
- 0   500 m

- Võru & Otepää

1.3 | ESTONIA | Eastern Estonia

129

Antonius Ülikooli 15 ☏ 737 0377, ⓦ www
.hotelantonius.ee. Classy, intimate choice in a
nineteenth-century building right opposite the
university, offering rooms with retro furniture, rich
fabrics and all the creature comforts. ⑥

Barclay Ülikooli 8 ☏ 744 7100, ⓦ www.barclay
.ee. It's hard to imagine that this handsome Art

Nouveau building once served as the regional HQ of
the Soviet army. The *Barclay* now has high-quality
en-suites and is well worth the money if you get an
east-facing room overlooking a leafy square. Suites
with private sauna cost more. ⑥–⑦

London Rüütli 9 ☏ 730 5555, ⓦ www
.londonhotel.ee. The only hotel in Tartu with

a water feature in the lobby offers compact, snazzy en-suites with TV, decorated in contemporary style. Deluxe doubles are slightly bigger and have bathtubs, while suites come with private sauna. ⑥–⑦

Pallas Riia 4 ☎730 1200, ⓦwww.pallas .ee; see Tartu map on p.128. Despite an unpromising location on the upper storeys of a grey block, the three-star *Pallas* maintains the heritage of the influential Pallas School of Fine Arts, which stood here until being destroyed in 1944. Decorated with reproductions of Pallas-era paintings, the rooms are refreshingly modern and those on the northern side have floor-to-ceiling windows with great city views. Breakfast is in the enjoyably kitschy *Big Ben* pub downstairs ⑤–⑥

Park Vallikraavi 23 ☎742 7000, ⓦwww .parkhotell.ee. Set amid trees on the western side of Toomemägi, this white-cube Modernist building dating from the 1930s is beginning to show its age, but the parquet floors and pastel decor are soothing enough. The simply decorated en-suites are slightly overpriced. ③–④

Tampere Maja Jaani 4 ☎738 6300, ⓦwww .tamperemaja.ee. A historic town house refurbished with money from the Finnish city of Tampere to serve as a cultural centre, art gallery

and guesthouse. Along with two four-bed family rooms with kitchens, there is a handful of en-suite doubles, all with wooden floors, muted colours and tasteful fabrics. ④

Tartu Hotell Soola 3 ☎731 4300, ⓦwww .tartuhotell.ee. Conveniently located opposite the bus station, this is a good-value choice, with functional, neat en-suites plus simpler triples and quads with shared facilities. Friendly staff and a fair-sized breakfast add to the appeal. ④

Vikerkaare külalistemaja Vikerkaare 40 ☎742 1190, ⓦwww.hot.ee/tdc; see Tartu map on p.128. A welcoming B&B in the peaceful Tähtvere suburb, 15–20min' walk west of the centre, with exceedingly comfy rooms, all with wooden furniture, shower and TV. Breakfast costs an extra €5. ③, with private sauna ④

Villa Margaretha Tähe 11/13 ☎731 1820, ⓦwww.margaretha.ee; see Tartu map on p.128. This restored Art Nouveau villa a short walk uphill from the centre offers plush rooms with Art Nouveau-style decoration. A handful of fancy apartments include the roomy top-floor Maria suite which has attic ceilings and access to a tower. A modern annexe at the back contains split-level suites with fold-out sofas. Suites from €60, doubles ④.

The City

Tartu's main point of reference is the Emajõgi River, which winds lazily through the city from northwest to southeast. The largely pedestrianized historic centre, arranged around the attractive **Raekoja plats**, lies on the west bank of the Emajõgi, while many of the set-piece **university** buildings are just uphill from here on **Toomemägi** ("Cathedral Hill"), a wonderfully leafy area that is bordered by atmospheric nineteenth-century suburbs.

The Raekoja plats

Tartu's focal point is the **Raekoja plats** (Town Hall Square), paved with lumpy cobblestones and surrounded by prim Neoclassical buildings, the most eye-catching of which is the lilac-and-orange **Town Hall** (Raekoda). It was designed in the 1780s by Rostock builder J.H.B. Walter, whose brief was to give the town a European flavour; he duly obliged with this Dutch-influenced edifice. The bell tower emits a shrill, music-box-like ditty on the hour – until about 10pm, after which it reverts to discreet bonging sounds.

In front of the Town Hall stands a fountain topped by a 3m-high statue of a young couple kissing under an umbrella. Unveiled in 1998 to provide Tartu with a millennial marker, it was criticized for spoiling the eighteenth-century character of the square – pictures of the statue have nevertheless found their way onto most of the mugs and T-shirts sold by nearby souvenir shops.

The Leaning House and the Tartu Art Museum

At the eastern end of the square, the house at no. 18 leans crookedly owing to a shifting of the water table. It was originally the *pied-à-terre* of **Mikhail Barclay de Tolly** (1761–1818), a Livonian baron of Scottish descent and one of Tsar Alexander I's top generals during the Napoleonic Wars. Roundly criticized by St Petersburg society for his strategy of retreating before Napoleon's advance in 1812, de Tolly was vindicated when the French ran out of steam, fleeing homewards with the onset of winter. The

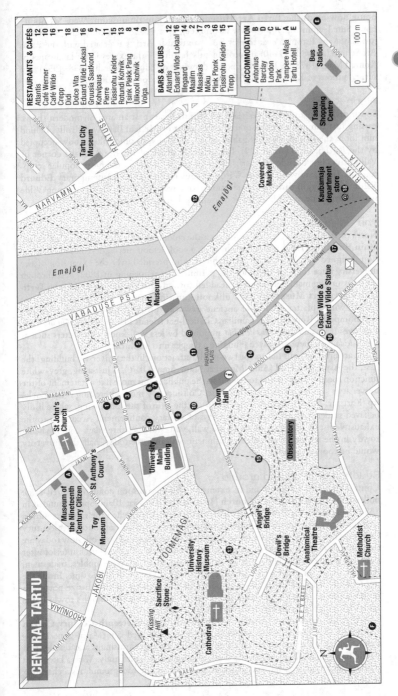

CENTRAL TARTU

RESTAURANTS & CAFÉS
Atlantis	12
Café Werner	10
Café Wilde	16
Crepp	1
Didi	18
Dolce Vita	5
Eduard Vilde Lokaal	16
Gruusia Saatkond	6
Kohvipaus	7
Pierre	11
Püssirohu Keider	15
Rotundi Kohvik	13
Tsink Plekk Pang	8
Ülikooli kohvik	4
Volga	9

BARS & CLUBS
Atlantis	12
Eduard Vilde Lokaal	16
Illegaard	14
Maailm	2
Maasikas	17
Möku	3
Plink Plonk	16
Püssirohu Keider	15
Trepp	1

ACCOMMODATION
Antonius	B
Barclay	D
London	C
Park	F
Tampere Maja	A
Tartu Hotell	E

house now holds the **Tartu Art Museum** (Tartu kunstimuuseum; Wed–Sat noon–6pm, Sun 1–6pm; €2.30; ⊛www.tartmus.ee), a vast collection embracing works by just about any Estonian ever to pick up a paintbrush. Artists associated with the Pallas Art School (active 1919–40) are prominently featured – the expressionist landscapes of Konrad Mägi (1878–1925), dense pencil drawings of Eduard Wiiralt (1898–1954), and surreal visions of Karin Luts (1904–93) are well worth looking out for.

Along Küüni

South of Raekoja plats, pedestrianized **Küüni** heads past an area of modern shops, passing first through a garden graced with a bust of Mikhail Barclay de Tolly. Behind him loom the Gothic-looking gables of an Art Nouveau office block, now occupied by the *Barclay* hotel (see p.129). Immediately south of the hotel on the corner of Vallikraavi (just outside the *Café Wilde*; see p.136) is one of the most popular sculptures in Tartu, showing **Oscar Wilde** and his Estonian near-contemporary **Eduard Vilde** (see p.79) in earnest conversation – one wonders what the shy retiring Vilde would have made of the high priest of camp had they ever met in real life.

The University Building

North of Raekoja plats, Ülikooli runs past the colonnaded facade of **Tartu University Main Building** (Tartu ülikooli peahoone), a cool, lemon meringue-coloured confection designed by J.W. Krause, the architect who presided over the expansion of the university once the Tsarist authorities permitted its reopening in 1802. Pass through the unassuming main doorway and head left towards the south wing to find the **Tartu University Art Museum** (Tartu ülikooli kunstimuuseum; Mon–Fri 11am–5pm; €1.30), where plaster replicas of ancient artworks throng a suite of galleries decked out in imperial Roman style. Familiar Classical-era friends like the *Discus Thrower*, the *Belvedere Apollo* and the *Venus de Milo* are joined by less well-known characters such as the *Suicidal Celt*, here portrayed plunging a dagger into his throat.

The art museum sells tickets for two public attractions in the university building: the first, the **Assembly Hall** (Aula; Mon–Fri 11am–5pm; €0.70), is just a big, grey-white function room – the decision to open it to the public seems more like a statement of the university's self-regard than anything else. Considerably more interesting is the **Lock-up** (Kartser; Mon–Fri 11am–5pm; €0.70), in the attic of the south wing, where badly behaved students had to endure a few days of solitary confinement. According to the exhaustive list of offences pinned to the wall, you could get three days here for being rowdy in the streets – were such punishments still in force today, half the university would be cooped up here.

St John's Church and around

Continuing along **Ülikooli** and its extension, **Jaani**, you soon come to the red-brick bulk of the Gothic **St John's Church** (Jaani kirik; Tues–Sat 10am–6pm), founded in 1330, bombed out in 1944 and left half-ruined until 1989, when the restorers moved in and added a new spire. The building is famous for the gallery of fourteenth-century terracotta heads arranged in niches around the main entrance. Those on show today are recently installed replicas – the originals will be displayed in the church interior after a spell at the restorers. They portray mostly medieval archetypes – nobles, tradesmen, peasants and so on – and were no doubt modelled on Tartu folk of the time. Inside the impressively bare red-brick nave are more terracotta figures, with full-size portrayals of saints perched in niches beneath the ceiling. You can scale the church's **tower** (same times; €1.30) for a bird's-eye view of the city centre.

Diagonally opposite the church, the **Museum of the Nineteenth-Century Citizen** at Jaani 16 (19 sajandi Tartu linnakodaniku muuseum; Wed–Sun; April–Sept 11am–6pm; Oct–March 10am–3pm; €0.70) features the kind of furnishings and textiles that would have graced the dwelling of a middle-ranking merchant family. With a kitchen lit by candlelight and a grandfather clock ticking away in the background, it's a charming period piece.

Tartu Toy Museum

Occupying a beautifully restored one-storey house just west of St John's Church at Lutsu 8, the **Tartu Toy Museum** (Mänguasjamuuseum; Wed–Sun 11am–6pm; €2; ⓦ www.mm.ee) is a compelling jumble of playthings through the ages, including dolls from around the world, board games, train sets, model spaceships and tin soldiers. A sizeable section is devoted to the Nukufilm animation studio founded in Tallinn by puppet film pioneer Elbert Tuganov in 1957. Many of the stars of Tuganov's films are on display, together with the puppets and film sets used by contemporary Estonian film-makers.

The Botanical Garden

Marking the northern boundary of Tartu's Old Town, the **Botanical Garden** at Lai 38 (Botanikaaed; daily: May–Sept 7am–9pm; Oct–April 7am–7pm; free) is one of the city's most popular outdoor spaces. Tropical and subtropical plants are packed into the central Palm House (Palmimaja; daily 10am–5pm; €1.70), behind which lies a small, but enormously varied, display of outdoor plants, occupying what's left of a defensive earthwork built to protect the northeastern corner of the (now disappeared) town wall. The most striking of the sculptures littering the garden is an imperious-looking Lithuanian fertility spirit carved from a tree trunk, presented to Tartu by Vilnius University in 1982.

Towards Toomemägi

From behind Tartu's Town Hall, Lossi tänav climbs **Toomemägi** ("Cathedral Hill"), site of a fortress and a cathedral during the Middle Ages, subsequently abandoned after damage in the Livonian Wars. The area was derelict until the refounding of the university in 1802, when it was chosen as the site of several key academic buildings and generously planted with the trees that make it such a relaxing spot today.

Presiding over the bottom end of Lossi is a bust of Russian medical hero **Nikolai Pirogov**, who taught at Tartu in the 1840s and went on to become a pioneer in modern surgical technique. A Florence Nightingale with whiskers, Pirogov introduced new standards of cleanliness and organization to Tsarist military hospitals during the Crimean War, and hordes of high-born Russian ladies thronged to Sevastopol to join his nursing staff. The steeply banked park behind the bust is a favourite place for lounging in summer – especially with students who, armed with take-out beers, turn the area into a vast outdoor bar.

From here, Lossi heads uphill beneath **Angel's Bridge** (Inglisild), a brightly painted wooden structure dating from the nineteenth century; carry on over the brow of the hill and you'll pass under its counterpart on the other side, the **Devil's Bridge**.

The Cathedral and the University History Museum

Dominating the summit of Toomemägi are the stark, skeletal remains of Tartu's red-brick **Cathedral** (Toomkirik; June–Aug daily 11am–7pm; May & Sept daily 11am–5pm; April Wed–Sun 11am–5pm; Oct & Nov Sat & Sun 11am–5pm), built by the Knights of the Sword during the thirteenth century. Although Tartu became a thoroughly Protestant city in the 1520s, the Poles returned the cathedral to the Catholic fold when they took control of Tartu in 1582, and the building's destruction by fire in 1624 – the result of sparks flying from a Midsummer Night's bonfire – was seen by many contemporaries as a sign of divine displeasure. It was J.W. Krause, the architect in charge of the redevelopment of Toomemägi at the beginning of the nineteenth century, who hit on the idea of leaving the bulk of the cathedral as a romantic ruin, while rebuilding the choir to serve as the university library – the charmingly lopsided results of which can be seen today.

Since 1979, the library has served as the **University History Museum** (Wed–Sun 11am–5pm; €1.70), a three-floor collection beginning (at the top) with portraits of the university's first rectors and a diorama of a seventeenth-century anatomical theatre, in which intestines hang from the table like a string of butcher's sausages. On the floor below, a stuffy display of professors through the ages is enlivened by the recreated physics lab of Rector Georg Friedrich Parrot (1765–1852), where a host of beauti-fully crafted instruments includes an electrostatic generator constructed from Karelian birchwood and turquoise glass tubes. On the same floor, one hall is preserved as it was in the nineteenth century, with rows of musty books and an unlabelled dummy of what looks suspiciously like the library's founder, Professor J.K.S. Morgenstern, who also established the University Art Museum (see p.132). Nearby are the sabres and flags brandished by nineteenth-century student fraternities – predominantly German-speaking affairs until 1870, when the first Estonian student association emerged. All the fraternities had tricolour banners, and in 1884 the Estonians chose a blue, black and white colour scheme (by this time it was the only combination left), subsequently adopted as Estonia's national flag.

The Sacrifice Stone and Kissing Hill

Toomemägi's main landmark north of the museum is a monument to one of Tartu University's most famous alumni, **Karl Ernst von Baer** (1792–1876), whose pioneering work in the field of embryology was credited by Charles Darwin as being a major step towards the development of evolutionary theory. West from here, it's easy to miss the so-called **Sacrifice Stone** (Ohvrikivi), an unobtrusive lump of rock where pre-Christian Estonians would place offerings to the departed – and where present-day students come to burn their exam papers. Behind it rises a knoll known as **Musumägi**, or "Kissing Hill", possibly because the path leading up it is barely wide enough to allow two people to walk side by side without rubbing up against each other.

The Anatomical Theatre and the University Observatory

At the southern end of Toomemägi stands the impressive, barrel-shaped **Anatomical Theatre**, designed by J.W. Krause in 1803. In many ways the university's trademark – medicine has always been one of the most prestigious subjects taught here – the building was in use as an anatomical theatre right up until 1999. It now houses the Medical Faculty Collections (Tues–Sat 11am–5pm; €1.30), a small but compelling col-lection of medical specimens in antiquated bottles, human skulls, and primitive surgical instruments. Pondering the parkscape just in front of the theatre is a bust of **Friedrich Robert Faehlmann** (1798–1850), the Germanized Estonian who played a leading role in the founding of the Estonian Learned Society (see p.127), and whose enthusiasm for collecting old folk tales inspired F.R. Kreuzwald (see p.142) to compile Estonia's epic, *Kalevipoeg*. A short distance south, a building that looks like a decapitated windmill turns out to be the **University Observatory**, also designed by the ubiquitous Krause. Best known among the astronomers who came to ogle celestial bodies here was F.W. Struve (1793–1864), one of the first scientists to accurately measure the distances of various stars from the earth – he's celebrated by an angular concrete monument out front.

The Estonian National Museum

Founded in 1905 by local Estonian patriots, the **Estonian National Museum** (Eesti rahva muuseum; Wed–Sun 11am–6pm; €3.50; Ⓦwww.erm.ee) west of Toomemägi at Kuperjanovi 9 is another Tartu-based national institution that has resisted the temptation to move to Tallinn. It contains an exemplary overview of the nation's ethnography, with a stunning array of regional handicrafts and good English labelling. Rakes the size of small trees serve as a reminder of how haymaking and preparation of winter fodder was a matter of life and death to the average Estonian farmstead, while a sizeable collection of carved wooden beer tankards introduces a section on village feasts and holidays. The hand-woven textiles on display look far more exotic than the bland linen tablecloths sold in the Estonian souvenir shops of today: look out for embroidered skirts from the Halliste region, featuring archaic star- and sun-shapes in bright greens and blues. A section on domestic interiors features a recreated living room from 1978 filled with the dull-brown furniture that was standard issue in the Soviet Union. Pencilled in for 2014, the museum will be moving to a new building at **Raadi**, a former airfield some 4km northeast of the city centre.

The KGB Cells Museum

The **KGB Cells Museum**, Riia 15B (KGB kongid; Wed–Sat 11am–4pm; €1.30) is in the so-called "Grey House" (Hallis majas), former regional headquarters of the Soviet secret police. As well as preserving the basement cells in their original state, the museum offers a history lesson in Soviet methods of control. Any lack of English-language labelling is more than made up for by the narrative power of the grainy photographs on display, recalling the deportations of 1941 and 1949, as well as the gruelling conditions of life in Siberia experienced by the victims. Most poignant of all are the pictures of idealistic schoolchildren who joined secret patriotic organizations like the Tartu-based Blue-Black-and-White (named after the colours of the Estonian flag), only to be confined in the cells here before being sent to work camps in the east.

St Paul's Church and the Oskar Luts Museum

Just southwest, the red-brick **St Paul's Church** (Paulusekirik) on Riia is a highly individual piece of Estonian interwar architecture, its central tower resembling a bloated Egyptian obelisk thrust skywards by rocket boosters. Continuing along Riia for another five minutes brings you to the **House Museum of Oskar Luts**, Riia 38 (Oskar Lutsu majamuuseum; Wed–Sat 11am–5pm, Sun 1–5pm; €0.60), celebrating the Tartu-trained pharmacist and author (1887–1953), best known for the semi-autobiographical *Kevade* ("Spring"), a classic account of growing up in the Estonian countryside. The house where he lived from 1918 until his death is packed with interwar furnishings, old photographs of Tartu and the hideous-looking puppets used in animated films based on Luts's children's story "Forest Fairytale". Luts was one of the pillars of the interwar literary establishment, and a 1937 newsreel shows the great and the good flocking to his fiftieth birthday party.

Returning back to town along Riia, it's worth making a southward detour along streets like Tähe or Kalevi into the suburb of **Karlova**, famous for its handsome array of nineteenth-century wooden houses. Some of the best are to be found 750m southeast of Riia along Tolstoi.

Tähtvere, the Song Festival Grounds and Soup Town

There's enough interesting architecture in the northwestern suburbs of Tartu to justify a brief stroll up **Jakobi**, the street that connects the city centre with a plateau of residential streets above. The **Children's Art School** at Jakobi is a wonderful example of a pre-World War I timber mansion, with a fanciful, medieval-style central tower, and lovingly carved door and window frames. Jakobi's extension, Kreuzwaldi, enters **Tähtvere**, an elite suburb built for university professors in the 1920s and packed with the kind of Bauhaus-influenced houses that were all the rage with the interwar Estonian middle class. The best known of these is the white-cube **Villa Tammekann** at Kreuzwaldi 6, designed by Alvar Aalto in 1932 and now occupied by a university research institute. From here it's only a ten-minute walk to the **Song Festival Grounds** (Laululava), on the very edge of Tartu, where a stage capable of accommodating ten thousand singers shelters under a sea-shell canopy. Built in 1994 to symbolize Tartu's place in Estonian choral culture (the first national song festival was held here), it's nowadays the venue for pop concerts, musicals and folk-singing performances. From here, you can either dally in the adjacent amusement park, or return to the centre via the streets of **Supilinn** immediately to the east, a ramshackle residential area of old wooden houses and vegetable plots. Thoroughfare names such as Oa ("Bean Street"), Kartuli ("Potato Street") and Herne ("Pea Street") help explain how the suburb got its name – "Soup Town".

The Stone Bridge and Tartu City Museum

At the eastern end of Raekoja plats, pedestrian traffic bustles across the River Emajõgi on a small bridge built in modest commemoration of the earlier Stone Bridge, an elegant eighteenth-century structure and a symbol of the city until the retreating Red Army destroyed it in 1941. A five-minute walk through parkland on the opposite bank takes you to the **Tartu City Museum** at Narva mnt 23 (Tartu linnamuuseum; Tues–Sun 11am–6pm; €1.70), an easy-on-the-eye display of furniture, prints and porcelain in a lusciously restored eighteenth-century mansion. Highlights include a round table of truly Arthurian proportions, around which the Estonian–Soviet Peace Treaty was signed on February 2, 1920, and a fascinating model of Tartu as it was in 1940 – free of the Soviet-era tower blocks that now clutter the suburbs.

The open-air market and AHHAA Science Centre

Taking the riverside path east from Raekoja plats takes you along an attractive stretch of the Emajõgi, reaching the **Sadamateater** cultural centre after about fifteen minutes. Behind the theatre is Tartu's main outdoor **market**, home to fresh fruit and veg stores as well as cheap clothes and household goods. Immediately south are two of Tartu's most distinctive contemporary buildings, the spiral-form apartment block known as the **Snail Tower**, and the domed **AHHAA Science Centre** (daily 10am–7pm; €3.50, family ticket €8.50; ⓦwww.ahhaa.ee), geared towards kids with its numerous interactive exhibits on changing themes and a "4D" cinema.

Eating and drinking

Tartu has Estonia's widest range of **cafés and restaurants** outside Tallinn, with plenty of ethnic and vegetarian options alongside the more standard north European favourites. As you would expect from a university town, there are plenty of **pubs and bars**, many of which offer a full food menu.

Unless otherwise stated, the following places are shown on the Central Tartu map on p.131.

Cafés

Café Werner Ülikooli 11. Dating back to 1895, this was a hangout for quarrelsome intellectuals during the Soviet period. A recent modernization, however, has brought it firmly into the twenty-first century; and it still has superior coffee and sweets, with fruity cheesecakes and Napoleon millefeuilles. The upstairs section has frilly-apron table service, a full menu of substantial salads, and main meals. Outdoor courtyard seating in summer. Mon–Thurs 7.30am–11pm, Fri & Sat 8am–1am, Sun 9am–9pm.

Café Wilde Vallikraavi 4. Housed in a former print works – some old presses are on display – this relaxing café features big red chairs that look like thrones, and serves up good coffee and toothsome cakes. Mon–Fri 9am–7pm, Sat 10am–6pm.

Crepp Rüütli 16. Chunky wooden tables and candlelight provide a fitting setting for a French-inspired menu of filling, sweet and savoury crepes, as well as quiches, baguettes and large salads. Daily 11am–midnight.

Didi Riia 1. Welcoming haven for ailing shoppers on the second floor of the Kaubamaja Shopping Centre, with big floor-to-ceiling windows providing good views of neighbouring parks. Hot buffet with salad bar in one half; a café serving quiche and cakes in the other. Mon–Sat 9am–9pm, Sun 10am–7pm.

Kohvipaus Rüütli 8. Counter café with a good choice of sit-down or take-away sandwiches,

wraps and salads. Also breakfast cereals, traditional Estonian drinks like *kama* (sour milk with healthy grains), and coffee. Mon–Fri 7am–7pm, Sat 10am–6pm.

Pierre Chocolaterie Raekoja 12. Sister operation to the café in Tallinn (see p.82), *Pierre* has a distinct 1930s air, with extravagant silk tablecloths and elegant table lamps. Simply delicious range of handmade chocolate truffles. Mon–Thurs 8am–11pm, Fri 8am–1am, Sat 10am–1am, Sun 10am–11pm.

Rotundi Kohvik Toomemägi. A summer-only café in a cosy, octagonal pavilion, with outdoor seating beneath the trees of Toomemägi. A small menu of Estonian staples makes it a good spot for an inexpensive lunch. Daily 10am–6pm.

Shakespeare Vanemuise 6; see Tartu map on p.128. A roomy establishment inside the Vanemuine theatre and concert hall offering drinks, reasonably priced salads and meat-and-potatoes main courses. There's often live music in the evenings. Sun–Thurs 11am–11pm, Fri & Sat 11am–1am.

Ülikooli Kohvik Ülikooli 20. In a suite of lovingly restored rooms in a historic house, next door to the main university building, this relaxing café has near-antique furnishings, an outdoor terrace, and tempting cakes and truffles. The ground-floor buffet (till 7pm) is arguably the best of the order-at-the-counter options in town, with a good choice of salads and mains. Mon–Thurs 11am–11pm, Fri & Sat 11am–1am, Sun 11am–9pm.

Restaurants

Atlantis Narva mnt 2. Civilized but not over-expensive dining in a curved, glass-fronted building overlooking the river. You'll get the same pork, chicken and beef as elsewhere, but with more stylish service and presentation. Sun–Thurs noon–midnight, Fri & Sat noon–1am.

Dolce Vita Kompanii 10. This chilled-out Italian, its whitewashed walls decorated with Federico Fellini movie posters, dishes up good thin-crust pizzas, soups and salads. Mon–Thurs 11.30am–11pm, Fri & Sat 11.30am–midnight, Sun noon–11pm.

Eduard Vilde Lokaal Vallikraavi 4. Pub-restaurant with meaty main courses featuring steak, lamb and moose in the €10–14 range, alongside cheaper pastas and risottos. The main bar has the feel of a traditional pub cluttered with bric-a-brac, while adjoining areas have a more formal dining-room feel. Mon–Thurs noon–midnight, Fri & Sat till 2am, Sun till 11pm.

Gruusia Saatkond Rüütli 8. In a minimally decorated apartment, the "Georgian Embassy" has long been popular with fans of Caucasian cuisine. Appetizing dishes include beef in walnut sauce, lamb shish kebabs and beef and aubergine stew. The freshly baked *hachapuri* (bread with cheese and egg filling) is delicious, and there is a good range of reasonably priced lunch options.

Tsink Plekk Pang Küütri 6. This popular local haunt – whose name, somewhat bizarrely, is Estonian for "zinc-plated bucket" – serves up tasty Chinese- and Indian-influenced food in relaxed, loungey surroundings. A good venue for an evening drink, with DJs at the weekends. Sun–Wed noon–11pm, Thurs–Sat till midnight..

Volga Küütri 1 ☎730 5444. Classy restaurant with a Russian theme, although the menu runs through fairly traditional north European culinary territory. Mains range from pork hock (€9) to Chateaubriand steak (€16), with salmon, lamb and duck dishes too. Daily noon–midnight.

Bars and pubs

Genialistide klubi Corner of Lai and Magasini (entrance via the alleyway that leads behind Lai 37) ⓦ www.genklubi.ee; see Tartu map on p.128. Near-legendary alternative-culture institution, occupying a rambling building with a bar downstairs and a performance room for gigs, DJs, theatre and art events. There's a choice of good cheap food during the day, with vegetarian choices well represented. Mon–Sat noon–4am.

Illegaard Ülikooli 5. Occupying an atmospheric barrel-vaulted basement, *Illegaard* manages to combine being a jazzy-flavoured bar, big-screen football pub, and weekend student drinking den all rolled into one. Mon–Fri 11am–3am, Sat & Sun 2pm–3am.

Maailm Rüütli 12. A bar-restaurant with an eccentric twist – you can sit on an indoor swing and read the newspaper and magazine clippings that decorate the walls – and a wide range of international dishes. Daily 6pm–3am.

Möku Rüütli 18. Convivial basement bar not much bigger than a cupboard, which still succeeds in doling out a wide range of beers and spirits to a regular stream of customers, accompanied by an indie-rock and underground-dance playlist. The pavement outside is always packed. Daily 6pm–3am.

Püssirohu Kelder Lossi 28. In a cavernous, red-brick armoury built under Peter the Great, *Püssirohu Kelder* is a suitably atmospheric place in which to swig beer at big wooden tables and tuck into platefuls of pork and sauerkraut. Occasional live music, when there may be a cover charge. Mon–Thurs noon–2am, Fri & Sat noon–3am, Sun noon–midnight.

Trepp Rüütli 16. Upstairs from *Crepp* (see opposite) this typically Tartu-esque slice of student bohemia features bare wooden floors, matt black furnishings, paintings that look like the work of an art-hooligan, and sculptures of giant weeds. Mon–Sat 5pm–2am.

Zavood Lai 30; see Tartu map on p.128. Legendary student hangout near the Botanical Garden with post-industrial decor, late hours, table football and eccentric indie sounds. An inexpensive menu of filling Estonian meals is chalked up on the blackboard opposite the bar. Mon–Fri 11am–4am, Sat & Sun 7pm–4am.

Nightlife and entertainment

Tartu's main **theatre** and **concert** venue, the Vanemuine, Vanemuise 6 (box office Mon–Sat 10am–7pm; ☎744 0165, ⓦ www.vanemuine.ee), is one of the most prestigious in the country, presenting top-quality drama, classical music, opera and dance performed by top acts from Tallinn or abroad – either in the comfortable modern main building, or in the smaller but equally stylish nineteenth-century auditorium just uphill at Vanemuise 45A. A range of broadly contemporary theatre and dance performances also take takes place in the modern auditorium of the riverside Sadamateater, Soola 5B (box office Mon–Sat noon–5pm & 1hr before performance; ☎734 4248,

The University Spring Days and other annual events

The best-known and probably most enjoyable of Tartu's annual events is the **Student Spring Days** (Ülikooli kevadpaevad; ⓦ www.studentdays.ee), a five-day fiesta straddling May 1, when the town is transformed into a vast open-air student party. Highlights include a fund-raising rubber-boat regatta on the Emajõgi River, and the night of May 1 itself, when the town's pubs are allowed (nay, expected) to stay open all night. The Student Autumn Days (Sügispaevad) involve similar high-jinks in mid-October.

Tartu's other major festival is the feast of medieval-themed dressing-up that is the **Hansa Days** (ⓦ www.hansapaevad.ee) in mid-June, when tournaments take place in city squares and handicraft sellers set up stalls throughout the centre.

Other festivals include the **tARTuFF Film Festival** (ⓦ www.tartuff.ee) in August when art films with a love-story narrative are screened in the open on Raekoja plats; and the **Draama Theatre Festival** (ⓦ www.festival.ee) in early September, showcasing the best new work by Estonia's leading theatre companies in a variety of venues around town.

A broad range of classical and jazz concerts take place in summer; the tourist office (see p.127) has further information and sells tickets to most events.

ⓦ www.vanemuine.ee/sadamateater). Big operatic and musical productions are staged at the Song Festival Grounds in summer; check posters around town or ⓦ www .visittartu.com. The Toy Museum's **Teatri Kodu** (Theatre House), Lutsu 8 (☎ 746 1061; ⓦ www.teatrikodu.ee) stages kids' performances.

Cinamon in the Tasku Shopping Centre (☎ 630 4113, ⓦ www.cinamon.ee) is the city's prime multi-screen **cinema**; the two-screen Ekraan, Riia 14 (ⓦ www.superkinod.ee), is the only other central option.

Clubs

In addition to the **clubs** reviewed below, check the club nights and DJ evenings at *Genialistide klubi*, *Tsink Plekk Pang*, and the Sadamateater (all on p.137). Unless otherwise stated the following places are shown on the "Central Tartu" map on p.131.

Atlantis Narva mnt 2 ⓦ www.atlantis.ee. A riverside disco of many years' standing that packs in a youngish, hedonistic crowd. Tues–Sat 11pm–4am.

Club Tallinn Narva mnt 27 ⓦ www.clubtallinn. ee; see Tartu map on p.128. One of Estonia's best clubs, this is the main gathering point for the more style-conscious music freaks, offering cutting-edge sounds and the best big-name DJs. Wed–Sat 11pm–4am.

Illusion Raatuse 97 ⓦ www.illusion.ee; see Tartu map on p.128. Housed in an old cinema, *Illusion* is now among the most popular – and the priciest –

clubs in Tartu, with a good range of hip-hop, house, drum'n'bass and disco. Wed–Sat 11pm–4am.

Maasikas Küüni 7 ⓦ www.maasikas.com. *Maasikas* – "strawberry" in Estonian – attracts a slightly older (mid-20s) crowd than the other clubs in town. Cool and kitsch, it plays an eclectic mix of music – from live jazz to DJ sets. Fri–Sun 11pm–3.30am.

Plink Plonk Vallikraavi 4 ⓦ www.plinkplonk .ee. Studenty club showcasing indie rock and edgy dance music, beneath the *Vilde Lokaal* pub-restaurant (see p.136). Thurs–Sat 10pm–4am.

Shopping

For souvenirs and handicrafts you need look no further than **St Anthony's Court** at Lutsu 5 (Antoniuse Õu; ⓦ www.antonius.ee; Wed–Fri 11am–5pm, Sat & Sun 11am–3pm), where weavers, potters, milliners and ironmongers have open workshops and items for sale.

Big city-centre shopping **malls** include Kaubamaja and Tasku, diagonally opposite each other at the junction of Riia and Turu streets. The Kaubamaja's **supermarket** (Mon–Sat 9am–10pm, Sun 10am–8pm) has the widest choice, although Rimi (Mon–Sat 10am–9pm, Sun 10am–6pm) in Tasku is not far behind. Best for fresh fruit and veg is the open-air **market** behind the Sadamateater, where local seasonal produce is the main attraction. The covered market on Vabaduse offers more of the same plus meat, bread and dairy products.

For the biggest range of maps, local guidebooks and English-language paperbacks, head for the Apollo **bookshop** in Kaubamaja, or Rahva Raamat in the Tasku Centre. The secondhand bookstores at Riia 7 and Rüütli 12 are well worth a rummage.

Listings

Bicycle rental Jalgratas, Laulupeo 19 ☎742 1731; Velospets, Riia 130 ☎738 0406, ⓦwww .velospets.ee.

Ferry trips Tartu Sadam, Soola 5 (☎734 0066, ⓦwww.transcom.ee) organizes short cruises on the Emajõgi, as well as longer excursions to Lake Peipsi.

Hospital Puusepa tee, 2km west of the centre (for an ambulance call ☎112).

Internet Tourist Office, Raekoja plats; Kaubamaja Meestemaalim, Riia 1.

Left luggage At the bus station (24hr; from €1.30/day).

Pharmacy Raekoja Apteek, Town Hall, Raekoja plats (24hr).

Police Raekoja plats 7. In emergencies call ☎112.

Post office Vanemuise 7 (Mon–Fri 9am–7pm, Sat 9am–3pm).

Swimming Aura, just beyond the bus station at Turu 14 (Mon–Fri 7am–10pm, Sat & Sun 9am–10pm; ⓦwww.aurakeskus.ee), is a massively popular indoor complex with a 50m pool, paddling sections and water slides. For outdoor bathing, head for the stretch of the River Emajõgi northwest of town (walk along Ujula from the Kroonuaia bridge).

Travel agents Baltic Tours, Ülikooli 10 (☎740 0000, ⓦwww.baltictours.ee) and Estravel, Vallikraavi 2 (☎744 0300, ⓦwww.estravel.ee).

South of Tartu

South of Tartu is the one genuinely hilly region in Estonia, a glacier-sculpted landscape of smooth, dome-shaped heights and lake-filled depressions that stretches all the way to the Latvian border. With few summits exceeding 300m above sea level, there's little for ambitious hillwalkers to get excited about, but it's a visually arresting area all the same, with swathes of pine forest, deciduous woodland, arable land and pasture combining to produce a crowded palette of greens. The principal destination is **Otepää**, an endearing small town set among rippling hills that's an important centre for downhill and cross-country skiing in winter. Further south, the larger, but equally laid-back, town of **Võru** has a lakeside beach, but is really a staging-post en route to attractive villages like **Haanja** and **Rõuge**.

Otepää

Although known as Estonia's "winter capital", **OTEPÄÄ** is a great place to enjoy the region's landscape all year round. Just 45km southwest of Tartu and reached by regular bus, this country town has been a favourite holiday retreat for urban Estonians since the interwar years. As the only place in the country with a sufficient number of slopes to make downhill skiing worthwhile, it is much frequented on winter weekends, when the pubs and hotel bars take on a new lease of life. The mellow beauty of the surrounding area – and the presence of **Lake Pühajärv** 3km south of town – has also helped turn Otepää into one of Estonia's most popular inland summer resorts.

The town is full to bursting for the **Tartu Marathon** (ⓦwww.tartumaraton.ee), a cross-country skiing race on the first or second Sunday in February, starting at the Otepää ski stadium and winding up 63km later in the town of Elva, southwest of Tartu. The same course is pressed into service for the Tartu Cycle Marathon in mid-September.

Otepää's **bus station** is behind the Town Hall, inside which you'll find a helpful **tourist office** (mid-May to mid-Sept Mon–Fri 10am–5pm, Sat & Sun 10am–4pm; mid-Sept to mid-May Tues–Fri 10am–5pm, Sat 10am–4pm; ☎766 1200, ⓦwww .otepaa.ee), well stocked with local maps and brochures.

Accommodation

Its popularity as a resort means a handsome choice of **hotels** in Otepää and the surrounding region, and the tourist office can book you into local **B&Bs** (①–②), in town or in the countryside. The price codes below refer to the rates charged during Otepää's two high seasons (Jan–Feb & July–Aug). Some hotels officially drop their prices outside these periods, and others may well be open to bargaining, especially midweek.

Bernhard Kolga 22A ☎766 9601, ⓦwww .bernhard.ee. A classy place 3km southeast of town and a short walk from Lake Pühajärv, with balconied en-suites decked out in warm reds and browns, an indoor pool, spa facilities and bike rental. ⑤

Karupesa Hotell Tehvandi 1A ☎766 1500, ⓦwww .karupesa.ee. Mid-sized hotel with all the creature comforts, a 5min walk south of the centre. Carpeted en-suites have satellite TV and slightly chintzy decor; some also offer views towards Linnamägi and the parish church. Plus a restaurant, bar, and tennis court (or ice-rink in winter). ④

Lille Lille 6B ☎766 3999, ⓦwww.lillehotel.ee. This big suburban house, in a quiet residential area just off the main street, has plain, homely en-suites with TV. Sauna on site. ③

Nuustaku Nüpli ☎766 8208, ⓦwww.nuustaku .ee. A B&B attached to the popular pub of the same name, perched above the Pühajärv shore – perfect if you want a lakeside location and a party scene. En-suite rooms come with woody furnishings; those with lake views cost a little more. ③

Pühajärve Spa Pühajärve ☎766 5500, ⓦwww .pyhajarve.com. Fourteenth-century manor house with modern annexes, offering a superb lakeshore position and spa facilities. Pleasant rooms have chic, Nordic-style furnishings. Standard en-suites ④, with private sauna ⑤

The Town

Otepää's ridge-top town centre looks out towards a series of pudding-shaped hills. The first of these to the east is crowned by the **parish church** (mid-May to mid-Sept Tues–Sun 10am–5pm; donation), a dainty neo-Gothic edifice whose exterior is decorated with plaques recalling the one historical event for which Otepää is famous: on June 4, 1884, members of Tartu University's Estonian student fraternity came here to consecrate the blue-black-and-white tricolour they had chosen as their banner. After the tricolour was adopted as the Estonian state flag Otepää became a low-key patriotic pilgrimage centre. The interior is decorated with some fine pre-World War I woodwork, including an ornate pulpit and lacy-patterned ceiling timbers.

South of the parish church, paths curl their way towards the summit of **Linnamägi**, a low wooded hill that served from the Iron Age Estonian chieftains as a natural stronghold until German crusading knights expelled them from it in the thirteenth century. Apart from a few stretches of reconstructed wall there's little to see here now, but the bare hilltop offers excellent views back towards the church and the rippling hills to the south, where you'll see the summit of Otepää's ski-jump ramp poking up above the trees.

Lake Pühajärv

From the centre of Otepää it's an easy thirty-minute walk to the northern shore of **Lake Pühajärv** – you can also get there by bus (12 daily, destination Kariku or Valga), which drop off beside the *Pühajärve* hotel. About 3km from north to south and 1km across, this serene stretch of water occupies an important place in Estonian folklore – according to legend, it was formed by the tears of a mother grieving for five sons killed in battle and its waters have had healing powers ever since – especially if drunk on Midsummer's Eve. Most visitors only get as far as the northern end, where there's a sizeable sandy beach, pedalos for rent and a couple of waterfront cafés. To get away from the throng it's well worth exploring the 13km-long **hiking route** that follows the lake's heavily indented shoreline (partly on asphalt road, partly off-road), passing through a landscape of coastal meadows and golden-brown reed beds. You'll probably catch sight of plenty of grebes and ducks on the way, with sandpipers, kingfishers and herons occasionally making an appearance towards the quieter, southern end of the lake. Branching off from the lake path just south of the *Pühajärve* hotel, the

Murrumetsa Nature Path takes you on a 3.5km circuit through a lakeside forest of fir, birch and aspen, beginning with a boardwalk trail across seasonally squelchy meadow and marsh. According to the English-language signboards along the way, this part of the shore is popular with otter, beaver and mink – although you're unlikely to find these secretive twilight creatures posing for passing tourists.

Skiing around Otepää

The main **downhill skiing** areas around Otepää are at Väike Munamägi, 3km southeast of the town centre, and Kuutsemäe, 11km southwest. At both places you'll find an undemanding range of 150m- to 250m-long slopes served by simple draglifts, and kiosks renting out gear. There's also an impressive network of **cross-country skiing** routes, many of them fanning out from the Winter Sports Stadium on the southeastern outskirts of town. You can rent ski gear here, and from most of the bigger hotels in and around Otepää; ski and snowboard rental costs around €25–35 per day.

Eating and drinking

There's a welcoming handful of **pub-restaurants** around Otepää's central T-junction. *Oti Pubi*, in a glass-fronted decahedron at Lipuväljak 26 (daily 10am–midnight), does reliable, cheap set lunches as well as substantial main meat-with-fries meals, while *Hermanni*, opposite the Town Hall at Lipuväljak 10 (daily 11am–11pm, 1am at weekends), offers more of the same in an enjoyable pub-like interior plastered with ski memorabilia. *Edgari Trahter*, Lipuväljak 3 (daily 9am–7pm), is a cheap and friendly café dishing up savoury pies, soups, salads, and pork-and-potato main courses. Further afield, *Nuustaku*, on the eastern shore of Pühajärv lake (daily 11am–midnight), is a roomy wooden-floor pub with a big veranda overlooking the lake and serving a good choice of pork and freshwater fish dishes, while the *Karupesa Hotell* (see opposite) and *Bernhard* (opposite) have more upmarket restaurants.

Võru

Ranged along the eastern edge of Lake Tamula, **VÕRU** is a quiet provincial town with leafy parks and a stretch of sandy shoreline. It was founded by decree of Catherine the Great in 1784, which helps explain the neat, grid-plan appearance. The long, straight strip of **Jüri tänav** runs through the centre, separating the modern, concrete parts of town to the northeast from an altogether more charming neighbourhood of timber houses to the southwest. Heading into the latter along Katariina brings you to the **Võrumaa County Museum** at no. 11 (Võrumaa muuseum; Wed–Sun 11am–6pm; €1), a fairly traditional display with little English-language labelling. The most venerable item in the collection is the skull of a Stone Age woman, thought to date from the fourth millennium BC, making it the oldest human remains to be found in Estonia. There's also a history of the Võru region as told through old photos, domestic knick-knacks and an at times eccentric choice of artefacts: a display case devoted to the political confusion that followed World War I contains the visiting card of local Bolshevik leader Oskar Leegen and the noose used by German occupying forces to hang him.

At the bottom of Katariina, turn left onto Kreuzwaldi and after ten minutes you come to the **F.R. Kreuzwald Memorial Museum** at no. 31 (F.R. Kreuzwaldi memoriaalmuuseum; Wed–Sun 11am–6pm; €1), occupying the property where the author of Estonia's national epic, *Kalevipoeg* ("Son of Kalev"), practised as a doctor from 1833 until his retirement in 1877. The exhibition opens with a stolid, text-based survey of Kreuzwald's life, and it's something of a relief to move on to the barn in the courtyard, where works of art inspired by his writings are displayed – look out for Kristjan Raud's celebrated illustrations for the interwar editions of *Kalevipoeg*. Finally, visitors are ushered into Kreuzwald's waiting room and surgery. An inkpot in the form of a dragon is the only artefact on display that Kreuzwald actually owned, but the period furnishings convey a strong flavour of nineteenth-century life.

F. R. Kreuzwald 1803–82

Throughout the nineteenth century, many ambitious Estonians turned their backs on their native heritage, regarding it as a mark of peasant backwardness from which they had been lucky to escape. By providing Estonians with a literary heritage they could be proud of, **Friedrich Reinhold Kreuzwald** was one of the first to buck this trend.

Kreuzwald was born to a family of Estonian serfs in Jõepere near Rakvere. After doing well at school Kreuzwald found work as a private tutor, saving enough to enter Tartu University's medical faculty in 1826. Receiving a Third Class Physician's Licence (insufficient to become a doctor to gentlefolk) he set up a modest practice in Võru in 1833.

Kreuzwald's enthusiasm for folklore had been nurtured through contact with other young intellectuals in Tartu, notably Friedrich Robert Faehlmann, who set up the Estonian Learned Society in 1838. Inspired by the example of Elias Lönnrot, who had created a Finnish national epic in the 1830s by bundling together traditional folk tales to form the *Kalevala*, Faehlmann came up with the idea of collecting indigenous Estonian material to the same end. The project was enthusiastically taken up by Kreuzwald, and **Kalevipoeg** ("Son of Kalev") was the result.

Published in serial form between 1857 and 1859, *Kalevipoeg* immediately made Kreuzwald's reputation and has enjoyed a sacred position in Estonian culture ever since. It was initially believed that *Kalevipoeg* was a compilation of genuine folk tales – it only emerged later that Kreuzwald had made most of the story up, by which time the reading public had already embraced the epic and were unwilling to question its value.

Despite the success of *Kalevipoeg* among educated Estonians, Kreuzwald never earned much from writing it. He resented contemporaries like Johann Woldemar Jannsen (editor of *Postimees*; see p.109), who managed to make a living from journalism, while the great intellectual Kreuzwald continued to languish as a country doctor in Võru. Despite remaining aloof from the emerging cultural scene in Tartu and Tallinn, Kreuzwald exerted a strong influence over young, educated Estonians – not least Jannsen's poetry-writing daughter Lydia Koidula (see p.109). The pair exchanged over ninety letters from 1867 onwards, a touchingly intimate correspondence full of mutual intellectual admiration. When Koidula married Eduard Michelson – a Latvian doctor who didn't speak Estonian – in 1873, Kreuzwald regarded it as a betrayal of her cultural mission, and never wrote to her again.

Southwest of here, streets slope down to the sandy shores of **Tamula järv** (lake) a popular year-round strolling area, with a sandy beach, seasonal cafés, and good views of the low green hills to the southwest.

Practicalities

Võru's **bus station** is on the northeastern side of town, about five minutes' walk downhill from the main Jüri tänav. The **tourist office**, on the southwestern side of Jüri at Tartu 31 (mid-May to mid-Sept Mon–Fri 9am–6pm, Sat & Sun 9am–3pm; mid-Sept to mid-May closed Sun; ℡782 1881, ⓦwww.visitvoru.ee), has plenty of local brochures and can help find **B&Bs** in the villages south of town. The best of the town's **hotels** is the *Tamula*, right on the beach at Vee 4 (℡783 0430, ⓦwww.tamula.ee; ❺), offering swish en-suites in a stylish, modern building; ask for one facing the lake. *Õlle Nr. 17*, Jüri 17, is a wonderfully relaxed **pub** with a wide choice of cheap meat and fish dishes, while *Mõisa Ait*, in the courtyard behind Jüri 20, is a two-level pub-restaurant serving trusty Estonian pork-and-potatoes. In mid-July, the **Võru Folklore Festival** (ⓦwww.werro.ee/folkloor) attracts a variety of Estonian and international ensembles for three days of parades, dancing and concerts.

Suur-Munamägi and around

The wooded dome of **Suur-Munamägi** ("Great Egg Hill"), 12km south of Võru, would barely register as a bump in most other European countries, but at 318m above sea level it's the highest point in the Baltic States – and a popular focus for Estonian day-trippers. The surrounding landscape of farmsteads, hump-backed hills and forests is as attractive as any in the region, and the lanes are perfect for cycle rides and undemanding hikes. There's a lot of off-the-beaten-track **B&B accommodation** in the area – ask the tourist offices in Võru (see above) or Rõuge (see below) to reserve a place for you, as few vowels speak English. Regular **buses** make their way from Võru to **HAANJA**, an uneventful village, 1km north of the hill. There's also a daily bus to Haanja from Tallinn (passing through Tartu on the way), which arrives in the early afternoon and heads back after about ninety minutes – giving you ample time to clamber up and down Suur-Munamägi.

The path to Suur-Munamägi's summit heads uphill about 1km south of Haanja, starting from a roadside monument recording an episode from the War of Independence, when a clash with Bolsheviks on March 20, 1919, left seven Estonians dead. It takes just five minutes to reach the fir-tree-carpeted hilltop, where a 1939 Art Deco **viewing tower** (Vaatetorn; mid-April to Sept daily 10am–8pm; Oct Sat & Sun 10am–5pm; mid-Nov to mid-April Sat & Sun noon–3pm; €4 elevator, €2 by steps) offers a superb panorama of the surrounding countryside.

Rõuge

Some 9km west of Haanja, **RÕUGE** is famous for being one of Estonia's most picturesque villages, offering more of the gently hilly terrain that seems a world away from the flatlands that make up most of Estonia. Its buildings are scattered haphazardly on the slopes above Rõuge Suurjärv lake – which, at 38m, is the deepest in the country. Suurjärv is the most central of a string of lakes lying in the **Rõuge Primeval Valley** (Ürgorg), a broad trough carved by a glacier during the last Ice Age. Feeding into the valley is the **Ööbikuorg** ("Valley of Nightingales", so-called because it's a favourite nesting area of the birds in spring), a twisting, steep-sided dell that lies behind the village's whitewashed, eighteenth-century church. A well-signed hiking trail into the dell and onwards to the lakes of the Primeval Valley begins just outside the village beside the Haanja road. Looming above the start of the trail is an eight-storey wooden viewing tower, providing a stirring panorama of the Rõuge landscape.

Buses from Võru pick up and drop off at a T-junction beside Suurjärv lake, near a basic provisions store. The **tourist office**, in a timber hut at the start of the Ööbikuorg trail (☎785 9245, ⓦwww.rauge.ee), can fix you up with farmhouse **accommodation**; otherwise try *Suurjärve külalistemaja*, a tastefully renovated farmstead overlooking the lake at Metsa 5 (☎785 9273, ⓦwww.hot.ee/maremajutus; ②), which has simply decorated rooms with shared facilities, more modern en-suites and a log-built smoke sauna in the garden. Near the bus stop, the *Ala-Rõuge külalistemaja* at Võru 13 (☎785 9236, ⓦwww.alarouge.ee; ②) offers en-suite doubles and bunk-bed triples and quads in a converted weir-side mill. If you've got your own transport, you can choose from plenty of **B&Bs** within a short drive of Rõuge, including the *Lätte Turismitalu*, 5km northwest near Nursi village (☎786 0706, ⓦwww.hot.ee/lattetalu; ②), with rustic wood-panelled rooms in the main house or its two annexes, right beside Kahvila lake. There's no restaurant in Rõuge and the *Saarsilla* **café** midway between bus stop and church is only open at weekends – most B&B hosts will prepare meals if you enquire in advance.

Lake Peipsi

Lake Peipsi, measuring 3555 square kilometres, forms a large stretch of Estonia's border with Russia. Despite ranking as the fifth-biggest lake in Europe, Lake Peipsi is a low-key area of sleepy fishing settlements, thick reed beds and quiet, sandy beaches, offering little in the way of tourist facilities. If you have a taste for simple rusticity, however, you'll find a visit here rewarding, not least because of Lake Peipsi's ethnographic peculiarities. Many of the shoreline villages are home to members of the Russian Orthodox sect of **Old Believers**, who came here in the early eighteenth century to escape persecution at home and settled down to catch fish and grow onions.

The Old Believers

The origins of the **Old Believers** – or *Staroviertsii* as they are known in Russian – lie in the liturgical reforms introduced into the Russian Orthodox Church by Nikon, the mid-seventeenth-century patriarch of Moscow. Faced with the task of systematizing the divergent practices then in use in the national church, Nikon opted to follow the contemporary Greek model, adopting the use of three fingers instead of two when making the sign of the cross and introducing Greek ecclesiastical dress. Priests who opposed the reforms were removed from office, but many of their congregations persisted with the old practices and were dubbed "Old Believers" by a church hierarchy eager to see them marginalized. Peter the Great was particularly keen to get rid of them and it was under his rule that groups of Old Believers moved to Lake Peipsi – and other areas on the western fringes of the empire – where they continue to practice their religion as they wish. They are more egalitarian than mainstream Orthodox churches, choosing clergy from among the local community rather than relying on a priesthood. Services are conducted in Old Church Slavonic – the medieval tongue into which the Scriptures were originally translated – rather than in modern Russian.

An estimated fifteen thousand Old Believers still live in Estonia, most of whom remain in the Lake Peipsi region. Strict adherence to their beliefs has traditionally prevented them from being assimilated by post-World War II Russian migrants, although their numbers are now in decline – largely owing to the migration of the young to the towns and their intermarriage with other groups.

Renowned for their wooden houses and timber churches, Old Believer settlements like Nina, Kasepää, Varnja, and most of all **Kolkja**, exude an untroubled tranquillity that probably hasn't changed much since the community first arrived.

Lake Peipsi is easy to access **from Tartu**: the main road passes through Kallaste, the chief settlement and service centre on the central part of the lake, before wheeling north towards Narva (see p.123). The principal Old Believer villages are a short detour away from this route, but a handful of Kallaste-bound buses pass through Kolkja en route.

About 35km from Tartu, the Kallaste-bound road passes through the village of **KOOSA**, where an eastbound turn-off leads to a string of Old Believer villages occupying a reedy stretch of the Lake Peipsi shoreline. The first of these is **VARNJA**, a largely nondescript huddle of houses grouped around a church with a tower shaped like a spear. **KASEPÄÄ**, 3km up the shore to the north, is more picturesque, its jaunty pea-green church surrounded by a thicket of graveyard crosses.

The northern end of Kasepää runs imperceptibly into **KOLKJA**, a 4km shoreline stretch of brightly painted wooden houses, most of which are surrounded by neat onion plots. Set back from the shore in the modern part of the village, the **Museum of Old Believers** (April–Sept Wed–Sun 11am–6pm; Oct–March Sat & Sun 11am–5pm; €1.70) occupies a back room of the village school. Inside lies an incandescent display of beautifully embroidered traditional costumes, including some especially attractive pink caftans – which turn out to be burial shrouds. There's a cabinet full of liturgical books in Old Church Slavonic – a handful of local schoolchildren still receive lessons in the language. *Kolkja Camping*, in the west part of the village (☎5648 5274 ⊛www .kolkjacampingmajad.ee), has two- to four-person chalets from €13 per person. The *Kala-Sibula* **restaurant** (summer daily noon–6pm; in winter ring in advance; ☎745 3445), midway between the museum and the lakeshore, serves up *sudak* (pike-perch) and other local fish, often garnished with sauces featuring the local onions.

Setumaa

East of Võru, rolling hills give way to a gently undulating landscape, with broad pastures and arable land broken up by occasional wedges of forest. This southeastern corner of the country is known as **Setumaa** or "land of the Setu" – a branch of the

Estonian nation that has preserved distinctive ethnographical features and an archaic dialect. The historic isolation of the **Setu** from the rest of the country owes much to the fact that the region was under the jurisdiction of the Russian principalities of Pskov and Novgorod during the Middle Ages and, unlike the rest of Estonia, was Christianized by the eastern Orthodox Church.

The grammar and pronunciation of the Setu dialect is sufficiently close to that of the nearby Võru region for local linguists to group the two together, claiming the existence of a Võro-Seto language which is distinct from modern Estonian. Although Võro-Seto is yet to be officially recognized, Estonian society is much more tolerant towards this kind of regional particularism than it was during the Soviet period – when cultural and linguistic unity was considered essential to the nation's survival. Indeed, the Setu region is increasingly seen as a source of ethnographic riches, not least because of the survival of archaic **folk-singing** techniques that have died out elsewhere. Often featuring partly improvised epic narratives, Setu songs or *leelos* are usually sung by a group of five or six women, one of whom sings a semitone higher than the others – producing a discordant, haunting polyphony. Traditional Setu dress is also distinctive, with dark red the dominant colour, augmented by plenty of heavy, metal jewellery – notably the vast metal breastplates worn by unmarried women. What makes the Setu heritage particularly precious to present-day Estonia is the fact that of the twelve *nulks*, or tribal units, into which Setumaa is divided, four lie across the border in the Russian Federation – a division made all the more galling by the knowledge that they were all part of Estonia until the Soviets arbitrarily redrew the frontier in 1940. Setumaa's main market centre, **Pečory** (Petseri in Estonian), now lies 3km on the wrong side of the border, leaving the Estonian Setu without an urban focus. Nowadays, the main centres of Setu culture are the villages of **Obinitsa** (served by regular buses from Võru) and **Värska** (reached by bus from Tartu).

Värska

VÄRSKA, 90km southeast of Tartu, is a forest-shrouded village on the southwestern shores of Lake Pihkva, a southern extension of Lake Peipsi. Set in an attractive, reedy landscape frequented by herons and other waterfowl, it's an undramatic place, its only real sight being the charming **Setu Farm Museum**, Pikk 40 (mid-May to mid-Sept Tues–Sun 10am–5pm; mid-Sept to mid-May Tues–Sat 10am–4pm; ⓦ www.setomuuseum.ee; €2). With old tools, farm machinery, textiles and traditional handicrafts from the late nineteenth century displayed in original reed-thatched buildings around a common yard, the museum also offers traditional cookery and handicraft workshops.

Värska's **tourist office**, on the main street at Pikk 12 (mid-May to mid-Sept daily 10am–6pm; mid-Sept to mid-May Mon–Fri 8.30am–4.30pm; ⓣ796 4782, ⓦwww .verska.ee), can advise on local **B&Bs**. Otherwise, try the *Hirvemäe Holiday Centre*, near the centre at Silla 2A (ⓣ797 6105, ⓦwww.hirvemae.ee; ❸), which has modern en-suites with pine furnishings and attic ceilings. You can **camp** in the grounds for €1.60 per tent, plus €1.60 per vehicle. The centre's **café** is the best place to eat, although it closes at 4pm or so out of season.

Obinitsa and around

The quiet agricultural settlement of **OBINITSA** lies 20km southwest of Värska and 25km east of Võru. Buses from Võru pick up and drop off just south of the staggered central crossroads, where a signed alley leads east to the **Setu Museum House** (Seto muuseumitare; mid-May to mid-Sept Mon–Fri 10am–5pm, Sat & Sun 11am–5pm; mid-Sept to mid-May Mon–Fri 10am–5pm; €1.70). Housed in a traditional timber building, the museum gives an insight into Setu family life from the 1920s to the 1940s, with beautiful embroidered folk costumes, religious icons and intricate handicrafts. To sample a traditional Setu meal, contact the Obinitsa **tourist office** inside the museum in advance (same times; ⓣ785 4190, ⓦwww.obinitsamuuseum.ee).

If you continue east from here, you'll arrive after five minutes at an artificial lake with a beach. Overlooking the lake from its unmissable hillside position is the granite statue of the **Setu Song-Mother** (Setu Lauluimä), a stylized tribute to the female singers who have kept the tradition of epic narrative songs alive. Scattered in the grass around the statue are boulders engraved with the names of individual performers who were bestowed with the honorific title of Lauluimä during their lifetime. About 500m north of the central crossroads is Obinitsa's wooden **church**, built in 1905 and largely destroyed after World War II, but returned to use in the early 1950s, when the communist authorities turned a blind eye to its reconstruction. **Transfiguration Day** (Paasapäev) on August 6 is one of the biggest feast days in Setumaa: thousands of Orthodox descend on Obinitsa church to commemorate the dead, and local families tuck into picnics on top of their ancestors' graves in the adjoining cemetery.

Piusa Sand Caves

The **Piusa Sand Caves** (Piusa koopad), one of the country's more offbeat tourist attractions, lie 5km north of Obinitsa. The "caves" (really a single chamber) were excavated between 1922 and 1970 to extract sand for use in the glassmaking industry. The area became a protected nature reserve in 1999, largely owing to the caves' importance as a habitat for bats – the creatures have flourished since the end of mining activities, and Piusa now harbours one of the biggest colonies in the Baltics. You're free to enter the excavations at any time, although some sections are boarded off for fear of cave-ins. Once inside it's a marvellously atmospheric place, with rows of sand-carved arches bringing to mind some kind of abandoned subterranean cathedral. The section nearest the entrance is hauntingly illuminated by the daylight leaking in from outside; if you want to venture further in you'll need to bring a torch. Round the back of the caves, paths lead around the edges of the Piusa Sandpit (Piusa liivakarjäär), a Sahara-like expanse of sand edged by rare grasses and shrubs.

Travel details

Trains

Narva to: St Petersburg (3 weekly; 3hr 30min).
Tallinn to: Narva (1 daily; 3hr 30min).

Buses

Narva to: Narva-Jõesuu (every 20–30min; 20min); Otepää (2 daily; 4hr 30min); Rakvere (7 daily; 2hr 20min); Sillamäe (hourly; 30–40min); Tartu (11 daily; 2hr 50min–3hr 35min).
Otepää to: Narva (2 daily; 4hr 30min); Tallinn (2 daily; 3hr 30min); Tartu (10 daily; 1hr 10min–2hr); Võru (3 daily; 1hr 10min).
Rakvere to: Käsmu (Mon–Fri 4 daily, Sat 3 daily, Sun 2 daily; 1hr 15min); Narva (7 daily; 2hr 20min); Palmse (Mon, Wed, Fri & Sun 1 daily; 40min); Võsu (Mon–Fri 4 daily, Sat 3 daily, Sun 2 daily; 1hr).
Tallinn to: Haanja (1 daily; 4hr); Käsmu (June–Aug 1 daily; 1hr 30min); Narva (hourly; 3hr 15min); Tartu (every 30min; 2hr 20min–3hr); Võsu (June–Aug 3 daily, Sept–May 1 daily; 4hr 15min).

Tartu to: Haanja (2 daily; 1hr 30min); Kallaste (Mon–Fri 5 daily, Sat & Sun 3 daily; 1hr 20min–1hr 50min); Käsmu (mid-May to mid-Sept 1 daily; 2hr 50min); Kolkja (Mon–Fri 4 daily, Sat 1 daily, Sun 2 daily; 1hr 20min); Kuressaare (2–3 daily; 6hr); Narva-Jõesuu (2 daily; 3hr 30min); Otepää (10 daily; 1hr 10min–2hr); Põlva (10 daily; 40min); Rakvere (8 daily; 2hr 10min–3hr); Rõuge (2 daily; 2hr); Sillamäe (3 daily; 2hr 30min); Värska (3 daily; 2hr); Viljandi (8 daily; 1hr–1hr 20min); Võsu (mid-May to mid-Sept 1 daily; 2hr 40min).
Võru to: Haanja (5 daily; 25min); Obinitsa (Mon–Sat 4 daily, Sun 3 daily; 40min–1hr 30min); Rõuge (Mon–Fri 8 daily, Sat & Sun 5 daily; 25min); Tallinn (12 daily; 3hr 45min); Tartu (every 30min–1hr; 1hr 20min).

International buses

Narva to: St Petersburg (7 daily; 3hr).
Tartu to: Rīga (2 daily; 4hr); St Petersburg (2 daily; 8hr).

Latvia

Latvia highlights

✳ **Rīga Old Town** A nest of narrow streets lined with an engaging ensemble of buildings reflecting eight centuries of history. See p.166

✳ **Art Nouveau architecture, Rīga** Nymphs, caryatids and a host of other creatures peer down from the richly ornamented facades of Rīga's nineteenth-century centre. See p.178

✳ **Rundāle** A veritable Versailles of the north, this stupendous eighteenth-century palace is filled to the rafters with sumptuous Baroque and Rococo furnishings. See p.196

✳ **Cape Kolka** Hauntingly beautiful horn of land extending into the Baltic Sea and flanked by semi-deserted sandy beaches. See p.198

✳ **Kuldīga** An attractive huddle of half-timbered houses set beside the foaming River Venta, Kuldīga represents small-town Latvia at its most picturesque. See p.203

✳ **Gauja National Park** The River Gauja cuts its way through pine-carpeted sandstone hills to create this paradise for hikers, canoeists and nature lovers. See p.217

✳ **Latgale** This sparsely populated area of rustic villages and rolling hills is one of the most delightful rural landscapes in the region. See p.226

△ Three Brothers, Rīga

Introduction and basics

Contemporary Latvia presents two very contrasting faces to visitors. The first is provided by the bustling capital city of Rīga, where several centuries of fine architecture rub shoulders with a brash, rapidly developing commercial culture. Outside Rīga, however, Latvia comes across rather differently, as a restful country of market towns, farmsteads, forests and bogs. The Latvian landscape also offers stately homes, ruined castles and historic churches aplenty, although most of these bear witness to the waves of foreign occupiers who put down roots in Latvian soil. A Baltic tribe closely related to their Lithuanian neighbours, the Latvians were overwhelmed at the start of the thirteenth century by German crusading knights, who massacred and enslaved them in the name of Christianity. The Germans continued to dominate both land and trade even after political control passed to the Polish-Lithuanian Commonwealth, then Sweden and finally Russia. Despite a brief period of independence between 1918 and 1940, Russian power returned in 1940 when all three Baltic republics were annexed by the Soviet Union. Latvian language and culture have re-established themselves in the years following the regaining of independence in 1991, although certain aspects of the Soviet legacy still remain. Most obvious of these is the presence of a large Russian minority on Latvian soil: originally encouraged to settle here as industrial workers in the 1950s and 1960s, Russians now make up an estimated thirty percent of the population.

Where to go

The most obvious destination in Latvia is its capital, **Rīga**, a boisterous, mercantile city whose Gothic red-brick heart is girdled by one of the richest collections of Art Nouveau apartment blocks anywhere in Europe. The Latvian capital is also known for its varied and often wild nightlife, and offers easy access to the sands of **Jūrmala**, a seaside suburb northwest of the city.

One of the most scenic stretches of the Latvian countryside lies just east of Rīga, where the River Gauja winds its way through wooded sandstone hills, passing medieval castles at **Sigulda** and **Cēsis** en route. Further southeast, Latvia's gritty second city **Daugavpils** is very much an acquired taste, but it does possess an enchanting rustic hinterland in **Latgale**, a region of rippling hills and beguiling villages, of which **Aglona** – Latvia's most popular Catholic pilgrimage centre – is the most obvious target.

South of Rīga lies a flat-as-a-pancake region of rich farmland, dotted with the country palaces of the eighteenth-century Baltic aristocracy, with the Rococo **Rundāle Palace** making a rewarding day-trip from the capital. On the west coast, the port city of **Ventspils** offers museums and sandy beaches, although **Liepāja** has more in terms of historical heritage and nightlife. Just inland, the riverside settlement of **Kuldīga** can't be beaten for countryside charm. For the best in deserted beaches, dunes and sea views, head for **Cape Kolka** in the far northwest.

Getting around

Latvia's public transport network is, on the whole, efficient and comprehensive. Travelling by bus is generally slightly quicker, but also a little more expensive, than by train. For details of travelling between Latvia and the other Baltic States, see p.34.

Buses

Latvia is covered by a comprehensive **bus** network; frequent services run between the main cities and even the smallest villages see at least one bus a day. Buses on the

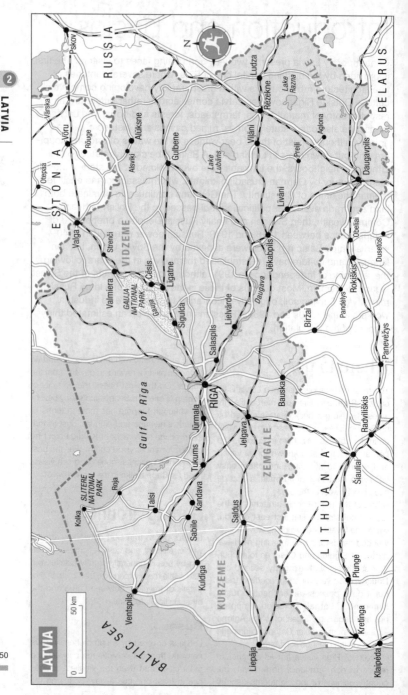

LATVIA

intercity routes are reasonably comfortable; those plying rural routes may well be ancient contraptions with sagging seats. At the bigger stations **tickets** should be bought in advance wherever possible; if you're catching the bus from an intermediate stop-off rather than its point of origin, you'll have to pay the driver. Large bags are stowed in the luggage compartment. **Fares** are reasonable: cross-country journeys like Rīga–Liepāja or Rīga–Daugavpils weigh in at around 6Ls, while Rīga–Sigulda costs around 2.50Ls. Note that some inter-city routes (such as Liepāja–Ventspils) are operated by small minibuses that fill up quickly at weekends – so book your tickets early to avoid getting stranded.

Departure boards at bus stations are fairly easy to understand, with most of the terminology the same as that used in train stations (see below). Express buses are usually shown on timetables with the letter "E"; buses that only travel on a certain day of the week are marked with an initial denoting the day in question ("P" means *pirmdiena* or Monday, for example; see p.396 for a full list of days in Latvian).

However, information provided in bus stations rarely covers the times of return buses from the particular place you're heading for, making it difficult to plan day-trips with any certainty – a problem made worse by the fact that station staff outside Rīga rarely speak any English. If in doubt, telephone the tourist office of the place you're aiming for and ask them for advice on how to get there and back – they're usually quite happy to help. **Timetable information** is available on ⓦ www.1188.lv.

Trains

Latvia's **train** network is exceedingly useful if you're making short trips in and around the Rīga region: there are regular services to Jūrmala, the Gauja National Park and the Daugava Valley towns, putting lots of destinations within comfortable day-trip range. Many carriages feature hard, wooden or plastic seating, so bring a cushion if you're accustomed to travelling in comfort. Services to southeastern destinations like Daugavpils and Ludza take four or more hours and don't have a buffet car – so you'll need to bring your own food and drink. **Prices** are slightly lower than buses, with Rīga–Sigulda

tickets costing around 2Ls, Rīga–Daugavpils 5.50Ls.

Train **tickets** (*biļete*) should be bought in advance if the ticket office is open – if not, pay the conductor. All but the smallest of train stations will have the **timetable** (*kustības saraksts*) written up on a board – departures are listed under *atiešana* or *atiet*, arrivals under *pienākšana* or *pienāk*. *Darbdienās* means on working days, *brīvdienās* or *svētdienās* means on Sundays and public holidays; the words *nepietur stacijās* mean "doesn't stop at". Trains with four-digit route numbers stop at virtually every halt; those with three-digit route numbers are "fast" trains that miss some of the smaller stations out – although even these are unlikely to travel at speeds exceeding 60km/hr.

Driving

Road conditions in Latvia can vary dramatically. There are no two-lane highways, apart from a brief stretch between Rīga and Jūrmala. Roads linking major towns are usually reasonable, but off the beaten track, conditions deteriorate rapidly. The biggest hazard is reckless drivers – Latvia's road casualty rate is shocking.

Speed limits are 50kph in built-up areas, 90kph on the open road and 100kph on highways. In towns it's forbidden to overtake stationary trams. The wearing of **seatbelts** is compulsory, and **headlights** should be switched on at all times. It's illegal to drive with more than 0.05mg of **alcohol** in the blood (which is roughly equivalent to a pint and a half of beer). Though most towns and major highways are well provided with round-the-clock petrol stations (*degvielas stacija*),

Addresses

In Latvia the street name always comes before the number, and the word for "street" (*iela*) is often omitted; Barona 28 is 28 Barona Street. A street number comprising two figures separated by slash (7/2 or 9/25 for example) means that the building is on a corner or intersection – the first number denotes its position in the main street, while the second number refers to its position in the street being intersected.

there are few in rural areas – carry a spare can. **Petrol** costs around 1Ls for a litre.

Accommodation

The last decades have seen a hotel-building boom in Rīga, ensuring that the mid-range and business ends of the market are increasingly well catered for. There's a shortage of **budget** hotels, but plenty of B&Bs and backpacker-oriented hostels have emerged to fill the gap. Outside the capital things are less predictable, although the number of affordable B&Bs and rural homestays is increasing, and there are plenty of idyllic camping opportunities if you don't mind roughing it a bit.

Hotels

The cheapest **hotels** tend to come with functional furnishings and en-suite shower and WC, although a few places have a handful of cheaper rooms with shared toilet facilities in the hallway. For a double in this type of hotel you'd expect to pay 30–50Ls in Rīga, 20–25Ls in the provinces.

In the capital at least, and increasingly in provincial cities and popular areas like Jūrmala and the Gauja Valley, there's a broad range of mid-priced hotels. Either reconditioned Soviet-era places or establishments built in the last twenty years, these will invariably have plush carpets, TV and a modern bathroom. A double will cost 60–80Ls in the capital, 30–40Ls elsewhere.

Latvia also has a good choice of upmarket hotels that would merit four or more stars in any other European country, and charge rates to match. Some Rīga hotels cut their prices at weekends and off-season, such as in autumn and early spring – it always pays to ask.

Guesthouses and rural homestays

Outside the big cities there's an increasing number of family-run places calling themselves a **guesthouse**, or *viesu nams*. Standards vary widely – some guesthouses are small hotels in all but name, while others are simply suburban houses or rural farmsteads that rent out rooms and are similar to B&Bs. They're usually a good deal cheaper than mid-range hotels at around 20-30Ls a double and offer a friendlier, more intimate atmosphere to boot.

Most tourist offices outside Rīga will have a list of local households offering **B&B** accommodation, and in most cases will make reservations on your behalf – the hosts themselves rarely speak much English. Many of these B&Bs are in rural areas and may indeed be run by a farming family – as such they represent a great way to experience the countryside, but you'll probably need your own transport to make full use of them. One **agency** that deals exclusively with rural homestays throughout Latvia and the rest of the Baltics, and can fix up your whole holiday in advance is Lauku ceļotajs, Kalnciema 40, Rīga (℡6761 7600, Ⓦwww.celotajs.lv).

Hostels

There's an impressive array of backpacker-friendly **hostels** in Rīga, although they are less easy to find outside the capital. Conditions can be cramped in summer, but prices – at 7–10Ls a bed – are reasonable.

The most basic form of **campsite** in Latvia is a tent site (*telšu vieta*), which, as its name suggests, is basically a meadow where you're allowed to pitch a tent for around 1Ls or 1.50Ls – facilities such as earth toilets or a water tap may or may not be provided. Several national parks (notably the Gauja

Accommodation price codes

The hotels and guesthouses listed in the Latvian chapters of this guide have been graded according to the following price bands, based on the cost of the least expensive double room in summer.

❶ 18Ls and under
❷ 19–24Ls
❸ 25–32Ls
❹ 33–44Ls
❺ 45–60Ls
❻ 61–80Ls
❼ 81–120Ls
❽ 121Ls and over

National Park; see p.217) provide tent sites free of charge, and even supply wood for bonfires – the idea being that this prevents campers from illegally chopping timber themselves.

One step up from a *telšu vieta* is a **kempings** (campsite), where – alongside tent and caravan space – accommodation consists of two- or four-person cabins, with shared toilets and washing facilities. On average, a two-person cabin costs 15–20Ls.

Food and drink

Traditionally, Latvian cuisine is rich in **meat** and **dairy**, with pork, cheese and sour cream forming the mainstay of the national diet. In recent years, however, chicken, fish and fresh salads have started appearing on menus. As you'd expect, Rīga boasts the best range of restaurants, cafés, bars and pubs, along with a growing stable of ethnic-influenced places; the further away you travel from the capital, the narrower the choice, with most establishments concentrating on a tried-and-tested repertoire of traditional Latvian food.

The word **restorāns** (restaurant) usually denotes a smartish, starched-tablecloth establishment – and although there are plenty of these in Rīga, many Latvians prefer to eat in the more informal (and cheaper) surroundings of a **krogs** or *krodziņš* (pub-like taverns often decked out in folksy wooden furnishings), or in a **kafejnīca** (a catch-all term covering anything from a greasy spoon to an elegant coffee-and-cakes café). Many *kafejnīcas* are in fact sizeable, self-service restaurants in which a handsome selection of traditional eats is displayed at the counter and you simply point to what you want – an excellent, affordable way to fill up. A two-course meal with drink will cost you 12–20Ls in a restaurant, or well under 10Ls in a *kafejnīca*.

What to eat

Latvian staples that function superbly as **snacks** or quick **lunches** begin with *pīrāgi* or *pīradziņi* (parcels of dough with various stuffings, usually cabbage and/or bacon bits), and *pelmeņi* (meat-filled pockets of pastry akin to ravioli). Also common are savoury pancakes (*pankūkas*), usually filled

with cheese or ham – *kartupeļu pankūkas* are potato pancakes.

One typically Latvian dish that is frequently ordered with a round of beers but works perfectly well as a snack on its own is *pelēkie zirņi* (mushy yellow peas cooked in smoky-bacon fat). Other indigenous specialities include pork in aspic (*cūkas galerts*) and smoked sausage (*žāvēta desa*). Fish dishes that make good **starters** or snacks include sprats with onions (*šprotes ar sēpoliem*), herring (*siļķe*) and fried, smoked or salted eel (*zutis*). Popular **soups** (*zupas*) include *aukstā zupa* (cold borscht), and *solanka*, a meat, vegetable and gherkin broth of Russian origin.

Whatever you order it will come with several slices of bread (*maize*), including some of the delicious, dark rye bread (*rupjmaize*) for which the Baltic region is famed.

Main courses

A main course based on **meat** (*gaļa*) usually comes in the form either of a *fileja* (fillet) or *karbonāde* (chop, often a lightly battered schnitzel). *Cūkas fileja* is a pork fillet, *teļa* veal, *liellopu* beef and *cālīšu* chicken. Cuts of pork and other meats usually come edged with fatty rind – giving people only lean meat was traditionally considered rather rude.

Common varieties of **fish** (*zivs*) include *lasis* (salmon), *forele* (trout) and *zandarts* (pike-perch). Main courses are usually served with boiled potatoes or french fries, accompanied by a coleslaw-style salad or a pile of pickled vegetables. Popular garnishes include lashings of sour cream (*krējums*), or a ladleful of mushroom sauce (*sēņu merce*).

Desserts

One traditional Latvian **dessert** that crops up everywhere is *ķīselis*, oat porridge sweetened with seasonal fruit and forest berries. Otherwise, dessert menus concentrate on more familiar items such as ice cream (*saldējums*), gateau (*torte*) and all manner of cakes (*kūkas*). Pancakes (*pankūkas*) come with a variety of fillings, notably *biezpiens* or curd cheese, which is slightly sweetened to achieve a cheesecake-ish taste. Tasty little chocolate-coated cubes of *biezpiens* (Kārums is the best-known make) can be picked up from supermarket chiller cabinets.

Drinking

Traditionally Latvian drinking culture revolves around the **kafejnīca** or café, which serves both alcoholic and non-alcoholic drinks and closes early in the evening, and the **krogs** or tavern for serious evening boozing sessions. Nowadays, the range of internationally styled bars and pubs in Rīga and other big cities has massively broadened – as has the choice of drinks.

The main alcoholic drink in Latvia is *alus* (**beer**), which comes either as *gaišs alus* (the regular, lager-like brew) or as *tumšs alus* (a strong dark porter). The biggest mass-market breweries are Aldaris from Rīga, and Cēsu from Cēsis, although tastier regional brews abound: Bauskas, Užavas, Valmiermuižas and Tervetes are among those worth trying.

One Latvian spirit you should definitely try is Rīgas melnais balzāms, or **Rīga black balsam**, a bitter-tasting potion brewed according to a 250-year-old recipe that combines various roots, grasses and herbs. It's an acquired taste when drunk neat, but combines rather well with mixers. The local **sparkling wine**, Rīgas šampanietis, is both potent and cheap.

One traditional **non-alcoholic** beverage making something of a comeback is *kvass*, a drink made from malt extract, resembling cola in colour and just as popular locally. **Coffee** (*kafija*) and **tea** (*tēja*) are usually served black – if you want milk (*piens*), you'll have to ask. *Ar cukuru* means with sugar, *bez cukura* means without.

The media

For a country containing little over 1.5 million native speakers, Latvia can boast an astonishing array of **newspapers** and magazines. Best by far of the national dailies is *Diena* ("The Day"; ⓦ www.diena.lv), a well-designed and -written broadsheet. Latvia's Russian-speaking inhabitants have a handful of tabloid-style dailies of their own, and at least one influential business daily in the shape of *Biznes & Baltija*.

As for **magazines**, *Rīgas laiks* is a good-looking but intellectually obscure cultural monthly; it's more a fashion accessory than something you would ever dream of reading. More down-to-earth, but impeccably stylish with it, *Pastaiga* and *Ieva* are the most broad-based of the women's interest titles. If you're interested in architecture and interior design, *Latvijas Architektūra* is worth getting just for the photos, while *Studija* (ⓦ www .studija.lv) is a highly recommended fine arts magazine with English-language summaries.

When it comes to **television**, most people tune in to state-owned terrestrial channels LTV1 and LTV7 for serious news and culture, and to privately owned LNT and TV3 for game shows and imported dramas. English-language films are shown in the original language with Latvian subtitles on LTV7 only – all other Latvian channels show them dubbed. Many hotels and households are equipped with a multitude of cable channels, offering a broad range of English-, German- and Russian-language programming.

Festivals

In pagan times, Latvian **festivals** were closely related to the position of the sun, with solstices and equinoxes providing the main occasions for ritual celebration. Many of these practices still exist, although they dovetail so neatly with the Christian calendar that they're no longer recognizable as the pagan holidays they originally were.

The run-up to **Easter** (*Lieldiena*) is marked by hawkers selling bunches of catkins (*pūpoli*), which, as well as serving as a symbol of the coming spring, are also used to thrash your nearest and dearest on the morning of **Palm Sunday** (*Pūpolsvētdiena*). In days gone by, rural communities celebrated Easter itself by gathering beside the village swing – a huge wooden platform capable of bearing whole families – and taking it in turns to swoop up and down to the accompaniment of suitably rhythmic chants. A fertility ritual of ancient, pre-Christian origins, the practice is kept alive by folklore societies.

The one big ritual event that is still celebrated en masse is **Jāņi**, or **Midsummer's Eve**, when urban Latvians head for the countryside to spend the whole night drinking beer around a bonfire and singing ancient

Remembrance days

A number of dates in the Latvian calendar are set aside for remembering specific events or particular groups of people who made some contribution to the nation. Commemorative events are organized, and wreaths are laid at monuments.

March 16 Latvian Legion
March 25 Deportations of 1949
May 8 Victims of World War II
June 14 Victims of Communist Terror
July 4 Holocaust Day
November 11 Lāčplēšis Day (Marking the defence of Rīga from the Baltic Germans; 1919)

---

sun-worshipping songs known as *līgotne* – named after the swaying "*līgo, līgo*" refrain that almost all of them feature. Traditionally, *Jāņi* represented the last chance for a booze-up before the hard work of the harvest season began, and it's the hedonistic aspect of the occasion that has made it enduringly popular – and also explains why there are so many drunk drivers careering around Latvia's roads on midsummer morning.

At some stage in summer or autumn, each town and village has a **graveyard festival** (*kapu svētki*), when family plots are tidied up and picnics are eaten beside the graves – urban dwellers often go back to their home village to take part. Latvian **Christmas** (*Ziemassvētki*) is nowadays the commercialized occasion that it is in the rest of Europe, and few families still celebrate Christmas Eve by tucking into the traditional boiled pig's head and peas. A couple of practices connected to the winter solstice are still enacted by folklore societies, especially at the open-air museum in Rīga (see p.183), where you can see mummers masked as bears, horses, cranes, goats or the grim reaper going from house to house to drive away evil, and a yule log (*bļuks*), symbolizing the misfortunes of the previous year, is dragged around by celebrants before being ritually burned. **New Year** (*Jaungads*) is marked by the familiar round of boozing, partying and firework displays.

For a list of **cultural festivals** see the events calendar on p.34.

Entertainment

Although most Latvian cities can muster a theatre, a cinema and the odd music venue, the bulk of the country's entertainment options are concentrated in Rīga, a culture-saturated metropolis with something to satisfy most tastes. Details of where to catch opera, ballet, orchestral music and theatre in the capital can be found on p.187.

Choral and classical music

Choral singing has played a central role in Latvian culture since 1868, when 150 singers attended the first-ever national song festival in Valka. The nurturing of an indigenous folk-song tradition was seen as an important way of opposing the domination of German-language culture and it helped to keep Latvian traditions alive during the Soviet period. Nowadays, there's hardly a village, factory or government department without a choir, most of them performing material deeply rooted in Latvia's rich folk tradition (for more on folk music, see p.380). The nation's choirs get together every five years to participate in the **All-Latvian Song and Dance Festival**, when the sound of thousands of massed voices issuing forth from the open-air song bowl in Rīga's Mežaparks can be a truly visceral experience. If you can't make it to the festival (next due in July 2013), there are plenty of opportunities to hear top-quality **choirs** in Rīga. Prominent among these are the all-female Dzintars, and the mixed choir, Ave Sol, both of whom perform startlingly modern arrangements of archaic Latvian songs, as well as specially commissioned contemporary compositions.

One outstanding modern composer known for his choral as well as orchestral works is **Pēteris Vasks** (b.1946), whose journeys into contemplative, deeply spiritual territory have earned him comparisons with the likes of Gorecki, Tavener and Pärt. His works are regularly performed in Rīga, and the city's record shops are full of his CDs. One of the best-known interpreters of Vasks's work is the Rīga-born violin virtuoso **Gidon Kremer** (b.1947), whose multinational chamber ensemble **Kremerata Baltica** has garnered an international reputation for its

155

performances of contemporary classical music. Tickets for performances sell out fast in Rīga – again, there are plenty of CDs in the shops if you miss out.

Clubbing and pop music

Rīga's **club scene** offers a bit of everything, from cavernous mega-clubs pumping out frenetic techno to thousands, to more intimate alternative spaces where you can hear anything from hip-hop and reggae to post-industrial noise. A lot of the latter places offer live music, so the **underground** gig scene is slightly more vibrant here than in Tallinn or Vilnius. There's also a range of mid-sized venues hosting performances by Latvia's homegrown pop-rock acts.

Ever since the 1960s, Latvia has developed a strain of melodic, lyrical **pop** which, going against the grain of both Soviet showbiz culture and Western rock, has become an important element in national identity. Central to its evolution has been **Imants Kalniņš**, a classically trained composer (his symphony no. 4 is widely held to be on a par with most contemporary classical production), who has written songs for just about every Latvian pop performer of consequence from the late 1960s onwards. His 1967 song *Dziesma par četriem baltiem krekliem* ("Song About Four White Shirts") – recorded by the group Menuets for the cult film *Elpojiet Dziļi* ("Breathe Deeply") – was banned because the shirts in question were taken as a metaphor for Latvian dignity in the face of Soviet oppression, and Kalniņš has been a symbol of national integrity ever since. His wide-ranging oeuvre is difficult to pin down, but if you crossed Paul McCartney with Leonard Cohen and Burt Bacharach, something resembling Kalniņš would probably come out the other end. Your best bet is to get hold of best-of compilation *Dziesmu izlase* and make up your own mind.

Few subsequent songwriters have enjoyed similar stature, save perhaps for **Ainars Mielavs**, originally lead singer with rousing folk-pop practitioners Jauns Mēness – their early 1990s albums represent the high point of Latvian rock. Mielavs is now a solo performer of adult-oriented, mellow songs and also heads leading folk label Upe records. Latvian pop's main international standard bearers are Brainstorm, one of the few groups to appear in the Eurovision Song Contest (they came third in 2000) and survive with their career unscathed. They have recorded numerous albums of bright, infectious, indie-influenced melodies, some of which come in both Latvian and English versions, and they have a sizeable fan base in central Europe and Scandinavia.

No discussion of Latvian music would be complete without a mention of composer, impresario and all-round national institution **Raimonds Pauls**. His album *Tik Dzintars Vien* – recorded in 1970 but recalling European popular songs of the 1950s – was a landmark in Latvian easy-listening. He went on to become a big star in the Soviet Union, penning albums for variety-show warblers like (Latvian) Laima Vaikule and (Russian) Alla Pugacheva. You might want to give his latter-day work a wide berth, though, ranging as it does from Eurovision-style pop-pap to cocktail-bar piano-tinkling of the queasiest kind.

Cinema

Latvian **cinemas** show feature films in the original language – with subtitles in both Latvian and Russian blotting out the bottom third of the screen. During the Soviet period, Rīga's film studio turned out an average of eight features a year, but with the collapse of state funding after 1990 the tally has shrunk to one or two low-budget affairs. Ask locals to name their favourite Latvian film of all time and they'd probably plump for 1973's "Blow, Wind!" (*Pūt Vējiņi!*), a lavishly costumed tale of love and death set in pre-Christian Latvia, and featuring a rousing score by Imants Kalniņš – the soundtrack CD is worth having on its own.

Internationally, Latvia is more famous for its documentaries than its feature films. This is almost entirely due to the career of **Juris Podnieks**, whose 1986 work *Is It Easy To Be Young?* – an unflinching investigation into the lives of directionless, delinquent youth in Rīga – eloquently stripped bare the inner psychoses of a disintegrating society and attracted massive audiences throughout the Soviet Union as a result. He subsequently devoted his efforts to documenting the death throes of Soviet communism – his TV series *Hello, Can You Hear Us?* (1989) was a disturbing portrait of a multinational empire on the skids, while *Homeland* (1992) dealt movingly with the drive to independence in the Baltic States. Production of the latter was marred by the deaths of two of Podnieks's cameramen – shot while filming the Soviet attack on the Latvian Interior Ministry in January 1991 (see p.176). Podnieks himself died in a freak scuba-diving accident in 1992.

A major showcase for new Latvian films of all kinds is the **Lielais Kristaps festival** (Ⓦ lielais-kristaps.filmas.lv), held every odd-numbered year.

Sport

Of all international team games it's **ice hockey** that generates most enthusiasm in Latvia. The sport's big breakthrough in the public consciousness came during the world championships of 2000, when an unfancied Latvian team defeated title-favourites Russia in the group stages, sending thousands of Latvians out onto the streets of Rīga in celebration. The Latvians have remained in or around the world's top ten ever since, but are yet to break through to the medal-winning stages of a major competition. League games in Latvia itself are lacklustre affairs (the best Latvian players ply their trade in North America), and the best way to enjoy the sport is to catch a major international encounter on the big screen in a crowded pub. The distinctive maroon Latvian hockey jerseys make desirable souvenirs, and can be bought from some of the Rīga souvenir shops listed on p.189. Latvia also has a couple of decent **bobsleigh** crews, and the national track at Sigulda is used for international world cup meetings.

Travel essentials

Internet

Wi-fi access is the rule in hotels and increasingly in cafés too. Often it's free, although you may have to buy a Lattelekom pre-paid card at the café in question. The number of

internet cafés (*interneta kafejnīca*) has fallen as a result of wi-fi availability, although you can still find them in Rīga and major cities. Internet access is also available in public libraries, although you may have to wait to use a terminal. Thirty minutes of surfing time rarely costs more than 1Ls.

Left luggage

Most bus stations have a left-luggage counter (*Bagāžas novietne* or *Rokas bagāžas glabātava*), charging around 0.50–1Ls daily per item, depending on size.

Mail

The Latvian postal service (*Latvijas pasts*) is reasonably reliable, even if post offices themselves tend to be gloomy and disorganized places, with a confusing array of counters. Opening times are generally Mon–Fri 8am–7/8pm, Sat 8am–4pm. City-centre post offices may also be open Sat 8am–6pm and Sun 8am–4pm. Cards (0.50Ls) and letters (0.70Ls) to Europe take about seven days; cards (0.60Ls) and letters (0.80Ls) to North America or Australasia take fourteen days. Most post offices have a fax (*fakss*) counter where you can send documents for a few santimi.

Money

The Latvian capital, Rīga, has the highest cost of living of any city in the Baltics, and your daily spend here will be greater than in Vilnius or Tallinn. Things are different outside Rīga, where you can live well on very little. For an idea of accommodation, food and transport costs, see the relevant sections on p.152, p.153 and p.149.

Latvia's unit of currency is the lats (plural lati), abbreviated to Ls and divided into 100 santimi. Coins come in denominations of 0.01, 0.02, 0.05, 0.10, 0.20, 0.50, 1 and 2Ls, and notes in 5, 10, 20, 50, 100 and 500Ls.

Major banks (*banka*) like Hansabanka, Latvijas Krājbanka and Unibanka will change money and cash travellers' cheques (Thomas Cook and American Express preferred), and some give advances on major credit cards. Opening times are usually Mon–Fri 9/10am–5/6pm, with some banks in big cities opening 10am–3pm on Saturday. Outside these hours you can change cash in currency exchange offices (*valūtas* maiņa), many of which are little more than kiosks found in unlikely locations like food shops or gambling arcades. These are often open until around 10pm, and one or two in Rīga are open 24 hours. You'll find ATM cash machines (automāts) liberally dotted around most town centres. Credit cards can be used in a growing number of bars, restaurants and shops in Rīga and other cities, as well as in most petrol stations, but are not widely accepted in small towns and villages.

Opening hours

Shops are usually open Mon–Fri 10am–7/8pm, Sat 10am–4/5pm, though some close for an hour around lunchtime. Supermarkets and food shops often stay open until 10pm and also open on Sunday.

Museums and galleries are usually open Tues–Sun or Wed–Sun 10am–5pm, with the addition of the odd extra hour or two in summer. Latvia's Lutheran churches can be very hard to get into outside Sunday service times, unless – like those in central Rīga for example – they're of particular cultural and historic importance, in which case they'll be open from 9am to 5pm daily. Orthodox churches are far more accessible, and there's usually an attendant selling candles and icon-bearing postcards during the day.

Public holidays

All banks and offices, as well as most shops, are closed on the following public holidays. Big supermarkets and food stores in Rīga may well stay open, apart from on January 1, when there is a genuine national shutdown.

January 1 New Year's Day

March/April (variable) Good Friday Easter Sunday, Easter Monday

May 1 Labour Day

May 4 Declaration of Independence (1990)

May (second Sunday) Mothers' Day

June 23–24 Midsummer celebrations

November 18 Declaration of Independence (1918)

December 24–26 Christmas

December 31 New Year's Eve

For post office and bank opening hours, see "Mail" and "Money" (p.157) respectively.

Phones

The Latvian telephone system is generally easy to use: there are no separate area codes. Direct international calls are possible from all phones – dial 00 followed by the country code, area code and number. Town centres are well supplied with public telephone boxes, operated using credit cards or pre-paid cards (telekarte or zvanu karte). These come in 2, 5 and 10Ls denominations and can be bought at the post office or from newspaper kiosks. A 2Ls card should just about stretch to a three-minute call to Europe, the US or Australasia.

For general information on using mobile phones in the Baltic States, see p.42. If you have a GSM mobile phone it's possible to avoid heavy call costs by buying a pre-paid SIM card from one of the local operators such as Bite, LMT or Tele2. This will provide you with a Latvian telephone number and allow you to make local calls at the local rate. In each case it costs 5–6Ls for the SIM card and your first few minutes of airtime, after which you can buy top-ups in increments of 2, 5, 10Ls and above. Starter packs and top-up cards can be bought from newspaper kiosks and supermarket checkouts throughout the country.

Smoking

Smoking is banned from all public places, including hotels, restaurants, cafés and the majority of bars. Smoking on café or restaurant terraces in summer may also be restricted, although there are usually a few outdoor tables reserved for smokers. Some drinking and nightlife venues provide a smoking zone in a separate room, although this is the exception.

Tipping

Tipping is only expected in restaurants or in the smarter cafés with waited tables, in which case you add ten percent to the bill or round it up to the nearest convenient figure.

Toilets

Public toilets can be found at most bus stations. Ladies are dāmas; gents are kungi.

2.1

Rīga and around

With just over 709,000 inhabitants, almost one third of the country's population, **RĪGA** is the biggest city in the Baltics, offering a degree of cosmopolitan bustle, sophistication and sheer urban chaos that neither Tallinn nor Vilnius can really compete with. It's also one of the best-looking Baltic cities, with medieval red-brick churches and gabled merchants' houses rising above the alleyways of the Old Town, and some remarkable examples of Art Nouveau in the surrounding nineteenth-century streets.

Ever since its thirteenth-century foundation, Rīga has been a melting pot of different ethnic groups. Today, half of the inhabitants are Latvian, while the other half are either Russian or Russian-speaking, giving the city a strangely schizophrenic character. The two communities get on peaceably enough, but tend to lead separate lives, reading their own newspapers and watching their own TV stations, and often displaying a staggering indifference to each other's language and culture.

Boasting historic buildings on almost every corner and a strong hand of set-piece museums, **downtown Rīga** can easily fill two or three days of your time – longer if you're drawn to the offbeat attractions of the city's **suburbs**, such as the Open-air Ethnographic Museum. Also within easy reach are the beguiling beach resort of **Jūrmala**, 20km west, and the Holocaust memorial sites at **Rumbula** and **Salaspils**, just outside the city to the southeast. You could even use Rīga as a base for exploring sizeable chunks of north and central Latvia.

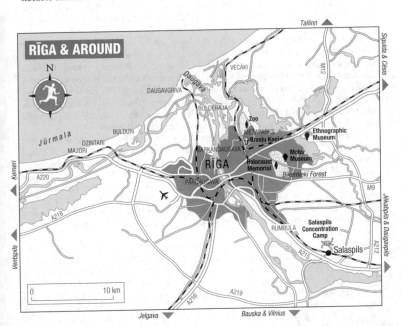

Rīga was founded by **Albert von Buxhoeveden**, a priest from Bremen who arrived in 1201 with twenty shiploads of crusaders to convert the Baltic tribes to Christianity. Taking over a site previously occupied by Liv fishermen, Albert lost no time in building a fortified settlement, and civilians from northern Europe flocked to Rīga to take advantage of new opportunities for trade. As the headquarters of the crusading effort in the Baltics, Rīga was home to three often quarrelsome groups – the church, the knights of the Livonian Order and the increasingly assertive citizenry. With the last refusing to put up with the dictates of the other two, Rīga became a self-governing municipality owing symbolic fealty to the Order, whose Grand Master continued to base himself in Rīga's castle. Eager to exploit this new freedom of manoeuvre, the city joined the **Hanseatic League**, a loose alliance of north German trading cities, in 1282. Civic life was to remain in the hands of a German-speaking mercantile elite for the next six hundred years.

Rīga grew rich on the trade of timber, furs and flax, which were floated down the Daugava River on enormous rafts before being loaded onto ships and exported west. Perennially suspicious of the grasping Baltic clergy, the citizenry provided fertile ground for the spread of **Protestantism** in the early sixteenth century, and Rīga became a bastion of the new creed. The city's remaining monks were chased out in 1524, and most of the churches were vandalized by Protestant mobs at around the same time – little medieval religious art survives today.

Squeezed between the expanding states of Russia, Sweden and Poland, the Livonian Order collapsed in 1562 and Rīga briefly became an independent city-state before being absorbed into the **Polish-Lithuanian Commonwealth** by King Stefan Bathory in 1582. The Poles kicked out by the **Swedes** in 1621 and Rīga became the main base for Swedish military campaigns in the Baltics, filling the coffers of the city's merchants. The Swedes met their nemesis, however, in the shape of **Peter the Great of Russia**, who captured Rīga in 1709 after a nine-month siege. Even under the Russians, Rīga remained culturally a German city, although the seventeenth century saw an influx of **Latvian-speaking** peasants from the countryside. The German and Latvian populations were largely segregated, and knowledge of German remained the only route to social advancement. It wasn't until the 1780s that the right of Latvians to own property in the city was recognized.

During the nineteenth century, Rīga developed into a major industrial centre, the population growing to half a million by the century's close. Significant numbers of Russians were brought to Rīga to work in the factories, and Russian was made the main language in schools. Although denied any real political influence, the burgeoning Latvian population was determined to make its presence felt, with events like the first all-Latvian song festival (held in June 1873) signalling their increasing cultural self-confidence. On the eve of World War I the Latvians were the biggest ethnic group in the city – the Germans had in the meantime been pushed into third place behind the Russians.

Latvia spent much of World War I as a front-line city and the end of the war ushered in a period of extreme chaos. Latvian independence was proclaimed in the National Theatre on November 18, but with no army at their disposal, the new government surrendered the city to the **Bolsheviks** on January 3, 1919. Home-grown Latvian revolutionary Pēteris Stučka presided over four months of communist terror, before being chased out by a combined force of Latvians, White Russians and Germans. This marriage of convenience didn't last long, however, and the White Russians and Germans were finally seen off by the Latvians in November, 1919, helped by a British naval bombardment.

Now the capital of an independent Latvia, Rīga entered the new era massively changed. Industry was in ruins, and the population had fallen by half since 1914. The city recovered quickly, however, and for much of the 1920s and 1930s enjoyed something of a belle époque. The city's cosmopolitan mix was boosted by an influx of anti-Bolshevik refugees from Russia, with their taste for old-world etiquette and lavish entertaining.

World War II – during which Rīga was occupied by the Soviets, then by the Germans – once again left the city impoverished, a situation that didn't radically improve when the Soviets returned in October 1944. The communists dedicated themselves to the development of heavy industry in Rīga and radically changed the city's ethnic profile by importing a (largely Russian-speaking) workforce from all over the Soviet Union. By the late 1980s the influx of Russian immigrants had reduced the Latvians to a minority in their own capital. Most of Rīga's non-Latvians were unenthusiastic about leaving the Soviet Union when the independence drive took off in the late 1980s, but few supported the use of OMON troops and tanks to seize control of key buildings in January 1991, an action which cost five innocent lives and destroyed any shred of credibility communist rule still had.

By the turn of the millennium Rīga had become something of a boom town, with gleaming office blocks sprouting up on vacant lots and real estate prices going through the roof. The financial crisis of 2008 slowed this process down considerably, and revealed just how little of Rīga's new wealth had trickled down to the majority of its citizens.

Arrival

Rīga's **airport** (Rīgas lidosta) is 12km southwest of the Old Town. Head straight out of the arrivals hall and cross the car park to find the bus stop, from where bus #22 (2–3/hr; 0.70Ls; pay the driver) runs to Abrenes iela on the southeastern fringes of the centre, passing the bus and train stations on the way. A taxi to the centre will cost around 9–11Ls.

Rīga's main **train station** (Centrālā stacija) and **bus station** (Autoosta) are within 200m of each other, five minutes' walk south of the Old Town. Taxi drivers outside both stations aren't keen on ferrying passengers short distances, and will demand a minimum of 5–6Ls to take you anywhere in the city centre.

Moving on from Rīga

Rīga is a major transport hub, with **bus** routes fanning out across the Baltic region and beyond. There are several daily buses to Vilnius and Tallinn and plenty of direct services to Germany, France, the Netherlands and Great Britain. There are also overnight **trains** to Russia, the Ukraine and Belarus, as well as **car ferries** to Scandinavia and Germany.

The **bus station** (ⓦ www.autoosta.lv) is relatively user-friendly, with easy-to-read departure listings and an English-speaking information office in the main ticket hall. Domestic tickets are sold from the counters opposite the main entrance; international services are handled by a cluster of offices just around the corner on the right. The main **agents** for international tickets are Eurolines Lux Express (ⓣ 6778 1350, ⓦ www .luxexpress.eu), Ecolines (ⓣ 6721 4512, ⓦ www.ecolines.net) and Nordeka (ⓣ 6746 4620, ⓦ www.nordeka.lv); all have outlets at the station.

With all its cafés and bakeries, Rīga's **central station** feels more like a vast shopping mall than somewhere to get a train. There are daily or thrice-weekly services to Moscow, St Petersburg, Minsk, Vitebsk, L'viv and beyond – all of which require at least one night on the train. Buy **tickets** for international services at the "Starptautiskie vilcieni" counters; or for journeys within Latvia from windows marked "Iekšzemes vilcienu biļešu kases".

The **ferry terminal** at Eksporta iela 3A (tram #7 from the bus station or National Opera to Ausekla iela) has ticket counters, an exchange office and a duty-free shop – but little else. The daily ferry **to Stockholm** is operated by Tallink, which has a ticket office at the terminal (ⓣ 6709 9700, ⓦ www.tallink.lv). Ave Line, Zivju 1 (ⓣ 2944 4999, ⓦ www.aveline.lt), sells tickets for the twice-weekly ferry **to Lübeck**.

Rīga's **airport** (ⓣ 1187, from abroad +371 2931 1187, ⓦ www.riga-airport.com) is 12km southwest of the centre, at the end of bus route #22.

Of **travel agents**, Latvia Tours, Kaļķu 8 (ⓣ 6708 5030, ⓦ www.latviatours.lv), and Kaleva, Barona 7/9 (ⓣ 6781 2624, ⓦ www.viariga.lv), are good for international airline and ferry tickets, car rental and excursions within Latvia.

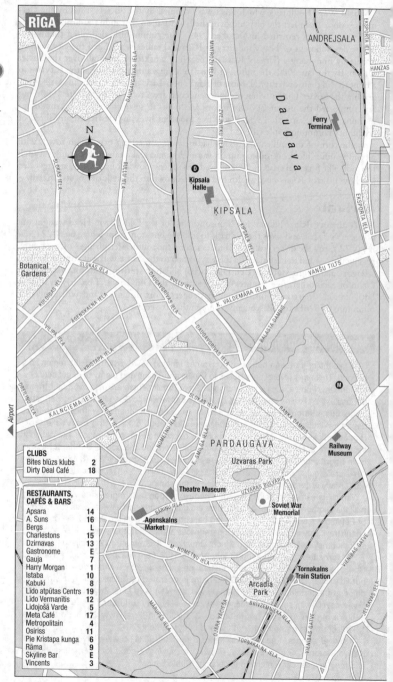

ANDREJSALA

HANZAS

D a u g a v a

Ferry Terminal

D Kipsala Halle

KIPSALA

VANŠU TILTS

Botanical Gardens

PARDAUGAVA

Uzvaras Park

Railway Museum

Theatre Museum

CLUBS

Bites blūzs klubs	2
Dirty Deal Café	18

Soviet War Memorial

Agenskalns Market

RESTAURANTS, CAFÉS & BARS

Apsara	14
A. Suns	16
Bergs	L
Charlestons	15
Dzirnavas	13
Gastronome	E
Gauja	7
Harry Morgan	1
Istaba	10
Kabuki	8
Lido atpūtas Centrs	19
Lido Vermanïtis	12
Lidojošā Varde	5
Meta Café	17
Metropolitain	4
Osiriss	11
Pie Kristapa kunga	6
Rāma	9
Skyline Bar	E
Vincents	3

Tornakalns Train Station

Arcadia Park

▲ Airport

Hospital

Skonto Stadium

Daile Theatre

Art Nouveau Museum & Rozentāls Museum

A

IELA

RODNIECIBAS IELA

PILKVEŽA BRIEZA IELA

SKANSTES IELA

SPORTA IELA

HANZAS IELA

K. VALDEMARA IELA

A. BRIĀNA IELA

BRIVIBAS IELA

BRUNINIEKU IELA

STABU IELA

TALLINAS IELA

TALLINAS IELA

MIERA IELA

TERBATAS IELA

ALBERTA IELA

DZIRNAVU IELA

ELIZABETES IELA

See "Riga Old Town" map for details

St Gertrude's Church

Corner House

Jewish Museum

A. Kenins Highschool

Cathedral of the Nativity

Suta & Belcova Museum

CENTRS

A. Čaks Museum

Kronvalds Park

Esplanāde

City Park

KRONVALDA BULVARIS

K. VALDEMARA IELA

BASTEJA BULVARIS

ELIZABETES IELA

BRIVIBAS IELA

GERTRUDES IELA

K. BARONA IELA

A. ČAKA IELA

MATĪSA IELA

BRUNINIEKU IELA

STABU IELA

AVOTU IELA

Vērmane's Garden

K. Barons Museum

Patricia Agency

DZIRNAVU IELA

TERBATAS IELA

E. BIRNICKA UPĪŠA IELA

VECRĪGA

Natural History Museum

Train Station

MARIJAS SATEKLES IELA

11 NOVEMBRA

AKMENS TILTS

KRASTMALA

13 JANVARA IELA

KRASTA IELA

Bus Station

Central Market

Academy of Sciences

Spikeri

Church of the Annunciation

Former Synagogue

Jesus Church

MOSCOW SUBURB

N

MASKAVAS IELA

TURGENEVA IELA

GOGOL IELA

LACPLESA IELA

SADOVNIKOVA IELA

LAZDONAS KALNA IELA

MASKAVAS IELA

MASKAVAS IELA

Daugava

MIKUSALAS IELA

BURU IELA

BIEKENSALAS IELA

SALU TILTS

KRASTA IELA

Grebenshchikov Church

K. ULMANA GATVE

ACCOMMODATION	
Alberts Hotel	B
B&B Riga	H
Bergs	L
Dodo	N
Europa Royale	K
Funky Hostel	J
House Hostel	I
Jakob Lenz	A
KB	G
Krišjānis & Ģertrūde	F
Laine	C
Radisson Blu Daugava	M
Radisson Blu Latvija	E
Riga City Camping	D

0   500 m

The **ferry terminal** (Jūras pasažieru stacija) is 1500m north of the Old Town at the end of Eksporta iela. Trams #5, #7 or #9 run from the stop 100m east of the terminal on Ausekļa iela to the edge of the Old Town (two stops; tickets 0.70Ls from the driver or 0.50Ls if bought from a kiosk).

Information

The main **tourist office** is on the Old Town's main square, Rātslaukums (Mon–Sat 10am–6pm; ☎6703 7900, ⓦwww.rigatourism.com). In addition, there are information booths at the bus station (Tues–Sat 9am–6pm; ☎6722 0555) and the train station (Tues–Sat 10am–6pm; ☎6723 3815). All three are a mine of information, and can provide accommodation lists, although they don't book hotels on your behalf. They also sell the **Rīga Card** (10Ls for 24hr, 14Ls for 48hr, 18Ls for 72hr; ⓦwww .rigacard.lv), which allows unlimited use of public transport, entry to the major museums, a guided tour of the city and discounts in some restaurants – worth it if you intend to do a fair amount of sightseeing. *Rīga in Your Pocket* (from news kiosks or their office at Laipu 8; 2Ls; ⓦwww.inyourpocket.com) is the most reliable source of well-written and up-to-date information on eating, drinking and shopping.

City transport

The centre of Rīga is easily walkable and outlying attractions are served by **bus**, **tram** or **trolleybus** (all around 5am until 11pm), with a few night buses between the city centre and key suburbs. Single-journey **tickets** cost 0.50Ls if bought from newspaper kiosks, or 0.70Ls from the driver. Tickets for one form of transport are not valid on any other; validate them by swiping them across the electronic reader on entering the vehicle.

Taxis are generally cheap: the basic fare is around 0.50Ls plus an additional charge of 0.50Ls/km during the day and 0.60Ls between 10pm and 6am. A few drivers may take advantage of foreigners by switching the meter off and demanding a set price. You'll find taxi ranks at all the main entry points to the Old Town, although it's usually cheaper to phone in advance; see p.190 for recommended firms.

Another good way to see Rīga is via the **canal** that runs just east of the Old Town through the Kronvalda and Bastejkalns parks. The Canal Motorboat Company (ⓦwww.kmk.lv) offers a circuit around the canal and along the connecting stretch of the Daugava river; you can hop on and off at any of the six stops en route (every 30min 9am–11pm; single-circuit 5Ls, multi-circuit day ticket 10Ls).

Of the many **bike rental** outlets BalticBike (1Ls/hr, 8Ls/24hr; ⓦwww.balticbike.lv) is the most versatile, with six stands throughout the centre and one in Jūrmala (near Majori train station). You pay by phoning and quoting your card details, and can return the bike to any of the stands.

Accommodation

Rīga has undergone a hotel-building boom in the years since independence, and there are lots of places to stay, from upper-bracket establishments to backpacker-friendly hostels. Little more than a field with factory views, *Riga City Camping*, behind the Ķipsala exhibition hall at Ķipsalas 8 (☎6706 5000, ⓦwww.rigacamping.lv) is the most conveniently located **campsite**, just twenty minutes' walk from the Old Town. The seaside site of *Nemo* in Vaivari, Jūrmāla (see p.190) is a forty-minute drive or train ride from central Rīga.

Hostels

Unless otherwise stated, the following hostels are on the "Rīga Old Town" map on p.167.

Franks 11 Novembra krastmala 29 ☎2599 0612 or 6722 0040, ⓦwww.franks.lv. Decked out in bright but tolerable orange, *Franks* is a big 180-bed hostel on the second floor of a riverside block, with multi-bunk dorms and a handful of doubles. The main advantages are the roomy kitchen/diner and a bar/common-room with fantastic views of the Daugava bridges. Coin-operated laundry, six computer terminals, and free wi-fi in the reception area. Doubles ❶, dorm beds from 8Ls.

Funky Baroṇa 25 ☎ 2910 5939, Ⓦ www .funkyhostel.com; see the "Rīga" map on p.162. Homely fifth-floor apartment offering a pair of 6-bed dorms, a couple of triples and one private double. The pleasant sitting room comes with big-screen TV and a library of DVDs. Basic breakfast included in the price. They also offer two-person apartments nearby. Doubles ❷, dorm beds 8Ls.

House Baroṇa 44 ☎ 2649 1235, Ⓦ www.riga-hostel .com; see the "Rīga" map on p.162. Friendly place offering the kind of comfy sitting room and well-equipped kitchen where you'll feel at home. Instead of big dorms they offer quads and private doubles, giving the place an intimate feel, and the bathroom boasts a claw-foot tub. Doubles ❷, dorm beds 9Ls.

Naughty Squirrel Kalēju 50 ☎ 6722 0073, Ⓦ www.thenaughtysquirrel.com. Two floors of high-ceilinged pine-bunk dorms and a few quads and doubles, with backpacker-friendly staff, a home-from-home living room, and free coffee and tea in a small kitchen area. Wi-fi in the reception area. Rooms ❷, dorms from 8Ls.

Old Town Hostel Valṇu 43 ☎ 6722 3406, Ⓦ www .rigaoldtownhostel.lv. Airy, bright, clean dorms in an ideal location, with a lively ground-floor bar, a kitchen and a sauna in the basement. Doubles ❷, dorms from 8Ls.

Rīga Hostel Marstaḷu 12 ☎ 2233 7884 or 6722 4520, Ⓦ www.rigahostel.com.lv. Convenient, central hostel on the upper floors of a nineteenth-century apartment block. Bunks in 10- to 15-person dorms, some attractive doubles and quads in the attic, and basic breakfast in the kitchen/common room. Wi-fi. Doubles ❷, dorms from 8Ls.

Hotels

There are many hotels in and around the Old Town, with a glut of mid-price establishments offering neat, bland rooms. Places of charm and character do exist, however – typically in the more expensive categories. You'll be hard-pushed to find a double room in the Old Town for less than 50Ls, though there are cheaper deals in the Centre district, and a growing choice of decent accommodation in the suburbs. Some hotels cut their prices in winter (typically Oct–March), while others offer weekend **discounts** – always ask. **Breakfast** is included in the rates for the places below unless otherwise stated.

The Old Town and around

Ainavas Peldu 23 ☎ 6781 4316, Ⓦ www.ainavas .lv. A small, intimate and characterful hotel in a restored medieval house, offering attractive en-suite rooms, each decorated in different pastel colours – hence the place's name, which means "Landscapes". ❼

Centra Audēju 1 ☎ 6722 6441, Ⓦ hotelcentra.lv. Spacious, smart rooms, decorated in modern, minimalist style, with shower and TV, each offering good views of the Audēju iela street scene below. Good value for the location. ❼

Grand Palace Pils 12 ☎ 6704 4000, Ⓦ www .grandpalaceriga.com. A luxury hotel in a wonderful old building, stuffed full of antique-effect furniture, just off Doma laukums. Rooms from 160Ls. ❽

Gutenbergs Doma laukums 1 ☎ 6781 4090, Ⓦ www.gutenbergs.eu. Affordable and superbly situated, this comfy, mid-sized place fills fast. Faux-rustic rooms in one wing, more chintzy affairs in the other. The restaurant's summer terrace, with views of the Old Town's roofscape, is a major plus. ❼

Konventa Sēta Kalēju iela 9/11 ☎ 6708 7507, Ⓦ www.konventa.lv. A charming, 140-room hotel in the heart of the Old Town, with modern en-suites surrounding the beautifully restored courtyard of a former convent. Some apartment-style doubles with kitchenettes. ❻

Monte Kristo Kalēju 56 ☎ 6735 9100, Ⓦ www .hotelmontekristo.lv. This reliable, mid-sized three-star on the fringes of the Old Town offers en-suites – and couldn't be better placed for the bus and train stations. ❺

Neiburgs Jauniela 25 ☎ 6711 5522, Ⓦ www .neiburgs.com. A lovely blend of cool modern design and original Art Nouveau fittings, this swanky apart-ment hotel offers mostly two-person studios, plus four-person apartments and split-level suites. ❻

Old City Hotel Teātra 10 ☎ 6735 6060, Ⓦ oldcityhotel.lv. Sensitively renovated medieval house on a cobbled Old Town street, its thirteen rooms mixing folksy furnishings with snazzy modern bathrooms. Buffet breakfast is served in the stone-lined cellar. ❻

Radi un Draugi Mārstaḷu iela 1/3 ☎ 6782 0200, Ⓦ www.draugi.lv. Neat, cosy en-suites, a little bland but in an excellent location. It's superb value, so reservations are essential. ❺

Outside the Old Town

Albert Hotel Dzirnavu 33 ☎ 6733 1717, Ⓦ www .alberthotel.lv. Modern ten-storey slab popular with

tourist groups and conferences, and close to the Art Nouveau buildings of Alberta iela. Rooms have an amusing Albert Einstein theme. The top-floor lounge bar offers excellent views of the city. ❻
B&B Riga Gertrudes 43 ☎6727 8505, ⓦwww .bb-riga.lv. Eighteen en-suites in a nineteenth-century apartment block, decorated in different styles – from funky split-level studio apartments to cosy doubles with wooden floors. Breakfast is in the café across the road. ❹–❺
Bergs Elizabetes 83/85 ☎6777 0900, ⓦwww .hotelbergs.lv. Rooms in this unabashedly contemporary hotel are either studio apartments or multi-room suites, each with matt-black floorboards, swish bathroom, kitchenette and an arty mix of ethnic fabrics and designer fittings. Free use of the sauna and gym, and wi-fi throughout. Studios from 130Ls, apartments from 180Ls. ❻
Dodo Jesikas 1 ☎6724 0220, ⓦwww.dodohotel .com. Modern budget hotel on the cobbled streets of the Moscow Suburb, 2km east of the Old Town. En-suite rooms are small but neat, and there are four-person family rooms with bunks for the kids. *Dodo* is over-popular with stag groups at weekends, but perfectly peaceful at other times. Discounts for internet bookings. Trams #3, #7 and #9 from Maskavas iela. ❹
Europa Royale Barona 12 ☎6707 9444, ⓦwww .europaroyale.com. Classy accommodation in an opulent nineteenth-century mansion. Rooms are spacious and regally furnished, providing you steer clear of the modern annexe tacked onto the back, where low ceilings and small windows conspire to spoil the four-star ambience. Breakfast is served in the neo-Baroque restaurant on the first floor. ❼

Jakob Lenz Lenču 2 ☎6733 3343, ⓦwww .guesthouselenz.lv. B&B with small but neat doubles occupying several floors of an apartment block steps away from the Art Nouveau district and within walking distance of the Old Town. ❸
KB Barona 37 ☎6731 2323, ⓦwww.kbhotel.lv. This eight-room B&B on the fifth floor of an apartment block is reached via a wonderfully ornate stairwell. Rooms – on the plain side – are mostly en suite, although a couple share facilities. There's a pleasant breakfast room, and guests are free to use the kitchen. ❹
Krišjānis & Gertrūde Barona 39/1 ☎6750 6604, ⓦwww.kg.lv. Charming B&B with a handful of chinzy en-suites, a cosy breakfast room, free internet and friendly hosts. ❺
Laine Skolas iela 11 ☎6728 8816, ⓦwww.laine.lv. Entered via the courtyard of an anonymous-looking apartment block, the mid-sized *Laine* is much more welcoming than its surroundings suggest, with simple, spacious rooms (many with bathtubs), plants in the corridors and obliging staff. Just 10min walk northeast of the Old Town. ❺
Radisson Blu Daugava Kuģu 24 ☎6706 1111, ⓦwww.radissonblu.com. Comfortable 350-room monster with good-quality business-class rooms and great views of the Old Town skyline. There's a covered pool, and a couple of rooms equipped for wheelchair-users. ❼
Radisson Blu Latvija Elizabetes 55 ☎6777 2222, ⓦwww.radissonblu.com. A 27-floor block, once part of the Soviet state-run Intourist organization, now refurbished with neat en-suites and great views from the upper floors. Some rooms equipped for wheelchair-user. ❼

The City

The majority of Rīga's historical buildings are in the **Old Town** (Vecrīga), a compact web of narrow, cobbled streets, medieval merchant houses and brick-built churches squatting on the eastern bank of the broad **River Daugava**. To the east, the spacious belt of **parkland**, with its sedate nineteenth-century buildings sheltering beneath beech, elm and lime trees, couldn't be more different. Beyond here, streets radiate outwards through the so-called **Centre** (Centrs), the nineteenth- and early twentieth-century extension of the city and its commercial and administrative heart – a gritty, grey area redeemed by the innumerable gems of Art Nouveau architecture lining its streets. Further afield, Rīga's suburban sprawl harbours the engaging Open-air Ethnographic Museum and the fascinating Motor Museum, while sizeable stretches of park in **Pārdaugava** and **Mežaparks**, and woodland around **Biķernieki**, present opportunities for strolling. Southeast of the city lie the sombre Holocaust memorial sites at **Rumbula** and **Salaspils**.

The Old Town

World War II bombardment and insensitive postwar restoration notwithstanding, Rīga's **Old Town** still looks and feels like the warren it was in the Middle Ages. Nineteenth-century German guidebook writer J.G. Kohl could have been writing today

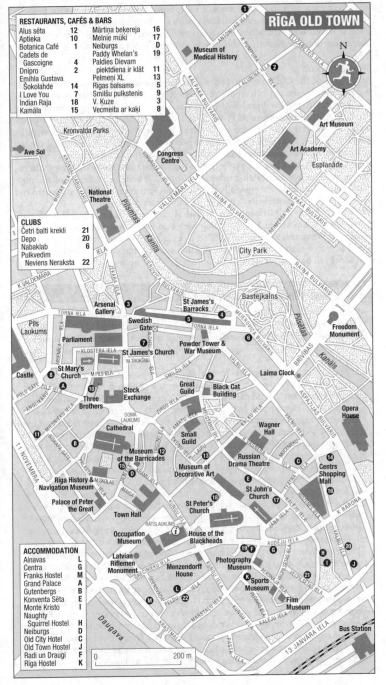

RĪGA OLD TOWN

N

RESTAURANTS, CAFÉS & BARS

Alus sēta	12
Aptieka	10
Botanica Café	1
Cadets de Gascoigne	4
Dnipro	2
Emihla Gustava Šokolahde	14
I Love You	7
Indian Raja	18
Kamāla	15
Mārtina beķereja	16
Melnie mūķi	17
Neiburgs	D
Paddy Whelan's	19
Paldies Dievam piektdiena ir klāt	11
Pelmeni XL	13
Rigas balsams	5
Smilšu pulkstenis	9
V. Ķuze	3
Vecmeita ar kaķi	8

CLUBS

Četri balti krekli	21
Depo	20
Nabaklab	6
Pulkvedim Neviens Neraksta	22

ACCOMMODATION

Ainavas	L
Centra	G
Franks Hostel	M
Grand Palace	A
Gutenbergs	B
Konventa Sēta	E
Monte Kristo	I
Naughty Squirrel Hostel	H
Neiburgs	D
Old City Hotel	C
Old Town Hostel	J
Radi un Draugi	F
Rīga Hostel	K

Museum of Medical History

Art Museum

Art Academy

Esplanāde

Kronvalda Parks

Ave Sol

Congress Centre

National Theatre

City Park

Bastejkalns

Freedom Monument

Arsenal Gallery

St James's Barracks

Swedish Gate

Parliament

St James's Church

Powder Tower & War Museum

Laima Clock

St Mary's Church

Castle

Three Brothers

Stock Exchange

Great Guild

Black Cat Building

Cathedral

Small Guild

Wagner Hall

Opera House

Museum of the Barricades

Russian Drama Theatre

Centrs Shopping Mall

Rīga History & Navigation Museum

Museum of Decorative Art

St John's Church

Palace of Peter the Great

Town Hall

St Peter's Church

Occupation Museum

House of the Blackheads

Latvian Riflemen Monument

Photography Museum

Menzendorff House

Sports Museum

Film Museum

Bus Station

Daugava

0   200 m

Pils Laukums

Castle

when he compared it to a "huge mass of rock, bored through, with holes for houses", parts of which "the sun has not seen for centuries". The main thoroughfare is the dead-straight **Kaļķu iela**, which cuts through the Old Town from northeast to southwest; many attractions are away from this strip in a maze of crooked alleyways.

Doma laukums

At the core of the Old Town, just off Kaļķu iela, **Doma laukums** (Cathedral Square) is dominated by the red-brick bulk of Rīga's Romanesque **Cathedral** (Rīgas dome; Sat–Tues & Thurs 9am–6pm, Wed & Fri 9am–5pm; 2Ls). The biggest cathedral in the Baltics, it was begun in 1211 by Albert von Buxhoeveden, the warrior-priest who founded Rīga and became its first bishop. Although much tinkered with by his successors, it remains an exuberant expression of medieval ecclesiastical power, bowling successive generations over with its combination of sheer size and decorative finesse – particularly fine are the intricate brickwork chevrons and zigzag patterns that cover the outer walls. Post-medieval add-ons have bestowed a degree of eccentric grandeur on the building – especially the enormous Renaissance gable at its eastern end and the bulbous Baroque belfry rising improbably from the roof.

In true Lutheran style, the **interior** is relatively austere, its most eye-catching feature being a florid pulpit from 1641, bristling with statues of saints and trumpet-wielding angels. The magnificent organ with 6768 pipes is said to be the fourth largest in the world (it was *the* largest in the world when it was first installed in 1884); its stentorian tones can be heard at weekly organ recitals – pick up a schedule at the cathedral

Johann Gottfried von Herder (1744–1803)

Although ruled by a German-speaking aristocracy for seven hundred years, the Latvians retained a rich national culture, including a vast repertoire of folk songs that were passed down orally from one generation to the next. Ironically, the first person systematically to put these songs down in writing was a German, **Johann Gottfried von Herder**.

Born in the small East Prussian town of Mohrungen (now Morąg in Poland), Herder studied medicine and theology in Königsberg before arriving in Rīga to teach at the cathedral school in 1764. Herder's interest in folklore was initially focused on Germany, a country then divided into petty principalities, each ruled by an aristocratic elite that preferred French manners and culture to their own. Herder maintained that the rediscovery and propagation of authentic folklore would provide the German people with the cultural confidence that they lacked. The five years Herder spent in Rīga were enough to persuade him that the folk cultures of other nations – including the Latvians and Estonians – deserved to be taken just as seriously.

Believing that the very soul of a nation resided in its folk poetry, Herder spent the rest of his life collating traditional songs of peasant cultures, from the Baltics to the Balkans. Many of these were collected together in his *Stimmen der Völker in Liedern* ("Voices of the Peoples in Song"). A large number of these songs were of an epic nature, recalling heroic struggles against powerful enemies or foreign occupiers, and they went down a storm with a Europe-wide public hungry for an exotic, romantic read.

When an ethnic Latvian intelligentsia began to emerge in the late nineteenth century, Herder's work provided the foundations upon which a modern national culture could be built. The poet and journalist Andrējs Pumpurs came up with just the kind of national epic that Herder had been so enthusiastic about and concocted the tale of superhuman warrior *Lāčplēsis* (published in 1888) by weaving several folk tales into a single narrative and adding his own material. His near-contemporary Krišjānis Barons (see p.180 & p.381) carried out the more painstaking task of systematically collecting over one million folk songs, thereby bequeathing a vast library of indigenous literature to the nation. The songs collected by Barons still form the staple diet of Latvia's choral societies, and remain central to the country's self-image to this day.

entrance or at the tourist office. Occupying a pinnacle-capped niche on the left-hand side of the choir is the gravestone of Meinhard, Bishop of Uexküll, the first German ecclesiastic to make his way to Latvia in an attempt to convert the local heathens, building the region's first church southeast of Rīga in 1188, and paving the way for Albert von Buxhoeveden's crusading hordes.

Doma laukums extends around the western side of the cathedral and runs into **Herdera laukums**, a small triangular space named after the German philosopher Johann Gottfried von Herder (see opposite), who once taught in the cathedral school. Herder was a well-known critic of the harsh feudal system under which the Latvian peasantry lived, and notoriously likened the German presence in the Baltics to the Spanish conquest of Peru in terms of the damage done to indigenous culture. A bust placed here in his honour was removed after World War II in an attempt to de-Germanize Rīga's history – only to be returned to its pedestal in 1959 when a fraternal delegation from the GDR flew into town.

The Rīga History and Navigation Museum

On the eastern side of Herdera laukums is the grilled entrance to the cloister known as the **Cross Gallery** (Krusteja; April–Oct daily 10am–5pm; 0.50Ls), a surviving part of the monastery that was attached to the cathedral before the Reformation. Its rib-vaulted arcades are stuffed with all manner of post-medieval junk, from coats of arms to seventeenth-century cannons. Much of this is overspill from the adjacent **Rīga History and Navigation Museum** (Rīgas vestures un kugniecības muzejs; Tues–Sun 10am–5pm; 3Ls), which charts the importance of seafaring in Rīga's development through an impressive collection of model ships. These range from the Viking longboats that visited the Daugava estuary in the ninth century to the tugs, tankers and trawlers turned out by the local shipyards some thousand years later. A further section of the museum is devoted to twentieth-century urban life, vividly recalled through old photographs, theatre posters and interwar fashions.

The Palace of Peter the Great

Running west of Doma laukums is the narrow Palasta iela and the former **Palace of Peter the Great** at no. 9, a plain-looking building where the tsar lived for all of three months in 1711. Peter first visited Rīga in 1697 during the so-called Grand Embassy, when he traversed northern and western Europe accumulating the kind of technological and military knowledge that would help Russia become a great power. He was prevented from studying Rīga's fortifications by local officials, an incident (subsequently dubbed the "insult at Rīga") which so rankled that Peter is said to have hurled the first grenade at the city himself when besieging it twelve years later. When Princess Sophie von Anhalt-Zerbst (the future Catherine the Great) stayed in the palace in 1744, her guard of honour was commanded by a certain Hieronymus Karl Friedrich von Munchhausen (1720–97), the bogus baron who went on to regale European society with improbable tales of his adventures while in imperial service.

Rīga Castle, Foreign Art Museum and Latvian History Museum

From Doma laukums, Pils iela runs west to leafy **Pils laukums** (Castle Square), the site of Rīga's **Castle** (Rīgaspils). The castle began life as the headquarters of the Livonian Order, and now serves as the official residence of the Latvian president and also accommodates several museums. It has had a somewhat chequered history: the original thirteenth-century construction was demolished in 1484 by Rīga's municipal authorities, who were eager to celebrate the Livonian Order's declining influence over life in the city, and even sent individual bricks to other Hanseatic cities as a mark of their success. In 1491, the Order forced the townsfolk to rebuild it, and after numerous later additions, the castle ended up looking like the rather nondescript office block it is today. Beyond the discreet front door lies the first of the two museums, the **Foreign Art Museum** (Ārzemju mākslas muzejs; Tues, Wed & Fri–Sun 11am–5pm, Thurs 1–7pm; 1Ls); its occasional visiting exhibitions are usually more interesting than its permanent collection – which comprises plaster copies of Greek and Roman sculptures plus a smattering of minor Flemish and Dutch paintings. The museum's one star turn is Hans Makart's *Fight Between Lapiths and Centaurs* (1888), which fills a whole wall with writhing nude forms.

A couple of floors above is the considerably more colourful **Latvian History Museum** (Latvijas vēstures muzejs; Tues–Sun 11am–5pm; 1Ls), which contains a well-presented display of Neolithic pots, early Latvian weaponry and medieval jewellery. A room full of ploughs, rakes and wicker baskets evokes the back-breaking toil endured by nineteenth-century villagers, although the traditional Latvian taste for the fine things in life is evident in the display of folk costumes from all over the country – exquisitely embroidered belts and bonnets for the ladies, sober grey or blue tunics for the blokes.

From the Three Brothers to the Swedish Gate

Heading back east from Pils laukums along Mazā Pils iela takes you past the trio of venerable houses known as the **Three Brothers** (Trīs brāli). The first of the three, at no. 17, which looks like a Cubist painter's nightmare and appears to be toppling into its neighbours, is also the oldest, dating from the early 1400s. While the slight, green brother at no. 21 is a little unassuming, the middle sibling at no. 19 is a handsome, yellow-ochre structure with an elegant Renaissance portal and a wood-beamed interior that harbours the **Latvian Architecture Museum** (Latvijas architektūras muzejs; Mon–Fri 9am–5pm; donation requested), hosting small but worthwhile temporary exhibitions.

A left turn into Jēkaba iela at the end of Mazā Pils iela leads to the thirteenth-century red-brick **St James's Church** (Jēkaba baznīca), the seat of Rīga's Roman Catholic archbishop. As the centre of efforts to re-Catholicize Rīga in the late sixteenth century, St James's was trashed by the townsfolk on Christmas Day, 1584, and its rich inventory of Renaissance artworks destroyed. In a totally unconnected piece of urban lore, the church was famous for possessing bells that would supposedly peal of their own accord whenever a two-timing woman walked past. (Said bells were melted down to provide Russia with munitions in World War I and the church has been chime-free ever since.)

Next door, at Jēkaba 11, is Latvia's **Parliament** (Saeima), a workmanlike neo-Renaissance building that you wouldn't notice were it not for the discreet purr of ministerial motorcars on the cobbled street outside. Built in 1867 as an assembly hall for the Barons of Vidzeme (a region in eastern Latvia), and accordingly dubbed the Ritterhaus, or "Knights' House", it became the headquarters of Peteris Stučka's Bolsheviks during their brief reign over Rīga in spring 1919, only to be taken over by the British Mission to the Baltic States when the Reds retreated. Stučka's headed notepaper was still on the desks when the mission moved in, and its members immediately used it to write jokey letters home. Attendance at the mission's not infrequent parties was considered de rigueur by any party animal still left standing in the war-scarred city. When mission head Stephen Tallents held a reception for Latvian parliamentarians in May 1920, he commented drily that "the drinks were vodka, port and beer. Some of our guests drank them separately, others preferred them mixed."

At its northern end, Jēkaba iela opens out onto Torṇa iela, where a left turn brings you to the **Arsenal Gallery** (Arsenāls; Tues, Wed & Fri noon–6pm, Thurs noon–8pm, Sat & Sun noon–5pm; 2.50Ls), the place to catch high-profile contemporary art shows. Heading in the opposite direction along Torṇa iela takes you past **St James's Barracks** (Jēkaba kazarmas), a 200m-long block built in the seventeenth century by the Swedes and now occupied by upmarket shops and offices. Fired by cultural patriotism and revolutionary fervour, Latvian units of the Russian army invited Rīga's artists to establish a commune in the barracks in 1917. It was closed by the city authorities, but its members went on to dominate the Latvian cultural scene during the interwar years.

Over the road from the barracks is another legacy of Swedish rule, the **Swedish Gate** (Zviedru vārti), a simple archway beneath a three-storey town house. The only surviving city gate, it no longer leads anywhere in particular, although the alleyways on the other side – Aldaru iela and Trokšņu iela – are as picturesque as any in this part of town.

The Powder Tower and the Latvian War Museum

At the end of Torņa iela is the **Powder Tower** (Pulvertornis), a portly fourteenth-century bastion whose red-brick walls are still embedded with cannonballs from various sieges. Somewhat appropriately, the tower now forms part of the adjacent **Latvian War Museum** (Latvijas kara muzejs; Wed–Sun 10am–5pm; free), a well-presented, four-storey array of guns, uniforms and photographs that provides a thorough introduction to modern Latvian history. The narrative kicks off with World War I and the Latvian Riflemen – local units who fought with the Tsarist armies before defecting to the Bolsheviks (see p.174). The establishment of the interwar state (when both Germans and Bolsheviks had to be beaten off) gets equally thorough coverage: it comes as a bit of a surprise to see Latvian aeroplanes of the 1920s sporting swastikas until you learn that this common folk symbol was politically neutral at the time. Most poignant display is that devoted to the anti-Soviet partisans of the 1944–56 period: cheery black-and-white portraits of optimistic young fighters are juxtaposed with Russian intelligence photographs of those who were later captured and summarily shot.

The Great and Small Guilds

From the Powder Tower, Meistaru iela runs down to the **Great Guild** (Lielā Gilde) on the corner of Meistaru and Amatu, once the centre of commercial life in Hanseatic Rīga. The building owes its present neo-Gothic appearance to a nineteenth-century facelift, its main hall now pressed into service as the major venue for concerts by the Latvian National Symphony Orchestra. Next door is the smaller but infinitely more arresting **Small Guild** (Mazā Gilde), a playfully asymmetrical building with a castellated turret on one side and a jaunty spire on the other. A statue of the guild's patron, St John, occupies a niche beneath the spire. Rīga's business class had been divided into these two guilds since the fourteenth century, when the richer traders organized the Great Guild in order to differentiate themselves from shop-keepers and artisans, who quickly formed themselves into the Small Guild. Both guilds were exclusively German institutions – Latvian-speaking Rīgans had to make do with the significantly less prestigious Guild of Fishermen and Boatmen, which collected together all those who worked on and around the Daugava River.

Opposite the Great and Small Guilds stands a yellow building known as the **Black Cat** (Melnais Kaķis), a wonderfully fluid piece of late Art Nouveau named after the lithe feline forms that ornament its two fanciful turrets. According to urban legend, the building's owner, black-balled by the Great Guild, arranged for a cat statuette to be placed on his rooftop and proffering its behind in the guild's general direction. After a successful legal action by the guild, the beast had to be repositioned with its cheeks pointing the opposite way.

The Decorative and Applied Arts Museum

The austere stone interior of the thirteenth-century chapel of St George at Skārņu 10 provides a suitably atmospheric home for the **Decorative and Applied Arts Museum** (Dekoratīvi lietišķās mākslas muzejs; Tues & Thurs–Sun 11am–5pm, Weds 11am–7pm; 3Ls), which showcases crafts as diverse as textile-weaving, glassware and book-binding. During the interwar years, Rīga's crockery factories employed some of the country's best artists to design their tableware, and plates by the likes of Aleksandra Beļcova, Romans Suta and Sigismund Vindbergs – imaginatively mixing folksy Latvian motifs with more modern abstract forms – deservedly occupy centre stage here.

St John's Church

Next door to the Applied Arts Museum is the thirteenth-century **St John's Church** (Jāņa baznīca; Tues–Sun 11am–6pm; donation requested), the red and green brickwork of its stepped gable catching the late afternoon sun to spectacular effect. Legend has it that two monks chose to be immured in the southern facade during the church's construction, where they lived on food delivered through a hole in the wall – an extreme act of ascetic piety not unknown in the Middle Ages. The Gothic interior, whose rib-vaulted ceiling has been repainted in jolly primary colours, hosts popular chamber concerts.

St Peter's Church

Looming up on the western side of Skārņu iela is the imposing red-brick **St Peter's Church** (Pētera baznīca; Tues–Sun 10am–5pm; donation requested), whose graceful three-tiered spire is the city's trademark symbol. Although of thirteenth-century origins, the main body of the church acquired its present shape in the early 1400s and, notwithstanding the addition of some Baroque statues on either side of the main door, has remained pretty much the same since. The history of the spire is another story, however, beginning in 1491 with the construction of a 137m-high wooden spire – the highest in Europe at the time. It collapsed just under two hundred years later and was rebuilt twice in Baroque style before being destroyed by German shelling in 1941. Today's 123m-high spire is a steel replica of the eighteenth-century version, its three slender tiers seeming to sprout from a succession of onion domes. A lift (3Ls) takes you to a gallery in its upper reaches, where you can enjoy a panoramic view of the city. The lofty church interior itself is a bit of a come-down, rioting Protestants having destroyed its original medieval furnishings in the 1520s.

Rātslaukums and the House of the Blackheads

From the main door of St Peter's you look directly across Kungu iela towards **Rātslaukums** (Town Hall Square), whose buildings were largely destroyed in World War II and subsequently replaced by ponderous, Soviet-style blocks. Since independence, however, the square has been the focus of an ambitious rebuilding effort centred on the late-Gothic **House of the Blackheads** (Melngalvju nams), shelled by the Germans in 1941 and totally demolished by the Soviets at the war's end. Beginning in 1995, the house was rebuilt from scratch in time for Rīga's eight-hundredth birthday celebrations in 2001. It's a wackily asymmetrical affair, comprising two joined buildings, one set back slightly from the other, both of which boast enormous stepped gables studded with statue-bearing niches. Although you wouldn't know from the present-day replicas, the building on the right was originally the older of the two, begun in the fourteenth century and progressively tinkered with over the next two hundred years; the one on the left was tacked on in 1891, in conscious imitation of the original.

The house was used as a meeting place by the group of unmarried merchants that took the name "Blackheads" in honour of their patron, the Roman warrior-saint of North African origin, Maurice. A rowdy bachelors' drinking club, and the scene of grandiose feasts such as the Fasnachtsdrunken ("Carnival Drinking Bout"), celebrated on the Saturday before Shrove Tuesday, the house was both a focus of civic life and a symbol of Rīga's cosmopolitan, mercantile identity. For centuries it was a magnet for tourists and foreign conquerors alike – both Peter the Great of Russia (in 1709) and Kaiser Wilhelm of Germany (in 1917) made it their first port of call in order to stamp their authority on the city. Since it was the smartest auditorium in Rīga, the House was also a major concert venue – as musical director of the City Theatre in the late 1830s, Richard Wagner frequently brandished his baton here, sometimes conducting his composition *Nikolai: Hymn of the People* (written in honour of Tsar Nicholas I) as a show-stopping finale. Today, the house is resuming something of its former social role; its main hall hosts regular chamber concerts.

On the other side of the square, the similarly war-ravaged **Town Hall** was also rebuilt in 2001, although without the same commitment to accuracy – it's essentially a twenty-first-century office block with a Neoclassical portal tacked on for good measure. Presiding over the flagstoned square between the Town Hall and the House of the Blackheads is a **statue of Roland**, the legendary eighth-century knight who died defending a Pyrenean mountain pass against invading Arabs – an act immortalized in the epic medieval romance *The Song of Roland*. The cult of Roland was immensely popular in northern Europe, and Rīga honoured him with a statue on this spot in the fourteenth century – the current version is a modern replica of a nineteenth-century incarnation.

The Occupation Museum

The western end of Rātslaukums is dominated by a squat grey structure built to house the now-defunct Museum of the Latvian Riflemen, local troops who fought with the Bolsheviks during the Russian Civil War (see p.174). After independence it was transformed into the **Museum of Latvia's Occupation** (Latvijas okupācijas muzejs; daily 11am–6pm; donation requested; Ⓦ www.occupationmuseum.lv), a moving and in parts disturbing display devoted to Latvia's occupation by the Nazis and the Soviets respectively. Portraits of Hitler and Stalin hover above the entrance to the exhibition – it was their decision to parcel up Eastern Europe into mutually agreed spheres of influence in 1939 that condemned Latvia (along with Estonia and Lithuania) to the first period of Soviet occupation, which began in June 1940. Germany's declaration of war on the Soviet Union a year later ushered in four years of Nazi control (a photograph shows Latvian girls in national costume welcoming the German troops with flowers), after which the Soviets returned in 1944 – and stayed for another 45 years. Photographs and propaganda posters recall these events in punchily effective style. The Soviets tried to rob Latvia of its ethnic identity by deporting a large proportion of its citizens to Siberia, implementing a first wave of mass arrests in June 1941, and a second in March 1949. The victims were often chosen arbitrarily – one of the Soviet warrants on display gives the reason for arrest as simply "belonging to the Latvian nationality". Most of the deportees lived in log-cabin work camps that they had to build themselves – the reconstructed interior of a typical barrack block gives an idea of the harshness of camp life. Display cases contain examples of the artefacts made by deportees to make exile bearable – beautiful hand-drawn Christmas cards, carved wooden chess sets and, most poignantly of all, the balaclava-like face masks fashioned from scraps of material in a desperate attempt to ward off the Siberian winter.

Latvian Riflemen's Square and 11 Novembra Krastmala

A further echo of Soviet culture can be found in the windswept car park immediately west of the museum, which still bears the heroically communist name of **Latvian Riflemen's Square** (Latviešu strēlnieku laukums), and where the riflemen are commemorated with a suitably red, granite monument. Depicting three stern figures buried in enormous greatcoats, it is one of the last examples of ideological sculpture left in the city. The natural gathering point for pro-communist, anti-independence protesters in 1991, the square is nowadays just a bus stop.

Northwest of the Riflemen's Square, along the right bank of the Daugava extends the traffic-choked strip of **11. Novembra Krastmala**, named in commemoration of the defeat of von der Goltz's Germans outside Rīga in November 1919, rather than the end of World War I in November 1918. The pleasant riverside walkway on the far side of the road is punctuated with steps leading down to the water's edge and provides a good vantage point from which to observe the traffic pulsing across Rīga's bridges – with the futuristic Vanšu tilts suspension bridge to the north and the elegant five-arched span of the railway bridge to the south. Until the building of the latter in 1872, the only Daugava crossing was a pontoon affair, laid out every spring and packed up again in the autumn. In winter, people simply drove their carts across the ice.

Heading along 11. Novembra towards Vanšu tilts, you'll come across a glass-covered shrine holding a wooden statue of St Christopher bearing the Christ Child on his broad shoulders. Known as **Lielais Kristaps**, or "Big Christopher", it's very much a symbol of the city.

The Latvian Riflemen

Considered heroes by Latvian patriots and Soviet loyalists alike, the **Latvian Riflemen** (Latviešu strēlnieki) continue to occupy a paradoxical place in the nation's heritage. Made up of local recruits, the unit was created by the Russians in 1915 and charged with the task of defending central Latvia against the advancing Germans. The Russian military authorities considered the creation of ethnic Latvian infantry units an effective way of harnessing local patriotism to the Tsarist cause and, initially at least, were not disappointed. The riflemen often bore the brunt of the heaviest fighting and soon became a symbol of military pride to the folks back home. Increasingly aware that they were being used as cannon-fodder by their Tsarist commanders, however, the riflemen came under the sway of revolutionary propaganda as the war dragged on. Radicalized by Bolshevik agitators, Latvian Riflemen played a key role in Lenin's seizure of power in November 1917.

Many of the riflemen simply drifted back to Latvia as World War I drew to an end, but those who remained loyal to the new Soviet state soon became a byword for Bolshevik discipline and were regarded by Lenin as the only revolutionary troops he could really trust. When anti-Bolsheviks attempted a coup in June 1918, the Latvians were charged with defending the Kremlin – and saved the regime in the process.

The importance of the Latvian Riflemen to the Soviet regime was not lost on the Western powers, and in summer 1918 the British representative in Moscow, Robert Bruce Lockhart, aided by Sidney "Ace of Spies" Riley, briefly entertained the idea of bribing the Latvians into deserting the Bolsheviks. Agents of the Soviet security services, or Cheka (which counted numerous Latvians among its leaders), soon infiltrated the Lockhart plot and it was quickly abandoned.

The Menzendorff House and Grēcinieku iela

Immediately east of Rātslaukums, on the corner of Grēcinieku and Kungu, is the so-called **Menzendorff House** (Mencendorfa nams; Wed & Fri–Sun 11am–5pm, Thurs noon–7pm; 2Ls), an impeccably restored merchant's house decorated in grand style and adorned with period furniture and artefacts. Built by alderman Jürgen Helm in 1695, the house got its name from the luxury Menzendorff delicatessen, which occupied the ground floor of the building in the years before World War I. The four-storey interior was turned into flats after World War II and allowed to decay, but was completely renovated in the 1980s and pretty much restored to its eighteenth-century self – complete with creaky pine floors, mullioned windows and chunky Baroque wardrobes.

East of the Menzendorff House, **Grēcinieku iela** threads its way past a clutch of shops and bars. With a name that translates as "Sinners' Street", Grēcinieku was for a long time Rīga's pleasure quarter, a tradition that still holds true today if excessive alcohol consumption counts among the major vices – several of the Old Town's most popular bars are located here.

The Photography Museum and the Film Museum

On the southern side of Grēcinieku and its extension Audēju lies a warren of narrow streets lined with Gothic merchants' houses. The **Photography Museum** (Fotogrāfijas muzejs; Tues, Fri & Sat 10am–5pm, Wed & Thurs noon–7pm; 1.50Ls), on Alksnāja iela, offers an entertaining jaunt through the history of photography in Latvia. Things get under way with Tsarist-era family portraits and a photojournalist's record of President Ulmanis's arrival in Rīga in 1919, greeted by head of the British Mission (and temporarily governor of Rīga) Steven Tallents. Moving on to the 1920s and 1930s, glamour photos and publicity shots of Latvian actresses reveal what an exciting place interwar Rīga must have been. There's a small section devoted to the desirably sleek and silvery Minox, a miniature camera developed by Rīga's VEF factory in the 1930s and displayed – with pride – as a shining example of how technologically advanced the Latvian republic was before the Soviets took over.

Hidden in an unassuming courtyard off the southeastern end of Alksnāja iela, the **Rīga Film Museum**, Māza Peitavas iela (Tues–Sat 11am–6pm; 2Ls), mounts temporary exhibitions devoted to different aspects of Latvian cinema history – they're usually highly colourful and entertaining affairs, accompanied by screenings of historic films.

The Central Market

Southeast of the Old Town on the opposite side of 13 Janvāra iela sprawls the **Central Market** (Centrāltirgus), an animated, seven-days-a-week affair housed in five hulking pavilions, each the size of a small football pitch. The pavilions are reconditioned World War I Zeppelin hangars, built near Liepāja by the Germans and re-erected here in the 1920s, with ochre Art Deco facades tacked on at each end lending an air of architectural extravagance. Inside, stallholders sell top-quality farm produce from all over Latvia; as well as excellent honey and cheeses, you'll come across rows of animal carcasses waiting to be carved into cutlets in the meat hall (gaļu pavilions), and gurgling tanks full of eels and carp in the fish hall (zivu pavilions). Outside the hangars, Rīgans who can't afford supermarket prices throng around the fruit, veg and flower stalls, or peer into the jumbled window displays of kiosks selling everything from alarm clocks to zebra-print underwear.

Immediately south of the market, a group of nineteenth-century brick warehouses known as **Spīķeri** is being renovated and transformed into an arts and entertainment quarter – a number of bars, cafes and cultural institutions have already moved in.

East of the Old Town: the park belt

From the eastern edge of the Old Town, the broad asphalt stripe of **Brīvības bulvaris** (Freedom Boulevard) and its extension, Brīvības iela, forge a path out to the suburbs and beyond, cutting through a sequence of parks marking the boundary between medieval Rīga and the nineteenth-century parts of town to the east. The parks come in two parallel strips running roughly northwest to southeast: the first, comprising **City Park** and **Kronvalds Park**, is bordered to the east by **Raiņa bulvaris**, a busy street lined with imposing nineteenth-century mansions – mostly occupied by banks, foreign embassies and Rīga University. Beyond Raiņa lies the second strip of parkland, made up of **Esplanāde** and **Vērmane's Garden**. Landscaped when the city walls were demolished in the 1850s, the whole area is now a much-loved green belt, characterized by well-tended lawns, stately rows of trees and the odd formal flowerbed. It's packed with promenaders whatever the season.

Marking the start of Brīvības on the corner of Aspazijas bulvaris is the **Laima Clock**, an unassuming 4m-high pillar erected in the 1930s to advertise the Laima chocolate factory, and still sporting its original Art Deco logo. A much-loved monument to interwar Rīga, it's also the place at which half the city agrees to meet in the evening.

The Freedom Monument

Dominating the view as you head east along Brīvības bulvaris is the defiantly Modernist **Freedom Monument** (Brīvības piemineklis). Unveiled on November 18, 1935, it's a soaring allegory of Latvian independence and has occupied an important place in the national psyche ever since. A red granite pedestal bearing reliefs of Latvian heroes and inscribed with the words *Tevzemei un brīvībai* ("for fatherland and freedom") provides the base for a slender 50m-high column, crowned by a stylized female figure affectionately known as "Milda" – the most popular female first name in the country between the wars, Milda became emblematic of Latvia as a whole. She holds aloft three stars symbolizing the three regions of Latvia – Kurzeme, Vidzeme and Latgale.

Oddly, the Soviets never attempted to demolish this rallying point for Latvian patriotism – unsurprisingly, it was the scene of the first pro-independence demonstrations in August 1987. During the 1990s it became the focus for gatherings of former SS Latvian volunteers on **March 16** – the official day of remembrance for World War II veterans. A government keen to ingratiate itself with both NATO and the EU banned the event after 2001, although the public still gravitate towards the monument to lay flowers on the same date.

The City Park and Bastejkalns

On either side of Brīvības, paths dive into the **City Park** (Pilsētas parks), the first of the wedges of greenery that extend along the eastern boundaries of the Old Town. A ribbon of well-tended lawns patrolled by ducks, it's split by the serpentine form of the **City Canal** (Pilsētas kanāls) – what's left of Rīga's moat. The main feature of the park on the southeastern side of Brīvības is the coolly imperious Rīga **Opera House**, built in 1887 and recently restored to something approaching its belle époque splendour.

Northwest of Brīvības, paths wind their way around **Bastejkalns** (Bastion Hill), a low knoll which began life as a pile of left-over rubble after the city defences were dismantled and was subsequently grassed over. It is also a reminder of Rīga's more recent history: on January 20, 1991, five people were killed here by sniper fire as Soviet OMON troops stormed the Latvian Ministry of the Interior on nearby Raiņa bulvaris during an attempted crackdown on Latvia's independence drive. Stones on the northern side of the hill mark the spots where they fell. Further northwest, progress through the park is briefly broken by the busy thoroughfare of **Valdemāra iela**, the far side of which is overlooked by the **National Theatre** (Nacionālais teātris), a pair of muscular Titans bearing the weight of its renovated, neo-Baroque facade. It was here that Latvian independence was proclaimed on November 18, 1918, although the nation's new leaders had hastily to evacuate a city that was soon overrun by the Bolsheviks. The resolutely modern **Rīga Congress Centre** (Rīgas kongresu nams), which stands at the corner of Kronvalds Park (Kronvalda parks) 200m further north, played host to another generation of Latvian leaders in 1988, when it served as the venue for the first-ever congress of the Latvian Popular Front.

Museum of Medical History

One of Rīga's most compelling museums, the **Stradiņš Museum of Medical History** (Stradiņa medicīnas muzejs; Tues, Wed, Fri & Sat 10am–5pm, Thurs 10am–7pm; closed last Fri of month; 1.50Ls), stands on the corner of Kalpaka and Antonijas iela. Based on the collection of the Latvian physician Pauls Stradiņš (1896–1958), it's packed with eccentric oddities, beginning with a series of dioramas illustrating man's first forays into medicine; in one of them, a witch-doctor is trepanning a patient by hammering a pointed stick into his skull with a rock. A re-creation of a medieval street scene includes a mannequin having its leg sawn off with the aid of a prayer book rather than an anaesthetic. Upstairs, a display of dental instruments through the ages will probably have you vowing never to visit the dentist's again, while a fascinating top-floor section on the Soviet space programme includes spacesuits, models of rockets, and the cabin built to accommodate space dog Veterok ("Breeze") – who orbited the earth in 1966 before returning safely to terra firma. The canine theme concludes with the museum's most notorious exhibit, the (stuffed) **two-headed dog** of Dr Demihov, the eccentric Soviet scientist who pioneered a range of organ transplants in animals, few of which lived to tell the tale. Looking more like a creature from the novels of Mikhail Bulgakov than a monument to scientific progress, this specimen was produced by grafting the head and torso of a small dog onto the back of a larger one, ostensibly in order to see whether the vital functions of a weakened animal could be sustained by attaching it to a stronger host.

The National Art Museum

The stern, red-brick bulk of the **Art Academy** (Mākslas akademija), on Kalpaka, is a building so perfectly neo-Gothic that it was used to represent London locations in Soviet-made Sherlock Holmes adventures. Immediately northeast of the Academy, the junction of Valdemāra and Elizabetes is dominated by the **National Art Museum** (Latvijas nacionālais mākslas muzejs; Tues–Thurs 11am–6pm, Fri 11am–8pm, Sat & Sun noon–5pm; ⓦ www.lnmm.lv; 3Ls), a grandiose Neoclassical edifice with an imperious-looking Athena gazing down from above the entrance.

The **ground floor** contains a largely uninvolving collection of nineteenth-century Russian and German canvases, although you should on no account miss the Roerich room. Blending Art Nouveau, Russian folk art and eastern mysticism, **Nicholas**

Roerich (1874–1947) was one of the best-loved Russian artists of the twentieth century. Consisting mostly of moody purple Himalayan landscapes, this collection is an excellent introduction to his work.

A grand staircase ascends to the **first-floor galleries**, where you'll find an exhaustive overview of Latvian painting and sculpture through the ages. Prime among the past masters is the St Petersburg-educated **Jānis Rozentāls** (1866–1916), who employed a lively Impressionistic style in documenting the Latvian landscape and its people – although the most famous of his works on show here (and one that most Latvians would instantly recognize) is the comparatively dour *Coming from Church after the Service* (1894), depicting sober village folk togged up in their Sunday best. Others who sought to capture the character of the Latvian landscape were **Jānis Valters** (1869–1932) and **Vilhelms Purvītis** (1872–1945) – the latter was a master at depicting the changing face of the countryside during the spring thaw.

The diversity of Latvian interwar art on display owes a lot to the activities of the **Rīga Artists' Group**, an association that brought together most of the painters who had been involved in the St James's Barracks commune (see p.170) – look out for the brooding expressionist works of **Jēkabs Kazaks** (1895–1920) and the angular, Cubist pictures of **Niklāvs Strunke** (1894–1966). The most revolutionary artist of the period was **Gustavs Klucis** (1895–1938), an enthusiastic Bolshevik who chose a career in the Soviet Union rather than life in interwar Latvia. A room is devoted to his propagandist collages and photomontages, with an absorbing 50-minute documentary about his place in the Soviet avant-garde. The leading Latvian female artist of the twentieth century, Russian-born **Aleksandra Beļcova** (1892–1981), is represented by a striking series of female portraits, combining the glamour of glossy magazines with a palpable atmosphere of listlessness and boredom.

Esplanāde

Stretching southeast of the State Art Museum is the **Esplanāde**, a park planted with rows of lime trees at the close of the nineteenth century and popular with strollers and pram-wielding parents ever since. Rising above the trees at its southeastern end are the neo-Byzantine domes of the **Cathedral of the Nativity** (Kristus dzimsanas katedrāle), built for the city's expanding Russian community in 1884 and turned into a planetarium during the Soviet period, when its café was a popular hangout for the city's bohemian intelligentsia. Restored and repainted since being returned to the church in 1990, the cathedral boasts some wonderfully expressive Byzantine-style frescoes.

A little way west of the cathedral is a pink granite statue of **Jānis Rainis** (1865–1929), the poet and playwright whose dour, socially engaged works form the staple diet of Latvian schoolchildren. Gracing a pedestal on the eastern side of the cathedral is a statue of **General Barclay de Tolly**, the Livonian baron of Scottish descent who was commander-in-chief of the Russian armies during the Napoleonic Wars. The statue itself was evacuated – along with other Tsarist-era public sculptures – by the retreating Russian army in World War I, only to enjoy something of a second coming in 2001, when local businessman Yevgeny Gomberg commissioned a replica of the work and campaigned for its reinstatement.

Vērmane's Garden and the Natural History Museum

Continuing southeast along Elizabetes iela, you soon come to the next park, **Vērmane's Garden** (Vērmanes dārzs), occupied by residential houses until 1812, when the Tsarist authorities burnt them down to provide the army with a field of fire from which to defend the city against the advancing French. This may have been a huge miscalculation – it's said that one of the Russian scouts saw dust rising from a herd of cattle just south of the city and mistook it for Napoleon's cavalry. Five years later, the wasteland was redeveloped as a park by the wife of Rīga merchant, A. Wöhrmann (transliterated as "Vērmane" in Latvian, hence the park's name), although for decades it was reserved for Rīga's elite – the plebs had to content themselves with observing the Sunday promenade from behind the railings. Nowadays, the park is a favoured meeting point for elderly chess-players, who hog the benches of an outdoor theatre in the park's northwestern corner.

The Romans Suta and Aleksandra Beļcova Museum

Just north of Vērmane's Garden is one of Rīga's most intimate and charming art attractions, the **Romans Suta and Aleksandra Beļcova Museum** (Romana Sutas un Aleksandras Beļcovas muzejs; Wed–Sun 11am–6pm; 1Ls). Located in the couple's former fifth-floor apartment in the courtyard behind Elizabetes 57a, the museum provides a fascinating insight into the Art Deco tastes of Rīga's interwar cultural elite. Like the majority of the city's art students during World War I, Suta (1896–1944) was evacuated to the Russian city of Penza, where he met fellow student Aleksandra Beļcova (1892–1981), and participated in the Russian revolution. The couple returned to Rīga in 1920 full of new ideas, opening a ceramics studio and branching out into stage design as well as churning out paintings and graphics. Examples are on display, alongside mementos relating to their ballet-dancing daughter Tatjana, who was instrumental in establishing this museum.

The Centre (Centrs)

East of the Vērmane's Garden and Esplanāde parks is the district known as the **Centre** (Centrs) – a name that never fails to confuse first-time visitors, who, not unreasonably, assume that Rīga's centre is somewhere in the Old Town. Although it's largely residential, it also contains the city's most important shopping and commercial district – concentrated in the region enclosed by **Valdemāra iela** to the northwest and **Čaka iela** to the southeast. The boulevards that characterize the Centre bear witness to a period of rapid urban expansion that began in the mid-1800s and lasted right up until World War I.

The Centre's long lines of nineteenth-century apartment blocks look a little grey and unwelcoming on first sight, but as you get close a wealth of **Art Nouveau** embellishments comes to light: florid stucco swirls adorning doorways, stylized human faces incorporated into facades and towers fancifully placed on top of buildings.

The Art Nouveau district

The biggest concentration of Art Nouveau buildings lies in the northwestern corner of the Centre, the majority of them designed by **Mikhail Eisenstein**, the architect father of cinema pioneer Sergei (see opposite). One of Eisenstein *père*'s most famous creations lies just north of the Esplanāde park at **Elizabetes 10A and 10B**, an apartment building adorned with plaster flourishes and gargoyles and topped by two vast, impassive faces. Eisenstein was also responsible for just about everything on the even-numbered side of **Alberta iela**, one block north of here, a uniquely exotic terrace of town houses, each of which is stylistically different from the next. The most extrovert of the lot is the florid neo-Egyptian affair at no. 2A; the facade is slightly higher than the building itself, which makes it look more like a film set than a real building. At ground level things are more reassuring, with a brace of contented-looking sphynxes standing guard on either side of the entrance.

The most striking of the buildings on the opposite side of the street is the dark-grey apartment block at no. 11 designed by Eižens Laube, the prime exponent of **National Romanticism**. Following hard on the heels of Art Nouveau in Rīga, this new style sought to establish a truly Latvian form of architecture through the inclusion of folksy touches like shingled roofs, irregular window frames and pointy gables – all of which are employed here to monumental effect.

The Art Nouveau Museum

Occupying a restored ground-floor apartment at Alberta iela 12, the **Art Nouveau Museum** (entered round the corner on Strēlnieku iela; Tues–Sun 10am–6pm; 2.50Ls) provides the opportunity to explore a typical domestic interior of the period. The sizeable family apartment has retained much of its original parquet flooring, stained glass

Sergei Mikhailevich Eisenstein (1898–1948)

Rīga-born cinema pioneer **Sergei Eisenstein** grew up at Valdemāra 6 (a plaque outside the Zvaigzne bookshop marks the spot), and was educated at the gymnasium just down the road at Valdemāra 1 (which is still a high school). His report cards gave little indication of his future calling – he received average marks for art and his best subject was theology. However, the development of Eisenstein's visual imagination is apparent in the letters he wrote to his mother, who had moved to St Petersburg in 1909 – in these, Eisenstein recounts the events of the week in vivid film-storyboard style, with cartoon strips and caricatures.

During World War I, the Eisensteins were evacuated to Russia, Sergei going on to study art in Moscow before specializing in film. Many observers have interpreted his enthusiasm for the new art of cinema as a rebellion against the florid style of his architect father. His cinematic trademark – the employment of a vigorous, jump-cut editing style – he called "the montage of attractions".

Cinema was regarded as the most politically effective art form of all by Soviet Russia's new rulers, and Eisenstein quickly established himself as its greatest practitioner. His first feature film, **Strike** (1924), was an attack on the evils of capitalism, while **October** (1928) offered an over-dramatized reconstruction of the Bolshevik seizure of power – it's said that more people were injured during the making of the film than during the event itself.

During the interwar years Eisenstein's films were rarely seen in the city of his birth. Playwright and socialist MP, Jānis Rainis (see p.191), campaigned successfully to have Eisenstein's greatest masterpiece **Battleship Potemkin** (1925) shown in Rīga, despite the hostility of government censors towards such outright Soviet propaganda. Things changed when Latvia was sucked into the Soviet sphere of influence in 1939, and Eisenstein's epic of medieval Russia's struggle against the Germans, **Alexander Nevsky**, arrived in local cinemas at a time of growing anti-German feeling. "At each reverse suffered by the Teutonic Knights," wrote British diplomat's wife Peggie Benton, "the Latvian audience stamped their feet and clapped until the management had to silence them by turning on the lights."

and stucco ceiling decoration. Wall coverings and window curtains have been recreated from original patterns, while antique furniture collected from other locations provides visitors with a taste of how a pre-World War I professional family might have lived. Clad in period costume, staff are on hand to explain what's on display.

The Rozentāls and Blaumanis Museum

Occupying the top floor of the residential block at Alberta 12, the **Jānis Rozentāls and Rudolfs Blaumanis Museum** (Jāņa Rozentāla un Rudolfa Blaumaņa memoriālais muzejs; Wed–Sun 11am–6pm; 1Ls) is in the former apartment of painter Jānis Rozentāls (1866–1916), where the writer Rudolfs Blaumanis (1863–1908) was a frequent guest. The museum is packed with period furnishings and evocative pictures of Rīga in the early twentieth century. Rozentāls is primarily known for his large-format landscapes, although the smaller canvases gathered together here are full of intimacy and warmth – especially the pictures of family and friends that fill the light-flooded attic studio. The room next door was set aside by Rozentāls for his friend Blaumanis, the critically acclaimed novelist who never earned enough money to rent his own big-city pad. The space is largely bare save for a few facsimile manuscripts and a glass case containing a huge bearskin coat – donated by Rozentāls to help the tubercular Blaumanis ward off the winter chill.

The Museum of Latvia's Jews

The small but compelling **Museum of Latvia's Jews** (Muzejs Ebreji Latvijā; Sun–Thurs noon–5pm; donation requested) is on the third floor of the Jewish community's cultural centre at Skolas 6. Built around documents amassed over many years by two Rīga-based Holocaust survivors, Zalman Elelson and Margers Vestermanis, the display commemorates a community that on the eve of World War II made up eleven percent of Rīga's population – the second-largest ethnic group in the city after the Latvians themselves – before being all but wiped out by the Nazis.

Until the twentieth century there was little evidence of anti-Semitism in Latvia, a point pressed home by the following quote from the 1881 article, *A Word on the Baltic Jews*, by nineteenth-century national ideologue Krišjanis Valdemārs: "Not one Latvian, neither wise nor fool, in the townlet or on the land, neither thought nor spoke about Jews being injurious to them. I myself perceived that Jews do somewhat to the benefit of Christians but nothing to the detriment." As photographs in the exhibition show, Jewish volunteers fought on the Latvian side in the 1918–20 War of Independence and Jewish politicians stood for mainstream Latvian parties in the years that followed. When the Germans moved into Latvia in 1941, most of the city's Jews were herded into ghettos southeast of the Old Town, then taken to forests outside the city and shot. Viewed against this background, the museum's photos of Jewish life in the 1930s – banal pictures of football teams, trips to the beach and family picnics – assume a profoundly moving significance. There are also some disturbing pictures of the Holocaust itself, including images of a massacre of Jews on Liepāja beach in July 1941, filmed dispassionately by a German cameraman.

Barona iela and the Barons Museum

One of the Centre's main arteries is **Barona iela**, home to some of the area's smarter shops. Hogging most of the architectural limelight is the deliciously gaudy Art Nouveau office block at the junction of Barona and Blaumaņa, a veritable bestiary in vertical form, the facade of which features bat-like demons just above ground level, lions and hogs further up and dragons crowning the battlements at the top. Providing an escape from the daytime bustle is the **Krišjānis Barons Memorial Museum** (Krišjāņa Barona memoriālais muzejs; Wed–Sun 11am–6pm; 0.70Ls) at no. 3, the flat where the eponymous writer and ethnographer lived for four years following World War I. Barons' great service to Latvian culture was the cataloguing of over one million traditional Latvian *dainas* – four-line folk poems that country people knew by heart but had never been systematically recorded. Barons wrote each *daina* on a tiny piece of paper, bundles of which were then placed in specially made chests of drawers – a pair of which are preserved here. Elsewhere are pictures of people and places associated with Barons, although it's the chance to see the flat's well-preserved 1920s interiors that make a visit worthwhile.

Čaka iela and the Čaks Museum

Easternmost of the Centre's big lateral boulevards is **Čaka iela** and its extension, Marijas iela. Čaka takes its name from the poet Aleksandrs Čaks (1901–50), who broke with Latvian literature's traditional obsession with the countryside to pen eulogies to the edgy urban landscape of interwar Rīga. He was particularly enthralled by the low-life atmosphere of the street that now bears his name, calling it "forever the merchant…buying and selling anything from a piece of junk to human flesh". From 1937 until his death, Čaks lived in a flat at the junction of Čaka iela and Lāčplēša iela, now the **Aleksandrs Čaks Memorial Museum** (A. Čaka memoriālais muzejs; entrance at Lāčplēša 48/50; Tues–Sat 11am–5pm; 0.60Ls). The poet's cosy sitting room, stuffed with prints, paintings and other objets d'art, is a charming period piece.

Southeast of the Old Town

Immediately southeast of the Old Town, the bustling area around the Central Market gives way to a quiet, run-down district seemingly untouched by the post-Soviet economic changes so evident in other parts of the centre. Many of the sights, however, have a deep historical resonance.

The principal landmark in this area of greying, nineteenth-century apartment blocks is the **Academy of Sciences** (Latvijas zinātņu akademija) at the junction of Turgeņeva and

Gogoļa, built during the early 1960s and nicknamed "Stalin's Birthday Cake" because of its resemblance to the monumental, pseudo-Baroque structures that sprang up all over Moscow in the 1940s and 1950s. Constructed from enormous, gingerbread-coloured chunks of stone, this unloved communist heirloom radiates a melancholy beauty.

Immediately southeast of the academy on Elijas iela is the ochre-painted **Jesus Church** (Jēzus baznīca), surrounded by a horseshoe of grubby flats. Dating back to 1635, this is Rīga's oldest wooden church, though it's been rebuilt following fires a couple of times since then. The interior is unusual, with a circular central hall supported by wooden pillars.

The Great Synagogue and the Moscow Suburb

At the intersection of Gogoļa and Dzirnavu stand the remains of Rīga's **Great Synagogue**, set alight on the night of July 4, 1941 (just three days after the Germans entered the city) with, it is thought, about a hundred worshippers still inside. The attack was thought to be the work of Viktors Arājs, leader of the Latvian security team that worked with the German SS and played a major role in murdering Rīga's Jews. Living in Germany under an assumed name after the war, Arājs was unmasked in 1979, extradited to Latvia and sentenced to life imprisonment (he died in 1988). The walls of the synagogue have been reconstructed to a height of a few metres to serve as a memorial and there's a lone boulder in the adjoining park simply inscribed "1941. 4/VII".

East of here stretches the **Moscow Suburb** (Maskavas forštate), so named because the main road to Moscow ran through it. The area was inhabited by many of Rīga's Jews and is the site of the wartime ghetto to which they were confined by the Nazis. The erstwhile core of the ghetto is a good 400m east of the Great Synagogue, in the area now bounded by Lāčplēša, Maskavas, Lauvas and Kalna ielas. The Nazis started clearing the ghetto almost immediately after its establishment in September 1941 and by December of the same year almost all of its 25,000 inhabitants had met their deaths in the Rumbula and Biķernieki forests, just east of the city. The ghetto was then repopulated by Jews from Western Europe, brought here to work as slave labourers, until they, too, were considered surplus to Nazi requirements and murdered. It's now an area of gritty apartment blocks and warehouses, with a dearth of memorials to those who lived and suffered here, save for a lone inscription at the entrance to the former **Jewish cemetery** (Ebreju kapi; tram #3, #7 or #9 from the Central Market to the Balvu iela stop) at the corner of Maskavas iela and Ebreju iela. Shorn of its gravestones in World War II, it's now a grassy park.

The Grebenshchikov Church

On the southern edge of the former ghetto at Krasta 73 is the gold-domed **Grebenshchikov Church** (Grebenščikova baznīca), built in 1814 for the Old Believers, a dissenting sect that broke away from the Orthodox Church during the seventeenth century and many of whose members fled Russia to escape persecution (see p.144). There are still enough Old Believers around in Rīga to maintain a small congregation, although the church is rarely open outside prayer times – 7/9am and 5pm are your best bets.

Pārdaugava

Immediately west of the Old Town, trams #2, #4, #5 and #10 rattle across the Akmens tilts ("Stone Bridge") towards the downbeat suburb of **Pārdaugava** (literally "Across the Daugava"), characterized by rickety old wooden houses, post-World War II housing blocks and extensive parks. The Pārdaugava riverbank affords majestic **views** back towards the city centre – revealing a spire-studded skyline that appeared to Laurens van der Post in the early 1960s "as tranquil and translucent as any of Vermeer's views of Delft".

The Railway Museum, Uzvaras Park and the Latvian Theatre Museum

Some 400m beyond the western end of Akmens tilts, an unassuming brick warehouse at Uzvaras 2/4 accommodates the **Latvian Railway Museum** (Latvijas dzelzceļa muzejs;

Tues–Sat 10am–5pm; ⓦ www.railwaymuseum.lv; 1Ls), a small collection of old train tickets, station paraphernalia and railway uniforms, enlivened by a model railway featuring a faithful reconstruction of Lĭvberže station (on the Rīga–Ventspils line).

Bāriņu iela forges west across the grassy expanse of **Uzvaras Park** ("Victory Park"), passing the most overstated of Rīga's Soviet-era monuments, erected in honour of the Red Army's victory in World War II. Its giant concrete needle spangled with shiny five-pointed stars might at first glance be taken for some outsize advertisement for a nightclub – though at ground level there's no mistaking the political message hinted at by the statue of Victory being saluted by machine-gun-toting Soviet soldiers. West of the park, Bāriņu iela leads to **Agenskalns covered market** (Agenskalņa tirgus), a deliciously doom-laden, red-brick pavilion that looks like something out of a horror movie.

Arcadia Park and Torņakalns

At its southern end, Uzvaras parks runs into **Arcadia Park** (Arkādijas parks), a smaller but prettier stretch of greenery arranged around a winding waterway popular with ducks. Just across the rail tracks to the east, **Torņakalns train station** was a key embarcation point in the deportations of 1941 and 1949, when thousands of Latvians were loaded into cattle trucks and shipped to Siberia. A cluster of knobbly granite shapes, erected behind the station by sculptor Pauls Jaunzems, serves as their memorial.

North and east of the city centre

North and east of the city centre sprawl industrial estates and concrete residential zones, softened here and there by sizeable patches of woodland. A great deal of interest is hidden away in these suburban areas. To the north lie the monumental interwar sculptures of the **Braļu kapi cemetery** and the dense woodland of the **Mežaparks** recreation area, both on the same tram route. To the east are an engaging **Motor Museum** and a moving **Holocaust Memorial**, each beside the deep-green swathe of Biķernieku forest. Further out are the former presidential summer house, now an intriguing museum of interwar life, at Dauderi, and the enthralling collection of village architecture at the **Open-air Ethnographic Museum** near Lake Jugla.

Braļu Kapi and around

Some 4km northeast of the centre, **Braļu kapi** ("Brothers' cemetery"; tram #11 from Radio iela) was planned in 1915 as a shrine to the Latvian soldiers then serving in the Tsarist army; by the time it was finished a decade later, it had become a powerful symbol of the newly independent Latvian state and the price in blood that had been required to build it. It remains a strongly evocative spot, its rows of graves guarded by the muscular creations of sculptor Kārlis Zāle, who blended folkloric traditions with Modernism to produce a heroic national style. His monumental *Mother Latvia* (Māte Latvijā) towers over one end of the cemetery, with accompanying pieces *Divi Braļi* ("Two Brothers") and *Ievainotais Jatnieks* ("Wounded Horseman") driving home the message of comradeship and sacrifice.

On either side of Braļu kapi lie larger, rambling civilian cemeteries set in pleasant, park-like woodland. On the northern side, **Meža kapi** (Woodland cemetery) is full of wooden benches, provided so that Latvians can sit and commune with their ancestors. South of Braļu kapi, many of Latvia's leading writers, artists and stage performers are buried in **Raiņa kapi**, so named because it centres on the granite tomb of Latvia's most respected man of letters, Jānis Rainis (see p.191).

Mežaparks and the zoo

From Braļu kapi, tram #11 meanders through northeastern Rīga for another 3km before terminating at **Mežaparks**, a prosperous garden suburb that has been popular with the city's upper crust for well over a century. Occupying a wooded, hilly site right beside the tram stop is Rīga's **zoo** (Rīgas zoologiskais dārzs; daily: mid-April to mid-Oct 10am–6pm; rest of year 10am–4pm; 4Ls), with a pleasant if predictable collection of elephants, camels and zebras enlivened by a pair of rare Amur tigers. Beyond the zoo, you can follow paths into a sizeable expanse of woodland and park, in the middle of which sit a funfair and the **Song Stadium**, built to accommodate the mind-bogglingly enormous choirs that perform at the National Song Festivals every five years – when over ten thousand people might be singing their hearts out at any one time.

The Motor Museum

Some 6km east of the centre, a sleek brick-and-glass pavilion on the edge of Bikernieki forest holds the **Motor Museum** (Rīgas motormuzejs; Tues–Sun 10am–6pm; 1.50Ls) at Eizensteina 6, an eye-opening round-up of Latvian – and Soviet – transport history. The easiest way to get there is to catch bus #21 from Stacijas laukums or opposite Katedrāle to Pansionāts. The wide-ranging collection's most venerable exhibit is the fire engine made by Rīga's Russko-Baltiiski engineering factory in 1912. The Ford family cars made under licence by the Latvian Vairogs ("Shield") firm in the 1930s look frumpily utilitarian in comparison with the luxury motors favoured by Bolshevik Russian fat cats during the same period: note the 1939 Rolls Royce Wraith used by Stalin's foreign minister, Molotov. Eloquently summing up the Kremlin's love affair with big cars is the somewhat crumpled 1966 Rolls-Royce Silver Shadow owned by notorious speed freak Leonid Brezhnev, who pranged it himself during one of his customary nocturnal drives around Moscow.

Biķernieku forest and the Holocaust Memorial

Behind the Motor Museum, paths lead into the deep evergreen cover of the **Biķernieku forest** (Biķernieku mežs), site of the winding racetrack where Soviet motorcycling championships were once held. The southwestern end of the forest, traversed by the dead-straight Biķernieku iela, was used by the Nazis as a mass murder and burial ground in World War II – thousands of Jews from all over Europe were shot here between 1941 and 1944. The sixtieth anniversary of the first wave of exterminations (which actually began not here but in Rumbula forest; see p.184) was marked on November 30, 2001, by the unveiling of an impressive **Holocaust Memorial**, just off the southwestern side of Biķernieku iela. A profoundly beautiful piece of *plein-air* sculpture, its central feature is an angular concrete canopy covering a black slab, on which an inscription in Latvian, German, Hebrew and Russian quotes Job 16.18: "Oh earth, cover not my blood, and let my cry have no peace". Radiating out from the slab is a garden of jagged stones marked out into plots – each inscribed with the name of the European city the victims came from. Some visitors place pebbles on or around individual stones in a personal act of remembrance. In the surrounding forest, mass graves are marked by raised beds of grass, each with a rough-hewn rock planted in the middle.

Trolleybus #14 (from opposite Katedrāle) goes past the memorial, but there's no stop beside the site itself – you need to get off at the Keguma iela stop and continue east along Biķernieku iela on foot (1km), or stay on the bus until the Eizenšteina iela stop and walk back along the same road (1.5km). If you've just been to the Motor Museum, you can walk to the memorial by following forest paths from the former racetrack, although you'll need a decent Rīga city map to navigate your way through the woods – there aren't any signs.

The Ethnographic Museum

The **Latvian Open-air Ethnographic Museum** (Latvijas etnogrāfiskais brīvdabas muzejs; daily 10am–5pm; 2Ls), 12km east of the centre on the Tallinn road, brings together over a hundred traditional buildings from all over Latvia, reassembled in a partly forested setting by the shores of Lake Jugla. It's a big site, and you'll need a couple of hours and an appetite for woodland strolling to get the best of it. Consider buying the English-language plan (0.80Ls) at the entrance – you could quite easily get lost in the eastern reaches of the museum without it. The display captures perfectly the atmosphere of nineteenth-century rural life, when the majority of Latvians lived in isolated farmsteads. Although most of the timber-built houses look comfortably large, much of the space was devoted to grain or animals, and families lived in cramped, spartan quarters at one end of the building. Open hearths were used for smoking meats and drying hay, which was then stored in the loft. Farmsteads had to be self-sufficient – the recreated kitchen gardens are full of every manner of vegetable, fruit tree and medicinal herb. The oldest of the buildings is a sixteenth-century church from Vecborne near Daugavpils, its interior featuring a painted, wooden ceiling filled with jovial-looking angels.

On **summer** weekends, craftsmen demonstrate their work, while around **Christmas**, folk groups from all over Latvia converge here to perform Yuletide songs and dances. There's a traditional-style **inn** near the entrance serving Latvian specialities such as *zirņi* (grey peas with bacon), along with coffee and cakes. To get to the museum, take **bus** #1 from Brīvības iela, and get off at the first stop after passing the shores of Lake Jugla on your right.

Rumbula forest

Some 11km from the city centre, **Rumbula forest**, a once dense area of woodland, is now broken up by a patchwork of postwar factories, housing projects and vegetable plots. As many as 28,000 Latvian and Lithuanian Jews were brought to be shot in Rumbula on November 30, 1941, and mass killings continued here throughout the war. A **memorial site** now occupies a wooded knoll beside the road, the entrance to the access path marked by a striking modern stone-and-steel sculpture that looks like a swooning tree. A restful place surrounded by birches, the site consists of a central plaza, the main focus for the laying of wreaths, and a surrounding parkland where raised grassy beds, each sprouting with rough-hewn rocks, mark individual massacre sites.

To get here **by car**, head southeast from central Rīga along Maskavas iela (the main highway to Daugavpils) for 11km and you'll find the site right at the city limits, just beyond a used car lot and opposite a petrol station. The easiest way to get here **by public transport** is to take trams #7 and #9 from the Central Market to the Kvadrāts terminus, followed by bus #15 to the Rumbula terminus (from where you walk back the way you came for 100m and cross the road). Rumbula train station, just east of the memorial, is no more than an unmarked wayside halt in the middle of a meadow and you could easily miss it altogether.

Salaspils

Between October 1941 and October 1944 an estimated 100,000 people met their deaths in **Salaspils concentration camp**, hidden in dense woodland 14km southeast of Rīga and 3km short of the town of Salaspils itself. Although intended as a transitional camp in which Jews from Germany, Austria and Czechoslovakia could be held before their deportation to work camps and extermination sites elsewhere, Salaspils was increasingly used as a killing zone.

At the centre of the site is a long, concrete hall, mounted on pillars and slightly tilted to form a gently ascending processional way, intended to evoke the journey from life to death. At the end of the hall a staircase drops down into a small museum space, containing a series of gripping illustrations evoking the harshness of camp life by K. Būss, a Latvian political prisoner interned here. Outside, a long, black concrete slab containing a slowly ticking metronome is the main focus for wreath-laying, remembrance and prayer. The surrounding terrain is peppered with concrete tablets marking the locations of the barrack buildings where the prisoners were held. An ensemble of heroic statues intended to depict the uncrushable human spirit comes across as tastelessly Soviet – one angular-jawed example is entitled "Red Front", as if to suggest that resistance to Nazi barbarity was entirely the preserve of the communists.

You can get to the memorial by taking a suburban **train** to the Dārziņi stop – there's currently no station signboard in evidence, but it's the first station out of Rīga that is completely surrounded by pine forest. From here a signed path leads to the memorial site – a fifteen-minute walk through peaceful woodland. Approaching the site **by car** along the Daugavpils-bound highway, you'll see a long concrete slab 15km out on the northern side of the road pointing the way to the site – assuming you're in the eastbound lane, however, you'll have to carry on for another couple of kilometres and do a U-turn.

Food and drink

The calorie-rich Baltic diet provides perfect insulation against long north European winters, but may not do your waistline any favours. It's a diet very much determined by local landscape, with rye fields lending flavour to the distinctively rich Baltic bread, seas and rivers yielding culinary treats from salted herring to smoked eel, and meadow-grazing dairy herds providing the raw materials for delicious sour cream and cheese. Pork is the most popular of the locally reared meats. Although global culinary trends are increasingly making their presence felt, these staple foodstuffs still form the mainstay of the eating-out experience.

скумбрija
ук
1 кg 7. 30

Pork

If there's one dish that appears on absolutely every Baltic restaurant menu, it is the **pork chop** (*karbonaad* in Estonia, *karbonāde* in Latvia, *karbonadas* in Lithuania). At its most basic, this is a simple slice of (often fatty) meat thrown into a pan for a brief sizzle, although the classic Baltic chop – cooked in tasty beer-batter and accompanied by a tangy mound of sauerkraut – can be a real treat.

Fish

Pork chops with cranberries ▲

Fish stall, Rīga Central Market ▼

As you'd expect in a region with a long coastline and a wealth of freshwater lakes, fish plays a crucial role in the Baltic diet. Traditionally, fishermen would home-cure a large part of their catch by smoking it in sheds (which often doubled as the family sauna). **Smoked fish** is still a delicacy, offered as a starter in restaurants or as a snack in street cafés. Usually you'll be given the whole fish, complete with head, skin and bones, served on a plate but with no cutlery – picking out the flesh with your fingers is part of the ritual. All kinds of salt- and freshwater fish are seen as suitable for smoking, although **eel** is considered the real delicacy. Peeling the succulent white meat from the rubbery skin is a laborious, but rewarding experience.

Freshwater fish from the Baltic lakes and rivers – especially **trout**, **pike** and **pike-perch** – feature regularly on menus throughout the region. Some of the most distinctive recipes are found in the shoreline settlements of Lake Peipsi in Estonia, where the local catch is stewed or baked with lashings of local onions. Another Baltic standby is salted or marinated **herring**: universally available as a starter, it is also served as a snack to accompany vodka or other spirit shots.

Potatoes

Nowhere is the Baltic love affair with the potato more profound than in Lithuania, where this outwardly unassuming vegetable plays a starring role in the national cuisine. Widest known – and most immediately recognizable – of the potato-based dishes is **cepelinai** (literally "zeppelins"), in which finely grated potato mush is formed into cylinders, stuffed with minced meat and then boiled to produce glutinous blobs. They aren't to everyone's liking, but can be tasty.

Potato pancakes (*bulviniai blynai*), made by dropping big dollops of shredded potato into hot oil, are an important part of the culinary repertoire and often quite delicious when served with mushroom sauce, smoked salmon, or, most traditionally of all, savoury bacon bits swimming in thick sour cream. There are many regional variations on the potato pancake theme, *Žemaičių blynai* (stuffed with meat and moulded into a heart shape) being among the most satisfying.

▲ Potato dumplings

▼ Rye bread

Bread

Considered as something of an occasional treat in other European countries, **black rye bread** (*leib* in Estonia, *rupjmaize* in Latvia, *duona* in Lithuania) is an everyday staple in the Baltic States, and accompanies every meal from breakfast onwards. Made from a mixture of rye and wheat flour (the proportion differs from bakery to bakery), and often flavoured with caraway seeds or other natural goodies (Lithuanian *ajerų duona* is baked on a bed of bulrushes), Baltic bread is extraordinarily rich in nutrients and has the added advantage of staying fresh and springy for days.

Cold borscht

Opinions differ as to the precise origin of borscht, the beetroot-based **soup** that has for centuries been a popular staple across the whole of northeastern Europe, particularly in the peasant communities. The form of borscht most closely associated with the Baltic States is the cold, summer variety, which goes under the name of *šaltibarščiai* in Lithuania and *aukstā zupa* in Latvia.

Comprising shredded beetroot, sour milk or yoghurt, garlic, gherkin – and maybe a hard-boiled egg if you're lucky – and garnished with sour cream and chopped herbs, it's alarmingly pink in colour and looks more like a fancy pudding than a savoury dish. If you're after a refreshing summer lunch with a local twist, however, you can't do much better. A side dish of boiled potatoes is the perfect accompaniment.

Cold borscht ▲

Rīga Balsam ▼

Rīga Balsam

Few Baltic spirits are as immediately recognizable as **Rīga Balsam** (*Rīgas balzams*), the sticky black syrup sold in traditional, black-labelled clay bottles. Brewed in the city since the eighteenth century, the 45-percent-proof firewater tastes rather like cough medicine and is made from an appropriately healthy-sounding list of ingredients – which include a reputed 24 different herbs, along with forest berries, ginger and birch buds. Downing the stuff neat can be something of an ordeal, although combined with hot blackcurrant juice or coffee, it becomes the perfect winter warmer.

The same company distils **Ķimelis**, a nectar-sweet liqueur made from caraway seeds which has many Latvian adherents – foreigners, however, may find it something of an acquired taste.

Eating

The majority of Rīga's **restaurants** serve international cuisine, while a crop of self-service **cafeterias** offer filling and cheap meat-and-potatoes meals. Restaurant **prices** are on the whole higher than in Vilnius or Tallinn, but still significantly lower than in Western European capitals; on average, a three-course meal with drinks will be somewhere around 20 or 30Ls – more if you're ordering bottles of wine. We've included telephone numbers for those restaurants where reservations are recommended at weekends.

For livelier eating options check out the **bars** listed under "Drinking" below – many offer substantial eats at reasonable prices. Most of Rīga's **cafés** also offer a range of hot meals, which can often be as good as anything in a restaurant, and cheaper to boot. You can pick up fruit, veg and other **basics** at the Central Market just beyond the bus station, or at supermarkets like Rimi, at Audēju 16 and Matīsa 27.

Cafés

Old Town

The places listed below are marked on the "Rīga Old Town" map on p.167.

Cadets de Gascoigne Basteja 8. A French patisserie right opposite Bastejkalns hill, where you can pig out on melt-in-the-mouth croissants and brie-filled baguettes. Daily 7am–10pm.

Emihla Gustava Šokolahde Aspazijas 24. Coffee, cakes and gourmet chocolates in restful, waitress-service surroundings. In the same building as the Valters un Rapa bookshop (see p.190). Mon–Sat 9am–11pm, Sun 11am–11pm.

Martiņa beķereja Valnu. If you want to eat your way through the traditional Latvian repertoire of *pirāgi* (doughy pies with savoury fillings) then this unpretentious bakery-cum-café is probably the best place to do it. Daily 8am–9pm.

Smilšu pulkstenis Corner of Meistaru iela and Mazā smilsu iela. A cosy café conveniently located just off Livu laukums, serving decent tea and coffee, delightful pastries and an impressive array of cakes. Mon–Fri 8.30am–9pm, Sat 10am–8pm.

V. Ķuze Jēkaba 20/22. Delicious cakes and handmade chocolates in an atmospheric recreation of an interwar coffee shop. The decor and staff uniforms are all suitably retro; the prices, unfortunately, are bang up to date and still rising. Daily 10am–9pm.

Outside the Old Town

The places listed below are marked on the "Rīga" map on p.162.

Apsara Elizabetes iela. Quaint wooden pavilion on the eastern side of Vērmane's Garden, with a big range of speciality teas, and comfy cushions to sit on. Popular with school-age teenagers in the late afternoon, but quiet at other times of day. Daily 10am–10pm.

Charlestons Café Blaumaņa 38/40. Great coffee, excellent salads and dangerously delicious cakes and sweets straight from the kitchens of the *Charlestons* restaurant next door (see p.186). Mon–Fri 8am–midnight, Sat & Sun 10am–midnight.

Osīriss Barona 31. A stylish, intimate café in the Centre, with coffee, cakes, breakfasts, salads and a full menu of mouth-watering international main courses. Candlelit at night, it's a popular place for an intimate tête-à-tête. Mon–Fri 8am–midnight, Sat & Sun 10am–midnight.

Canteens and order-at-the-counter restaurants

Old Town and around

The places listed below are marked on the "Rīga Old Town" map on p.167.

Alus Sēta Tirgotu iela 6. A justifiably popular pub with huge meals served from the grill. A good place to sample good, cheap Latvian ales accompanied by the national beer-snack – *zirņi* (grey peas with bacon). Outdoor seating in warm weather. Daily 11am–1am.

Dņipro Alunāna 6. Lovely little Ukrainian restaurant with folksy wooden furnishings, staff in embroidered Carpathian blouses, and a tapestry portrait of national novelist Ivan Franko on one wall. Cheap, filling dishes include Ukrainian borscht and *vareniki* (boiled pastry parcels of meat or potato similar to Russian *pelmeni* or Polish *pierogi*). Mon–Fri 10am–9pm, Sat & Sun noon–8pm.

Pelmeņi XL Kalķu 7. A popular self-service joint on the Old Town's main street offering *pelmeņi* (Russian ravioli) filled with meat or cheese, alongside *soļanka* (Russian meat-and-vegetable soup), borscht and other Eastern European staples. Daily 9am–4am.

Outside the Old Town

The places listed below are marked on the "Rīga" map on p.162.

Dzirnavas Dzirnavu 76. Solid repertoire of Latvian fish, pork- and potato-based meals, in a self-service restaurant decorated in enjoyably over-the-top folk style. Mon–Sat 8am–11pm, Sun 9am–10pm.

Līdo Atpūtas Centrs Krasta 76. A vast self-service restaurant complex 3km southeast of the centre on the Daugavpils road. Huge choice of belly-filling Latvian cuisine, local draught beers, a children's play area and a real-size reproduction windmill. Daily 10am–11pm.

Līdo Vērmanītis Elizabetes 65. Cafeteria serving all manner of tasty Latvian meat-and-potato dishes, pancakes and salads, with an interior decked out in country-cottage style. Mon–Sat 8am–11pm, Sun 8am–10pm.

Metropolitain Antonijas 13. This roomy café-restaurant is the most versatile of several places in the Art Nouveau district, with an inexpensive daytime buffet (Mon–Fri 11.30am–7pm), and an à la carte selection of international food at other times. Mon–Thurs 8am–11pm, Fri 8am till last client, Sat 10am till last client.

Rāma Barona 56. A vegetarian bistro run by Hare Krishna devotees that's often crowded at lunchtimes. The food can be unexciting, but it's wholesome, filling and cheap. Mon–Fri 10am–7.30pm, Sat 11am–7.30pm, Sun 11am–7pm.

Restaurants

Old Town and around

The places listed below are marked on the "Rīga Old Town" map on p.167.

Botanica Café Antonijas 9. Delicious vegetarian food served in a cool interior with dark furnishings, amber-coloured walls and jazzy tunes; a popular street-corner terrace opens in summer. Mon–Thurs 11am–11pm, Fri & Sat 11am–2am, Sun noon–10pm.

Indian Raja Vecpilsētas 3 ☎6722 1617. Authentic Indian food, good service and an atmospheric warren of rooms. Daily noon–11pm.

Kamāla Jauniela 14. Smart, but not overpriced, vegetarian restaurant just round the corner from Doma laukums, serving Indian and Middle Eastern dishes in a room stuffed with cushions and exotic textiles. Mon–Sat noon–11pm, Sun 2–10pm.

Melnie mūki Jāņa sēta 1 ☎6721 5006. An elegantly converted medieval building offering an imaginative range of top-notch, reasonably priced international food. Daily noon–midnight.

Neiburgs Jauniela 25 ☎6711 5522. Lurking behind one of the Old Town's most famous Art Nouveau portals, this light-filled restaurant offers a stylish Latvian-European menu and attentive service. There are plenty of salads and pastas for light-biters, but excellent baked fish and roast meats form the core of the menu. Mains 10–12Ls, with some cheaper set-price lunches (11am–3pm), and a drinks list strong on cocktails. Daily 11am–11pm.

Vecmeita ar kaķi Mazā pils 1. An informal cellar restaurant just off Doma laukums, the "Grandma with Cat" offers pork-based Latvian favourites alongside healthy salads and pasta. Nicely priced for the area. Daily 11am–11pm.

Outside the Old Town

The places listed below are marked on the "Rīga" map on p.162.

Bergs *Bergs* hotel (see p.166) ☎6777 0957. Inside the ultra-chic hotel of the same name, this ultra-chic restaurant has a calming modern interior and a terrace overlooking the comings and goings in the upmarket Berga bazārs shopping precinct. Changing menu of imaginative, modern European dishes, at high, but not stratospheric, prices. Daily noon–11pm.

Charlestons Blaumaņa 38 ☎6777 0572. Quality food in relaxingly informal surroundings, with a menu that offers a range of global eats, from steak through ribs to pasta. Consistently reliable quality, good service and desserts to die for. Daily noon–midnight.

Gastronome Brīvības 31 ☎6777 2391. In a mall beneath the *Reval Hotel Latvia*, *Gastronome* makes up for what it lacks in atmosphere with some of the best fish and seafood in the city. Mains around 15–20Ls; inexpensive lunchtime specials are chalked up on a board at the door. Daily 11am–11pm.

Istaba Barona 31A. Cosy, chic and quirky café tucked into the second floor of an enjoyably odd art gallery-cum-gift shop. Coffee, tea and cakes are tip-top, and there's a range of meals – the menu is not written down, and you'll be asked what kind of food you like by a waiter-cum-chef. Mon–Sat noon–midnight.

Kabuki Tērbatas 46 (entrance from Mārtas). One of the most pleasant and reliable among the crop of sushi restaurants that has opened in Rīga in recent years, with a functional but chic interior, a big choice of sushi and noodle dishes, generous pots of tea and reasonable prices. Daily 11am–10.30pm.

Lidojošā Varde Elizabetes 31A ☎6732 1184. A bright basement restaurant with a profusion of frog motifs, and a wildly popular terrace on the street outside. The eclectic international menu features salads, pastas and vegetarian choices, alongside more substantial steak and fish dishes. Mains 8–9Ls. Daily 10am–1am.

Pie Kristapa Kunga Baznīcas 27/29. This roomy restaurant with a vaguely medieval theme has a pair of ground-floor dining rooms and several stone-lined chambers below. A good place to tuck into hearty meat and fish swilled down with good local beer on tap. Daily 11am–11pm.

Vincents Elizabetes 19 ☎6733 2634. Long-standing gourmet destination with formal service, über-cool interior and modern European menu. Main meals include steaks and some extremely good grilled and baked fish dishes. Entrees 15–20Ls. Mon–Sat 6–11pm.

Drinking

Rīga, and especially the **Old Town**, offers lots of opportunities for bar-hopping. There's a healthy scattering of characterful bars in the **Centre**, although they're more spread out – it's best to aim for one rather than expect to crawl your way through several. Most places are open until midnight or later on weekdays, 2am or later on Fridays and Saturdays. Drinks are affordable even in the most stylish places, and there's usually some sort of food menu. Bars that feature live music or DJs are listed under "Clubs and live music" (see below).

Old Town

The places listed below are marked on the "Rīga Old Town" map on p.167.

Aptieka Mazā Miesnieku 1. Blue and white tiles, a pill theme and probably the only jukebox in town that stretches from the Rolling Stones to Sonic Youth. Sun–Thurs 5pm–1am, Fri & Sat 5pm–3am.

I Love You Aldaru 9. Mildly bohemian drinking den with a nice mix of old and new furnishings: choose a wooden table in the medieval brick cellar or perch in a plush armchair upstairs. Salads, sandwiches and burgers make it a good lunch spot. Daily 11am–midnight.

Paddy Whelan's Grēcinieku 4. A big, lively Irish pub occupying lovely stucco-ceilinged rooms, popular with young locals and ex-pats alike. Head upstairs to the laid-back *Paddy Go Easy* bar for a quiet pint.

Paldies Dievam piektdiena ir klāt 11 Novembra krastmala 9. Translating as "Thank God it's Friday" (although it is most certainly not part of the global chain), this is an enjoyably brash bar with excellent cocktails, kaleidoscope-coloured interior and Caribbean-themed food. Sun–Thurs till 2am, Fri & Sat till 4am.

Rīgas balzams Torņa 4. Chic, roomy cellar bar serving Rīga's favourite firewater – the black, syrupy *balzams* – either solo or in a mind-boggling number of mixer combinations. Daily 11am–midnight.

Outside the Old Town

The places listed below are marked on the "Rīga" map on p.162.

A.Suns Elizabetes 83–85. Named after *Un Chien Andalou*, the Surrealist film made by Salvador Dalí and Luis Buñuel, this roomy café-bar is equally suited to an evening meal or a beery night out. The menu lists some eclectic dishes, with main courses from around 8Ls and some considerably cheaper omelettes and pastas. Sun–Wed till 1am, Thurs–Sat till 3am.

Gauja Tērbatas 56. Loving recreation of a Latvian domestic interior circa 1973, complete with mismatching furniture, frumpy textiles, old-style board games and shelves of boring-looking books. Good draught beer. Daily noon–11pm.

Skyline Bar in the *Radisson Blu Latvija* (see p.166). Up on the twenty-sixth floor of central Rīga's tallest hotel, and offering mesmerizing views of the Old Town skyline. Retro 1960s and '70s furnishings and a long list of cocktails add an air of camp luxury to the proceedings, although none of it comes cheap. Daily 3pm–2am.

Nightlife and entertainment

Rīga in Your Pocket carries advance **information** on classical music and theatre events. If you can read Latvian, you'll find a comprehensive run-down of concerts, plays and club nights hidden away in the *Diena* newspaper's TV supplement, which appears on Friday.

Clubs and live music

Most **dance venues** offer a commercial diet of techno, Euro-hits and golden oldies, although you might get more variety in the smaller clubs, especially on week-nights. **Live music** is largely limited to the middle-of-the-road pop-rock groups that Latvia seems to churn out in ever greater numbers, with gigs in a wide range of music bars and clubs. International touring acts perform at the **Sapņu Fabrika**, a post-industrial venue for alternative music, theatre and dance at Lāčplēša 101 (Ⓦwww.sapnufabrika.lv), or **Arena Rīga**, a much bigger auditorium for mega-bands at Skanstes 13 (Ⓦwww.arenariga.com). Clubs and music venues charge an entry fee of anything from 1–5Ls; drinks shouldn't be that much more expensive than in regular bars.

Unless otherwise stated, the places listed below are on the "Rīga Old Town" map on p.167.

Bites blūzs klubs Dzirnavu 34A; see Rīga map on p.162. Relaxed music pub with live acts most nights – performed by visiting bluesmen or by the house band. Fri & Sat till 2am. Sun–Thurs till 1am.

Četri Balti Krekli Vecpilsētas 12. Large, upmarket cellar bar, restaurant and disco known for its Latvian-only music policy (the better-known domestic bands perform here) and thus popular with an older crowd keen to escape the techno on offer elsewhere. Strictly no trainers. Daily 8pm–3am.

Depo Valnu 32 Ⓦ www.klubsdepo.lv. Post-industrial cellar space with alternative DJ nights and live bands. A laid-back café during the day. Daily 8pm–3am.

Diry Deal Cafe Spīķeri, Maskavas 12 Ⓦ www .dirtydeal.lv; see Rīga map on p.162. This restored brick warehouse in the Spīķeri complex is a prime venue for dance events and cutting-edge gigs from across the musical spectrum. There's an art gallery upstairs, and outdoor seating in the huge courtyard. Tues–Sat 4pm–late.

Nabaklab Z.A. Meierovica bulv 12 Ⓦ www .nabaklab.lv. Live rock and alternative DJ nights in a club co-founded by independent radio station Naba and Latvian University. Excellent draught beers, affordable shots, and the added advantage of a vintage secondhand clothing store on site. Noon–2am.

Pulkvedim Neviens Neraksta Peldu 26/28 Ⓦ www.pulkvedis.lv. Taking its name from the Gabriel García Márquez novel *Nobody Writes to the Colonel*, this hip bar with industrial-chic decor hosts different breeds of DJ on different nights of the week, as well as occasional live bands, attracting a laid-back artsy crowd. Mon–Thurs 8pm–3am, Fri & Sat 8pm–5am.

Classical music and theatre

Classical music in Rīga is of an exceptionally high standard. Performances are reasonably accessible – tickets, except for opera, cost between 7Ls and 10Ls, and rarely need booking weeks in advance. The Latvian National Symphony Orchestra and the Latvian National Opera are the biggest shows in town, but look out too for performances by Kremerata Baltica, a chamber ensemble put together by the Rīga-born violinist Gidon Kremer, and the world-famous choral group, Ave Sol. The best of the previous season's opera productions are reprised during the **Rīga Opera Festival** (middle fortnight of June; Ⓦ www.opera.lv). Rīga offers a rich and varied diet of **theatre**, although you'll need a working knowledge of Latvian or Russian to appreciate it fully.

Tickets can be bought at the venues themselves or booked through Biļešu paradize (☏ 9000 2000, Ⓦ www.bilesuparadize.lv) – box offices at the Great Guild, National Theatre and National Opera act as their agents.

Concert venues and companies

Ave Sol Concert Hall (Koncertzāle Ave Sol) Citadeles 7 ☏ 6718 1130. Home to Ave Sol, one of the best choral ensembles in the Baltic States. Also hosts concerts by other choirs and chamber musicians.

Great Guild (Lielā Ģilde) Amatu 6 ☏ 6721 3643, Ⓦ www.lnso.lv. Main venue for the Latvian National Symphony Orchestra, who usually play on Saturday evenings except when on tour. Frequent Saturday- or Sunday-lunchtime concerts aimed at children and families, featuring popular classics. Box office Mon–Thurs noon–7pm.

Latvian National Opera (Latvijas Nacionālā Opera) Aspazijas bulvaris 3 ☏ 6707 3777, Ⓦ www.opera.lv. The main auditorium – lavishly refurbished in late nineteenth-century style – stages classic operatic productions and is also home to the Rīga Ballet (Rīgas Balets). The New Hall (Jaunajā zāle) hosts anything from chamber music to civilized, sit-down pop-rock. Tickets in the stalls start at 17Ls, although there may be cheaper options way back in the upper tiers. Box office Mon–Fri 11am–6pm.

Rīga Cathedral (Rīgas Doms) Doma laukums ☏ 6721 3213, Ⓦ www.doms.lv. Recitals by world-class musicians on the sonorous cathedral organ several times a week, daily in summer. Tickets 5–10Ls. Box office Mon–Sat 10am–5pm and 1hr before performance.

Rīga Sinfonietta Maskavas 4 ☏ 6721 5018, Ⓦ www.sinfoniettariga.lv. Latvia's national chamber orchestra, performing at their own hall in the Spīķeri warehouse at Maskavas 4; or at the Small Guild (Mazā Ģilde), Amatu 3.

Theatres

Daile Theatre (Dailes Teātris) Brīvības 75 ☏ 6729 4444, Ⓦ www.dailesteatris.lv. Big, modern auditorium hosting a mixture of classical drama, musicals and comedy. Small-scale productions in the adjoining Mazā zāle, or "small hall". Box office Mon–Fri 10am–7pm, Sat & Sun 11am–6pm.

National Theatre (Nacionālais Teātris) Kronvalda bulvaris 2 ☏ 6700 6338. Elegant pre-World War I building with mainstream classical drama on the main stage, and more experimental stuff in the Aktieru zāle studio theatre. Box office Mon–Fri 11am–6pm, Sat 11am–4pm.

New Rīga Theatre (Jaunais Rīgas Teātris) Lāčplēša 25 ☎ 6728 0765, ⓦ www.jrt.lv. Generally considered the best place to see contemporary plays, this is the home theatre of internationally acclaimed director Alvis Hermanis – anything

bearing his imprint is well worth seeing. Box office Mon–Sat 10am–7pm, Sun noon–7pm.

Puppet Theate (Leļļu teātris) Barona 16/18 ☎ 6728 5355, ⓦ www.puppet.lv. Great puppets, great stage designs, great fun for children of all ages. Productions usually kick off at 11am or 3pm.

Cinema

Big-name movies arrive in Rīga almost immediately after their release in Western Europe. **Films** are usually shown in the original language with Latvian and Russian subtitles, though art-house movies that are in Rīga for a short run only will have Latvian-language voice-over.

Tickets cost around 3.50Ls to 5Ls, although most cinemas reduce their rates by up to fifty percent at least one day a week – usually Mondays or Tuesdays.

Forum 13 janvāra 8 ⓦ www.forumcinemas.lv. Modern multi-screen next to the train station with shopping mall, cafes and bars right on the doorstep.
Kino Suns Elizabetes 83/85 ⓦ www.kinogalerija .lv. Mainstream films and art-house flicks.
Rīga Elizabetes 61 ⓦ www.kino.riga.lv. The oldest of Rīga's surviving cinemas (formerly the

Splendid Palace), and still a plush, atmospheric place. Commercial films and the occasional art-house offering. One of the few cinemas that still hires an artist to paint the coming-attraction advertisements rather than simply putting up posters.

Shopping

Rīga's Old Town possesses a reasonable selection of boutiques, souvenir **shops** and bookstores. The more mainstream high-street stores are concentrated in the streets east of here – Čaka, Barona, Tērbatas and Brīvības ielas. The vast **Central Market** (Centraltirgus; see p.175) is great for browsing for cheap clothes, fake designer watches and Russian fur hats, though you're unlikely to turn up anything of quality.

You will, however, find excellent traditional, **hand-knitted woollens** throughout Rīga. Many are decorated with traditional Latvian geometric patterns – often sun, star and fir-tree shapes, symbolizing nature's bounty. The same designs crop up on tablecloths, linens and other textiles, many of which are hand-embroidered. You'll find them in souvenir shops and on the occasional street stall, alongside pendants, necklaces and bracelets made from the ubiquitous Baltic amber, and handmade ceramics – including lanterns in the form of tiny clay houses.

Souvenirs and gifts
Art Nouveau Rīga Strēlnieku 9. Textiles, ceramics and other knick-knacks made to traditional Art Nouveau designs. Daily 10am–6pm.
Hobbywool Maža Pils iela 6. Hand-knitted hats, socks, mittens and sweaters, in a range of trad-folksy and cool-designer styles. Mon–Fri 10am–7pm, Sat & Sun 11am–5pm.
Istaba Barona 31A. Funky gallery-shop selling T-shirts, prints, artist-designed cards and off-the-wall gifts. Good café-restaurant upstairs (see p.186). Mon–Fri noon–8pm.
Laipa Laipu 2/4. Reasonable across-the-board selection of linens, woollens, amber jewellery and wooden toys. Mon–Fri 10am–6pm, Sat 10am–3pm.

Senā Klēts Rātslaukums 1. A treasure trove of Latvian ethnography, with traditional folk costumes, tablecloths, bedspreads and more. Quality handiwork, high prices. Mon–Fri 10am–7pm, Sat & Sun 10am–5pm.
Tine Vaļņu 2. Large store selling ceramics, amber trinkets, linen goods and plenty of woolly mittens and socks. Mon–Sat 9am–7pm, Sun 10am–5pm.
Upe Vāgnera 5. Wooden craft toys and traditional folk instruments, plus Latvian folk CDs. Mon–Fri 11am–7pm, Sat 11am–4pm.

Books and music
Jāņa Rozes Barona 5. Good choice of tourist-oriented guidebooks and photo albums, and a

decent range of English-language paperbacks. Mon–Fri 10am–8pm, Sat 10am–7pm.

Jāņa Sēta Elizabetes 83/85. The best place in the Baltics for maps and travel guidebooks. Mon–Fri 10am–7pm, Sat 10am–5pm.

Lukabuka National Opera ticket hall, Aspazijas bulvāris 3. Specialist art, architecture and design bookseller with an excellent range of highly desirable titles. Also stocks Latvian alternative comic-strip magazine *Kuš*. Mon–Fri 11am–7pm, Sat 11am–4pm.

Upe Vāgnera 5. Folk and world music store run by the Upe record label, and the best place to seek out many of the CDs in our "Baltic Folk Music" section (see p.383). Branches at Valnu 26 and Barona 37 are good for rock, classical and jazz. Mon–Fri 11am–7pm, Sat 11am–4pm.

Valters un Rapa Aspazijas 24. Big bookstore selling stationery, calendars and coffee-table books about Rīga. Mon–Fri 9am–9pm, Sat 10am–9pm, Sun 10am–4pm.

Listings

Airlines Aeroflot, Skolas 9 ☎6724 0226; AirBaltic, at the airport ☎900 1100, from abroad ☎+371 6700 6006; Finnair, at the airport ☎6720 7010; Lufthansa, at the airport ☎6750 7711; SAS, see AirBaltic.

Embassies and consulates Belarus, Jēzusbaznīcas 12 ☎6722 2560, ☜www .belembassy.org; Canada, Baznīcas 20/22 ☎6781 3945, ☜www.latvia.gc.ca; Ireland, Alberta 13 ☎6703 9370, ☜www.embassyofireland.lv; Russia, Antonijas 2 ☎6733 2151, ☜www.latvia.mid.ru; UK, Alunāna 5 ☎6777 4700, ☜www.ukinlatvia .fco.gov.uk; US, Raiņa 7 ☎6703 6200, ☜riga .usembassy.gov.

Exchange Round-the-clock service at Marika, Dzirnavu 96, Brīvības 30.

Hospital The main emergency department is at Hospital No. 1 (Rīgas pirmaja slimnīca) on Bruņinieku iela, although for all but the most urgent complaints you'd do better to book an appointment with an English-speaking doctor at Diplomatic Service Medical Centre, Elizabetes 57 (☎6722

9942, ☜www.dsmc.lv) or Ars, Skolas 5 (☎6720 1007, ☜www.ars-med.lv).

Internet access Elik, Kaļķu 11 (24hr).

Left luggage In the basement of the train station (daily 4.30am–midnight) and at the bus station (24hr).

Parking 24hr guarded car parks at Prāgas 2, Z.A Meierovica bul. 8.

Pharmacies Ģimenes aptieka, Audēju 16 (daily 8am–8pm) & Tallinas 57b (24hr).

Police Emergency number ☎02 or ☎110.

Post office Brīvības 32 (Mon–Fri 7.30am–8pm, Sat 8am–6pm, Sun 10am–4pm).

Taxis Ranks at the junction of Kaļķu and Aspazias, and at the junction of Audēju and Aspazijas. Otherwise call Rīga Taxi (☎800 1010) or Rīgas taksometru parks (☎800 1313 or 8383).

Tours Skaisto skatu aģentūra, Kungu 8 (☎6722 1767, ☜www.skaistieskati.lv) organizes excursions throughout Latvia – tours will probably be in Latvian only but the sights themselves will be pretty self-explanatory.

Jūrmala

JŪRMALA, or "Seashore", is the collective name for a string of small seaside resorts that begins just beyond the estuary of the River Lielupe, 15km west of Rīga, and straggles along the Baltic coast for 20km. Originally favoured by the Tsarist nobility, Jūrmala had become a virtual suburb of Rīga by the 1920s and 1930s, when anyone who could afford it would rent a holiday house here for the summer. Jūrmala's seasonal citizens would commute to Rīga by train every morning, returning late in the afternoon to change into sanatorium-style pyjamas in which they would then promenade down to the beach. After World War II, Jūrmala became popular with Soviet citizens from all over the USSR; it was considered more Westernized and sophisticated than resorts elsewhere in the Union. Today, its sandy beaches backed by dunes and pinewoods seethe with people at weekends and on holidays. Despite a few decaying Soviet-era hotels, it's a delightfully low-rise area on the whole, with brightly painted wooden houses and tasteful modern holiday homes nestling beneath the trees. The main centre is the small town of **Majori**, 20km west of Rīga, where a busy strip of outdoor cafés caters for the stream of summer visitors; elsewhere, Jūrmala is wonderfully underdeveloped and laid-back.

Trains to Jūrmala leave from platforms 3 and 4 of Rīga's central station (every 30min, 5am–11pm). The **tourist office**, just off Majori's main street at Lienes 5 (Mon–Fri

9am–7pm, Sat 10am–5pm, Sun 10am–3pm; ☎6714 7900, ⓦwww.jurmala.lv), can arrange **private rooms** (❷) and give advice on **hotels** throughout the region.

Majori and Dzintari

At the centre of Jūrmala's string of beachside settlements, **MAJORI** is the area's most urbanized resort and main service centre. Cafés and boutiques line Jomas iela, the pedestrianized main street that conveys new arrivals from the station square northeast towards the beach. Just off Jomas to the south on Tirgoņu iela, the **Jūrmala City Museum** (Wed–Sun 11am–5pm; 1Ls) hosts excellent contemporary art exhibitions in the light-filled space upstairs, although the permanent collection of nautical bric-a-brac is a bit of a let-down. About 800m further down Jomas, a left turn into Pliekšāna iela brings you to the **Rainis and Aspazija Memorial Summer House** (Raiņa un Aspazijas memoriālā vasarnica; Wed–Sun 11am–6pm; 0.70Ls), in which Latvia's leading literary couple, Jānis Rainis (1865–1929) and Elza "Aspazija" Rozenberga (1865–1943), spent three summers in the late 1920s. Rainis was an anti-Tsarist newspaper editor before World War I, who suffered exile in Siberia as a result of his support for the 1905 Revolution, before going on to write poetry, novels and plays, becoming Latvia's "national" writer in the process. His wife Elza was his equal as a playwright, her allegorical drama Sidabra Šķidrauts ("The Silver Veil") causing riots in 1905 because of its perceived anti-Tsarist message. There's an absorbing collection of heirlooms, photographs and manuscripts relating to the pair, and a chance to peruse the relaxing, sun-lit veranda where Rainis scribbled his verse.

Another five minutes' walk down Jomas brings you to **DZINTARI** – allegedly a separate town, although there's no appreciable boundary between the two – a locality rich in pre-World War I holiday villas, many adorned with mock-medieval spires and towers. Bang in the middle of Dzintari is the **Forest Park** (Dzintaru mežaparks), a dense rectangle of pine forest criss-crossed by footpaths, with a playground and space for rollerskating and skateboarding. Skates can be hired from the Skrituļslidu noma **kiosk** at the park's western end (Mon–Fri 5–9pm, Sat & Sun noon–8pm). A **viewing tower** in the middle of the park provides a sweeping view of Jūrmala, the Lielupe river and the coast.

The beach and the aquapark

Wherever you are in Majori or Dzintari it's just a short walk north to the dune-backed **beach**, a grey-gold ribbon of sand that stretches as far as the eye can see in either direction. Despite being prone to strong winds, it's packed in July and August with people sunbathing, playing volleyball or drinking in alfresco cafés, and is a popular – if bracing – place for a stroll throughout the year.

Some of the most beautiful, least crowded parts of the beach are at the eastern end of Jūrmala, near the point at which the Lielupe River curves round to meet the sea. You can get here by alighting from the train at **BULDURI**, 4km east of Majori, and walking northeast through the pines. Bulduri itself was once named "Edinburg" after Prince Alfred, Duke of Edinburgh and second son of Queen Victoria (he married Marie, daughter of Tsar Alexander II of Russia, in 1874); always considered to be Jūrmala's upmarket end, it's currently home to some of the most expensive real estate in Latvia.

On the southern side of Bulduri, beside the Lielupe River at Viestura iela 24, and a fifteen-minute walk from either Bulduri or Lielupe train stations, **Livu Akvaparks** (Mon–Fri noon–10pm, Sat & Sun 10am–10pm; 2hr 7Ls, day pass 13Ls; ⓦwww .akvaparks.lv) is Latvia's biggest swimming complex, with a variety of indoor pools and plummet-down waterslides. Wave pools, palm trees and a replica pirate ship provide fun for the kids.

Eating, drinking and entertainment

Bars and restaurants are buzzing in **peak season**, when Jomas iela in particular is lined with places serving Caucasian-style šašliki kebabs to the accompaniment of blaring

Russian pop music. Many places work limited hours in spring and autumn and may close altogether in winter. The open-air stage next to the concert hall at Dzintari hosts **performances** over the summer ranging from Russian-language crooners to the Latvian Symphony Orchestra – check the tourist offices or street posters to find out what's on.

Eco Café Tirgoņu iela 29, Majori. Housed in the same building as Jūrmala museum, this charmingly restful café serves organic coffees and health-food snacks in a bright space sprinkled with settees and pot plants. Wed–Sun 11am–5pm.

Park Café Dzintaru mežaparks, Dzintari. Drinks and snacks in an angular glass-and-metal box in the middle of the Dzintari Forest Park. June–Sept daily 10am–10pm.

Sue's Indian Asia Jomas 74, Majori. Satisfyingly spicy Thai and Indian dishes, including plenty of vegetarian options, with mains around 8-10Ls. Daily noon–11pm.

Zanzegur Jomas 80, Majori. Armenian restaurant with a Caucasian menu of skewer kebabs, spicy meat stews, and *hinkali* (boiled pastry parcels filled with minced meat). Daily 11am–11pm.

Travel details

Trains

Rīga to: Cēsis (4 daily; 2hr); Daugavpils (4 daily; 3hr 20min–4hr); Majori (every 20–30min; 45min); Rēzekne (2 daily; 4hr); Salaspils (every 30min–1hr; 30min); Sigulda (10 daily; 1hr 5min–1hr 20min).

Buses

Rīga to: Aglona (3 weekly; 4hr 30min); Bauska (every 30–40min; 1hr 10min); Cēsis (hourly; 1hr 50min–2hr 5min); Daugavpils (8 daily; 3hr 30min–4hr); Kolka (3 daily; 3hr 30min–4hr 30min); Kuldīga (Mon–Sat 9 daily, Sun 6 daily; 2hr 30min–3hr 45min); Liepāja (14 daily; 3hr 30min–4hr); Rēzekne (4 daily; 4hr); Sigulda (hourly; 1hr 10min); Ventspils (14 daily; 3–4hr).

International trains

Rīga to: Moscow (2 daily; 16–17hr); St Petersburg (1 daily; 13hr).

International buses

Rīga to: Berlin (1 daily; 20hr); Hamburg (4 weekly; 24hr); Kaliningrad (2 daily; 10hr); Kaunas (3 daily; 4hr 30min–5hr 20min); Klaipēda (2 daily; 5hr 30min–6hr); Köln (1 daily; 32hr); Minsk (1 daily; 12–14hr); Moscow (2 daily; 12hr); Paris (2 weekly; 40hr); Pärnu (4 daily; 3hr 30min); St Petersburg (2 daily; 12hr); Šiauliai (4 daily; 3hr 15min); Stuttgart (2 weekly; 32hr); Tallinn (6 daily; 5–6hr); Tartu (2 daily; 5hr); Vilnius (4 daily; 5hr–5hr 30min); Warsaw (4 weekly; 12hr).

International flights

Rīga to: Amsterdam (2 daily; 2hr 30min); Berlin (1 daily; 1hr 45min); Brussels (1 daily; 2hr 30min); Copenhagen (4 daily; 1hr 30min); Dublin (3 daily; 3hr); Frankfurt (2 daily; 2hr 20min); Hamburg (1 daily; 1hr 45min); Helsinki (4 daily; 1hr 10min); Kiev (1 daily; 4hr); Liverpool (1 daily; 3hr); London (3 daily; 3hr); Milan (1 daily; 3hr); Moscow (2 daily; 1hr 45min); Oslo (1 daily; 1hr 45min); Prague (2 daily; 2hr); Stockholm (4 daily; 1hr 30min); Tallinn (2 daily; 50min); Vienna (1 daily; 2hr); Warsaw (1 daily; 1hr 30min).

International ferries

Rīga to: Lübeck (2 weekly; 36hr); Stockholm (daily; 16hr).

2.2
Western Latvia

Western Latvia's rich variety of attractions extend from vibrant port cities to quirky market towns, not to mention long, sandy beaches – the region's 320km-long coastline amounts to virtually one long, continuous strand. Inland, there are innumerable areas of genuine wilderness, especially in the north, where squelchy bogs and deep forest break up crops and grazing land. The southwest is made up of Latvia's most fertile arable land, its farms producing bountiful harvests of grain, potatoes and sugar beet.

The region consists of two ethnographically distinct areas. **Zemgale**, extending south from Rīga to the Lithuanian border, is named after the Zemgaļi (Semgallians), one of the original Baltic tribes that subsequently coalesced to form the Latvian nation. Over to the west, **Kurzeme** – usually rendered into English as **Courland** – gets its name from the Kurši (Cours), a tribe that established the area's enduring reputation for fishing, seamanship and trade. From the 1560s onwards, Zemgale and Kurzeme were united to form the **Duchy of Courland**, which exploited Polish, Swedish and Russian rivalries to ensure over two centuries of semi-independence.

Much of western Latvia is within day-trip distance of Rīga. Easily reached are the Baroque palaces at **Rundāle** and **Jelgava** south of Rīga, providing some insight into the lavish tastes of Courland's eighteenth-century dukes. Nearby, the aristocratic seat

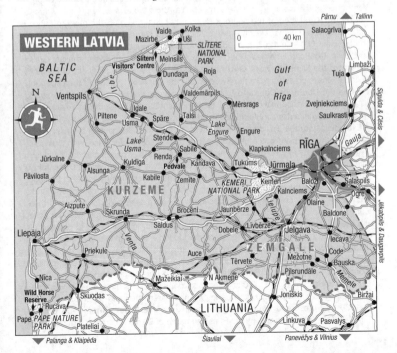

of **Mežotne** provides a cool Neoclassical riposte. West of the capital, the green, rolling countryside of Kurzeme enfolds attractive rural centres like **Kandava** and **Kuldīga**, both offering an authentic taste of small-town Latvia. All this contrasts with the hurly-burly of western Kurzeme's great port cities, **Ventspils** and **Liepāja**. The best of the region's wild, unspoiled nature is to be found in the beaches and forests of the **Slītere National Park** around Kurzeme's northernmost point; the desolate beauty of **Cape Kolka**; the bogs of the **Ķemeri National Park** just west of Rīga; and the reedy environs of the **Lake Pape Nature Reserve** south of Liepāja.

Zemgale

The region of **Zemgale** occupies central Latvia, cut through by the busy Rīga–Vilnius road. The landscape is largely flat and unremarkable, made up of arable farmland, but whatever Zemgale lacks in terms of natural beauty is more than made up for by the presence of two sumptuous palaces: park-girdled, Neoclassical **Mežotne** and the splendid Baroque–Rococo confection that is **Rundāle**. Both lie just outside the small town of **Bauska**, the major transport hub for the area. All three places can be visited as a day-trip from Rīga, providing you make an early start.

Zemgale's only real city – and a more exciting urban prospect than Bauska – is **Jelgava**, 55km southwest of Rīga. One-time capital of the Duchy of Courland, it's home to a fine ducal palace, though sadly many of its other venerable buildings were destroyed in World War II.

The Duchy of Courland: a brief history

The original inhabitants of Courland were the **Livs** (see p.200), a Finno-Ugric tribe related to the Estonians who arrived in the wake of the last Ice Age and are still around – albeit on the verge of extinction – in the isolated fishing villages of the extreme north. Very much in the majority until the early Middle Ages, the Livs were gradually forced out by the **Kurši**, one of the bedrock Baltic tribes that make up the modern Latvian and Lithuanian nations. Despite giving Courland its name, the Kurši succumbed to the Livonian Order in 1267, and power passed to a new class of German-speaking landlords. Courland emerged as a distinct political entity in 1562, when the last Grand Master of the Livonian Order, **Gottfried Kettler**, faced with the prospect of Livonia's collapse under pressure from the Swedes and the Russians, dissolved the Order and created the **Duchy of Courland** to serve as a new power base. In need of a strong ally, Kettler made Courland a vassal of the Polish-Lithuanian Commonwealth, while retaining internal autonomy for himself and his successors.

Extending from the Baltic coast in the west to the River Daugava in the east, Courland under the Kettlers was a generally peaceful and prosperous place, with towns like Jelgava, Ventspils and Kuldīga growing fat on the profits of expanding trade. The duchy even enjoyed a brief spell as a transatlantic trading power when ambitious **Duke Jakob** (ruled 1642–82) received an unusual gift from his godfather, King Charles I of England, in the shape of the Caribbean island of **Tobago**. Merchantmen bearing Courland's standard – a black crayfish on a red background – were seen in ports all over northern Europe. Jakob's dreams of empire soon faded, however: the Swedes, unwilling to tolerate the existence of a rival maritime power in the Baltic, forced Jakob to disband his fleet in 1658. The overseas colonies were abandoned – although the waters around the Tobagan town of Plymouth are still known as Great Courland Bay.

Eventually, the rise of Russia and the decline of Poland seriously compromised Courland's independence. **Peter the Great** married his niece, **Anna Ioannovna**, to Duke Frederick Wilhelm in 1710 and sent his troops to take control of the region when the duke died childless two months later. Anna herself became Empress of Russia in 1730 and presented the dukedom to court favourite **Ernst Johann von Bühren** (1690–1772) – better known by his Russified name of **Biron** – marrying him off to one

Bauska

The main road to Vilnius ploughs right through the bland market town of **BAUSKA**, 75km south of Rīga. As well as offering public transport links to Rundāle and Mežotne, Bauska can also boast a substantial aristocratic seat of its own. Looming over parkland fifteen minutes' walk west of the town's main T-junction, **Bauska Castle** (Bauskas pils; May–Oct daily 9am–7pm; 1.50Ls) began life as a Livonian-order strongpoint commanding the confluence of the Mēmele and Mūsa rivers. Subsequently used by the dukes of Courland as a temporary residence, it was destroyed by order of Peter the Great in 1706. The fifteenth-century parts of the castle have been faithfully restored and now hold a museum display rich in Renaissance stove tiles, pot fragments, cannon-balls and the like. The older, thirteenth-century wing of the castle is largely a ruin save for one reconstructed tower, which affords sweeping views of the Mēmele and Mūsa; they converge just upstream to become the Lielupe ("Great River"), which flows into the Baltic Sea just west of Rīga. If you've got a bit of time to kill, check out the **Museum of Regional Studies and Art** (Bauskas novadpētniecības un mākslas muzejs; Tues–Fri 10am–5pm, Sat & Sun 10am–4pm; 0.50Ls), just off the flagstoned main square at Kalna 6. Its old sepia photographs of firemen, brass bands and schoolchildren eloquently sum up Bauska's small-town sense of community.

Practicalities

Bauska's **bus station** is at the southeastern end of town. Ten minutes' walk away is the **tourist office** on the main square, Rātslaukums 1 (May–Sept Mon–Fri 9am–6pm,

of her ladies-in-waiting, Benigna Gottlieb von Trotta-Treyden. Flush with wealth and success, Biron commissioned Italian architect Rastrelli to design sumptuous palaces at **Rundāle** and **Jelgava**. With the death of Anna Ioannovna in 1740, Biron fell from grace and was exiled to Siberia by new Empress Elizabeth. Finding favour again under **Catherine the Great** and resuming his ducal office in 1764, he went on to supervise the completion of Rundāle Palace and presided over a glittering court at Jelgava. Before long, Jelgava's palace had become a popular stop-off for society folk travelling from Western Europe to St Petersburg. One house guest was Casanova, whose ability to sound off on subjects he knew nothing about tricked Biron into believing he was an internationally recognized authority on mining techniques – somewhat improbably, Biron paid the Venetian charmer 200 ducats to write a report on the minerals of Courland. Biron's son and successor Peter was no less gullible a host, giving board, lodging and lavish gifts to bogus faith-healer Cagliostro.

With Courland's formal incorporation into the Russian Empire in 1795, the duchy was finally extinguished. Shifts in sovereignty made little difference to local society, with the Latvian-speaking majority remaining subject to a Germanized landowning elite. Life continued to be centred on the great manor houses, and the nobles themselves overcame isolation by devising a busy round of social events, attending society gatherings in provincial towns like Jelgava and Aizpute (where balls usually lasted three days in order to justify the travelling involved) and decamping to the seaside in July. Their easy-going, hospitable nature was much appreciated by German guidebook writer J.G. Kohl, who summed up a visit to Courland in the 1840s by asking, "What gentleman or lady values time? The whole day is made up of leisure. No one looks at the clock, except to know when it will be dinner time, or whether tea may soon be ordered."

The duchy was briefly resurrected in March 1918 by Kaiser Wilhelm, who believed that a chain of German-dominated states could be established along the Baltic seaboard prior to their outright incorporation into the Reich. Even after the defeat of Germany in November 1918, this dream was kept alive by a Baltic German army of General von der Goltz, who based themselves at Liepāja, then Jelgava, before finally being beaten off by the Latvians in November 1919.

Sat & Sun 1.30am–3.30pm; Oct–April Mon–Fri 9am–5pm; ☎6392 3797, ⒲www
.tourism.bauska.lv), stocked with information on sights and accommodation
throughout Zemgale. *Kafejnīca pie Rātslaukuma* (daily 8am–8pm), on the main square at
Plūdoņa 38, is a good place for a cheap, filling **meal**.

② Rundāle Palace

Rising above rich farmland 13km west of Bauska, **Rundāle Palace** (Rundāles pils;
daily: June–Aug 10am–7pm; May & Sept 10am–6pm; Oct–April 10am–5pm; 3.50Ls;
⒲www.rpm.apollo.lv) is one of the architectural wonders of Latvia, a haughty slab
of Baroque masonry filled with Rococo furnishings. This monument to eighteenth-
century aristocratic excess is all the more impressive for its situation – plonked
incongruously among the more modestly proportioned farmhouses and cottages of the
Latvian countryside. The site was bought in 1735 by Empress Anna's fancy-man, Duke
of Courland **Ernst Johann von Biron**, who named it *Ruhetal* (German for "Vale of
Peace") and engaged Francesco Bartolomeo Rastrelli, architect of the Winter Palace in
St Petersburg, to build the 138-room summer hideaway that you see today. Most of the
construction work was completed by 1740, but Biron was exiled to Siberia in the same
year, and it wasn't until his return in the 1760s that the interiors were finally decorated in
the opulent Rococo style that was all the rage at the time. On the abolition of the duchy
in 1795, Biron's son Peter was thrown out of Rundāle (he took most of the movable
furnishings to Żagań in Silesia, where they were destroyed in World War II), and the
palace was given to Catherine the Great's favourite, Platon Zubov. It remained in private
hands until 1920 and thereafter fell into disrepair, but meticulous restoration, begun in
1972, has returned large chunks of the palace to their former glory. With approximately a
third of the palace open to the public, Rundāle is very much a work in progress.

The grandeur of Rundāle unfolds gradually: after you've passed through a belt of
orchards and crossed a small moat, a wine-red gatehouse heralds the entrance to an oval-
shaped outer courtyard. At the far end of this, a brace of regal-looking lions guard the
entrance to the inner courtyard, closed off on three sides by the ochre wings of the palace
itself. Once inside, you ascend to the **staterooms of the east wing**, where the original
decorations – wall and ceiling paintings by St Petersburg-based Italians Francesco Mar-
tini and Carlo Zucchi, stucco by Johann Michael Graff – have been faithfully recreated.

First up is the **Gilded Hall**, a long, showpiece chamber intended for ceremonial recep-
tions, with exuberant ceiling frescoes swirling above a row of mirrors, each topped by a
relief of birds fighting over berries. From here the Grand Gallery, featuring an animated
ceiling fresco of the god Apollo, leads on to the **White Hall**. A ballroom the size of a
basketball court, the hall features a grandiose stucco frieze depicting cherubs in a range
of rather unlikely pastoral situations – tooling away on flutes, riding goats or ward-
ing off big-tusked boars. Side chambers are devoted to displays of fancy porcelain, the
asymmetrical Rococo shelving so ornate that it upstages the vases themselves.

Return the way you came and proceed to the south wing and you will come to the
Rose Room, with its fanciful ceiling painting of Flora (goddess of spring) surrounded
by fleshy attendants, and the **Lord's Bedchamber**, whose gargantuan pair of tiled
stoves give some idea of how difficult it must have been to keep the palace warm during
the dark Baltic nights. Next up is the florid pink wallpaper of the **Audience Room**,
where family portraits include a radiant depiction of Peter von Biron's stepdaughter
Dorothea, a famed beauty and bedroom-hopper whose lovers included French states-
man Talleyrand (who married her off to his nephew). Passing through the **Shuvalov
Room**, filled with portraits of the Russian family who inherited the palace after the
death of Platon Zubov, you arrive in the west wing, where a set of smaller rooms are
rounded off with the **Lady's Boudoir**, **Bedchamber** and **Washroom** with its fanciful
floral wall decorations and cherub-encrusted stucco work.

Practicalities

Getting to the palace is easy enough: it's a well-signed 13km drive west of Bauska
on the Eleja road. There are five daily buses (four on Sundays) from Bauska – make

sure you catch a service that's going to Pilsrundāle or Rundāles pils ("Rundāle Palace") rather than simply the village of Rundāle, which is 3km west. Get off when you see a big hedge: the palace gates are hidden just behind it. You can eat well at the rather formal **restaurant** in the palace basement, which serves up superb cuts of veal and steak in the former kitchen – where spits big enough to skewer an entire family of buffalo are lined up in front of gaping fire grates. A more modest **café**, also in the basement and decorated with stuffed animals, serves simpler food at half the price.

Next to the palace car park, the *Baltā Māja* has a folksy café-restaurant and is also a characterful **place to stay** (☎6396 2140 or 2912 1374, ⊛www.hotelbaltamaja.lv; ❷–❸), offering rooms in a lovingly restored nineteenth-century house full of trad furnishings – most come with shared facilities although there is one en-suite double with Jacuzzi-style bathtub.

Mežotne Palace

Some 10km northwest of Bauska and another easy jaunt by local bus, the cool, lemon-yellow bulk of **Mežotne Palace** (Mežotnes pils; daily 9am–5pm; 1Ls) could almost be seen as a restrained neoclassical response to the lavish ostentation of Rundāle. It began life as the country estate of Princess Charlotte von Lieven, who was given the land by Catherine the Great in 1795 in recognition of her services as governess to the imperial children. The princess visited Mežotne only once, but the palace stayed with the Lieven family until the Land Reform of 1920 (when most Baltic German aristocrats were kicked off their lands), after which it became an agricultural college. It was badly damaged in World War II and subsequently various parts of the building served as a library, post office and residential flats. Now lavishly restored, it functions primarily as a hotel and conference centre, although several staterooms are open to the public. Decked out in pastel shades of ochre, pink and eau-de-nil, the interiors exude an easygoing elegance, with decoration limited to stuccoed floral motifs and friezes of personable gryphons, their paws raised as if in friendly greeting. A small display of engravings shows how the estate looked at the time of the Lievens and there's a forest-green ballroom framed at each end by Ionic columns. One space you'll want to return to is the **Cupola Room**, a light-filled chamber said to be modelled on the Pantheon in Rome and featuring a dome held up by Titans – it also offers panoramic views of the palace park from its windows. The park itself is a terrific place for a stroll, stretching away along the bank of the River Lielupe and densely wooded at its far end.

The palace **hotel** (☎6396 0711 or 2200 8086, ⊛www.mezotnespils.lv; ❺–❻) is one of the most charming in Latvia, offering eight doubles and five three- to four-person apartments, each decorated in olde-worlde style – expect things like cast-iron bedsteads and Thonet furniture. The hotel's **restaurant** serves up quality Latvian food, including excellent freshwater fish.

Jelgava

Straddling the road between Rīga and Kaliningrad, **JELGAVA** is a predominantly postwar, concrete city, although a reconstructed ducal palace and a smattering of other old buildings make a short stop-off here worthwhile. Jelgava was founded in 1265 by the Livonian Order, who named it Mitau and used it as a base from which to mount successive campaigns against the pagans of Zemgale just to the south. In the seventeenth and eighteenth centuries, it was the capital of the Duchy of Courland and became an important social centre: Duke Jakob resided here for at least part of the year, and his successor Friedrich Casimir founded an (albeit short-lived) opera house. By the nineteenth century, most of Courland's German barons owned town houses in Jelgava and spent the coldest months here rather than on their country estates, turning winter into one long round of parties and balls. Sadly, little architectural evidence of Jelgava's golden age survives today: Baltic German forces under General von der Goltz put much of the town to the torch in November 1919 and World War II bombing raids largely put paid to what was left.

The City

Twice rebuilt almost from scratch following devastation in both world wars, the Baroque **Jelgava Palace**, with its dignified, maroon-and-cream facade, graces the riverbank just east of the city centre, next to the main Rīga road. The palace, built by Rastrelli for Count Ernst Johann von Biron in 1738, was intended as an urban equivalent to the edifice then taking shape at Rundāle. Now part of the Latvian University of Agriculture, its student-tramped rooms retain little in the way of original features. For an idea of what it looked like before World War I, visit the small **palace museum** (May–Oct daily 9am–4pm; Nov–April closed Sun; 0.50Ls), displaying photographs and prints recalling the days when Jelgava was a popular stop-off for society folk travelling from Western Europe to St Petersburg.

Beneath the east wing of the palace and accessible from a doorway outside the gates, the **Burial Vault of the Dukes of Courland** (May–Oct daily 9am–5pm; 1Ls), is where all the duchy's rulers, from Gottfried Kettler to Peter Biron, are lined up in a series of richly decorated caskets. Hogging the limelight is the burnished copper affair belonging to Ernst Johann von Biron, adorned with a dull-grey death's head and mounted on feet in the form of snarling lions. The adjoining anteroom displays the richly embroidered burial shrouds in which seventeenth-century dukes were originally laid to rest, and a fetching pair of felt pantaloons once worn by Ernst Johann von Biron.

Practicalities

Jelgava is an easy half-day trip from Rīga; trains leave hourly from the central station and minibuses every fifteen to thirty minutes from the bus station. Jelgava's **bus station** is in the city centre, about 400m west of the tower of the Church of the Holy Trinity. The **train station** is about 1km to the south: bear left down Zemgales prospekts to reach the centre. The **tourist office**, Pasta 37 (Mon 8am–6pm, Tues–Thurs 8am–5pm, Fri 8am–3.30pm; ☏6302 2751, ⓦwww.jrp.lv) hands out free maps and gives advice on accommodation.

Good for a relaxing sit-down **meal**, *Tobago*, overlooking the Lielupe at Čakstes bul. 7, has all manner of steak and fish, and an attractive riverside position. More informal is *Silva*, opposite the bus station on the pedestrianized Driksas iela, a stylish canteen with the added advantage of a bar and an outdoor terrace.

Cape Kolka and around

Separating the Gulf of Rīga from the open Baltic Sea, the horn-shaped land mass of **northern Kurzeme** is endowed with one of the most captivating stretches of coast in the country: an almost uninterrupted ribbon of white sand backed by pines and spruce trees. The main focus for visitors is **Cape Kolka**, at the northernmost tip, a short, sandy spit jutting out into the Baltic Sea, backed by an enchanting hinterland of dunes, bogs and forests. A 10km belt of territory around the cape is protected by the **Slītere National Park**, the well-maintained walking trails of which provide access to the best of the local landscape. Despite the presence of a few thriving fishing ports, most of the settlements in Latvia's far northwest have an eerie, semi-abandoned air – the result of decades of rural depopulation. During the Soviet period, the entire shore was a sensitive border area, and resources like schools and hospitals were concentrated inland in order to dissuade people from moving to the coast.

The best way to get to northern Kurzeme from Rīga **by car** is to head for Jūrmala (see p.190) and simply keep going – the scenic coastal road goes all the way to Cape Kolka. You could easily see the cape and be back in Rīga by nightfall, though it's worth sticking around for a day or so. If you're reliant on public transport you'll have to stay overnight – the three daily **buses** from Rīga all set off in the afternoon (and a couple of them seem to travel all over Kurzeme before arriving). It's best to book accommodation in advance, especially at weekends, as places to stay are thin on the ground – the tourist office in the regional capital Talsi (☏6322 4165; ⓦtalsitourism.lv) can help. Jāņa

Sēta's 1:100,000 **map** of the Talsi region (Talsu rajons) covers the whole of northern Kurzeme and is essential if you're exploring the area in any depth.

The Gulf of Rīga

The road from Rīga to Cape Kolka sticks to the coast for most of its 150km length, providing plenty of opportunities for scenic stop-offs. After leaving the urbanized sprawl of Jūrmala, the road passes through a series of small settlements popular with day-trippers keen to escape the more crowded beaches further east. The first of these, some 10km out of Jūrmala, is **Lapmežciems**, a fishing village renowned for its smoked fish – which can be sampled at a string of roadside cafés. The village also abuts the eastern corner of Lake Kanieris, a brackish stretch of water separated from the Gulf of Rīga by a 1km-long, thick bar of sand. The marshy shores of the lake attract white-tailed eagles, ospreys and bitterns, and are particularly popular with migrating cranes in the autumn. Further on, the stretch of coast between **Ragaciems** and **Klapkalnciems** is particularly beautiful, with a wonderful beach backed by pines – and a couple of secure car parks along the road.

Cape Kolka and around

Buses from Rīga stop 2km short of **Cape Kolka** in **KOLKA** village, which, like most settlements in these parts, consists of a single street running parallel to the coast. To reach the cape, head to the northern end of the street and turn right. There's nothing much here, but it's a uniquely beautiful spot nevertheless, with a desolate, end-of-the-world feel. Looking out to sea, you'll catch sight of the Kolka lighthouse rising up from a small island 6km to the northeast. In certain conditions, currents from the Gulf of Rīga meet counter-currents from the Baltic Sea to produce a chevron pattern of wavelets. In spring, the cape is an important collection point for migrating birds, with thousands of geese and ducks joined by herons, buzzards and eagles.

There's a lot more in the vicinity to enjoy, whether it's the fishing villages west of the cape, **Vaide**, **Košrags** and **Mazirbe** (see p.200), where time seems to have stopped, or the distinctive landscape inland, shaped over millions of years: at the end of the last Ice Age, the sea extended all the way to the Zilie Kalni (Blue Hills), a 70m-high escarpment that lies about 10km inland from the present-day coast. Since then the sea has been in slow retreat, leaving behind the rippling succession of duney ridges that characterize the landscape today. Many of these ridges are covered in forest, but there are also large tracts of heath and bog – notably Bažu bog (Bažu purvs), just off the main Rīga–Kolka road, though it's a protected reserve and is closed to the public. The whole area falls under the protection of the **Slītere National Park** (Slīteres nacionlais parks), which maintains a modest visitors' centre at Slītere lighthouse. The park is also a haven for roe deer, elk, wild boar and lynx.

One of the best sea views is from **Ēvaži cliff** (Ēvažu stāvkrasts), a bank of moss- and tree-covered dunes that rises above the seashore 5km south of Kolka, just off the Rīga road, and is reached by a short trail just opposite the Novakari bus stop. From the top, you get a great view of the coast all the way down to Roja. Walking back to Kolka along the beach is a great way of taking in the pines-and-sands landscape.

The **Cape Kolka Visitors' Centre** on the approach road to the cape's tip (☎2914 9105, ⓦwww.kolkasrags.lv) handles information. **Accommodation** in Kolka is limited to the *Zītari*, next to a supermarket of the same name at the southern entrance to town (☎6327 7145; ❷), with acceptable en-suites but indifferent service; and the more basic but much friendlier *Ūši*, at the northern end of the main street (☎6327 6507 or 2947 5692; ❶), offering two sparsely furnished rooms, a communal kitchen and tent space. There's a **café** serving meat-and-two-veg main courses at the *Zītari*.

West of Kolka

West of Kolka, the main Ventspils-bound road runs a couple of kilometres inland to a string of sleepy fishing villages, connected to the outside world by a dirt road. The first you come to is **VAIDE**, a dune-encircled collection of fishermen's cottages and holiday houses about 7.5km west of Kolka. Aside from another glorious stretch of white sand, Vaide's main attraction is the **Horn Museum** (Ragu kolekcija; daily 9am–8pm; 0.70Ls), a forest ranger's collection of elk and stag antlers, gleaned from the forest and artfully arranged in an attic.

From Vaide you can continue westwards via a dirt road – a great ride through coastal heath and forest (if your suspension's up to it) – or return to the main road, turning off again after 6km for the village of **KOŠRAGS**, where wooden fishermen's houses huddle around sand-paved streets. There's a highly attractive **B&B** here, *Jauntilmači viesu nams* (℡2941 2974; ❸), offering smart rooms and an on-site sauna. A further 3km beyond Košrags lies the village of **MAZIRBE**, set back from a beautiful stretch of dune-backed beach. Like all the villages along this part of the coast, Mazirbe is inhabited by descendants of the **Livs** – a Finno-Ugric people closely related to the Estonians, who settled in Latvia just after the last Ice Age – although you're unlikely to find anyone here who speaks the rapidly disappearing language. The **Liv House** (Lībiešu Tautas Nams/Līvlist Roukuoda), a Modernist white cube built in 1939 with financial support from other Finno-Ugric nations, valiantly attempts to keep the study of Liv culture alive, but prospects are bleak. Towards the southern end of the village, the **Rāndali Ethnographic Collection** (Etnogrāfiska kolekcija Rāndali) has a small display of Liv costumes, while a little further on, on the far side of the Kolka–Ventspils road, Mazirbe **parish church** sports a pebble-dashed exterior and a lovely wooded cemetery. Back in the village, there's a cosy **B&B**, *Kalēji* (℡6324 8374; ❷), with tent space in the grounds, and a **food shop** opposite the Liv House.

Beyond Mazirbe the main road continues southwest towards Ventspils, while another route forks south towards Talsi, climbing up the Zilie Kalni escarpment. Taking the latter route, you'll pass a sign to the **Pēterezers Nature Trail** (Pēterezera dabas taka) on your right after about 4km. This enjoyable boardwalk trail takes you up and down some of the region's trademark dune ridges and across heath before arriving at Pēterezers, a shallow lake edged by dark pines. Returning to the road and continuing up the hill for another 5km brings you to **Slītere lighthouse** (Slīteres bāka; Wed–Sun 10am–6pm; 0.50Ls), a stocky cylinder dating from 1849 and now containing a display of photographs of lighthouses throughout the world. You aren't allowed all the way to the top of the lighthouse, but you get a good view of the surrounding countryside from the penultimate floor, with a lush plateau of farmland to the south and wooded wilderness stretching seawards to the north. On the ground floor is the **Slītere National Park Visitors' Centre** (same times), where you can buy brochures and rudimentary maps. Behind the lighthouse, a wooden stairway leads down the escarpment towards the **Slītere Nature Trail** (Slīteres dabas taka), which winds through a lush expanse of mixed forest with occasional stretches of semi-bog, the undergrowth thick with bird's-eye primrose and ferns. The trail's only drawback is its short length, taking barely thirty minutes to complete.

Ķemeri and around

The commuter rail line that loops northwest out of Rīga via Jūrmala puts a couple of worthwhile destinations within day-trip range of the capital. Around 50km out of Rīga, **Ķemeri** was one of the show-pieces of the interwar Latvian state – a high-society spa resort, which, despite several decades of decay, still retains something of its former elegance. More importantly, the town is the centre of the **Ķemeri National Park** and provides access to the **Great Ķemeri Bog**, one of the most captivating wetland landscapes in the country.

Drivers should note that although a town in its own right, Ķemeri is in administrative terms part of Jūrmala – this accounts for the rather confusing signs reading "Jūrmala" which you'll see if you enter Ķemeri by road.

Ķemeri

An upmarket resort in the interwar years and a popular health spa during the Soviet era, **ĶEMERI** has fallen off the tourist map since Latvia regained independence and nowadays has a rather abandoned air. However, a tangible sense of grandeur still lingers in the **spa park** (a fifteen-minute walk northeast across town from the train station), where manicured lawns and flowerbeds and elegant, tree-lined avenues seem tailor-made for hours of recuperative walks. At its centre stands the **Ķemeri Hotel**, a stately ocean liner of a building whose smooth curves and castellated towers bring to mind some sort of Art Deco Camelot. Designed in the early 1930s by leading National Romantic architect Eižens Laube, it seems a world away from the Gotham City-style apartment blocks he built in central Rīga. The hotel is currently being restored and looks set to resume its role as playground of the Rīga elite when it reopens.

Ķemeri National Park

Northeast of the hotel, a path leads off through densely forested parkland, arriving after 1km at the Meža Māja, or Forest House, where the **Ķemeri National Park Visitors' Centre** (Mon–Fri 9am–5pm; ☎6714 6819, ⓦwww.kemeri.gov.lv) sells maps and advises on walks. Immediately north of here lies the start of the **Black Alder Wetland Path** (Melnalkšņu dumbrāja taka), an 800m-long boardwalk trail through dense and leafy woodland and over soggy (and sometimes rather smelly) soil, fed by the same sulphurous springs that provide the Ķemeri spa with its restorative waters. For a slightly longer walk, the **Lake Sloka Trail** (Slokas ezera taka) heads northeast from the visitors' centre to the Sloka swamp, which runs around the western shores of the aforementioned lake. Half an hour out from the Visitors' Centre you hit a boardwalk trail that takes you on a 3km circuit of the most untouched parts of the swamp, rich in mosses, berries and squelchy sulphurous mud.

Great Ķemeri Bog

Lovers of bleak wilderness landscapes will want to make the trip to **Great Ķemeri Bog** (Lielais Ķemeru tīrelis), a 6000-hectare expanse of bog covered in springy sphagnum moss and punctuated by stunted birch trees and conifers. Leading out into the bog is a 3km-long boardwalk trail, which starts a good 4km south of Ķemeri itself. To get there, head south from Ķemeri train station to the main Rīga–Ventspils road, turn right and follow it for 800m before turning left down a dirt road that leads past Ķemeri cemetery. Curving through the forest, the road eventually arrives at a national park signboard, where you veer right and follow the "laipa" sign to find the start of the trail.

The boardwalk leads out onto a patchwork of greens and tawny browns, and, further along, a glinting archipelago of ponds. Local flora worth looking out for include cranberries (picking them is strictly forbidden) and sundews, which use the sticky red hairs on their lower leaves to trap insects – that's if the creepy crawlies haven't already been gobbled up by the bog's wood sandpipers.

The Abava Valley

The glacier-carved, U-shaped **Abava Valley** is one of the most picturesque spots in western Latvia – not least because it offers a welcome change from the flat arable landscape that dominates elsewhere. Quaint country towns like **Kandava** and **Sabile** provide reason to pause – the latter is a short hike away from the open-air art museum at **Pedvāle**. Further west lies **Kuldīga**, arguably Latvia's most appealing provincial town.

Five daily Rīga–Kuldīga **buses** run through the Abava Valley, along with a handful of additional Rīga–Sabile and Sabile–Kuldīga services.

Kandava

Some 30km west of Rīga, **KANDAVA** drapes itself between a trio of hillocks just above the main Kuldīga-bound road. Boasting a handsome collection of two-storey houses, and with central streets still paved with their original nineteenth-century cobblestones, it's a lovely place for a stop-off. The hillock nearest to the road is **Bruņinieku pilskalns**, the easily scaled site of a Livonian Order castle that still preserves the remnants of its thirteenth-century fortifications. Behind Bruņinieku pilskalns lies a neat town square overlooked by a curious nineteenth-century fire station with fortress-like lookout tower. A little way further up the main Lielā iela, at no. 51, a whitewashed former **synagogue** (and subsequently town cinema) stands in mute commemoration of the fact that fifty percent of Kandava's population was Jewish prior to World War I – after which mass emigration in the 1920s and 30s, followed by the murder by Nazis of those that remained, put paid to their presence in the town. The **Town Museum**, Talsu iela 11 (Tues–Fri 9am–4pm, Sat 10am–2pm; 0.50Ls) displays photographs documenting Courland's tragic role in World War II's closing stages, when Latvian volunteers were used as cannon fodder by Germans desperate to stem the Soviet advance. There's also a "red corner" filled with objects – Soviet flag, bust of Lenin – that date back to the building's former role as a branch of the Soviet state bank. East of the centre, on the far side of the main Tukums–Kuldiga road, a dainty four-arched **bridge** spans the Abava River – built in 1873, it has been a beloved local landmark ever since.

Kandava's **tourist office**, behind the main bus stop at Kūrortu iela 1B (mid-July to Sept Tues–Fri 8.30am–noon & 1–6pm, Sat 9am–1pm; Oct to mid-July Mon–Fri 8.30am–noon & 1–5pm; ☎6318 1150, ✉info@kandava.lv), will provide a free town map and regional information. The charming *Tējas bode* teahouse, Lielā 30 (Mon–Fri till 8pm, Sat till 10pm, Sun till 6pm), is the place for a refreshing brew.

Sabile

Sheltering beneath a south-facing escarpment 16km west of Kandava, **SABILE** is famous for being the northernmost location at which vines are cultivated. On the hill just north of town, **Sabile vineyard** (Sabiles vīnakalns) was founded in the seventeenth century by Duke Jakob of Courland, one of many pet schemes designed to lessen the duchy's dependence on foreign imports. It never produced much in the way of wine and soon fell into disuse, but was re-established in 1936 in order to carry out research into hardy strains of vine – the hundred or so bottles of plonk produced here annually are unlikely to make it as far as the supermarket shelves. To inspect the wine terraces at close hand, and enjoy the view across Sabile's rooftops, you need to buy a ticket from the tourist office (0.15Ls). Back on the main street, Rīgas, it's hard to miss the stately apricot-coloured form of Sabile's nineteenth-century **synagogue**, restored and pressed into service as a contemporary art space managed by the Open-air Museum at nearby Pedvāle (opening hours vary). At the western end of town, the seventeenth-century **Lutheran Church** (Luteranu baznīca) harbours a striking Baroque pulpit held up by a quartet of gryphon-headed snakes. Behind the church, a brisk five-minute ascent brings you to the summit of the pudding-shaped **Castle Hill** (Sabiles pilskalns), site of an ancient Latvian fortress and affording excellent views across the valley.

The **tourist office** in the town council building at Pilskalna 6 (Mon–Fri 10am–3pm; ☎6325 2344, ⊛www.sabile.lv) will put you in touch with local **B&B** hosts (❶–❷), few of whom speak English. For something to eat, try one of the decent **cafés** along Rīgas: *Sabiles vīnakalns*, no. 11, does a good line in pork and chicken standards, while *Kafejnīca Zane*, no. 8, has more salads and soups.

Pedvāle

Up on the ridge on the opposite side of the valley to Sabile lies Pedvāle Manor, an abandoned estate entrusted to sculptor Ojārs Feldbergs in the early 1990s on condition that he restore the buildings and open them up as a cultural centre. The result of his labours is the **Pedvāle Open-air Art Museum** (Pedvāles brīvdabas mākslas muzejs; daily: May to mid-Oct 10am–6pm; mid-Oct to April 10am–4pm; 2Ls; ⊛www .pedvale.lv), a sculpture park set in part-agricultural, part-virgin countryside. The park functions wonderfully well as a nature trail, too, whether you're interested in sculptures or not, with paths taking you down beside densely wooded streams and up over wildflower-carpeted hills, with several storks' nests scattered around for good measure.

To get to Pedvāle, cross the river from Sabile and head uphill – a left turn takes you to the **main entrance** at Firkspedvāle manor house, where there's a window selling tickets. Spread over 2km are well over a hundred works, ranging from the profound to the pretentious, donated by abstract and conceptual sculptors from all over the world. Many of the more memorable works are by **Ojārs Feldbergs** himself – an expanding collection of brooding, deeply mysterious granite lumps. The collection of rocks dangling from poles that make up his *51 Heartstones* (51 sirdsakmens) is the most impressive work in the park, although the quietly enigmatic stone hut that is Ryan Hoover's and Kerin Rozycki's *Fire Inside* (Iekšējā uguns) comes a close second.

If you want **to stay**, the restored manor house at Firkspedvāle (℡6325 2249) has a handful of atmospheric doubles, triples and quads, all at 12Ls per person – all have wooden floors and beams, with showers/WCs in the hallway. You can **camp** in the field outside for 1.50Ls. The nearby *Krodziņš Dāre* **pub-restaurant** serves everything from simple salads to steak and trout dishes.

Along the Abava to Renda

There are a couple of much-frequented local beauty spots just west of Sabile, beginning with the **Abava Falls** (Abavas rumba), 4km west of town and 500m from the road, a series of frothing rapids where the river descends what looks like a stairway of stratified rock. Back on the main road, another 15km brings you to the turn-off (near the Kaleši bus stop) for **Māra's Chambers** (Māras kambari), a series of sandstone hollows 2km away on the banks of the Abava, where it's thought that ancient Latvians made sacrifices to Māra the Earth Mother. Some 5km beyond, the main road traverses the river at the village of **Renda** and leaves the Abava Valley, crossing low hills before dropping down towards Kuldīga.

Kuldīga

If you visit just one provincial town in Latvia then it really should be **KULDĪGA**, 155km west of Rīga, a pretty little town of cobbled streets and half-timbered houses on the banks of the Venta. Kuldīga also boasts one of the natural wonders of Latvia right on its doorstep – a set of rapids known as the **Venta Falls**. Thanks to the navigability of the Venta River, Kuldīga was once one of most important trading towns in Kurzeme and a member of the Hanseatic League. The birthplace of Duke Jakob, Kuldīga's castle was a favourite residence of the dukes of Courland until its destruction by the Russians in the Great Northern War, after which Kuldīga settled back into the state of small-town tranquillity that still characterizes the place today.

Arrival, information and accommodation

Kuldīga's **bus station** is a few paces southwest of the town centre, hidden behind two large supermarkets. The **tourist office** at Baznīcas 5 (Mon–Fri 9am–5pm; July & Aug also Sat 10am–4pm & Sun 10am–2pm; ℡6332 2259, ⒲www.kuldiga.lv) is a good source of information on Kurzeme as a whole. They rent bikes, too, as does the*Ventas Rumba* hostel (see below).

Of the handful of **hotels**, one of the nicest is *Aleksis*, Pasta iela 5 (℡6332 2153; ❸), offering sweet little doubles with modern furniture and jazzy colour schemes, all with shower, and some with TV. Also good is *Jāņa Nams*, Liepājas 36 (℡6332 3456, ⒲www.jananams.lv; ❸), with neat, simply furnished en-suites in a quiet courtyard. The *Metropole*, Baznīcas 11 (℡6335 0588, ⒲www.hotel-metropole.lv; ❹), offers smart modern rooms in a nicely renovated nineteenth-century building overlooking the town centre's main junction. Alternatively, snuggle down in one of the en-suites with wooden floors and furnishings at the ⚘ *Sauleskalni B&B* (℡2680 6054 or 6332 2850, ⒲www.sauleskalni.com; ❸), in idyllic countryside south of Kuldīga. **Hostel** beds are available at *Virkas Muiža*, twenty minutes' walk northwest of the centre at Virkas iela 27 (℡6332 2787, ⒲www.hotelvirka.lv; 7–18Ls per person), and *Ventas Rumba*, across the river from town beside the Venta Falls (℡6332 4168 or 2643 8250, ⒲www.ventasrumba.lv) – an attractive, shingle-roofed old house offering doubles with shared facilities (❷), en-suites (❸) and some quads (35Ls) – and you can pitch tents on the lawn outside. Breakfast (extra) is in the nearby *Pīlādzītis* café. The nearest **campsite** is the *Nabīte*,

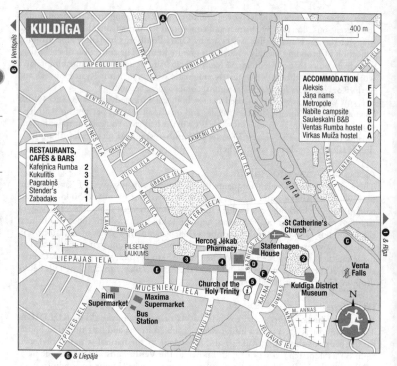

KULDĪGA

B & Ventspils

0   400 m

A

1 & Rīga

C

G & Liepāja

ACCOMMODATION

Aleksis	F
Jāņa nams	E
Metropole	D
Nabīte campsite	B
Sauleskalni B&B	G
Ventas Rumba hostel	C
Virkas Muiža hostel	A

RESTAURANTS, CAFÉS & BARS

Kafejnīca Rumba	2
Kukulītis	3
Pagrabiņš	5
Stender's	4
Zabadaks	1

St Catherine's Church

Hercog Jēkab Pharmacy

Stafenhagen House

Venta Falls

Kuldīga District Museum

Church of the Holy Trinity

Rimi Supermarket

Maxima Supermarket

Bus Station

N

about 12km northwest of town (signed off the Ventspils road; ☎2945 8904, ⓦwww .nabite.viss.lv), offering four-person cabins (15Ls) on the wooded shores of Nabes lake.

The Town

Central Kuldīga is such a compact place that you can probably see all its sights in half an hour and still have time for a coffee, although the relaxing effect of its quiet streets and gingerbread-style buildings will make you want to stay longer. The most attractive of its well-preserved houses are concentrated around the junction of Baznīcas iela, Liepājas iela and Pasta iela. The creamy-yellow house on the corner of Baznīcas and Pasta is supposedly the oldest surviving wooden building in Kurzeme, dating from 1632, although it has been much rebuilt since. Heading east along Liepājas and taking the first left down Raiņa iela brings you to the seventeenth-century Catholic **Church of the Holy Trinity** (Sv Trīsvienības baznīca; Mon 3–7pm, Tues, Wed & Fri 11am–7pm, Thurs & Sat 11am–4pm, Sun 9.30am–4pm), a delightful stone building, sheltering in a neat garden square. The main focus inside is a nineteenth-century altar rich with Neoclassical detail, with smooth-skinned angels framing a much older statue of the Virgin. On the right side of the nave, look out for a seventeenth-century confessional booth decorated with jolly floral squiggles.

Returning to Baznīcas iela and heading north, you'll pass a string of old stone houses, including at no. 17 which hosted Swedish King Charles XII in 1701; when not preoccupied with planning military campaigns against Peter the Great, he enjoyed hunting in the local forests. At its northern end, Baznīcas curves its way around **St Catherine's Church** (Sv Katrīnas baznīca), an oft-rebuilt structure where Duke Jakob of Courland was baptized and later married to Princess Louisa Charlotte of Brandenburg. The church doesn't have regular opening times but if you do find it open, look out for an exquisitely carved wooden altar by seventeenth-century Ventspils sculptor Nicholas Soffrens.

The bridge across the Venta affords a superb view of the **Venta Falls** (Ventas rumba) immediately upstream. At less than 2m in height, they're not exactly Niagara, but provide a memorable spectacle nevertheless, curving across the 250m-wide river in an elegant S-bend. Occupying high ground on the south side of the bridge is a grassy park covering the site of the (now demolished) castle. In the middle stands the **Kuldīga District Museum** (Kuldīgas novada muzejs; Tues–Sun 11am–6pm; 1Ls), in a wooden house built in 1900 to serve as the Russian pavilion at the Exposition Universelle in Paris. Intended to show off prefabricated house-building techniques, it was successfully dismantled and re-erected here by a Liepāja businessman eager to impress his Kuldīga-born fiancée. The creaky-floored interior harbours a scale model of Kuldīga castle as it looked in its sixteenth-century heyday, and a colourful display of playing cards through the ages.

Eating and drinking

There are plenty of places **to eat** in town. For a relaxing drink and a great view, try *Kafejnīca Rumba*, a kiosk near the museum with an outdoor terrace overlooking the Venta Falls. *Kukulītis*, Liepājas 35, is the best place for take-away pastries. *Stender's*, a two-tier wooden pavilion at Liepājas 3, has the full range of meat-and-potato dishes and is an enjoyable place for an evening **drink**, as is *Pagrabiņš*, occupying a cellar behind the tourist office at Baznīcas 5 and featuring steaks, salmon and trout. Check posters to see if anything is happening at alternative **club** *Zabadaks*, on the eastern side of the Venta at Vijolīšu 24, one of the few places outside Rīga or Liepāja to host live bands.

Ventspils

Once the most hard-edged of port cities, **VENTSPILS** has spent the last decade reinventing itself as a tourist-friendly city, and now enjoys the enviable status of being the number-one day-trip destination in Latvia, with a restored medieval castle, a white-sand beach, an open-air ethnographic museum and lots of attractions for kids. While a stark industrial landscape of warehouses and cranes still dominates the north bank of the River Venta, the southern bank is characterized by cutely cobbled pavements, neat flowerbeds and sculpture-scattered parks.

Arrival, information and accommodation

Ventspils **bus station** is conveniently located on the southeastern fringes of the centre on Kuldīgas iela. **Ferries** from Västervik and Lübeck dock some 400m from the centre, at the eastern end of Ostas iela. The **tourist office** in the ferry terminal (Mon–Fri 8am–5pm, Sat 10am–3pm; ☎6362 2263, ⓦwww.tourism.ventspils.lv) hands out town maps. Although good-value, quality **accommodation** in Ventspils is on the rise, there's still not enough of it to go round – book ahead if you can. **Campers** should head for the year-round *Piejūras kempings*, Vasarnīcu 56 (☎6362 7925, ⓦwww.camping.ventspils.lv), a large, well-tended site with tent and trailer pitches (3–5Ls) and timber cottages sleeping four (10Ls, 20Ls en suite).

Hotels and guesthouses

Jūras brīze Vasarnīcu 34 ☎6362 2524, ⓦwww.hoteljurasbrize.lv. Small hotel in a traditional-style house close to the Aquapark and beach, offering en-suites with laminate floors. Family-sized suites (38–48Ls) sleep three or four, and room #14 (reached by a wobbly spiral staircase) offers cosy quarters beneath a steeply sloping attic ceiling. ❸

Karlīnes nams Karlīnes 28 ☎6362 0114, ⓦwww.karlinesnams.viss.lv. Cute guesthouse in the Ostgals quarter offering a handful of en-suite doubles and quads with small TVs. Optional breakfast is 3Ls extra. ❸

Olympic Centre (Olimpiskā centra viesnīca) Lielais prospekts 33 ☎6362 8032, ⓦwww.ocventspils.lv. A former housing block, 10min walk south of the bus station, converted into a bright, modern hotel, offering functional, plain en-suites. No breakfast, but there's a small café on site. ❸

Raibie logi Lielais prospects 61 ☎2914 2327, ⓦwww.raibielogi.lv. Charming timber house offering a handful of traditionally decorated en-suites with TV. Plenty of triples and quads make this a good choice for families. ❸

VENTSPILS

▲ Riga

RESTAURANTS, CAFES & BARS
Don Basil — 2
Kafejnīca Buģiņš — 3
Melnais Sivens — 1
Pankoki — 4

ACCOMMODATION
Jūras brīze — D
Karlīnes nams — A
Olympic Centre — C
Piejūras kempings campsite — E
Raibie logi — B

0 ___ 500 m

N

Venta

South Pier

Town Beach

Observation Tower

Aquapark

OSTGALS

A Karlīnes

Children's City

Seaside Open-Air Museum

D

E

B

Livonian Order Castle

Hercogs Jēkabs

Ferry Terminal

Former Synagogue

Baptist Church

St Nicholas's Church

Orthodox Church

Bus Station

Olympic Centre Sports Hall

C

DURBES IELA

LĀCPLĒŠA IELA

BRĪVĪBAS IELA

LIELAIS PROSPEKTS

SARKANMUIŽAS DAMBIS

KULDĪGAS IELA

SAULES IELA

KATOĻU IELA

LIELAIS PROSPEKTS

VAIGZNU IELA

SPORTA IELA

BĒRZU IELA

GANĪBU IELA

PUTNU IELA

PLAVAS IELA

VĪTOLU IELA

PRIEŽU IELA

PURU IELA

DZIRNAVU IELA

PĀVILA IELA

MENESS

PĒTERA IELA

LIELĀ DZIRNAVU IELA

RAINA IELA

JŪRAS IELA

ALEKSANDRA IELA

LAUKU IELA

KULDĪGAS IELA

PILS IELA

OSTAS IELA

RĀTSLAUKUMS

LIEPU

MEŽA IELA

PLATĀ

LIEPĀJAS

RĪGAS IELA

KATOĻU IELA

AVOTU IELA

LĪVU

K. VALDEMĀRA

KRONU IELA

VIĻŅU IELA

MEDŅU IELA

LŌDU IELA

PARKA IELA

VASARNĪCU IELA

PĒTERA IELA

PĻAVINU IELA

PĒRĶŌNA

INŽENIERU IELA

TĀLIVALŽA

JŪRKALNES

INŽENIERU IELA

TĒRANDES

SAULES IELA

MEŽA IELA

BĒRZU IELA

GANĪBU IELA

DZINTARU IELA

DZINTARU IELA

TĀRGAS

LŌKSTGALU

RINKA IELA

APŠU IELA

STRĀDU

OZOLU

TORŅA

LĀMAS

AFĪJAS

Venta

The City

Most of Ventspils' sights are spread out over 2km along the south side of the Venta estuary. Starting at the eastern end of this strip, there's a handsome collection of nineteenth-century buildings around **Rātslaukums**, the historic centre of the city. From here your best bet is to proceed westwards along the waterfront, taking in views of the bustling container port before arriving at the superbly restored **Livonian Order Castle**, now home to an absorbing history museum. Strolling west then south through the picturesque nineteenth-century suburb of **Ostgals** brings you eventually to the vast, green, open spaces of the **Children's City** play area, **Seaside Open-air Museum** and **Seashore Park**.

Rātslaukums and the waterfront

At the centre of Ventspils lies a tangle of narrow streets zeroing in on an unassuming **Town Hall Square** (Rātslaukums). On the square's eastern edge is the nineteenth-century **St Nicholas's Church** (Sv Nikolaja baznīca), the principal Lutheran place of worship in the city. It looks rather like a Greek temple with an observatory growing out of its roof, and has a beautifully proportioned balustraded interior. From here, Tirgus iela leads north to a market square thronging with shoppers on weekday mornings.

Beyond the market square lies **Ostas iela**, a waterfront promenade running along the southern bank of the River Venta and dotted with an impressive array of public sculpture. The eastern end starts with the *Sea Stone* (Jūras akmens), a rough-hewn lump of grey rock mounted on granite supports, and continues with several similarly inscrutable abstract pieces by local artists. Looking no less sculptural are the immense loading chutes and cranes of the cargo port on the opposite bank of the river. For a closer look at the port facilities, including the oil terminal just north of town, take a 45-minute trip with the **Hercogs Jēkabs excursion boat** (May–Sept roughly hourly between 10am & 6pm; Oct 5 daily; 1Ls), which departs from a mooring just to the east of the Sea Stone.

The Livonian Order Castle

At the western end of Ostas iela, lanes lead back inland towards the egg-yolk-coloured bulk of the **Livonian Order Castle** (Livonijas ordeņa pils; daily: May–Sept 9am–6pm; Oct–April 10am–5pm; 1.50Ls), a medieval fortress and, later, Tsarist prison that has become a Ventspils landmark in the wake of its much-publicized restoration in 2001. Inside is a well-designed **museum of the city's history**, which makes up for a lack of genuinely dramatic artefacts through imaginative use of diagrams and touch-screen computers. The castle's renovated halls and galleries are a major attraction in themselves, especially the beautifully lit central courtyard overlooked by arched, red-brick galleries. Seasonal arts and crafts exhibitions are held in the main tower, where you'll also chance upon a clumsily painted fresco featuring weightlifters – a reminder that this part of the castle was used as a Soviet army gym in the 1960s.

West of the castle

Ten minutes' walk west of the castle lies a grid of cobbled streets and wooden single-storey houses known as **Ostgals** ("Port's End"), an attractively sleepy suburb dating from the mid-nineteenth century, when the Tsarist authorities encouraged local fishermen and farmers to build homes in the area, in order to prevent the Sahara-like encroachment of nearby dunes. Head south from here and you'll find it hard to avoid the hordes of little ones making a bee-line for **Children's City** (Bērnu pilsētiņa; free), a kiddies' playpark featuring all manner of slides, climbing frames and sandpits.

From here it's a five-minute walk southwest along Vasarnīcu iela, lined with Tsarist-era summer houses, to the **Seaside Open-air Museum** (Piejūras brīvdabas muzejs; May–Sept daily 11am–6pm; Oct–April Wed–Sun 11am–5pm; 1.50Ls). Alongside a display of beached fishing boats of all eras and sizes, there's a street of fishermen's cottages (each with a pair of crotch-high wading boots hung up in the hallway) and a nineteenth-century windmill whose mechanism is driven by wood-carved cogs. One of the museum's most popular attractions is the **narrow-gauge railway** (Mazbānītis), on which a steam-hauled train (0.50Ls extra) takes passengers on a brief circuit of the lawns and trees of the adjacent **Seashore Park** (Jūrmalas parks), its shrill whistle audible all over the western side of the city.

North of the museum lie the outdoor pools and waterslides of the **Aquapark** (Akvaparks; May–Sept daily 10am–9pm; 4Ls/90min, 7Ls/day), while over to the west lies a glorious stretch of white-sand **beach**, with yet more swings and climbing frames for the kids. Following the road north of here will bring you to a harbourside **observation tower**, offering good views of cargo ships lumbering their way into Ventspils' port, and the beginning of the 800m-long **South Pier** (Dienvidu mols) – the lighthouse at the end makes for an obligatory stroll.

Eating and drinking

Although culinary culture in Ventspils has yet to catch up with the rapid modernization elsewhere in the city, the generous sprinkling of **cafés and restaurants** in the centre is perfectly adequate if you're simply after a functional meal and a relaxing drink.

Don Basil Annas iela 5 ℗2680 9086. Cosy bistro-style place with wooden tables and earthy colours. They offer lots of the usual pork, chicken and freshwater fish dishes, with a fair selection of pastas and risottos to broaden out the menu. Main courses 8–10Ls. Small but varied wine list. Daily 11am–11pm.

Kafejnīca Bugiņš Lielā iela 1/3. This cosy café-bar, decked out like a log cabin, is a good place to tuck into inexpensive pork-based favourites or snuggle down for an evening's drinking session. Daily 11am–midnight.

Melnais Sīvens Jāņa 17 ℗6362 2396. In the basement of Ventspils Castle, this restaurant has a vaguely medieval feel, with wooden floors, stone walls and candlelight. In summer the terrace provides good views of the portside cranes on the north bank of the Venta. Mains – slabs of pork, chicken or salmon – are around 10Ls. Daily 10am–11pm.

Pankoki Vasarnīcu 17. An old-fashioned and rather basic order-at-the-counter café in a timber-built villa, specializing in sweet and savoury pancakes. Handy for the Open-Air Museum. Daily 10am–7pm.

Liepāja

Squeezed between a sandy seashore and the marshy Lake Liepāja (Liepājas ezers), the port city of **LIEPĀJA** has undergone several shifts in identity over the last century or so: bustling mercantile centre, then genteel bathing resort, Soviet garrison town and now cultural and commercial capital of Latvia's southwest. Its history is reflected in the city's engaging hodge-podge of architectural styles: wooden seaside villas rub shoulders with red-brick industrial buildings and dockside cranes. Attractions extend to leafy seaside gardens and long sandy beaches, a handful of museums and the grimly fascinating northern suburb of **Karosta**, once a Tsarist naval fortress and then a Soviet submarine base – virtually a walk-through history lesson.

Although served by regular **buses** from Rīga, Liepāja is too far from the capital (220km) to make a comfortable day-trip. Luckily, there's more than enough here to warrant an enjoyable couple of days' stay – not least its proximity to Latvia's south coast, notably the nature reserve at **Lake Pape**.

Some history

Liepāja grew out of the village of Līva, a medieval fishing settlement subsequently taken over by the Livonian Order in the thirteenth century; they renamed it Libau and used it as a base from which to extend their rule over the Curonian coast. As one of the region's few ice-free ports, the city was developed by Tsarist Russia as a naval base in the late nineteenth century and was also one of the main departure points for passenger liners heading for the US, taking thousands of Latvian, Estonian and Lithuanian migrants with them.

In 1919, with Rīga in the hands of the Bolsheviks, Liepāja became the seat of the Latvian Provisional Government. Unfortunately, it had to share the town with an army of Baltic Germans under General von der Goltz, who still entertained the dream

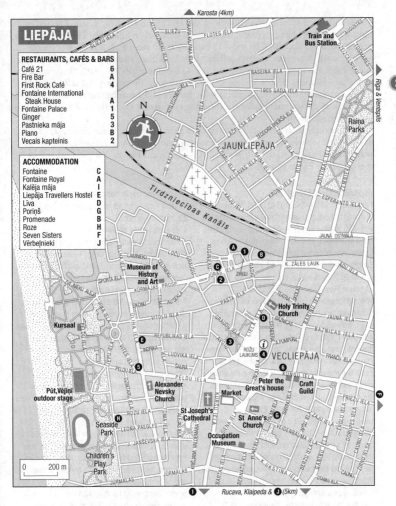

LIEPĀJA

▲ Karosta (4km)

Train and
Bus Station

▶ Rīga & Ventspils

RESTAURANTS, CAFÉS & BARS

Café 21	6
Fire Bar	A
First Rock Café	4
Fontaine International Steak House	A
Fontaine Palace	1
Ginger	5
Pastnieka māja	3
Piano	B
Vecais kapteinis	2

ACCOMMODATION

Fontaine	C
Fontaine Royal	A
Kalēja māja	I
Liepāja Travellers Hostel	E
Līva	D
Poriņš	G
Promenade	B
Roze	H
Seven Sisters	F
Vērbeļnieki	J

JAUNLIEPĀJA

Raina Parks

Tirdzniecības Kanāls

Museum of History and Art

Holy Trinity Church

Kursaal

VECLIEPĀJA

Pūt, Vējiņi outdoor stage

Alexander Nevsky Church

Market

Peter the Great's house

Craft Guild

Seaside Park

St Joseph's Cathedral

St Anne's Church

Occupation Museum

Children's Play Park

0   200 m

▼ ● Rucava, Klaipeda & ● (5km) ▼

of turning Latvia into a German-dominated statelet. The British, who needed both the Latvians and the Germans to stave off the westward advance of Bolshevism, sent the Royal Navy to Liepāja to keep the peace. A period of uneasy cohabitation unfolded, with British and German troops patrolling different parts of the city. Liepāja's brief period in the political limelight ended when von der Goltz marched off to occupy Rīga in May 1919 – although he was kicked out of the capital by the Latvians a few months later.

The Soviet navy established itself in Liepāja after World War II and the city was virtually closed to foreigners until 1990 – which goes some way to explaining why the tourist potential of its long, sandy beaches has waited until now to be exploited.

Arrival, information and accommodation

Liepāja's **bus and train stations** occupy the same building at the northern end of Rīgas iela, some 1500m from the town centre. Catch any tram heading down Rīgas iela to reach the centre (tickets 0.25Ls from kiosks, 0.30Ls from the driver) – get off when you see the grey spire of the Church of the Holy Trinity on your left. **Ferries** from Rostock and Karlshamn arrive at the Brīvosta terminal on Siļķu iela, 2km north of the centre and buses #3, #6, #10 and #15 run into town from Kalpaka iela, just inland.

The South Kurzeme **tourist office** (Lejaskurzemes tūrisma informācijas birojs; Mon–Fri 9am–5pm, Sat 10am–4pm, Sun 11am–3pm; ☎6348 0808, ⓦwww.liepaja .lv), Rožu laukums 5/6, is a mine of information on the region and sells city maps. There's a rapidly improving collection of **hotels and hostels**; the tourist office can also book **B&B** accommodation in the villages scattered along the coast from here to the Lithuanian border.

Campers can pitch a tent or park a caravan 5km south of town at *Verbelnieki* (☎2913 8565, www.verbelnieki.lv), a holiday complex with guesthouse accommodation (❷), a playpark and a long stretch of beach. Liepāja-Nica and Liepāja-Klaipēda buses pass by (get off at the Pērkone stop).

Hotels and hostels

Fontaine Jūras iela 24 ☎6342 0956, ⓦwww .fontaine.lv. Lovingly restored nineteenth-century villa with original timber features and rooms decorated in a variety of styles – some display folksy Latvian touches while others come with Middle Eastern fabrics or brash pop-art. The "Elvis Room" should be booked well in advance. ❷–❸

Fontaine Royal Stūrmaņu 1 ☎6348 9777, ⓦwww.fontaine.lv. Portside blockhouse given an extravagantly kitsch make-over by the Fontaine team, with luscious fabrics and fittings contrasting with bare concrete ceilings. With an all-night bar in the lobby and a pet iguana on the third-floor landing, wannabe rock-star types with an appetite for camp will feel right at home. Most en-suite doubles come with views of the harbour; "budget" rooms are extremely small with shared WC/shower in the hallway. Breakfast is 3Ls extra. ❷–❸

Kalēja māja Kalēju iela 8 ☎2648 8200, ⓦwww .kalejamaja.et.lv. Charming nineteenth-century house on a residential street, with three snug rooms in the attic, each decorated with traditional furniture and fabrics. Toilet, shower, kitchenette and fridge are shared. You can rent the whole house if travelling as a family or group. ❷

Liepāja Travellers Hostel Republikas iela 25 ☎2869 0106, ⓦwww.liepajahostel.lv. Relaxing, homely hostel a block from the seaside park, with a 12-bed dorm, a brace of four-bed rooms, and a couple of private doubles. There's a

common-room with basic kitchen facilities and an outdoor terrace for summer barbecues. Doubles ❶, dorm beds 8Ls.

Līva Lielā iela 11 ☎6342 0102, ⓦwww.liva.lv. A conveniently central block offering a mixed bag of en-suites – "business class" rooms feature new carpets, warm colours and satellite TV, while "economy" rooms still proudly display their grey-brown, Soviet-era colour schemes. ❸–❺

Poriņš Palmu iela 5 ☎2915 0596, ⓦwww.porins .lv. A renovated nineteenth-century town house on a cobbled street, with nine comfy rooms, each with en-suite shower. The homely atmosphere makes this very popular with the foreign business community, so it's best to book. ❺

Promenade Vecā ostmala 40 ☎6348 8288, ⓦwww.promenadehotel.lv. Attractively restored grain warehouse on a nineteenth-century quayside. Expect stylish en-suites with hardwood floors, exposed brickwork and flat-screen TVs. ❻

Roze Rožu 37 ☎6342 1155, ⓦwww.parkhotel -roze.lv. A pair of renovated villas beside the Seafront Park offering repro furniture, roomy doubles with spacious bathrooms and a handful of swish self-catering apartments. ❹–❼

Seven Sisters Egļu 8 ☎6348 1140, ⓦwww .sevensisters.lv. Friendly B&B in an attractive red-brick house 20min walk east of the centre, offering crisply decorated rooms and a walled garden. ❷

The City

The obvious place to start exploring Liepāja is **Lielā iela**, the main north–south thoroughfare. Its principal landmark is the **Holy Trinity Church** (Sv Trīsvienības baznīca), with its distinctive, four-tiered bell tower. The church's weather-beaten exterior certainly doesn't prepare you for the Rococo delights inside, where there's an exuberantly decorated high altar, a pulpit held up Atlas-like by the figure of an angel and an organ built by H.A. Contius in 1779 (and said to be the largest mechanical organ in the world until 1912), the clustered pipes of which appear to be dripping with molten gold. You can climb the **tower** (daily 10am–6pm; donation requested) for views of the town.

The city centre

South of the church, the pedestrian **Zivju** and **Stendera streets** break off from Lielā to pass through the main shopping area of town. There's a scattering of picturesque old buildings in the side streets off to the east, including a half-timbered former inn at Kungu 24 where Peter the Great allegedly stayed in 1697. The visit formed part of the so-called Great Embassy, when Peter led a 250-man mission to Western Europe in order to study modern techniques in shipbuilding and fortress construction. It's not known whether he learned much in Liepāja, but he was back here as a conqueror ten years later. Across the road from the house is the workshop of Liepāja's **craft guild** (Aušanas darbnīca), worth visiting for the small shop (Mon–Fri 9am–4pm) and the chance to watch weavers at work.

Another 200m south, the neo-Gothic **St Anne's Church** (Sv Annas baznīca) contains a wonderfully delicate Baroque altar carved by Nicholas Soffrens in 1697. A three-tiered affair with a scene of the Crucifixion at the bottom, the Deposition in the middle and the Ascension at the top, the whole ensemble radiates a honey-coloured glow that is in marked contrast to the plain grey tones of the rest of the – largely unadorned – interior.

One block south of the church at Kļava Ukstiņa, **Liepāja Occupation Museum** (Liepājas okupacijas muzejs; Wed, Thurs, Sat & Sun 10am–6pm, Fri 11am–7pm; donation requested) commemorates those locals who were deported to Siberia by the Soviets in the 1940s, with a moving display of photographs. Head north along Kuršu iela and left past Liepāja's animated covered **market** to find the Roman Catholic **St Joseph's Cathedral** (Sv Jāzepa katedrāle), whose pinnacle-encrusted towers are a fanciful nineteenth-century addition to a structure of much older vintage. It's as ornate inside as it is out, its walls covered with floral designs, saints and harp-strumming angels, all rendered in bright reds and greens. To the right of the high altar there's a stunning Art-Nouveau side chapel hung with an intricate model ship.

The Seaside Park and around

Peldu iela heads west from the city centre towards the beach, passing through a residential zone of timber villas where nineteenth-century industrialists spent their summers – some have been lovingly restored, others are slowly crumbling into the ground. At the junction with Ūliha iela you'll catch sight of the brittle spire of the Russian **Orthodox Church of St Alexander Nevsky** on your right; it's rarely open, but the turquoise exterior is pure eye-candy. Continuing west along Peldu and turning right into Hika iela brings you face to face with some of the best preserved of Liepāja's belle époque villas, their filigree wooden window frames giving them the appearance of festive doily-trimmed cakes.

Down an alley from a swan-stocked pond lies Liepāja's derelict **Kursaal** (Kūrmāja), a colonnaded, Neoclassical facade hinting at its former grandeur. Extending south of the Kursaal is the **Seaside Park** (Jūrmalas parks), a well-tended area of lawns and leafy promenades separated by a line of dunes from the beach itself – as pristine a stretch of sand as you're likely to find on Latvia's west coast and a good spot for amber-hunting after storms.

Returning towards the town centre via the lime-tree-shaded Kūrmājas prospekts will take you past the **Museum of History and Art** at no. 9 (Vestures un mākslas muzejs; Tues, Thurs, Sat & Sun 10am–6pm, Fri 11am–7pm; 1Ls), a didactically arranged assemblage of local artefacts occupying a villa built in 1901 for the Katzenelson family. The inlaid wooden floors and stuccoed ceilings of the interior provide an attractive setting for models of the Neolithic villages and fortresses that were once scattered along this stretch of coast, and a rather magnificent display of the eighteenth-century pewter tankards that were made for the town's guilds – encrusted with heraldic emblems and topped with statuettes of mermaids, they look like trophies awarded for some long-forgotten exotic sport. A words-and-pictures romp through Liepāja's history includes family snapshots of generations of Liepājans at work and play, and chilling photographs of Latvians shot dead by Stalin's NKVD in 1941. There's also a colourful display of traditional Kurzeme costumes.

Karosta

Some 4km north of the Old Town lies **Karosta** (a contraction of "kara osta", which means simply "naval port"), a military suburb developed by Tsarist Russia in the late nineteenth century in order to guard against the growing threat of German sea power. Paradoxically, Karosta's expensively fortified port facilities and gun batteries were never put to the test – on the outbreak of war in 1914 the Russians withdrew their Baltic fleet to Tallinn and Helsinki and sank blockships in Karosta harbour in order to dissuade the Germans from bothering to capture it. Subsequently adopted by the Soviets as a submarine base, Karosta grew into a self-contained, Russian-speaking city inhabited by naval ratings, ancillary workers and their families. Many of the civilians are still here, left stranded by the pull-out of the military machine they served.

The best way to **get here** is to take bus #10, #11 or #15 from Lielā iela to the **Kalpaks Bridge** (Kalpaka tilts), the elegant pre–World War I swing bridge that marks the southern entrance to Karosta. From here, the broad Atmodas bulvaris heads north through a landscape of imposing Tsarist-era buildings, semi-ruined barracks and grey lines of run-down housing blocks. Dominating the skyline to the east are the yellow domes of Karosta's finest Tsarist-era heirloom, the **Orthodox Cathedral of St Nicholas** (Sv Nikolaja pareizticīgo katedrāle), with a striking facade of ochre-coloured bricks speckled with turquoise, blue and green tiles. The main object of veneration in the sparsely furnished interior is an icon depicting a placid Madonna and Child flanked by angelic beings bearing gifts. About 1km south at Invalīdu 4 lies the forbidding red-brick **Karosta Prison** (Karostas cietums; May–Sept daily 10am–6pm, Oct–April on request; ℡2636 9470; 2Ls), a punishment block for unruly sailors used successively by Tsarist, interwar Latvian, then Soviet navies. Visitors are given an atmospheric tour of the grim-looking cells, as well as the red-flag-draped offices once occupied by Soviet administrators. One prison experience you'll have to book in advance is the popular interactive show "**Behind Bars**" (Aiz restem; ℡2636 9470, @www.karostascietums.lv; 2Ls), which involves actors dressed as Soviet prison guards herding groups of visitors into the cells at gunpoint, bellowing orders and initiating rounds of repeat-after-me Leninist sloganeering. The show is normally conducted in Latvian or Russian, but if you book well in advance someone will be on hand to translate. Night performances (5Ls) involve bedding down in the cells.

At the northern end of Karosta, lanes lead west to the seashore, where the **Northern Pier** (Ziemeļu mols) extends into the Baltic, providing amateur fisherfolk with a 1.5km-long perch. Beyond the pier, paths lead north along a sandy shore overlooked by gun emplacements built by the Russians between 1894 and 1908. Long abandoned, they're now collapsing slowly into the sea.

Eating, drinking and entertainment

Liepāja boasts a decent variety of places to **eat and drink**, mostly concentrated on or around Lielā iela and Graudu iela. Additionally, in summer, a handful of relaxing outdoor cafés open up in the Seaside Park, near the western end of Peldu iela. This is the only Latvian city outside Rīga to have a **symphony orchestra** – it performs regularly at the Filharmonija, Graudu iela 50 (℡6342 5588, @www.lso.lv). You can also hear music – mostly musicals and rock opera – at Liepāja's **theatre**, Teātra 4 (℡6342 2406, @liepajasteatris.lv). In summer, all kinds of concerts take place at the Seaside Park.

Cafés and restaurants

Café 21 Kungu iela 21. Comfortable and inexpensive café offering several varieties of *karbonade*, chicken dishes, and substantial savoury pancakes. Mon–Sat 11am–7pm.

Fontaine International Steak House Stūrmaņu 1 ℡6348 3843. Occupying the ground floor of the *Fontaine Royal* hotel and decked out in customarily garish style, this is the place for substantial

and none-too-expensive grill-steaks – although the accompanying salad bar serves as a tasty reminder that there may be more to life than red meat. The outdoor terrace looks towards canalside ship moorings. Sun–Thurs noon–10pm, Fri & Sat noon–midnight.

Ginger Peldu 54 ℡6342 0293. This half-timbered parkside pavilion is a relaxing place to work your way through a familiar menu of Chinese food done

the European way, with mains around 5–6Ls. Sun–Thurs 11am–10pm, Fri & Sat 11am–11pm.
Pastnieka māja Brīvzemnieka 53 ☏ 6340 7521. A reconditioned red-brick and timber building harbouring a snazzy pub-restaurant with a large outdoor terrace. Alongside good-quality pork and fish there are always several vegetarian main courses; the extravagant puddings are worth leaving room for. Daily noon–midnight.
Piano Vecā ostmala 40 ☏ 6348 3805. In atmospheric red-brick rooms on the ground floor of the *Promenade* hotel, *Piano* is a good option for a refined meal, with impeccably prepared beef, duck and carp served by aproned wait-staff. Prices are moderate, and inexpensive lunchtime specials are chalked up daily. Sun–Thurs noon–10pm, Fri & Sat til 11pm.
Vecais Kapteinis Dubulšteina 14 ☏ 6342 5522. Tastefully restored timber house with a mouth-watering menu of steak, duck, trout and salmon dishes, as well as the usual pork-based staples. It's atmospheric too, with wooden beams, an open fireplace and a model ship hanging from the ceiling. More expensive than other places, but still reasonable. Daily 11am–11pm.

Bars and clubs

Fire Bar Stūrmaņu 1. Dark, cosy hotel bar in the *Fontaine Royal*, furnished with a pleasing jumble of lived-in sofas and old chairs. The gas-mask design motif provides an alternative edge. Regular themed nights from live gigs through Latin dancing to film shows.
First Rock Café Stendera 18/20. A social hub, with an enjoyable pub-restaurant at ground level, decorated with memorabilia donated by local rock performers, a café with roof terrace upstairs, and a basement nightclub, *Pablo* (ⓦ www.pablo.lv), which regularly features live bands. Sun–Wed 9am–midnight, Thurs–Sat till 6am.
Fontaine Palace Dzirnavu 4 ⓦ www.fontaine.lv. Featuring a lofty red-brick interior, huge wooden-beam pillars and an impressively high stage, this converted canalside warehouse is Latvia's leading mid-sized rock venue. Live bands and/or DJs appear at weekends – the *Palace* functions as a round-the-clock music bar on other nights. There's an all-night burger bar outside. Open 24hr.

Lake Pape

Beyond Liepāja, a sandy sliver of beach backed by forest and coastal heath continues all the way to the Lithuanian border, some 60km to the south. There are any number of picturesque spots where you could stop off along the way, although it's the nature reserve at **Lake Pape** (ⓦ www.pdf-pape.lv), just short of the border, that shows this part of the coast at its unspoilt, desolate best. Cut off from the sea by a bar of sand, the lake is surrounded by reeds, wetland forest and grassy meadow, grazed by a herd of wild horses, the only such herd in the country and one of the reserve's main attractions. The area also offers some rewarding walks; the best start from the lake's main settlement, **Pape village**, and wend along the seashore.

Lake Pape is best explored with your own transport, though getting to the lake by bus is just about possible. The main entry point to the region is the village of **RUCAVA**, on the main Liepāja–Klaipēda highway, 7km east of the lake. International Rīga–Liepāja–Klaipēda **buses** stop in Rucava, but the timetable information displayed at Rucava's tiny bus station is only approximate – allow twenty minutes either side when moving on. From Rucava you could feasibly walk to the lake's main sights in the space of a day, though it's a hard slog.

The lake's eastern shore

Since 1999, the eastern shore of Lake Pape has been the centre of a project to reintroduce **wild horses** to Latvia. Wild horses died out in the area in the eighteenth century and the aim of the project is to recreate the kind of naturally grazed landscape that would have existed all over the Baltic States before the Middle Ages. Eighteen stocky, grey *konnik polski* (a type of horse with wild traits selectively bred in Poland in the 1930s) were imported initially and there are now over fifty horses living in five or six so-called "harems" or social units – with new groups being formed every time older males drive younger ones away to form harems of their own.

The best way to reach them if you're coming by car is from **Kalnišķi** on the main southbound highway. Take the signed dirt road that branches off from Kalnišķi, and after ploughing through forest for about 5km the road arrives at a ticket barrier (May–Sept daily 9am–5pm; 1.50Ls), where a warden will either guide you through the lakeside meadows, or simply give you advice on where you can walk and leave you to get on with it. Although they're far from tame, the horses are relatively unfazed by humans and are unlikely to scamper off on your arrival – they're certainly a delight to watch. The rush-shrouded shores of the lake itself lie about 1km west of the ticket barrier and are favoured by all kinds of **migrating birds** in spring. The arrival of the horses has helped to increase the numbers of visiting greylag geese, who favour the short-grass habitat created by grazing animals.

Pape village

On the low sandy ridge that separates the lake from the sea, the wind-battered village of **PAPE** was a thriving fishing port until the communist period (when the Soviet military sank ships in the narrow coastal waters and used the wrecks for target practice), and is now a sleepy, dune-enclosed settlement, with a largely Lithuanian-speaking population. You can walk from the horse reserve to Pape in about two hours by following paths running southwestwards beside the irrigation dykes. If you're driving, return to the main road and head south to Rucava and the Pape turn-off. Just before arriving at the village from the Rucava direction, you'll pass a wooden observation tower offering panoramic views of the lake's reedy south shore – but don't be surprised if the bulk of Pape's birdlife is away at the quieter, northern end of the lake.

Pape itself is the starting point for wonderful seashore walks in either direction, particularly to the south, where the signed **Path of Natural Processes** (Dabas procesu taka) takes you through landscape of meadow, forest and dunes before returning to Pape along the beach – a circuit of 9km in all. About 1.5km into the trail (and just about accessible by car), a delightful **Vītolnieki Fishermen's Homestead Museum** ("Vītolnieki" zvejnieku sēta; May–Oct daily except Mon & Thurs; 0.50Ls) occupies the private house of a woman who has kept everything pretty much as it was in her grandfather's time. It somehow makes a difference to know that the simple wooden furnishings, cast-iron kitchenware and trunk-sized bedstead are still in use. There's more of a museum-style display in the outbuildings, with a collection of traps and baskets in the net-mending shed and a thousand-year-old, carved tree-trunk canoe in the granary.

Practicalities

The **tourist offices** in Liepāja (see p.210) and Rucava (Mon–Fri 9am–5pm; ☎2913 4903) can book you into local **B&Bs** (❶). The *Pūķarags* campsite (☎2837 8625, ⓦwww.pukarags.lv) north of Pape village has space for tents and caravans and bright, cosy en-suite rooms in its guesthouse (❷).

There are a couple of **food and drink** shops on Rucava's main square and a rudimentary daytime café in the nearby town hall. If you're planning on doing a lot of walking in the area, invest in **map** no. 3113 in the 1:50,000 Latvias satelitkarte series, available from the Jāņa Sēta shop in Rīga (see p.190).

Travel details

Trains

Rīga to: Jelgava (hourly; 50min); Ķemeri (every 40–50min; 1hr 5min).

Buses

Bauska to: Jelgava (6 daily; 1hr 20min); Mežotne (Mon–Fri 6 daily, Sat & Sun 4 daily; 25min);

Rundāles pils (Mon–Fri 12 daily, Sat 10 daily, Sun 5 daily; 25min).
Jelgava to: Bauska (6 daily; 1hr 20min); Rīga (every 20min; 50min); Tērvete (6 daily; 30min).
Kuldīga to: Liepāja (Mon–Sat 5 daily, Sun 3 daily; 1hr 40min); Rīga (Mon–Sat 9 daily, Sun 6 daily; 2hr 30min–3hr 45min); Sabile (Mon–Sat 11 daily, Sun 7 daily; 1hr); Ventspils (Mon–Sat 5 daily, Sun 3 daily; 1hr 20min).

Liepāja to: Rīga (14 daily; 3hr 30min–4hr); Rucava (5 daily; 40–50min); Sabile (4 daily; 3hr); Ventspils (Mon–Sat 6 daily, Sun 4 daily; 1hr 50min–3hr).

Rīga to: Bauska (every 30min; 1hr 10min–1hr 30min); Jelgava (every 30min; 50min); Kolka (3 daily; 3hr 15min–4hr 30min); Kuldīga (5 daily; 2hr 30min–3hr 30min); Liepāja (14 daily; 3hr 30min–4hr); Mazirbe (2 daily; 4hr); Rucava (4 daily; 4hr 30min); Sabile (Mon–Sat 13 daily, Sun 6 daily; 2hr); Ventspils (14 daily; 3–4hr).

Sabile to: Kuldīga (Mon–Sat 11 daily, Sun 7 daily; 1hr); Liepāja (4 daily; 3hr); Rīga (Mon–Sat 13 daily, Sun 6 daily; 2hr).

Ventspils to: Kuldīga (Mon–Sat 4 daily, Sun 2 daily; 1hr 20min); Liepāja (Mon–Sat 6 daily, Sun 4 daily; 3hr); Rīga (14 daily; 3–4hr); Talsi (Mon–Sat 6 daily, Sun 4 daily; 1hr 40min).

International buses

Liepāja to: Klaipēda (4 daily; 2hr 30min); Palanga (4 daily; 1hr 45min).

2.3

Eastern Latvia

T he dominant geographical features of **eastern Latvia** are its two main river valleys: the gloriously unspoilt **Gauja**, northeast of Rīga, and the broad **Daugava**, to the southeast, the main transport corridor to the province of Latgale and beyond. The combination of cliff-lined riverscapes and forest-clad hills make the **Gauja National Park** the one must-see natural attraction in the country, with the relaxing resort of **Sigulda** and the historic market town of **Cēsis** making ideal entry points. Offering sports ranging from bob-sledding to bungee-jumping, Sigulda in particular enjoys a well-deserved reputation as Latvia's **outdoor-activity** capital. Main settlement of southeastern Latvia, the brooding industrial city of **Daugavpils** is very much an acquired taste, and a totally misleading introduction to the surrounding province of **Latgale** – a rustic paradise of forests and lakes which counts the Catholic pilgrimage centre of **Aglona** and the tranquil country town of **Ludza** among its highlights.

Rail and bus links from Rīga are plentiful, and the whole area is theoretically within day-trip distance of the capital – although a few overnight stops here and there will ensure you get the best out of the region.

The Gauja Valley

Rising in an area of rolling uplands 90km due east of Rīga, the **River Gauja** winds its way through most of northeastern Latvia before emptying into the Baltic Sea a short way north of the capital. The most exciting stretch of the valley is between the towns of **Sigulda** and **Cēsis**, where the river carves its way through hills of Devonian sandstone, leaving ruddy cliffs and steep, forest-covered banks in its wake. Even though the highest peaks in the region barely scrape altitudes of 100m above sea level, it's a spectacularly lumpy region by local standards – so much so that the Baltic Germans were moved to call it the "Livonian Switzerland".

Much of the Sigulda–Cēsis stretch falls within the boundaries of the **Gauja National Park** (Gaujas nacionālais parks; ⓦwww.gnp.gov.lv), founded in 1973 to protect the region's diverse flora and fauna and establish a well-maintained network of walking routes. Regular trains and buses leave Rīga for **Sigulda** and the next major town upriver, **Cēsis**, either of which serves as a handy, attractive base. Midway between the two, the **Ligatne Nature Trail** allows you to see the park's flora and fauna at close quarters, while the reconstructed lake-village at **Āraiši**, just south of Cēsis, provides a fascinating insight into the lives of the Latvians' ancient forebears.

Throughout the park you'll find many **forest and riverbank trails** suitable for exploring by foot or bike, while **canoeing** down the Gauja itself is a particularly invigorating way of enjoying the scenery. Although the pistes at Sigulda and Cēsis are puny by alpine standards, the potential of the area as a low-level, laid-back **skiing** centre shouldn't be overlooked – given the rigours of the Baltic winter, at least snow cover is guaranteed. Jāņa sēta's 1:100,000 *Gaujas nacionālais parks* **map**, sold in local tourist

---

Canoeing down the Gauja Valley

To experience the Gauja landscape at its best, you have to see it from the river itself, and **canoeing down the Gauja** has become one of Latvia's most popular outdoor holiday activities. True aficionados start at Strenči, northeast of Valmiera, and spend four to five days paddling their way downstream to Sigulda – a distance of 95km. However, the more scenic 35km stretch between Cēsis and Sigulda is the busiest, especially on summer weekends. Most people do the Cēsis–Sigulda trip in two to three days, overnighting at designated national park campsites spaced at convenient intervals along the way. The easiest way to start is simply to rent a canoe (and a tent if you don't have one) and set off; you could also opt for a guided canoe trip organized by one of the adventure tourism agencies listed below. The season lasts from early June to the end of August.

It's best to organize canoe rental and trips a few days in advance – things get booked up quickly at summer weekends. We've listed a few of the best agencies below; tourist offices in Sigulda and Cēsis can advise on others. Expect to pay 15Ls a day for canoe rental, 20Ls per person per day for a guided canoe tour.

Canoe rental contacts
Campo Kroņu iela 25D, Rīga ☎6750 5322, ⓦwww.campo.laivas.lv. Canoe rental, advice and guided canoe trips on the Gauja. They can also organize the transport of your canoe to and from the Gauja.

Cīrulīši Mūrlejas iela 12, Cēsis ☎2626 6266, ⓦwww.zagarkalns.lv. Canoe and tent rental.

Eži Raiņa iela 26/28, Cēsis ☎6410 7022, ⓦwww.ezi.lv. Canoe rental and guided one- to three-day tours.

Makars Peldu 2, Sigulda ☎2924 4948, ⓦwww.makars.lv. Canoes (15–20Ls/day), rowing boats (1Ls/hr) and tents (1.50Ls/day) for rent. Guided one- to seven-day tours.

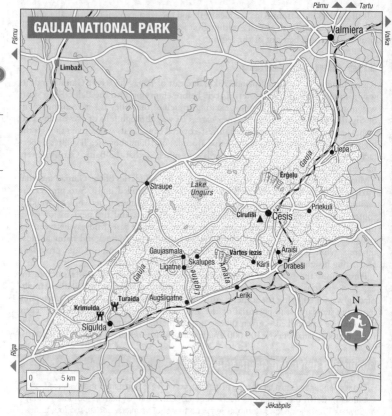

offices, covers the region, and comes with smaller-scale inset maps of Līgatne, Āraiši and other key localities.

Sigulda and around

Sprawled across a plateau on the south bank of the River Gauja, **SIGULDA** is not so much a town as a vast leafy park tastefully scattered with a few houses and apartment blocks. Close to some of the most beautiful stretches of the Gauja Valley, it has been Latvia's most popular inland resort since the mid-nineteenth century, when the construction of the Rīga–Valka railway line put it within reach of vacationing St Petersburg folk. It's a great base for short- and mid-range walking, with a variety of woodland and river-bank trails within easy striking distance of the centre. It's also the obvious starting point for visits to the reconstructed castle at **Turaida** and the nineteenth-century aristocratic seat of **Krimulda**, both of which adorn hilltops on the opposite side of the valley. With the recent construction of high-wire forest parks, all-weather toboggan runs and an Aerodium wind tunnel, Sigulda has emerged as Latvia's premier destination for outdoor **adventure sports**. In the colder months, **winter-sports** enthusiasts flock here to experience the thrills of the country's only Olympic-standard bobsleigh track and its downhill ski runs.

Arrival, information and accommodation

Sigulda is an easy day-trip from Rīga, with **buses** and **trains** running almost hourly. If you're approaching from the east, catch a Cēsis–Rīga bus – these don't actually pass through the town centre, but pick up and drop off on the main highway 1km south.

Sigulda's **tourist office**, next door to the bus station at Raiņa 3 (May–Oct daily 9am–7pm, Nov–April Mon–Fri 9am–6pm, Sat & Sun 10am–4pm; ☏6797 1335, ⒲www .sigulda.lv) is a good source of advice on local sights, accommodation and activities, while the **Gauja National Park Visitors' Centre**, Baznīcas 3 (daily: April–Oct 9.30am–6pm, Nov–March 10am–4pm; ☏6780 0388, ⒲www.gnp.gov.lv), has information about hiking trails and sells a wide range of maps. You can rent **bikes** from Buru sports, 1km south of the centre at the junction of Gāles iela and the main Rīga–Cēsis highway (☏6797 2051, ⒲www.burusports.lv) and Tridens, Cēsu 15 (☏2964 4800). For **canoe** and rowing boat rentals see the box on p.217.

There is a small but good selection of **hotels** in and around town, and the tourist office can book you into **B&B** accommodation in private houses from 8Ls per person. The *Siguldas pludmale* **campsite**, Peldu 1 (☏2924 4948, ⒲www.makars.lv) occupies an attractive, tree-shaded stretch of riverbank and is equipped with toilet blocks but no other facilities.

Hotels

Līvkalns Pēter013 ☏6797 0916, ⒲www .livkalns.lv. Traditional-style, reed-thatched house with a lovely lakeside garden, offering eight pine-furnished en-suites. Within easy striking distance of Satzele Castle Mound and numerous forest trails. **❸**

Parks Atbrivotaju 1 ☏6797 2684 or 2659 6816, ⒲www.parks-inn.lv. Six-room guesthouse offering brightly furnished en-suites, on-site sauna, and a garden with a lawn. **❸**

Melnais kaķis Pils iela 8 ☏6787 0272 or 2915 0104, ⒲www.cathouse.lv. Mid-sized hotel on the main street offering contemporary en-suites decorated in warm colours. **❹**

Sigulda Pils iela 6 ☏6797 2263, ⒲www .hotelsigulda.lv. Central, nineteenth-century building with modern add-ons, including a tiny indoor pool. The en-suite rooms are smart but not particularly spacious. **❹**

Western Sigulda: activities and adventures

The western side of Sigulda is fast becoming a major centre for all kinds of **outdoor experiences and activities**. Longest-established of these attractions is the **cable car** (Gaisa trosu ceļš; May–Sept 10am–6pm; 2.50Ls; ⒲www.lgk.lv) built by Georgian technicians in the 1960s, which sets off from the terminal on Poruka iela five minutes' walk west of Raiņa iela. Hourly departures take you across the Gauja to Krimulda (see p.222), offering superb views of the valley along the way. Bungee jumps (15Ls) from the mid-point of the route can be booked in advance. A little way further west, the ferris-style **Panoramic Wheel** (Panorāmas rats; May–Oct daily 10am–6pm; 1Ls) provides another way to enjoy the Gauja landscape.

Just southwest of the wheel, **Sigulda Adventure Park** (Siguldas piedzīvojumu parks; ⒲www.tarzans.lv) offers three main activities: a chairlift (0.50Ls each way) that descends to the Siguldas pludmale campsite (see above) on the Gauja riverfront; a summer toboggan (2Ls); and a Tarzan high-wire park (12Ls), offering six harness-assisted treetop routes of varying degrees of difficulty. You can also sign up for a **rafting trip** (12–15Ls/person) organized by Makars at the *Siguldas pludmale* campsite. Gently drifting affairs rather than white-water thrill rides, these usually involve one- or two-hour trips in scenic stretches of the valley upstream from Sigulda.

South of the Adventure Park is a west-facing escarpment that becomes a ski piste in winter and is also the site of the town's state-of-the-art **toboggan and bobsleigh track** (Kamaniņu un bobsleja trase). As well as hosting World Cup luge and bobsleigh events in winter, it's put to good use from May to October when you can descend the course in a "summer bob" – a thick-tyred, futuristic-looking silver kart – for 5Ls per person.

High-wire adventures are on offer at the **Mežakaķis Adventure Park** (Mežakaķis piedzīvojumu parks; 10am–10pm; ⒲www.mezakakis.lv; 12Ls), 1km further west, which has six treetop routes, while 5km west of town, just off the main Rīga road, the **Sigulda Aerodium** (April–Oct: daily noon–9pm; Nov–March: Fri–Sun noon–8pm; ⒲www .aerodium.lv; "flights" from 15Ls for 2 minutes) offers the exhilarating opportunity to hover in a stream of air blasted upwards from a vertical wind tunnel.

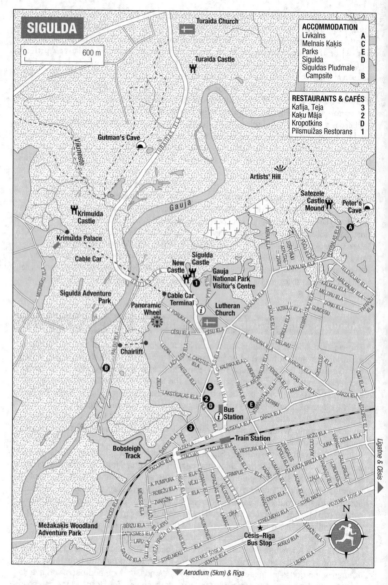

Ligatne & Cēsis ▶

SIGULDA

0 _____ 600 m

ACCOMMODATION
Lībkalns — A
Melnais Kaķis — C
Parks — E
Sigulda — D
Siguldas Pludmale
Campsite — B

RESTAURANTS & CAFÉS
Kafija, Teja — 3
Kaku Māja — 2
Kropotkins — D
Pilsmuižas Restorans — 1

Turaida Church

Turaida Castle

Gutman's Cave

Artists' Hill

Krimulda Castle

Satezele Castle Mound

Peter's Cave

Krimulda Palace

Gauja

Cable Car

Sigulda Adventure Park

New Castle

Sigulda Castle

Gauja National Park Visitor's Centre

Cable Car Terminal

Lutheran Church

Panoramic Wheel

Chairlift

Bus Station

Bobsleigh Track

Train Station

Cēsis–Rīga Bus Stop

Mežakaķis Woodland Adventure Park

N

▼ Aerodium (5km) & Rīga

The Town

From the train station, **Raiņa iela** runs north through the town centre, passing the bus station before forging through a swathe of parkland shaded by limes, oaks and maples. After about 800m, a right turn into **Baznīcas iela** takes you past the brilliant-white spire of the **Lutheran church** (Luterānu baznīca) and on to **Sigulda New Castle** (Siguldas Jaunā Pils), a nineteenth-century manor house with medieval pretensions, sporting an ostentatiously crenellated turret and now used as council offices. In front, neat flowerbeds lie in the shade of a monument to Atis Kronvalds (1837–75), the nineteenth-century publicist who energetically promoted Latvian-language education at a time when knowledge of German was seen as the only passport to a successful career.

Immediately north of the New Castle, a path leads across a long-dried-up moat to the ruins of **Sigulda Castle** (Siguldas Pilsdrupas), a thirteenth-century Livonian Order stronghold built from rough-hewn blocks of honey-coloured stone. Behind it lies an outdoor stage which is put to good use during the summer opera festival, and beyond that a knobbly hillock that affords sweeping views of the Gauja Valley. More fine valley views can be savoured by following footpaths east from the castle ruins to Miera iela, through the enchantingly shrubby town cemetery, then northeast along the ridge known as **Artists' Hill** (Gleznotāju kalns). The viewpoint at the end of the ridge offers an expansive panorama of Turaida, Krimulda and the surrounding woodland – unsurprisingly, it was a favourite spot with early twentieth-century landscape painters Jānis Rozentāls and Vilhelms Purvītis. Southeast of here, paths descend steeply to meet the Vējupite stream, which flows into the Gauja a few hundred metres to the north. Sticking to the high ground and heading south will bring you to the **Satezele Castle Mound** (Satezeles pilskalns), a Liv stronghold associated with semi-legendary chieftain Dabrelis, who fought unsuccessfully to stem the Teutonic advance in the early thirteenth century.

From Sigulda to Turaida

From central Sigulda, Gaujas iela descends towards the bridge over the Gauja, and then heads north along the northern bank of the river before climbing up to **Turaida Castle**, some 3km distant. Sigulda–Krimulda buses pass along this route roughly every hour, but you're unlikely to take in much of the scenery through the window – walking at least part of the way seems a good idea.

Starting on the far side of the bridge from Sigulda, paths lead away from the main road and into the shadow of the densely forested escarpment that overlooks the valley from the northwest. Here, all kinds of alternative trails and interesting detours present themselves: you can head due west up to Krimulda (see p.222), or follow the path that winds its way up the enchanting, wooded gully of the Vikmeste stream before emerging at the top of the ridge midway between Turaida and Krimulda. Alternatively, you can stick to the valley floor, following a level trail that runs past a sequence of small lakes and several sandstone caves. Despite its small, unexciting proportions, **Gūtman's Cave** (Gūtmaņa ala) is the most famous of these fissures, not least because of the key role it plays in the story of *Turaida Rose* – a heady tale of love, death and Latvian virtue. National poet Jānis Rainis based his play *Love is Stronger than Death* (Mīla stiprāka pār nāvi) on the story, and most Latvian schoolchildren know the plot by heart. The rose in question was a seventeenth-century local maiden named Maija, who fell in love with the Turaida castle gardener Viktor, while at the same time being subject to the unwanted advances of Polish army deserter, Adam Jakubovsky (some versions have him as a Swedish officer). When Jakubovsky trapped her in Gūtman's Cave, she wound a scarf given to her by Viktor around her neck in the hope that it would shield her from evil. When the Pole struck out with his sword, however, the scarf unsurprisingly failed to provide the degree of protection expected. Maija's murder was initially pinned on Viktor, but he was released when a guilt-tormented Jakubovsky committed suicide.

Beyond the cave, the path rejoins the main road for the final 800m climb to the **Turaida Museum Reserve** (Turaidas muzejrezervāts; daily: May–Oct 10am–6pm; Nov–April 10am–5pm; ⓦ www.turaida-muzejs.lv; 2Ls), which comprises a partially reconstructed castle and extensive grounds scattered with outbuildings. Built on the site of a Liv stockade fort, Turaida was one of the bishop of Rīga's key strongholds from 1214 onwards, surviving numerous wars until finally reduced to rubble when lightning hit its gunpowder magazine in the early eighteenth century. With a handful of towers and halls now open to the public, the castle's museum spaces are short on actual exhibits but strong on atmosphere. Nearby, the eighteenth-century **Turaida Church** (Turaidas baznīca), an appealing shingle-roofed building with a Baroque tower, contains a small but alluring display of thirteenth-century Latvian jewellery. Just outside the church, a plaque honouring the Turaida Rose is one of the most popular venues in the country for the post-wedding photo shoot. From here, grassy parkland scattered with modern sculptures stretches east along the ridge-top overlooking the Gauja valley. North of the church, a restored nineteenth-century **manorial complex** (Muižas saimnieciskais centrs), comprising stables, fishpond, smithy and bath house (the latter filled with fragrant dried herbs) recalls life on the agricultural estates of yore.

Krimulda

Commanding superb views of the Gauja Valley 2.5km southwest of Turaida is the custard-coloured, Neoclassical **Krimulda Palace** (Krimuldas pils), seat of the Baltic German Lieven family in the nineteenth century and now a sanatorium. Though the palace is closed to visitors, the wooded ridge-top setting provides reason enough to visit. There's a neat park with flowerbeds on the western side of the building, while over to the east lie the fragmentary remains of **Krimulda Castle** (Krimuldas pilsdrupas), a thirteenth-century stronghold perched dramatically on a rocky bluff overlooking over the valley.

As well as being served by Sigulda–Krimulda buses, the sanatorium can also be reached by paths from the Gauja Valley (notably from the Vikmeste stream path). The most stylish way to arrive, though, is by **cable car** from Sigulda (see p.219).

Eating and drinking

The *Kropotkins* **restaurant** (closed Mon) inside the *Sigulda* hotel (see p.219) is an elegant but not over-posh place to enjoy a relaxing sit-down meal, with freshwater fish enjoying pride of place on the menu. *Kafija Teja*, Valdemara 3 (10am–8pm), is a comfortable coffee-and-cake stop and has a small but well-chosen menu of quality main courses too. For fans of faded charm, *Pilsmuizas Restorans* (daily 10am–11pm) in the New Castle (see p.220) offers substantial pork, trout and salmon dishes in a charmingly old-fashioned wood-panelled interior. For a quicker, on-your-feet meal, try *Kaķu Māja*, Pils 8 (daily 8am–9pm), which offers canteen food and also sells delicious cakes and pastries in the adjoining bakery.

Līgatne Nature Trail and around

Some 12km northeast of Sigulda, the **Līgatne Nature Trail** (Līgatnes dabas takas) provides one of the best ways to sample the sheer variety of the Gauja Valley landscape. Located on the south bank of the river, the trail meanders through a changing landscape of dense pinewoods, evergreen forest and meadow clearings, and gives access to some cliff-lined stretches of the riverbank itself. Entrance to the trail is 2km west of the village of **Gaujasmala** and 3km northwest of the village of **Līgatne**, which in turn is 5.5km north of its sister settlement on the main Rīga–Cēsis highway – variously called Augšlīgatne ("Upper Līgatne"), Līgatnes stacija ("Līgatne Station") or simply "Līgatne", depending on which map you look at. It's this place that Rīga–Cēsis **trains and buses** serve: once here, you can either walk to Līgatne proper (1hr), or wait for one of the six daily buses (three at weekends) which start at the train station, then call at Augšlīgatne's main bus stop before continuing to Līgatne proper, terminating at Gaujasmala. If you're approaching from the Cēsis direction, you can take one of the Cēsis–Līgatne–Gaujasmala buses (3 daily Mon–Fri only).

Līgatne and Gaujasmala

LĪGATNE village is a pretty little place hugging the banks of the Līgatne stream, a tributary of the Gauja, here overlooked by a handsome set of the region's trademark red sandstone cliffs. Līgatne is also the site of one of Latvia's oldest paper mills, which explains the attractive complex of nineteenth-century industrial buildings just east of the village centre and the red-brick workers' houses that cluster around it. The village possesses a modest **café** and a couple of food shops. From the main crossroads, Dārza iela winds west then north before coming to a T-junction after 2km: a left turn takes you to the Līgatne Nature Trail (see below), while a right turn leads directly into grubby **GAUJASMALA**, a village of Soviet-era apartment blocks, worth visiting for its **ferry** (pārceltuve; May–Sept: shuttle service 6am–11pm; 0.20Ls per person; 1Ls per vehicle). Basically a small open-topped raft, guided across the river by a fixed chain, it's one of the last such contraptions still in use in the Baltics. There's a free **campsite** next to the riverbank, with a couple of rudimentary earth toilets.

Līgatne Nature Trail

Established in 1975, **Līgatne Nature Trail** (May–Sept Mon–Fri 9am–6pm, Sat & Sun till 7pm; 2.50Ls) is basically an open-plan zoo of indigenous fauna, including brown bears and bobcats, with several large enclosures scattered, safari-park-style, over a wide area. The animals spend the summer roaming their spacious quarters at Līgatne, returning to Rīga zoo for the winter. Getting from one enclosure to another involves passing through undulating terrain carpeted in sweet-smelling forest, which is the trail's main appeal. There are two circular routes about 6km long – one for cars, one for pedestrians – both of which pass the principal enclosures; the information desk at the entrance will give you a map. Things are well signposted and it's easy to find the most popular way-stations: a field full of aurochs (European bison) on the eastern side of the circuit, and a wooded hillside over to the west populated by brown bears – although extinct in Latvia by the late nineteenth century, the creatures began migrating back from Estonia in the 1970s. Elsewhere you'll see wild boar, roe deer, red deer and (if you're very lucky) lynx. A couple of footpaths leading off the main trail are well worth exploring: one (the Gaujmalas taka, or "Gauja bank trail") heads west from the information kiosk towards the riverbank, where you can admire the **Gūdu iezis** sandstone outcrop on the opposite bank, while another (the Neskartās dabas taka, or "wild nature trail") branches off just south of the brownbear enclosure and heads down **Paparžu grava**, a leafy gully whose name – "fern glen" – is self-explanatory.

Some 2km northwest of Līgatne on the way to the nature trail, the *Lāču Miga*, Gaujas iela 22 (☎2913 3713, ⓦwww.lacumiga.lv; ❸) is an attractive, rustic **guesthouse** offering thirteen en-suite rooms and a **café-restaurant**. There's a free riverside **campsite** at Katrīnas iezis, 500m north of the trail entrance.

The Rehabilitation Centre and the underground bunkers

Some 3km northeast of Līgatne village on the road to Zvārtes iezis, the **Vidzeme Regional Rehabilitation Centre** (Rehabilitācijas centrs) at Skaļupes once served as the holiday retreat of high-ranking members of the communist regime. It was also the cover for a top-secret complex of **underground bunkers** (pazemes bunkuri; ⓦwww.bunkurs.lv), to which Soviet Latvia's civilian and military leadership were to be evacuated in the event of nuclear war. Entered via an anonymous-looking staircase in the Rehabilitation Centre's lobby, the bunker complex, which, with its lino floors and plywood furniture resembles a sinister underground high school, was begun in 1968 and consists of 89 rooms 9m below ground level (guided tours only; English-language tours bookable 24hr in advance; prices start at 20Ls; ☎6416 1915). The tour takes in military command rooms hung with maps and flags, and equipped with some of the earliest computers produced in the Soviet Union (data was stored on reel-to-reel tape). You can also see a pumping system designed to keep the complex supplied with air for three months – how the Soviet top brass aimed to stay alive beyond this period remains unclear.

The Rehabilitation Centre itself (☎6416 1917, ⓦwww.rehcentrsligatne.lv; ❸) is open as a sanatorium and spa **hotel**. With the sandy banks of the Gauja River just a five-minute walk away through the forest, it's an undeniably restful spot.

Cēsis and around

The well-preserved, laid-back market town of **CĒSIS**, on a hillside 35km northeast of Sigulda, is as close as you'll get to prewar, small-town Latvia. The knot of narrow streets at its heart, characterized by sturdy stone houses and one-storey timber dwellings, was largely undamaged in World War II and spared any significant modernization in the

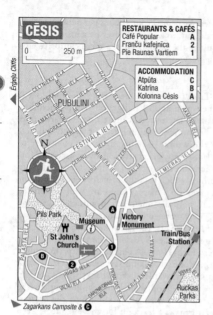

CĒSIS

RESTAURANTS & CAFÉS	
Café Popular	A
Franču kafejnica	2
Pie Raunas Vartiem	1

ACCOMMODATION	
Atpūta	C
Katrīna	B
Kolonna Cèsis	A

0   250 m

Ērgeļu Cliffs

PUBULINI

N

Pils Park

Museum

St John's Church

Victory Monument

Train/Bus Station

Ruckas Parks

Zagarkans Campsite & **C**

years that followed. The town's other main draws are its moody **castle ruins**, fine **museum** and convenience as a base for the rest of the Gauja Valley; particularly close at hand are Līgatne, the Iron Age settlement at **Āraiši** and **Ērgeļu Cliff**. The Gauja riverbank 3km west of town is one of the main starting points for canoe trips heading downstream (see p.217), while the steep escarpment above it is the raison d'être of the popular downhill skiing resort of **Žagarkalns**.

Arrival, information and accommodation

Buses and trains use the **station** 500m east of the main square, Vienības laukums: bus timetables and ticket windows are on the left-hand side as you enter from the street; train timetables and tickets are on the other. The helpful **tourist office** lies five minutes west of the square in the entrance lobby of the Cēsis Castle complex (June–Sept Mon–Fri 9am–6pm, Sat & Sun 10am–5pm; Oct–May Mon–Fri 9am–5pm; ℡6412 1815, Ⓦwww.turisms.cesis.lv). You can rent **bikes** from Eži, Raiņa iela 26/28 (℡6410 7022, Ⓦwww.ezi.lv).

Cēsis has a decent range of **hotels**, with a handful of stylishly modern establishments in the centre of town and a scattering of cheap, simple options in the suburbs.

Hotels

Atpūta Cīrulīšu iela 49 ℡6412 7811, Ⓦwww .hotelatputa.lv. Intimate eleven-room hotel in an attractive modern building with colonnaded porch. Smart en-suite rooms, on-site sauna and bike rental. **③**

Katrīna Maza Katrīnas iela 8 ℡2000 8870, Ⓦwww.hotelkatrina.com. A modern but cosy eight-room place on a quiet street in the heart of historic Cēsis. Rooms are smallish with shower and TV, each decorated in a different colour. **④**

Kolonna Cēsis Vienības laukums 1 ℡6412 0122, Ⓦwww.hotel.kolonna.com. A modernized interwar hotel on the main square, offering thick-carpeted en-suites with bathtubs and high standards of service. **④**

The Town

Marking the eastern entrance to the town centre of Cēsis is the broad square **Vienības laukums**, dominated by the impressive if eccentric **Victory Monument**, an obelisk licked by concrete flames and topped by what looks like a golden ping-pong ball. Erected in the 1920s, demolished by the Soviets in the 1950s (presumably for political rather than aesthetic reasons) and reconstructed in the 1990s, it commemorates June 1919's **Battle of Cēsis**, in which an Estonian army, backed up by Latvian volunteers, defeated the Iron Division of German General von der Goltz. The Estonians chased von der Goltz all the way back to Rīga, only to be dissuaded from finishing his army off entirely by the British, who argued that German troops might still come in useful in fighting the Bolsheviks, who were proving difficult to dislodge from Latvia's south-eastern corner.

Southwest of the square, Skolas iela descends towards the thirteenth-century **St John's Church** (Sv Jāņa Baznīca), a heavily buttressed structure containing the tombs of several masters of the Livonian Order, most notably Walter von Plettenberg (1494–1535).

Something of a national hero among Baltic Germans, Plettenberg pushed back seemingly unstoppable Russian offensives at the beginning of the sixteenth century, winning a brief but significant respite for the Livonian Order – which struggled on for another fifty years before bequeathing its territories to the Poles and the Swedes. The narrow streets just west of the church are among Cēsis's most atmospheric, with one-storey wooden dwellings huddled over the cobbles.

Cēsis Castle (Cēsu pils; mid–May to mid–Sept Tues–Sun 10am–5pm; 2Ls) was built by the crusading Knights of the Sword in 1207 and subsequently inherited by their successor organization, the Livonian Order – whose first Grand Master, Hermann Balk, moved here in 1239. It continued to serve intermittently as the master's residence until the mid-sixteenth century, after which the conquering Swedes turned it into an administrative centre for the whole of northeastern Latvia. The Russians took the castle in 1703, severely damaging it in the process and leaving it to fall into ruin. The castle's stout, barrel-like towers and central keep have been partially reconstructed, leaving an impressively moody collection of walk-around grey ruins. A couple of towers can be scaled via unlit spiral staircases – you'll be provided with lanterns when buying your ticket. The same ticket allows access to the **Cēsis Museum of History and Art** (Cēsu vēstures un mākslas muzejs; same times) in the "New Castle", the stately home built for Cēsis's nineteenth-century owner Karl Gustav von Sievers. It's one of the country's more entertaining historical collections, getting under way with intricately fashioned jewellery unearthed from twelfth-century Latvian graves – including necklaces festooned with bronze toggles and miniature horse shapes. After rooms devoted to local landscape painters and grainy photographs of the 1919 Battle of Cēsis, steps climb to the summit of the Ladermacher tower, a fifteenth-century bastion affording sweeping views of the surrounding hills.

On a forest-fringed bluff overlooking the Gauja Valley, 2.5km southwest of the town centre, **Žagarkalns** (Ⓦwww.zagarkalns.lv; reached by minibus #5 or #9) is the most popular downhill skiing resort in Latvia after Sigulda, although its three short pistes and small snowboard park (all served by drag lift; passes 3Ls/hr) are unlikely to set the pulse racing.

Eating and drinking

In the basement of the *Kolonna Cēsis* hotel, *Café Popular* offers cheap and filling Latvian meat-and-two-veg meals, alongside workmanlike pizzas and some superb sweets. *Pie Raunas Vārtiem*, Rigas iela 3, is another dependable source of salads, pork chops, pancakes and the like. For decent coffee, croissants and crêpes head for *Franču kafejnīca* on Rožu laukums. There are also a couple of beer gardens on Rožu laukums in summer.

Ērgeļu Cliff

Of all the rocky outcrops overhanging the waters of the Gauja, **Ērgeļu Cliff** (Ērgeļu klintis), 7km north of Cēsis, is probably the most dramatic, a wavy line of sandstone some 500m long and topped with dark-green conifers. To get there, take Lenču iela from Cēsis's main square and keep going as far as Pieškalni – a car park on the far side of the village marks the end of the road. A further five minutes on foot brings you to the top of the cliff, from where you can follow trails either east or west along the summit.

Āraiši

Some 7km south of Cēsis, the rustic lakeside village of **ĀRAIŠI** would be a charming enough spot for a stroll even without the **Āraiši Lake Fortress** (Āraišu ezerpils; May to mid-Oct daily 10am–6pm; 2Ls), a modern-day reconstruction of an Iron Age settlement. Built on a man-made island and joined to the lakeshore by a causeway, it's an exact replica of the ninth-century original that once stood on this site. It's not really a "fortress", rather a compact village with fifteen dwellings, rendered defensible by its watery location. Shrouded by reeds and with the ruddy roof of Āraiši village church in the background, it couldn't be more picturesque. Locally available trees provided the raw material for almost everything in the lake dwelling, with the tiny log-built houses with bark roofs huddled together on wooden decking.

A few minor attractions justify lingering a while, including the ruins of **Āraiši Castle** (Āraišu pilsdrupas), on a hillock immediately to the southeast. Built by the Livonian Order in the thirteenth century, it was abandoned after Ivan the Terrible's Russians sacked it in 1577. Heading northwards around the lake, you come to **Āraiši village** and its slender-spired parish church, erected in the thirteenth century and rebuilt in the eighteenth – when a human skeleton was found bricked up in the wall. The discovery soon entered local folklore, with villagers claiming that the church's original architect had pledged to ensure the structure's longevity by immuring the next human being he saw, unaware that his own daughter was at that moment advancing up the street with his lunch. Finally, for a great view back towards lake, fortress and village, it's worth walking as far as the **windmill** on the low hill to the west, its overhanging wooden canopy looking like an upturned boat.

At least one daily Rīga–Cēsis **bus** passes through Āraiši itself; most other Rīga–Cēsis services use the main road 1km west of the site – get off at the Betes stop and walk via the windmill, clearly visible on the brow of the hill above the road. In addition, four daily Rīga–Cēsis **trains** call at the Āraiši stop, although it's 2.5km southeast of the village.

Latgale

Extending east from the Daugava river to the Russian border, the region of **Latgale** (Ⓦ www.latgale.lv) offers some of the most enchanting landscapes in the country: pleasantly rolling upland studded with lakes, girdled with a mixture of reed beds, pine trees and birch. Along with Vidzeme, Kurzeme and Zemgale, it's one of the four main historical regions of Latvia and, although it no longer exists as an administrative unit, preserves a stronger sense of local identity than any other part of the country. The region's name comes from the Latgalians, one of the original Baltic tribes who settled in Latvia four millennia ago. Latgale still preserves an archaic dialect that differs sufficiently from standard Latvian for some to consider it a separate language.

Latgale's uniqueness is largely due to the fact that it was cut off from the rest of Latvia for large chunks of its history, thereby missing out on the process of cultural and linguistic unification that bound the other three regions together as a nation. Most significantly, it was part of the Polish-Lithuanian state from 1561 until the first partition of Poland in 1772. During this period the tribes living in northern and western Latvia gradually standardized their languages into a mutually intelligible national tongue, while the isolated Latgalians stuck to their own archaic dialect. Latgale was also cut off from the Protestant culture then developing in the rest of Latvia, remaining under the sway of the **Catholic Church** – a faith to which the Latgalians are still passionately devoted to this day. Under Russian rule from 1772, Latgale was attached to the Vitebsk Gubernia (covering what is now most of eastern Belarus), distancing it even further from the main currents of Latvian culture. The Latgalian intelligentsia always regarded themselves as a legitimate branch of the Latvian national family, however, and in April 1917 the **Latvian–Latgalian Congress** convened in Rēzekne to declare Latgale's "independence" from Vitebsk and its unification with Latvian territories governed by Rīga. For the next three years Latgale was the scene of fierce battles between pro-Latvian forces and Bolsheviks invading from the east and it wasn't until 1920 that real political unity was achieved.

Latgale was always an **ethnically mixed** area, with Latgalian Latvians dominating the countryside and Russians and Poles in the towns. Jews made up forty to fifty percent of the population in urban areas like Daugavpils, Ludza and Krāslava, though Nazi terror in World War II destroyed this centuries-old presence at a stroke. After the war, Latgale's cities were earmarked for industrialization, encouraging mass immigration from other parts of the Soviet Union – with the result that Russians are now the largest ethnic group in the region, making up some 43.5 percent of the population.

Daugavpils and **Rēzekne** are the main transport hubs and service centres, although neither city will hold your attention for long. Rural Latgale is another matter, however, with the Catholic pilgrimage site of **Aglona** and the drowsy market town of **Ludza** providing access to the best of the lakeland scenery.

Daugavpils

Latvia's second city, **DAUGAVPILS** is usually dismissed by the rest of the country as an economically depressed backwater with few redeeming features. It's true that this erstwhile industrial powerhouse has fallen on hard times, but it remains – in parts at least – a ruggedly handsome place whose historical resonances run deep. If there is so much prejudice against Daugavpils it's probably because so few Latvian-speakers actually live there: over ninety percent of the population is Russian-speaking and although the street signs are in Latvian, you'll rarely hear the language used in everyday conversation.

Perhaps appropriately for a town with such a large Russian population, Daugavpils appears to have been founded by marauding Muscovite Ivan the Terrible, who sacked the Livonian Order fortress of Dünaburg, 19km upstream, and ordered its reconstruction on the site of the present-day city. An important garrison town under successive rulers, Daugavpils experienced its most rapid period of growth in the years before World War I, when a developing manufacturing industry sucked in migrant workers from all over the Russian Empire. The process repeated itself after 1945, when the Soviet authorities deliberately imported a non-Latvian workforce to feed the city's expanding factories, which produced everything from landmines to lawnmowers. Daugavpils took an economic battering in the immediate post-independence years, with mass unemployment engendering a despondent atmosphere that is only now beginning to lift. However, it's by no means the unremittingly ugly city that many Latvians claim it to be, and with a

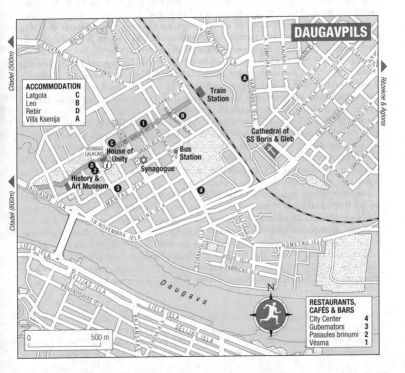

downtown full of robust nineteenth-century buildings, it has enough in the way of gruff charm to reward even the briefest of visits.

Arrival, information and accommodation

Daugavpils' **train station** lies at the northeastern end of the main street, Rīgas iela, while the **bus station** is a few blocks south; both are within easy reach of the helpful **tourist office** at Rīgas 22A – the entrance is round the back of the building (Mon–Fri 9am–6pm, Sat 10am–4pm; ☏6542 2818, ✉ourinfo@daugavpils.apollo.lv). With an improving stock of **hotels** in Daugavpils, you shouldn't have any problems finding a central place to stay.

Hotels

Latgola Gimnazijas 46 ☏6540 4900, ⓦwww
.hoteldaugavpils.lv. Ten-storey slab in the centre, offering comfortable, if cramped, en-suites. Views from the upper floors are excellent, and breakfast is eaten in the pop-art, panoramic top-floor café-restaurant. ⑤–⑥

Leo Krāslavas 58 ☏6542 6565. Unpretentious B&B in a residential courtyard between the bus and train stations. Homely en-suites come with

chintzy fittings; there are only five rooms, so call in advance. ④

Rebir Vienības 19 ☏6542 1857, ✉rebir_d@inbox
.lv. Central guesthouse with a handful of doubles and triples, plainly furnished but comfortable. ③

Villa Ksenija Varšavas 17 ☏6543 4317, ⓦwww
.villaks.lv. Pre-World War I mansion 20min walk uphill from the centre, behind the Orthodox cathedral. Slightly cramped but comfy and stylish en-suite doubles, and a handful of swish apartments. ⑥

The Town

Slicing straight through the middle of Daugavpils' city centre grid is **Rīgas iela**, a stately, pedestrianized strip lined with tastefully restored nineteenth-century apartment blocks. Midway along the street's 1.5km length, the tree-fringed open spaces of **Vienības laukums** provide downtown Daugavpils with some kind of focus. Squatting immediately opposite the ten-storey bulk of the **Hotel Latgola** is the grey-brown **House of Unity** (Vienības nams), a combined theatre and administrative building that holds the dubious distinction of being the largest construction project undertaken by the interwar Latvian state. From here it's a short hop southwest to the **Regional History and Art Museum** at Rīgas 8 (Daugavpils novadpētniecības un makslas muzejs; Tues–Sat 10am–6pm; 1Ls), with a words-and-pictures historical display enlivened by colourful local costumes. Upstairs, the **Mark Rothko Room** (same times; additional 1Ls) is devoted to the master abstract painter, born Markus Rothkowitz in Daugavpils in 1903. He was only 10 years old when his family left for Portland, Oregon, and there's consequently little of Daugavpils in the man's work, or indeed the man's work here in Daugavpils – although reproductions of his paintings help to provide this display with some focus. A further reminder of the town's once-thriving Jewish community is provided by the smart **synagogue** four blocks northeast on the corner of Cietokšņa and Lāčplēša – with fewer than four hundred Jews left in the city, it's rarely open outside prayer times.

Dominating the high ground east of the city centre is the **Orthodox Cathedral of SS Boris and Gleb** (Borisa un Gļeba pareizticīgo katedrāle) – head northeast along 18 Novembra iela, cross the railway tracks and you can't miss it. The cathedral is an outstanding example of nineteenth-century Muscovite exuberance, its shiny bauble-like domes impaled on lilac spires. Russian armies marched into Daugavpils on the feast day of Boris and Gleb in 1656, and renamed it "Borisoglebsk" in their honour, and though the Poles recaptured the town twelve years later, the medieval warrior saints have been the patrons of Daugavpils' Russian-speaking population ever since.

The Citadel

Following Cietokšņa iela northeast from the centre brings you after twenty minutes to the **Citadel** (Cietoksnis; undergoing long-term renovation; contact tourist office for details), a self-contained suburb of barrack blocks surrounded by red-brick bastions and grassy earthworks. This area was the town centre until the 1770s, when the Tsarist authorities decided to turn it into a garrisoned military stronghold and relocated civilian activities to the southeast. The French captured it in 1812 and proceeded to demolish what they found – most of what you see today dates from the mid-nineteenth century and after. The Citadel survived the twentieth century relatively unscathed: the Russians evacuated it without a fight in World War I, and having failed to do much damage to it in World War II, the Soviet Air Force turned it into an Aviation High School – which it remained until 1990. Today it's one of the most bizarre places in Latvia (topped only by Karosta in Liepāja; see p.212), its long, grey lines of peeling buildings enlivened by the odd patch of greenery or ornamental artillery piece.

Eating and drinking

There are plenty of **cafés** along Rīgas iela, especially at the train-station end. *Vēsma*, Rīgas 49, has an order-at-the-counter canteen with a good salad bar, a cakes-and-ice cream section, sushi bar, and a summer-only roof terrace with grill-restaurant. *Pasaules brinumi*, just off the main square at Vienības 17, does a good line in salads, pork chops and pancakes, but the attractive, cellar-bound *Gubernators*, Lāčplēša 10, offers the best in the way of traditional Latvian pork-chop cuisine, and is also a lively place to **drink**. The *City Center* bowling alley, southeast of the bus station at Viestura 8 (Ⓦwww.citycenter .lv) boasts a smart café-bar with a snack menu and a weekend-only nightclub.

Aglona

Nestling picturesquely between a pair of lakes 45km northeast of Daugavpils and 10km east of the Daugavpils–Rēzekne highway, the one-horse village of **AGLONA** is dwarfed by the twin-towered, late-Baroque basilica that stands on its outskirts. The most important Catholic shrine in Latvia, it can draw anything from 100,000 to 150,000 celebrants for the Feast of the Assumption on August 15, and remains popular with pilgrims throughout the year – Easter, Pentecost and September 8 (Birth of the Virgin) being the other key dates. Aglona's importance as a religious centre dates back to 1699, when Dominicans chose to settle in this tranquil spot, bringing with them a seventeenth-century image of the Virgin that soon developed a reputation for miraculous healing powers. The first (wooden) monastery burnt down in 1766 and Aglona's burgeoning popularity with the faithful was considered sufficient reason to justify construction of the impressive basilica. Aglona's holy aura was boosted further when a local woman claimed to have seen a vision of the Virgin on the hillock beside the basilica in 1798. During the Soviet period the monastery was closed and pilgrimages discouraged, although the basilica was allowed to publicly celebrate its bicentennial in 1980. Thoroughgoing restoration was carried out in time for Pope John Paul II's visit in September 1993, when a massive paved area was laid down for outdoor Masses.

The **basilica** has the severe appearance of a freshly iced, but otherwise undecorated, cake. Its distinguishing feature is the pair of chunky 60m-high towers on either side of the main door – the basilica was by far the highest man-made object in the vicinity until the erection of the next-door TV transmission mast. It doesn't keep regular opening hours, and unless you arrive on Sundays, getting in is a matter of luck. Inside, the icon-like image of the Virgin that graces the high altar is hidden behind a curtain – and only unveiled on holy days. If all this is a bit of a let-down, you can always enjoy the scenery by following the paths around Lake Aglona immediately east of the basilica, or the larger, reed-fringed expanse of Cirīss to the west.

Getting to Aglona

Buses stop on what passes for a main square, 500m uphill from the basilica. If you're coming **from Rīga**, aim for the market town of **Preiļi**, 25km northwest of Aglona, and pick up a local bus from there – you should be able to see Aglona as a day-trip providing you set off early and double-check return times at each stage of the journey. Preiļi's bus station is on the central square, across from a **tourist office** at Tirgus laukums 1 (Mon–Fri 9am–5pm; Ⓣ6532 2041, Ⓦwww.preili.lv).

From Daugavpils or Rēzekne, Daugavpils–Rēzekne buses *don't* pass through Aglona itself, not matter what staff in local bus stations may say; they stop instead in the similarly named Aglonas stacija ("Aglona Station") on the main highway, a hamlet huddled around a barely used railway halt and not the kind of place where you want to get stranded. A handful of Daugavpils–Aglona and Rēzekne–Aglona services do exist, but they tend to set off too late to allow enough time to look around and get back to town.

Driving to Aglona is far less complicated: the main turn-off from the Daugavpils–Rēzekne highway at Aglonas stacija is marked by a huge white cross. For a more picturesque approach, turn off the highway at **Spogi**, 30km out of Daugavpils, and head east via the tiny lake resort of **Viški** – not all the road is tarmacked, but it's a lovely ride through rolling, partly forested countryside.

Information, accommodation and eating

Aglona's helpful **tourist office** is at Somersētas 34 (☎2911 8597, ⓦwww.visitaglona .lv). Ask here about the welcoming **B&Bs** in and around town – hosts may speak Russian or German but not much English. Most offer half- or full-board arrangements for a few extra lati – well worth considering as the quality of cooking is generally excellent and other eating and drinking opportunities are few. **Campers** will find tent and caravan space at *Pussala*, a lakeside site 2km northwest of the village off the Preiļi road (☎2644 7747), and at *Aglonas Alpi*, 4km south on the shores of the Ciriša reservoir (☎2919 4362 and 6532 1465, ⓦwww.aglonasalpi.viss.lv) – the latter also has en-suite cottages (four-person cottages from 37Ls, two-person ❹).

The **café** opposite the bus stop serves soups, salads and pork cutlets; and the *Aglonas maize* **bakery** at Daugavpils iela 7 (Mon–Fri 8am–6pm, Sat & Sun 9am–4pm) sells fresh rye bread – including the speciality loaf Veistuklis which contains tasty chunks of bacon fat.

B&Bs

Aglonas Cakuli Ezera 4 ☎6537 5465 or 2919 4362, ⓦwww.aglonascakuli.lv. Lakeside house in the centre of Aglona with small, simply furnished rooms, some with tiny bathrooms. There's usually local fish on the menu for those that choose half-board. ❷–❸

Aglonas maize Daugavpils iela 7 ☎2928 7044 or 6532 1905, ⓦwww.aglonasmaize.viss.lv. Five rooms above the *Aglonas maize* bakery, each with attic ceilings, original timber features, bright cake-icing colours and bread-baking smells wafting up from below. Shared WC & shower in the hallway. ❷

Mežnieku mājas Gūteņi ☎2923 4425, ⓦwww .mezniekumajas.viss.lv. Secluded farmstead 7km west of Aglona, at the end of a well-signed forest track just off the Viški road, with neat, simple wood-panelled rooms spread over a couple of buildings, and a communal kitchen and sauna. Idyllic surroundings include birch groves, woodland trails and a "druidic zodiac park" planted with the talismanic trees associated with each group of birthdates. ❸

Upenīte Tartakas 7 ☎2631 2456, ⓔa.upenite @inbox.lv. Farmstead 2km west of town on the Viški road, offering snug rooms (one double and one quad) with painted floorboards, wooden ceilings and old-fashioned textiles. Lake Cirišs is a few metres downhill. Ponies, a traditional smoke sauna and tasty home cooking provide additional incentives to stay. ❸

Rēzekne

Despite being fortified by both Latgalian chieftains and the Livonian Order, **RĒZEKNE**, 90km northeast of Daugavpils, didn't really take shape until the nineteenth century, when it was laid out in the grid pattern beloved of the Tsarist Empire's town planners. Unfortunately, few historic buildings survive from any era: Rēzekne found itself among the most artillery-pummelled towns in Latvia in World War II, and its buildings are unremittingly grey and modern. That said, it's a relatively relaxing, leafy city, and with a decent museum and a couple of other cultural oddities to its name, it's worth a brief stop.

Rēzekne's main street, **Atbrīvošanas aleja** ("Liberation Alley"), runs north–south through the centre. Half-way along, at a roundabout, stands the region's most famous resident, **Māra of Latgale** (Latgales Māra), a statue of a woman brandishing a cross in celebration of victory over the godless Bolsheviks in 1920 and Latgale's subsequent absorption into the state of Latvia. The inscription on the pedestal reads *Vienoti Latvijai* ("For Latvian Unity!").

Photographs of the local woman who modelled for the sculpture are on display at the **Latgale Museum of History and Culture** (Latgales kultūrvēstures muzejs; Tues–Fri 10am–5pm, Sat 10am–4pm; 1Ls), just north of the roundabout at Atbrīvošanas 102. The collection is a nostalgic evocation of the Rēzekne of old, with sepia photos of the handsome brick buildings that used to line the main street before World War I and re-creations of shop interiors. Several rooms are devoted to traditional Latgale ceramics – look out for the many-branched candlesticks, very much a local trademark.

Practicalities

Rēzekne has two **train stations**: Rēzekne II, just off the northern end of Atbrīvošanas aleja and about twenty minutes' walk north of the central roundabout, handles trains to and from Rīga and Ludza, while Rēzekne I, fifteen minutes southwest of the roundabout, is currently served by the Vilnius–St Petersburg express only, which passes through three times a week in each direction. The **bus station** is ten minutes' walk south of the roundabout. Overlooking the roundabout, and offering good views of the city from its upper floors, the tower-block *Latgale* **hotel** (℡ 6462 2180, ⓦ www .hotellatgale.lv; ❹), Atbrīvošanas aleja 98, offers bright, modern en-suites. The best place for a quick bite is *Mols* (daily 10am–10pm), near the bus station at Latgales 22/24, a combined **café**, gallery and craft shop which serves salads, soups and pork chops on traditional Latgalian ceramic plates. *Little Italy* (daily 11am–11pm), beside the roundabout at Atbrīvošanas aleja 100, serves pizza, pasta and pork and chicken dishes in an elegant but not-too-formal environment.

Ludza

A short 25km ride from Rēzekne across a pleasing landscape of low hills and lakes, **LUDZA** is one of the most attractive small towns in Latvia, with neat rows of wooden houses draped across a neck of land separating three lakes. Overlooking the scene from a small hill is the pert, twin-towered Catholic church, accompanied by a free-standing half-timbered bell tower. Immediately to the north are the ruins of Ludza's red-brick fortress, built by the Livonian Order to keep Russian invaders at bay. Head to the rugged shell of the three-storey keep to enjoy a sweeping panorama of the lakes, with Mazais Ludzas ezers ("Little Ludza Lake") over to the west, Lielais Ludzas ezers ("Great Ludza Lake") to the northeast and Dunakļu ezers further away to the north.

North of the fortress, on the far side of a bridge, the **Ludza District Museum** (Ludzas novadpētniecības muzejs; Tues–Fri 9am–5pm, Sat 10am–5pm; 1Ls), at Kuļņeva 2, occupies the former villa of Yakov Petrovich Kulnev (1763–1812), a dashing cavalry officer who was the first Russian general to be killed defending the homeland during Napoleon's invasion of Russia of 1812 and became a national hero as a result. Alongside Latgale ceramics, the display includes a fine collection of spiral headbands, necklaces and bracelets found in locally excavated tenth-century graves. Presiding over a fishpond in the yard are a pair of typical Latgale timber farm buildings and a small windmill.

Behind the museum, Soikāna iela leads uphill onto a ridge running along the north side of the lake, arriving after ten minutes at an atmospheric, tree-canopied **Jewish cemetery**, with hundreds of Hebrew-engraved tombstones amid the long grass. In the eighteenth century, an estimated 59 percent of the town's population was Jewish, earning Ludza the title of "Latvian Jerusalem" – although the community thinned out in the 1930s owing to emigration to Rīga or America, and was annihilated completely by the Nazis in summer 1941. In town, there's an unused synagogue on the lakeside Ezerkrasta iela, behind the tourist office, although there's nothing to indicate its former function.

If you're shopping for authentic handmade souvenirs, head for the **Ludza Craft Centre**, Tālavijas 27a (Ludzas amatnieku centrs; Mon–Fri 9am–5pm, Sat 9am–3pm), which has an outstanding selection of Latgale ceramics, linen shirts and embroidered bedspreads.

Practicalities

Ludza can be reached by two daily trains (mid-May to mid-Sept only) and two daily buses from Rīga; otherwise public transport comes from Rēzekne. The **bus station** is right in the town centre, while the **train station** is a good twenty-minute walk south, at the top of Stacijas iela. The enthusiastic **tourist office**, Baznīcas 42 (Mon–Fri 8am–5pm; ☎6570 7202, ⊛www.ludza.lv), supplies brochures and town plans and can book you into B&B accommodation in villages throughout the district. The *Valensija* **hotel**, centrally located at Baroņa 20 (☎2862 9829, ⊜valensija.ludza@inbox.lv; ❸), has en-suite doubles and triples and an on-site sauna. *Kafejnīca Kristīne* (Sun–Thurs 10am–9pm, Fri & Sat till 11pm), opposite the tourist office at Baznīcas 25, serves supremely tasty pork-and-potato dishes.

Travel details

Trains

Rīga to: Cēsis (4 daily; 2hr); Daugavpils (4 daily; 3hr 20min–4hr); Līgatne (4 daily; 1hr 15min); Ludza (summer only; 2 daily; 4hr 40min); Rēzekne (2 daily; 4hr); Sigulda (10 daily; 1hr 5min–1hr 20min).

Buses

Cēsis to: Erģeļu klintis (Mon–Fri 2 daily, Sat 5 daily, Sun 4 daily; 30min); Līgatne (Mon–Fri 3 daily; 40min).
Daugavpils to: Aglona (3 daily; 1hr 20min); Ludza (Mon–Sat 2 daily; 2hr 30min); Rēzekne (7 daily; 2hr 10min).
Līgatne train station to: Līgatne village (Mon–Fri 6 daily, Sat 3 daily, Sun 5 daily; 15min).
Preiļi to: Aglona (6 daily; 55min).

Rēzekne to: Aglona (2 daily; 1hr 30min); Daugavpils (7 daily; 2hr 10min); Ludza (5 daily; 30–50min); Rīga (8 daily; 5hr).
Rīga to: Cēsis (hourly; 2hr); Daugavpils (7 daily; 3hr 30min–4hr); Preiļi (6 daily; 3hr 30min); Sigulda (Mon–Sat 15 daily, Sun 7 daily; 1hr 10min).
Sigulda to: Krīmulda (9 daily; 20min); Rīga (Mon–Sat 15 daily, Sun 7 daily; 1hr 10min); Saulkrasti (4 daily; 1hr); Turaida (10 daily; 15min).

International trains

Daugavpils to: Vilnius (3 weekly; 3hr 30min).

International buses

Daugavpils to: Vilnius (2–3 daily; 3hr).

Lithuania

Lithuania highlights

✳ **St Casimir's Fair, Vilnius** A colourful craft fair attracting just about every woodcarver, ironmonger and basket-weaver in the country. See p.256

✳ **Vilnius Old Town** Inviting warren of alleyways overlooked by a handsome collection of Baroque and neoclassical churches. See p.258

✳ **National Art Gallery, Vilnius** Lithuanian art gets the showcase it deserves in this superbly renovated modernist building. See p.272

✳ **Trakai** This beautifully restored fourteenth-century fortress, set in serene lakeland, is one of the finest in the Baltics. See p.283

✳ **Museum of Lithuanian Life at Rumšiškės** A rambling, enormously enjoyable collection of nineteenth-century wooden homes from all over the country. See p.310

✳ **Dzūkija National Park** Rural Lithuania at its most unspoiled, with tumbledown villages and sandy-soiled pine forests teeming with mushrooms and berries. See p.314

✳ **Hill of Crosses** Set amid the green pasturelands of the northwest, this is a compelling memorial to faith, national suffering and hope. See p.325

✳ **Nida** A relaxing village of fishermen's cottages at the foot of towering, tawny dunes. See p.338

✳ **Palanga** There's something for everyone at this resort, from bucket-and-spade beach culture to dance-till-dawn nightlife. See p.343

△ Trakai castle

Introduction and basics

Boasting the best rye-based black bread in the world, a unique range of herb-infused alcoholic spirits and a distinctive cuisine in which the humble potato is elevated to sacred status, Lithuania possesses plenty in the way of identity. Such character owes a lot to the fact that, unlike its Baltic neighbours, Lithuania once enjoyed a period of sustained international greatness, building a medieval empire that stretched south and east across modern Belarus, Russia and the Ukraine. Such strength allowed Lithuania to remain a nature-worshipping pagan state until well into the fourteenth century, and a mystical relationship with the lakes and forests marks out the Lithuanian character to this day. Christianity came to Lithuania after dynastic union with the Kingdom of Poland in 1386, and Polish Catholic culture went on to exert an increasing influence over the country, especially after the creation of the so-called Polish-Lithuanian Commonwealth in 1569. After 1795, Tsarist Russia became the dominant power. Despite successive waves of Polonization and Russification, however, Lithuanian culture was preserved in villages and farmsteads, and the country remains extraordinarily rich in folk art, rural festivals and traditional song. Lithuania can also claim to be the first Baltic State to declare its independence from Moscow, breaking free in 1990 and forcing the pace of change that led to the collapse of the Soviet Union, the spread of civil society and free-market economics – and, ultimately, the accession of all three Baltic States to the European Union in 2004.

Where to go

The Lithuanian capital **Vilnius**, with its cobbled alleys and Baroque churches, is arguably the most architecturally beautiful of the Baltic capitals. Easily reached from the capital is the imposing island fortress of **Trakai**, perhaps the country's best-known landmark and something of a national symbol. The rest of eastern Lithuania is characterized by deep forest, sandy-soiled pine woods and lakes, the most scenic stretches of which fall within the **Aukštaitija National Park** and **Dzūkija National Park**. Close to the latter are the relaxing spa resorts of **Druskininkai** and **Birštonas**, each of which offers the opportunity to splash around in invigorating spring water or embark on long woodland walks.

Set amid the green farmland of central Lithuania is its second city, **Kaunas**, with its attractive old town and set-piece museums. The main city in the northwest is **Šiauliai**, rather workaday, but a convenient base from which to visit the Hill of Crosses, a remarkable monument to Catholic piety and native Lithuanian mysticism.

On the coast, the busy port city of **Klaipėda** has something of an old quarter and a handful of lively bars and clubs. It's also the gateway to the **Curonian Spit**, a uniquely beautiful offshore strip of sand dune and forest that shields Lithuania from the open Baltic Sea.

Up the coast from Klaipėda, **Palanga** is an inviting cross between family beach resort and bar crawler's paradise, while the **Žemaitija National Park**, inland, offers an engaging mixture of pretty rural villages and forested wilderness.

Getting around

Buses provide the most convenient way of getting around Lithuania: there are frequent services between the main cities and at least one or two daily departures to the remotest of villages. **Trains** are slightly cheaper, but although they connect the major towns, departures are infrequent and journey times painfully slow. For details of travel from one Baltic state to another, see p.34.

Buses

Lithuania's bus network is run by an at times confusing array of local companies – **Toks**

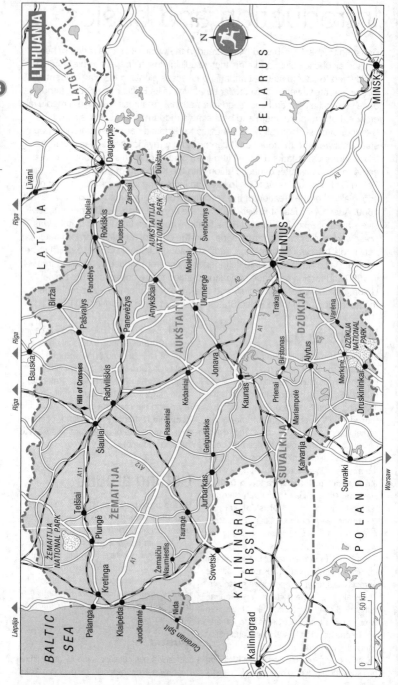

LITHUANIA

(🌐www.toks.lt) in Vilnius and **Kautra** (🌐www
.kautra.lt) in Kaunas being two of the biggest – but services are well integrated and
bus stations (*autobusų stotis*) are generally
well organized, with clearly marked departure
boards and ticket counters allowing you to
book your seats in advance. Smaller towns
and villages will have a simple bus stop
(*stotelė*) with no timetable information, so it's
best to enquire about timings at one of the
bigger bus stations before heading out into
rural areas. The **website** 🌐www.autobilietai
.lt is a useful timetable resource. On **inter-city
routes** you might have a choice between regular buses, which stop at innumerable places
en route, and **expresses** (*ekspresas*, usually
marked on timetables by the letter E), which
travel more or less directly to their destination
and cost a few litai extra. Short routes (such
as Vilnius to Kaunas, Klaipėda to Nida, and
Klaipėda to Palanga) are often operated by
minibuses (*mikroautobusas*) – timetable information is usually displayed in bus stations.

Fares are reasonable: travelling from Vilnius
to Trakai will set you back around 6Lt, while
a ticket from Vilnius to Kaunas weighs in at
around 25Lt. Moving across country from
Vilnius to Klaipėda costs about 75Lt. At big-
city bus stations, you usually buy your **ticket**
from ticket windows before boarding the bus.
Tickets show the departure time (*laikas*), platform number (*aikštė*) and seat number (*vieta*)
and will probably carry the name of the bus
company you're travelling with – useful to
know if two companies are running services
to the same destination at around the same
time. If you're catching a bus from some
intermediate point on the route, it's often
impossible to buy tickets in advance – pay
the driver or conductor instead. Small items
of luggage are taken on board; large bags
are stowed in the luggage compartment, for
which you might have to pay an extra 3–5Lt.

Buses on the major inter-city routes can
get busy on summer weekends, so it's worth
reserving seats a day or two in advance.

Trains

Services run by **Lithuanian Railways** have
been cut back considerably in recent years.
Commuter lines running in and out of Vilnius
and to Kaunas are still served by frequent
trains, but longer routes (Vilnius to Šiauliai,

or Vilnius to Klaipėda, for example) only see
a couple of departures a day – they're also
slower than the much more frequent buses.

Tickets (*bilietas*) have to be bought before
you board. Train stations (*geležinkelio stotis*)
often have separate windows for long-distance (*priemiestinis*) and suburban (*vietinis*)
trains. **Long-distance services** are divided
into two categories: passenger (*keleivinis
traukinys*) and fast (*greitas*). Both are in fact
painfully slow, but the latter at least won't stop
at every second village. Most international
trains (*tarptautinis*) travel overnight and offer
couchette or sleeping-car accommodation.

Printed **timetables** (*tvarkaraštis*) are few
and far between, so you'll have to rely on
departure boards for information, or consult
the Lithuanian railway's website 🌐www.litrail
.lt. "Departure" is written *išvyksta*, *išvykimas* or
išvykimo laikas; and "arrival" *atvyksta*, *atvyki-
mas* or *atvykimo laikas*. Trains that operate
on working days (ie Mon–Sat) are marked
with the words *darbų dienomis*; those running
on Sundays and public holidays are marked
švenčių dienomis. Otherwise, numbers 1–7
are used to denote the days of the week
on which a particular service operates (1
is Monday, 2 is Tuesday, and so on), often
accompanied by the word *kursuoja* ("it is running") or *nekursuoja* ("it isn't running").

Driving

Driving in Lithuania throws up an assortment
of hazards. Along with high-powered Western
cars and four-wheel drives, you'll see some
spectacularly decrepit cars on the roads, and
in country areas you may have to contend
with slow-moving tractors, horses and carts,
stray farm animals and the odd wandering

Addresses

In Lithuania the street name always
comes before the number, and the word
for "street" (*gatvė*) is often omitted, for
example Pilies 28 would be 28 Pilies
Street. A street number comprising two
figures separated by slash (7/2 or 9/25
for example) means that the building
is on a corner or intersection – the first
number denotes its position in the main
street, while the second number refers to
its position in the street being intersected.

drunk. The **roads** from Vilnius to Panevėžys, and from Vilnius to Klaipėda via Kaunas, are fairly respectable two-lane highways for much of their length. Most other main roads are in reasonable repair, but many minor roads are little more than dirt tracks. How much of the road network is passable depends on the time of year; in winter you may need a four-wheel drive to access country areas. Snow is the main problem; although the main routes are regularly ploughed and only become impassable during the heaviest blizzards, secondary roads are often left with a covering of snow throughout the winter season.

Petrol (*degalinė*) costs roughly €1/£0.85/$1.20 per litre. Though most towns and highways have plenty of 24hr petrol stations, there are few in rural areas, where it is a good idea to carry a spare can.

The use of **seatbelts** is compulsory, **headlights** must be on at all times, and It is illegal to drive after drinking even the tiniest drop of **alcohol**. **Speed limits** are 50kph in built-up areas and 90kph on the open road. The limit on two-lane highways is 130kph (April–Sept) and 100kph (Oct–March). The police are extremely vigilant, and will spot-fine you for any transgressions.

Car rental costs around €60–80/£50–67/$72–100 per day from one of the big companies, slightly less from local firms – though with the latter, insurance coverage may be sketchy and the cars may not be well maintained. Contact details of major car rental firms are given on p.34.

Accommodation

There's a growing range and diversity of accommodation in Lithuania, especially at the top end of the scale, with new, **business-oriented** hotels and international franchises moving in; in addition, many old, state-run establishments are being privatized and refurbished. The overall effect of these developments has been to push prices up. That said, however, bargains are still easy to come by – especially if you're staying in hotels and **guesthouses** on the coast or in the provinces. There are also plenty of inexpensive, good-value **rooms** in private houses and on rural farmstays. A handful of backpacker-oriented **hostels** exist in Vilnius, though they're

few and far between in the rest of the country. Most **campsites** tend to be rather basic, but are usually set in idyllic rural surroundings.

Hotels

Most hotels in Lithuania have been graded according to the international five-star system, although ratings tend to be on the optimistic side and may not be an accurate indication of quality.

You'll find plenty of competitively priced **mid-range hotels** offering en-suite showers, TV and breakfast – establishments that would fit comfortably into the international two- and three-star brackets. Prices and quality vary considerably in this category: the majority are of post-1991 vintage, often occupying renovated town houses and featuring new furniture. Expect to pay 300–400Lt for a mid-range double in Vilnius, slightly less in Kaunas. Elsewhere, doubles are more likely to fall somewhere in the 200–250Lt range.

In international **business-class** hotels, you'll get a range of familiar comforts for 400–500Lt: satellite TV, air conditioning, minibar and a lavish buffet breakfast.

Private rooms

Private rooms (*kambariai*) with local families are available in Vilnius, Kaunas, Klaipėda and Palanga, and in the resorts of the Curonian Spit. Conditions vary from place to place: some hosts have refurbished their flats and installed new furniture with guests in mind; others will plonk you in a bedroom recently vacated by their grown-up offspring. In most cases you'll be sharing your host's bathroom and whether or not you'll be allowed access to tea/coffee-making facilities is a matter of luck. Staying in private rooms isn't necessarily a great way of meeting the locals: some hosts will brew you a welcome glass of tea and want to talk; others will simply give you a set of keys and leave you to get on with it.

Local tourist offices can sometimes help you secure a room, but the only nationwide booking agency is **Litinterp**, with offices in Vilnius, Kaunas and Klaipėda (the latter also deals with Palanga and Nida) – see the relevant sections of the Guide for contact details. Rooms arranged through Litinterp cost 90–110Lt per person and an additional 10–15Lt gets you breakfast.

Accommodation price codes

The hotels and guesthouses listed in the Lithuanian chapters of this guide have been graded according to the following price bands, based on the cost of the least expensive double room in summer.

❶ 90Lt and under
❷ 91–120Lt
❸ 121–160Lt

❹ 161–220Lt
❺ 221–300Lt
❻ 301–400Lt

❼ 401–600Lt
❽ 601Lt and over

Cheaper rooms are available in Palanga and Nida if you're prepared to tramp the streets looking for vacancies – signs advertising *kambarių nuoma* ("rooms for rent") and *laisvos vietos* ("vacancies") are posted outside individual houses.

Rural homestays

In an attempt to stimulate the provincial economy, authorities are encouraging the development of rural **homestays** (*poilsis kaime*), where you stay on working farms or in village houses and eat locally produced food and drink. Room quality varies, although most are neat little en suites, often with a rustic feel. Some hosts offer self-contained apartments with catering facilities.

Prices start from as little as 60Lt per person, rising to about 120Lt if the property has been swankily modernized. Half- or full-board featuring tasty, home-cooked food is often available for an extra 20–30Lt per person. While offering a wonderful taste of rural life, most of these homestays are a long way from regular bus routes – so you'll need your own transport to get around.

Local tourist offices are keen to push this form of tourism and will always help you secure a room in their region, although it pays to contact them a few days in advance. The **Lithuanian Rural Tourism Association** (Lietuvos kaimo turizmo asociacija; Lietuvos respublikos žemės ūkio rūmai, Donelaičio 2, LT-3000 Kaunas; ☎37/400 354, ⓦwww .atostogoskaime.lt) publishes a catalogue of properties throughout the country and also handles advance reservations.

Hostels and camping

Backpacker-oriented **hostels** can be found in Vilnius and Klaipėda, offering dorm accommodation for as little as 40Lt a night, although they're oversubscribed in summer, so it's a good idea to reserve in advance. Vilnius also has a couple of students' and teachers' hostels that rent out rooms throughout the year when there's space – expect to pay around 40Lt for a bed in a double or triple room. The **Lithuanian Youth Hostelling Association**'s website, ⓦwww .lha.lt, provides contact details for hostels in Vilnius, Klaipėda and Druskininkai.

Lithuania boasts a handful of well-appointed **campsites** (*kempingas*) with toilet blocks, washing facilities and electric power points for caravans, the main locations being Trakai, Druskininkai and Nida. Expect to pay 15Lt per pitch, 15Lt per person and 10Lt per vehicle in these places. Elsewhere in the country, camping can be a wonderfully idyllic experience if you're prepared to rough it; in many cases campsites are nothing more than grassy areas supplied with picnic benches and (if you're lucky) simple outhouse toilets, which will probably just be a hole in the ground. National park areas are particularly well supplied with these sites, charging as little as 5Lt for a tent space.

Food and drink

Lithuanian cuisine is based around a traditional repertoire of hearty peasant dishes, in which potatoes and pork play the starring roles. Main meals tend to be heavy and calorie-laden – perfect for the long winters. International and ethnic cuisine is beginning to appear in the cities, and pizzerias are popping up almost everywhere. Although vegetarianism has yet to establish itself, it's possible to find meat-free options on most menus – mushroom- or cheese-filled pancakes being the most common.

Lithuanian **restaurants** (*restoranas*) range from swanky city-centre places, with starched napkins and pan-European menus, to unpretentious eateries offering a cheap range of Lithuanian standards. Most Lithuanians like to combine eating and drinking in the same venue. Many **cafés** (*kavinė*), for example, are restaurants in all but name, serving inexpensive and simple Lithuanian standards alongside the coffee and cakes, and most places that describe themselves as **bars and pubs** (see "Drinking", opposite) also offer a full menu of hot food. In addition, there's a growing number of homely establishments featuring folksy wooden furnishings and a big choice of drinks and local specialities at mid-range prices – these places often go under names such as *užeiga* ("inn") or *smuklė* ("tavern"), underlining the cosy, bucolic theme.

Even in a fairly upmarket restaurant, a meal shouldn't be much more expensive than in a mid-range establishment in Western Europe, and it's possible to eat really well for much less if you head for the inns and cafés, where a main course often costs less than 15Lt. Wherever you eat, though, be prepared for **slow service**. You'll find a **glossary** of food and drink terms on p.401.

What to eat

Most Lithuanians tuck straight into a **main course** (usually listed under *karšti patiekalai* or "hot meals"), although menus invariably include a short list of starters that would also do as light snacks (*šalti užkandžiai* are cold starters; *karšti užkandžiai* are hot starters) – typical choices include marinated mushrooms (*marinuoti grybai*), herring (*silkė*) and smoked sausage (*rūkyta dešra*). Soup (*sriuba*) is sometimes offered as a starter, although it's more commonly treated as a quick and cheap lunchtime meal in its own right. Cold beetroot soup (*šaltibarščiai*) is a Lithuanian speciality, and can be deliciously refreshing in summer.

Typical Lithuanian staples

The mainstay of the nation's cuisine is the **potato**, which not only serves as the staple accompaniment to most main courses, but also forms the central ingredient in a series of typical Lithuanian specialities. Raw potatoes are passed through the fine end of a grater, mixed with egg and then dropped in hot oil to form *bulviniai blynai* (potato pancakes)

– they're delicious on their own, or are sometimes filled with meat. The same grated-potato mixture forms the basis of *cepelinai*, Zeppelin-shaped parcels stuffed with minced meat, mushrooms or cheese and then boiled, while *kugelis* (also known as *bulvių plokštainis* or "potato slab") is a brick-shaped helping of grated or mashed potato baked in the oven. Another favourite is *žemaičių blynai* (*Žemaitija* pancakes) – mashed potato moulded into heart shapes, stuffed with minced meat and then fried. One dish that is definitely tastier than it sounds is *vedarai*: sausage made from pig's intestine and filled with potato pieces.

Common **potato-free dishes** include *koldūnai* (ravioli-like pasta stuffed with minced pork), *balandeliai* (cabbage leaves stuffed with meat and rice) and all manner of crepe-style pancakes (*blynai*, *blyneliai* or *lietiniai*), containing ham, cheese, mushrooms and other savoury fillings.

All of the above are usually served without accompanying vegetables or bread, but can be enormously filling in their own right – not least because they're invariably garnished with pieces of fried bacon fat, lashings of sour cream (*grietinė*), or a tasty mixture of both.

Meat and fish dishes

Meat (*mėsa*) in Lithuanian restaurants usually comes in the form of *kepsnys*, a chop or cutlet that is either roasted or pan-fried (menus find it difficult to specify which, because the expressions "to fry" and "to roast" are covered by the same verb: *kepti*). A *kepsnys* traditionally consists of a fat slice of pork (*kiauliena*), although cuts of beef (*jautiena*), veal (*veršiena*), chicken (*vištiena*) and turkey (*kalakutiena*) are increasingly common. A *kepsnys* might come garnished with a sauce (*su padažu*), mushroom sauce (*grybų padažas*) being the most common.

Other common meat dishes include sausages (*dešrelės*), usually made from spicy, heavily seasoned pork rather than the bland, boiled variety. Stew (*troškinys*) may come in the form of a satisfying meat-and-vegetable meal, but might equally be a thin soup with a few bits of beef floating around in it. Lamb (*aviena*) rarely figures on menus, except in recipes borrowed from other republics of the former Soviet Union – notably in the form of *šašlykai* (grilled kebabs) from the Caucasus.

The commonest kinds of **fish** (*žuvis*) are trout (*upėtakis*), pike-perch (*sterkas*), cod (*menkė*) and salmon (*lašiša*); all are usually pan-fried or baked, although salmon steaks are sometimes prepared *ant grotelių* ("grilled"). A speciality of the Nida region is smoked eel (*rukytas unguris*), sliced and eaten cold.

Meat and fish main courses are usually accompanied by (often quite small) portions of potatoes and seasonal vegetables, alongside generous amounts of bread.

Desserts and cakes

Typical restaurant **desserts** include ice cream (*ledai*), cakes (*pyragai*), cottage cheese (*varškė*) with fruit, and innumerable fruit-filled varieties of pancake (*blyneliai* or *lietiniai*). One of the most popular pastries you'll come across in cafés and bakeries are Lithuanian doughnuts (*spurgos*), which look like deep-fried tennis balls with neither a hole nor jam in the middle – they're delightfully fluffy when fresh. More spectacular are *šakotis*, a large, honey-coloured cake in the shape of a spiky fir tree; and *skruzdėlynas* (literally "ant-hill"), a pyramid of pastry pieces covered in syrup. These two creations are usually consumed at family feasts and birthday parties and hardly ever appear on menus – you can always buy a small one from a supermarket or a bakery and scoff it in your room.

Breakfasts and snacks

Unless you're staying in a budget hotel, hostel or private room, **breakfast** will almost always be included in the cost of your accommodation. At its simplest, it will consist of bread, cheese, ham and tea or coffee. Mid- and top-range hotels will offer a buffet breakfast, complete with a range of cereals, scrambled eggs and bacon. Pastries (*bandelės*) can be picked up from bakeries, cafés and street kiosks.

Basic self-catering and **picnic ingredients** can be bought at a food store (*maisto prekės*), supermarket (*prekybos centras*) or open-air market (*turgus*). You can buy **bread** (*duona*) from any of the above or from a bakery (*kepykla*). Lithuania's delicious bread is of the brown, rye-flour variety found across the Baltics. It's often baked in big square blocks, and you're more likely to buy a quarter (*ketvirtas*) or half (*pusė*) than a whole

loaf (*kepalas*). White bread is much less common, and is usually produced in French-style, baton form (*batonas*).

Lithuanian **street-food** culture revolves around kiosks (often located near markets or bus stations), selling *čeburekai* or *kibinai* (pies stuffed with spicy minced meat).

Drinking

Cafés (*kavinė*) come in all shapes and sizes: from modern places with a varied food menu to chintzy venues serving pastries and cakes. Most offer a full range of alcoholic as well as soft drinks. **Coffee** (*kava*) and **tea** (*arbata*) are usually served black, unless you specify *su grietinele* ("with cream") or *su pienu* ("with milk"). *Su cukrumi* is with sugar, *be cukraus* is without.

City centres and resorts feature a growing range of lively **bars** – many aping American or Irish models, although there are also plenty of folksy Lithuanian places with wooden benches and rustic decor. **Beer** (*alus*) is the most popular alcoholic drink. The biggest local **brewers** – Utenos, Švyturys and Kalnapilis – produce eminently drinkable, light, lager-type beer (*šviesus alus*), as well as a dark porter (*tamsus alus*). It's worth seeking out the more characterful brews produced by Lithuania's many small breweries – Biržų alus, Rinkuškiai and Ponoras (all from the Biržai region) being among the best. It's common to nibble **bar-snacks** (*užkandžiai prie alaus*) alongside your drinks – *kepta duona* (fingers of brown bread fried with garlic) being the standard order.

An increasingly impressive range of imported **wines** (*vynas*) is available in bars and shops. Alita, the locally produced brand of sparkling, champagne-style wine (*šampanas*) is extremely palatable and very cheap – a bottle costs around €6/£5/$7 in supermarkets.

Vodka (*degtinė*) is widely consumed, alongside more traditional firewaters like Starka, Trejos devynerios and Medžiotojų – invigorating, amber-coloured spirits flavoured with herbs and leaves. Lithuanian **mead** (*midus*) is particularly potent. Strongest of all the spirits is **samanė**, a clear, grain-based spirit which is often brewed illicitly in the countryside and incapacitates the brains of all who drink it; a weaker version is available in shops.

The media

For details of **English-language publications** common to all three Baltic States, see p.41.

The biggest-selling and most influential of Lithuania's daily **newspapers** is *Lietuvos Rytas* ("Lithuanian Morning"; Ⓦ www.lrytas .lt), a self-consciously serious publication famous for stodgy reporting and tortuously long sentences. The lifestyle supplements with the weekend editions provide light relief, and Friday's entertainment listings are pretty thorough. Tabloid-sized *Respublika* is a bright and breezy alternative, while evening paper *Vakaro Žinios* is an entertainingly downmarket scandal rag.

News **magazines** and special-interest periodicals are pretty uninspiring, and it's in the women's market that you'll find most in the way of good design and visual style: avoid the Lithuanian-language versions of international titles like *Cosmopolitan* and look instead at home-grown monthlies like *Laima* ("Fortune") and *Moterys* ("Woman") to get an idea of how contemporary Lithuanians really see themselves. Interior-design magazines like *Namas ir Aš* convey a Scandinavian sense of contemporary cool and may well provide you with a few make-over ideas into the bargain.

Most hotel-room **televisions** will probably offer a handful of German- and English-language channels in addition to national networks like state-owned LRT and private stations LNK and TV3. All the national TV channels show plenty of English-language films and dramas, but they're almost always dubbed into Lithuanian, usually with a single actor reading all the parts.

Festivals

The Lithuanian year is peppered with traditional events and celebrations that mix ancient pagan tradition, Catholic ritual and the simple need for a knees-up. Falling into the last category are the **Sartai horse races** on the first weekend of February, a contest of nineteenth-century origins involving horse-and-trap teams racing on the frozen surface of Lake Sartai, 150km north of Vilnius. It's one of the most important social events of the winter, attracting high-profile bigwigs from Vilnius. If the ice isn't thick enough, the races are moved to the hippodrome in the nearby village of Dusetos.

The promise of approaching spring brings people out onto the streets of Vilnius on the weekend nearest March 4, St Casimir's Day, to take part in **Kaziuko Mugė** (St Casimir's Fair), an enormous handicrafts market at which artisans from all over Lithuania display and sell their wares. At around the same time, **Užgavėnės** (Shrove Tuesday) marks the beginning of the Lenten fast – as in the rest of Europe, it's celebrated by the over-consumption of pancakes. However, Užgavėnės in Lithuania bears characteristics that are clearly pre-Christian in origin – children in animal masks pass from house to house bringing good luck for the coming agricultural year (they're given sweets or small gifts in return), and the symbolic ending of winter is marked by burning an effigy of the Morė – an archetypal scapegoat figure – on a bonfire. Užgavėnės celebrations are organized in Vilnius on Shrove Tuesday, while the Museum of Lithuanian Life at Rumšiškės (see p.310) organizes a day of Užgavėnės-related events that usually fall on the nearest Sunday.

Most Lithuanians mark the arrival of spring by decorating their home with a sprig of **catkins** (*kačiukai*). This practice is closely related to **Verbų sekmadienis** (Palm Sunday), when *verbos* (colourful wands bound from dried grasses, corn stalks and flowers) are bought from street vendors – they're usually on sale from St Casimir's Day onwards – and proudly displayed in the home for the rest of the year. **Velykos** (Easter Day) is marked with a large family meal – usually ham accompanied by a sharp-tasting horseradish purée (*krienas*).

The biggest event of the year for many is the night of June 23–24, which is a pagan summer solstice celebration in origin, despite being known by its Christian name of **Joninės** – after St John's Day, June 24. The festival is also known in some quarters as Rasos ("Dew") on account of the magical healing properties attached to the dew collected at sunrise on June 24. Most people celebrate Joninės by heading for the countryside, where they either sing songs around a bonfire until dawn or head off into the woods with a loved one – deities attached to fertility are supposedly particularly powerful on this night.

As in the rest of Catholic Europe, November 1 and 2 (**All Saints'** and **All Souls'** days respectively) are marked by mass visits to cemeteries to honour the dead. Full of flowers and lit up by innumerable candles, they can be atmospheric places to visit at dusk.

The central event of **Kalėdos** (Christmas) is the Christmas Eve meal (*kučios*), when the whole family gathers to eat twelve courses (symbolizing the twelve apostles), none of which should contain meat or dairy – pies stuffed with mushrooms, and top-quality fish (notably carp) feature heavily. Also gracing the Christmas table are *kučiukai*, tiny, hard biscuits which are sold in shops in the weeks before Christmas, and dipped into poppy-seed milk before eating.

Sport

The country's most popular spectator sport by far is **basketball** (*krepšinis*). Lithuania has been a basketball superpower ever since the 1930s, when the national team won the first-ever European championships in Rīga in 1937, and retained the title on their home turf two years later. During the communist period, Lithuania's leading club team, Žalgiris Kaunas, was a major force in the Soviet league and served as an important symbol of national pride at a time when outright manifestations of Lithuanian patriotism were officially discouraged. With the restoration of independence in 1991, Lithuania bounced back onto the international basketball scene, winning the Olympic bronze in 1992, 1996 and 2000, and winning the European championships in Sweden in 2003.

In domestic competition, Žalgiris Kaunas remains the top side, although Lietuvos Rytas Vilnius has offered stiff competition in recent years – matches between the two can be intensely heated affairs. The season runs from October through to April, with a regular diet of Lithuanian league matches (on Sat or Sun) augmented by midweek games featuring Lithuanian representatives in one of two international leagues – the Euroleague, which is the continent's premier club competition, and the North European Basketball League (NEBL), which features teams from the Ukraine to the UK. Lithuanian **football** (*futbolas*) is in a comparatively sorry state,

with top-league matches frequently attracting crowds of under a hundred and most fans contenting themselves instead with TV broadcasts of top European games.

Entertainment and the arts

Lithuania offers a broad spectrum of entertainment, including a lot of serious music and drama. It's all very accessible: tickets for even the most prestigious events are rarely impossible to come by, and prices are cheap by European standards. Almost every branch of culture is marked by at least one major festival – see the events calendar on p.34 and the "Nightlife and entertainment" section of the Vilnius chapter (see p.279) for a thorough run-down.

Classical music and opera

Between them, Vilnius and Kaunas ensure a rich programme of music year-round. **Vilnius** boasts two symphony orchestras, an opera and a ballet company, while **Kaunas** has a chamber orchestra and highly rated choir. The capital attracts many top international conductors and soloists during the concert season, while the Vilnius Festival (June) and Trakai Festival (Aug) feature star performers playing in the open air.

The one "national" composer who features regularly in the repertoire is **Mikalojus Konstantinis Čiurlionis** (1875–1911), whose tone poems *Jūra* ("The Sea") and *Miške* ("In the Forest") were the first full-length symphonic pieces to be composed by a Lithuanian and the first to attempt a symbolic evocation of the country's unspoiled landscapes. Less regularly performed, but creating waves internationally, are works by an impressive stable of **contemporary composers** led by Bronius Kutavičius, Mindaugas Urbaitis and Ona Narbutienė, who mix the mystical sounds of Lithuanian folklore with minimalism and contemporary instrumentation. The **Gaida Festival of Contemporary Classical Music** (see p.280) is one occasion when you can bank on hearing a wide selection of their music. ⊛ www.mic.lt is a site devoted to Lithuanian contemporary composers, with biogs, scores and downloads.

Clubbing and pop music

Lithuanians love dancing, and are much less self-conscious about what they strut their stuff to than their modish north European counterparts. Mainstream **discos** are hugely enjoyable affairs featuring everything from Eminem to Boney-M – but you're unlikely to chance upon niche dance music outside a handful of specialist clubs in Vilnius.

Plenty of bars host **live bands** who play rock-pop covers, but there's little in the way of a serious gig circuit, and many local groups restrict themselves to ad hoc performances in unofficial spaces. Unsurprisingly then, there's not a big local rock scene (and any scene that does exist will be so far underground that you probably won't find it), although several semi-legendary names still mean a great deal to local fans. In the late 1980s and early 1990s, the angular, experimental band Bix seemed to personify Lithuania's break-out from the Soviet cultural straightjacket. At around the same time, Fojė imported a stylish new-wave sensibility to Lithuanian pop – since going solo, its lead singer Andrijus Mamantovas has proved to be the country's most enduring rock-pop performer. Lithuania's brightest hope for the future, however, is singer-songwriter **Alina Orlova** (handled by French indie label Fargo), whose happy-sad shards of musical poetry feature lyrics in Lithuanian, Russian and English. Her gigs are like intimate chamber concerts and are well worth catching.

Jazz

A handful of venues stage regular **jazz** gigs in Vilnius and Klaipėda, and there are good festivals involving international guests in Vilnius, Birštonas and Kaunas (see p.310). In the 1970s and 80s, Vilnius was home to the **Ganelin-Chekasin-Tarasov Trio**, the greatest – and perhaps the only – avant-garde jazz ensemble in the Soviet Union, still enjoying legendary status. Keyboardist Ganelin emigrated years ago, but saxophone-bellower Vladimir Chekasin and drummer Vladimir Tarasov are still around, working on a variety of (no longer connected) musical projects. Other contemporary performers to look out for are sax-player **Petras Vyšniauskas**, a pioneer in the field of jazz–folk crossover, and younger-generation vocalist **Neda**, a far

more stirring live performer than her bland MOR albums would suggest.

Drama

The Lithuanian capital is currently home to some of the most critically acclaimed **directors** in Europe – their works are regularly staged in Vilnius and if you're at all interested in theatre it's well worth making the effort to find out what's on in the city during your stay. English-language earphone commentary is sometimes provided in the bigger theatres, although there's usually enough happening on stage to make a visit worthwhile whether there's a translation or not.

Godfather of the Vilnius drama scene is **Eimuntas Nekrošius**, who spent most of the 1980s as director of the Vilnius Youth Theatre (see p.281) and now heads a production company of his own, Meno Fortas ("Art Fortress"). His lengthy performances (4–5 hours being typical) feature minimal stage props and repetitive, ritualistic movement. A generation younger, **Oskaras Koršunovas** is something of an antidote to this, combining an experimental approach (strongly influenced by Russian avant-gardists Daniil Kharms and Aleksandar Vvedensky) with a thoroughly contemporary taste for bright lights, big noises and visual jokes – he's probably one of the few directors who could stage a version of *Hamlet* in which the inclusion of a giant white rat fails to detract from the tragic sense of the original. Koršunovas has turned his hand to everything from intense studio performances to musicals, and has become something of a one-man national industry, with numerous productions on the go at any one time.

One other name worth looking out for is **Rimas Tuminas**, founder of Vilnius Little Theatre (see p.281); his understated but innovative productions of contemporary pieces and Shakespearean classics have earned him Europe-wide critical acclaim.

Cinema

Lithuanian **cinemas** show English-language films soon after their release in Western Europe – in the original language with Lithuanian subtitles. During the Soviet period, Lithuania's film studios churned out a respectable handful of local-language movies every year, and their facilities are currently very much in demand, with Western production companies seeking to employ skilled technicians on the cheap; domestic film production, meanwhile, has shrivelled to nothing.

One hugely popular Lithuanian cinema classic which you'll see in video stores – and might be tempted to buy if you have a taste for the bizarre – is Arūnas Žebriūnas's 1973 film *Velnio Nuotaka* ("Devil's Bride"), a lavish musical based on Lithuanian folk tales and featuring the cream of theatrical and artistic talent of the time. Featuring an overblown screenplay by poet Sigitas Geda (see "Books", p.376) and a prog-rock-meets-Europap score courtesy of keyboard-bashing groovster Vyacheslav Ganelin (see "Jazz", opposite), it's a one-of-its-kind experience.

Travel essentials

Internet

There's a good choice of internet cafés in Vilnius, Kaunas and Klaipėda, but they're still pretty rare elsewhere; expect to pay around 5–6Lt for an hour's surfing. Wi-fi is widespread in Vilnius's hotels, restaurants and cafés, and increasingly common in other cities too. Sometimes it is free, at other times it is supplied by a local provider such as Zebra (5Lt/24hr, payable by sending a text message via your mobile phone).

Laundry

Dry-cleaners (*cheminis valymas*) are reasonably common, but self-service launderettes are almost non-existent in Lithuania – you may have to resort to washing your smalls in the hotel sink.

Left luggage

Most train and bus stations have a left-luggage office (*bagažinė*). The daily charge per item is rarely more than 3–4Lt.

Mail

Lithuanian postal and telephone services are generally well organized and easy to use. In

major towns, post offices (*paštas*) are usually open Monday to Friday 8am to 6/7pm, Saturday 8am to 3pm; in smaller places hours are more restricted. Larger post offices often have a confusing array of counters: if you just want to buy a stamp, head for the counter marked *laiškai* ("letters"). Airmail takes about four days to reach Britain, eight to reach North America; surface mail takes twice as long.

Money

Most of life's essentials – including food, drink and travel – are relatively cheap in Lithuania, and even if you're on a strict budget you shouldn't have too much trouble enjoying yourself. The only real exception is the price of accommodation, which is slowly creeping up towards Western European levels. For an idea of accommodation, food and transport costs, see the relevant sections on p.238, p.240 and p.237.

Lithuania's unit of currency is the litas (usually abbreviated to Lt), which is divided into 100 centai. Coins come in denominations of 0.01, 0.02, 0.05, 0.10, 0.20, 0.50, 1, 2 and 5Lt and bank notes in 1, 10, 20, 50, 100 and 200Lt denominations.

The main high-street banks (*bankas*) are Vilniaus bankas, Lietuvos taupomasis bankas, Lietuvos žemes ukio bankas, Hansabankas and Snoras bankas – this last, despite operating out of a chain of pre-fabricated blue kiosks, is a perfectly respectable outfit. Branches of all the above can change money, give cash advances on Visa, MasterCard or American Express cards, and cash travellers' cheques (for a commission of 2–3 percent). Opening hours vary, with most branches operating Monday to Friday 8am to 5/7pm. Big-city branches may well open on Saturday (typically 8am–3pm or 10am–5pm), and in rare cases for a few hours on Sunday too. ATMs are scattered liberally throughout central Vilnius, Kaunas and Klaipėda, and you'll find one or two in most other town centres. If you want to change cash outside banking hours, head for an exchange office (*valiutos keitykla*), often just a counter in a corner of a high-street department store. They only deal in cash, but they're usually open in the evenings and at weekends.

Credit cards are widely accepted in hotels, restaurants, big shops and petrol stations in Vilnius and other major urban centres. In small towns and villages, you're unlikely to have much luck.

Opening hours

Shops are typically open from Monday to Friday, 10/11am to 6/7pm, and on Saturdays from 10/11am to 3/4pm. Food stores and supermarkets in the cities usually keep longer hours, opening as early as 7am and working through to 8pm or 10pm, even at weekends. In rural areas, shops may break for lunch and close earlier in the evenings.

Opening times of museums, galleries and other tourist attractions vary. Generally, they're open from Tuesday to Sunday (in some cases Wed–Sun) from around 11am to 5/6pm – although some museums work on a Monday-to-Friday basis.

Churches in city centres may be open daily from 7am until around 7pm, but elsewhere they only open their doors for holy Mass (times of which are posted outside).

Phones

Public telephones use phonecards (*telefono kortelė*; 9Lt, 13Lt, 16Lt and 30Lt) available from post offices and newspaper kiosks – a 9Lt card will suffice for a handful of local calls; a 13Lt card should cover a short international call.

For all local calls from landlines, simply dial the subscriber number. To make a long-distance call within Lithuania, first dial 8, before dialling the area code and phone number. If you're using a mobile phone inside Lithuania, all numbers have to be preceded by 8 and the area code, even if you're in the same city as the recipient. When calling Lithuania from abroad on any phone, the initial 8 is omitted. For international calls from Lithuania, dial 8, wait for the tone, then dial 10, then the country code, area code and subscriber number.

For general information on using mobile phones in the Baltic States, see p.42. Lithuania's three mobile phone operators, Bitė, Omnitel and Tele2, run schemes that allow you to make calls within the country at local rates and receive calls without the caller incurring international charges. To get on one of these schemes, you need to buy a local SIM card for your GSM phone – this costs as little as 13Lt – after which you can buy pre-payment top-ups from newspaper kiosks in increments of 10Lt and upwards. Tele2 allows you to go roaming in Latvia and Estonia, too, where your calls will cost only slightly more than the local Lithuanian rate. Starter packs including SIM card and subsequent top-up cards, can be bought from newspaper kiosks.

Public toilets

Public toilets (*tualetas*) are rare outside bus and train stations (where a small fee, normally no more than 1Lt, is charged), although almost every café, restaurant and bar will have one. Gents are marked with a letter V or a ▲ symbol; ladies with an M or a ▼ symbol.

Smoking

Smoking is forbidden in public places, including all bars, restaurants and clubs. An increasing number of small and mid-sized hotels are strictly non-smoking throughout, although some larger establishments may still allow nicotine addicts to puff away in the privacy of their rooms.

Tipping

Tipping is not always expected in Lithuania, especially if you've only had a cup of coffee or a snack. After a round of drinks or a full meal, however, it's polite to leave roughly ten percent or to round up the bill to a convenient figure.

Public holidays

Most shops and museums and all banks are closed on the following public holidays:

January 1 New Year's Day
Febuary 16 Independence Day
March 11 Restoration of Independence Day
March/April (variable) Easter Sunday Easter Monday
May 1 May Day
May (first Sunday) Mothers Day
June 24 Midsummer
July 6 Coronation of King Mindaugas
August 15 Assumption
November 1 All Saints' Day
December 25 and 26 Christmas

3.1

Vilnius and around

" **N**arrow cobblestone streets and an orgy of Baroque: almost like a Jesuit city somewhere in the middle of Latin America," wrote the author Czesław Miłosz of prewar **VILNIUS** – a description that in many ways still holds true. Laid out in a bowl carved by the winding River Neris and surrounded by pine-covered hills, central Vilnius remains largely untainted by the high-rise development that characterizes the postwar suburbs and boasts perhaps the most impressive concentration of Baroque architecture in northern Europe, its skyline of domes and belfries making a lasting impression on visitors to the city. At ground level,

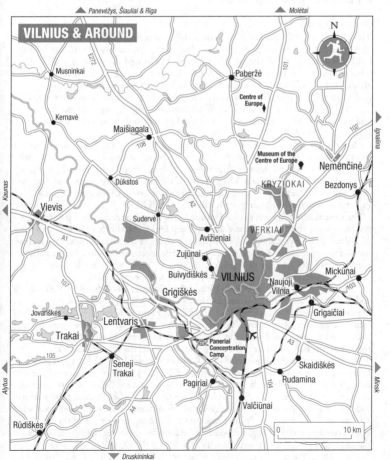

VILNIUS & AROUND

▲ *Panevėžys, Šiauliai & Riga*   ▲ *Molėtai*

N

Musninkai

Paberžė

Centre of Europe

Kernavė

Maišiagala

Museum of the Centre of Europe

Nemenčinė

Dūkstos

KRYŽIOKAI

Bezdonys

Kaunas

Vievis

Sudervė

VERKIAI

Avižieniai

Zujūnai

Buivydiškės

VILNIUS

Naujoji Vilnia

Mickūnai

Grigiškės

Jovariškės

Lentvaris

Grigaičiai

Trakai

Paneriai Concentration Camp

Minsk

Seneji Trakai

Skaidiškės

Pagiriai

Rudamina

Valčiūnai

Rūdiškės

0   10 km

▼ *Druskininkai*

247

the centre is a maze of atmospheric alleyways lined with solid, eighteenth-century town houses, punctuated by archways leading through to cobbled backyards.

Despite the impression of continuity given by its well-preserved architecture, Vilnius's history is as fragmented as any in Eastern Europe. Since the city's emergence as capital of the Lithuanian dukes in the Middle Ages, Russians, Belarussians, Jews and Poles have all left their mark, and Vilnius has been an important cultural centre to each in turn. The city is particularly cherished in Polish hearts: as well as Nobel prizewinner Miłosz, literary figures as diverse as Adam Mickiewicz, Juliusz Słowacki and Tadeusz Konwicki all spent their formative years here. Vilnius is still a cosmopolitan place – around twenty percent of its population is Polish and another fifteen percent is Russian – though with just under 550,000 inhabitants it has an almost village-like atmosphere, making it an easy place to get to know.

Vilnius's single most important attraction is the **Old Town**, an ensemble of winding, narrow streets and stately churches, with an engaging clutch of museums that includes some gripping displays recounting both the Nazi and Soviet occupations. Vilnius is also a good base from which to explore much of eastern Lithuania; the medieval fortress at lake-bound **Trakai**, the Iron Age hill-forts of **Kernavė** and the **Museum of the Centre of Europe** are easy day-trips, and Lithuania's second city **Kaunas** (see p.294) can also be reached in under two hours.

Some history

The city of Vilnius was born some time in the eleventh century when the sandy hills overlooking the confluence of the Vilija and Neris rivers became key strongholds for Lithuanian chieftains. Vilnius probably hosted the court of Mindaugas, who united the Lithuanian tribes into a centralized state in the thirteenth century, although it was his grandson, Gediminas, who made it a permanent power base. Although still a pagan, Gediminas encouraged the settlement of **Christian peoples** – notably German traders from Rīga and Russian-speaking nobles from the east – and many of Vilnius's churches pre-date the Lithuanian state's official acceptance of Christianity in 1386.

After the dynastic union between Lithuania and Poland in 1387, real power shifted towards Kraków (and subsequently Warsaw), where the kings of the new **Polish-Lithuanian state** spent most of their time – although Vilnius remained the capital of the Grand Duchy of Lithuania. The nobility of the Grand Duchy increasingly adopted the language and manners of their more sophisticated Polish neighbours, turning Vilnius into a culturally (if not necessarily ethnically) Polish city.

The close relationship with Poland ensured that Vilnius remained in touch with central European culture. Sigismund August (Grand Duke of Lithuania 1544–72 and King of Poland 1548–72) maintained a magnificent court in the city, encouraging learned minds from the rest of Europe to settle here. His successor-but-one, Stefan Bathory, presided over the creation of Vilnius University in 1579, and it has been one of the most prestigious seats of learning in northeastern Europe ever since.

When the creation of the **Polish-Lithuanian Commonwealth** in 1569 effectively ended the autonomy of the Grand Duchy, Vilnius lost some of its pre-eminence and increasingly became a peripheral, provincial city. Nevertheless, the Grand Duchy's leading magnates – drawn from powerful families such as the Radvilas, Sapiehas and Pacs – continued to build palaces in Vilnius and fund the building of churches, often in the exuberant Baroque style that became the town's architectural trademark.

The incorporation of Vilnius into the **Russian Empire** in 1795 led to an influx of Russians, a renewed wave of Orthodox-church building and the expansion of the city beyond its Old Town boundaries. The key Russian legacy was the construction of Gedimino prospektas, the showpiece boulevard around which the principal administrative and business districts subsequently developed. If anything, Tsarist rule only reinforced Vilnius's role as a centre of Polish patriotism and culture, however, and the university was closed down in 1831 (and remained closed for over eighty years) in order to prevent the nurturing of a seditious anti-Russian elite.

By the end of the **nineteenth century**, Vilnius was an amazingly diverse city, with the Jews making up 40 percent of the population, followed by Poles at 31 percent and Russians at 20 percent; Lithuanians had been reduced to a tiny minority. Notwithstanding, the Lithuanians still regarded Vilnius as their historical capital, and based most of their cultural institutions here. The opportunity for them to flex their political muscle came with the withdrawal of the Russian authorities in **World War I**. Vilnius's new German masters encouraged Lithuanian sentiment as a counterbalance to the other nations competing for the city, and on February 16, 1918, community leaders declared Lithuania's **independence**. World War I was followed by two years of confused three-way fighting, with Lithuanian and Polish armies fighting both against each other and the Bolsheviks, who were advancing into Central Europe in an attempt to export the Russian Revolution. In 1920, the Polish leader Marshal Piłsudski – himself a native of the countryside outside Vilnius – encouraged the maverick General Lucjan Żeligowski to seize the city once and for all.

World War II saw Vilnius occupied by the Soviets, the Germans and then the Soviets again; the Polish resistance played a major part in the liberation of Vilnius from the Germans, only to see their leaders arrested by the victorious Red Army and deported to Siberia. With Vilnius becoming the capital of the Soviet Republic of Lithuania after 1945, the majority of Vilnius's Poles left for Poland, although in many cases their place was taken by immigrant Polish-speakers from the surrounding villages – with the paradoxical result that the Polish population of Vilnius today is just as numerous as it was in 1939.

Despite the straitjacket of Soviet rule, Vilnius soon became the focus of Lithuanian political and cultural activity, and it was inevitable that the struggle for **independence from the Soviet Union** was concentrated here at the close of the 1980s. The attempt by Soviet forces to gain control of strategic buildings on January 13, 1991 was met by mass unarmed resistance from Vilnius's citizens – twelve died under the wheels of Soviet tanks in an attempt to defend the TV Tower (see p.275), provoking a flood of international sympathy and paving the way for full Lithuanian independence.

While many of the outlying high-rise suburbs still bear the imprint of post-Soviet decay, parts of the city centre easily compare with some of the more prosperous central European capitals. Filled with banks and snazzy shops, and spruced up by a succession of ambitious mayors, the heart of old Vilnius is now an island of wealth in a country which, as a whole, is still to reap the benefits of post-communist change.

Arrival and information

Vilnius **airport** (Oro Uostas) is around 5km south of the city centre on Rodūnios kelias. A train runs from the small station 100m east of the arrivals hall to the main

Moving on from Vilnius

Several daily buses run from Vilnius to Rīga, Tallinn, Warsaw, Minsk and Kaliningrad, and there are a fair number to Western Europe, including direct services to Berlin, London, Paris and Amsterdam. Numerous other destinations are accessible by changing in Warsaw – you can buy tickets covering the whole journey in Vilnius from either the Eurolines or Toks counters in the bus station. See Travel details on p.287 for frequency of departures and journey times.

International **trains** are fewer, and services are usually slower than buses. There are daily trains to Warsaw, Kaliningrad, Minsk, Moscow and St Petersburg; the latter two both entail an overnight journey.

To reach the **airport**, 5km south of the centre at Rodūnios kelias 2 (☎8-5/230 6666, ⓦ www.vno.lt), take a train from the main station (7am–7pm); bus #1 from the train station (roughly hourly) or bus #2 from Lukiškiū aikštė (roughly 2 per hour).

The **travel agent** AAA Wrislit, Rūdninkū 16 (☎8-5/210 7661, ⓦ www.wrislit.lt), deals in tickets for international airlines and ferries from Klaipėda to Scandinavia.

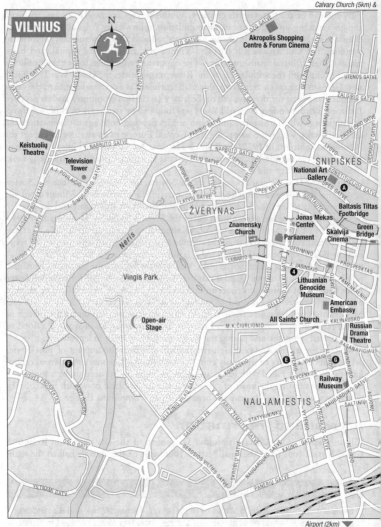

Calvary Church (5km) &

VILNIUS

N

Akropolis Shopping
Centre & Forum Cinema

Keistuolių
Theatre

Television
Tower

SNIPIŠKĖS

National Art
Gallery

ŽVĖRYNAS

Baltasis Tiltas
Footbridge

Jonas Mekas
Center

Znamensky
Church

Parliament

Skalvija
Cinema

Green
Bridge

Neris

Vingis Park

Lithuanian
Genocide
Museum

American
Embassy

All Saints' Church

Russian
Drama
Theatre

Open-air
Stage

Railway
Museum

NAUJAMIESTIS

Airport (2km) ▼

station (every 30min; 6.30am–9.30pm; 6Lt), otherwise bus #2 runs from outside the
arrivals hall a couple of times an hour to Lukiškių aikštė, handy for the downtown area
around Gedimino prospektas, and bus #1 (roughly hourly) will take you to the train
and bus station area, from where you can walk into the Old Town – buy bus tickets
(2.50Lt) from the driver. One **taxi** firm has a monopoly on the airport-city centre
route and charges 80Lt/€25 for the journey to the Old Town.

The main **train station** (Geležinkelio stotis) is just south of the Old Town, and the
main **bus station** (Autobusų stotis) is across the road. You could walk into the Old
Town from here or catch trolleybus #2 from the square in front of the train station to
Katedros aikštė, the main square. Station-based taxi drivers don't like picking up short-
distance fares and may overcharge.

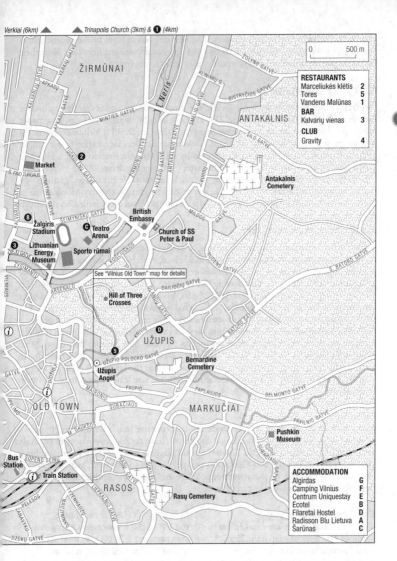

Verkiai (6km) ▲ ▲ Trinapolis Church (3km) & ❶ (4km)

0   500 m

RESTAURANTS
Marceliukės klėtis   2
Tores   5
Vandens Malūnas   1
BAR
Kalvarijų vienas   3
CLUB
Gravity   4

3

3.1 | **LITHUANIA** | Vilnius and around

ŽIRMŪNAI

ANTAKALNIS

Market

British Embassy

Antakalnis Cemetery

Žalgiris Stadium

Teatro Arena

Church of SS Peter & Paul

Lithuanian Energy Museum

Sporto rūmai

See "Vilnius Old Town" map for details

Hill of Three Crosses

UŽUPIS

Bernardine Cemetery

Užupis Angel

OLD TOWN

MARKUČIAI

Pushkin Museum

Bus Station

Train Station

RASOS

Rasų Cemetery

ACCOMMODATION
Algirdas   G
Camping Vilnius   F
Centrum Uniquestay   E
Ecotel   B
Filaretai Hostel   D
Radisson Blu Lietuva   A
Šarūnas   C

Information

There are branches of the municipal **tourist office** at the train station (Mon–Fri 9am–6pm, Sat & Sun 10am–4pm), the Town Hall on Rotušės aikštė (Mon–Fri 9am–6pm, Sat & Sun 10am–4pm), and at Vilniaus 22 (April–Oct Mon–Fri 9am–6pm, Sat & Sun 10am–4pm; Nov–March closed Sun; ☏8-5/262 9660, Ⓦwww.vilnius-tourism.lt). All sell maps, guidebooks and concert tickets, can book accommodation for a 6Lt fee, and sell the Vilnius City Card (52Lt for 24hr; 110Lt for 72hr), which offers free public transport and entry to museums and galleries, along with discounts in some hotels, restaurants and shops. It's good value if you are seriously "doing" all the museums, less so otherwise.

The *Vilnius in Your Pocket* city guide (6Lt from newspaper kiosks and bookshops; Ⓦwww.inyourpocket.com) provides entertaining restaurant and bar listings, as well as addresses of all kinds of useful services. The best city **maps** (sold in the tourist offices and bigger bookstores) are produced by the Rīga-based cartographers Jāņa Sēta; their 1:25,000 plan includes public transport routes and a street index.

City transport

Central Vilnius is easily walkable, while the more far-flung sights can be reached by **bus** or trolleybus. **Tickets**, costing 2Lt, are best bought in advance from newspaper kiosks (*kioskas*); you can also get them from the driver for 2.50Lt. Validate your ticket by punching it in the machine on board. Ticketless travellers face a spot-fine if caught by an inspector. Some routes are also served by minibuses (*maršrutinis taxi*), which halt at the same stops as buses, but tend to be faster (3Lt; pay the driver).

Taxi prices are reasonable, providing you stick to reputable firms (see "Listings" on p.282). Expect to pay around 1.50–2Lt per kilometre during the day, double that at night. Taxis ordered by phone are almost always cheaper than those hailed on the street.

Accommodation

Vilnius has a reasonable amount of **hotels**, although budget choices are relatively thin on the ground and should be booked well in advance, especially in summer. Other inexpensive options include an increasing number of **hostels** and **B&Bs** – the cheapest way of staying in or close to the Old Town. The Litinterp agency, Bernardinų 7-2 (Mon–Fri 8.30am–10pm, Sat 9am–3pm; ☎8-5/212 3850, ⓦwww.litinterp.lt) charges from 90Lt for a single room, 160Lt for a double, and also has its own guesthouse (see opposite). The tourist offices (see p.251) have lists of local families offering homestays at similar prices.

There's a summer-only **campsite** 3km west of the city centre, in the grounds of the Litexpo exhibition centre at Laisvės prospektas 5 (June to mid-Sept; ☎8-6/803 2452, ⓦwww.camping.lt/vilniuscity); take trolleybus #16 from the train and bus stations to the Parodų rumai stop. The nearest all-year campsite is the lakeside *Kempingas Slėnyje*, near Trakai (see p.284), 25km southwest of Vilnius – you'll need your own transport to get there.

Hotels

Many of Vilnius's growing crop of moderate-to-expensive hotels are modern, business-oriented affairs, but there's also a nice choice of characterful, cosy places in stylishly restored old buildings. The Old Town is a good place to look, or the area around Naujamiestis ("New Town") and Gedimino prospektas just to the west, which is within easy walking distance of the attractions. There are also a few options on the rapidly developing north bank of the river Neris.

Old Town and around

The following hotels are marked on the "Vilnius Old Town" map on p.255.

Alexa Pylimo 53 ☎8-5/219 1780, ⓦwww .hotelalexa.eu. Inexpensive choice conveniently placed between Old Town and the stations. Simple but smart doubles with en-suite shower, TV and – if you have a east-facing room – views of the main market. A handful of triples are also on offer. ❸

Apia Šv. Ignoto 12 ☎8-5/212 3426, ⓦwww.apia.lt. Cosy, intimate place in the heart of the Old Town offering eleven differently furnished but equally charming rooms. Most come with hardwood floors and pastel colour schemes; those on the top floor have sloping ceilings and skylights. Breakfast is in the café next door. ❺

Bernardinu Guest House Bernardinų 5 ☎8-5/261 5134, ⓦwww.avevita.lt. Converted town house on a quiet Old Town street offering a range of rooms, most with en-suite bath, TV and hardwood floors. A couple have foldout sofa beds and can sleep 3 or 4. Continental breakfast costs a few extra litai. En suites ❺, shared WC/shower ❹

Domus Maria Aušros vartų 12 ☎8-5/264 4880, ⓦwww.domusmaria.lt. Friendly hotel occupying one large wing of the Vilnius Archbishopric, and offering roomy en-suites with TV and smart, Scandinavian-style furnishings. Good-value triples and quads too. Long, high-ceilinged corridors and views of the Archbishopric courtyard add to the atmosphere. ❺

Europa Royale Vilnius Aušros vartų 6 ☎8-5/266 0770, ⓦwww.europaroyale.com. A mid-sized hotel in an attractive building. En-suite doubles come with TV and desk, and some boast small, street-facing balconies. The top-floor suites, with barrel-vaulted ceilings and lunette windows, ooze character. For something out of the ordinary take cylinder-shaped room 401, which has a round bed and panoramic, floor-to-ceiling windows. ❻/❽

Grotthuss Ligoninės 7 ☎8-5/266 0322, ⓦwww.grotthushotel.com. Intimate and luxurious hotel in an attractively restored town house, featuring stuccoed ceilings, rich fabrics and dark-wood furniture. Contemporary Lithuanian artwork adds a touch of class to the hallways, and excellent international food can be had in the *La Pergola* restaurant. ❼/❽

Grybas House Aušros Vartų 3a ☎8-5/261 9695, ⓦwww.grybashouse.com. A congenial, family-run place occupying an attractive old house in the heart of the Old Town. Rooms are decked out in soothing colours, each featuring TV, wi-fi and well-equipped bathroom. Only ten rooms and four suites, so reservations essential. ❻/❺

Litinterp Guest House Bernardinų 7 ☎8-5/212 3850, ⒺVilnius@litinterp.lt. Neat little rooms – en-suite and shared – with simple pine furnishings and pastel decor, in the apartment block just above the Litinterp B&B agency. Breakfast is brought to your door on a tray, and fridges and kettles are positioned strategically between every few rooms. It's deservedly popular, and reservations are essential in summer. If you're going to be arriving outside Litinterp office hours (see opposite), you'll have to ring or email in advance. ❸

Mabre Residence Maironio 13 ☎8-5/212 2087, ⓦwww.mabre.lt. Elegant quarters in the colonnaded courtyard of a converted Orthodox monastery, just around the corner from St Anne's Church. Standard doubles boast plush carpets and rich colour schemes; suites (one of which features a kitchenette), from 950Lt, include a presidential suite with timber-beamed ceiling and palatial lounge. Breakfast is served across the courtyard in the brick-vaulted *Hazienda* restaurant. ❼/❽

Narutis Pilies 24 ☎8-5/212 2894, ⓦwww.narutis.com. A central, intimate hotel housed in a much-modernized sixteenth-century building, with plain but elegant rooms around a glass-roofed courtyard. Those on the top floor have low attic ceilings. Breakfast is served in an atmospheric medieval cellar. ❼

Novotel Vilnius Gedimino prospektas 16 ☎8-5/266 6200, ⓦwww.novotel.com. This 150-room monolith is a temple to contemporary design, with light-filled rooms boasting matt-black desks, bold bed linen and trough-shaped bathroom sinks.

Those on the eastern side of the building offer fantastic Old Town vistas, and the floor-to-ceiling windows of the breakfast room provide a bird's-eye view of Gedimino prospektas. ❼

Radisson Blu Astoria Didžioji 35/2 ☎8-5/212 0110, ⓦwww.radissonblu.com. Popular with businessmen, large tour groups and visiting dignitaries, this hotel occupies a commanding position on the Old Town's main thoroughfare. Standard rooms are on the small side; those on the sixth floor do at least offer hardwood floors and good views. Business-class rooms have smarter bathrooms and bedside espresso machines. Hallways in the west wing boast replicas of the Art Deco wall paintings that decorated the place when it was a Jewish community savings bank in the 1920s and 1930s. ❽

Rinno Vingrių 25 ☎8-5/262 2828, ⓦwww.rinno.lt. Clean and cosy place on a quiet side street, offering "standard" rooms with TV and en-suite shower, and more spacious "superior" rooms with minibars and bathtubs. Strictly speaking, this isn't really in the Old Town, but it's close enough – just across the road. ❺–❻

Scandic Neringa Gedimino 23 ☎8-5/268 1910, ⓦwww.scandichotels.com. Relatively spacious rooms decked out in warm colours. Top-floor "superior" rooms have hardwood floors and bigger bathrooms. The hotel restaurant – long famous for its chicken Kiev – was the birthplace of Soviet jazz in the late 1960s (see p.244), although the polo-neck-wearing crowd moved on years ago. Ask about weekend reductions. ❻–❼

Shakespeare Bernardinų 8 ☎8-5/266 5885, ⓦwww.shakespeare.lt. On a narrow alley, this attractively renovated town house has fifteen rooms – each named and themed after a famous writer. Rooms feature original timber beams, oriental rugs and spacious bathrooms. ❼

Outside the Old Town

The following hotels are marked on the Vilnius map on p.250.

Algirdas Algirdo 24 ☎8-5/232 6650, ⓦwww.algirdashotel.lt. Three-star comforts and soothingly decorated rooms in a handsome nineteenth-century brick building 10min walk uphill from the Old Town. Wi-fi. ❺

Centrum Uniquestay Vytenio 9/25 ☎8-5/268 3310, ⓦwww.uniquestay.com. A newish building within walking distance of Gedimino prospektas and the Old Town. Rooms are simple but stylish, each with internet-connected computers and large bathtubs. Kooky ceramics and minimalist furniture in the hallways lend a chic, modernist feel. There's a small pool and fitness room. ❼

Ecotel Slucko 8 ☎8-5/210 2700, ⓦwww.ecotel.lt. In a mixed area of residential apartments and office blocks north of the river, but still within walking distance of the Old Town, *Ecotel* offers minimally furnished, smart en-suites. Most have shower cabins; some come with bathtub. Triples available. Ask about weekend reductions. ❹

Radisson Blu Lietuva Konstitucijos 20 ☎8-5/272 6272, ⓦwww.radissonblu.com. In the heart of Vilnius's emergent business district, this smart tower block offers four-star comforts and expansive views, along with the panoramic top-floor *SkyBar*. ❻

Šarūnas Raitininkų 4 ☎8-5/272 3888, ⓦwww .hotelsarunas.lt. A modern hotel on the north bank of the river, owned by former Sacramento Kings basketball player Šarūnas Marčiulionis. Far enough from the main road to be peaceful, and set around a quiet courtyard, the hotel offers comfy rooms, a gym and a bar stuffed with NBA memorabilia. ❺

Hostels

Hostels in Vilnius are basic compared to their counterparts in Western Europe: rooms are often cramped and very simply furnished, though invariably clean, and the staff usually enthusiastic and friendly.

Filaretai Filaretų 17 ☎8-5/215 4627, ⓦwww .filaretaihostel.lt. See Vilnius map on p.250. A simple but clean and well-run hostel about a 15min walk from the Old Town in the atmospherically shabby Užupis district; take bus #34 from bus/ train stations to the Filaretų stop. Options include two-bed rooms (❷), eight-bed dorms (30Lt per person) and a swanky self-catering apartment across the yard. Breakfast is sometimes available in summer for an extra charge. Well-equipped kitchen, common-room with TV, and washing machines (10Lt/load). There's a 2Lt surcharge for non-HI members.

Hostel Gate Šv. Mikalojaus 3 ☎8-6/383 2818, ⓦwww.hostelgate.lt. See Vilnius Old Town map opposite. Comprising a trio of neat, bright bunk-bed dorms, one spacious double, and a brace of self-catering apartments, this hostel combines a central location with a laid-back vibe. There's a spacious kitchen with cooking facilities and free hot drinks, and you can do your laundry for a few extra litai. Doubles ❷, dorms 42Lt per person.

Old Town Hostel (HI) Aušros Vartų 20-15A ☎8-5/262 5357, ⓦwww.lithuanianhostels.org. See Vilnius Old Town map opposite. Small, friendly place that fills up quickly owing to its prime location, midway between the train station and the Old Town. With functional, clean, six- and eight-bed dorms, a double and a triple room (book well in advance), and a cosy kitchen, this is a good place to stay if you want to meet other travellers and don't mind co-hostellers rolling home in the early hours. Double ❷, dorms 35Lt per person; 2Lt surcharge for non-HI members.

The City

Most of Vilnius's sights are concentrated in a compact area on the south bank of the River Neris. At the centre of the city is the main square, **Katedros aikštė**, site of the **cathedral**. South of here extends the atmospheric **Old Town**, with its impressive collection of Baroque churches and venerable university, while to the west stretches the long, straight boulevard of **Gedimino prospektas**, the focus of the city's commercial and administrative life. Running towards Gedimino prospektas along the eastern side of the Old Town is **Pylimo gatvė**, bearing just a few traces of the sizeable Jewish community that once lived here. Beyond the centre lie a handful of suburban sights, most of which are easily accessible by brisk walk, public transport or taxi.

Katedros aikštė and around

Lording it over the broad, flagstoned expanse of **Cathedral Square** (Katedros aikštė) is the off-white, colonnaded **Cathedral** (Arkikatedros bazilika; daily 7am–7pm), described as "a cross between a Greek temple and a Polish civic theatre" by the German Expressionist writer Alfred Döblin, who passed through town in the early 1920s. The site was originally a shrine to Perkūnas, the Lithuanian god of thunder, and Mindaugas the Great chose to build a simple brick church here in the thirteenth century – a move which didn't go down well with the resolutely pagan Lithuanian nobles, who had him murdered in 1263. The spot wasn't associated with Christianity again until the

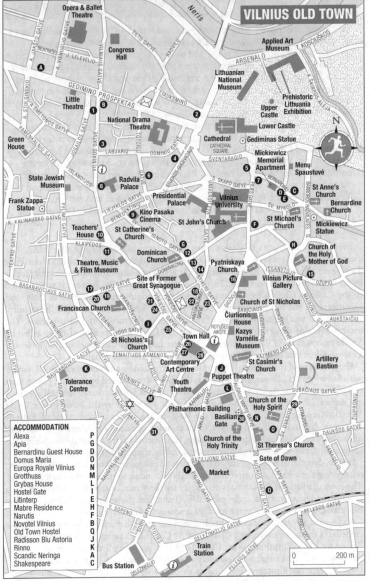

VILNIUS OLD TOWN

ACCOMMODATION

Alexa	P
Apia	G
Bernardinu Guest House	D
Domus Maria	O
Europa Royale Vilnius	N
Grotthuss	M
Grybas House	L
Hostel Gate	I
Litinterp	E
Mabre Residence	H
Narutis	F
Novotel Vilnius	B
Old Town Hostel	Q
Radisson Blu Astoria	J
Rinno	K
Scandic Neringa	A
Shakespeare	C

0   200 m

RESTAURANTS & CAFÉS

Balti drambliai	11
La Boheme	9
Čili kaimas	25
Coffee Inn (Pilies)	5
Coffee Inn (Traku)	19
Coffee Inn (Vilniaus)	1
Lokys	23
Mano guru	3
Markus ir Ko	22
Pilies menė	7
Ponių Laimė	18
La Provence	24
Skonis ir kvapas	17
Stikliai	14
Tres Mexicanos	2
Žemaičiai	21

BARS, CLUBS & PUBS

Brodvėjus	27
Café de Paris	16
Cozy	12
In Vino	30
Neringa	A
Pabo Latino	20
The Pub	13
Savas kampas	26
Šnekutis	31
Šuolaikinio meno centras (ŠMC)	28
Tamsta	29
Tappo d'oro	4
Transylvania	6
Užupio kavinė	15
Vasaros terasa	10
Woo	8

St Casimir and the Kaziukas Fair

St Casimir, the patron saint of Lithuania, was born in 1458, the second son of Casimir IV, King of Poland and Grand Duke of Lithuania. Intensely spiritual, he devoted himself to study and prayer and seemed singularly ill-suited to the dynastic role marked out for him. His reputation for purity and holiness blossomed into a full-blown popular cult after his death from illness at the age of 26. Fuelled by court propagandists eager to ensure local support for the ruling dynasty, the cult grew quickly in the Grand Duchy of Lithuania, and he was worshipped as a saint here long before his official canonization by Pope Clement VIII in 1602.

In the second half of the nineteenth century St Casimir's Day (March 4), traditionally the occasion of ceremonial Masses and processions, began metamorphosing into the **Kaziukas Fair** ("Kaziukas" being the diminutive form of Casimir in Lithuanian). Peasants from the surrounding villages would throng the square, selling handicrafts – particularly wicker boxes and baskets. The tradition continued under the communists, although it was shorn of its religious significance. Straddling the nearest weekend to St Casimir's Day, the fair has now grown to huge proportions, with stalls running the length of Gedimino prospektas and threading through the Old Town to Rotušės aikštė.

conversion of Lithuania to Catholicism under Grand Duke Jogaila after 1387. The church Jogaila built was constantly added to and reconstructed over the next four hundred years, and today's building is largely the result of a late-eighteenth-century facelift by Laurynas Stuoka-Gucevičius. Turned into a museum by the Soviets, it was restored to the Catholic Church by a reform-minded local communist leadership in 1988, and reconsecrated the following year. As the symbolic heart of Lithuanian Christianity, the cathedral was the natural focus of mass rallies in the run-up to independence. The most moving of these took place in January 1991, when the coffins of those killed by Soviet troops at the TV Tower (see p.275) were laid on the flagstones of the square for a memorial service that united tens of thousands in grief and defiance.

The pediment of the cathedral's main **facade** is crowned by a trio of monumental statues, with St Helena brandishing a huge cross at the apex, accompanied by Casimir, patron saint of Lithuania, on the right, and Stanislas, patron saint of Poland, on the left. All are modern replicas of early nineteenth-century originals, destroyed by the Soviets after World War II. Running round the sides of the building are statues of past rulers of Poland-Lithuania, caught in stiff mid-gesture, often to unintentionally comic effect. To the right of the main entrance looms the freestanding, three-tiered **belfry** (Arkikatedros varpinė), a coffee-and-cream-coloured cylinder that resembles a stranded Baroque lighthouse.

Inside, devotional paintings crowd the walls and pillars, and locals kneel deep in prayer, reinforcing the aura of devotion and spirituality found in so many Lithuanian churches. The most dramatic of the canvases on display are the scenes of the life of Christ running around the ambulatory, a cycle painted by Franciszek Smugliewicz, Vilnius's leading Neoclassicist and professor at the local art academy in the early nineteenth century.

A constant stream of pilgrims heads down the right-hand ambulatory towards the cathedral's main attraction, the **Chapel of St Casimir** (Kazimiero koplyčia), commissioned by King Sigismund Wasa III in 1623 in a propagandistic attempt to associate the Wasas (a dynasty that was relatively new to the throne of Poland-Lithuania) with their rather more illustrious Jagiellonian predecessors – the family to which fifteenth-century royal Prince Casimir (see above) belonged. A riot of marble, stucco and silver statuary, the chapel is Vilnius's most complete Baroque statement – and was one of the few parts of the cathedral untouched by Stuoka-Gucevičius's refurbishments. Designed by Italian architect Costante Tencalla, the chapel consists of a black, marble-lined square chamber, with a second octagonal tier on top supporting a richly decorated cupola. On the south-facing wall is the ornate silver-plated casket containing the bones of St Casimir, a relic that was returned to the cathedral with much pomp in 1989 after being exiled to the Church of SS Peter and Paul during the Soviet period. The icon-like image of the saint below depicts Casimir with three hands, probably because the artist painted two versions of the saint's right arm and when the painting was subsequently cleaned the first arm miraculously re-emerged. Occupying niches in the walls of the chapel are eight silver-plated statues of Jagiellonian and Wasa rulers, while frescoes on the ceilings and side walls show episodes from the saint's life. Two of the larger scenes, painted by Michelangelo Palloni in 1692, portray the miracle cures experienced by those praying at St Casimir's grave.

The Gediminas Statue
At the east side of the square, a tall, grey plinth bears a statue of the Grand Duke of Lithuania and legendary founder of Vilnius, **Gediminas** (1271–1341), depicted here as a lean, martial figure gesturing towards the city with an outstretched sword. Below the duke and his horse crouches a wolf – a reference to the popular folk tale that seeks to explain Vilnius's origins. Gediminas, so the story goes, was taking a rest while hunting in the hills above the Vilnia River when he dreamed of an iron wolf howling in the night. Asked to explain this dream, the duke's head priest suggested that the wolf's howling represented the fame of a great city built on this site that would one day reverberate around the world. Suitably impressed, Gediminas ordered the construction of a new capital here without delay.

The Lower Castle
Immediately behind the cathedral rises the cool grey bulk of the so-called **Lower Castle** (Žemutinės pilis), where the Grand Dukes of Lithuania once held court. Demolished by the Russians in the eighteenth century, the castle was reconstructed at great expense at the beginning of the twenty-first, using archeological evidence and period engravings as a guide to what the original must have looked like. The castle's most famous resident was Sigismund Augustus (1520–72), King of Poland and Grand Duke of Lithuania, who maintained a glittering ducal court complete with orchestra, art collection and a library of over four thousand books, enhancing Vilnius's reputation as an important cultural centre. A **museum** in the castle will display a sequence of historic interiors containing the kind of furnishings, fabrics and paintings that a monarch of Sigismund's stature would have owned. The castle is a work in progress – ask at the tourist office about the possibility of guided tours.

The Upper Castle
The tree-clad hill immediately behind the Lower Castle was originally crowned by the **Upper Castle** (Aukštutinės pilis), a tenth-century stockade fort subsequently strengthened in stone by Gediminas and his successors. An easy ten-minute stroll up from the park behind the cathedral, the Upper Castle can also be reached by a **funicular** (keltuvas; Tues–Sun 10am–6pm; 3Lt return), which shuttles up and down from behind the Prehistoric Lithuania exhibition (see p.258). The only bit of the Upper Castle left standing – and one of the city's best-known landmarks – is the **Gediminas Tower** (Gedimino bokštas), a red-brick octagon that rises sand-castle-like from the brow of the hill. It retains little original stonework from Gediminas's time, having been rebuilt in the nineteenth century to provide recreational strollers with a viewing platform. You can get an idea, though, of what the castle looked like in medieval times by examining the impressive array of scale models in the **Upper Castle Museum** (Aukštutinės pilies muziejus; Wed–Sun 11am–5pm; 5Lt; free on Wed in winter) inside the tower. There's a superb panorama of the Old Town's church spires and towers from the top.

The Lithuanian National Museum
A hundred metres or so north of the cathedral lie the arsenal buildings, a pair of creamy-yellow barrack blocks built in the sixteenth century and given a touch of Neoclassical grandeur by the Russians some three hundred years later. The first of these, at Arsenalo 1, is now home to the **Lithuanian National Museum** (Lietuvos Nacionalinis muziejus; Wed–Sun: May–Sept 11am–6pm; Oct–April 11am–5pm; 6Lt; free Wed in

winter), containing an engaging jumble of artefacts ranging from old prints of Vilnius to recreated farmhouse interiors from the eighteenth and nineteenth centuries. Traditional Lithuanian crafts are represented by wicker baskets, chequered bedspreads and the wood-carved figures of saints used to decorate wayside shrines in the countryside.

An annexe (enter a little further north on Arsenalo) houses the extremely well-presented **Prehistoric Lithuania exhibition** (same times; 6Lt), with explanations in English, on the history of Lithuania up to the twelfth century. It begins with the flint and bone tools and distinctive boat-shaped battle-axes used by the Baltic region's earliest inhabitants – the ancestors of today's Lithuanians and Latvians arrived in the area sometime on the cusp of the second and third millennia BC. You can also see models of the stockaded hill-forts, dating from the tenth to the twelfth centuries, in which tribal leaders held sway. Isolated from the rest of Europe by thick forests, the Lithuanians were slow to develop unified state structures, and lived in loosely bound tribal units until well into the Middle Ages. Also on display are reproductions of sumptuous Iron Age Lithuanian costumes and some delicate silver jewellery.

The Applied Art Museum

The **Applied Art Museum,** Arsenalo 3 (Taikomosios Dailės muziejus; Tues–Sat 11am–6pm, Sun 11am–4pm; 6Lt), displays chalices, reliquaries and Baroque paintings – including a fleshy *Lot and his Daughters* by the Austrian master Johann-Michael Rottmayr – taken from the region's churches. There's also a wide-ranging display of folk art, with several examples of the wooden wayside crosses (still a common feature of rural Lithuania) that typically combine Christian imagery with older pagan sun motifs, as well as bunches of colourful *verbos* – the bundles of dried grasses and flowers traditionally prepared in the run-up to Palm Sunday.

The Old Town

Just south of Cathedral Square lies the **Old Town** (Senamiestis), a dense network of narrow, largely pedestrianized streets that invites aimless wandering. The main reference points are **Pilies gatvė** (Castle Street), which ascends gently from Cathedral Square, and its extensions **Didžioji** and **Aušros Vartų**, which cut south through the heart of historic Vilnius. Almost everything you'll want to see in the Old Town lies on or just off this artery.

Bernardinų gatvė

Leading off Pilies to the east is **Bernardinų gatvė**, one of the Old Town's most appealing back streets, a narrow lane lined with seventeenth- and eighteenth-century houses. Occupying no. 11 is the **Adam Mickiewicz Memorial Apartment** (Adomo Mickevičiaus memorialininis butas; Tues–Fri 10am–5pm, Sat & Sun 10am–2pm; free), where the Polish poet (see opposite) lived for a few months in 1822. The paltry collection of exhibits includes a couple of period chairs, a desk once owned by Mickiewicz and a number of Polish and Lithuanian first editions of his works.

The Church Heritage Museum

At the far end of Bernardinų, the stately ochre bulk of **St Michael's Church** (Šv Mykolo bažnyčia) peeks out from its walled enclosure. The twin towers of its seventeenth-century facade are complemented by a freestanding belfry, the main gateway into the church courtyard. The church is now home to the **Church Heritage Museum** (Bažnyčinio paveldo muziejus; Tues–Sat 11am–6pm; 9Lt), a glittering collection of vestments and silverware – including a fourteenth-century arm reliquary of St Stanislas, at the end of which sprout five delicate half-clenched fingers. However the star turn is the church itself, with beautifully restored stuccowork rich in rosettes and heart shapes, and an impressive clutch of funerary monuments. Most impressive is the granite-coloured memorial of **Leo Sapieha** (1557–1633), who is depicted in relief clad in impressively voluminous pantaloons and ruff, while his two wives lie obediently on either side. A typical product of the Grand Duchy of Lithuania's cosmopolitan elite, Sapieha was a nobleman of Belorussian origin who converted from the Orthodox faith

Litwo! Ojczyzno moja! ty jesteś jak zdrowie;
Ile cię trzeba cenić, ten tylko się dowie,
Kto się stracił

(O Lithuania, my homeland, thou art like health itself;
I never knew till now, how precious,
Till I lost thee)

The opening lines of Adam Mickiewicz's *Pan Tadeusz* (1834)

It's paradoxical that the most famous lines ever written about Lithuania were the work of a Polish poet, yet **Adam Mickiewicz** (or Adomas Mickevičius, as he is known in Lithuania) is one of the few literary figures whose words have been adopted as rallying cries by both nations. Above all, Mickiewicz embodies the nostalgia shared by both Lithuanians and Poles for the **Grand Duchy of Lithuania**, the multi-ethnic and multilingual territory carved out by Lithuanian rulers in the Middle Ages, and subsequently a key component (some would say equal partner) in the Polish-Lithuanian Commonwealth.

Mickiewicz himself was a typical product of the Grand Duchy, born to an impoverished Polish gentry family in the countryside near Novogrudok (now in Belarus). In 1815, Mickiewicz went to study at Vilnius University, and was a founder of the **Philomaths**, a pseudo-masonic organization dedicated to fighting Tsarist rule through the promotion of local culture. In November 1823, he was arrested along with fellow members on suspicion of "spreading Polish nationalism", and imprisoned in the Basilian monastery (see p.264) before being deported to Russia where he remained, mostly in Moscow, for the rest of the decade.

Following the failure of the November 1830 Polish Uprising, Mickiewicz, like many Polish intellectuals, went into exile in Paris and quickly immersed himself in émigré politics. It was here that Mickiewicz wrote *Pan Tadeusz* (1834), his greatest epic poem; modelled on the novels of Walter Scott, it's a masterful, richly lyrical depiction of traditional gentry life in the multi-ethnic borderlands east of Vilnius. As in all of Mickiewicz's works, Lithuania is represented as a wild, mythic land of dark forests – a seductive contrast to the urban world of Warsaw or Kraków.

Banned from re-entering the Tsarist Empire, Mickiewicz never returned to Poland or Lithuania. For the next two decades he taught Slavonic literature at Lausanne and Paris, canvassing the courts of Europe for support in Poland's struggle against the Russians. The writer's life came abruptly to an end in 1855 when Prince Adam Czartoryski, a leader of the Paris exile community, sent him on a mission to Turkey to organize Polish volunteer forces in the approaching Crimean War: having contracted typhus soon after his arrival, Mickiewicz died in November 1855 in Istanbul. He was already a national hero of almost mythic proportions, and his remains were eventually brought back to Poland and placed, along with other Polish "greats", in the crypt of Kraków's Wawel Cathedral.

Although Mickiewicz was never a Lithuanian patriot in the modern sense (he believed that the country's destiny was inextricably bound up with that of Poland), his heritage was readily appropriated by the Lithuanian national movement. His fascination with the history and traditions of the Grand Duchy helped to provide Lithuanians with a sense of their own past greatness, and his lyrical descriptions of the Lithuanian countryside inspired hordes of local imitators. Translations of Mickiewicz's works were very popular in late nineteenth-century Lithuania, and nationalist ideologue Vincas Kudirka adapted the opening words of *Pan Tadeusz* to form the first line of a patriotic hymn – which is still in use as the Lithuanian National Anthem. However *Pan Tadeusz* was always treated with suspicion by a Lithuanian elite who felt that it over-romanticized the Polish-speaking gentry. It wasn't translated in its entirety until 1927, and even then most of the references to "Poland" were left out – sparking the inevitable protests from Warsaw.

to Protestantism and then to Catholicism in an attempt to retain his political influence in the shifting religious landscape of sixteenth-century Europe.

St Anne's Church

Opposite St Michael's Church soar the fairytale, pinnacle-encrusted towers of **St Anne's** (Šv Onos bažnyčia; daily 10am–3pm), the church that so impressed Napoleon Bonaparte that he's said to have wanted to take it back to Paris in the palm of his hand. Intricate, red-brick traceries weave like intertwined thorn branches across its tall, narrow facade. The most outstanding Gothic building in Lithuania, it's nevertheless a relatively late example of the style: the facade is thought to have been completed only in 1582, by which time Baroque was already beginning to make its presence felt in Vilnius. Inside, spindly lines of red-brick rib vaulting extend across a white ceiling, sheltering a relatively undistinguished ensemble of altars bunched up at the end of the small nave.

The Bernardine Church

Rising directly behind St Anne's is the considerably more restrained facade of the much larger **Bernardine Church** (Bernardinų vienuolyno bažnyčia), built at around the same time as its neighbour, together with the adjoining Bernardine **monastery** (now occupied by the Vilnius Art Academy). According to communist folklore, the church cellar was where Vilnius high-school student and future founder of the KGB, Felix Dzerzhinsky (see p.273), established an underground printing press, confident that the Tsarist police would never think of looking for it here. The church's **interior**, rich in Baroque furnishings and medieval frescoes, was neglected during the Soviet era and is currently undergoing restoration. Among the few things that have escaped damage are the two fine seventeenth-century funerary monuments (that of Stanislaus Radziwiłł on the north side, Petras Veselovskis on the south) that face each other across the nave – their incumbents are depicted in relief, reclining contentedly as if on a country picnic.

The Mickiewicz statue and the Church of the Holy Mother of God

Just south of the Bernardine Church is a modern **statue** of poet Adam Mickiewicz (see p.259), leaning authoritatively on a lectern as if to launch into a reading of his verse. The statue was the site of one of the first Glasnost-era demonstrations against Soviet power in Lithuania, when on August 23, 1987, a few hundred people gathered to demand the publication of the **Molotov-Ribbentrop Pact**, the secret agreement in which the Soviets and Germans carved out spheres of influence in the Baltics and Poland in 1939.

South of here, Mairono gatvė swings around the **Church of the Holy Mother of God** (Skaisčiausios dievo motinos cerkvė; daily 8am–6pm), Vilnius's largest Orthodox place of worship, an off-white nineteenth-century cube topped by a fat central cupola and four fortress-like towers. Beside the church a small bridge leads across the River Vilnia to the inner-city suburb of Užupis. West of Mairono, the network of crooked alleys made up of Rusų, Volano, Literatų and Šv Mykolo provides numerous opportunities for zipping back towards Pilies.

The University and St John's Church

Occupying a jumble of buildings constructed between the sixteenth and eighteenth centuries around nine linked courtyards, **Vilnius University** (Vilniaus Universitetas; access to the courtyards Mon–Fri 9am–5pm, Sat 9am–noon) squeezes into a neat quadrant of land between Pilies and Universiteto gatvė. In response to the spread of Calvinism in Vilnius, a college was established here by Bishop Walerijan Protasewicz in 1569 to serve as a Jesuit-run vehicle for the propagation of Catholic ideals. Despite resistance from Protestant nobles, the King of Poland and Grand Duke of Lithuania **Stefan Bathory** upgraded the college to university status ten years later. Tuition was initially in Latin, but by the early nineteenth century the university enjoyed a growing reputation as one of the Polish-speaking world's leading educational institutions. It also became a hotbed of Polish resistance to Tsarist rule: students formed conspiratorial societies such as the Philomaths (Towarzystwie Filomatów), dedicated to raising the anti-Russian consciousness of the

The university interiors

For a glimpse of the university buildings' interiors you'll have to sign up for one of the tours organized by the University Library, which is entered from Universiteto gatvė outside the main gate. There are plenty of English-language tours during the summer but you should call first to reserve a place (☎8-5/268 7103; price varies). Highlights include the barrel-vaulted **Smugliewicz Hall** (originally the refectory, now the library's rare books department), decorated with Smugliewicz frescoes depicting Jesuit theologians sheltering under the Virgin Mary's cape; and the Neoclassical **White Hall**, crammed with old telescopes and celestial globes, and featuring an ornate portal by Carlo Sampari straddled by figures of Diana and Urania. A tightly wound staircase ascends from the White Hall to the **observatory tower**, offering a fine panorama of the Old Town.

locals by the promotion of Polish and Lithuanian culture. However, it was broken up by the authorities in November 1823 and its leading lights – including young poet **Adam Mickiewicz** (see box, p.259) – exiled from the city. The Russians closed the university altogether in 1832 in the wake of the failed anti-Tsarist rebellion of 1830–31, and it wasn't reopened until after World War I when it once more resumed its position as one of Poland's top universities. Before long it was back in the political fray: right-wing students periodically mounted anti-Semitic raids on the nearby Jewish districts of town, while nonconformists gravitated towards left-of-centre groupings such as the Vagabonds' Club (Akademicky klub Włóczęgów), whose members, among them future Nobel laureate **Czesław Miłosz**, advertised their bohemian leanings by wearing floppy black berets. Thoroughly "Lithuanianized" after World War II, the university survived the Soviet era with its academic reputation intact, and is now the country's undisputed centre of learning, with over fourteen thousand students.

The **main entrance** is on Universiteto gatvė, where an office beside the main gate sells tickets (4Lt) and hands out plans. You're then free to wander around the courtyards. In the rather plain Sarbiewski courtyard an archway leads through to the **Grand Courtyard** (Didysis kiemas). This arcaded quadrangle is dominated by the scrumptious wedding-cake facade of **St John's Church** (Šv Jono bažnyčia), its three custard-coloured tiers seemingly held aloft by slender Corinthian pilasters arranged in clusters of two or three. Although of fourteenth-century origin, the church's outer appearance is due to a mid-eighteenth-century facelift by Jan Krzysztof Glaubitz, architect of more than a few of Vilnius's Baroque buildings. The church was closed in 1948 and pressed into service as a warehouse for the newpaper *Tiesa* ("Truth"), the Lithuanian Communist Party's answer to *Pravda*. Vilnius University managed to get the church back in 1963, and turned it into a science museum. It wasn't reconsecrated until 1991.

Inside, at the far end of the church, is a cluster of altars in no-holds-barred Baroque. The high altar resembles a vast gateway, guarded by statues of St John Chrysostom, St Gregory the Great, St Anselm and St Augustine, and through which a small statue of the Virgin is barely visible on the far side. Archways on either side of the nave lead off to richly decorated chapels – often locked – some of which still hold books and manuscripts from the church's days as a science museum. Over to the left as you face the altar is the **Guild of Musicians' Chapel**, with a fresco of robed academic figures in the cupola, and a richly gilded Madonna, credited with miracle-working powers, on the altar. Cherubs wrestling with pointy-eared demons frame the doorway to the adjacent **St Anne's Chapel**, which houses a brightly painted, eighteenth-century wooden altar showing Christ on the Cross, the disciples represented as bunches of grapes.

Turning to leave the church, you'll see the slender pipes of the organ above the main door, topped by trumpeting angels and fronted by a bust of Stanisław Moniuszko (1819–72), the Polish composer who was the organist here before becoming a big-time conductor in Warsaw, and penning *Halka*, Poland's first important national opera. Standing apart from the main body of the church is the stout bell tower, capped with a collection of tiny urns that look like sporting trophies. At 68m, it's the tallest belfry in the Old Town. Next to the tower is a stately, barrel-roofed structure that looks as if it ought to be a chapel or an oratory; actually it's a rather swish daytime café for university students.

The Presidential Palace

Stretching west of Universiteto gatvė, the neat, flagstoned triangle of **Daukanto aikštė** is overlooked by the regal facade of the **Presidential Palace** (Prezidentūra), a former merchant's house remodelled in its present Neoclassical form at the end of the eighteenth century, when it served as the comfortable downtown residence of the Bishop of Vilnius. It became the home of the Russian governor general soon afterwards, and it's likely that Adam Mickiewicz was interrogated here prior to his imprisonment in the Basilian monastery. The building's most despised denizen was Governor General Muravyev, nicknamed "the hangman" for his brutal suppression of the anti-Tsarist revolt of 1863–64. Despite being right at the heart of the Lithuanian state, the square is a restrained, sober place free of ideological or national symbols – save for the yellow, green and red Lithuanian tricolours fluttering gamely from a trio of flagpoles.

The Pyatnitskaya Church

From the university you can cut back east along the broad, park-like space of Syrvido skveras to the northern end of Pilies, which culminates in a triangular piazza occupied by a year-round craft market selling paintings, amber jewellery and wicker baskets. Hidden behind the street stalls is the Orthodox **Pyatnitskaya Church** (Pjatnickajos cerkvė), a modest piece of mid-nineteenth-century architecture, rather like a domed brick shed. A Russian-language inscription on the outside wall relates the (admittedly apocryphal) tale that the poet Alexander Pushkin's grandfather Hannibal – an African slave presented to Tsar Peter the Great by the Turkish sultan – was baptized here in 1704. Inside, a carved iconostasis places peacock motifs amid vegetal swirls, while a huge chandelier crowned with a double-headed eagle dangles from the ceiling.

Vilnius Picture Gallery

Further south, Pilies gives way to **Didžioji gatvė** or "Main Street". Kicking off the sights along here is the Chodkiewicz Palace at no. 4, an opulent pied-à-terre built three centuries ago for one of the Grand Duchy's most prominent families and now occupied by the **Vilnius Picture Gallery**, home to the permanent collection of the Lithuanian Art Museum (Tues–Sat noon–6pm, Sun noon–5pm; 5Lt; free Wed in winter). Second-Empire furnishings and creaky parquet floors provide an elegant backdrop to the somewhat patchy overview of local painters through the ages. **Franciszek Smugliewicz** (1745–1807), the doyen of Vilnius's Neoclassicists, is particularly well represented, with numerous overblown canvases depicting biblical and historical subjects – look out for the pseudo-oriental pantomime costumes worn by the protagonists of his *Scythian Messengers with Darius, King of Persia*. There's little of note among the other artists featured, but temporary exhibitions help to raise the interest level.

The Orthodox Church of St Nicholas

South of the gallery, it's impossible to miss the eye-catching jumble of architectural styles that makes up the Orthodox **Church of St Nicholas** (Šv Mikalojaus cerkvė), remodelled in the wake of the brutal suppression of the 1863–64 rebellion by the Tsar's governor general in Vilnius, General Muravyev, to serve as a propagandist statement of the virtues of Russian culture. Framed by a squat, Byzantine-style chapel on one side and a tapering Muscovite spire on the other, the facade is resplendently decked out in bright ochre with brick-red trimmings. The interior boasts lively floral-patterned murals, and stoves decorated with oriental-style tiles.

Rotušės aikštė

Immediately beyond the Church of St Nicholas, Didžioji opens out into **Rotušės aikštė**, or "Town Hall Square", the hub around which life in the Old Town revolves. Little changed since the late eighteenth century, the square is a pretty assemblage of two- and three-storey town houses colourwashed in blue, orange and burgundy. Standing at its southern end is the old **Town Hall** (Rotušė) itself, an imposing, off-white pile fronted by a dignified colonnade, built in 1799 by Laurynas Stuoka Gucevičius, the architect of Vilnius Cathedral.

On the eastern side of the square, a seventeenth-century merchant's house at Didžioji 26 provides an atmospheric venue for the **Kazys Varnėlis Museum** (Tues–Sat 9am–5pm; booking necessary; ☎8-5/279 1644), a rambling collection of prints, furniture and sculpture collected by artist and art teacher Varnėlis (born in 1917, he emigrated to the US after World War II), alongside the striking abstract paintings he produced himself. Highlights include Dürer and Goya engravings in barrel- vaulted rooms near the entrance, and nineteenth-century Japanese woodcuts in the high-ceilinged galleries upstairs. Varnėlis's own work, involving organic and geometric shapes painted in bright pop-art colours, ranges from the hypnotic to the headache-inducing.

The Ciurlionis House and around

The **Čiurlionis House** (Čiurliono namai; Mon–Fri 10am–4pm; donation requested), Savičiaus gatvė 11, is where Lithuania's most celebrated artist and composer, Mikalojus Konstantinas Čiurlionis (see p.303), spent the winter of 1907–8 trying to promote Lithuanian culture in the city. Helping to organize the first-ever group exhibitions by Lithuanian artists, Čiurlionis was disheartened by the low cultural horizons of the people who came to the shows but failed to buy any of his paintings: "As far as art is concerned," he notoriously grumbled, "Vilnius is still in nappies!" There's not a great deal to see here, though, apart from a few prints, family photographs and coffee-table books showing reproductions of his artwork.

A few paces beyond the Čiurlionis House at Savičiaus 5, the five-storey, rocket-like belfry of the eighteenth-century **Augustine Church** (Augustijonų bažnyčia; closed for restoration) is one of the most exhilarating architectural sights in the city.

The Contemporary Art Centre

The pale, concrete building marking the southwest corner of Rotušės aikštė, just behind the Town Hall, is the **Contemporary Art Centre** (Šiuolaikinio Meno Centras; ⓦ www.cac.lt; Tues–Sun 11am–7pm; 4Lt, free Wed in winter), which hosts high-profile exhibitions of artists from Lithuania and elsewhere. The one permanent exhibit is the **Fluxus Cabinet** (ask at the ticket desk for it to be opened), a small first-floor room devoted to the Dada-influenced art movement formed by Lithuanian-born, New-York based avant-garde prankster George Maciunas (1931–1978). Inside are numerous Fluxus posters, photographs and documents, including the Maciunas-penned scores for Fluxus concerts – which usually involved the systematic destruction of the instruments.

St Casimir's Church

Hogging the eastern shoulder of Rotušės aikštė, **St Casimir's Church** (Šv Kazimiero bažnyčia; Mon–Fri 4–6.30pm, Sun 8am–2pm) boasts an arresting facade of homely pink broken up by vertical cream stripes. Built for the Jesuits in the early seventeenth century, the church was turned into a grain store by the Napoleonic French, transformed into an Orthodox church by Tsarist Russia, handed over to the Lutheran congregation by the Germans in World War I and used to house a museum of atheism by the Soviets after World War II, before being finally returned to the Catholic Church in 1987. The church's most striking exterior feature is the elaborate crown and cross on top of the central dome. Representing the ducal crown of the Grand Duchy of Lithuania, it was placed here in 1942 to symbolize Lithuanian sovereignty over the city of Vilnius – which was under Nazi occupation at the time. The towers flanking the building house a series of bells which chime gently whenever the striking mechanism is stirred by the wind – a sound sculpture designed by erstwhile giant of the Soviet jazz scene Vladimir Tarasov. Unsurprisingly, given the church's chequered history, the interior is largely bare, save for a trio of lovingly restored eighteenth-century altars, their gilded capitals appearing to drip down the sombre, grey pillars. The **organ** is one of the city's finest – and frequently features in weekend concerts (see posters at the church entrance for dates and times).

Along Didžioji and Aušros Vartų

Continuing south along Didžioji, you come to the **Philharmonic building**, whose sober, grey-green Neoclassical front hides a charmingly old-fashioned, chandelier-studded interior. It was here in 1909 that Jascha Heifetz gave his famous performance of Mendelssohn's Violin Concerto in E minor at the age of 8, before leaving his native Vilnius for St Petersburg, then the West, where he became one of the most celebrated virtuosi of the twentieth century – a musician so perfect that George Bernard Shaw once advised him to play "one wrong note every night before you go to bed". Now home to the Lithuanian National Philharmonic Orchestra, the building has hosted an impressive number of top international soloists and conductors since 1990; before this all visiting artists had to be approved by the stiflingly bureaucratic ministry of culture in Moscow.

The Basilian Gate and the Church of the Holy Trinity

Didžioji gives way to **Aušros Vartų gatvė**, which curves gently south past the **Basilian Gate**, an ornate coffee-and-cream archway which leads through to the courtyard of the long-defunct Basilian monastery. The monastery was a major centre of learning in the sixteenth and seventeenth centuries, when it served as the headquarters of the Uniate (also known as Greek-Catholic) community. Created by the Union of Brest in 1596 to accommodate those Orthodox believers prepared to accept the primacy of the pope, the Uniate Church was conceived as a handy way of allowing the Grand Duchy's many Russian and Belorussian nobles access to the country's Catholic-dominated elite. The hulking grey form of the monastery's **Church of the Holy Trinity** (Šv Trejybės cerkvė) still serves the city's small community of Ukrainian Greek-Catholics. Devastated during the Soviet era, the interior is largely bare, although the grave plaque of sixteenth-century Vilnius mayor Antanas Baga, on the right hand side of the nave as you face the altar, features some delightful floral carvings. The surrounding monastery buildings (now belonging to a technical college) were used as a prison during the Tsarist period – the poet Adam Mickiewicz (see p.259) was one of the many Polish intellectuals incarcerated here following the round-ups of October 1823.

The Church of the Holy Spirit

A gateway off **Aušros Vartų** leads to the **Church of the Holy Spirit** (Šv Dvasios cerkvė), one of the oldest Orthodox churches in Lithuania and the most popular city-centre place of worship for Vilnius's Russians. Inside the lofty, light-filled interior, rich with the smell of incense and candles, you're immediately drawn to the Baroque iconostasis in three stunning tiers of frivolous bright greens, blues and pinks, designed by the city's outstanding architect of the time, Jan Krzysztof Glaubitz. In front of the iconostasis, the bodies of three fourteenth-century martyrs, Anthony, Ioan and Eustachius, are displayed in a glass casket, dressed in red velvet robes (white at Christmas, and black during Lent). According to tradition, the trio were hanged from an oak tree on the orders of the rigidly pagan Grand Duke Algirdas in 1347, although the latter subsequently married an Orthodox Russian princess, converted to Christianity, and ordered the construction of a chapel (the forerunner of today's church) on the execution site before retiring to become a monk.

St Theresa's Church

The stately orange-and-grey **St Theresa's Church** (Šv Teresės bažnyčia), further south on Aušros Vartų, is another soaring testament to the city's dominant architectural style. Founded in the mid-1600s by the Grand Duchy's treasurer, Stephen Christopher Pac, the church didn't receive its vibrant, salmon-pink rococo interior until over a century later, when local painter Mateusz Suszczański provided the exuberant ceiling frescoes depicting scenes from the life of St Theresa.

The Gate of Dawn

The southern border of the Old Town is marked by the **Gate of Dawn** (Aušros Vartai), the sole survivor of nine city gates that once studded the walls of Vilnius. In 1671, Carmelite monks from nearby St Theresa's Church built a **chapel** inside the gate to house the most revered of the city's many sacred images, the **Madonna of the Gate of Dawn** (Aušros vartų Marija), and it has been a place of pilgrimage for Lithuanians and Poles ever since. The Madonna is just about visible through a trio of arched windows directly above the gate; it's rare for locals not to look up at the image and cross themselves as they pass underneath it.

Entrance to the chapel is via a doorway at the rear end of St Theresa's, from where a narrow staircase leads up to the chamber where the image is kept. It's an intimate space, filled with kneeling supplicants whispering prayers, the aura of sanctity strangely undisturbed by the steady shuffle of visitors' footsteps. Her slender fingers splayed in a stylized gesture of grace, the Madonna herself is all but hidden by an extravagant silver-plated covering that emits a beckoning sparkle to those approaching the gate along the street below. The air of glittering opulence is enhanced by the panels on either side of the image, covered with the heart-shaped ex votos left by grateful pilgrims.

The southern side of the gate is surprisingly plain, save for a relief depicting a horse-borne knight known as the **Vytis**, which served as the symbol of the Grand Duchy of Lithuania from the times of Vytautas the Great onwards, and was resurrected after 1991 to feature on the newly independent republic's coat of arms.

The Artillery Bastion

The **Artillery Bastion** (Artilerijos Bastėja; Tues–Sun 10am–5pm; 5Lt), Boksto 20/18, is a semicircular, red-brick cannon battery built in the seventeenth century to defend the (no longer standing) Subačiaus gate nearby. There's a modest display of weapons and armour inside, although the museum is more interesting for its setting than its contents: visitors descend via a long brick passageway into the bowels of the building, where cannons similar to those used to defend the city have been placed in the embrasures. A door at the top of the passageway leads to a viewing terrace, from where you can gaze across towards the crowd of Old Town belfries to the northwest and the narrow streets of the hilly Užupis district to the northeast.

Vokiečių gatvė and the former Jewish ghetto

Before World War II, Vilnius was one of the most important centres of Jewish life and culture in Eastern Europe and was known as the "Jerusalem of the North" – a name allegedly bestowed on it by Napoleon Bonaparte when he paused in the city in 1812. First invited to settle in 1410 by Grand Duke Vytautas, the Jews made up a third of the city's population by the nineteenth century, inhabiting a sizeable chunk of the Old Town. The **Jewish quarter** was concentrated in the warren of alleyways either side of **Vokiečių gatvė**, an area vividly remembered by Czesław Miłosz in his book *Beginning with my Streets* (see p.376) as "a labyrinth of absolutely medieval, narrow little streets, the houses connected by arcades, the uneven pavements two or three metres wide". Little of this world now survives: the 70,000-strong community that once lived here was almost totally wiped out during the Nazi occupation, and few survivors chose to move back after 1945. A handful of the streets still retain something of their pre-World War II appearance, although most were reduced to rubble during the war and overlaid with parking lots and office blocks.

The Jewish quarter was carved into two **ghettos** by the Germans in 1941, with the streets north of Vokiečių becoming the so-called **Ghetto no. 1** (which was cleared in September 1941), and those to the south becoming **Ghetto no. 2** (cleared in September 1943). After the war, the ghettos were rebuilt and repopulated with Lithuanians from the countryside, and the area's past was quietly forgotten. The Soviet regime drew a veil over the true extent of Jewish suffering, preferring to present the "Soviet people" as the sole victim of Nazi terror. Vilnius's Jews remained without monuments or memorials until the 1990s, when a scattering of inconspicuous plaques were put up to help fill the yawning gap in the city's collective memory.

On the eve of World War II the **Jewish** community constituted the biggest single ethnic group in Vilnius, making the city one of the most important centres of Jewish culture in northeastern Europe. Although they had been present in the city since at least the time of Vytautas the Great, their numbers rose significantly after 1795, when the western territories of the Tsarist Empire (of which Lithuania was now a part) were specifically earmarked for Jewish colonization – a ruse designed to keep them out of the Russian heartlands of the east.

As the main urban centre for Jews living in the territories of present-day Lithuania and northern Belarus, Vilnius became a hot-house of intellectual activity towards the end of the nineteenth century. In 1897, the city saw the birth of the **Bund**, the international Jewish socialist movement which had a major influence on the development of left-wing ideas in the Tsarist Empire and beyond. The city also enjoyed a rich artistic life: the painter **Chaim Soutine** and the sculptor **Jacques Lipchitz** passed through Vilnius Art School in the years before World War I, while violin virtuoso **Jascha Heifetz** attended the city's Music Academy.

The interwar period saw an upsurge in Yiddish culture, Yiddish being the first language of the majority of Vilnius's Jews. In the 1930s, the literary periodical **Yung Vilne** ("Young Vilnius") provided an outlet for a new generation of Jewish poetry and prose writers, of whom Chaim Grade (best known for the autobiographical short-story collection *My Mother's Sabbath Days*; see p.378) is the most famous. The idea of Yiddish as a national Jewish language equal in importance to Hebrew was promoted by the **YIVO** (Yidisher Visnshaflekher Institut or Yiddish Scientific Institute), founded here in 1925 to conduct research into the ethnology and folklore of Yiddish-speaking communities throughout Eastern Europe.

However, Vilnius was not immune from the waves of **anti-Semitism** that swept across Central Europe in the wake of World War I. Already in 1919, units of the Polish Legion – in Vilnius to defend the region against the Bolsheviks – had run amok in the Jewish-inhabited parts of the Old Town, leaving many dead. In the late 1930s, Jewish students at Vilnius University were made to sit at the back of the lecture hall in order to prevent them "contaminating the morals" of their Catholic classmates.

None of this, however, prepared Vilnius's Jews for the fate that lay ahead under the **Nazi occupation**, which began with the German army's arrival in the city on June 24, 1941. Within weeks of taking control of the city, the Nazi authorities were joined by special units known as the Einsatzkommandos, who were charged with the job of ridding the German-controlled areas of Eastern Europe of their Jewish inhabitants. From July 8 onwards, the Einsatzkommando responsible for the Vilnius region – aided by Lithuanian auxiliaries – started taking an average of five hundred Jews a day to the Paneriai forest on the outskirts of town, where they were shot and thrown into pits. On September 6, 1941, the Jewish quarter of Vilnius's Old Town was divided into two **ghettos**, in which the city's surviving Jews were confined. The smaller of the two ("Ghetto no. 1"), comprising the narrow streets on the northeastern side of Vokiečių gatvė, contained about eleven thousand people, most of whom were killed

Vokiečių and around

Vokiečių gatvė curves northwestwards from Rotušės aikštė, its name (literally "German Street") a relic of the medieval period when merchants from various countries were allowed to settle in different quarters of the city. The Vokiečių of today, however, has little in common with its pre-World War II incarnation, when it served as the main commercial artery of Vilnius's Jewish community and would have been a chaotic jumble of carts, stalls and bilingual Yiddish and Polish shop signs. A broad, tree-lined boulevard with a slim ribbon of park running down the middle, it's busy on summer evenings, when young Vilniusians congregate in open-air cafés or sprawl on park benches to swig their takeout beers.

over the next two weeks. The larger ghetto ("Ghetto no. 2"), which occupied the streets southwest of Vokiečių, initially held 29,000 inhabitants (mostly able-bodied Jews considered fit for work, together with their families), although this number was gradually reduced over the next two years as more and more people were taken away – either to provide slave labour elsewhere, or to be killed at Paneriai.

Despite the lack of food and the spirit-sapping fear of Nazi round-ups, Ghetto no. 2 continued to function as an urban community with a semblance of normality, boasting a hospital (jammed between Ligoninės and Pylimo), a public library and sports club (both at Žemaitijos 4) and even a theatre (Arklių 3), where a drama troupe, choir and symphony orchestra performed. The ghetto also had a **resistance movement** in the shape of the United Partisan Organization (Fareinikte Partisaner Organizatsie or **FPO**), formed in January 1942 with the aim of smuggling Jews out of the ghetto and into the forests outside Vilnius, where partisan groups were active throughout the war. After an escape attempt in summer 1943, in which twelve made it out of the ghetto (another nine were caught and shot), the Germans announced that they would execute all family members of anyone who tried to flee. The FPO henceforth concentrated on arming itself, which it did by bringing in weapons through the sewers. In July 1943, the Germans declared that they would liquidate the ghetto forthwith unless the FPO leader, Iztak Witenberg, was handed over to the Gestapo. He gave himself up immediately.

On September 1, increased military activity around the ghetto persuaded the remaining FPO leaders that it was about to be cleared and its inhabitants relocated to concentration camps. Barricades were set up at either end of Žemaitijos gatvė in an attempt to protect the FPO headquarters (at Žemaitijos 4) and buy time. Approaching German troops were fired on from a building at the eastern end of Žemaitijos and forced to retreat before returning to blow the building up. This act of resistance was no more than a minor inconvenience to the Germans, but it did persuade them to postpone the full clearing of the ghetto for a couple of weeks, allowing several FPO members and other young Jews to escape (either through the sewers, or via gates in the ghetto wall which were supervised by slack Lithuanian police). One of those who got away was **Abraham Sutskever**, a member of the prewar Yung Vilne literary set who went on to become one of the major postwar writers in the Yiddish language.

However, the vast majority of the ghetto's remaining ten thousand inhabitants were rounded up on September 23 and dispatched to a variety of destinations: able-bodied adults were sent to labour camps in Estonia and Latvia; most of the women and children were delivered to the death camps. Those too sick to be transported were taken to the Paneriai forest to be shot.

Today, Vilnius has a Jewish population of around 3000, although most of these belong to families who moved to the city from other parts of Lithuania after 1945. Many of the Vilnius-born Jews who survived the Holocaust simply couldn't bear the pain of living here after 1945 and left for North America or Israel – consigning the cosmopolitan world of prewar Vilnius to the realm of history books and reminiscences.

Something of the Jewish quarter's original warren-like street plan has been preserved off the southwestern side of Vokiečių, where Mėsinių ("Butchers' St") leads into the heart of the former site of **Ghetto no. 2**. About 150m up the street, near the junction with Ašmenos, a modest granite memorial bears a Hebrew and Lithuanian text reading: "In remembrance of those who suffered and struggled in the Vilnius ghetto". A few steps away at the junction of Mėsinių and Dysnos is a monument to much-loved nineteenth-century doctor Tsemach Shabad, famous for treating the Vilnius poor free of charge. Across a grassy park to the east lies Rūdninkų gatvė, where the main gate to Ghetto no. 2 was located – it was through here that work details left in the morning, and were locked back in at night.

West of Mėsinių, at Žemaitijos gatvė 12, a plaque marks the spot where the armed Jewish underground put up barricades on September 1, 1943, in a desperate attempt to prevent German troops from clearing the ghetto. From here, Šv Mikalojaus gatvė spins back north to rejoin Vokiečių, on the way passing the Gothic **St Nicholas's Church** (Šv Mikalojaus bažnyčia), whose red-brick, stepped gable peers over a white courtyard wall. During the interwar period this was the only Lithuanian-speaking church in Vilnius – services in all the other Catholic establishments were conducted in Polish. Inside, the ceiling boasts attractive ribbed vaulting and an unusual sunburst motif.

Opposite St Nicholas's, Pranciškonų darts north towards the eighteenth-century **Franciscan Church** (Pranciškonų bažnyčia), whose lofty interior is once more open for worship after serving as a storehouse during the communist period. Harbouring little other than a marble statue of the Madonna, this draughty, semi-devastated space packs a spiritual punch more powerful than many of the better-preserved places of worship.

Žydų gatvė and around

The historical heart of Jewish Vilnius lay on the northeastern side of Vokiečių around **Žydų gatvė**, or "Jews' Street" ("Yidishe gas" to its pre-World War II inhabitants), site of the **Great Synagogue** and the labyrinth of courtyards and alleyways that once surrounded it. Seriously damaged in World War II, the synagogue was levelled by the Soviets, and its place is now occupied by a kindergarten tucked between postwar apartment blocks. Outwardly unassuming, the synagogue was built slightly underground, possibly to prevent its grandeur from inviting the envy of local Christians. "It took my breath away, for I had never expected it to be so grand," wrote Lucy Dawidowicz, whose book *At that Time and Place* (see p.377) describes the year she spent as an American student in pre-World War II Vilnius. "Outside, the synagogue looked to be about three stories tall, but inside it soared to over five stories." It's said that congregations of five thousand people crammed the cavernous, domed interior on major religious holidays.

There's no plaque marking the location of the synagogue, but squeezed between the kindergarten and a neighbouring house is a bust of the **Gaon of Vilnius**, Elijah ben Solomon (1720–97), the renowned Talmudic scholar who lived and taught here. The Gaon was one of the main opponents of Hasidism (the ecstatic, mystical sect which spread throughout the Jewish communities of Eastern Europe in the mid-eighteenth century), and his reputation as an authority on all aspects of doctrine added to Vilnius's prestige as a centre of Jewish learning.

Between Žydų and Antokolskio to the east there once existed a warren of courtyards and tiny alleys (now it's just a car park), home to the poorest of Vilnius's Jewish poor, who would eke out a living by selling old clothes and flea-market junk from makeshift stalls. It was here that Dawidowicz came across the "Durkhoyf" or "Through-Yard", which she called "the most dismal place of poverty I knew in Vilna", where the air "was close, musty and fetid with the odor of old clothes, the stink of refuse, and the rank odor emanating from the buildings' moldering walls".

The Dominican Church

At the northern end of Vokiečių, Dominikonų heads back east into the heart of the Old Town, passing after 100m or so the **Dominican Church** (Dominikonų bažnyčia), yet another medieval edifice rebuilt in Baroque style by the ubiquitous Jan Krzystof Glaubitz in the 1770s. Given the narrowness of the street, it's difficult to get a good look at the church's most arresting external feature – the broad cupola squatting atop a hefty octagonal drum. Approaching or leaving along Stiklių gatvė, just to the southeast, should do the trick.

The macabre Last Judgement scenes covering the walls of the porch provide little warning of the pink and mauve tones in the church's effervescent interior. Beyond a pulpit decked with sprightly angels and cherubs lies a vivacious cluster of altars, from which gesticulating saints appear poised to leap into the congregation. Up above, a dizzying swirl of frescoes depicting the Apotheosis of the Holy Spirit run around the cupola in celestial comic-strip style.

The congregation is largely drawn from the city's Polish community, many of whom come to linger in the side chapels dedicated to an assortment of miracle-working Virgins and saints. Most, however, gravitate towards an unremarkable-looking painting, roughly halfway down the nave, which portrays a robed Christ with divine rays emanating from his chest – a work inspired by the visions experienced by Sister Faustyna Helena Kowalska, a celebrated Catholic mystic of the interwar period. A local rector encouraged Sister Faustyna to describe what she'd seen to the painter Eugeniusz Kazimirowski in 1934, and the resulting canvas has been the focus of a cult ever since. Sister Faustyna herself was beatified in April 1993 on the occasion of Pope John Paul II's visit to Vilnius.

Pylimo Gatvė

Running parallel to Vokiečių to the southwest, **Pylimo gatvė** follows the line of the former town walls, and still acts as an unofficial boundary between the Old Town and the nineteenth-century Naujamiestis, or "New Town", beyond. A slightly scruffy thoroughfare traversed by lumbering trolleybuses, it's nevertheless rich in memories of Jewish Vilnius.

The State Vilnius Gaon Jewish Museum

At Pylimo's northern end, the **main branch of the State Vilnius Gaon Jewish Museum** at no. 4 (Valstybinis Vilniaus Gaono Žydų muziejus; Mon–Thurs 9.30am–5.30pm, Fri 9.30am–4.30pm; 1Lt, free Wed in winter) occupies a labyrinthine building housing numerous Jewish cultural organizations. A fragmentary display located in several rooms in different parts of the building kicks off with a tribute to the anti-Nazi resistance groups in the wartime ghettos of Vilnius and Kaunas, and the smuggling operations that allowed a small number of Jews to escape to the forests where they could link up with the partisans. Elsewhere, there are words-and-pictures displays devoted to Vilnius-born cultural figures, notably Yiddish writer Avrom Karpinowicz (1918–2004), sculptor Mark Antokolski, and the fiddle-playing phenomenon Jascha Haifetz. Upstairs is the Gallery of the Righteous (Teisuolių galerija), a large hall containing photographs of Lithuanians who were honoured by postwar Israel for their help in sheltering Jews from the Germans, alongside the moving testimonies of those they saved.

The Green House

At Pamėnkalnio 12 is another site of the Jewish Museum, the **Catastrophe Exhibition** (ekspozicija "Katastrofa"; Mon–Thurs 9am–5pm, Fri 9am–4pm; same ticket). Housed in a building colloquially known as the "**Green House**" on account of its colourful timber construction, this contains a harrowing display about the fate of Lithuania's Jews during the war. An English-language leaflet guides you around the photographs and documents – most chilling of which are the matter-of-fact reports submitted by Einsatzkommando leaders in December 1941, detailing how the killing of Jews had been organized and the numbers involved. Most of Lithuania's Jews were murdered within months of the Nazi takeover, although a few exhibits hint at the remarkable tales of the few who survived.

The Tolerance Centre

Another branch of the Jewish Museum, the so-called **Tolerance Centre** (Tolerancijos centras; Mon–Thurs 10am–6pm, Sun 10am–4pm), occupies a former Yiddish-language theatre on Naugarduko. The display begins on the uppermost of three floors with artworks by Lithuanian-Jewish artists, including a fine set of abstract lithographs by Druskininkai-born Jacques Lipchitz (see p.320). Items rescued from the Vilnius Great Synagogue include the doors of the Aron Ha Kodesh (the ark in which the Torah scrolls are kept) and fragments of the reader's lectern. The most delightful exhibit is the series of puppets made by Aaron Chasit of Kelmė in the early twentieth century. Depicting King Solomon and members of his court, they are a unique example of Lithuanian-Jewish folk art. The second floor features a chronological words-and-pictures account of the history of Jews in Lithuania.

The synagogue

At Pilymo 39 is the city's one surviving **synagogue** (Mon–Thurs 8am–10am, Sun 7pm–9pm), a Moorish-style structure built in 1903 to serve a congregation that belonged to the Haskalah ("Enlightenment") tradition – a nineteenth-century movement that aimed to bring Judaism into line with modern secularism. Originally known as the Choral Synagogue, owing to the (then innovative) use of a boys' choir during services, it was a popular place of worship for wealthier, westernized Jews pre-World War II, and now serves the whole of Vilnius's remaining Jewish community.

The Frank Zappa Statue

One of the city's more unexpected cultural monuments is tucked away in the car park of a hospital on Kalinausko. Mounted on a soaring pillar, this bust of the American rock avant-gardist **Frank Zappa** was erected in 1995 on the initiative of local jazz musician Saulius Paukstys. The choice of Zappa – a widely understood symbol of non-conformity perhaps, but hardly a Lithuanian icon – seemed to be a wryly ironic gesture in a country that had seen enough of ideologically charged public monuments, and the project was supported by many people who had never heard a note of his music.

Vilniaus gatvė

An alternative to Pylimo as a route through the western fringes of the Old Town is offered by **Vilniaus gatvė**, a sinuous street that starts at the northwestern end of Vokiečių and works its way up towards the bustling shops of Gedimino prospektas. There's a smattering of sights along its length, beginning with the gorgeous strawberries-and-cream exterior of **St Catherine's Church** (Šv Kotrynos bažnyčia), an elegant twin-towered structure that serves as a wonderfully atmospheric concert hall. Opposite the church, the two-storey town house at no. 41 provides a suitably refined home for the **Lithuanian Theatre, Music and Film Museum** (Lietuvos teatro, muzikos ir kino muziejus; Tues–Fri 11am–6pm, Sat 11am–4pm; 5Lt), which harbours an alluring jumble of posters, costumes and antiquated cameras.

A little further along, at no. 39, the **Teachers' House** (Mokytojų namai), overlooking the junction of Vilniaus and Klaipėdos, is occupied by a multitude of cultural organizations – including the **Vartai Art Gallery** (Tues–Fri noon–6pm, Sat noon–4pm; free), which quite apart from putting on some of the best contemporary art shows in the capital, retains some spectacular Art Nouveau stucco work in its high-ceilinged rooms.

Radvila Palace

A squat, ochre-plastered block at Vilniaus 22 is the one surviving wing of the seventeenth-century **Radvila Palace** (Radvilų rūmai; Tues–Sat 11am–6pm; 5Lt), the downtown pad of one of the Grand Duchy of Lithuania's leading aristocratic families. Rising to prominence in the fifteenth century, the Radvilas (more widely known by their Polonized name of Radziwiłł) went on to provide the duchy with many of its most outstanding military commanders, diplomats and bishops. Their palace now contains a rather mundane collection of paintings and furniture, enlivened only by occasional visiting exhibitions, and a downstairs room plastered with 165 oddly compelling prints from the Radvila family album. Commissioned by Mykolas "My Dear Fishy" Radvila (depicted in portrait no. 157, he was so nicknamed because those were the over-familiar words he used to address bemused fellow aristocrats), the series portrays all the prominent family members through the ages, starting with the mysterious, semi-mythical founder of the Radvila dynasty, Vaišunda, and culminating with Karol Stanisław Radvila (1734–90), who – despite being pictured here as a foppish aristocrat – was a shaven-headed drunkard and hooligan accused by contemporary chroniclers of shooting his own servants for sport.

Gedimino prospektas

Gedimino prospektas, running west from Cathedral Square, was the main thoroughfare of nineteenth-century Vilnius, and remains the city's most important commercial street. A broad, cobbled boulevard, overlooked by trolleybus wires and spruced-up, stuccoed buildings, it has been variously named after St George, Mickiewicz, Stalin and Lenin, reflecting the succession of different regimes. It's a place to shop or do business rather than sightsee, although few of its buildings are without deep historical associations.

Around 600m west of Cathedral Square is the **Hotel Neringa**, whose restaurant was the favoured haunt of the city's artistic elite during the brief golden age of relative cultural freedom in the late 1960s and early 1970s. The Russian dissident poet and Nobel Prize-winner, Jozef Brodsky, whiled away the evenings here when visiting Lithuanian literary colleague Tomas Venclova, and the avant-garde Ganelin-Tarasov-Chekasin jazz trio (which went on to achieve world renown) played four-hour sets to appreciative crowds of coffee-swilling intellectuals. Perhaps inevitably, the *Neringa* was also a stronghold of the local KGB: foreign visitors were invariably ushered towards private booths fitted with listening devices. The trend-setting crowd moved away from the *Neringa* decades ago, and the restaurant nowadays caters to fat cats rather than hep cats, but it still preserves much of its original decor, notably the famous murals featuring idealized scenes of fisherfolk from Neringa, the sandy peninsula after which the hotel is named.

Nearby, the broad open space of **Lukiškių aikštė** has played an infamous role in the city's history. After the 1863–64 uprising against the Tsarist regime, a number of rebels were publicly hanged here by the hardline Russian governor Muravyev. From 1952 to 1991 it was graced by a monumental **statue of Lenin**, unceremoniously carted away in August 1991 as the collapse of the Moscow coup signalled the final break-up of the Soviet Union. Preserved as a warning to future generations, the statue can still be seen in the Grūtas sculpture park outside Druskininkai (see p.322).

The Lithuanian Genocide Museum

On the southern side of Lukiškių aikštė, the forbidding grey Neoclassical building at no. 40 is the former site of Lithuania's KGB headquarters and now the educative and moving **Lithuanian Genocide Museum** (Lietuvos genocido aukų muziejus; entrance on Aukų 2A; mid-May to mid-Sept Wed–Sun 10am–5pm; mid-Sept to mid-May Wed–Sun 10am–4pm; donation expected; English-language leaflet 2Lt, tape commentary 8Lt). Built in 1899 to serve as the city courthouse, the building was taken over by the NKVD (as the KGB was initially known) during the first Soviet occupation of Lithuania in 1940. It then served as the HQ of the Gestapo when the Germans took over in July the following year, and reverted to the Soviets in 1944. The word "genocide" in the museum's title refers to the sufferings of the Lithuanians under Soviet rule – no mention is made of the Nazi genocide against the Jews in World War II.

The ground floor contains an imaginative multimedia display relating the history of the Soviet occupation, complete with English-language captions. In the basement, the dank cells where the KGB incarcerated and tortured their prisoners have been preserved in their pre-1991 state. There are texts and photographs relating to some of the more famous prisoners to have passed through here – notably the Catholic Bishop Borisevičius, shot in the basement in 1946, and partisan leaders Jonas Žemaitis and Adolfas Ramanauskas, who survived for years in the forests of Soviet Lithuania before being captured – and executed – in the mid-1950s. Particularly chilling are the water isolation cells, in which prisoners had to stand on precarious concrete perches for hours – or risk falling into a dirty pool of freezing water. On the first floor, the reassembled remnants of the KGB's own museum (a propagandistic affair that was only open to KGB members) illustrate the self-celebratory mindset of the Soviet Union's secret police.

The Parliament Building

At the extreme western end of Gedimino prospektas stands Lithuania's **Parliament Building** (Seimas), a graceless modern structure built in the 1980s to serve as the home of the Lithuanian republic's Supreme Soviet – a toothless assembly of party appointees. The first free elections to the Soviet in February 1990 transformed this bastion of communist authority into a focus of Lithuanian patriotism overnight, and it was here that the restoration of Lithuanian independence was declared on March 11 of the same year – to the intense annoyance of Mikhail Gorbachev, who was on an official visit to

Vilnius at the time. When the Kremlin moved to crush the Lithuanian independence movement on January 13, 1991, thousands of ordinary citizens descended on the parliament to prevent its capture by Soviet forces, who had already killed twelve unarmed civilians while storming Vilnius's TV Tower. On the side of the parliament facing the river some of the barricades built to defend the building have been preserved; there's also a moving memorial of traditional wooden crosses commemorating those who died at the TV Tower, and the seven border guards killed at Medininkai by Soviet special forces six months later.

The Jonas Mekas Visual Arts Center

Occupying the second floor of a modern office block just north of the Parliament building, the **Jonas Mekas Visual Arts Center** (Tues–Sun noon–6pm; ⓦmekas.lt) hosts a variety of contemporary art exhibitions, many with international avant-garde connections. The centre gets its name from Lithuanian-born experimental film maker Jonas Mekas (born 1922), a stalwart of the New York arts scene since his arrival there in 1949. Mekas for a time lived in the Fluxus artists' cooperative building established by fellow-Lithuanian George Maciunas (see p.306) – Mekas and Maciunas have always been powerful symbols of the Lithuanian avant-garde spirit, although their artistic activities were virtually unknown in their native land until after 1990.

The centre also contains a scale model of the proposed Guggenheim-Hermitage Museum, a high-profile, high-cost art gallery designed by Zaha Hadid and planned for the north bank of Vilnius's River Neris.

North of the river Neris

North of the River Neris lies the one part of Vilnius whose skyline has radically changed in the years following independence. The huddle of sleek office towers and brash shopping malls along Konstitucijos prospektas seems a deliberate corporate-age challenge to the baroque belfries of the Old Town just to the southeast. A couple of museums and the opportunity for a riverside stroll provide the main reasons to visit. From the Gedimino prospektas end of town you can walk across the **Baltasis Tiltas** footbridge towards the National Art Gallery. Otherwise the **Žaliasis Tiltas** ("Green Bridge") further east is an attraction in itself, decorated with the city centre's last remaining collection of Soviet-era statues – with heroic workers, peasants and soldiers well to the fore.

The National Art Gallery

Dominating the ridge just west of the Baltasis Tiltas bridge, the **National Art Gallery** (Nacionalinė dailės galerija; ⓦwww.ndg.lt; Tues, Wed, Fri & Sat noon–7pm, Thurs 1–8pm, Sun noon–5pm; 6Lt) occupies an angular grey building that originally served as Soviet Lithuania's Museum of the Revolution. Designed by Gediminas Baravykas and Vytautas Vielius in the late 1960s, it's a fine example of cool modernist minimalism, demonstrating that the kind of contemporary architecture frowned upon in Moscow was occasionally allowed to flourish on the Soviet empire's Baltic fringes.

The collection concentrates on local art from the early twentieth century onwards (the earlier stuff is on display at the Vilnius Picture Gallery; see p.262), starting with the two artists who dragged Lithuanian painting into the modern era – dreamy symbolist Mikalojus Konstantinas Čiurlionis (see p.303) and his impressionistic contemporary Antanas Žmuidzinavičius. No less exciting are the cubist- and constructivist-inspired artists of the 1920s, with Vytautas Kairiukštis, Vladas Drėma and Stasys Ušinskas leading the way. Despite being smothered by socialist dictates in the 1940s and 50s, Lithuanian avant-garde instincts blossomed again in the Sixties, although many of the mould-breaking experimental works on display here were considered decadent and unexhibitable at the time they were made. Look out for the quietly moving abstract works of Kazė Zimblytė (1933–99), an artist whose creations were rarely seen outside her own home during the Soviet period.

Regular temporary exhibitions are a major added attraction, and the café boasts attractive views back across the river.

The Lithuanian Energy Museum

About 1.5km east along the riverbank from the National Art Gallery, the **Lithuanian Energy Museum** (Lietuvos energetikos muziejus; Tues–Sat 10am–5pm; 10Lt) is housed in a handsome pre-World War I industrial building that served from 1902 until 2003 as the city's main heating plant. You can still inspect the main boiler, which sprouts a fantastic collection of multi-coloured pipes, alongside a collection of electricity-generating turbines. There's also a scale model of the Ignalina nuclear power station, a Soviet-built installation that was closed down on EU insistence in January 2010. An adjoining pavilion contains a collection of vintage cars, with a scarlet-coloured 1942 Mercedes effortlessly upstaging the Soviet-built family cars of the 1970s.

East of the Old Town

From Maironio gatvė, which marks the eastern boundary of the Old Town, a narrow bridge leads over the fast-flowing Vilnia River towards the district of **UŽUPIS** (literally "beyond the river"), an attractive hillside heap of nineteenth-century houses whose mixed population of arty bohemians, nouveaux-riches and traditional working class has made it one of central Vilnius's most characterful areas. It's the artier types that are largely responsible for the **Užupis Republic** (Užupio respublika), which declared its independence from the rest of Vilnius on April 1, 2000. Intended as a wry comment on the very notion of independence in the era of globalization, the "republic" also represents a serious attempt to build a sense of community in the district and to stimulate local culture.

The *Užupio kavinė* (see p.278), just over the bridge from the Old Town, has long been the Republic's main social centre. North of here, a path runs along the riverbank, passing artists' studios and a brace of alternative galleries. To the east, the gently ascending Užupio gatvė leads to a triangular piazza and a tall pillar topped by the trumpet-blowing **Užupis Angel** – unveiled in April 2001 to mark the first birthday of the republic.

One of the more infamous former residents of this part of town was **"Iron" Felix Dzerzhinsky**, the Lithuanian-born Pole who went on to become a committed Bolshevik and one of Lenin's closest collaborators. Dzerzhinsky lived at Užupio 14 (roughly level with the angel) while a high-school student, before moving on to become a socialist agitator in Kaunas. After the Russian revolution Dzerzhinsky was entrusted with setting up the Cheka, the much-feared state security service that later metamorphosed into the KGB. Unsurprisingly, there's no commemorative plaque.

The Hill of Three Crosses

Pathways on the northern side of the Užupis district lead up onto a group of sandy, pine-covered knolls known by the collective name of Kalnų parkas ("Hill Park"), a peaceful area light years away from the bustle of the city below. The most prominent – and most visited – of the heights is the **Hill of Three Crosses** (Tryų kryžių kalnas), reached more conveniently from its northern side, where an asphalted road climbs up from Kosciuškos gatvė, near the Applied Art Museum (see p.258). According to popular tradition, it's here that Jogaila erected three crosses in memory of the seven Franciscan monks executed on this spot by his grandfather, Grand Duke Algirdas. Whatever their origins, a trio of crosses did exist here until Russian Governor General Muravyev's decision to remove them – a reprisal for the 1863–64 uprising. Vilnius town council celebrated the departure of the Russians in 1915 by building three new crosses in gleaming white stone, a much-loved landmark on the city's eastern skyline until the Soviets dynamited them in 1950. The replicas erected after 1990 have quickly re-established themselves as popular targets for weekend strollers. Those who make it up here are rewarded with excellent city views, with the Old Town laid out in the foreground and more distant landmarks, such as the green cupolas of All Saints' Church and the spear-like form of the TV Tower, further to the east.

The Church of SS Peter and Paul

Past the Hill of Three Crosses, Kosciuškos continues 800m northeast towards the **Church of SS Peter and Paul** (Šv Petro ir Povilo bažnyčia), its twin-towered facade presiding over a busy traffic roundabout. Of fifteenth-century origin, the church was rebuilt as a three-aisled basilica in 1668 on the initiative of Lithuania's Grand Hetman (military commander-in-chief and second only to the Grand Duke in times of war), Michael Casimir Pac. Pac intended the church to be a celebration of Vilnius's deliverance from the Russians, who had just vacated the city after a thirteen-year occupation.

The **interior** looks cold and grey at first, but on closer inspection comes alive with gloriously over-the-top stucco work, featuring cavorting cherubs, rich foliage and exotic plants laden with fruit. The whole ensemble was conceived by Italian craftsmen Pietro Perti and Giovanni Maria Galli, who spent eleven years cramming every available centimetre of the upper walls and ceiling with over two thousand mouldings. Some of the most complex work is around the dome, where angels twang away on musical instruments and contorted human forms appear to be holding up the central lantern. Of the several richly decorated chapels on either side of the nave, the most famous is the altar of the Madonna of Misericord in the left-hand transept, where an image of the Virgin supposedly protects parishioners from ill health and disease. Donated to the church by Bishop Jerzy Tyszkiewicz in 1647, it became the focus of a serious cult during the plague epidemic of 1708–10, when Bishop Brzostowski began holding forty-hour Masses at the altar in an attempt to soothe the anxieties of his flock. On leaving the church, look out for the stucco figure of Death prancing mischievously on one side of the main doorway – a memento mori said to mark the grave of Pac himself.

The outskirts

There's a handful of isolated attractions outside central Vilnius, each of which could be seen in half a day. On the eastern margins of the city, both the **Alexander Pushkin Museum** in Markučiai and the **cemetery** in the suburb of **Rasos** are reasonably short hops from the centre and provide a glimpse of its semi-rustic, forest-fringed outskirts. Further west, the **Television Tower** is an engaging attraction in its own right, as well as a powerful reminder of Lithuania's resistance to the Soviet aggression of January 1991. Historical memories of a more harrowing kind are attached to the forest of **Paneriai**, 10km southwest of town, where the bulk of Vilnius's prewar Jewish population were brutally murdered by the Nazis.

The Alexander Pushkin Museum

In the suburb of Markučiai, 2km east of the Old Town, the **Alexander Pushkin Museum** (Aleksandro Puškino muziejus; Wed–Sun 10am–5pm; 4Lt) is a bit of a fake, bearing in mind that it was the home of Pushkin's son rather than that of the great Russian poet himself. Such details shouldn't put you off, however – the timber building in which the museum is housed harbours the best-preserved nineteenth-century interior in the city, and the surrounding woods make it a lovely place for a short stroll. Built for the Russian General Melnikov in 1867, the house was inherited by his daughter, Varvara, who married Pushkin's youngest son Grigorii. Chunky period furniture and reproduction wallpaper provide the backdrop to a display (texts in Lithuanian and Russian only) about the poet's life and work, including several references to Adam Mickiewicz (see p.259); the poets knew each other in Moscow, and Pushkin's enthusiasm for his colleague's writings contributed greatly to Mickiewicz's growing international reputation. Outside the house, paths lead through deciduous forest to the small onion-domed chapel beside which Grigorii and Varvara lie buried. To get to the museum, take bus #10 from the Užupio stop on Maironio gatvė to the Markučiai terminus – the house is on a knoll straight ahead.

Rasų cemetery

A forest of predominantly nineteenth-century funerary monuments ranged across tree-shaded hillocks, **Rasų cemetery** is an important place of pilgrimage for Lithuanians and Poles alike, owing to the unusually large number of historical figures buried here. It lies in otherwise undistinguished suburbs about 1600m southeast of the Old Town:

from Rotušės aikštė, walk east along Subačiaus then south along Rasų gatvė; otherwise take bus #31 from the train station. Prime among the remains laid to rest here is the **heart of Marshal Józef Piłsudski**, leader of the Polish independence movement at the beginning of the twentieth century and that country's first president after 1918. Born into an impoverished gentry family in the Polish-Lithuanian borderlands, Piłsudski went to school in Vilnius, and owned land outside the town in the 1920s. He long entertained the romantic notion that the Polish-Lithuanian Commonwealth of old could be restored (a Commonwealth in which the Poles, of course, would play the leading role), and was genuinely disappointed that the strength of Lithuanian national sentiment after World War I rendered such a dream impossible. He gave tacit support to the Żeligowski coup that restored Vilnius to Poland in 1920, and remained sentimentally attached to the Vilnius region throughout his life – hence the desire to have at least one portion of himself laid to rest here. Buried with much pomp on May 12, 1936, the marshal's heart lies underneath a black granite slab just to the left of the cemetery's main entrance, surrounded by the graves of Polish soldiers who defended Vilnius against Bolshevik forces in 1919. Piłsudski's remaining body parts can be found in the crypt of Kraków's Wawel Cathedral.

One of the few prominent Lithuanians who chose to stay in Vilnius during the Piłsudski era was **Jonas Basanavičius** (1851–1927), the publicist and patriot who had become the leader of the Lithuanian national movement at the close of the nineteenth century. A simple obelisk marks his final resting place opposite the cemetery's main chapel, which is uphill and to the right of the Piłsudski memorial. Basanavičius was one of the prime movers behind the Lithuanian Declaration of Independence on February 16, 1918, and wreaths are laid here on the anniversary. A Lithuanian cultural icon of equal stature – the painter and composer **Mikalojus Konstantinis Čiurlionis** (see p.303) – lies a short distance away in the northern part of the cemetery, marked by an angular grey tombstone.

The Television Tower

Perched on high ground 3km west of the centre in the suburb of Karoliniškės, the slender form of the 326m **Television Tower** (Televizijos bokštas; daily 10am–9pm; 22Lt) soars gracefully above the surrounding pines. On January 13, 1991, the Kremlin ordered its troops to seize control of the TV Tower and other key public buildings in a ham-fisted attempt to reassert authority over the wayward republic. When unarmed civilians gathered to defend the tower, twelve of them died under the tracks of Soviet tanks. Once in control of the tower, the Soviets closed down the Lithuanian TV service – which simply continued broadcasting from its studios in Kaunas. Fearful of causing further casualties, the Soviets backed off from their plans to storm the Seimas, where many thousands more civilians had gathered. The events of January 13 provoked international outrage (irredeemably tarnishing the image of Soviet leader Mikhail Gorbachev) and only served to boost the prestige of the Lithuanian independence movement.

Today, the dead are commemorated by a group of **wooden crosses** at the tower's base, while a photographic exhibition on the ground floor inside vividly captures the drama and heroism of the time. Lifts convey visitors to the rather drab café-restaurant near the summit; there's a superb panorama of the city from the slowly revolving viewing deck.

To get to the tower, take trolleybus #16 or bus #54 from the train station, or trolleybus #11 from Lukiškių aikštė; alight at the Televizijos bokštas stop on Sausio 13-Osios gatvė.

Paneriai

PANERIAI, the forested site where the Nazis and their Lithuanian accomplices murdered 100,000 people during World War II, lies among nondescript suburbs 10km southwest of the centre. The site was initially used by the Soviet army, who dug oil storage pits here in 1941. The Nazis, who arrived in July the same year, found the pits especially convenient. Political undesirables from all over Europe were among those killed and buried here, although the vast majority (an estimated seventy thousand) were the Jews of Vilnius, who were systematically exterminated from July 8, 1941 onwards.

The killing grounds are about 1km into the woods due west of Paneriai train station and marshalling yards. The entrance to the site is marked by two stone slabs dating from the communist period, whose Russian and Lithuanian inscriptions refer to murdered "Soviet citizens" rather than Jews – a typical example of how the Soviet authorities exploited the Holocaust for their own political ends. A central slab with an inscription in Hebrew commemorating "seventy thousand Jewish men, women and children" was only added in 1990. From the memorial, a path leads to the **Paneriai Memorial Museum** (Panerių memorialinis muziejus, Agrastų 15; officially Sun–Thurs noon–6pm, Sat & Sun 11am–6pm, but call ☎8-5/260 2001 to check), which holds a small display detailing what happened here. From the museum, paths lead to the pits into which the Nazis initially threw their victims; the bodies of many were later exhumed and burned when the advance of Soviet armies prompted the Germans to start hiding the evidence of their crimes. This latter task was carried out by an eighty-man, corpse-burning team composed of Jews and Russian POWs. They were kept chained at all times and slept in a heavily defended bunker accessible by a ladder that was removed at night. After spending three months digging a tunnel with spoons and bare hands, forty of the corpse burners escaped on April 15, 1944. Twenty-five of them were caught and killed immediately, while the rest broke through to join partisan groups in the forest. The forty corpse burners who had stayed behind were executed five days later.

To get to Paneriai, take a southwest-bound suburban train from Vilnius station and alight at Paneriai. From the station platform descend onto Agrastų gatvė, turn right and follow the road through the woods for about 1km.

Eating and drinking

Vilnius has a rapidly growing choice of **restaurants**, offering everything from Lithuanian to Lebanese cuisine in all budgets. **Cafés**, offering snacks and cheap meals, as well as the full range of alcoholic and non-alcoholic drinks, may stay open until late, but most night-time drinking happens in the **bars**, many of which keep going until the early hours. Most bars and restaurants are concentrated around Gedimino or in the Old Town, though there are a few characterful suburban establishments.

Picnic supplies can be bought from big stores like Rimi, opposite the town hall at Didžioji 28 (daily 8am–10pm); Iki, in the same building as the bus station (daily 8am–10pm); or the mega-supermarket Maxima, just west of the Old Town at Mindaugo 11 (daily 8am–midnight).

Restaurants

Many Vilnius **restaurants** serve the kind of cuisine you find in most northern European countries: meat-and-potatoes, schnitzels and chops. An increasing number, however, are serving traditional Lithuanian food, such as *cepelinai*, *koldūnai* and *blynai*, in folksy surroundings. In addition, there's no end of pizzerias and a handful of ethnic restaurants around the centre.

Prices for main courses are usually around 20–35Lt, although speciality dishes, especially in the posher places, often cost more. Telephone numbers are included below where it's necessary to book at weekends.

Old Town and around

The restaurants listed below are marked on the "Vilnius Old Town" map on p.255.

Balti drambliai Vilniaus 41. Vegetarian restaurant with a loyal clientele of mildly bohemian youth, located in a many-chambered, red-brick basement decorated with pictures of various deities. Tasty, inexpensive tofu-based stews with couscous or rice form the backbone of the menu. The tusk-like sculpture in the bar refers to the restaurant's name, which means "White Elephant". Mon–Fri 11am–midnight, Sat & Sun noon–midnight.

La Boheme Šv Ignoto 4/3 ☎8-5/212 1087. Wine bar-cum-restaurant that enjoys a fine barrel-vaulted setting. Food is modern European with a Mediterranean slant, including some excellent salads and risottos. Lived-in wooden furnishings and candles add to the atmosphere. Sun–Thurs noon–midnight, Fri & Sat noon–2am.

Čili kaimas Vokiečių 8 ☎8-5/231 2536. Labyrinthine temple to Lithuanian kitsch decorated with antlers, saddles, antiquated brass instruments, a whole tree and even a fishpond. The menu features everything from boiled pigs' ears to roast chicken, along with national dishes like *cepelinai* and *koldūnai*. The food is on the ordinary side, but the fun factor keeps locals and tourists coming back in their droves – reserve, or be prepared to queue, at weekends. Sun–Thurs 10am–midnight, Fri & Sat 10am–2pm.

Lokys Stiklių 8/10 ☎8-5/262 9046. Long-established Lithuanian cellar restaurant serving boar, elk and a wide range of pork and beef standards in atmospheric, almost dungeon-like surroundings. Prices are creeping up but remain affordable. Daily noon–midnight.

Mano Guru Vilniaus. Snazzy salad restaurant with innumerable permutations of fresh crunchy things. Hearty eaters may prefer to give it a miss, but with the menu rounded out with some excellent soups and desserts, this is an excellent place for a light, healthy meal. Mon–Fri 8am–9pm, Sat 10am–7pm.

Markus ir Ko Antokolskio 11 ☎8-5/262 3185. Cosy restaurant in informal, bar-like surroundings, drawing a loyal clientele of eager carnivores with its superb steaks – filet mignon is the house speciality – plus generous salads. Mains hover around 30–40Lt. Reserve at weekends, when there's live jazz or piano. Daily noon–midnight.

La Provence Vokiečių 22 ☎8-5/262 0257. French and south European cuisine in a formal environment. Faultless cooking and service, and a more extensive (and pricey) wine list than is usual for Vilnius. Twice as expensive as anything else in the Old Town, but worth the treat. Daily 11am–midnight.

Stikliai Gaono 7 ☎8-5/262 4501. French food in the posh restaurant upstairs, homely, cheaper Lithuanian fare in the beer-cellar-style room downstairs. The latter hosts live Lithuanian folk music nightly except Sunday. Daily noon–midnight.

Tres Mexicanos Tilto 2. Tucked away in a side street diagonally opposite the cathedral, this bright little space decked out in mood-enhancing citrus colours delivers a fairly authentic range of spicy dishes, with prices lurking well below the norm. 11am–11pm.

Žemaičiai Vokiečių 24 ☎8-5/261 6573. Subterranean labyrinth specializing in Žemaitijan (west Lithuanian) cuisine. An excellent place to try *cepelinai*, smoked fish or *Žemaičių blynai* (potato pancakes stuffed with mincemeat), as well as tasty pork and beef dishes. The drinks list features some strong speciality beers, as well as an array of Lithuanian spirits. Head for the wooden-bench courtyard in summer. A tourist favourite, but prices remain affordable. Daily 1pm–midnight.

Outside the Old Town

The restaurants listed below are marked on the "Vilnius" map on p.250.

Marceliukės Klėtis Tuskulėnų 35 ☎8-5/272 5087. Traditional Lithuanian favourites in a folksy tavern-style pavilion jammed between tower blocks north of the River Neris. The top-quality food is not too expensive, and there's live folk music most nights. Daily 11am–midnight.

Tores Užupio 40 ☎8-5/262 9309. Modern European cuisine with the emphasis on steaks and grilled fish. Renowned for the panoramic view of Vilnius's Old Town from its outdoor terrace. Daily 11am–11pm.

Vandens Malūnas Verkių 100 ☎8-5/271 1666. Traditional meaty Lithuanian fare and quality international dishes in an old mill 6km north of the centre, set between suburban houses and meadows. Three storeys of wooden-beamed rooms, with antiquated milling machines dotted around the place and dried herbs hanging from the rafters. Daily 11am–midnight.

Cafés

Many of Vilnius's **cafés** offer much the same food as those places that call themselves restaurants, but in more informal surroundings and at sometimes significantly cheaper prices. All of the cafés listed below are marked on the "Vilnius Old Town" map on p.255.

Coffee Inn Trakų 7. A domestic high-street coffee chain, *Coffee Inn* retains a certain quirky character – probably due to the odd mix of furnishings in idiosyncratic Old Town interiors. Decent coffee and sandwiches, and first-rate cheesecakes. Also at Vilniaus 17 and Pilies 3. Mon–Fri 7am–10pm, Sat & Sun 9am–10pm.

Pilies Menė Pilies 8. Flash, modern café-bar renowned for its extensive menu of sweet and savoury pancakes. Good place for a daytime coffee or night-time drink. Daily 10am–midnight.

Ponių Laimė Stiklių. One of the more refined order-at-the-counter cafés, perfectly located for a quick Old Town coffee break or lunch. Treats include a salad bar, savoury pastries and pies (including the excellent *daržovių pyragas* or vegetable bake), and a colourful array of cakes. Mon–Fri 9am–10pm, Sat 10am–10pm, Sun 11am–6pm.

Skonis ir Kvapas Trakų 8. Relaxing café occupying an elegant suite of barrel-vaulted rooms, and offering big pots of properly brewed tea, excellent coffee and an affordable range of hot meals. The cakes are top-notch too. Daily 9.30am–midnight.

Bars and pubs

Watering holes in central Vilnius, especially in the Old Town, range from faux-rustic taverns with wooden benches to swish designer bars with minimalist decor. Several call themselves "pubs", although few really try to ape British or Irish styles, preferring instead to cultivate a cosmopolitan, fun atmosphere that wouldn't be out of place in any large, hedonism-driven city. Most places serve a wide range of food, and the locals are as likely to visit them for lunch or dinner as for a session of serious drinking. A few close at 11pm or midnight, although the majority stay open into the early hours, especially at weekends. Unless otherwise stated, all of the places listed below are marked on the "Vilnius Old Town" map on p.255.

Café de Paris Didžioji 1. The café next to the French Cultural Centre functions as a coffee-and-crêpes venue during the day and turns into a mildly arty DJ bar at night, featuring offbeat styles of music and occasional acoustic gigs. It's oddly shaped and impossible to navigate without bumping into people, but an enjoyable crush. Sun–Tues noon–midnight, Wed–Sat noon–2am or later.

Cozy Dominikonų 10. One of those wonderfully multi-functional Vilnius locales that serves as a relaxing café during the day and cool DJ bar in the evening. The matt-black floor and tangerine-coloured chairs might have you jotting down interior-design notes. Daily 9am–2am or later.

In Vino Aušros vartų 7. Wine bar and much more besides, with candlelight and wooden chairs and tables creating a nineteenth-century French-farmhouse-kitchen feel in the main room, and a more loungey area around the corner. Background jazz and chansons create a bit of extra class. Sun–Thurs 4pm–2am, Fri & Sat 4pm–4am.

Kalvarių vienas Kalvarių 1; see Vilnius map on p.250. Located in a riverside folly that looks like a castle, this chic but laid-back café/bar/restaurant is arguably the only really inspiring drinking destination north of the river. The sophisticated menu runs to fish dishes and steaks, and the desserts are always worth a try.

The Pub Dominikonų 9. Enduringly popular bar with wooden interior and pub grub that takes in everything from shepherd's pie to chicken curry. The covered courtyard frequently hosts live music, discos and big-screen basketball. Sun–Thurs 11am–1am, Fri & Sat 11am–3am or later.

Savas Kampas Vokiečių 4. A long-standing favourite with a broad cross-section of drinkers, not least because of its prime location. Choose between the front room with mildly rustic wooden tables, and the two back rooms with their sofas, standard lamps and olde-worlde living-room feel. Food-wise, there are passable pizzas and lots of sweet and savoury pancakes. Mon–Thurs 8.30am–1am, Fri 8.30am–4am, Sat 10am–4am, Sun 10am–1am.

Šnekutis Sv Stepono 8. A favourite with the real ale drinkers, serving draught beers from small-town breweries in a semi-rustic environment. Pub food, Lithuanian-style, comes in the form of *cepelinai*, goulash and *zirnai* (peas topped with bacon bits). Mon–Sat noon–11pm.

Šuolaikinio Meno Centras (ŠMC) Inside the Contemporary Art Centre at Vokiečių 2. This dark, minimally decorated café-bar has long been a meeting point for arty types and nonconformists. The lunches and light meals are cheap and tasty, although it's as an offbeat evening drinking venue that *ŠMC* really comes into its own. Large and popular summer terrace. Mon–Thurs 11am–midnight, Fri & Sat 11am–1am or later, Sun noon–midnight.

Tappo d'Oro Stuokos-Gucevičiaus 7. A well-stocked wine bar with soothing Mediterranean-style white walls. The patio is packed in summer – arrive early or end up standing in the street outside. Daily 11am–11pm.

Transylvania Totorių. Convivial pub with medieval-Dracula theme (expect pictures of Romanian warlord Vlad the Impaler rather than Bela Lugosi), unobtrusive rock music in the background and a good cross-section of local drinkers. Lithuanian and international beers on tap, and a solid menu of food and beer snacks. Sun–Thurs 11am–midnight; Fri & Sat 11am–2am.

Užupio kavinė Užupio 2. A comfortable café-bar just over the Užupio bridge from the Old Town, catering for a mixed crowd of youngish professionals and the arty denizens of the bohemian Užupis district (see p.273). The moderately priced food includes ribs, fish, a couple of vegetarian offerings and above-average potato pancakes. The

Stebuklas ("Miracle") apple pie fully deserves its moniker. Madly popular in summer, with a shady outdoor terrace overlooking the Vilnia River. Daily 10am–11pm.

Vasaros Terasa ("Summer Terrace"), Vilniaus 39. The capacious courtyard of the Mokytojų namai ("Teachers' House") turns into an outdoor café-bar in summer, hosting frequent DJ events, film nights, and concerts of all kinds (when there's an entrance fee). Daily noon–2am.

Woo Vilniaus 22. Basement bar and diner with a white-walled, minimalist interior and DJ-driven club events at weekends. Alongside a good selection of cocktails and a solid wine list, there's a full menu of Asian-influenced foods – with Vietnamese soups, Japanese sushi and Thai curries geared to suit most appetites and pockets. Mon–Thurs noon–2am, Fri noon–5am, Sat 5pm–5am, Sun 5pm–midnight.

Nightlife and entertainment

There's an ever-changing roster of **clubs** in Vilnius, although many of the best nights out are in late-opening **bars** rather than in designated DJ spaces. Contemporary **drama** and quality **classical music** are the big draws in a city known for its high-brow culture; the tourist office has programme details. In general, *Vilnius in your Pocket* or the *Baltic Times* are your best source of **listings**, unless you can read Lithuanian, in which case the local daily *Lietuvos Rytas* or cerebral arts weekly *Literatūra ir menas* carry more detail.

Clubs and live music

Vilnius has several large **mainstream clubs** attracting a friendly, relaxed crowd with an unsophisticated mixture of Western, commercial dance tunes and Lithuanian and Russian techno. In addition, many of the establishments listed under "Bars and pubs" (see opposite) have DJs or live music at weekends. Entry fees are on the whole reasonable: anything between 10 and 35Lt.

There are always a few local bars or restaurants hosting gigs by local **jazz** musicians; decent live **rock**, on the other hand, is harder to find. Local bands play at venues such as *Brodvėjus/Broadway* or *Tamsta*; details of upcoming events are posted on the door. Traditional **folk** music is conspicuous by its absence unless you head for one of the more touristy restaurants or come during the annual **Skamba Skamba Kankliai** festival in late May, when bands from all over Lithuania play in Old Town courtyards and parks.

Unless otherwise stated the following places are on the "Old Town" map on p.255.

Brodvėjus (aka "Broadway") Mėsinių 4 ⓦ www.brodvejus.lt. A Vilnius classic, this popular drinking-and-dancing venue is in a long, galleried space packed with tables – with a stage at one end for live bands (Thurs–Sun) and bopping. Full menu of snacks and hot meals; lunchtime specials are chalked up on a board outside. Sun & Mon noon–2am, Tues noon–3am, Wed–Sat noon–4am.

Gravity Jasinskio 16 ⓦ www.clubgravity.lt. See Vilnius map on p.250. Minimalist decor and DJs from the wilder frontiers of dance culture have made this a favourite with young hedonists who know a thing or two about cutting-edge house and techno. Fri & Sat 10pm–4/5am.

Neringa Gedimino 23. An elegant and intimate dance-bar beneath the *Neringa* hotel attracting a slightly older crowd with its weekend discos. Broad range of danceable pop classics and occasional cover bands. Mon–Thurs noon–midnight; Fri & Sat till 3am.

Pabo Latino Trakų 3/2 ☏ 8-5/262 1045, ⓦ www .pabolatino.lt. Hugely enjoyable Latin music club attracting a healthy cross-section of students, business types and vivacious clubbers. Door staff can be choosy at weekends, and if you want a seat you'll have to reserve a table in advance. Wed–Sun 8pm–3am or later.

Tamsta Subačiaus 11a ☏ 8-5/212 4498, ⓦ www .tamstaclub.lt. Live music club where leading lights of the local rock-pop scene play to good-natured audiences. It's a chairs-and-tables kind of place, so arrive early if you want a seat. Schedule posted on the door. Wed–Sat 7pm–2am or later.

Classical music, opera and ballet

Vilnius boasts two symphony orchestras, of which the **Lithuanian National Philharmonic Orchestra** (Lietuvos nacionalinis simfoninis orkestras) is marginally the more prestigious, receiving the lion's share of visiting soloists and also embarking on major international tours in its own right. The **Lithuanian State Symphony Orchestra** (Lietuvos valstybinis simfoninis orkestras) is a newer outfit that doesn't have quite the same pedigree, but is nonetheless of the highest quality, as is the other jewel in Vilnius's musical crown, the **Lithuanian National Opera and Ballet Theatre** (Nacionalinis operos ir baleto teatras). All three perform throughout the year, except for short periods (notably in July and/or Aug). In addition, look out for numerous chamber concerts and solo recitals.

A wide range of national and international musicians pack the programme of the **Vilnius Festival** (late May to early July), while the **St Christopher Summer Music Festival** in July features local and international chamber ensembles, with most performances taking place in St Ignatius's Church on Šv Ignoto gatvė. In August, city folk head out to the summer festival in the nearby town of **Trakai** (see p.286) to enjoy concerts, opera and ballet in the romantic setting of the castle courtyard. The biggest events of the autumn are the **Vilnius Jazz Festival** (October; ⊛ www.vilniusjazz.lt); and the **Gaida Festival of Contemporary Classical Music** in October. For further information on festivals in the city, see ⊛ www.vilniusfestivals.lt.

National Philharmonic (Nacionalinė filharmonija) Aušros Vartų 5 ☎ 8-5/266 5233 or 266 5216, ⊛ www.filharmonija.lt. The elegant but not over-formal home of the country's premier orchestra. Symphonic concerts on most Saturdays, frequently featuring appearances by international soloists and conductors. Also "family" concerts of popular classics on Sunday lunchtimes, and a regular programme of chamber music. Box office Tues–Sat 11am–7pm, Sun 10am–noon.

Opera and Ballet Theatre (Operos ir baleto teatras) Vienuolio 1 ☎ 8-5/262 0727, ⊛ www .opera.lt. A modern auditorium with a busy programme of top-notch productions. Performances take place four or five times a week and are hugely popular, so book well in advance. Box office Mon–Fri 10am–7pm, Sat 10am–6pm, Sun 10am–3pm.

St Catherine's Church (Šv Kotrynos bažnyčia) Vilniaus ☎ 8-5/261 2691. A wide range of music from classical recitals to jazz, in a beautifully restored Baroque church.

St John's Church (Šv Jono Bažnyčia) Vilnius University main courtyard. Organ and choral concerts every Sunday: check posters in and around the university, or ask at the tourist office.

Vilnius Congress Hall (Vilniaus kongresų rūmai) Vilniaus 6/16 ☎ 8-5/261 8828, ⊛ www .lvso.lt. A modern venue hosting performances by the Lithuanian State Symphony Orchestra about once a fortnight, as well as chamber concerts and occasional musicals. Box office Mon–Fri noon–7pm, Sat 11am–4pm.

Theatre

Vilnius's **theatre scene** is interesting and varied, although performances are invariably in Lithuanian (or Russian) except on the rare occasions when visiting companies are in town. However, the language barrier shouldn't prevent you from enjoying shows by the best of the contemporary drama companies, for whom movement and stagecraft are often just as important as the text. Lithuanian directors of worldwide renown whose performances should not be missed include Eimundas Nekrošius, Rimas Tuminas, Gintaras Varnas and Oskaras Koršunovas.

The **Sirenos Festival** (⊛ www.sirenos.lt) brings genre-defining international drama companies to town in early October.

Lėlė Puppet Theatre (Lėlių teatras) Arklių 5 ☎ 8-5/262 8678. Top-quality children's entertainment featuring superbly designed puppets and enchanting stage sets. Performances at lunchtime or mid-afternoon. Box office Tues–Sun 10am–4pm.

Lithuanian National Drama Theatre (Lietuvos nacionalinis dramos teatras) Gedimino 4 ☎ 8-5/262 9771, ⊛ www.teatras.lt. Flagship of

Lithuanian theatre with a comfortable, modern auditorium. As well as being home to the state drama company, it also hosts productions by prestigious independent drama troupes and high-profile performances from abroad. Some performances take place in the Small Hall (Mažoji salė), entered via Odminių gatvė round the back. Box office Mon & Fri 11am–2pm & 3–7pm, Tues–Thurs 11am–6pm, Sat & Sun 11am–1pm & 2–6pm.

Meno fortas ⓦ www.menofortas.lt. Eimundas Nekrošius's theatre company. Productions are staged in different venues throughout the city, so check the site for performance details.

Meno spaustuvė Šiltaradžio 6 ☎ 8-5/204 0832, ⓦ www.menuspaustuve.lt. The "Art Printing House" is an arts centre in a former warehouse in the Old Town, hosting boundary-pushing theatre, contemporary dance and off-the-wall music.

OKT/Vilnius City Theatre ⓦ www.okt.lt. The production house of director Oskaras Koršunovas. Venues change, so check the site for details.

Russian Drama Theatre (Rusų dramos teatras) Basanavičiaus ☎ 8-5/262 7133. Mixed programme of Russian-language classics and modern experimental work in a lovely 150-year-old building in sore need of renovation. It's an atmospheric place with good acoustics, but the glitzy theatre crowd tends to hang out elsewhere. Box office Tues–Sun 1–7pm.

Teatro arena Olimpiečių ☎ 683 77357, ⓦ www .teatroarena.lt. Cavernous space just north of the river, currently hosting Oskaras Koršunovas productions as well as dance performances and concerts.

Vilnius Little Theatre (Vilniaus mažasis teatras) Gedimino 22 ☎ 8-5/249 9869, ⓦ www.vmt .lt. Serious contemporary work in a marvellously old-world auditorium. Box office Tues–Sat 11am–6.30pm, Sun 1–6.30pm.

Youth Theatre (Jaunimo teatras) Arklių 5 ☎ 8-5/261 6126, ⓦ www.jaunimoteatras.lt. A mixture of classical and experimental productions performed by youth companies. Box office Tues–Sun 11am–2pm & 3.30–7.30pm.

Cinema

Films are usually shown in the original language with Lithuanian subtitles. Tickets cost around 12–20Lt except on Mondays, when most cinemas drop their prices. The only **film festival** of real note is Kino Pavasaris ("Cinema Spring"), which falls in the last week of March and screens the odd new Lithuanian film alongside recent international releases.

Kino Pasaka Šv Ignoto 4/3. Lovely small rep cinema in the heart of the Old Town showing international, mostly non-mainstream films. The *La Bohème* wine bar (see p.276) is immediately below.

Skalvija Goštauto 2/15. A good place to catch international art-house movies, within easy walking distance of the Old Town.

Shopping

Retail culture has wrought major changes on central Vilnius over the last decade, and streets like Gedimino prospektas, Pilies gatvė and Vokiečių gatvė are lined with the kind of high-street stores that you'd expect to find in any European city. However, many locals still buy food and household essentials from vast, bustling **markets**, where stallholders sell top-quality farm produce alongside small-time traders dealing in all manner of contraband. The most central of these are on Bazilionų gatvė (daily till 1/2pm), just north of the train and bus stations, and on Kalvarijų gatvė (Tues–Sun till 1/2pm), north of the River Neris but still within walking distance of the centre.

For souvenirs, you should head first to the outdoor **crafts market** at the junction of Didžioji and Pilies, where a gaggle of stalls sell traditional wicker baskets, wooden handicrafts and amber jewellery. The goods on display here are of variable quality, but may well be cheaper than those in souvenir shops, of which there are a growing number in the more tourist-trodden streets of the Old Town.

Souvenirs and gifts

Amber Museum Gallery Šv Mykolo 8. Amber shops are ten a penny in Vilnius, but this one is a bit special, presenting well-designed (and pricey) jewellery and rare stones in a chic, gallery-style environment. Daily 9am–6pm.

Linen and Amber Studio Stiklių 3. Linen shirts and dresses, as well as bed sheets and tablecloths, alongside other traditional textiles. Mon–Sat 10am–7pm, Sun 10am–5pm.

Sauluva Šv Mykolo 4 & Literatų 3. A variety of gifts, including *verbos,* or "palms", the wand-like bundles of dried flowers and grasses used to decorate homes in the run-up to Palm Sunday. Mon–Sat 10am–7pm.

Šokoladino namai Trakų 13. Highly individual range of locally produced gourmet chocolates, in all sorts of flavours and shapes. Mon–Fri 10am–8pm, Sat & Sun 11am–6pm.

Verpstė Žydų 2. A good selection of linen, wooden toys and pottery. Mon–Fri 10am–6pm, Sat 11am–3pm.

Books and music

Akademinė Knyga Universiteto 4. An academic bookstore with English-language books about Lithuania on the ground floor and English-language fiction in the basement. Mon–Fri 10am–7pm, Sat 10am–3pm.

Littera Šv Jono 12. In the main courtyard of Vilnius University. Worth checking out for the neo-Baroque ceiling paintings as well as the books. Mon–Fri 9am–6pm, Sat 10am–3pm.

Muzikos Bomba Corner of Jakšto and Goštauto. A wide selection of Lithuanian classical CDs, as well as international rock and pop. Mon–Fri 10am–7pm, Sat 10am–4pm.

Prie Halės Corner of Pylimo and Sodų. Good choice of guidebooks and large-format art titles. Mon–Fri 11am–6pm, Sat 10am–3pm.

Thelonious Second Hand Music Stikliū 12. A cellar-full of secondhand CDs and old vinyl – a good place to browse for local jazz and folk. Mon–Fri 11am–7pm, Sat 11am–3pm.

Vaga Gedimino 50. One of the bigger downtown bookstores, with a small selection of English-language fiction and tourist-oriented titles. Mon–Fri 10am–7pm, Sat 11am–4pm.

Listings

Airlines Aeroflot, Pylimo 8/2 ☎8-5/212 4189; Air Baltic (and SAS), Universiteto 10-7 ☎1825; Austrian Airlines, at the airport ☎8-5/232 9377; Finnair, at the airport ☎8-5/252 5210; LOT, at the airport ☎8-5/273 9000; Lufthansa, at the airport ☎8-5/232 9292; Star 1, Pelesos 1/2 8-5/247 7744.

Car rental In addition to national chains, local firms include A & A Litinterp, Bernardinų 7-2 (☎8-5/212 3850, ⓦwww.litinterp.lt) and Aunela, Vytenio 6-110 (☎686 63444, ⓦwww.aunela.lt).

Embassies and consulates Australia, Vilniaus 23 ☎8-5/212 3369; Belarus, Muitinės 41 ☎8-5/213 2255, ⓦwww.belarus.lt; Canada, Jogailos 4 ☎8-5/249 0950, ⓦwww.canada.lt; Ireland, Gedimino 1 ☎8-5/262 9460; Russia, Latvių 53/54 ☎8-5/272 1763, ⓦwww.rusemb.lt (visas Mon–Fri 8.30am–noon); UK, Antakalnio 2 ☎8-5/246 2900, ⓦwww.britain.lt; Ukraine, Teatro 4 ☎8-5/212 1536; US, Akmenų 6 ☎8-5/266 5500, ⓦwww .usembassy.lt. The nearest New Zealand embassy is in Warsaw, Poland ☎+48 22/521 0500.

Exchange ATMs are located throughout the city. The Parex Bankas exchange office outside the train station at Geležinkelio 8 is open 24hr.

Hospitals The main emergency department is at Vilnius University Emergency Hospital (Vilniaus universitetinė greitosios pagalbos ligoninė) Šiltnamių 29 ☎8-5/216 9212. For private,

English-speaking care, Baltic-American Clinic, Nemenčinės 54A ☎8-5/234 2020, ⓦwww.bak.lt.

Internet access Many cafes and bars offer wi-fi access although this may be a pay-to-use service rather than free. Most central of the internet cafés is Collegium, Pilies 22 (Mon–Fri 9am–7pm, Sat 11am–7pm).

Laundry Joglė, in the Maxima supermarket at Mindaugo 11, for service washes and dry-cleaning (Mon–Fri 10am–10pm, Sat 10am–6pm).

Left luggage At the bus station (Mon–Fri 5.30am–9.45pm, Sat & Sun 7am–8.45pm). Luggage lockers (from 5Lt) can be found in the basement of the train station.

Pharmacies Gedimino Vaistinė, Gedimino 27 (Mon–Fri 8am–9pm, Sat 9am–5pm, Sun 10am–5pm); Vokiečių Vaistinė, Didžioji 13 (Mon–Fri 9am–8pm, Sat & Sun 10am–6pm).

Photo developing and supplies Foto servisas, Pilies 23, process snaps, print from digital files, sell film and offer developing services (Mon–Fri 10am–7pm, Sat 10am–3pm).

Police ☎112.

Post office Gedimino 7 (Mon–Fri 7am–7pm, Sat 9am–4pm).

Taxis Ranks on Rotūšės aikštė, although overcharging of foreigners is rife. You'll do better booking a taxi in advance – try Eipažas (☎8-5/239 5539) or Martono (☎8-5/240 0004).

Around Vilnius

An appealing mixture of gently rolling agricultural land, pine forests and lakes, the countryside around Vilnius is fairly typical of much of Lithuania and makes a good introduction to the country as a whole. Within easy day-trip distance of the capital are **Trakai**, the much-visited site of a major medieval fortress; the Iron Age site of **Kernavė**; and the open-air sculpture park that goes under the modest name of the

Museum of the Centre of Europe, just under 20km north. Trakai and Kernavė are easily accessible by bus; to get to the museum, however, you need your own transport.

Trakai

Some 25km west of the capital, lakeside **TRAKAI** once rivalled Vilnius as a hub of political and military power. The town's imposing island castle, completed during the reign of Vytautas the Great, is arguably the single best-known monument in the country – an instantly recognizable national symbol that receives a year-round stream of visitors. The surrounding lakes and forests further enhance Trakai's status as a beauty spot, and it's an ideal place for a lazy day of swimming, boating or strolling.

Served by regular **buses** and minibuses from Vilnius, Trakai is an easy day-trip from the capital, though the beauty of the countryside – coupled with some good accommodation – makes it a nice spot for a longer rural break. Indeed, the growing range of **accommodation** here means that you could easily use Trakai as a base in preference to Vilnius.

Some history

Together with Vilnius and Kernavė, Trakai was one of the earliest military strongholds in Lithuania, and occupied a crucial position in the ring of castles that protected the heartland of the Grand Duchy from the expansionist forays of the Teutons. The first fortified settlement here was located 3km southeast of the current town, where the village of Senieji Trakai ("Old Trakai") now stands. Senieji Trakai was the ruling stronghold of **Grand Duke Gediminas** before he moved his capital to Vilnius, and it is also thought to be the birthplace of Gediminas's grandson, **Vytautas the Great**, under whom Lithuanian power reached its apogee in the early fifteenth century. It was Vytautas's father, Kęstutis, who founded modern-day Trakai, choosing an island in Lake Galvė to build his impressive **castle**. Vytautas the Great resided here when not on campaign, and invited the **Karaim** (a Judaic sect from the Crimea; see p.284) to settle here and serve as his personal bodyguards. A couple of hundred Karaim still live in Trakai, their distinctive wooden cottages lining the main street. After the reign of Vytautas, Trakai continued to be second only to Vilnius in political importance: the whole of south-central Lithuania was governed from here, and whoever controlled Trakai castle was effectively the vice-ruler of the Lithuanian state. The town's significance declined in the sixteenth century, and the castle itself was abandoned after being sacked by the Cossacks in the war of 1654–67, to be rediscovered in the twentieth century as a potent symbol of the country's medieval greatness.

Arrival, information and accommodation

Trakai's friendly **tourist office** (Mon–Fri 8am–noon & 1–5pm, Sat 10am–3pm; ☎8-528/51934, ⓦwww.trakai.lt), about 800m north of the train and bus stations at Vytauto 69, sells local maps. **Bikes** can be rented from the tourist office, or the *Slėnyje* campsite (see below).

There's a fair selection of hotels and guesthouses in and around Trakai; you'll need your own transport to get to the out-of-town places. The tourist office can organize **B&B** (❶) with local families, although vacancies disappear fast in summer. *Slėnyje* campsite also offers **guesthouse** accommodation.

Hotels and guesthouses

Akmeninė Rezidencija Bražuolės village ☎8-528/25186, ⓦwww.akmenineuzeiga.lt. Swish waterside retreat on the shores of Lake Akmeninė, 5km north of town just beyond the turn-off for Užutrakis. A central, thatched-roof cottage offers snug doubles with log-cabin decor, iron bedsteads and modern bathrooms. Outlying two-person villas offer self-catering, and super-stylish modern furnishings made from natural materials. There's a restaurant on site, and a separate bathhouse with a Russian-style, log-fired sauna. Villas from 795Lt, hotel rooms ❻

Karaimų 13 Karaimų 13 ☎8-5/285 1911 or 8-6/562 4562, ⓦwww.karaimai.lt. Guesthouse with six simple, supremely comfy en-suite rooms featuring pine floors and ceiling beams and small TV. Breakfast is not included, but can be ordered

from the downstairs café – which boasts an outdoor lake-facing terrace. ④
Margis Penkininkai village ☎8-528/21717, ⓦwww.margis.lt. Classy option located in pinewoods beside Lake Margis, 8km west of Trakai on the Aukštadvaris road. Rooms feature designer furniture, earthy or pastel colour schemes, plenty of desk space and modern bathrooms. Outlying bungalows contain two- or three-person split-level apartments with snazzy modern furnishings and floor-to-ceiling windows. Bungalows 900–1250Lt, doubles ⑤–⑥
Salos Kranto ☎8-528/53990, ⓦwww.salos.lt. Small, central hotel on the shores of Lake Totoriškų, offering simple, cosy en-suites with TV or swanky

split-level studios with wooden beams. There's a sauna and plunge-pool on site (100Lt/hr) and a basement DJ bar open at weekends. ④–⑤

Campsite
Kempingas Slėnyje Slėnio 1 ☎8-5/285 3880 or 8-6/861 1136, ⓦwww.camptrakai.lt. Some 7km by road from Trakai on the far side of Lake Galvė, this is a well-equipped affair with plenty of space, power points for trailers, a restaurant and access to lovely lakeside walks. It also has two small guesthouses offering en-suite rooms with TV, one with wooden floors, rustic furnishings and lake views (④), the other with slightly chintzier decor (③).

The Town

Trakai extends over a long, narrow peninsula that touches on three lakes: Bernardinų to the east, Totoriškų to the west and the biggest, Galvė, to the north. From the **train** and **bus stations** follow Vytauto gatvė north to reach the main sights, which kick off after about 1000m with the Orthodox **Church of the Holy Mother of God** (Skaisčiausios dievo motinos gimimo cerkvė), a creamy-brown building topped with a Russian spire. Squatting on high ground a couple of hundred metres further on is the twin-towered **Church of the Visitation** (Šv Mergelės Marijos apsilankymo bažnyčia), a fairly unprepossessing place rebuilt many times since its original foundation by Grand Duke Vytautas in 1407. The church is an important pilgrimage site thanks to the presence of a fourteenth-century icon of the Virgin, presented to Vytautas the Great by Byzantine Emperor Manuel II Paleologos in 1391. Set on a glittering gilded side altar, the icon pictures a dusky beauty who could have jumped straight from the pages of *Vogue Italia*.

The Karaim

A Turkic-speaking group practising a branch of Judaism, the **Karaim** are thought to be descended from the Khazars, a Central Asian people who held sway over a steppe empire stretching between the Black and Caspian seas in the seventh and eighth centuries AD. It's thought that the Khazar rulers invited Christian, Islamic and Jewish missionaries to their court, and eventually chose Judaism as the religion of the Khazarian elite. Although the Khazar empire was swallowed up by rivals some time in the ninth century, the Khazar language and culture were preserved by individual groups, one of which is believed to be the Karaim.

Whatever their origins, Karaim had by the eleventh century settled in the Crimea, which was then ruled by the Tatars – another Central Asian group who spoke a similar language. It was here that they came into contact with the Lithuanian ruler Vytautas, who after campaigning in the region in 1397 invited several Karaim and Tatar families to Trakai in order to form an elite guard loyal only to the Grand Duke. Karaim migration to the Grand Duchy of Lithuania continued over the next few centuries, with families often coming to Trakai first before moving on to new centres. One such place was Lutsk (now in the Ukraine), which became an important centre of Karaim learning and book publishing. At the beginning of the twentieth century there were thought to be over five thousand Karaim in the Crimea and about eight hundred in Lithuania. Since then numbers have steadily declined, largely owing to intermarriage and assimilation. There are now an estimated 300 Karaim in Lithuania, just over a hundred of whom are in Trakai – numbers so small that any real Karaim cultural renaissance must remain outside the realms of possibility.

After another 500m, turn right down Kęstučio gatvė to find the remains of the **Peninsula Castle** (Pusiasalio pilis), thought to have been built by Duke Kęstutis, son of Gediminas and father of Vytautas. Only the walls, rebuilt to a height of about 1–2m, remain, penning in an inner courtyard given over to wild grasses. A former monastery chapel near the entrance to the castle is nowadays occupied by the **Sacral Art Museum** (Sakralinio meno paroda; Wed–Sun 10am–6pm; 4Lt), which boasts a small display of church silver and priestly regalia.

From here the main street changes its name to Karaimų gatvė and continues north through the part of town traditionally inhabited by the Karaim, their bright yellow and green timber-clad houses set end-on to the road, each sporting three ground-floor windows – "one for God, one for oneself, and one for Grand Duke Vytautas", as the local saying has it. At Karaimų 22 is the **Karaim Ethnographic Exhibition** (Karaimu etnografinė paroda; Wed–Sun 10am–6pm; 4Lt), a modern pavilion with sepia photographs of nineteenth-century Karaim families (see opposite), the men in their dark kaftans and black-and-white felt hats, the women in embroidered velvet jackets and ornate clogs. Filigree jugs and coffee cups add further to the oriental flavour, aided somewhat incongruously by medieval Persian swords and a suit of samurai armour. Further on, at no. 30, is the nineteenth-century **Kenessa** (Kenesa), or Karaim prayer house, a simple ochre cube with a greening roof.

The Island Castle

A hundred metres or so beyond the Kenessa, Karaimų descends to the shores of Lake Galvė, where stalls selling amber jewellery and hawkers renting out rowing boats and pedalos vie for your attention. Forming a wondrous backdrop to the waterfront scene is the **Island Castle** (Šalos pilis), about 500m offshore, a satisfyingly romantic cluster of red-brick watchtowers and squat round turrets topped with spindly weathercocks, grouped around a central, sky-scraping keep. The whole place was a ruin intil 1962, when the Lithuanian government decided to rebuild the castle as it must have looked in Vytautas the Great's time. It was a display of national pride to which Moscow chose to turn a blind eye, although Nikita Khrushchev was said to be infuriated by the project.

Two wooden footbridges lead across the water to the castle, now home to a **museum** (Tues–Sun: May–Sept 10am–7pm; Oct–April 10am–5pm; Ⓦ www.trakaimuziejus.lt; 10Lt), which interweaves the castle's history with local ethnography. The most important exhibits are in the warren of halls within the central **keep**, separated from the rest of the castle by an inner moat, and holding within its sturdy frame a surprisingly delicate, galleried courtyard. Inside are scale models of the castle at different stages of its development, medieval weaponry, and mannequins dressed in the traditional local dress – white smocks and straw hats for the men, full skirts with black aprons embroidered with flowers for the women. Exhibits in the outer courtyard evoke medieval castle life: there are wild-boar skins, drinking horns and a jumble of furniture, including a bizarre table-and-chair set fashioned from stag antlers.

In summer, a **lake steamer** (10Lt return) runs from the castle to the northern end of Lake Galvė (also accessible by road), where the Tyszkiewicz family built the summer residence of **Užutrakis Palace**, and called in French landscape gardener Edouard André (who also worked for the family in Palanga) to lay out a wooded park. The palace is not open to the public, but the leafy park is a pleasant place for a wander, with good views back towards Trakai.

Eating, drinking and entertainment

Trakai's main claim to culinary fame is the Karaim-introduced *kibinas*, a crescent-shaped pastry filled with meat that unleashes a deadly drip of hot fat after a few bites. The traditional *kibinas* contains chopped lamb and fried onion, although you can get beef, pork and veggie variants. *Kibinai* can be bought from stalls and cafés throughout the town; there is also a respectable handful of restaurants offering familiar Lithuanian and north European food.

In August, Lithuania's National Philharmonic and National Opera come to take part in the **Trakai Festival**, a series of outdoor performances in the courtyards of both the Island and Peninsula castles. The tourist offices in Vilnius and Trakai sell tickets – advance booking is essential.

Cafés and restaurants

Apvalaus stalo klubas Karaimų 53A ☎8-528/55595. Smart lakeside pavilion offering views of Trakai castle and quality international cuisine, with mains around 45Lt. Choose between steaks, duck breast, or excellent freshwater fish, and leave room for the desserts. Daily 11am–10pm.

Kybynlar Karaimų 29 ☎8-528/55179. A lakeside restaurant with a Karaim-influenced, oriental theme (which extends to the costumed staff), this is probably the best place to sample *kibinai* – which come in several flavours, cheese- or vegetable-filled versions included. The menu is also strong on Near Eastern food such as stuffed vine leaves, spicy meatballs and skewer-grilled kebabs. Daily 11am–10pm.

Senoji kibininė Karaimų. One of the older *kibinai* outlets, in a wooden hut decorated with domestic knick-knacks at the northern end of town, about 1km south of the castle. The chewy-grey-meat-filled *kibinai* here are an acquired taste, but there's plenty in the way of inexpensive mainstream Lithuanian food – marinated-herring salads, potato pancakes and *koldūnai* included. Daily 10am–10pm.

Šokolado sostinė Corner of Vytauto and Birutės. Chocolate specialists serving delicious, handmade truffles, all manner of cookies and cakes, good coffee and speciality teas. Daily 11am–6pm.

Kernavė

Just outside the village of **KERNAVĖ**, 30km northwest of Vilnius, a cluster of four flat-topped hills overlooking the River Neris once made up the military and administrative centre of the pre-Christian Lithuanian state. Originally crowned with wooden stockade forts, the hills almost certainly served as the main power base of Mindaugas, the thirteenth-century strongman who welded the Lithuanian tribes into a unified and expansionist state. The site was abandoned at the end of the fourteenth century after repeated sackings by the Teutonic Knights – the last of which, in 1390, probably included volunteer crusader Henry Bolingbroke, the future King Henry IV of England. Now protected as an **archeological reserve**, the hills can be scaled by means of wooden stairways for sweeping views of the surrounding terrain.

The site's combination of historical pedigree and natural beauty has ensured its popularity with present-day neo-pagans, who congregate here for summer solstice bonfires on the night of June 23/24. Another good time to visit is the first or second weekend in July, when the **Kernavė Festival of Experimental Archeology** (Eksperimentinės archeologijos festivalis) provides enthusiasts with the chance to dress up as medieval Lithuanian warriors and peasants and give demonstrations of pottery and metalwork.

Kernavė is a well-signed, 12km journey west of the main Vilnius–Panevėžys highway. There are four to six daily **buses** to Kernavė from Vilnius, many of which leave uncomfortably early; catching the 1.30pm bus from Vilnius and returning at 6pm (5pm on Saturdays and Sundays) is currently your best option.

The Museum of the Centre of Europe

According to a study made by the French National Geographical Institute in 1989, the official centre of Europe is located at 25 degrees 19' longitude, 54 degrees 54' latitude – in other words 25km north of Vilnius just beside the main road to Utena. The exact spot is marked by a sundial about 400m west of the road, accessible via a (signed) track. A handful of passers-by stop to take a look, though there's little to detain you.

However, the institute's findings do serve as a handy raison d'être for the **Museum of the Centre of Europe** (Europos parkas; ⊛www.europosparkas.lt; 9am–dusk; 12Lt), a significantly more worthwhile destination, located – somewhat confusingly – 17km to the southeast (it's 19km out of Vilnius: leave town via Kalvarijų gatvė and it's well signed from there). Set amid forested hills, the museum is basically a huge open-air **sculpture park**, established on the initiative of local artist Gintaras Karosas in 1991, and featuring a growing display of more than 65 works by sculptors from all over the world. There's something for everyone in a collection that ranges from the impenetrably abstract to the facile. The main body of sculptures is 1km beyond the entrance, conveniently grouped around a café-restaurant (where you can pick up an English-language plan; 1Lt). Karosas's set-piece *Monument of the Centre of Europe*, a small pyramid with the names (and distances in kilometres) of various world capitals arranged around it, is less captivating than the title would suggest. Highlights elsewhere include Magdalena Abakanowicz's *Space of Unknown Growth*, a family of giant concrete eggs lurking in a small dell; Dennis Oppenheim's *Drinking Structure with Exposed Kidney Pool*, an unnerving cross between a caravan and an elephant; and Aleš Vesely's rather jolly *Sculpture idea – structure*, a metal, temple-like chamber on a spring-mounted floor, which slowly bounces up and down when you enter.

Travel details

Buses

Vilnius to: Anykščiai (3 daily Sat & Sun; 2hr); Birštonas (5 daily; 2hr 30min); Biržai (4 daily; 3hr 40min–4hr 20min); Druskininkai (6 daily; 2hr 5min–3hr 30min); Kaunas (every 15–30min; 1hr 30min–1hr 55min); Klaipėda (7 daily; 4hr); Nida (1 daily; 6hr); Palanga (7 daily; 4hr 15min); Panevėžys (10 daily; 1hr 50min–3hr); Šiauliai (8 daily; 3hr 15min); Šilutė (4 daily; 5hr 30min); Trakai (Mon–Fri 20 daily, Sat & Sun 15 daily; 40–50min).

Trains

Vilnius to: Ignalina (6 daily; 2hr); Kaunas (Mon–Fri 11 daily; Sat & Sun 8 daily; 1hr 40min–2hr); Klaipėda (2 daily; 5hr); Marcinkonys (Mon–Fri 3 daily; 2hr); Paneriai (Mon–Fri 24 daily; Sat & Sun 17 daily; 10min); Šeštokai (2 daily; 3hr 30min); Šiauliai (3 daily; 3hr 50min); Trakai (Mon–Fri 7 daily, Sat & Sun 4 daily; 40min).

International trains

Vilnius to: Daugavpils (3 weekly; 3hr); Kaliningrad (2 daily; 6hr 30min); L'viv (2 weekly; 16hr 10min);

Minsk (2 daily; 4hr 10min); Moscow (2 daily; 16hr); St Petersburg (3 weekly; 12hr); Warsaw (1 daily; 7hr).

International buses

Vilnius to: Amsterdam (1 weekly; 26hr); Berlin (1 daily; 18hr); Brussels (1 weekly; 30hr); Gdańsk (1 daily; 11hr); Kaliningrad (2 daily; 8hr); Kraków (2 weekly; 12hr); Minsk (3 daily; 4–6hr); Rīga (5 daily; 5hr); Tallinn (2 daily; 10hr 15min); Warsaw (3 daily; 9hr).

Flights

Vilnius to: Amsterdam (2 daily; 2hr 35min); Berlin (1 daily; 1hr 45min); Brussels (1 daily; 2hr 30min); Copenhagen (1 daily; 1hr 40min); Dublin (1 daily; 3hr 30min); Frankfurt (2 daily; 2hr 15min); Helsinki (2 daily; 1hr 25min); Kiev (1 daily; 1hr 40min); London (2 daily; 3hr); Moscow (2 daily; 1hr 55min); Paris (3 weekly; 3hr 20min); Prague (2 daily; 2hr 20min); Rīga (1 daily; 55min); Stockholm (1 daily; 1hr 10min); Tallinn (2 daily; 1hr 35min); Warsaw (1 daily; 1hr 10min).

3.2

Eastern and central Lithuania

A vast expanse of grazing land and cereal crops broken up by deep swathes of forest, eastern and central Lithuania make up the heartland of what is still a predominantly agricultural country. There's a modest scattering of fair-sized industrial cities, each filled with the energies one would expect from a fast-changing, post-communist country, but even these lie only kilometres away from bucolic market towns and isolated villages – the kind of communities that Lithuanian-born Polish novelist Tadeusz Konwicki described as "the desert islands of Central Europe".

Eastern and central Lithuania are traditionally made up of three distinct ethnographic areas: Aukštaitija in the north, Dzūkija in the southeast and Suvalkija in the southwest. **Aukštaitija** (which literally means "Uplands", although it's not particularly higher than any other part of the country) is such a big, amorphous region that it no longer serves as a common badge of identity to the people who live there – they're more likely to see themselves as inhabitants of a particular city or district. There's more in the way of local patriotism in **Dzūkija**, a densely forested region famous for its wild mushrooms, wood-carving and folk music – especially the unaccompanied narrative songs performed by women. The hard-working farming folk of **Suvalkija** (named after the regional centre of Suwałki, which is now just over the border in Poland) are said to speak the purest form of Lithuanian in the country – their dialect was chosen to form the basis of the official literary language by nineteenth-century reformers.

The region sees far fewer tourists than Vilnius or the Baltic coast, but there's a great deal to discover. With an absorbing Old Town and an impressive clutch of museums, Lithuania's second city of **Kaunas** is as rewarding as any of the big urban centres of the Baltics, and offers easy access to the unmissable open-air ethnographic museum at **Rumšiškės**. The region's remaining cities are largely modern, concrete affairs: Panevėžys is a transport hub for northern Lithuania, but offers far less in the way of attractions than **Šiauliai**, a youthful, energetic place that's the main jumping-off point for the pilgrim-tramped route to the mysterious **Hill of Crosses**. There's more in the way of atmosphere in the small towns of central Lithuania, with both **Biržai** and **Kėdainiai** boasting a wealth of historic monuments bequeathed by the aristocratic Radvila clan, and sleepy **Anykščiai** offering lazy woodland walks and a brace of quirky museums. For a taste of wild, unspoilt nature, the **Aukštaitija National Park** covers the most accessible chunk of northwestern Lithuania's extensive lakeland region, while, if you use the laid-back spa town of **Druskininkai** as a base, the **Dzūkija National Park** presents a superb opportunity to sample the enticing woodland environments of the south.

Getting around **by car** is relatively swift on the main highways (Vilnius–Kaunas–Klaipėda and Vilnius–Panevėžys–Rīga). Main roads elsewhere are mostly slow-going, single-lane affairs, although given the unspoilt countryside this is no great hardship. Vilnius, Kaunas and Panevėžys are the main nodes of an extensive **bus** network that covers all the places mentioned in this chapter – again, bear in mind that services on country roads can take an age. Many places can be accessed **by train** from Vilnius, with routes fanning out towards Kaunas, the Aukštaitija National Park, the Dzūkija National Park and Šiauliai.

Aukštaitija National Park

Northeast of Vilnius extends a rippling, green landscape scattered with a glittering archipelago of lakes, occupying the troughs and hollows gouged out of the Baltic plain by glaciers during the last Ice Age. Among the most attractive and easily visited of the lakeland regions is the **Aukštaitija National Park**, 100km northeast of Vilnius, where the River Žeimena and its tributaries feed over one hundred lakes. It's an understandably popular area with canoeists, who use the network of lakes and rivers as an aquatic highway traversing one of Lithuania's most unspoilt regions. It's prime walking territory, too, with waterside trails leading up into the low, rounded hills that cluster around the shores. Some seventy percent of the park is made up of forest – predominantly pine, spruce and birch. The densest woodland is in the sparsely populated northern parts of the park, where you're most likely to come across roe deer, red deer and wild boar, and more rarely elk, marten and beaver. Tickets (3Lt) to the park are available from the **information centre** in the main settlement, **Palūšė**. This centre, and the tourist office in nearby **Ignalina**, can provide details of the handful of small hotels and rural homestays in and around Palūšė, as well as the park's primitive campsites.

Ignalina

The park's main jumping-off point is **IGNALINA**, a small town of pastel-hued wooden houses just outside the park, on the Vilnius–Visaginas road and rail routes. **Train**

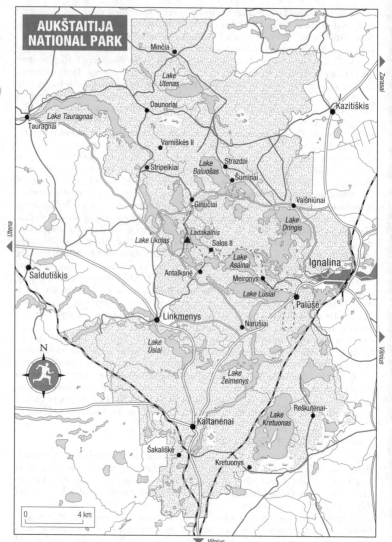

AUKŠTAITIJA
NATIONAL PARK

Minčia

Lake
Utenas

Daunoriai

Zarasai

Kazitiškis

Lake Tauragnas
Tauragnai

Varniškės II

Utena

Stripeikiai

Strazdai

Lake
Baluošas

Šuminai

Vaišniūnai

Ginučiai

Lake
Dringis

Ladakalnis

Lake Ūkojas

Salos II

Lake
Asainai

Ignalina

Antalksnė

Meironys

Lake Lūšiai

Palūšė

Saldutiškis

Linkmenys

Narušiai

N

Lake
Ūsiai

Lake
Žeimenys

Reškutėnai

Kaltanėnai

Lake
Kretuonas

Vilnius

Šakališkė

Kretuonys

0   4 km

Vilnius

and **bus stations** stand together just east of the centre, where the **tourist office** at Laisvės alėja 70 (Mon–Fri 9am–5pm; ☏8-386/52597, Ⓦwww.lsa.lt/ignalina) can book you into **rural homestays** (from 40Lt) all over the park. The *Žuvėdra* **hotel** at Mokyklos 11 (☏8-686 09069, Ⓦwww.zuvedra.com) offers neat en-suites in a lakeside location at the northwest end of town.

Palūšė

From Ignalina a minor road runs 5km west towards **PALŪŠĖ**, a village of dainty yellow houses grouped around the eastern end of Lake Lūšiai. There are 6–8 daily buses to Palūšė (it's a stop on routes to Anykščiai, Molėtai and Panevėžys), but the most enjoyable way to get there is to walk: from Ignalina train station head south-west along Turistų gatvė to pick up a foot- and cycle-path that takes you through some lovely countryside.

Slightly uphill from Palūšė's single street lies the wooden **Church of St Joseph** (Šv Jozefo bažnyčia), a mid-eighteenth-century structure with a squat, two-storey bell tower. A small pavilion nearby holds the **Pilkapis Exhibition** (Pilkapio ekspozicija; erratic opening times; ask at the National Park Information Centre), consisting of fifth-century-BC burial finds, namely a female skeleton accompanied by a trove of jewellery made from stones and animal bones.

Palūšė's main **beach** is at the eastern end of the lake. Several seasonal kiosks rent out rowing boats (6Lt/hr; 25Lt/day) and canoes (12Lt/hr; 35Lt/day). Behind the beach, the **Botanical Path** (Botanikos takas) is a 3.5km trail that takes you over a wooded hill, round the nearby Lake Tarama then back to Palūšė. Featuring tranquil forest and reed-cloaked wetland, it's an ideal introduction to the National Park's natural beauty.

Practicalities

Occupying a modern building downhill from the church, the **National Park Information Centre** (June–Aug Mon–Thurs 9am–5pm, Fri & Sat 9am–7pm, Sun 10am–2pm; Sept–May Mon–Fri 9am–5pm; ☎8-386/47478, ⊛www.anp.lt) sells maps and provides information on canoeing and rental; they can also book you B&B **accommodation** in the national park. If you don't have your own transport, try *Karolio Sodyba* (☎8-686 91547, ⊛www.karoliosodyba.lt; ❷) which offers neat en-suites in a timber building by the lake, or *Camping Palūšė* (☎8-386/52891, ⊛www.paluse.lt), which occupies a grassy, forest-fringed spot behind the church and has drinking water and shower/toilet facilities. Just west of Palūšė's church, the *Pirate Bar* offers basic food and drink, and there's a small provisions shop next door.

Around the park

The most renowned of the park's beauty spots is **Ladakalnis hill**, 9km northwest of Palūšė, the southernmost point of a ridge that extends between lakes Ūkojas and Link-menas. It was a place of sacrifice in pagan times, and it's easy to see why it might have appealed, with its commanding views of six surrounding lakes, their waters bisected by green fingers of forested land. Follow the ridge north to find **Ginučiai castle mound** (Ginučių piliakalnis), a tenth-century hill-fort whose summit is accessible via a wooden stairway. The forest cover is thicker here, but sweeping views occasionally open up between the trees. The easiest way to get to Ladakalnis is by car, heading northeast from Palūšė along the Tauragnai road and turning north onto a dirt road. Alterna-tively, you can walk from Palūšė (3–4hr), following a trail along the northern shores of Lake Lūšiai which takes you through a pair of wonderfully preserved villages full of timber houses, **Salos-I** and **Salos-II**.

GINUČIAI, 5km north of Ladakalnis, is a picturesque village of pea-green houses squeezed between lakes Alnajos and Sravinaitis. The nineteenth-century water mill in the centre is now a national park-operated guesthouse (☎8-616 29366; ❸), offering tasteful, wooden-floored rooms with shared facilities – there's no breakfast but you do get use of a kitchen. The former millpond is a popular bathing spot in summer, and you can rent boats. Ginučiai also boasts a simple **campsite** with a water supply and hole-in-the-ground toilets.

Ten kilometres east of Ginučiai, on the shores of Lake Dringis, **VAIŠNIŪNAI** is another lovely village of timber houses and granaries, watched over by a huge roadside Rupintojėlis figure sculpted by a local craftsman. Heading west from Ginučiai along dirt roads will bring you after 5km to **STRIPEIKAI**, where the **Ancient Beekeeping Museum** (Senovinės bitininkystės muziejus; May to mid-Oct daily 10am–7pm; 3Lt), displays an oddly riveting collection of traditional beehives, carved out of tree trunks into various shapes, and spread across a meadow like timber tombstones.

Anykščiai and around

ANYKŠČIAI (pronounced "A-*neeksh*-chey"), 110km northwest of Vilnius, is one of the most attractive towns in the Lithuanian northeast, nestling in a rolling patchwork of forest and green pasture either side of the River Šventoji. It makes a good base camp for woodland walks, and a convenient jumping-off point for **Niūronys** and its appealing horse museum.

The beauty of the region occupies a treasured place in the Lithuanian psyche, thanks largely to local-born priest **Antanas Baranauskas** (1835–1902) and his poem *Forest of Anykščiai (Anykščių Šilelis)* – a lyrical evocation of nature, regarded as one of the nation's most sacred texts. Perched on a hill just above the bus station, the **Baranauskas and Vienuolis-Žukauskas Memorial Museum**, Vienuolio 4 (Baranausko ir Vienuolio-Žukausko memorialinis muziejus; daily 8am–5pm; 4Lt) pays homage to both Baranauskas and the self-appointed keeper of his flame, Antanas Žukauskas (1882–1957), who wrote short stories under the pen-name of Vienuolis ("the monk"). The museum was originally the site of the Baranauskas family farmstead, which Vienuolis bought in 1922 with the express intention of turning its one surviving building – a log-built granary – into a national shrine. Now enclosed in a concrete-and-glass shell to protect it from the elements, the granary contains a chair and table belonging to Baranauskas and a few facsimile manuscripts, but little to convey the scale of his achievements – as well as being a prolific author, he was one of nineteenth-century Lithuania's leading ecclesiastics, rising to become Bishop of Seinai (now Sejny in Poland) in 1897. You can also look around the house Vienuolis built for himself next door to the granary; its mid-twentieth-century interior of floral wallpaper and ticking grandfather clocks has been lovingly preserved.

Across the river from the museum, Anykščiai's unassuming town centre is dominated by the neo-Gothic **Church of St Matthew** (Šv Mato bažnyčia), whose twin towers – at 79m each – are the tallest in the country. The cavernous interior features some lovely nineteenth-century, floral-motif wall coverings and brightly coloured stained glass by contemporary artist Anortė Mackelaitė. Diagonally opposite the church, the **Museum of Sacral Art** at Vilniaus 11 (Mon–Fri 10am–5pm, Sat 10am–4pm; 4Lt) contains a modest but rewarding collection of devotional paintings, including a handful of dreamy canvases by symbolist Kazys Simonis (1887–1978).

To reach what remains of the **forest** Baranauskas waxed so lyrically about, head southwest from the church along Vilniaus gatvė and keep going past the cemetery. The road soon turns into an asphalted path surrounded by dense woodland rich in pine, birch, oak and elm. Following the trail for 5km leads to the **Puntukas boulder** (Puntuko akmuo), a 6m-high lump of rock deposited by a retreating glacier some 12,000 years ago and nowadays a beloved landmark – no self-respecting local newlyweds would dream of having their photograph taken anywhere else. One side of the boulder is decorated with a bas-relief of pointy-helmeted pilots Darius and Girėnas, who plummeted to their deaths while attempting to fly from New York to Kaunas in 1933 (see p.302).

Anykščiai has one other attraction: the **narrow-gauge railway** (siaurukas; Ⓦwww .siaurukas.eu) that runs northwest to Panevėžys (see p.289) and east to Lake Rubikiai (Rubikių ežeras). Regular passenger services were discontinued in 2001 but the line has succesfully reinvented itself as a tourist attraction, operating weekend excursions to Rubikiai from late April to late October. Tickets (20Lt return) can be bought from the Anykščiai tourist office or from the conductor. Anykščiai's **train station**, ten minutes' walk north of the Baranauskas museum along Geguzės, is a handsome wooden building that hasn't changed much since the interwar years; there's a fascinating museum of narrow-gauge rolling stock in a former engine shed.

Practicalities

Anykščiai is an easy day-trip from Vilnius – if you miss one of the four or five daily **buses** from the capital, head for Ukmergė and change there. Anykščiai's **tourist office**, just below the Baranauskas museum at Gegužės 1 (daily 9am–5pm; ☎8-381/59177, ⓦwww.antour.lt), can book you into a clutch of rural homestays (❶–❷), including several around Lake Rubikiai, 10km east of town – you'll need a car. The best **hotel** is the *Keturi Kalnai*, just east of the centre at Liudiškių 18 (☎8-612 26439, ⓦwww .keturikalnai.lt; ❹), with cosy en-suites, gym and outdoor tennis courts. A cheaper option is the *Puntukas*, in the centre at Baranausko 8 (☎8-381/51345; ❷), offering frumpy rooms with shared facilities and a handful of more expensive, smarter en-suites with TV. The cosiest of the **cafés** is *Erdvė*, on the main square, offering a full menu of meat and fish and bench seating in the yard. *Bangelė*, occupying a weir-side building above the River Šventoji, is a good place for a drink.

Niūronys

Six kilometres north of Anykščiai, just off the Rokiškis road, the village of **NIŪRONYS** is the site of the delightful **Museum of the Horse** (Arklio muziejus; daily 10am–6pm; 6Lt), an ensemble of five timber buildings arranged farmstead-style beside the main crossroads. Lithuania's relationship with the beast is explored through photographs of working horses through the ages, a recreated village smithy and a barn full of horse-drawn ploughs. This is far from a tribute to a disappearing culture: in fact, the use of horses on Lithuanian farms has increased over the last two decades, the break-up of Soviet-era collective farms having led to fewer tractors in circulation. Between spring and autumn, you'll see plenty of characteristically stocky, Lithuanian farm horses grazing in the fields outside, and there's a paddock where kids can ride ponies. Horse-and-carriage excursions (horse-and-sledge in winter) are a great way to take in the local countryside, but should be booked in advance (☎8-381/51722; if you can't get through to an English-speaker, Anykščiai tourist office might be able to help).

Three **buses** a day run to **Niūronys** from Anykščiai, or you could walk back to town through the gently undulating landscape of forest and pastureland (1hr 20min). The *Pasagelė* **café** next to the museum doles out scrumptious potato pancakes, a soup of the day, and more substantial pork dishes.

Biržai

The border town of **BIRŽAI** lies 200km north of Vilnius and 20km east of the main Vilnius–Rīga highway. It was put on the map by the Radvila family, who owned the town from the fifteenth to the nineteenth centuries, turning it into a flourishing trade centre and key military stronghold in the process. Nowadays, Biržai is a pretty uneventful place, but it's worth visiting for its **fortress**, attractively set in a leafy park at the northern end of the town's main artery, Vytauto gatvė, and lapped by the waters of Lake Širvėna.

The fortress is actually a twentieth-century **reconstruction** of a sixteenth-century original, built by Kristupas Radvila, "the Thunderer" (1547–1603). Surrounded by grassy ramparts and reached via a dainty drawbridge, it's an elegantly arcaded, Renaissance-style building that looks more like a stately home than a castle. The Radvilas, who had plenty of estates elsewhere in Lithuania, abandoned it after it was blown up by the Swedes in

Bėk, bėk, žirgelį

Only a horse-mad nation like the Lithuanians could come up with a **festival** entitled **Bėk, bėk, žirgelį** ("Run, ye little horse!"), a celebration of all things equine which takes place in the field below the Museum of the Horse on the first or second weekend in June – the Anykščiai tourist office will have full details. Farmers from all over the region descend on the village with their horses and traps, and large crowds assemble to watch a day-long programme of races involving everything from donkeys to thoroughbreds. There's also plenty in the way of craft stalls, beer tents and grilled food. Extra buses from Anykščiai are laid on for the occasion.

1704; what remained was put to the torch seven decades later as part of a lavish theatrical entertainment put on by the hooligan-aristocrat Karol Stanisław Radvila.

The fortress now houses the **Biržai District Museum** (Biržų krašto muziejus; Wed–Sun 9am–5pm; 4Lt), which sets off with a daunting collection of ancient swords and axe heads. Things pick up with a scale model of the fortress as it looked in the time of "the Thunderer", overlooked by striking portraits of Augustus II "the Strong" of Poland-Lithuania and Peter the Great of Russia – the pair met here in 1701 to agree on a common front against the invading Swedes. Upstairs, wooden Catholic saints throng a room dedicated to folk art.

A short stroll southeast through the park brings you to the gleaming-white **Church of St John the Baptist**, its twin nineteenth-century towers piled wedding-cake-style in three tiers. From the church, head east along Basanavičiaus, cross the Apaščia River and turn left up Malūno gatvė to reach the most picturesque part of reed-shrouded **Lake Širvėna**. A rickety footbridge leads over the heads of inquisitive swans to the lake's northern shore, where a wooded park surrounds the stately **Astravas Palace** (Astravo dvaras) – a summer retreat built by the Tyszkiewicz family after the Radvilas sold them the town of Biržai in 1812. You can't go inside, but it's a lovely sight, its mock-Renaissance lookout tower giving it the appearance of a grandiose village fire station.

Practicalities

Biržai is served by a handful of direct **buses** from Vilnius and by more frequent services from Panevėžys and Pašvalys. The bus station is at the northern end of Vytauto gatvė, near the castle park. Once you've done the rounds of the sights there's little reason to stay, but if you do decide to stop over, ask at the **tourist office**, Janonio 2 (Mon–Fri 9am–5pm; ℡8-450/33496, Ⓦwww.birzai.lt), for details of rural homestays (❶) in outlying villages. Otherwise the *Tyla* **hotel**, 2km north of the centre at Tylos 2 (℡8-450/31191, Ⓦwww.tyla.lt; ❹), is the only sure-fire source of accommodation in town. There are a couple of serviceable **cafés** on the main strip and a handful of gloomy beer bars serving up the local tipple, Biržų alus (Biržai beer).

Kaunas and around

With a population of 355,000, **KAUNAS** is the fourth-biggest city in the Baltic States, a bustling, metropolitan place and a major commercial centre. It served as the temporary capital of Lithuania for twenty years following World War I, and contains museums and galleries of national importance, yet still seems overwhelmingly provincial and self-absorbed in relation to Vilnius.

Kaunas's medieval **Old Town** still boasts an enjoyable ensemble of red-brick buildings and ice-cream-coloured churches, gathered around a handsome main square. Extending east of here along the shop- and café-lined Laisvės alėja, the **New Town** is characterized by the Art Deco buildings hastily thrown up during the interwar period to make Kaunas look worthy of its capital-city status. Strewn along the way are museums offering everything from fine art to folk sculpture and carnival masks. Out-of-town attractions include the Baroque monastery of **Pažaislis** and the superb open-air Museum of Lithuanian Life at **Rumšiškės**. Traces of the Jewish community that once thrived in Kaunas are thin on the ground; many were executed by the Nazis at **Ninth Fort**, located northwest of the city and preserved as a grimly moving memorial.

Just 100km west of Vilnius and easily reached by **bus or rail**, Kaunas can be treated as a day-trip from the capital – although you'll need a few days to get the most out of it and to explore some of the outlying attractions. Good transport links also make it an ideal base for the whole of central Lithuania.

Some history

Kaunas started out as a key **border stronghold**, defending Lithuania from frequent incursions from the Teutonic Knights. After the Battle of Žalgiris in 1410, the Teutonic danger receded, leaving Kaunas free to grow rich from commerce – its position on the

Nemunas River providing access to a network of trade routes. Several centuries of prosperity followed, marred only briefly by the sacking of the town by the Russians in 1655. Kaunas also became an important ecclesiastical centre, the city's Catholic **seminary** producing many of the nation's spiritual leaders.

The Russians decided to make Kaunas the linchpin of their western defences in the 1880s, thoroughly redeveloping the place and building a new city centre around a long straight boulevard (now Laisvės alėja; see p.301). They also built a ring of **nine forts**, although these were in such a state of disrepair by 1914 that commander-in-chief Grand Duke Nikolai suggested that the city's name be changed from Kovno (Russian for "Kaunas") to Govno (Russian for "shit"). The fortifications were in any case never put to the test: scared witless by the German offensive of summer 1915, Kaunas's commander General Grigoriev fled to Vilnius rather than lead the city's defence, for which he was sentenced to eight years' hard labour.

After World War I, Vilnius was occupied by the Poles, and Kaunas was declared the **"provisional" capital** of Lithuania. It seemed an unlikely seat of power, not least because it lacked the set-piece administrative buildings that a national capital needed. Visiting in the early 1920s, British traveller Owen Rutter found Kaunas to be "not worthy of the name city and, quite frankly, it is filthy. Moreover, its hotels are the worst in the Baltic States." By the 1930s, however, Kaunas had been transformed, with a rash of construction turning the city into a showroom for **modern architecture** – the Resurrection Church, Vytautas the Great War Museum and main Post Office being the principal surviving monuments from this go-ahead era.

In the wake of World War II, Kaunas lost its political role, but gained an important place in the national psyche. Taking in fewer Russian immigrants than other big centres, Kaunas remained a Lithuanian-speaking city, proudly aware of its status as a repository of national values. It was here that art student **Romas Kalanta** burnt himself to death in 1972 to protest against Soviet power, sparking days of rioting.

Initially slow to reap the benefits of post-independence economic change, Kaunas is now transforming itself into a modern European city. Quirky souvenir shops in the Old Town and chic, glass-fronted cafés along Laisvės alėja lend the place a welcoming and animated air. One thing that hasn't changed is the city's deep-seated feeling of inferiority vis-à-vis near-neighbour Vilnius – comments about the culture and sophistication of the capital are usually met here with silence and a grinding of teeth.

Arrival and information

Kaunas's **airport** is 12km northeast of the centre – minibus #120 runs into town. A taxi should cost 30–40Lt, although many drivers charge more. The **bus and train stations** are within 400m of each other on Vytauto prospektas on the eastern edges of the city centre. Trolleybuses #1, #5 and #7 will take you to Vilniaus gatvė in the centre.

The **tourist information centre**, Laisvės alėja 36 (Kauno regiono turizmo informacijos centras; April–Sept Mon–Fri 9am–6pm, Sat 10am–3pm; Oct–March Mon–Fri 9am–6pm; ☎8-37/323436, ⓦwww.kaunastic.lt), handles information about the whole region, including Birštonas (see p.313), and can help with accommodation. You can also pick up a copy of *Kaunas in Your Pocket* here (ⓦwww.inyourpocket.com; 6Lt), a reliable source of accommodation, restaurant and bar listings that is updated yearly – it's also available from bookstores, newspaper kiosks and some hotel foyers.

Accommodation

Kaunas has plenty of business-class **hotels**, and although budget and mid-range choices are thinner on the ground, they're not impossible to find. Many of the more expensive hotels offer weekend discounts – it always pays to ask. The cheapest beds in town are in **private rooms** downtown (from 140Lt double); Litinterp, Gedimino 28-7 (☎8-37/228718, ⓦwww.litinterp.lt), can set you up in one of these. *Kaunas Camping*, northwest of the centre at Jonavos 51A (☎8-618 09407), is little more than a parking lot for mobile homes and caravans, and although there is a small strip of grass for tents, it's only really suitable for a one-night stopover.

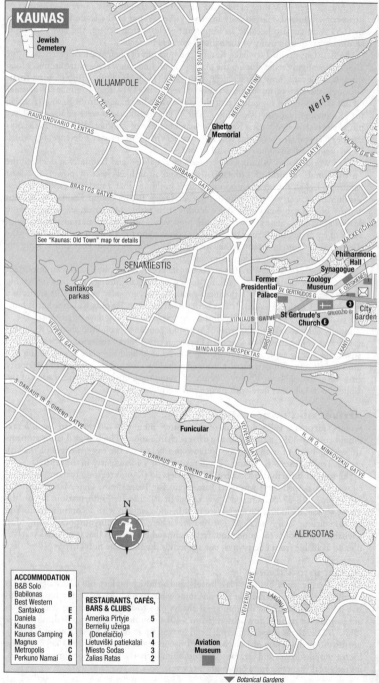

Ninth Fort & Klaipėda ▲

KAUNAS

Jewish
Cemetery

VILIJAMPOLE

LINKUVOS GATVĖ

PANERIU GATVĖ

TILŽES GATVĖ

NERIES KRANTINĖ

Neris

RAUDONDVARIO PLENTAS

**Ghetto
Memorial**

JURBARKO GATVĖ

JONAVOS GATVĖ

P. KALPOKO GATVĖ

BRASTOS GATVĖ

A. MACKEVIČIAUS

See "Kaunas: Old Town" map for details

SENAMIESTIS

**Philharmonic
Hall
Synagogue**

Former
Presidential
Palace

SV. GERTRUDOS G

**Zoology
Museum**

E. OŽEŠKIENĖS

Santakos
parkas

VILNIAUS GATVĖ

BIRŠTONO

**St Gertrude's
Church** E

GRUODŽIO G

3

**City
Garden**

VEIVERIU GATVĖ

MINDAUGO PROSPEKTAS

KANTO

S. DARIAUS IR S. GIRENO GATVĖ

Funicular

VEIVERIU GATVĖ

H. IR O. MINKOVSKIU GATVĖ

S. DARIAUS IR S. GIRENO GATVĖ

N

ALEKSOTAS

VEIVERIU GATVĖ

LAKUNU PL.

ACCOMMODATION	
B&B Solo	I
Babilonas	B
Best Western Santakos	E
Daniela	F
Kaunas	D
Kaunas Camping	A
Magnus	H
Metropolis	C
Perkuno Namai	G

RESTAURANTS, CAFÉS, BARS & CLUBS	
Amerika Pirtyje	5
Berneliu užeiga (Donelaičio)	1
Lietuviški patiekalai	4
Miesto Sodas	3
Žalias Ratas	2

**Aviation
Museum**

▼ Botanical Gardens

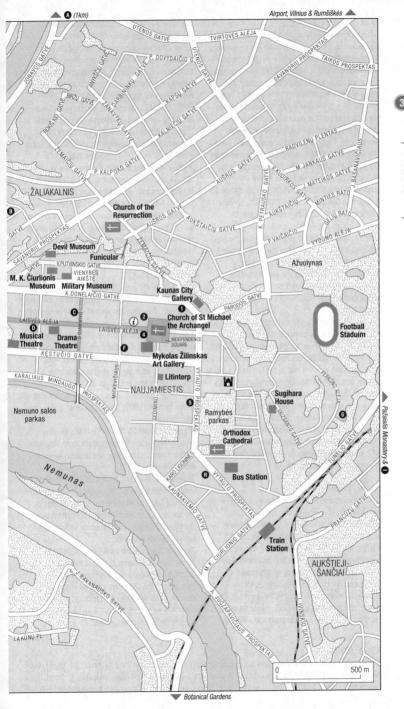

UTENOS GATVĖ
TVIRTOVĖS ALĖJA
JONAVOS GATVĖ
P. DOVYDAIČIO G.
SAVANORIŲ PROSPEKTAS
TAIKOS PROSPEKTAS
UTENOS GATVĖ
ANYKŠČIŲ GATVĖ
DARBININKŲ GATVĖ
BIRŽŲ GATVĖ
ŽANAVYKŲ GATVĖ
KAPSŲ GATVĖ
ROKIŠKIO GATVĖ
ŽEMAIČIŲ GATVĖ
KALNIEČIŲ GATVĖ
RADVILĖNŲ PLENTAS
M. JANKAUS GATVĖ
V. KUDIRKOS GATVĖ
J. MATEIKOS GATVĖ
J. BASANAVIČIAUS
P. KALPOKO GATVĖ
AUŠROS GATVĖ
K. PETRAUSKO GATVĖ
AUKŠTAIČIŲ
MINTIES RATO
GĖLIŲ RATO
ŽALIAKALNIS
Ⓑ
AUŠROS GATVĖ
AUKŠTAIČIŲ GATVĖ
P. VAIČAIČIO
VYDŪNO ALĖJA
GATVĖ
SAVANORIŲ PROSPEKTAS
GATVĖ
ŽEMAIČIŲ GATVĖ
Ažuolynas
Church of the Resurrection
✠
Devil Museum
Funicular
V. PUTVINSKIO GATVĖ
VIENYBĖS AIKŠTĖ
M. K. Čiurlionis Museum
Military Museum
K. DONELAIČIO GATVĖ
Kaunas City Gallery
❶
PARODOS GATVĖ
Football Staduim
LAISVĖS ALĖJA
Ⓒ
DAUKANTO
ⓘ
❷
Church of St Michael the Archangel
LAISVĖS ALĖJA
❹
✠
INDEPENDENCE SQUARE
Musical Theatre
Ⓓ
Drama Theatre
KĘSTUČIO GATVĖ
Ⓕ
Mykolas Žilinskas Art Gallery
KARALIAUS MINDAUGO
MICKEVIČIAUS
Litinterp
PERKŪNO ALĖJA
Ⓖ
KARALIAUS MINDAUGO PROSPEKTAS
GEDIMINO
NAUJAMIESTIS
🏠
Nemuno salos parkas
❺
VYTAUTO PROSPEKTAS
Ramybės parkas
Sugihara House
JUOZAPANTO GATVĖ
Nemunas
Orthodox Cathedral
✠
KARO LIGONINĖS
TUNELIO GATVĖ
Pažaislis Monastery & ❶ ▶
KAUNAKIEMIO GATVĖ
Ⓗ
VYTAUTO PROSPEKTAS
Bus Station
J. BAKANAUSKO GATVĖ
M. K. ČIURLIONIO GATVĖ
PRANCŪZŲ GATVĖ
Train Station
AUKŠTIEJI-ŠANČIAI
LAKŪNŲ PL.
A. JUOZAPAVIČIAUS PROSPEKTAS
LI VINSKIO GATVĖ

0   500 m

▼ *Botanical Gardens*

Old Town

The places reviewed below are marked on the Kaunas: Old Town map on opposite.

Apple Hotel Valančiaus 19 ☎8-37/321404, ⓦwww.applehotel.lt. Mid-sized hotel with welcoming green apple motifs adorning the lobby. The clean, bright en-suites come with small TV, pine furnishings and lino-like floors. Standard doubles are a bit cramped but most have attractive attic ceilings and skylights; "lux" doubles offer a bit more space. There are also a couple of four-person "family blocks": two adjacent doubles sharing a single WC/shower. The "museum of holiday souvenirs" in the stairwell is far cooler than it sounds. Breakfast costs a few litai extra. ❸–❹

Daugirdas Daugirdo 4 ☎8-37/301561, ⓦwww.daugirdas.lt. This hotel occupies a sixteenth-century house and its more modern neighbour – with a lofty, glass-roofed lobby occupying the gap between the two. Rooms offer the deep-carpeted comforts you'll find in any good international four-star. Bonuses include the barrel-vaulted, cellar-bound breakfast room, central location and attentive staff. Two rooms are wheelchair-accessible. ❼

Kaunas Archdiocesan Guesthouse (Kauno arkivyskupijos svečių namai) Rotušės aikštė 21 ☎8-37/322597, ⓦkaunas.lcn.lt/sveciunamai. Part of the seventeenth-century Kaunas archbishopric complex at the western end of the Old Town's main square, and used by the Soviet army before being returned to its original owners – who decided to turn it into a guesthouse. A selection of functional but well-cared-for singles, doubles, triples and quads, with high ceilings, parquet floors and small TVs. Most rooms are en-suite; some come with a WC/shower shared between two rooms. One room is wheelchair-accessible. ❷–❸

New Town

The accommodation reviewed below is marked on the Kaunas map on p.296.

B&B Solo Dysnos 10 ☎8-687 54443, ⓦwww.solohotel.lt. Suburban house in a quiet street, offering three self-contained studios with smart furnishings, fridge, TV, kettle and bathroom. The grassy back garden is also at your disposal. ❹

Babilonas Raseinių 25 ☎8-37/202545, ⓦwww.babilonas.lt. Lurking in the quiet streets of Žaliakalnis is this tall, thin hotel with five floors linked by a spiral staircase – hence the "Tower-of-Babel" moniker and the Babylon-inspired paintings in the rooms. The top-floor suite, with fireplace, circular dining table and fastastic views, is the most appealing, although the standard en-suites, with their pale pine furnishings, are attractive too. ❹–❻

Best Western Santakos Gruodžio 21 ☎8-37/302702, ⓦwww.santakahotel.eu. Swish hotel in a converted warehouse, offering atmospheric, spacious rooms with exposed brickwork and wood-beamed ceilings. Most feature bathtubs – ask for room #104 if you want to soak in an antique, claw-foot bathtub. Rooms in the modern annexe are smaller but just as classy – many have big windows with good downtown views. ❻

Daniela Mickevičiaus 28 ☎8-37/321505, ⓦwww.danielahotel.lt. Seventy-room downtown four-star just off the central Laisvės alėja, offering smallish, plush en-suites with primary-colour decor. More desirable are the top-floor, split-level suites with barrel-vaulted attic ceilings, and good views of the street below. ❻–❼

Kaunas Laisvės alėja 79 ☎8-37/750850, ⓦwww.kaunashotel.lt. Perfectly situated hotel on the main boulevard, occupying an elegant early-twentieth-century building with a modern metallic-cube annexe sprouting from the rear. Standard rooms feature primary colours and modern, pale-wood furnishings. Deluxe doubles are roomier – the upper-storey ones on the northern side offer a striking panorama of Laisvės alėja. Breakfast is in a folksy basement restaurant, and there's also a free gym and sauna (free at off-peak times) on site. ❺–❻

Magnus Vytauto 25 ☎8-37/340000, ⓦwww.magnushotel.com. Smart modern three-star, notable for its moderate prices and location opposite the bus station. ❸

Metropolis Daukanto 21 ☎8-37/205992, ⓦwww.metropolishotel.com. Charmingly old-world establishment that retains some fine period fittings in the public spaces, even though rooms themselves are bland. En-suites with TV, some with bathtubs rather than showers. ❸

Perkūno Namai Perkūno 61 ☎8-37/320230, ⓦwww.perkuno-namai.lt. One of the better business-class options if you don't mind being 2km east of the Old Town. Located in a quiet residential neighbourhood, it features roomy en-suites with Scandinavian-style furnishings, and friendly, attentive management. ❻

The City

Kaunas's medieval **Old Town** (Senamiestis) sits near the confluence of the rivers Nemunas and Neris; at its centre is the main square, **Rotušės aikštė**, graced by a splendid Town Hall. Within easy reach lie a handful of impressive medieval churches

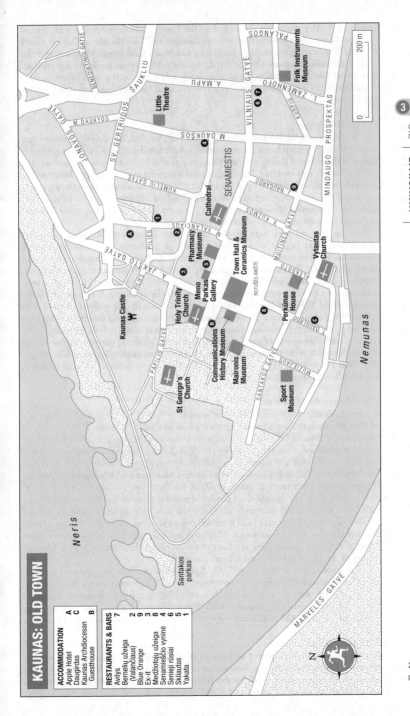

KAUNAS: OLD TOWN

ACCOMMODATION
Apple Hotel   A
Daugirdas   C
Kaunas Archdiocesan   B
Guesthouse

RESTAURANTS & BARS
Avilys   7
Bernelių užeiga   2
(Valančiaus)
Blue Orange   9
Ex-it   3
Medžiotojų užeiga   8
Senamiesčio vyninė   4
Senieji rūsiai   6
Skilautas   5
Yakata   1

Folk Instruments Museum

Little Theatre

Cathedral

SENAMIESTIS

Pharmacy Museum

Meno Parkas Gallery

Town Hall & Ceramics Museum

Holy Trinity Church

Kaunas Castle

Communications History Museum

Maironis Museum

St George's Church

Vytautas Church

Perkūnas House

ROTUŠĖS AIKŠTĖ

Sport Museum

Nemunas

Neris

Santakos parkas

MARVELES GATVE

200 m

0

Streets: BENEDIKTINŲ GATVE, M. DAUKŠOS, ŠV. GERTRUDOS, ŠAUKLIŲ, JONAKOS GATVE, M. DAUKOS, KUMELIŲ GATVE, M. VALANČIAUS, PILIES, A. JAKŠTO GATVE, PAPILIO GATVE, SANTAKOS GATVE, MUZIEJAUS, DAUGIRDO, ALEKSOTO, MUITINES GATVE, V. KUZMOS, V. NAUGARDO, MINDAUGO PROSPEKTAS, KURPIŲ, L. ZAMENHOFO, VILNIAUS GATVE, A. MAPŲ, PALANGOS and some quirky museums. East of the Old Town extends the nineteenth-century **New Town** (Naujamiestis), cut by pedestrianized **Laisvės alėja**. Off here lie a number of rewarding museums, including the **M.K. Čiurlionis Museum** and the eccentric **Devil Museum**. On the outskirts, leafy **Ąžuolynas park** and the tranquil **Botanical Gardens** provide pleasant retreats, while just to the west of the centre, the suburb of **Vilijampolė** preserves a few traces of the city's once-thriving Jewish community.

Rotušės aikštė

The broad expanse of **Rotušės aikštė** (Town Hall Square), lined with fifteenth- and sixteenth-century merchants' houses in pastel shades, is dominated by the magnificent **Town Hall**, its tiered Baroque facade rising to a graceful 53m-tall tower. Known as the "White Swan", this building dates back to the sixteenth century and has been used as an Orthodox church, a theatre and a university department, though these days it is best known as the city's main register office. The vaulted cellar provides an atmospheric home for a **Ceramics Museum** (Tues–Sun 11am–5pm; 4Lt), displaying work by some of the best of contemporary Lithuania's applied artists.

Over on the northern side of the square, the **Pharmacy Museum** (Tues–Sat 10am–5pm; 3Lt) begins with a dull history of medicine but picks up with a reconstructed nineteenth-century pharmacy, full of decorative storage cabinets and exotic glass vials. A few doors along at no. 26, the **Meno parkas** art gallery (Mon–Fri 10am–6pm, Sat 10am–4pm; free) is one of Kaunas's best venues for high-profile contemporary exhibitions. Looming towards you at the western end of the square is the Baroque **Holy Trinity Church**, its towers topped with cast-iron crosses adorned with sun motifs. Behind it lies a dignified group of creamy-coloured buildings belonging to Kaunas seminary, traditionally the most important seat of Catholic learning in the country, and a key centre of intellectual resistance to Tsarism in the years before World War I. Next door is the **Communications History Museum** (Ryšių istorijos muziejus; Wed–Sun 10am–4pm; 5Lt), home to a mildly diverting collection of postal uniforms and telephones through the ages.

The Maironis Museum and the Sport Museum

A smooth, granite statue just off the southwestern corner of Rotušės aikštė honours one of Kaunas seminary's most famous rectors, **Jonas Mačiulis-Maironis** (1862–1932), an enthusiastic patron of Lithuanian culture who also wrote lyric poetry suffused with love for the motherland – his *Voices of Spring* (1895) is the most widely read volume of verse in Lithuania. Behind the statue, the eighteenth-century town house where Maironis lived during his rectorship is now the **Maironis Museum of Lithuanian Literature** (Maironio lietuvių literatūros muziejus; Tues–Sat 9am–5pm; closed on last Friday of each month; 5Lt). The ground-floor display of materials chronicling the development of Lithuanian literature is frustratingly labelled in the local language only – and the sight of exhibits like Šatrijos Ragana's cello is unlikely to mean much to people who have never read her novellas. Upstairs, however, Maironis's perfectly preserved living quarters boast some of the most eye-catching interiors in the whole of the country, with a fabulous display of Art Deco and folk-inspired wall coverings.

A few steps south, at Muziejaus 7, the **Sport Museum** (Lietuvos sporto muziejus; Wed–Sat: summer 10am–6pm; winter 9am–5pm; 2Lt) presents a very different perspective on the nation's cultural history, with photographs of champion basketball teams and gold-medal Olympians – with discus throwers Romas Ubartas (Barcelona 1992) and Virgilius Alekna (Sydney 2000 and Athens 2004) – occupying centre stage.

The Cathedral

Just off the northeastern corner of Rotušės aikštė on Vilniaus gatvė, Kaunas's austere, red-brick **Cathedral** (Katedros Basilika) dates back to the reign of Vytautas the Great, although it has been much rebuilt since. After the plain exterior, the vivacious interior, full of brightly coloured frescoes and plaster cherubs looking down from pillars, comes as something of a surprise. There are nine altars in total, with the large, statue-adorned, Baroque high altar (1775) by Tomasz Podhayski stealing the limelight.

Kaunas Castle and around

Pre-dating the cathedral by several centuries is **Kaunas Castle** (Kauno pilis), the scant remains of which lie just northwest of the square. Little more than a restored tower and a couple of sections of wall are left, the rest having been washed away by the Neris, but in its day the fortification was a major obstacle to the Teutonic Knights. The fifteenth-century **St George's Church** (Šv Jurgio bažnyčia), next door, is an impressive Gothic pile in crumbling red brick, where restoration has so far done little to arrest fifty years of decay. West of here, foot- and cycle-paths converge on the spit of land where the river Neris flows into the Nemunas.

The Perkūnas House and the Vytautas Church

There's better-preserved Gothic finery south of the main square. The **Perkūnas House** (Perkūno namas) at Aleksoto 6 is an elaborately gabled, red-brick structure, thought to have been built as a merchants' meeting hall or possibly a Jesuit chapel, standing on the reputed site of a temple to Perkūnas, the pagan god of thunder (a statue of the god was found on the site in the nineteenth century). From here Aleksoto descends to the banks of the Nemunas and the glowering **Vytautas Church** (Vytauto bažnyčia), built by Vytautas the Great in around 1399 to give thanks for his deliverance from the armies of the Tatars. During its long existence it has suffered various indignities, including use as a munitions magazine and potato store, and, like many other Lithuanian churches, it also had a stint as an Orthodox place of worship.

Laisvės alėja and the Presidential Palace

Running east from the Old Town through Kaunas's **Naujamiestis** (New Town) is **Laisvės alėja** (Freedom Avenue), a broad, pedestrianized shopping street. The whole street was, bizarrely, a no-smoking zone from 1990 until 2000, when the city council finally gave up trying to enforce it. At the western end of Laisvės, near the junction with Vilniaus, an elegant, ochre mansion in a well-tended park served as the **Presidential Palace** (Prezidentūra; Tues–Sun 11am–5pm; ⓦ www.istorineprezidentura.lt; 4Lt) during Kaunas's period as the provisional capital, and now houses a history museum honouring its four interwar occupants – Antanas Smetona, Jonas Stamgaitis, Aleksandras Stulginskis and Antanas Merkys. Smetona enjoyed the longest stint in the presidential hot seat, and Smetona-related memorabilia unsurprisingly takes up most space in the elegant sequence of staterooms. However, the most revered relic in the collection – unsurprisingly for this basketball-mad country – is the ceremonial casket awarded to European champions Lithuania when they won the trophy for the second time in 1939.

St Gertrude's Church

Opposite the palace, a passageway leads off Laisvės into a yard containing **St Gertrude's Church** (Šv Gertrudos bažnyčia; Mon–Sat 10am–7pm, Sun 7.30am–noon), a fourteenth-century, red-brick structure so dwarfed by the surrounding apartment blocks that it looks more like a clay-house lantern souvenir than a church. Inside there's an ornate Baroque pulpit topped by a gesticulating statue of St John Nepomuk, and a much-venerated crucifix on the high altar – you'll see the devout crawling round it on their knees.

The Zoology Museum

Back on Laisvės, the **Tadas Ivanauskas Zoology Museum** (Kauno Tado Ivanausko zoologijos muziejus; Tues–Sun 11am–7pm; 5Lt) at no. 106 is a three-floor collection of stuffed and pickled creatures. It's all great fun and pretty self-explanatory, although the armadillo-to-zebra display of mammals on the ground floor is probably worth saving until last.

The City Garden

Opposite a bronze **statue of Vytautas the Great**, the fifteenth-century Grand Duke who extended Lithuania's borders as far as the Black Sea, the **City Garden** (Miesto sodas) is where, on May 14, 1972, the 19-year-old art student Romas Kalanta immolated himself in protest against Soviet rule. The act sparked several days of anti-Soviet rioting, and an estimated five hundred people were arrested. Kalanta's act is commemorated by local sculptor Robertas Antinis's memorial sculpture *Field of Sacrifice*, a rust-coloured assemblage of horizontal shards. The southern end of the park is marked by the **Musical Theatre**, the country's prime venue for operetta and the site – in May 1929 – of an attempt on the life of Prime Minister Augustinas Voldemaras. The assassin missed, killing the PM's grand-nephew instead.

The Choral Synagogue

Making a brief detour north from the City Garden up Sapiegos brings you to the nineteenth-century **Choral Synagogue** (Choralinė sinagoga; daily 6–6.30pm; Sat also 10am–noon) at Ožeškienės 17, the sole Jewish place of worship left in a city that could once boast them by the handful. The sky-blue, balustraded interior contains an intricately carved Aron ha Kodesh, or high altar, which somehow survived the Nazi occupation. In the yard behind the synagogue is another striking monument by Robertas Antinis, this time honouring the child victims of the Holocaust with a slab of metal studded with tiny stars.

Vienybės aikštė and the Military Museum

Kaunas celebrates its role in sustaining Lithuanian national identity on **Unity Square** (Vienybės aikštė), at the junction of S. Daukanto and K. Donelaičio, a block north of Laisvės. Here a **monument** depicting Liberty as a female figure faces an eternal flame flanked by traditional wooden crosses. Overlooking all this is the **Military Museum of Vytautas the Great** (Vytauto Didžiojo karo muziejus; Tues–Sun 9am–5pm; closed last Thurs of every month; 4Lt), a grey, angular symbol of interwar modernity

---

Darius and Girėnas

Most European nations had aviator heroes in the interwar years, and in **Darius and Girėnas**, Lithuania was not to be left out. Taken to live in the US at an early age, Steponas "Stephen" Darius (1896–1933) and Stasys "Stanley" Girėnas (1893–1933) both fought with US forces in World War I, learning to fly towards the war's end. Darius was the more flamboyant, winning a Purple Heart for bravery in 1918, and turning up in Lithuania to take part in the seizure of Klaipėda in 1923 (see p.330). A sports nut who excelled at just about every activity that involved kicking, throwing or hitting a ball, Darius was also influential in turning basketball into Lithuania's most popular team game.

Darius had long dreamed of flying non-stop from New York to Kaunas and enlisted Girėnas as his co-pilot. Money raised by the Lithuanian community in North America helped fund the purchase of a secondhand plane, which they named the *Lituanica*. They took off on July 15, 1933, only to crash two days later in an East Prussian forest, tantalizingly short of their target. As the first famous dead Lithuanians of the modern media age, Darius and Girėnas were quickly enshrined as national martyrs. Their embalmed bodies were on display until 1944, when they were banished to a storeroom by a Soviet regime that disapproved of patriotic cults. In 1964 they were finally laid to rest at Aukštieji Šančiai cemetery in the southeast of the city, but public remembrance of their exploits was broadly discouraged.

Post-independence, Lithuania has been quick to restore Darius and Girėnas to the national pantheon: the pair feature on the 10Lt banknote, and have been honoured with a monument next to the Kaunas sports stadium that bears their name. A scale model of the *Lituanica* hangs from the ceiling of the departure lounge of Vilnius airport, although it's not clear whether this is intended to inspire travellers or scare them witless.

completed in 1937. Inside, swords, pikes and scale models of stockade forts conjure up the martial vigour of the medieval Lithuanian state, while the independence struggles of 1918–20 are remembered in an impressive display of uniforms and weaponry. The museum also functions as a shrine to the Lithuanian pilots Darius and Girėnas (see opposite). One room displays poignant pictures of the pair being feted at farewell dinners before their departure from New York, while the ripped and blood-spattered shirts they were wearing when they crashed are kept in a case nearby. Preserved in an enormous glass box upstairs, the wreckage of their bright-orange plane, the *Lituanica*, looks more like a contemporary art installation than a tragic relic.

The M.K. Čiurlionis Art Museum
Part of the same building as the Military Museum, the **M.K. Čiurlionis Art Museum** (M.K. Čiurlionio dailės muziejus; Tues–Sun: summer noon–6pm; winter 11am–5pm;

Mikalojus Konstantinis Čiurlionis (1875–1911)

Born in the southeastern town of Varėna and raised in the spa resort of Druskininkai, Lithuania's **most famous painter and composer** was introduced to music by his father, who was the organist at Liškiava church (see p.322). The talented youth soon caught the attention of Count Michał Ogiński, who installed Čiurlionis in his private music school in Plungė, and went on to finance further study abroad. Čiurlionis graduated from the Warsaw Conservatoire in 1899, and was set to continue his studies in Leipzig when Ogiński died and the money dried up. Equipped with a sound grasp of musical theory however, Čiurlionis set about composing lengthy symphonic pieces, the best known of which are the tone poems *In the Forest* (*Miške*; 1900) and *The Sea* (*Jūra*; 1907). At the same time Čiurlionis was pursuing his career as an artist, enrolling in the newly opened Warsaw School of Fine Arts in 1904.

Čiurlionis held the Lithuanians to be a uniquely spiritual nation, who were closer to their Indo-European origins than many of their neighbours and therefore represented a bridge between European religions and Eastern mysticism. He believed that Lithuanian spirituality was expressed in its folk art, and – even though he didn't always use folk imagery in his own paintings – he strongly advocated a return to folk traditions in order to develop a true Lithuanian culture.

Like many urbanized Lithuanians of his generation however, Čiurlionis grew up speaking Polish, and only mastered Lithuanian after 1907 on the promptings of his fiancée, the essayist and critic Sofia Kymantaitė. In 1907 the couple helped to organize the first Lithuanian Art Exhibition in Vilnius, hoping to raise public perception of the arts in general and Čiurlionis's own paintings in particular. The response was disappointingly lukewarm. Unable to make a living from painting or composing in Vilnius, Čiurlionis headed for St Petersburg in 1909 in the hope of breaking into the flourishing art scene there. His work made a big impression on critics and fellow painters, but none of the local dealers offered him an exhibition. Back in Vilnius, lack of both money and an appreciative audience drove Čiurlionis into apathy, depression and, ultimately, serious mental illness. Thus weakened, he was unable to withstand the onslaught of pneumonia, and died at a sanatorium outside Warsaw on April 10, 1911.

Within a decade of his death, Lithuania was an independent state desperately in need of cultural icons, and Čiurlionis fitted the bill perfectly. An art museum bearing his name was established in 1925, and proceeded to buy all Čiurlionis's paintings from his widow. The symphonic poems, hardly ever performed during their composer's lifetime, became regular fixtures in the repertoire of the Lithuanian Philharmonic.

In the early years of the Soviet occupation, Čiurlionis's taste for mysticism was considered decadent and reactionary, and it wasn't until the late 1960s that the local communist party began to curry intellectual favour by readmitting Čiurlionis to the national pantheon. Nowadays, Čiurlionis's soulful, contemplative art is considered to be one of the most eloquent expressions of the Lithuanian national character.

closed last Tues of every month; 6Lt), houses an exhaustive collection of pictures by Lithuania's greatest artist. During his short career (he died of pneumonia at the age of 36 in 1911), Čiurlionis created a unique body of work, producing enigmatic paintings influenced by the French Symbolists, many of them suffused with religious imagery. A composer as well as a painter, Čiurlionis believed that the feelings aroused by symphonic music could also be expressed in two-dimensional art – the dreamy, pulsating and often hypnotic results of his labours are on show by the cartload here. He produced small-format watercolours and pastels for the most part, rendering them in hazy greens, yellows and blues, and giving them contemplative titles like *Sorrow*, *Truth* or *Thought*. Castles, mountains and rivers feature prominently in his works, but they're often lost in wavy washes of colour – leading some to claim him as a precursor of abstract art.

There's also a solid collection of Lithuanian art from the interwar years, when Kaunas was the site of the country's one art school. Particularly striking are the Expressionist landscapes of bendy trees and collapsing skies produced by Antanas Samuolis (1899–1942), and the Gauguin-esque portraits of Viktoras Vizgirda (1904–93). You'll also see a good deal of Lithuanian folk art, notably the wooden statuettes of saints that traditionally decorate wayside shrines.

The Devil Museum

Kaunas has a second unique art collection in the shape of the **A. Žmuidzinavičius Art Museum**, at Putvinskio 64 (A. Žmuidzinavičiaus kūrinių ir rinkinių muziejus; Tues–Sun: June–Sept noon–6pm; winter 11am–5pm; closed last Tues of every month; 6Lt). Better known as the **Devil Museum** (Velnių muziejus), this houses a vast collection of figures put together by the artist Antanas Žmuidzinavičius (1876–1966), who devoted his life to the collection of all kinds of folk art, specializing in the demonic masks worn by Lithuanian revellers at Shrovetide – when the spirit of winter is driven away by donning Hallowe'en-like disguises. There's an extensive display of the masks here, sporting fearsome horns, yellow teeth and lolling red tongues. Ranged elsewhere are all manner of devil-related objects donated to the museum by artists both domestic and foreign, including some rather desirable Latvian crockery decorated with cavorting, impish forms. Although there's a lot of disappointing junk, too (think pitchfork-wielding garden gnomes), some exhibits will stick in the memory – look out for Kazys Derškevičius's sinister representation of Hitler and Stalin as devils dancing on a Lithuania composed of skulls. The museum also has an impressive collection of more mainstream wooden folk sculpture, with several representations of the Rupintojėlis, or "Sorrowful Christ", a popular subject in Lithuanian folk art, in which Christ is traditionally depicted seated with his head in his hands. Other sculptures include a squadron of dragon-spearing St Georges, and numerous depictions of St Isidore – shown scattering seed from a flaxen bag, the sower-saint is a typical example of Lithuanian religious syncretism, mixing Catholic iconography with pagan fertility symbols of the pre-Christian era.

Church of St Michael the Archangel

Marking the eastern end of Laisvės alėja, the silver-domed **Church of St Michael the Archangel** (Igulos bažnyčia) stands imperiously over Nepriklausomybes aikštė ("Independence Square"). Originally an Orthodox church built for the Tsarist garrison in the 1890s, this neo-Byzantine structure has preserved its military associations despite several changes of regime and denomination, serving as the (Protestant) German army church in World War I, and becoming the (Catholic) Lithuanian army church immediately afterwards. Its bare interior is a reflection of the fact that it was an art gallery for most of the Soviet period. A garish modern altar painting of the Archangel adds a dash of colour, and a side altar to the right harbours a superb Rupintojėlis, or "Sorrowful Christ", sculpture. Downstairs, a so-called **Museum for the Blind**, initiated by Kaunas University students in 2005, aims to raise awareness about the problems of the unsighted by encouraging sighted people to spend time in a light-free environment in which they must survive by touch alone. Opening hours are irregular: ask at the Kaunas tourist office (see p.295).

The Mykolas Žilinskas Art Gallery

Occupying a contemporary building in the northeast corner of Nepriklausomybės aikštė, the **Mykolas Žilinskas Art Gallery** (Mykolo Žilinsko dailės galerija; June–Sept Tues–Sun noon–6pm; Oct–May 11am–5pm; closed last Tues of every month; 6Lt) showcases the globe-spanning collection of fine and applied art amassed by the Kaunas-born Žilinskas, who prospered in German business circles after 1945. Dominating a room of Egyptian amulets, Roman glassware and Ming vases is a show-stopping eighteenth-century set of over fifty ceramic figures representing the apotheosis of Catherine the Great – as well as the Empress herself, there are Greek gods, and figures in Turkish and Tatar garb representing the grateful subject nations of the Russian Empire. Less ostentatious, but still too good to eat your dinner off, are Art Deco plates from the 1920s and propagandist porcelain from Soviet Russia decorated with Cubist workers waving hammers and sickles. Among the paintings are several roomfuls of Flemish and Italian masters: Žilinskas's favourite painting was the turbulent maritime scene of *On the Coast of the Strong Sea* by Leonardo Coccarante (1680–1750), although visitors will also be drawn by Lithuania's only Rubens, a sombrely effective *Crucifixion*. Outside the gallery, Petras Mozūras's towering statue of an unabashedly naked man is something of a local talking point.

The Kaunas City Gallery

A short distance northeast of Nepriklausomybės aikštė, the **Kaunas City Gallery** (Kaono paveikslų galerja; Tues–Sun 11am–5pm; 4Lt) houses another artistic donation

Chiune Sugihara (1900–86)

A career diplomat and Russian specialist in the Japanese foreign ministry, **Chiune Sugihara** was posted to Kaunas as Japanese consul in March 1939 in order to report on Soviet intentions in the region. When Soviet forces occupied Lithuania in July 1940, most foreign diplomats were ordered to leave without delay, but Sugihara and the Dutch consul, Jan Zwartendijk, were allowed to stay for one more month.

At the time, thousands of Jewish refugees from Nazi-occupied western Poland were arriving in Kaunas, only to discover that the Soviet authorities refused to give them transit visas unless they first obtained valid visas for their next destination. As the only representative of a country bordering the Soviet Union left in the city, Sugihara was besieged with requests for help. However, he couldn't give the refugees normal Japanese entry visas because of objections from his ministry in Tokyo, so he opted instead to hand out Japanese transit visas – under the pretence that the refugees were ultimately bound for Dutch colonies in the east. Local Soviet officials turned a blind eye to Sugihara's scheme, but approval from Tokyo was slow in coming – so Sugihara simply went ahead on his own initiative, writing out the relevant documents by hand, thereby providing an estimated six thousand people with passage out of the country. When he finally left Kaunas on September 1, he presented his consular stamp to a refugee so that more visas could be issued on his behalf. Sugihara went on to serve in the Japanese embassy in Prague, but was sacked by the foreign ministry in 1945 – a belated punishment for his refusal to do things by the book in Kaunas.

Sugihara built a career as a businessman after the war and remained ignorant of the fate of those he had helped escape, until a survivor sought him out in 1969. Enthused by the renewal of old contacts, Sugihara visited Israel the same year. However, he remained largely unrecognized until 1984, when the Yad Vashem Institute declared him one of the "Righteous Among the Nations" – the title given to gentiles who took personal risks to save Jewish lives. See p.377 for details of Hillel Levine's warts-and-all biography of Sugihara, published in 1996.

by a rich local-born Lithuanian, Algimantas Miškinas – his collection takes in minor works by most twentieth-century Lithuanian artists, but lacks any real highlights. Rather more interesting are the pieces relating to the Fluxus movement of the 1960s, a loose group of avant-garde artists inspired by Lithuanian-born New Yorker George Maciunas. In the entrance hall, Ay-O's *Black Hole dedicated to George Maciunas* is an interactive piece you need to experience for yourself; the Fluxus Room upstairs contains more graphics by the same artist, plus plenty of other materials relating to the movement.

Žaliakalnis and the Church of the Resurrection

On the northern side of Putvinskio lies the lower station of a 1930s **funicular railway** (funikulierius; daily 7am–7pm; 0.50Lt), operated by a pair of beautifully maintained, almost museum-piece vehicles, each presided over by a red-uniformed conductor. The funicular climbs up to **Žaliakalnis** (Green Hill), a leafy residential area favoured by the Kaunas middle classes during the interwar years. Near the upper terminal is the **Church of the Resurrection** (Prisikėlimo bažnyčia), a masterpiece of 1930s architecture whose soaring tower is topped by a slender cross. Having served as a radio factory during the communist period, the church has undergone thorough restoration in the years since Soviet occupation, its bright-white paint job adding a touch of futuristic glamour to the Kaunas skyline. A lift (Mon–Fri noon–6pm, Sat & Sun 11am–6pm; 5Lt) ascends the first 30m of the 70m-high belfry to an expansive **viewing terrace** on the church's roof, affording panoramic views in every direction.

East of the centre: the Sugihara House and Ąžuolynas

Just east of the bus and train stations paths lead up to another prosperous area of quiet, residential streets – the kind of place where foreign diplomats set up home during the period when Kaunas was the provisional capital. One of these was Chiune Sugihara (see p.305), the unassuming consul who has been dubbed "Japan's Schindler" for his action in supplying thousands of Jewish refugees with Japanese visas – allowing them to escape a city threatened by Nazi invasion. The **Sugihara House** (May–Sept Mon–Fri 10am–5pm, Sat & Sun 11am–4pm; Oct–April Mon–Fri 11am–3pm; 10Lt), occupying the consul's former home at Vaizganto 30, displays fascinating photographic evidence of Sugihara's activities – one picture shows him still issuing visas from the window of a train compartment moments before his final departure from the city.

From the Sugihara House it's a short walk northeast to the **Darius and Girėnas Sports Stadium**, which, as the best equipped in the country, is where the Lithuanian football team play most of their matches. Immediately behind it lies **Ąžuolynas** ("oakwood"), a wonderfully leafy square-kilometre of park filled with ash, elm, lime and oak.

West of the centre: Vilijampolė

Before World War II, Kaunas, like Vilnius, had a large **Jewish population**. Nearly all were killed during the war and little remains of their presence. The main area of Jewish settlement was **Vilijampolė** (known for much of its history by the Russian name of Slobodka), a suburb just across the Neris from the Old Town, and it was here that the Nazis created a closed ghetto in July 1941. An attractive grid of timber houses, today's Vilijampolė contains little in the way of memorials to the people who once lived and died here. A granite obelisk at the junction of Linkuvos and Kriščiukaičio bears an inscription in Lithuanian and Hebrew stating simply that "on this spot stood the gates of the Kaunas ghetto 1941–44". From here you'll have to zigzag your way north through residential streets to find a small (and easily missed) plaque at Goštautų 4 that marks the former location of the ghetto hospital, burned down by the Nazis on October 4, 1941, with staff and patients still inside. Finally, there's an overgrown, barely accessible **Jewish cemetery** (Senosios žydų kapinės) clinging to a hillside in the northwest of the suburb, just off Kalnų.

Jewish Kaunas

Jews first came to Kaunas in the early fifteenth century at the invitation of Grand Duke Vytautas the Great, and were settled in **Vilijampolė** in order to keep them separate from the Lithuanian population of the city centre. Vilijampolė remained the focus of the Jewish community in Kaunas for the next five centuries, although they also settled in the Old Town in the years before World War I. On the eve of World War II, there were approximately 35,000 Jews in Kaunas (of which six thousand lived in Vilijampolė), about forty percent of the city's total.

Although there was little social integration between the Jewish and Lithuanian populations of prewar Kaunas, outbreaks of explicit anti-Semitism were rare. However, the arrival of the German troops on June 23, 1941 unleashed an unexpectedly ferocious wave of popular violence. On June 25, Lithuanian gangs ran riot in Vilijampolė, killing an estimated one thousand civilians and decapitating chief rabbi Zalman Ossovsky. Two days later in central Kaunas, a group of over fifty Jews was driven onto the forecourt of the Lietūkis garage and clubbed to death by the locals, with German soldiers looking on.

On July 10, all the city's Jews were herded into the newly established ghetto in Vilijampolė. Many were relieved by the move, thinking that this would protect them from the violence. However, regular "actions", in which arbitrarily chosen groups of Jews were rounded up and shot by the Germans, became commonplace as the autumn of 1941 wore on. The enthusiasm of the local Lithuanian population for anti-Semitic excesses continued to astound even the Germans. Colonel Jäger of Einsatzgruppe A, the organization charged with organizing mass killings throughout northeastern Europe, notoriously reported that Kaunas, "where trained Lithuanian volunteers are available in sufficient numbers, is comparatively speaking a shooting paradise."

From the start it was clear that those members of the community required by the Germans for work duty stood a good chance of surviving (for the time being), while the others were likely to be murdered. This placed Jewish leaders – who controlled the distribution of work permits – in the unenviable position of deciding who lived and died. Some argued that a refusal to issue any work permits at all would be the only morally correct action to take, until the new chief rabbi Abraham Dov Shapiro decreed that an attempt to save some Jewish lives was better than no attempt at all. On October 28, the Jews of Vilijampolė were assembled by their community leaders so that several thousand of them could be selected for work duties by the SS. Of the 20,000-plus that were surplus to requirements, approximately ten thousand were taken away and shot within weeks – most were murdered in the notorious Ninth Fort (see below) just outside the city.

Despite frequent actions and arbitrary shootings, Vilijampolė's surviving Jews attempted to preserve a semblance of normal life in the years that followed. The able-bodied continued to work in factories inside and outside the ghetto, squares were ploughed up and used to grow vegetables, and a 35-piece ghetto orchestra gave regular concerts. In April 1944, the Germans decided to clear the ghetto of its remaining eight thousand inhabitants. The women were sent to Stutthof, the men to Dachau, where 75 percent of them perished. By the time the Red Army arrived in August there were no Jews left in Kaunas – save for the fortunate handful who had found hiding places in the city or had escaped to join partisans in the surrounding forests. After the war, most survivors moved to Vilnius or emigrated entirely, and the local Jewish population currently stands at just over one thousand. The wonderfully restored synagogue on Ožeškienės gatvė (see p.302) functions as their social and spiritual centre.

The Ninth Fort

Many of Kaunas's Jews ended their lives at the **Ninth Fort** (Devintasis fortas) on the northwestern fringes of the city, one of several forts built around Kaunas by the Russians in the lead-up to World War II, and known by their numbers ever since. The Ninth Fort was used by the Lithuanians as a camp for political prisoners during the interwar years, was subsequently used by the Soviet NKVD in 1940, and then transformed into a holding prison and killing ground by the Nazis from June 1941 onwards. It's thought that as many as fifty thousand people lost their lives here over the next four years – at least thirty thousand of them were Jews from Kaunas or the surrounding region: the others came from locations as diverse as Munich and Marseilles.

Surrounded by banked-up earthworks, the fort forms the centrepiece of a large park criss-crossed by paths and planted with trees. A flagstoned avenue leads to a huge Soviet-era memorial, a jagged concrete outcrop pitted with the shapes of human faces and fists. Like all such monuments of the period, it's dedicated to the "victims of Fascism" and fails to mention the Jews by name – Soviet ideology always denied the true nature of the Holocaust in an attempt to portray Marxism-Leninism as the sole target of Nazi hatred. Nearby, smaller, post-1991 memorials honour particular communities of Jews who ended up here; a sign indicates one of the trenches where many of them were shot.

A doorway in a red-brick wall leads through to the **Ninth Fort Museum** (Wed–Sun 10am–4pm; 6Lt), which occupies a series of dark grey chambers that served as soldiers' dormitories during the Tsarist period, and prisoners' cells after that. Displays cover the fort's role as a Tsarist Russian garrison and its subsequent use as a Lithuanian political prison, before moving on to cover the Jewish experience in World War II. Among the poignant reminders of those incarcerated here is a section of glass-covered wall covered in graffiti by those about to be murdered – "we are 500 Frenchmen," wrote Abraham Wechsler of Limoges. An additional **"New Museum"** (same times, same ticket), in the concrete wedge-shaped building on the northeastern side of the complex, covers the Soviet occupation, deportations of 1941 and 1949, and the survival struggles of Lithuanian exiles in Siberia.

The Ninth Fort lies 4km northwest of central Kaunas, right beside the main highway to Klaipėda. **To get there**, catch any westbound inter-city service from the main bus station and get off when you see the memorial on your left.

Pažaislis monastery

Some 7km east of the city centre, the Baroque **Pažaislis monastery** (Pažaislio vienuolynas) is worth visiting as much for its location as for its architecture, situated as it is in a forest beside the shores of the so-called Kaunas Sea, or Kauno marios, an artificial lake created to feed a hydroelectric power station in the late 1950s. Surrounded by sandy shores shaded by pines, it's a popular recreation spot in summer and an invigorating place for a stroll whatever the season. **Getting there** is easy – take trolleybus #5 from opposite the bus station to the end of the line and carry on walking in the same direction, bearing left and under the railway tracks after about five minutes.

The monastery was built for the Camaldolese Order in 1667 by one of the Grand Duchy of Lithuania's leading aristocrats, Krzysztof Zygmunt Pac. Looted by Napoleon's troops in 1812 and closed down by the Tsarist authorities in 1832, it was subsequently used as an Orthodox church, a Lithuanian-American nunnery and a Soviet psychiatric hospital. The nuns returned in 1992. Presiding magisterially over a grassy courtyard, the monastery church is one of the most striking examples of the **Baroque** style in the country, with a twin-towered facade thrusting forward from a huge octagonal drum topped by a bulbous cupola. The **interior** (officially Tues–Sun 11am–5pm, but often closed) is vibrantly decorated with frescoes, with Giuseppe Rossi's *Coronation of the Virgin* filling the central dome, and Michelangelo Palloni's scenes from the lives of Christ and St Benedict covering the walls. The church's period as an Orthodox foundation is recalled by the tombstone of Aleksii Fedorovich Lvov (1798–1870), outside the main door and to the right – he penned the music to the Tsarist Empire's national anthem, *God Save the Tsar*. Summer **concerts** in the grounds often feature the Lithuanian Philharmonic Orchestra.

Eating and drinking

You needn't stray far from the **central strip**, formed by Laisvės alėja, Vilniaus gatvė and Rotušės aikštė, to find a convivial place to eat or drink in Kaunas. As usual in Lithuania, there's not always a clear boundary separating cafés, restaurants and bars, with many establishments catering for a coffee-swilling crowd during the daytime, serious diners in the evening and even more serious drinkers as the night draws on.

Old Town

The following places are marked on the "Kaunas Old Town" map on p.299.

Avilys Vilniaus 34. Upmarket pub in a tastefully renovated brick cellar that brews its own beer – including the light, lager-like Avylis, and the stronger, honey-flavoured and strangely addictive Medaus. There's a long list of beer cocktails (beer plus shots in the same glass) for those who favour the fast track to oblivion. The food menu features plenty of hearty meat dishes, augmented by desserts such as handmade chocolate truffles and fresh, locally-made ice cream. Sun–Thurs noon–midnight, Fri & Sat noon–2am.

Bernelių Užeiga Valančiaus 9. Lively restaurant in an attractive suite of rustic rooms, including an atmospheric, wood-beamed attic hung with dried herbs. The traditional Lithuanian menu doesn't restrict itself to the obvious (*cepelinai*, plus anything else made from potatoes), extending to deliciously flavoured stews and roasts rarely found outside the older recipe books. The drinks menu lists indigenous knock-you-for-six spirits like *samanė* alongside margaritas, piña coladas and other global concoctions. Very reasonable prices, too. Also at Donelaičio 11. Sun–Thurs 11am–10pm, Fri & Sat 11am–1am.

Blue Orange ("B.O.") Muitinės 9. Home-from-home drinking den drawing a cross-section of arty nonconformists and mainstream boozers eager to enjoy the laid-back vibe and vaguely alternative sounds on the CD player. An upstairs room hosts DJ nights and gigs at weekends, and cheap pizzas are available. Mon–Thurs 9.30am–2am, Fri 9.30am–3am, Sat 3pm–3am, Sun 3pm–1am.

Medžiotojų užeiga Rotušės aikštė 10. Upscale but not overpriced restaurant with a gamey theme that's reflected in the hunting trophies dotted around the walls. Chose between simple wooden tables or a more formal dining room. Meat-gluttons will be satisfied with whatever they order here, although venison and wild boar are the specialities. Desserts, too, are deeply satisfying. Daily 11am–midnight.

Senamiesčio vyninė Daukšos 23. Warm colours and the odd bit of exposed brickwork make this a civilized place to feast on mainstream Lithuanian food, bolstered by a good range of freshwater fish and an above-average choice of wines, with mains around 20–25Lt. There's usually a daily two-course lunch offer chalked up on a board outside. Large, globe-spanning wine list. Mon–Fri 11am–11pm, Sat & Sun noon–11pm.

Senieji rusiai Vilniaus 34. Candlelit, red-brick cellar with swords hanging theatrically from the walls. The international menu includes excellent grilled steaks and pan-fried and baked fish. With mains hovering around 30Lt, prices are reasonable. Daily noon–11pm.

Skliautas Rotušės aikštė 26. A cosy, barrel-vaulted chamber in an alleyway just off the Old Town's main square, decked out in sepia photos of prewar Kaunas. A good place for a cheap, filling lunch, although it is as a relaxing evening bar that *Skliautas* comes into its own. There's an outdoor bar and live music (Ⓦwww.skliautas.com) in the summer. Daily 10am–midnight.

Yakata Valančiaus 14. This small seven-table sushi restaurant is the perfect antidote to the meat-heavy stodge on offer elsewhere. Noodle soups and a serviceable teriyaki chicken round out the menu. Daily 11am–10pm.

Beyond the Old Town

The following places are marked on the "Kaunas" map on p.296.

Lietuviški patiekalai Laisvės 21. An order-at-the-counter café serving *cepelinai*, *bulvių plokštainis* and other reassuring stodgy Lithuanian favourites. Mon–Wed 9am–9pm Thurs–Sat 9am–11pm, Sun noon–9pm.

Miesto Sodas Laisvės alėja. Bright, roomy café-restaurant on the main strip with everything from T-bone steaks to salads. The big, street-side windows make this the perfect place for a people-watching lunch. Cocktails and jazzy piano-tinkling in the evenings. Sun–Wed 11am–11pm, Thurs–Sat 11am–midnight.

Žalias Ratas Laisvės 36B. In a building that looks like a country cottage, tucked incongruously in a yard behind the tourist office, you'll find moderately priced and homely, trad cooking, wooden benches, staff clad in traditional plaid and a big white stove in the middle of the room. A good place to try *cepelinai* (served until 3pm). Daily 11am–midnight.

Nightlife, entertainment and festivals

The popularity and hipness of Kaunas's **clubs** tends to change from one year to the next: long-standing fixtures include *Ex-it*, Maironio 19 (weekends only; Ⓦwww.exit.lt), which attracts big-name house and techno DJs from the Baltics and beyond, and the more popu-list *Amerika Pirtiye*. Vytauto 71, which concentrates on mainstream disco fun and live pop/rock acts.

There's a lot of serious **culture** on offer in Kaunas, too, much of it starting early – 5 or 6pm being the norm. The city's musical flagship is the **Kaunas Philharmonic** (Kauno Filharmonija), Sapiegos 5 (☎8-37/200478; box office daily 2–6pm), site of regular performances by the Kaunas Chamber Orchestra and the Kaunas State Choir (probably the top choral group in the country), as well as Friday-evening visits from the Vilnius-based Lithuanian National Symphony Orchestra. The **Musical Theatre** (Muzikinis teatras), Laisvės alėja 91 (☎8-37/200933; box office Tues–Sat 10am–1pm & 3–6pm, Sun 10am–3pm) is the venue for light opera and musicals.

Lithuanian-language **drama** – including major touring productions from Vilnius – can be seen at the Drama Theatre (Dramos teatras), Laisvės 71 (☎8-37/224064, ⓦwww.dramosteatras.lt; box office Tues–Sat 11am–2pm & 3–6.30pm, Sun 1hr before performance). Kaunas Little Theatre (Kauno Mažasis teatras), Daukšos 34 (☎8-37/206546; box office Wed–Fri 3–7pm, Sat 11am–6pm, Sun 1hr before performance), is the place to see contemporary drama in an intimate space. The Kaunas State Puppet Theatre (Kauno valstybinis lėlių teatras), Laisvės 87A (☎8-37/220061, ⓦwww.kaunoleles.lt) puts on performances for kiddies, usually starting at noon, with the occasional adult-oriented shows in the evening.

Festivals and events

The most prestigious of the year's culture-fests is the **Pažaislis Music Festival** (ⓦwww.pazaislis.lt) in July and August, when concerts featuring top classical performers from Lithuania and abroad are held in churches throughout the city centre and in the grounds of Pažaislis monastery – concerts held here are definitely worth attending if you have the chance. Information and tickets are available from Kaunas Philharmonic (see above).

The tourist office can provide details of other annual events: the **Kaunas Jazz Festival** (ⓦwww.kaunasjazz.lt) brings together the best Lithuanian musicians and several international guests during the last week of April, while the **Kaunas Modern Dance Festival** (ⓦwww.aura.lt) attracts a broad spectrum of innovative groups from the Baltic region in early October. **Days of Kaunas** (ⓦwww.kaunodienos.lt), held over a weekend in mid- or late May, culminates with a massive open-air pop concert in the Old Town's main square.

Listings

Car rental Budget, Savanorių 443A ☎8-37/490440, ⓦwww.budget.lt; Litinterp, Gedimino 28-7 ☎8-37/228718, ⓦwww.litinterp.lt.
Left luggage In the train station (daily 7am–7pm with a break for lunch).
Pharmacy Corner of Vytauto and Čiurlionio (open 24hr).
Post Office Laisvės alėja 102 (Mon–Fri 7am–7pm, Sat 7am–5pm).
Taxis Einesa ☎8-37/331533 or Kauno taxi ☎234444.

Travel agents Baltic Clipper, Laisvės 61–1 (☎8-37/320300), sells international plane tickets; Mūsų Odisėja, M.K. Čiurliono 15 (☎8-37/408410, ⓦwww.tourinfo.lt) organizes coach trips and hotel reservations throughout Lithuania; Studentų kelionės, Kęstučio 57–4 (☎8-37/220552, ⓦwww.studentukeliones.lt) deals in youth and student discount travel. Kautra, Laisvės 36 (☎8-37/209836, ⓦwww.kautra.lt) and at the bus station (☎8-37/322222) sells long-distance and international bus tickets.

Outside Kaunas: Rumšiškės

Twenty kilometres east of Kaunas, just off the main Vilnius-bound highway, **RUMŠIŠKĖS** is an unremarkable modern village built to accommodate locals whose homes were submerged by the creation of the Kaunas Sea (see p.308). However, the rolling green countryside just outside provides a perfect setting for the open-air **Museum of Lithuanian Life** (Lietuvos liaudies buities muziejus; Easter–Oct

Wed–Sun 10am–6pm; 6Lt), which gathers together approximately 150 original buildings – mostly from the nineteenth century – from all over Lithuania. It covers 175 hectares, so you'll need a couple of hours to do it justice – an English-language map (5Lt from the ticket office) will help you find your way around.

The buildings are arranged in groups representing Lithuania's principal ethnographic areas, with – roughly – Aukštaitija to the north, Žemaitija to the south, Suvalkija to the west and Dzūkija somewhere in the middle. Each group of buildings is separated from the next by stretches of farmland or forest, making the whole ensemble perfect for a countryside stroll. Many of the farmhouse interiors reveal how self-sufficient rustic households had to be, with furniture and farm tools crafted by the man of the house during the long winters, and bedspreads – very often the only sign of colour in the wood-floored, wood-panelled rooms – woven or embroidered by the women. At the northern end of the museum, an octagonal wooden church marks the approaches to an Aukštaitijan grid-plan village, its neat cottage gardens, porched houses and picket fences looking like an ideal piece of rural suburbia. Occupying a hill brow at the centre of the museum is the main street of a typical late-nineteenth-century town, its parallel rows of wooden buildings filled with craft workshops where you can watch woodcarvers, ceramicists and weavers at work – they'll have some of their handicrafts for sale here, too. You can pick up snacks and soft drinks at the town's *arbatinė*, or "tea room".

The museum is closed in winter except on the Sunday preceding **Shrove Tuesday** (Užgavėnės), when folklore enthusiasts dress up in mummers' costumes and burn an effigy known as the *morė* to mark the death of winter.

Rumšiškės is served by Kaunas–Vilnius **buses** (but not express minibuses), which pick up and drop off at the bus shelter on the main highway; from here it's a straightforward 25-minute walk south to the museum entrance.

Kėdainiai

With its well-preserved churches, surviving synagogues and elegantly proportioned main square, **KĖDAINIAI** exudes the religious tolerance and taste for fine architecture that characterized the courtly culture of early seventeenth-century Lithuania. It was then that this minor market town on the River Nevėžis became the property of the Calvinist branch of the Radvila family, who turned it into an important focus of Protestant culture. Kristupas Radvila (son of Kristupas "the Thunderer" of Biržai; see p.293), set the ball rolling, endowing Calvinist churches and encouraging merchants of various faiths to settle here, while his German-educated son Jonušas (who took first a Catholic, then an Orthodox wife in order to preserve his alliances with non-Protestant sections of the aristocracy) set up a printing press in the hope of weaning intellectuals away from Vilnius. Protestant emigrants from Scotland were particularly numerous, building the prosperous town houses that still surround the main square. This economic and cultural flowering was short-lived, however – Kėdainiai was repeatedly sacked during the Swedish-Russian wars of the 1650s, and didn't recover until the late nineteenth century, by which time its importance as a processing point for the local cucumber harvest had made it the pickled gherkin capital of the Baltics – a status it still enjoys.

Arrival, information and accommodation

Kėdainiai is an easy day-trip from Kaunas or a stop-off en route to Šiauliai. The **train station** is at the northern end of town, but as this is only served by three Vilnius–Šiauliai services a day, you're more likely to arrive at the **bus station** (hourly buses from Kaunas, and a handful from Vilnius and Šiauliai), 2km to the southwest, on the town's main road, **Basanavičiaus gatvė**.

Head up Basanavičiaus and turn left into Didžioji to find the **tourist office**, Didžioji 1 (Mon–Fri 9am–5pm; ☎8-347/60363, ⊛www.visitkedainiai.lt), which has English-language information and can book you into rural **B&Bs** in the region. Best of the **hotels** is ☀ *Grėjaus Namas*, Didžioji 36 (☎8-347/51500, ⊛www.grejausnamas.lt; ❹), a seventeenth-century structure built for Scottish settler Jacob Grey. Comfortable en-suites are decorated with photographs of Scottish castles, while cosy top-floor rooms have skylights. A worthy alternative is the *Smilga*, Senoji 16 (☎8-347/56626, ⓦwww .hotelsmilga.lt; ❹), which has neat, tidy doubles and a sauna.

The Town

Kėdainiai's historic heart stretches to either side of **Didžioji gatvė**, a largely pedestrianized shopping street that runs through a neat chequerboard of well-preserved buildings. The street culminates in **Didžioji rinka**, or Great Square, lined with the town houses built by Kėdainiai's seventeenth-century Calvinist community – most of them Scottish immigrants.

The Kėdainiai District Museum and around

Occupying a former Carmelite convent at Didžioji 19, the **Kėdainiai District Museum** (Tues–Sat 10am–5pm; 4Lt) offers an involving display of artefacts recalling the town's past glories. Alongside portraits of sundry Radvilas, there's a room full of nineteenth-century furniture made from antlers that has to be seen to be believed. Behind the museum, accessible via a narrow alleyway, the eighteenth-century **St Joseph's Church** (Šv. Juozapo bažnyčia) is a delightful wooden church with Baroque belfry, built by the Carmelites to wrest spiritual power away from the local Calvinists. Hidden away at the junction of Didžioji and Basanavičiaus on the second floor of the municipal council building, the **Vytautas Ulevičius Museum** (Mon–Fri 9am–5pm; 3LT) contains a fantastic collection of sculptures – including figures from Lithuanian pagan mythology or the Catholic pantheon of saints – carved from local oak by the self-taught Ulevičius.

The Reformed Church

A couple of blocks east of the District Museum at Senoji 1, the seventeenth-century **Reformed Church** (Reformatų bažnyčia; June–Sept Tues–Sat 11am–4pm; outside these months ask at the museum; 5Lt) is the town's trademark edifice, a high-sided oblong with a pair of ice-cream-cone towers either side of the main portal. Begun under Kristupas Radvila and finished under Jonušas, it's a wonderful exercise in ascetic religious architecture, its light, lofty and minimal interior designed to induce spiritual contemplation. The communists were so impressed by its spaciousness they turned it into a basketball court. Now used for occasional services attended by a dwindling congregation of local Protestants, the church is mainly visited for the Radvila family vault, which lies beneath the main altar. The grandest of the sarcophagi are a richly ornamented Baroque affair containing the remains of Jonušas Radvila and the adjacent casket of his grandfather Kristupas "the Thunderer", embossed with suitably fearsome lions' heads. The smaller coffins, each mounted on balled feet as if intended to be periodically rearranged by a macabre interior designer, belong to Jonušas's four siblings, all of whom died in infancy.

Didžioji Rinka

Immediately east of the church lies the **Didžioji rinka**, or Great Square, a broad, open space bordered by a handsome collection of oldish buildings. Most eye-catching are the merchants' houses at the square's northern end, their brightly painted, curvy gables resembling jellies at a children's party. In the middle of the square stands a **monument to Jonušas Radvila**, famous in Lithuania (and infamous in Poland) for attempting to rupture the Polish-Lithuanian Commonwealth in 1655 by allying the Grand Duchy of Lithuania with Sweden instead. Jonušas died in battle later the same year, and his projected political realignment remained a pipe dream.

Senoji Rinka

Moving north from the Didžioji rinka along Senoji gatvė brings you out onto another large square, **Senoji rinka**, or Old Square, once monopolized by the town's Jewish stall holders. Encouraged to settle in the area by the Radvilas in the seventeenth century, Kėdainiai's Jewish community played a prominent role in the town's social and economic

The great outdoors

Once you get beyond the capital cities, the Baltic States are predominantly rural in character, with isolated farmsteads and rustic market towns scattered across a landscape of grazing land, forest and bog-filled wilderness. The region's most dramatic natural feature is its coastline, however, with long sandy beaches stretching the length of Lithuania and Latvia, and on into southern Estonia. Occupying a prime position on north–south migration routes, the Baltic States are visited by hundreds of bird species every year, and its forests harbour a wide variety of fauna, from deer to wild boar to elk.

Lake Peipsi, Estonia ▲

Rowan tree, Matsalu Nature Reserve, Estonia ▼

Lakes and forests

Glaciers carved out a series of ruts and hollows in the Baltic interior, allowing the formation of the **lakes** which splash bright blue across any map of the region. Nowadays, large lakes at Trakai in Lithuania (see p.283) or Pühajärv in Estonia (see p.140) are places to head for the beach, hire a boat or dine at a shoreside restaurant, while the smaller, quieter lakes strewn across eastern Latvia and southern Estonia are the perfect places to get lost in solitary contemplation. The chance to commune with nature is also offered by the region's huge tracts of dense **forest**, predominantly made up of pine, spruce and silver birch, and providing protective cover to a large population of deer, elk, wild boar and other mammals. Forest-based activities such as mushroom-picking and berry-gathering still form an important part of village life, while the otherworldly stillness of the deep forest exerts a powerful hold over the nature-worshipping side of the Baltic character.

Bog-scape of Hare's-Tail Cottongrass, Estonia ▼

Bogs

Created by the gradual accumulation of moisture-bearing mosses, **bogs** can be starkly beautiful places. The archetypal Baltic bog-scape comprises a spongy green carpet of sphagnum moss, frequently punctuated by shimmering blue ponds and supporting a sprinkling of heathers, stunted conifers and spindly birches. Plants which relish the soggy conditions include cloudberries and cranberries, making the bog a popular feeding ground for birds and insects. Several Baltic bogs have been rendered accessible to visitors by wooden boardwalk trails, notably the Great Ķemeri Bog in Latvia (see p.200) and the Viru Bog in Estonia (see p.119).

Dunes

Arguably the most memorable landscape in the Baltics is provided by Lithuania's Curonian Spit, a 4km-wide strip of land composed almost entirely of **sand dunes**, formed over several millennia by the prevailing winds. Most of these dunes now have a sparse coverage of grasses or pine forest, producing a rhythmically undulating landscape in varying shades of green. Just south of the fishing village of **Nida**, however, significant stretches of dune remain beautifully bare. Rising up to 50m in height, and still classified as "live dunes" due to their wind-driven tendency to change shape from one generation to the next, the Nida dunes exude an almost Saharan majesty.

Wild animals

The **wild animals** you are most likely to see throughout the Baltic States are deer (roe or red), which can be seen foraging in open farmland, especially in the early morning or late evening. Wild boar rarely emerge from their woodland habitats, although you may catch sight of them in areas where they are concentrated, such as the the forests of the Curonian Spit in Lithuania. The other principal forest-dwelling animals – moose, elk, martens and lynx – are more secretive, and sightings are rare. Small numbers of bears live in the national parks of Estonia and occasionally make it as far south as Latvia, although the only ones you're likely to encounter are the captive examples held in enclosures at the Līgatne Nature Trail (see p.222). Freshly gnawed tree-trunks and log-built dams – evidence of beavers – are a frequent sight in Baltic national parks. You can learn more about these industrious creatures on the Oandu Beaver Trail in Lahemaa (see p.122).

▲ Nida dunes, Curonian Spit, Lithuania

▼ Wild moose

Birdwatching

The relatively unspoilt Baltic countryside supports a year-round profusion of **bird life**. Dense forests provide a habitat for woodpeckers, eagles and buzzards, while bogs and heaths offer inviting hunting grounds for sandpipers, grouse and cranes. The Baltic coastline forms part of one of the main north–south avian migration routes, and the skies are filled with birds on the move in spring and autumn. The marshes and lagoons of Matsalu Bay in Estonia (see p.94) are an important seasonal feeding ground for migrating geese and ducks, with mute swans, moorhens and corncrakes foraging among the coastal reeds. Slightly further northwest, the Vilsandi National Park on the island of Saaremaa (see p.104) is a major stopping-off point for greylag geese and Arctic terns.

Male Great Spotted Woodpecker ▲

Vilsandi National Park, Saaremaa, Estonia ▼

Top five nature trails

▶▶ **The Zackagiris Nature path** Marcinkonys, Lithuania. Explore the mysterious, sandy-soiled forests of Dzūkija in southern Lithuania. See p.316.

▶▶ **The Nida-Preila-Pervalka cycling route** Nida, Lithuania. Walk or cycle this coastal path passing a selection of the Curonian Spit's famous dunes. See p.341.

▶▶ **Great Ķemeri Bog** Ķemeri, Latvia. Boardwalk trail leading out across a starkly beautiful area of Baltic heath. See p.200.

▶▶ **Harilaid peninsula** Saaremaa, Estonia. Rocky shores, juniper heaths and lighthouses on Saarema Island's isolated northwestern tip. See p.104.

▶▶ **The Stone Plantation** Käsmu, Estonia. A huge collection of erratic boulders, covered by dense forest, just west of the famously pretty village of Käsmu. See p.120.

life until August 28, 1941, when the Nazis shot an estimated 2076 victims in one day. Two synagogues survive, standing end-to-end at the far side of the square. The larger of the two (colloquially known as the summer synagogue because it wasn't equipped with central heating) is now an arts school, while its smaller neighbour (the "winter synagogue", naturally) serves as the **Kėdainiai Multicultural Centre** (Daugiakultūris centras; Tues–Sat 10am–5pm; 4Lt), hosting seasonal exhibitions by contemporary artists and photographers. Whatever's on show, it's definitely worth having a peek at the spirit-soothing, light-blue interior, its ceiling held up by a quartet of spindly columns. The upstairs gallery, punctuated by twelve small windows symbolizing the twelve tribes of Israel, was where female members of the congregation followed services.

Eating and drinking

The best place **to eat** in the town centre is the restaurant of the *Grėjaus namos* hotel (see p.311), a barrel-vaulted, Baroque space offering solid international cuisine and courtyard seating in summer. The nearby *Nu, Blyn*, Didžioji 22, has an extensive menu of pancakes with all kinds of sweet and savoury fillings, and serviceable fresh salads – it turns into a fashionable bar at night.

Birštonas

Some 44km south of Kaunas, just off the main road to Druskininkai (see p.317), the spa town of **BIRŠTONAS** has been a popular getaway since the days of Vytautas the Great, when the Grand Duke and his entourage adopted the local castle as their favourite hunting lodge. The local mineral springs became fashionable in the 1920s, when Lithuania's leading spa town, Druskininkai, was occupied by Poland, and Birštonas was called upon to deputize. While spa tourism and the provision of rest cures remain Birštonas's raison d'être, the place retains a village-like feel and a rural pace. The settlement straggles along the banks of the River Nemunas, whose slow-moving meanderings have hereabouts produced a series of huge loops known as the **Nemunas Bends**. With the region's dense forest and wildlife under the protection of the **Nemunas Bends Regional Park** (Nemuno kilpų regioninio parkas), there are plenty of riverside paths to explore on foot or by bicycle.

The Town

Birštonas's focal point is the **Nemunas River**, which flows 2km west of town before looping back on itself and sweeping past Birštonas to the east. The town centre is on the eastern side of town, beside the river, with a sprinkling of spa buildings and a red-brick neo-Gothic parish church. Beside the church, the **Birštonas Sacral Museum** (Birštono sakralinis muziejus; Wed–Sun 10am–5pm; donation requested) honours local archbishop Teofilius Matulionis (1873–1962), who struggled to preserve religious freedoms during the Soviet occupation. It was in this house that Matulionis secretly consecrated Vincentas Sladkevičius (1920–2000) as bishop of Kaišiadorys, despite the opposition of the Soviet powers; Sladkevičius was subsequently made a cardinal by Pope John Paul II in 1988. Animated wooden statuettes of saints, previously displayed in wayside shrines, round off a charming display. Up the street, at Vytauto 9, the

---

Taking the cure in Birštonas

Birštonas has several **sanatoria**, of which the central **Tulpės** (☎8-319/65525, ⓦwww.tulpe.lt) is the best equipped. The modern indoor pool (Mon–Fri 8.30am–8.30pm, Sat & Sun 9am–8pm; 28Lt for 90min), fed by mineral water, also boasts water slides, kiddies' paddling areas, saunas and sweeping views towards the Nemunas river. Tulpės offers mineral baths, herbal baths and aromatherapy, as well as mud treatments for aching bones and muscles. All treatments (20–25Lt) can be booked at the main reception desk, although you may have to undergo a brief blood-pressure test before undergoing some procedures.

Birštonas Museum (Birštono muziejus; Wed–Sun 10am–5pm; free) has a modest collection of local agricultural implements and old spa-resort postcards, while a couple of blocks west, photographs in the **Nemunas Bends Regional Park Visitors' Centre** (Nemuno kilpų regioninio parko lankytojų centras; Mon–Fri 9am–5pm; free) provide a colourful introduction to the flora and fauna of the surrounding forests.

Into the park

The easiest way to access the Nemunas Bends Regional Park is to walk or cycle northwest along the riverbank from the centre of town and into the **Zverinčius Forest** (Žvėrinčiaus miškas), which extends for some 7km into a pocket of land almost encircled by the meandering river. Criss-crossed by trails (pick up a map from the tourist office), the forest is thick with soaring pines, although the ancient and knobbly conifer known as the Vytautas Oak, 4km out of Birštonas and a popular target for strollers, is thought to be one of the oldest trees in Lithuania. River islands lying off the northern end of the forest are an important nesting ground for little terns from May to August.

West of Birštonas, the road to Prienai runs beside the upstream loop of the Nemunas, passing after 2km one of the region's best-known beauty spots: the **Škėvonys Escarpment** (Škėvonių atodanga). Stretching north from the *Seklytėlė* café-restaurant (see below), this 500m-long sandstone cliff rises some 35m above the river, and provides an excellent view of the Nemunas below.

Practicalities

Birštonas is easily reached by half-hourly **bus** from Kaunas. Approaching from the Vilnius direction, the route via Trakai and Aukštiadvaris (served by five daily Vilnius–Prienai buses) ploughs through some of Lithuania's prettiest countryside, characterized by lakeside villages set amidst rolling hills.

The bus station is on the main street, Jaunimo gatvė, a short distance from the **tourist office** at Jaunimo 3 (☎8-319/65740, ⓦwww.birstonas.lt), where you can book accommodation and rent bikes. Among the handful of good hotels in town, the central *Audenis*, Lelijų 3 (☎8-319/61300, ⓦwww.audenis.lt; ④), offers nine roomy, unfussy en-suites and great attic rooms with skylight windows. *Sofijos Rezidencija*, near the tourist office at Jaunimo 6 (☎8-319/45200, ⓦwww.sofijosrezidencija.lt; ⑤), features gloriously over-the-top design touches, including copies of Renaissance paintings, loud and luscious fabrics and canopied beds. Both have good **restaurants**, although the most scenic option is *Seklytėlė*, Prienų 10, a rustic-style café-restaurant 2km west of town on the Škėvonys Escarpment (see above), with a sweeping panorama of the Nemunas from its terrace.

The Birštonas **Jazz Festival**, held on the last weekend of March on even-numbered years, is Lithuania's oldest such festival – initiated during the culturally stagnant Brezhnev era in 1980, it immediately attained cult status as a celebration of artistic freedom. Information and tickets are available from the tourist office.

Dzūkija National Park

With its vast tracts of sandy-soiled pine forest punctuated by the occasional one-street village, the **Dzūkija National Park** (Dzūkijos nacionalinis parkas;

Canoe trips

One of the best ways to enjoy Dzūkija's woodland scenery is to canoe down the Nemunas tributaries, Merkys and Ūla, although **permits** (available from the visitors' centre in Marcinkonys for a nominal fee) are required for the Ūla. You can only travel along the following national park-authorized **itineraries**: the half-day trip down the Merkys from Puvočiai to Merkinė; the one-day trip down the Ūla from Zervynos to Žiūrai; and the two-day trip down the Ūla from Zervynos to Puvočiai. Canoe **rental** (60Lt/day) and their transport to (and from) the river can be organized by the visitors' centre in Marcinkonys.

Ⓦ www.dzukijosparkas.lt) is about as far away from urban Lithuania as you can get. This 56,000-hectare stretch of rolling terrain on the east bank of the River Nemunas has never been a major agricultural area, most of the population making a living from forestry, beekeeping or gathering the berries and mushrooms for which the Dzūkijan woodland is famous. The local villages have preserved traditional features that elsewhere in the country can only be seen in ethnographic museums: timber houses adorned with intricate, filigree-effect window frames and gardens sporting boldly carved wooden crosses topped with shrines or sun symbols. The forest itself is teeming with animal life: eagles, buzzards and woodpeckers inhabit the canopy, while elk, deer and wild boar root around among the lichens and ferns below.

There are two main routes into the region: the main Vilnius–Druskininkai road runs along the park's northern boundaries, passing through **Merkinė** en route, while the Vilnius–**Marcinkonys** rail line cuts through the more densely forested southern section of the park. There are national park visitors' centres at Merkinė and Marcinkonys – the latter is marginally better as a base for woodland walks and is also within striking distance of the **Čepkelių bog reserve**, a protected area of marshland on the park's southern border.

A few village homestays and tent-pitching sites aside, the park doesn't offer much in the way of **accommodation**, and most visitors end up staying just outside the park in Druskininkai (see p.317).

Approaching the park along the main Vilnius–Druskininkai highway, you'll see a series of exquisitely carved roadside **shrine-poles** topped with all manner of faces and figures, which start just after Varėna, 82km out from the capital, and continue until well past Merkinė. They're based on themes in the Symbolist paintings and symphonic compositions of Mikalojus Konstantinis Čiurlionis (see p.303), who was born in Varėna and grew up in Druskininkai. The poles, sculpted by contemporary folk artists, were erected in 1976 to commemorate the centenary of his birth.

Merkinė

Some 25km beyond Varėna, Vilnius–Druskininkai buses stop at a dusty road junction at the eastern end of **MERKINĖ** – hardly the best of introductions to what turns out to be a neat country town of single-storey wooden dwellings and cottage gardens. There's a handful of incongruous concrete buildings on the main square, one of which houses the **National Park Visitors' Centre**, Vilniaus 3 (Mon–Fri 8am–noon & 1–5pm; ☎8-310/57245, ⓦwww.dzukijosparkas.lt); it sells maps and displays handicrafts – notably the locally made, dark-earthenware pottery, traditionally fired in a log-fuelled hole in the ground rather than a conventional kiln. The craft is still practised in the villages north of Merkinė, and most potters are eager to show visitors around their workshops (arrange through the visitors' centre a day or two in advance).

Opposite the information centre, a former Orthodox church now serves as the **Museum of Local Lore** (Merkinės kraštotyros muziejus; June–Sept Wed–Sun 11am–6pm; 2Lt), with wooden looms, spinning wheels and agricultural implements crammed into a junk-shop interior. Heading downhill along J. Bakšio, past the lipstick-bright Baroque facade of the Church of the Assumption, you soon arrive at the River Nemunas. Overlooking the north bank, a grassy **castle mound** (piliakalnis) was the site of a wooden stockade fort in the fourteenth century, an important link in a chain of fortifications protecting southern Lithuania from frequent incursions by the Teutonic Knights. Climbable via a wooden stairway, it's a great spot from which to contemplate the curve of the river and the grey-green forests beyond.

The visitors' centre can organize B&B **accommodation** in local farmhouses, and there are tent-pitching sites without facilities on the far bank of the river (cross the road bridge and turn right), and beside a pair of small lakes called Mergelės akelės ("little girls' eyes"), 2km east of town just off the Vilnius road. You can get **food and drink** from the supermarket on Merkinė's main square.

Marcinkonys

For a flavour of life in Dzūkija's backwoods, there are few better places than the mellow village of **MARCINKONYS** – and with three trains a day from Vilnius, it makes an easy day-trip. If you're approaching by car, take the Vilnius–Druskininkai highway and turn off at either Varėna or Merkinė.

Marcinkonys is a narrow, 2km-long village, built around a single street, Miškininkų gatvė, heading off north from the train station. After 100m or so it passes the **Ethnographic Museum** (Etnografinės muziejus; June–Sept Tues–Sat 9am–5pm; Oct–May Mon–Fri 11am–4pm; 4Lt), a wonderfully restored old farmhouse packed with domestic utensils, hand-woven textiles and practical pine furniture. Another 800m up the main street, the **National Park Visitors' Centre**, Miškininkų 61 (Mon–Fri 9am–5pm, Sat 10am–4pm; ☎8-310/44466, ⓦwww.dzukijosparkas.lt) sells maps, advises on local walks, and organizes canoeing trips on the Ūla river (see opposite). Continuing north along the main street brings you after another 1km to one of the most appealing wooden **parish churches** in the country, a twin-towered, canary-yellow building overlooking a pine-shaded graveyard. About 400m east of the church lies **Gaidžų kopa**, one of the most impressive of the local dunes.

The visitors' centre can book you into their own **guesthouse** with rooms above the office (❷), or rural homestays (❶–❷) throughout the park. There's a tent-pitching site, with no facilities, beside Lake Kastionis (Kastinio ežeras), 1km northeast of the train station. *Kavinė po liepa* **café**, midway between the visitors' centre and the ethnographic museum, sells simple snacks.

The Zackagiris Nature Path

The easiest walk in the area – which can be done in full or in part – is the **Zackagiris Nature Path** (Zackagirio gamtinis takas), a 13km-long circuit that starts at the visitors' centre and loops through the forest on either side of the village. For a short ninety-minute walk, head west along the trail to enjoy a quiet waterside trek along the Grūda river, where you'll see hives carved by beekeepers from living tree trunks. The eastern part of the circuit passes through thick pine forest growing on an undulating bed of sand dunes – areas of bog and beaver-created sunken forest can be seen along the way.

Čepkelių bog

Five kilometres southeast of Marcinkonys, the area's trademark sandy-floored pine forest suddenly gives way to the soggy terrain and stunted plants of **Čepkelių bog** (Čepkelių raistas). Although just outside the boundaries of the Dzūkija National Park, the bog is a state-protected area into which you are strictly forbidden to wander. However, you can get as far as the reserve's northwestern corner, where paths bordering the bog afford good views of the Čepkelių landscape. Bristling with heath plants, lichens and coniferous shrubs, it's a memorably stark spectacle. Keep still and you may catch sight of capercaillie strutting their way through the Čepkelių heather.

To get to the marshes, pick up the lane behind Marcinkonys train station and follow it southwest (ignore the sign to the left reading "Čepkelių" after 800m – this leads to the reserve's administration office), a lovely walk through blissfully quiet forest. After 4km you arrive at a picnic spot and a signboard that directs you to the edge of the bog.

The Ūla Valley

Running along the northeastern boundaries of the park, the **Ūla** is one of the park's most beautiful rivers, winding its way between sandy, tree-covered banks before emptying into the Merkys (which in turn joins the Nemunas at Merkinė). A good place to start exploring the valley is the picturesque, half-forgotten village of **ZERVYNOS**, 10km northeast of Marcinkonys and only one stop away on the train.

Six kilometres northwest of Zervynos and 2km beyond the river's-edge village of Mančiagirė, a wooden stairway leads down from the main Merkinė-bound road to a lovely wood-shrouded stretch of riverbank. A signed path leads off from here to the tiny lake known as **Ūlos akis** ("Eye of the Ūla"), where hot springwater agitates the dark sand on the lake bed to create a bubbling-cauldron effect.

A further 3km down the road from Ūlos akis lies the invitingly sleepy village of **ŽIŪRAI**, full of traditional wooden houses, their window frames carved into swirls and arabesques. The walk between Žiūrai and Marcinkonys, a two-hour trot along logging roads, is as atmospheric a woodland trek as you'll find. Whether you attempt the whole trail or not, be sure to make a short detour to forest-engulfed **BIŽAI**, a tiny village, 1.5km due south of Žiūrai; it's only accessible by dirt track and has a compelling end-of-the-world feel.

Druskininkai and around

Just west of the Dzūkija National Park, the spa resort of **DRUSKININKAI** is a strange mixture of modern town and rural getaway, its concrete buildings set incongruously in thick pine forest. The name of the town comes from the Lithuanian for salt (*druska*), a reference to the mineral-rich spring waters to which the town owes its health-retreat reputation. As well as being used in all kinds of physiotherapy, the waters are used to treat ailments ranging from arthritis to heart disease, bronchitis and asthma. Although the curative powers of the local waters had been well known to the locals for centuries (and King Stanisław August Poniatowski of Poland-Lithuania issued a decree recognizing this in 1794), Druskininkai's history as a spa really begins with the nineteenth-century craze for rest-cures. The first sanatorium was built here in 1838, and Druskininkai soon became the favoured summer retreat of Vilnius society – a status that to a large extent it still enjoys. During the Soviet period, when spa treatment was free to anyone who could talk a doctor into giving them the requisite sick-note, Druskininkai's sanatoria were receiving over 100,000 guests a year from all over the Soviet Union. These numbers fell after the Soviet Union's collapse, but Druskininkai is still the resort

ACCOMMODATION
Dalija	D
Druskininkai	F
Druskininkų kempingas campsite	H
Europa Royale	B
Medūna	C
Regina	A
Spa Vilnius	G
Violeta	E

RESTAURANTS, CAFÉS & BARS
Kolonada	2
Medūna	C
Senasis Nemunas	5
Sicilija	3
Širdelė	1
Sūkurys	4
Vido malūnas	6

DRUSKININKAI

Echo of the Forest (1km) & Grūtas Park (3km)

of choice for ailing Lithuanians – alongside a growing contingent of free-spending tourists who want to luxuriate in the resort's range of wellness and beauty treatments.

Served roughly hourly by **bus** from Vilnius, Druskininkai is just about do-able as a day-trip from the capital, although you'll need a night or two to allow its uniquely soothing, forest-shrouded ambience to take effect. There's plenty to see in the immediate surroundings, with the collection of Soviet-era sculptures at **Grūtas park** and the Baroque church at **Liškiava** both a short trip away.

Arrival, information and accommodation

Druskininkai's **bus station** lies a ten-minute walk south of the town centre at Gardino 1. The train station just beyond it is currently unused because the Vilnius–Druskininkai line – very popular in Soviet times – now runs through a corner of Belarus. The main **tourist office** is just southeast of the bus station building at Gardino 3 (Mon–Fri 8.30am–5.15pm; ☎8-313/60800, ⓦwww.info.druskininkai.lt), and there's an information booth on the corner of Dineikos and Čiurlionio (daily 10am–6.45pm; ☎8-313/51777). Both can book you into **B&Bs** (❶–❸) in Druskininkai and outlying villages. There's a wide choice of hotels in Druskininkai, including sanatoria – rooms are generally comfy and good value, so don't be put off by the institutionalized air of some of these places. The year-round *Druskininkų kempingas* **campsite**, Gardino 3A (☎8-313/60800; ⓦwww.info .druskininkai.lt), run by the tourist office, has a neat WC/shower block, electric power points for caravans and laundry facilities.

Marked bike trails lead out of town and into the forest: the tourist office has details of **bike rental outlets**.

Hotels and guesthouses

Dalija Vasario 16-osios 1 ☎8-313/51814, ⓦwww
.dalijahotel.lt. Homely eleven-room hotel in a
historic building opposite the Orthodox church,
offering functional en-suites with sinks, kettles and
cutlery. No breakfast. ❶–❸

Druskininkai Kudirkos 43 ☎8-313/52566,
ⓦwww.hotel-druskininkai.lt. Chic rooms with
four-star comforts. There's a range of roomy
suites (400–500Lt) on the fifth floor and a spa
centre with massage and beauty treatments in the
basement. ❺–❻

Europa Royale Vilniaus alėja 7 ☎8-313/42221,
ⓦwww.europaroyale.com. Converted nineteenth-
century mansion offering well-appointed rooms
with thick carpets and flat-screen TVs, and some
apartmetnts (from 600Lt). A covered corridor leads
to the next-door *Gydykla* (spa-treatment centre; see
below). Two rooms have been adapted for wheel-
chair users. Ask about weekend or seven-day packages including half-board and spa treatments. ❻

Medūna Liepų 2 ☎8-313/58033, ⓦwww
.meduna.lt. Resembling a traditional Lithuanian
house but with one wall comprised entirely of glass
– so you can admire the nearby Orthodox church

as you go up and down the stairs – this hotel
offers a range of en-suites: "mini" doubles are cosy
affairs with sloping attic ceilings, while regular
doubles offer more storage and desk space. ❸–❹

Regina T. Košciuškos 3 ☎8-313/59060, ⓦwww
.regina.lt. Modern, mid-sized hotel offering
top-quality accommodation in a central location.
Rooms are decked out in warm colours and feature
sizeable bathrooms with tubs. ❹–❼

Spa Vilnius Dineikos 1 ☎8-313/53811, ⓦwww
.spasana.lt. Former sanatorium refitted as a comfy
spa hotel. Regular rooms come with en-suite
shower, TV and small balcony, while the roomier
apartments offer loungey furnishings and a full-size
tub. Spa facilities on site (see below); ask about
accommodation-plus-spa packages. ❺

Violeta Kurorto 4 ☎8-313/60600, ⓦwww.violeta
.lt. Characterful building in the style of a
nineteenth-century spa pavilion, offering spacious
rooms with modern bathrooms. Three rooms have
fantastic views of the Nemunas; you can enjoy the
same panorama from the plant-filled lobby bar.
Fitness room, Jacuzzi pool and Turkish steam bath
in the basement, plus a massage centre. One room
is wheelchair-accessible. ❻

The Town

Although mostly made up of straight boulevards lined with modern buildings, Druskininkai can still muster some elegant reminders of the Tsarist era. There's a cluster of
attractive wooden villas on and near **Laisvės aikštė**, a central roundabout where traffic

Taking the cure

The easiest way to benefit from Druskininkai's health-giving waters is to drink a drop
of the stuff at the Pump Room or wallow in the pools of the Water Park (see p.320).
In addition, a range of mineral-water baths, massages and aromatherapy is offered
at the central Spa Centre (*Gydykla*) and many of the posher hotels. One of the most
effective ways to reinvigorate weary muscles and bones is to take a Druskininkai
mud bath, which involves a twenty-minute soak in a tub filled with peat from the
Dzūkija forest floor.

Mud baths and other treatments can be booked at the reception desks of the spa centres listed below. A brief medical consultation or blood-pressure test may be required
before you're allowed to take the treatment, although for most this is a formality.

Druskininkai Spa Centre (Druskininkų gydykla) Vilniaus alėja 11 ☎8-313/60508,
ⓦwww.gydykla.lt. Spa centre in the heart of the resort, offering mineral baths from
15Lt and mud baths from 26Lt. Also herbal bubble baths, and a plethora of mineral-
bath-plus-body-scrub-plus-massage packages.

Spa Vilnius Dineikos 1 ☎8-313/53811, ⓦwww.spasana.lt. Modern, relaxing spa
centre in the hotel of the same name (see above), with a mineral-water-fed pool and
a host of treatments. These include mineral baths from 20Lt, mud baths from 30Lt, an
array of beauty treatments and pretty much every variety of massage so far invented.

trundles around the nineteenth-century **Orthodox church** (Stačiatikių cerkvė) in the middle of the central reservation. Sprouting a forest of blue spires capped with purple domes, it's arguably the most extrovert building in the country. The interior, covered in what looks like Victorian wallpaper, conveys a strong sense of period.

The Jacques Lipchitz Museum

Just south of the square, at Šv Jokūbo 17, a single-storey house with intricately carved veranda screens now serves as the **Jacques Lipchitz Museum** (Žako Lipšico muziejus; mid-May to mid-Sept Tues–Fri noon–5pm; 2Lt), honouring the Druskininkai-born Lithuanian-Jewish artist with a modest display of mementos and period furnishings, as well as photographs of Druskininkai's once-thriving Jewish community. Born to a family of architects, Lipchitz (1891–1973) attended art school in Vilnius before heading for Paris, where he lived in the so-called "Beehive" – a famously buzzing artists' colony that also included fellow emigrés from Russia's western provinces, Chaim Soutine and Marc Chagall. Lipchitz made his name during World War I with a series of what he called "abstract architectural sculptures" – thrusting geometric forms that resemble scale models of yet-to-be-built skyscrapers.

The Pump Room and the Water Park

East of Laisvės aikštė, the pedestrianized Laisvės gatvė leads east to the historical centre of the resort, where you'll find a handsome collection of Neoclassical spa buildings holding the **Spa Centre** (*Gydykla*). Tacked on to the *Gydykla* is the bright, modern **Pump Room** (*biuvetė*; daily 8am–7pm), its minimalist, marble-effect interior providing a suitably clinical ambience in which to sample one of two local spa waters, the eggy-tasting Dzūkija and the bitter, brackish Druskininkai – the latter has a higher mineral content and is especially effective in treating the digestive system (and also goes down a treat as a hangover cure). North of here lies a futuristic grey tangle of concrete buildings built in the 1970s to serve as a spa treatment centre and expensively modernized in 2004–06. Now renamed the **Druskininkai Water Park** (Vandens parkas; Mon–Fri noon–10pm, Sat 10am–10pm, Sun noon–8pm; 40Lt/2hr; half-day and day tickets also available), the centre offers a mineral-water-fed swimming pool, spiralling water slides, Jacuzzi-style jet baths and paddling areas. A separate ticket (from 60Lt/2hr) gives you access to the Alita bath complex, where you can book a sauna, a Roman bath, or a steam bath – or drink cocktails in the wet bar.

The Town Museum and the Čiurlionis Museum

Heading south from the Pump Room along the flowerbed-lined **Vilniaus gatvė**, you come to the red-brick neo-Gothic **Church of the Virgin Mary of the Scapular** (Šv Mergelės Marijos Škaplierinės bažnyčia), before meeting up with Čiurlionio gatvė, which borders the kidney-shaped **Lake Druskonis**. Occupying a turreted, belle époque holiday home known as the Villa Linksma ("Happy Villa"), the **Town Museum** (Miesto muziejus; Mon–Sat 11am–5pm; 3Lt) at Čiurlionio 78 displays a marvellous collection of engravings showing nineteenth-century spa-town life, views of Druskininkai in old postcards, and photographs of the resort in the 1930s, when it was a pioneering centre of highly regimented health-camp tourism.

A few doors down at Čiurlionio 35, the **M.K. Čiurlionis Memorial Museum** (M.K. Čiurlionis memorialininis muziejus; Tues–Sun 11am–5pm; 4Lt) provides a fascinating insight into the life of the painter and composer (see p.303) who spent his early years in Druskininkai, and returned every summer in adulthood to brainstorm and brood. These seasonal visits certainly made an impression on the young Jacques Lipchitz (see above), who recalled later that he would watch Čiurlionis "passing like a shadow, always in deep thoughts…and I would dream to be like him." The exhibition begins with a modern pavilion filled with sepia photographs of Čiurlionis and family; behind it, the pastel-painted wooden house purchased by Čiurlionis's piano-teacher father in 1896 is crammed with nineteenth-century domestic knick-knacks. A second house immediately next door was bought by the family so they could rent holiday flats to tourists, although one room was kept as Čiurlionis's summer studio, preserved pretty much as he left it, complete with easel, writing desk and a couple of his paintings – devotional works intended for the family home, they reveal nothing of the Symbolist style for which he's famous.

The Jonynas Gallery and Lake Druskonis

A few steps west of the Čiurlionis Museum, the **Vytautas Kazimieras Jonynas Gallery** (Vytauto Kazimiero Jonyno galerija; Tues–Sun 11am–5pm) remembers the work of locally born Jonynas (1907–97), who taught at Kaunas art school prior to World War II, designed stamps for the West German postal services in the late 1940s, and went on to create stained-glass and devotional sculptures for Catholic churches throughout the US. The gallery displays a broad cross-section of Jonynas's work in a succession of chic, light-filled spaces. From here you can descend to Lake Druskonis, where there are **rowing boats and pedalos** for rent. On the far side of the lake, asphalt-ed foot- and cycle-paths present plenty of opportunities for exploring the forest.

The Echo of the Forest

About 1.5km east of the town centre, the **Echo of the Forest** natural history museum (Girios Aidas) at Čiurlionio 116 (Wed–Sun 10am–6pm; 6Lt) occupies a purpose-built wooden house of almost fairytale appearance, with doorposts in the form of giants and spindly balustrades carved into fir-branch shapes. It was constructed to replace an even odder original construction, which was suspended in the fork of a huge tree – both house and tree burnt down in 1992. The museum is divided into sections, each devoted to a particular tree typical of the region, with a display of the tools and furnishings traditionally made from it and information on its animal and bird life – unsurprisingly, there are a lot of stuffed pine martens.

Eating, drinking and entertainment

Druskininkai's **eating and drinking** scene is increasingly lively, with plenty in the way of Lithuanian meat-and-potato stodge and an increasing array of international options too.

Piano recitals are given at the Čiurlionis Museum every Sunday in summer, with performers tinkling away indoors while the audience sit on benches in the garden, watching and listening through a large open window. There's also a **Theatre Festival** in late July/early August – ask the tourist office for details. The **Druskininkai Autumn Poetry Festival** (Poetinis Druskininkų ruduo) is a must for literati from all over the country – English-language writers are occasionally included in the programme.

Restaurants, cafés and bars

Kolonada Kudirkos 22 ⓦwww.kolonada.lt. Park-side pavilion filled with potted palms, serving up good-quality international food, passable pizzas, and fancy cocktails. Frequent live jazz or pop-rock gigs, when there may be a cover charge. 10am–2am.

Medūna Liepų 2. Cosy, intimate restaurant squeezed into a corner of the *Medūna* hotel, with traditional meat and fish dishes given a stylish modern European twist. The weekday set lunches are a steal. Mon–Fri noon–11pm, Sat & Sun 1–11pm.

Senasis Nemunas Fonbergo 7. Hidden away in an unexciting courtyard behind the Maxima supermarket, this old, wood-panelled house serves up Lithuanian favourites *koldūnai* and *cepelinai*, and also offers salads made with the local marinated mushrooms. The Vilkmerges draught beer makes a nice change from the mass-market varieties on offer elsewhere. Daily 10am–11pm.

Sicilija Taikos 9. A café-restaurant in a chic, modern pavilion offering tasty, thin-crust pizzas, as well as traditional Lithuanian stomach-fillers – including divine potato pancakes drenched in sour cream. Sun–Thurs 10am–11pm, Fri & Sat 10am–midnight.

Širdelė Maironio 22. Rather old-fashioned café in a delightful wooden villa attached to the Dainava sanatorium, with simple pork and chicken dishes, cheap prices and a home-from-home atmosphere. Mon 11am–9.30pm, Tues–Sun 11am–11pm.

Sūkurys M.K. Čiurlionio 51 ⓦwww.sukurys .lt. Popular bowling alley with pool tables, whose adjacent lounge-style bar is a worthy drinking destination in its own right, with an inexpensive menu of hot food. Sun–Thurs 11am–midnight, Fri & Sat 11am–2am.

Vido malūnas Veisiejų 4. Atmospheric pub-restaurant in an old mill, with the rushing waters of a nearby stream providing the aural backdrop.

The reasonably priced menu takes in pancakes, *koldūnai* and pretty much everything in the pork-chop line. Daily 10am–11pm.

Grūtas park

Three kilometres northeast of Druskininkai on the Vilnius road just outside the village of Grūtas, **Grūtas park** (Grūto parkas; daily: May–Sept 9am–8pm; Oct–April 9am–5pm; ⓦwww.grutoparkas.lt; 20Lt) is the last resting place for many of the Soviet-era statues that were uprooted from town squares all over the land following the collapse of the Moscow Coup in August 1991. The park is the private initiative of mushroom magnate Viliumas Malinauskas, who has earned a fortune from exporting the local fungus since setting up shop here in the late 1980s. Malinauskas began buying up discarded Soviet-era statues in the mid-1990s, hoping to establish a park that would tell the story of Lithuania in the second half of the twentieth century. The fact that he also saw the collection as a commercial tourist attraction was, however, regarded as a sign of insensitivity to Lithuanian sufferings by many observers. Malinauskas's plan to include a train ride in cattle trucks similar to those used in the deportations of Lithuanians to Siberia in 1941 and 1949 had to be dropped when critics complained that he was creating a "Soviet Disneyland". Officially opened in spring 2001, the park swiftly became the number-one tourist draw in southern Lithuania – a status particularly valued by the hoteliers of nearby Druskininkai.

It takes a good hour to walk around Grūto parkas, with the **statues** themselves scattered throughout a superbly laid-out and landscaped park. Each statue is accompanied by a plaque in both Lithuanian and English explaining its significance, so the park functions both as enjoyable history lesson and *plein-air* sculpture gallery – not all Soviet-era statuary was as bad as you might think. Among the instantly recognizable pieces on display are a Stalin that once stood outside Vilnius railway station, and numerous Lenins in all shapes and sizes – including the one that dominated the capital's Lukiškių aikštė until being ceremonially hauled away by crane in August 1991 (note the join just below the knee – the lower legs were sliced off by demonstrators unable to detach the statue from its pedestal). Look out, too, for the stern visage of Felix Dzerzhinsky, the Vilnius-educated Polish communist who founded the Cheka (forerunner of the KGB) in 1918, and has been something of a pin-up for secret policemen the world over ever since. There are also plenty of statues honouring Lithuanian revolutionary heroes, including one of Vincas Mickevičius-Kapsukas, who led the short-lived Lithuanian Bolshevik dictatorship of 1919, and an ensemble piece depicting Požela, Greifendingeris, Giedrys and Čarna – the underground communist leaders who were shot in Kaunas in 1926 and commemorated with this angular monument some fifty years later. In the middle of the park stands a projection hall where you can watch boy-meets-tractor propaganda films and examine a range of old photographs, newspapers and agitprop posters – including one with a primary-school slogan that reads "Love the Party, child, as you love your own mother!"

Getting to Grutas is easy, with **bus** #1A trundling from central Druskininkai to the park seven times a day. There's a good **café-restaurant** just beyond the entrance, offering everything from potato pancakes to roast duck.

Liškiava

Perched on a bluff overlooking the River Nemunas, **LIŠKIAVA** occupies the extreme western corner of the Dzūkija National Park. Its main draw is the eighteenth-century **Church of the Holy Trinity** (Šv Trejybės bažnyčia), a pastel-pink structure crowned by a stately grey-green dome, built to serve a now-defunct Dominican monastery. The interior is one of the few examples of the florid Rococo style in Lithuania, with swirling ceiling frescoes overlooking a show-stopping line-up of seven gilded altars, each decorated with expressive statues. Once you've seen this you can tour the remains of a nearby fourteenth-century hill-fort, commanding views of the majestic sweep of the river.

Liškiava is usually approached from the Druskininkai direction – from where it's an easy 9km bus or cycle ride along the riverbank. It's also the target of popular **river cruises**, which set off from a jetty just east of Druskininkai town centre every afternoon in season (May to mid-Oct; timings and tickets from the tourist office).

Šiauliai and around

Although **ŠIAULIAI** (pronounced "Shyow-*ley*") is Lithuania's fourth-largest city and the administrative centre of the northwest, its historical origins remain a mystery. It's thought to have taken its name from a battle fought hereabouts in 1236 and known in German chronicles as the Battle of the Sun ("Saulės mūšis" in Lithuanian), when a Lithuanian-Žemaitijan army inflicted a crushing blow on the crusading army of the Knights of the Sword. Certainly by the mid-sixteenth century, Šiauliai had established itself as an important market town midway along the Königsberg–Rīga road – a position that also facilitated the arrival of successive waves of Swedish and Russian invaders. Emerging as a handsome and prosperous provincial centre under the Tsarist Empire, Šiauliai was so pummelled by Soviet artillery in World War II that it had to be almost completely rebuilt in the aftermath, and today's gridiron of concrete buildings is the result. However, there's an enjoyable clutch of **offbeat museums** to explore, and one of Lithuania's most important cult sights, the **Hill of Crosses**, lies just beyond the northern outskirts. The city also serves as a stepping-stone if you're journeying west towards the Žemaitija National Park (see p.347) and the Baltic coast. **Trains** on the Vilnius–Klaipėda line pass through Šiauliai (3 daily), and there are plenty of **buses** from Vilnius, Kaunas and Rīga.

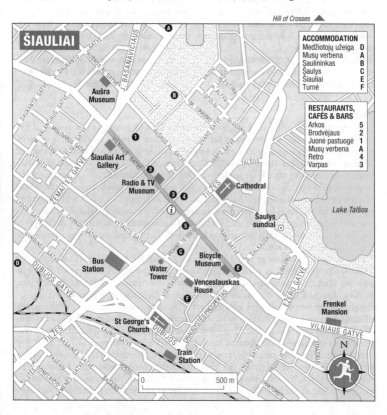

Arrival, information and accommodation

Šiauliai's main points of reference are the dead-straight **Tilžės gatvė**, which slices through the town northeast to southwest, and the pedestrianized **Vilniaus** gatvė, which cuts across Tilžės. The bus station is on Tilžės, about 500m southwest of Vilniaus, while the train station is slightly further out in the same direction, at the southwestern end of Draugystės prospektas. The friendly **tourist office**, Vilniaus 213 (July & Aug Mon–Fri 9am–6pm, Sat 10am–4pm, Sun 10am–3pm; Sept–June closed Sun; ☎8-41/523110, ⓦwww.siauliai.lt), has free town maps and can reserve accommodation on your behalf.

Hotels

Medžiotojų užeiga Dubijos 20 ☎8-41/524526, ⓦwww.medziotojuuzeiga.lt. Some way southwest of the centre on the far side of a major traffic intersection, but still within walking distance of the sights, this modern business-class hotel has a lofty, light-filled atrium stuffed with hunting trophies, and reasonably spacious rooms with all creature comforts. ④–⑥

Musų verbena Žemaitės 89 ☎8-41/211117, ⓦwww.verbena.lt. An attractively restored inter-war house just opposite the park with four rooms, each boasting pine floorboards, solid wooden beds and wardrobes, and embroidered linen pillows – along with TV and modern bathrooms. Room 2, with glass-enclosed balcony, is the best of an altogether charming bunch. ④–⑥

Saulininkas Lukausko 5A ☎8-41/436555, ⓦwww.saulininkas.com. A mid-sized place on a quiet street beside the park, offering functional

en-suites and a pair of "super-luxe" studio apartments with plush sofas and laminate floors. There's a sauna in the basement (90Lt/hr) and a gym. ④–⑤

Šaulys Vasario 16-osios 40 ☎8-41/520812, ⓦwww.saulys.lt. Stylish city-centre hotel centred on a nineteenth-century brick building with various new add-ons. Rooms feature deep carpets and bathtubs – although the slime-green colour scheme is a bit offputting. Gym and sauna (100Lt/hr) on site. ⑤–⑥

Šiauliai Draugystės 25 ☎8-41/437333. Grey, multistorey monument to Soviet-era tourism that now offers nicely renovated rooms with thick carpets and roomy bathrooms. Great views of the city from the west-facing side of the building. ③

Turnė Rūdės 9 ☎8-41/500150, ⓦwww.turne.lt. Central, but on a reasonably quiet street, this is a modern hotel with an intimate feel, attentive staff and simply furnished en-suites. ④

The City

Explorations of Šiauliai start with flagstoned **Vilniaus gatvė**, the shopping street where everyone wants to see and be seen in the evening. There's an absorbing array of museums along its length, starting at the southeastern end with the **Frenkel Mansion**, Vilniaus 74 (Tues–Fri 10am–6pm, Sat 11am–5pm; 6Lt). Built for a family of Jewish factory owners who ran a huge leather-tanning business, the mansion's rooms are richly decorated with delicate wood-panelling and florid stucco work, running the gamut of styles from neo-Baroque to Art Nouveau. Upstairs rooms are filled with furniture, porcelain and paintings from erstwhile aristocratic seats around Šiauliai, including several striking portraits of seventeenth- and eighteenth-century magnates – many sporting the extravagant moustaches, shaved heads and flowing oriental gowns favoured by the Polish-Lithuanian aristocracy of the period.

The **Bicycle Museum** at no. 139 (Dviračių muziejus; Tues–Fri 10am–6pm, Sat 11am–4pm; 6Lt) offers an entertaining round-up of two-wheeled transport throughout the ages, including just about every model ever produced by the local Vairas factory. Formed in 1948, Vairas was the Soviet Union's leading manufacturer of trendy chopper-style bikes for kids in the 1970s, and nowadays churns out thousands of mountain and racing bikes a year. At Vilniaus 174, the **Radio and TV Museum** (Radijo ir televizijos muziejus; Tues–Fri 10am–6pm, Sat 11am–4pm; 3Lt) was inaugurated to celebrate the output of local TV firm Tauras, although there's a lot else here besides, from old record players with enormous horns to Art Deco radiograms from the interwar years, and – as if to prove that consumer-oriented gimmickry wasn't entirely a Western invention – a portable radio in the form of a toy robot, made by a Rīga firm in 1980. A modern concrete structure at Vilniaus 245 harbours the **Šiauliai Art Gallery** (Šiaulių dailės galerija; Tues–Fri 10am–6pm, Sat 11am–4pm; 2Lt), a good place to catch contemporary art shows.

The gloomy corridors of the **Aušra Museum**, Aušros 47 (Aušros muziejus; Tues–Fri 9am–5pm, Sat 11am–4pm; 6Lt), are enlivened by a colourful display of folk costume from all over the country and a powerful collection of traditional sculpture, including a crowd of stern-faced saints and a riveting pietà. Down at the southeastern end of Aušros, the junction with Tilžės gatvė is dominated by the **Cathedral of SS Peter and Paul**. Built in 1625, it burned down along with just about everything else in the city in 1944. The current edifice dates from 1954, but is a faithful replica of the original, with a single white belfry (Lithuania's highest) rising up beside a supporting cast of tiny turrets – suggesting that it was originally intended as a fortified church capable of withstanding attacks by Swedes or Russians. Inside, all is light and purity, with a balustraded gallery overlooking a white-painted interior. A short stroll east along Aušros takas brings you face to face with the **Archer** (Šaulys), a gilded, bow-wielding statue atop a 20m-high concrete pillar. Built in 1986 to celebrate the 750th anniversary of the Battle of Saulė, the monument also functions as a huge sundial – the flagstoned expanse beneath it is marked with lines denoting the hours of the day.

The **Venclauskis House**, south of Vilniaus at Vytauto 89 (Venclauskių namai; Mon–Thurs 9am–5pm, Fri 10am–4pm; 6Lt), originally served as the opulent home of prominent nineteenth-century lawyer Kazimieras Venclauskis (1880–1940), who was mayor of Šiauliai in the immediate aftermath of World War I. His house is now given over to temporary exhibitions on local folklore and culture, alongside a memorial room commemorating Venceslauskis and his theatre-director wife Stanislava Jaskevičiutė.

Eating and drinking

Most of Šiauliai's eating and drinking venues are along or just off **Vilniaus gatvė**. Places here tend to go in and out of fashion at an alarming speed, but at least there are plenty to choose from. Šiauliai is not as a rule a big-spending city, and prices are generally reasonable.

Arkos Vilniaus 213. Roomy red-brick cellar with lots of cosy nooks and crannies, popular for quick lunches as well as more extended evening feasts. Lots of meat-and-potato main courses, plus pan-fried fish and a couple of veggie options. Also good just for a drink – especially at the weekend when there's live music and a cover charge. Daily 10am–midnight.

Brodvėjaus Vilniaus 146. Hedging its bets by offering both pizzas and pork-and-potatoes fare, *Brodvėjaus* is an unexciting place to eat but a great place to drink, with the staid bar-restaurant on the ground level leading to an animated downstairs bar, where fake leopard-print sofas and pop-rock sounds draw a loyal clientele of local youth. Sun–Thurs 10am–11pm, Sat & Sun 10am–midnight.

Juonė pastuogė Aušros 31A. In an alleyway midway between Aušros and Vilniaus, this barn-like venue with wooden-bench seating and a beamed attic ceiling is one of Šiauliai's more cosy, convivial venues. Lithuanian staples including *cepelinai*, pork chops and potato pancakes fill the menu. It's a

popular venue at weekends, with live country and western – Lithuanian style. Daily 11am–11pm.

Mūsų verbena Žemaitės. Charming teahouse on the ground floor of the *Mūsų verbena* B&B (see opposite), which serves traditional Lithuanian herbal teas alongside more familiar Indian and Chinese varieties. Full menu of main meals as well. Daily 11am–10pm.

Retro Vilniaus 146 (entrance around the corner on Varpo gatvė). This relaxing basement café-restaurant just about earns its name, thanks to an antique gramophone and the odd vintage clock. The wide-ranging menu takes in plenty of fish and vegetarian options, alongside the usual cuts of pork and chicken. Daily 11am–11pm.

Varpas Vilniaus 154. Another basement café-restaurant, this time with a vaguely Art-Nouveau interior with plush red couches and ornate wooden chairs. Strong on pork- or chicken-based main meals, the menu also offers a page of pancakes and a good choice of desserts. Sun–Weds 9am–11pm, Thurs–Sat 9am–midnight.

Hill of Crosses

The **Hill of Crosses** (Kryžų kalnas), 12km north of Šiauliai, just off the main road to Rīga, sums up the Lithuanian character more than any other sight in the country.

Combining evidence of profound Catholic piety, a deep appreciation for the simple forms of folk art and a fondness for contemplating the mysterious, it's a genuinely unique and strange attraction, and one that you should on no account miss.

Like many similar mounds dotting the Lithuanian countryside, the "hill" may have been associated with various forms of ancestor worship in the pre-Christian era, evolving naturally (with pagan totems replaced by crosses) as the centuries wore on. Tradition maintains that the rebellions of 1831 and 1863 were what turned the hill into a major focus of remembrance, with locals planting crosses out here in the countryside because the Tsarist authorities wouldn't have tolerated such an open display of national sentiment in an urban setting. It was certainly known as a focus of patriotic pilgrimage by the 1950s, when another round of cross-planting was undertaken by Lithuanians keen to preserve the memory of those who had died or disappeared as a result of the mass deportations to Siberia. Determined to discourage any further manifestations of religious or patriotic sentiment, the Soviet authorities had the site bulldozed repeatedly in the 1960s – each time, the locals responded by planting new crosses. A visit by Pope John Paul II in September 1993 helped to propel the hill into the premier league of pilgrimage destinations, with the construction of a brand-new Franciscan monastery just north of the site in 2001 underlining the place's growing spiritual stature.

Approaching the hill along an avenue of lime trees, it's initially difficult to work out what the bristling brown mass rising out of the flat green landscape actually is. It's only when you hit the coach-packed car park that you begin to pick out individual pilgrims and the strange collection of monuments they've come to visit. A cross presented by the Pope stands at the foot of the hill, its base inscribed with the words "Thank you Lithuanians for this Hill of Crosses, which testifies to the nations of Europe and the whole world the faith of the people of this land". Behind it, a towering wooden statue of Jesus, arms outstretched, seems to be ushering pilgrims onto the hill itself. It's an impressive sight, with every patch of ground planted with crosses of every conceivable size. There are even tiny crosses hanging by metal chains around the crosspieces of the larger ones – the jangling sound these make when the wind gets up is unearthly indeed. You'll see some marvellous examples of Lithuanian wood-carving, with totem-like pillars adorned with images of various saints, and numerous examples of the Rupintojélis, or Sorrowful Christ.

If you're **driving** to the hill, head out of town on the Rīga road and turn right when you see the sign for Kryžų kalnas about 6km beyond the city limits. By **bus**, Šiauliai–Joniškis services (7 daily) and Šiauliai–Rīga services (4 daily) stop right beside the Kryžų kalnas turn-off, from where it's a 2km walk to the hill itself – Šiauliai tourist office might be a more reliable source of English-language timetable information than the bus station.

Travel details

Buses

Anykščiai to: Biržai (1 daily; 2hr); Kaunas (10 daily; 2hr 30min); Panevėžys (8 daily; 1hr); Vilnius (4 daily; 2hr 20min).
Druskininkai to: Kaunas (7 daily; 2hr 15min); Vilnius (8 daily; 2hr).
Kaunas to: Anykščiai (10 daily; 2hr 30min); Biržai (3 daily; 3hr 30min); Druskininkai (7 daily; 2hr 15min); Klaipėda (12 daily; 3hr 30min); Kėdainiai (hourly; 1hr); Panevėžys (13 daily; 2hr 30min); Šiauliai (7 daily; 2hr 30min); Vilnius (every 15–30min; 1hr 30min).
Kėdainiai to: Biržai (4 daily; 3hr 30min); Kaunas (hourly; 1hr); Panevėžys (12 daily; 1hr 20min); Šiauliai (8 daily; 1hr 30min); Vilnius (3 daily; 2hr 20min).
Panevėžys to: Anykščiai (8 daily; 1hr); Biržai (16 daily; 1hr 20min); Kaunas (13 daily; 2hr 30min); Kėdainiai (13 daily; 1hr 20min); Šiauliai (11 daily; 2hr).
Šiauliai to: Kaunas (7 daily; 2hr 30min); Panevėžys (11 daily; 2hr); Vilnius (8 daily; 4hr).

Vilnius to: Biržai (4 daily; 3hr 40min–4hr 20min); Druskininkai (8 daily; 2hr); Kaunas (every 15–30min; 1hr 30min); Panevėžys (10 daily; 1hr 50min–3hr); Šiauliai (8 daily; 4hr).

Trains

Kaunas to: Klaipėda (2 daily; 6hr); Vilnius (10 daily; 1hr–1hr 15min).

Vilnius to: Ignalina (5 daily; 2hr); Marcinkonys (3 daily; 2hr); Šiauliai (3 daily; 4hr); Zervynos (3 daily; 1hr 50min).

International buses

Druskininkai to: Grodno (3 daily; 2hr); Kaliningrad (1 daily; 9hr); Warsaw (1 daily; 7hr).
Kaunas to: Rīga (3 daily; 5hr 20min).
Šiauliai to: Rīga (4 daily; 3hr 15min).

3.3

Western Lithuania

The undulating landscape of forests and lakes that characterizes much of **western Lithuania** rolls all the way to the Baltic Sea, where it culminates in a golden ribbon of sand backed by fragrant pines. With its long stretches of beach, towering dunes and church-topped hills, this part of Lithuania incorporates many of the country's most characteristic holiday-postcard images and is one of its most visited areas. There's a thriving resort culture along the seaboard, with plenty of accommodation and entertainment, but you're never too far away from semi-abandoned beaches and tranquil woodland paths. Strong folk art traditions survive in the villages: wooden farmsteads and fishermen's cottages sport intricately carved gables (the twin horse-head motif known as the *žirgelis* being one of the most typical designs), while totemic shrine-poles topped with statues of saints are commonly seen in gardens.

The region's unofficial capital is **Klaipėda**, a work-hard-play-hard port city with a medieval, German-flavoured Old Town at its heart. A short ferry ride away lies the **Curonian Spit** (also known as Neringa), an offshore sand bar boasting dense pine forests, rippling sand dunes and picturesque fishing villages, of which **Nida** is the most celebrated. Completely different in atmosphere is **Palanga**, just north of Klaipėda, a candyfloss-and-cocktails beach resort popular with families and fun-seeking teenagers. South of Klaipėda, the rustic, reed-fringed villages of the **Nemunas Delta** provide the perfect getaway from the holiday-resort crush, with plenty of bird-watching opportunities in spring and autumn. The main attraction inland is the **Žemaitija National Park**, where you can boat on tranquil Lake Plateliai or walk and cycle around the pretty villages.

Getting to the coast **by road** usually involves a less-than-inspiring 275km journey (3–4hr if driving; 4–5hr by bus) along the Vilnius–Kaunas–Klaipėda highway, which passes through an unchanging landscape of arable fields and pasture. A more scenic alternative – although it will add two or three hours to your journey – is to take the Kaunas–Jurbarkas–Šilutė–Klaipėda road, which for much of its length runs alongside the stately Nemunas River. The Vilnius–Klaipėda **rail line** loops northwards via Šiauliai before passing through **Plungė**, the main gateway to the Žemaitija National Park.

Some history: Žemaitijans, Curonians and Prussians

Western Lithuania is made up of two distinct areas: **Žemaitija** (sometimes called Samogitia in Western sources), which covers the rolling terrain in the northwestern corner of the country, and **Lithuania Minor** (Mažoji Lietuva), the lowlands around the Nemunas delta in the southwest and the whole of the coastal strip. Žemaitija is named after the Žemaitijans, one of the original tribes that came to the Baltic around four thousand years ago, providing the ethnic bedrock from which the Lithuanian nation emerged. The Žemaitijans held on to their tribal identity much longer than other Lithuanians, however, remaining independent of the medieval Lithuanian state that came into being in the thirteenth century. They joined Lithuanian ruler Mind-augas in defeating the Teutonic Knights at Šiauliai in 1236, but remained only loosely allied to Lithuania until the fifteenth century, when they were formally absorbed into the Grand Duchy. They missed out on Lithuania's conversion to Christianity in 1389, remaining pagan for a further half-century – as a result, Žemaitija is still regarded as a repository of ancient, pre-Christian, Lithuanian traditions.

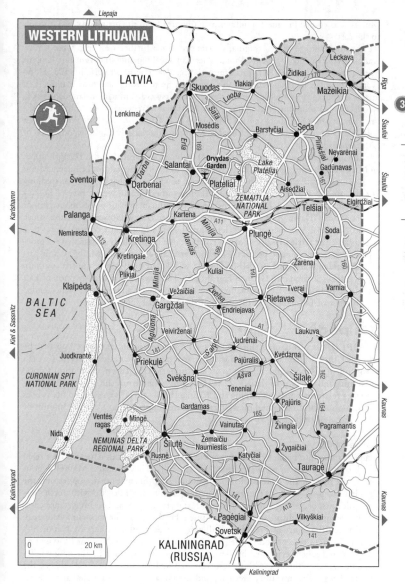

In the southwest were two other Baltic tribes: the **Curonians** (Kurši) on the coast and the **Prussians** (Prusai) on the banks of the Nemunas River. Both of these peoples were conquered by the Teutonic Knights in the thirteenth century and were either exterminated or driven into exile (the name "Prussia" survived though as a geographical label). The Teutons deliberately turned the whole of the seaboard into a wasteland, believing that this would deter attacks by the Žemaitijans and Lithuanians. By the fifteenth century, however, peasants from all over Lithuania were beginning to repopulate the area, assimilating any Curonians or Prussians who remained – the term "Lithuania

Minor" was coined in order to differentiate this area from the main body of Lithuania to the east.

Lithuania Minor – which originally extended much further west into what is now Kaliningrad Province – remained under German-speaking rule, the Teutonic Knights having transformed their territories into the secular state of Prussia in 1525. However, Lithuanian language and culture remained quite strong, and was – initially at least – encouraged by the Protestant clergy. The first-ever Lithuanian-language book, a collection of religious texts compiled by Martynas Mažvydas, was published in the Prussian city of Königsberg (now Kaliningrad) in 1547, in the hope that the Protestant faith could be exported from Lithuania Minor to the largely Catholic populace of Lithuania proper.

In the nineteenth century, when the rest of Lithuania was ruled by the Tsarist Empire, and Lithuanian-language publishing was subject to severe restrictions, Lithuania Minor enjoyed comparative cultural freedom. Prussian towns with a big Lithuanian-speaking population like Tilsit (now Sovetsk) and Ragnit (now Neman) were a hive of literary activity, and it was from Tilsit that the principal Lithuanian nationalist publication of the era, *Aušra* ("Dawn"), was smuggled into Tsarist territory. However, the area south of the Nemunas was increasingly Germanized as the nineteenth century drew to a close, while the territories north of the river became more solidly Lithuanian – a process accentuated by war and politics. This northern half of Lithuania Minor became part of independent Lithuania in 1918 (Klaipėda was added in 1923), while the southern half was incorporated into German East Prussia. The Soviet Union's absorption of East Prussia in 1945 and its transformation into the Russified Kaliningrad Province ended the presence of Lithuanian culture south of the Nemunas for good.

Klaipėda

KLAIPĖDA is Lithuania's third-largest city and the main transport hub for the whole of the Lithuanian coast. An easily manageable, yet energetic city, it's worth a stop-off in its own right, thanks to an atmospheric **Old Town**, a handful of good **museums** and a lively **nightlife** scene. Standing aloof from the rivalry that characterizes relations between Vilnius and Kaunas, it's a self-possessed place, its role as economic and cultural capital of western Lithuania engendering a certain amount of infectious civic pride.

Some history

Klaipėda came into being in 1252, when the Livonian Order built a fortress here from which to mount attacks on the heathens of Žemaitija. They named it **Memel** in honour of the river of the same name (the Nemunas in Lithuanian) that empties into the Curonian Lagoon 40km to the south. The settlement soon filled up with north German colonists, becoming a member of the Hanseatic League and an important centre for the export of Lithuanian timber. Despite a brief spell as the capital of Prussia in 1806, when the court of Frederick Wilhelm III was penned in here by Napoleon's armies, Memel's real period in the political limelight didn't come until the end of **World War I** when, evacuated by German troops, it was claimed by the newly independent state of Lithuania. Although surrounded by Lithuanian-speaking villages, the city itself was predominantly German, and the Great Powers assembled at the Paris Peace Conference didn't really know what to do with it. The French troops sent to garrison it turned a blind eye when the Lithuanians took matters into their own hands, seizing Memel by force in January 1923. The Lithuanians had already lost Vilnius to the Poles, and many in the international community saw their smash-and-grab raid on Memel as some form of compensation.

Renamed **Klaipėda**, the city retained its German population, and both German and Lithuanian were the official languages in local government. The two communities got on reasonably well until the 1930s, when local Nazis – emboldened by the aggressive foreign policy of Hitler's Germany – began to demand the city's reunification with the

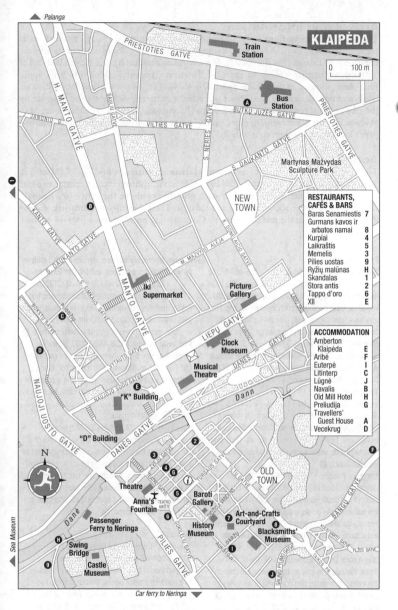

KLAIPĖDA

Palanga

Train Station

Bus Station

Martynas Mažvydas Sculpture Park

NEW TOWN

0   100 m

RESTAURANTS, CAFÉS & BARS
Baras Senamiestis	7
Gurmans kavos ir arbatos namai	8
Kurpiai	4
Laikraštis	5
Memelis	3
Pilies uostas	9
Ryžių malūnas	H
Skandalas	1
Stora antis	2
Tappo d'oro	6
XII	E

ACCOMMODATION
Amberton Klaipėda	E
Aribė	F
Euterpė	I
Litinterp	C
Lügne	J
Navalis	B
Old Mill Hotel	H
Preliudija	G
Travellers' Guest House	A
Vecekrug	D

Iki Supermarket

Picture Gallery

Clock Museum

Musical Theatre

"K" Building

"D" Building

Theatre

Anna's Fountain

Baroti Gallery

Art-and-Crafts Courtyard

History Museum

Blacksmiths' Museum

OLD TOWN

Passenger Ferry to Neringa

Swing Bridge

Castle Museum

Sea Museum

Car ferry to Neringa

Reich. On March 23, 1939, the Führer himself sailed into Klaipėda harbour aboard the battle cruiser *Deutschland* to take possession of the city. With the arrival of the Red Army in 1944, most of the Germans fled – there's now a mere handful of true Memelites left. Under the Soviets, Klaipėda was a strategic port that few foreigners were allowed to visit. Nowadays an economically buoyant, cosmopolitan place attracting its fair share of foreign investment, it's in much better shape than most provincial cities in the Baltics.

Arrival and information

The **train and bus stations** lie on opposite sides of Priestoties gatvė, ten minutes' walk north of the Old Town. A taxi from Klaipėda's small **airport**, 25km north of the city on the far side of Palanga (☎8-46/052020, ⌨www.palanga-airport.lt), will set you back 50Lt.

Klaipėda's **tourist office**, in the Old Town at Turgaus 7 (Mon–Fri 9am–6pm; June–Aug also Sat & Sun 9am–3pm; ☎8-46/412186, ⌨www.klaipedainfo.lt), can book accommodation. *In Your Pocket* publishes a characteristically thorough guide to the city's hotels, restaurants, bars and shops (Palanga and Nida in the same issue; 5Lt; ⌨www.inyourpocket.com), updated yearly and available from the tourist office, newspaper kiosks and hotel reception desks.

Accommodation

The city has a good range of **accommodation**. Litinterp, Puodžių 17 (Mon–Fri 9am–6pm, Sat 10am–4pm; ☎8-46/410644, ⌨www.litinterp.lt), has central **rooms**, either with local families or in their own guesthouse above the office (see below); they can also arrange rooms in Nida and Palanga. There's an all-year **campsite**, *Pajūrio* (☎8-67/773227), in the seaside village of Giruliai, 8km north of town (bus #4 or train to Giruliai station).

Hotels

Amberton Klaipėda Naujojo Sodo 1 ☎8-46/404372, ⌨www.ambertonhotel.lt. A prime example of a hotel that shouldn't be judged by its exterior, this angular red-brick lump harbours classy en-suite rooms. The spacious "lux" rooms, with Jacuzzi-bathtubs and flat-screen TVs, are worth the splurge. There's a gym and 20m pool on site. ⑤–⑥

Aribė Bangų 17A ☎8-46/490940, ⌨www.aribe.lt. A fifteen-room hotel a five-minute walk east of the Old Town, *Aribė* offers simple, neat en-suites with TVs and small desks. ⑥

Euterpė Daržų 9/Aukštoji 15 ☎8-46/474703, ⌨www.euterpe.lt. Historic building with modern add-ons, offering attractive en-suites with swish bathrooms. Extra-snug rooms on the top floor have attic skylights, while some deluxe doubles have wooden floors. ⑥

Litinterp Puodžių 17 ☎8-46/410644, ⌨www.litinterp.lt. Mixed bag of rooms above the Litinterp office, from small, airless singles with WC/shower in the hall to roomy en-suite doubles with natural wood furnishings and kitchenette. Call in advance if arriving outside Litinterp office hours (see above). ③

Lūgnė Galinio pylimo 16 ☎8-46/411884, ⌨www.lugne.lt. On the southeastern fringes of the Old Town, the *Lūgnė* is grey on the outside, but chic on the inside, with smart and comfortable en-suites aimed at an international business clientele. ④–⑤

Navalis Manto 23 ☎8-46/404200, ⌨www.navalis.lt. Business-class comforts in a mid-sized, charmingly intimate place in a handsome,

nineteenth-century building. Handily located midway between train/bus stations and the Old Town. ⑦

Old Mill Hotel Žvejų 22 ☎8-46/219215, ⌨www.oldmillhotel.lt. Modern construction with a medieval half-timbered look, right next to the pedestrian wing bridge. Most of the comfy, bright en-suite rooms come with great waterside views. ⑤

Preliudija Kepėjų 7 ☎8-46/310077, ⌨www.preliudija.com. Snug six-room B&B in a restored Old Town house. The en-suite rooms come in a variety of shapes and sizes – including a couple of L-shaped doubles that are quirkily cosy. Most have wooden floors, muted colour schemes and either a sofa or extra desk space. ⑤

Vecekrug Juros 23 ☎8-46/301002, ⌨www.vecekrug.lt. Modern hotel a short walk north of the centre on the edge of the container-port part of town, offering smart rooms. Most come with showers – if you fancy a Jacuzzi-style tub, ask for one of the roomy deluxe doubles. The rooftop summer terrace is an interesting spot to drink and gaze at Klaipėda's crane-scape. ⑥

Hostel

Travellers' Guest House Butkų Juzės 7–4 ☎8-65/594407 or 8-46/211879, ⌨www.klaipedahostel.com. Friendly backpackers' hostel in a residential block behind the bus station. Two cramped but neat bunk-bed dorms share a couple of toilets and a shower, and there's a little kitchen. It also rents out bikes. No breakfast, but *Café-Pizzeria Pipita* is just 2min walk away. 44Lt per person.

The City

Tucked into the right angle formed by the River Danė and the Curonian Lagoon, Klaipėda's **Old Town** (Senamiestis) has the cobbled streets and half-timbered houses of a provincial German town – which is essentially what Klaipėda was until 1944. Many of the buildings, however, were damaged in World War II and rebuilt in not quite authentic style, giving the centre a rather untidy, fragmented air. The medieval, gridiron street plan still survives though, and reminders of the trades once practised here live on in street names such as Kalvių (Blacksmiths'), Kurpių (Cobblers') and Vežėjų (Undertakers').

West of the Old Town lies the **Old Castle Port** (Senasis pilies uostas), a former dockland area being redeveloped as a waterside recreation spot – it already boasts a handful of restaurants and a marina. North of the River Danė, the nineteenth-century **New Town** (Naujamiestis) is the city's business and commercial centre.

The Old Town

At the heart of the Old Town, cobbled **Theatre Square** (Teatro aikštė) is named after the ornate Neoclassical theatre on its northern side. Hitler spoke from its balcony in March 1939 after Germany had annexed Klaipėda in its last act of territorial aggrandizement before the outbreak of war. In front of the theatre is **Anna's Fountain** (Anikės fontanas), a replica of a famous prewar monument to the German poet Simon Dach (1605–59), depicting the heroine of his folksong, *Ännchen von Tharau*.

Running northeast of the square, **Turgaus gatvė**, once Klaipėda's main market street, retains many of its fine pre-twentieth-century town houses. To the southeast lies a mixed area of nondescript modern buildings and picturesque, half-timbered warehouses. An imposing 200-year-old example of the latter, at Aukštoji 3, houses the commercial **Baroti Art Gallery** (Mon–Fri 11am–6pm, Sat 11am–4pm; ⓦwww .barotigalerija.lt; free), its contemporary paintings and sculptures spread across three floors of atmospheric, timber-beamed rooms.

Around the corner, at Didžioji vandens 6, the **History Museum of Lithuania Minor** (Mažosios Lietuvos istorijos muziejus; Tues–Sat 10am–6pm; 5Lt) presents a comprehensive chronological account of the region's history, including plenty of archeological interest, notably a scale model of a Lithuanian pagan sanctuary which once occupied Birutė's Hill, a well-known landmark in nearby Palanga (see p.345). The arrangement of the sanctuary reveals a high degree of astronomical knowledge, with the placing of totem-like poles dictated by the positions of the planets throughout the year, and the main axis of the ensemble aligned with the rays of the setting sun on April 23. The later, Christianized inhabitants of Lithuania Minor were obviously a sober, serious-minded bunch if the costumes on display here are anything to go by – greys and blacks predominate, with delicately embroidered belt-purses providing the only splash of colour. Finally, look out for photographs of Lithuania's seizure of Klaipėda in 1923, and a 1939 snap of Adolf Hitler riding down Manto gatvė in a motorcade, greeted by ranks of local Brown Shirts.

A few steps southeast at Šaltakalvių 2 is the **Blacksmiths' Museum** (Mažosios Lietuvos kalvystės muziejus; Tues–Sat 10am–6pm; 5Lt), based on the private collection of blacksmithery enthusiast Dionizas Varkalis, who made it his personal mission to collect and restore the neglected wrought-iron crosses found in graveyards across the region. These are a traditional Lithuanian folk art form, frequently featuring intricate sun-ray motifs that point to pre-Christian, pagan inspiration. Domestic oddities, including irons, kitchen tools and doorknobs, round off a fascinating collection.

The Old Castle Port

Southwest of the Old Town is the **Old Castle Port** (Senasis pilies uostas), a former industrial area that is being smartened up to create a swanky shoreline promenade. At its centre are the former ramparts of the original fortress built by Memel-Klaipėda's Teutonic founders, and a stretch of moat that has been turned into a marina. Two of the fortress's towers have been restored to house the **Castle Museum** (Pilies muziejus; Tues–Sat 10am–6pm; 6Lt), which tells the history of the city through a motley collection of exhibits – from mannequins dressed in medieval costumes to Renaissance ceramics and a scale model of sixteenth-century Memel. A wall of twentieth-century photographs includes an intriguing picture of a Red Army soldier hastening off with a (presumably) looted penny-farthing in 1945.

The Old Castle Port is reached by passing through the gates of Klaipėda's former shipyard (roughly opposite Daržų gatvė), or by approaching along Žvejų gatvė a little further north. The latter route involves a trip across the cast-iron **Swing Bridge**, an attractive nineteenth-century pedestrian bridge that is swung open (by manually operated cog mechanism) to allow boats into the marina once every hour.

The New Town

Klaipėda's largely twentieth-century **New Town** (Naujamiestis) is best accessed by crossing the bridge across the River Danė at the northeastern end of Tiltų gatvė. On the opposite side stands a modern, arch-shaped memorial symbolizing the reunification of Lithuania Minor with the rest of the country in the wake of World War II. Looming to the east, on the far side of the *Klaipėda* hotel, are two prominent symbols of contemporary Klaipėda – a huge red-brick office block in the shape of the letter K, standing beside a structure in the shape of a D. Completed in 2006, and clearly visible when approaching town by sea, the buildings are intended to provide modern-day Klaipėda with an instantly recognizable visual trademark.

Running northwest from the river Danė is the New Town's principal artery, the shop- and café-lined **Manto gatvė**. More interesting, though, is **Liepų gatvė**, which runs parallel to the river and on which stands Klaipėda's splendid, red-brick, Gothic-revival **post office**. Built between 1883 and 1893, it's a vivid reminder of German civic pride, not least because of the 48-bell carillon that rings out from the clock tower at noon every Saturday and Sunday. The post office is also famous for being the workplace of telephonist Erika Rostel, awarded the Iron Cross for staying at her post (and giving a running commentary on events to the German General Staff) when the Russian army raided the city in March, 1915 – most of the other civilians had taken to the Curonian Lagoon in boats. A few doors along at Liepų 12, the **Clock Museum** (Laikrodžių muziejus; Tues–Sat noon–6pm; Sun noon–5pm; 6Lt) is stuffed with timepieces from the earliest candle clocks onwards. As much as anything, the display provides a fascinating overview of changing fashions in clock design, with some magnificently over-the-top seventeenth- and eighteenth-century creations, and the odd Art Nouveau grandfather clock bringing up the rear.

Eating, drinking and entertainment

There's little distinction between eating and drinking venues in Klaipėda: **bars and pubs** usually offer a full food menu, while **restaurants** are frequently fun places in which to knock back a few beers. Most places are concentrated on or around the New Town's main thoroughfare, Manto gatvė, and its Old Town continuation, Tiltų gatvė. You can pick up **picnic** supplies from the Iki supermarket, on the corner of Mažvydo and Šiaulių (daily 8am–10pm).

Klaipėda's main cultural flagship is the **Drama Theatre**, Teatro 2 (Dramos teatras; box office Tues–Sun 10am–2pm & 4–6pm; ⑩www.kldteatras.lt); you'll encounter less of a language barrier at the **Musical Theatre** (Muzikinis teatras; box office Tues–Sun 11am–2pm & 3–6pm; ⑩www.klaipedosmuzikinis.lt), which hosts chamber concerts, musicals and occasional visits by Vilnius's symphony orchestras.

Cafés, restaurants and bars

Baras Senamiestis Bažnyčių 4/10. Unpretentious café-restaurant in a half-timbered house with original wooden features and Seventies' lounge furniture. The vaguely studenty clientele lend an arty vibe, while the basic pork-chop-and-fries menu keeps undemanding bellies satisfied. Plenty of outdoor bench space in summer. Daily 11am–11pm.

Gurmans kavos ir arbatos namai Fridriho pasaža, just off Tiltų gatvė. Refined two-storey café in the characterful alleyway that is Friedrich's Passage, offering excellent coffee, properly brewed tea and a hard-to-resist selection of salads and light meals, cakes and cookies. You can also stock up on speciality teas, freshly ground coffee and pipe tobacco from the retail counter. Mon–Fri 8.30am–11pm, Sat 9am–11pm, Sun 10am–10pm.

Kurpiai Kurpių 1A. A Klaipėda legend: a cosy brick-and-timber pub with good food, regular live bands (mostly jazz, but also rock-pop covers) and a regular crowd of easy-going punters. Tues–Sat noon–2am, Sun & Mon noon–midnight.

Laikraštis Turgaus 3. Right on the Old Town's main street, the "Newspaper" is a comfy, wood-floored, timber-panelled bar with a journalistic theme – note the pictures of local politicians, sportsmen and celebrities lining the walls. There's an extensive menu of main meals – and relatively early opening times make it a good spot for a breakfast fry-up. Mon–Sat 7am–midnight, Sun 10am–midnight.

Memelis Žvejų 4. A beautifully restored red-brick warehouse on the banks of the Danė River with hearty meat and fish dishes, delicious light, dark and wheat beers brewed on the premises, late-night drinking and dancing in the top-floor club. Tues–Thurs noon–2am, Fri & Sat noon–4am, Sun noon–midnight.

Pilies uostas Žvejų 24 ☎8-46/211887. At the increasingly swanky marina end of town, "Castle Port" is a something-for-everyone place serving passable pizzas and mainstream meat dishes in a roomy building decked out in nautical bric-a-brac. Best of all is the location, with a terrace facing Memel Castle's former moat. Daily 11am–11pm.

Ryžių malūnas Žvejų 22 ☎8-46/474764. Attached to the *Old Mill* hotel (see p.332) this is one of the best places on the coast for Italian-themed risotto, pasta and pizza. It enjoys an enviable location, with tables set out in ogling distance of the bobbing boats of Klaipėda's marina,

so arrive early or book on summer evenings. Daily noon–midnight.

Skandalas Kanto 44. Spacious, enduringly popular bar-restaurant some 20min walk northwest of the Old Town, worth investigating for its broad choice of international beers and lengthy menu of heavy-duty steaks, BBQ ribs and quality seafood. With human-sized effigies of the Statue of Liberty, a Native American and a US traffic cop, there's a strong Uncle Sam theme, although the vintage adverts covering the walls seem to have been plucked from all corners of the English-speaking world. Daily noon–1am.

Stora antis Tiltų 6 ☎8-46/493910. A cosy brick cellar whose arches are so low they're equipped with padded forehead buffers, the "Fat Duck" offers a lengthy menu of dishes from the Slavonic countries of Europe. It's best to stick to Russian and Ukrainian choices like *pelmeni* (stuffed pasta parcels), potato pancakes, *blini* and various types of borscht, rather than plumping for the "Croatian" or "Bulgarian" options – which don't have much to do with the cuisines of those countries. Daily noon–midnight.

Tappo d'oro Sikilelių 10. Dark, cosy wine bar with umpteen varietes of (mostly Italian) tipple, strong coffee, and a small menu of prosciutto-and-cheese-type nibbles. Outdoor seating on the edge of the main square. Daily 11am–midnight.

XII Top floor, *Amberton Klaipėda* hotel, Naujojo Sodo 1. Snazzy cocktail bar-cum-restaurant, with grilled steaks prepared in an open kitchen and loungey window-side seating offering fantastic city views. Mains around 30–35Lt. Daily noon–2am.

Listings

Hospital Red Cross Hospital (Raudonojo kryžiaus ligoninė) Nėries 3 ☎8-46/410 739.
International ferries Lisco, Perkėlos 10 ☎8-46/395050, ⓦwww.lisco.lt (ferries to Kiel and Sassnitz in Germany; also agents for the once-weekly DFDS ferry to Gdańsk); Scandlines (ferries to Åhus and Aabenraa), *Amberton Klaipėda* hotel, Naujojo Sodo 1 ☎8-46/310561, ⓦwww.scandlines.lt.

Pharmacy Vokiečių Vaistinė, Turgaus 22 (Mon–Fri 9am–7pm, Sat 10am–5pm).
Post office Liepų 16 ☎8-46/315022 (Mon–Fri 8am–7pm, Sat 9am–4pm).
Travel agents Baltic Clipper, Turgaus 2 ☎8-46/312312, ⓦwww.baltic-clipper.lt; Krantas Travel, Teatro 5 ☎8-46/395111, ⓦwww.krantas.lt.

The Curonian Spit

A short hop by ferry from Klaipėda's port, the long, sandy promontory which makes up the **Curonian Spit** (Kuršių nerija; aka "Neringa" after the sea goddess who allegedly built it) is one of the most exotic natural wonderlands in the Baltic. Formed over several millennia by deposits of wind- and wave-driven sand, the spit closed off the Nemunas delta from the open sea, forming the Curonian Lagoon in the process. Only the northernmost half of the 97km-long spit falls within Lithuania – the rest belongs to Kaliningrad Province, part of German East Prussia until 1945, but now governed by the Russian Federation.

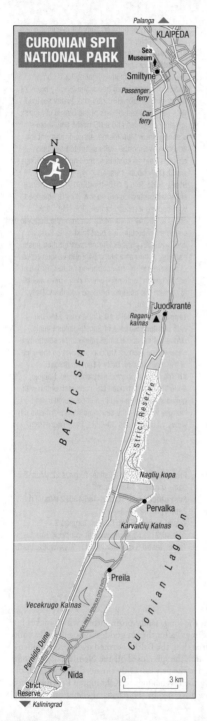

CURONIAN SPIT NATIONAL PARK

Palanga
KLAIPEDA
Sea Museum
Smiltyne
Passenger ferry
Car ferry
N
BALTIC SEA
Juodkrantė
Raganų kalnas
Strict Reserve
Naglių kopa
Pervalka
Karvaičių Kalnas
Curonian Lagoon
Preila
Vecekrugo Kalnas
Parnidis Dune
Nida
Strict Reserve
Kaliningrad
0   3 km

A sliver of land never more than 4km wide, the spit basically takes the form of an undulating line of huge, 50m-high sand dunes, some looking starkly Saharan in their bareness, but most covered in a dense carpet of dark-green pines, stately silver birches and skinny, soil-starved limes. It's an impermanent landscape, with sea breezes driving sand up the western slopes of the dunes and over the other side, causing a gradual eastward drift of the spit's central ridge. Deforestation in the seventeenth century sped this process up so much that villages had to be moved from one generation to the next as homes were progressively swallowed up by the sands. Systematic replanting of pines and grasses over the last century or so has served to stabilize the dunes. On the eastern side of the spit lies a scattering of villages that traditionally relied on the fish-teeming waters of the lagoon for a living (nowadays the main industry is tourism), while the western shore is one long, silky stretch of beach.

The whole of the Lithuanian part of the spit has been placed under the protective wing of the **Curonian Spit National Park** (Kuršių nerijos nacionalinis parkas). The northern parts of the promontory are nesting grounds for herons and cormorants, while some of the deeper forests harbour a handful of elk. Although most of the park is accessible, some areas of dune have been designated "strict reserves", closed to visitors in order to prevent erosion.

The best way to explore the spit is by bike or on foot: there's an extensive network of **forest trails** and surfaced **cycle paths**, as well as plenty of signboards with maps – the visitors' centre at the northern end of the spit (see below) can help with further information.

Ferries from Klaipėda arrive at **Smiltynė** at the northern end of the spit, the site of a hugely popular aquarium. However, the best of Neringa's scenery lies well south of here, around neat, timber-built resort villages like **Juodkrantė** and most of all **Nida**, which allows access to the most spectacular of the dunes. Although

Nida is do-able as a day-trip from Klaipėda, it makes sense to stick around – the village has an invigorating, Vilnius-by-the-sea feel in summer, and the surrounding sands-and-pines landscape is a joy to explore.

Getting there and information

Getting to Neringa involves taking one of two **ferries** from Klaipėda. The smaller one, for foot passengers (every 30min; 2.90Lt), departs from the Old Castle Port (Senasis pilies uostas), just outside the Old Town. A larger ferry leaves from the New Port (Naujasis uostas), 2km south of the Old Town (every 30min in summer, hourly in winter; foot passengers 2.90Lt, cars 40Lt). The ferry from the Old Castle Port arrives in Smyltinė, handy for both the Sea Museum and the bus stop – from here frequent **minibuses** run the length of the spit as far as Nida. The New Port ferry ends up a good 2km south of Smyltinė, convenient if you're driving straight down the spit. All visitors who come with a vehicle have to pay a national park **entrance fee** (20Lt/car, 7Lt/motorbike) at the road barrier 5km south of Smyltinė – keep the receipt for the return journey. The speed limit on the spit is 40km/hr.

The **National Park Visitors' Centre**, north of the passenger ferry landing at Smiltynės plentas 11 (May–Sept Tues–Sun 10am–6pm; ☎8-46/402257, ⊛www .nerija.lt), offers rudimentary **maps** and friendly advice; otherwise the tourist office in Nida (see p.338) is your best source of information.

Smiltynė

Lying a ten-minute ferry hop across the lagoon from Klaipėda, **SMILTYNĖ** is not a settlement as such – it's more of a rambling park, popular with Klaipėda folk as a recreation venue. Running along its eastern side, a promenade offers views of the merchant ships and loading cranes that crowd Klaipėda's port, while over to the west lies the start of the Curonian Spit's unbroken line of beach. Between the two lies a clutch of attractions, starting with the quaint **Fishermen's Farmstead** (Žvejų sodyba; free), north of the ferry landing, an ensemble of nineteenth-century, wooden buildings – a reed-roofed dwelling house (occasionally open), sauna, fish-smoking shed and potato cellar.

Another five minutes' walk north, a gun battery built to beef up Klaipėda's defences in the mid-nineteenth century provides the setting for Lithuania's most visited tourist attraction, the so-called **Sea Museum** (Jūrų muziejus; May–Sept Tues–Sun 11am–7pm; Oct–April Sat & Sun 11am–6pm; 10Lt; ⊛www.juru.muziejus.lt) – which is really an aquatic zoo with a few history-related displays tacked on. Resembling an enormous red-brick doughnut and surrounded by huge earthen ramparts, the former fortress is now garrisoned by all manner of water-dwellers – personable penguins and seals loll around in the inner moat, while the circular central enclosure accommodates everything from Black Sea sturgeon to piranha fish. Across the central courtyard, a display of nautical artefacts and model ships is less memorable than the atmospherically lit powder magazines in which it is housed. In summer, sea lions perform in an outdoor pool round the back of the main building (12Lt), while in the eternally popular **Dolphinarium** (shows May–Sept noon, 2pm & 4pm; Oct–April noon & 3pm; 15Lt) Black Sea bottlenose dolphins are put through the hoops. Even if you don't arrive in time for a show, you can observe the dolphins swimming from a large underwater window in the entrance hall. To get to Smiltynė's delicious, fine-sand **beach**, simply follow paths through the forest just west of the ferry landing – you'll hit it in fifteen minutes.

Juodkrantė and beyond

JUODKRANTĖ, 14km south of Smiltynė, was the favoured resort of well-to-do Klaipėda Germans during the interwar years and still has an air of gentility about it, with its trim, big-balconied, wooden villas, well-tended gardens and seafront park. At the southern end of the resort are a few rows of wooden fishermen's houses, watched over by a red-brick church, the strange, twisting spire of which looks as if it was designed to drill holes in the sky. Immediately opposite, a **gallery** (Tues–Sun 10am–6pm; free) displays several examples of the painted weather vanes for which Neringa's villages are famous.

From the centre of Juodkrantė a path winds up onto **Witches' Hill** (Raganų kalnas), a forested ridge dotted with wooden sculptures made by contemporary folk artists from all over the country and depicting sprites and demons from Lithuanian folklore. There are lots of sculptures of the sea goddess Neringa and her fisher-lover, although the most attention-grabbing work on display is a muscular St George slaying an intricately chiselled, fish-scaled dragon. Trails lead on further into the forest, continuing over the ridge towards the spit's western coast, where – after a good twenty-minute walk – you'll find Juodkrantė's **beach**. The coast around Juodkrantė is famous for being one of the prime Baltic nesting grounds for **cormorants**; they gorge themselves on the Curonian Lagoon's marine life – much to the chagrin of local fishermen.

Beyond Juodkrantė the southbound road heads inland and follows the spit's central wooded spine. Parking spaces have been strategically placed en route so you can pull over and admire the tawny-coloured dunes off to the east; most of these fall within one of the strict reserves, so you can't get up close on foot.

After 15km, a turn-off heads east to the sleepy village of **PERVALKA**, made up of a few (largely modern) holiday cottages and the odd café, and marking the northern end of the Nida–Preila–Pervalka cycle route (see p.341).

Juodkrantė practicalities

Smiltynė–Nida **minibuses** pick up and drop off on Rėzos, Juodkrantė's single main street. The **tourist office** at the northern end of the village at Rezos 8 (℡8-469/53490, Ⓦwww.visitneringa.com), can book you into private **rooms** (❷). The *Ąžuolynas* **hotel** (℡8-469/53310, Ⓦwww.hotelazuolynas.lt; ❻) is a concrete place with comfy en-suites in four large blocks and a small pool. More intimate is the *Kuršių Kiemas*, Miško 11 (℡8-469/53004, Ⓦwww.neringatravel.lt; ❸), a nicely renovated old building near the northern entrance to the village, offering neat en-suites with TV and minibar. The smartest place is the *Vila Flora*, at the northern end of the village at Kalno 7A (℡8-469/53024, Ⓦwww.vilaflora.lt; ❻), a modern structure in the style of a traditional, wooden villa. It also boasts the most varied **restaurant** menu, although the locally caught fish at *Žvejonė*, Rėzos 30, tastes all the better for being served in a flower-filled garden. Beside the pier at the southern end of town, *Vela Bianca* offers Baltic fish dishes and Mediterranean seafood in a building that combines a modern glass facade with a traditional thatched roof.

Nida

The ancient fishing village of **NIDA**, 35km or so south of Smiltynė, has been the main focus for tourism on the spit since the mid-nineteenth century, when the first German visitors were drawn here by the promise of unspoilt seaside rusticity. The Germans were quick to rediscover the place in the early 1990s, and it's now the country's most cosmopolitan resort, attracting a healthy cross-section of Lithuanians and outsiders. Despite some ugly Soviet architecture at its heart, it still possesses an impressive stock of traditional timber houses, many of their reed-thatched roofs sporting the wooden, horse-head crosspieces characteristic of Curonian homes.

Arrival and information

Minibuses arrive at the tiny bus station in the centre of the village. The **tourist office**, inside the cultural centre on the main square at Taikos 4 (mid-June to mid-Sept Mon–Fri 10am–7pm, Sat 10am–6pm, Sun 10am–3pm; mid-Sept to mid-June Mon–Fri 9am–1pm & 2–5pm, Sat 10am–3pm; ℡8-469/52345, Ⓦwww.visitneringa.com), can help with all kinds of information. Numerous ad-hoc establishments offering **bike rental** (dviračių nuoma) sprout up throughout the centre during the summer. Typical prices are 8Lt per hr, 30Lt per day.

Accommodation

Accommodation is expensive in July and early August; outside those periods rates may be considerably lower than those indicated below. The tourist office can book you a **room** in a private house (❷) for a 6Lt fee; for a little more, Litinterp in Klaipėda (see p.332) can also book rooms in advance. *Nidos kempingas* (Nida Camping; Taikos 45A ☎8-469/52045, ⓦwww.kempingas.lt) is a pine- and birch-shaded **campsite** 2km southeast of Nida, near the main Smyltinė–Kaliningrad road and handily placed for the beaches on the west side of the spit. There's an on-site café, sauna, swimming pool and limited cooking and clothes-washing facilities. It also offers **apartments** (180–460Lt), all boasting swanky minimalist decor and modern bathrooms with tub. Some have a groovy split-level layout, others boast small balconies; a few come with kitchenette.

Hotels and guesthouses

Banga Pamario 2 ☎8-469/51139 or 8-686/08073, ⓦwww.nidosbanga.lt. A thatched-roof cottage with fairytale exterior and simple, comfortable en-suite rooms inside. Top-floor apartments feature kitchenette, sitting room and fabulous lunette windows. Breakfast is included. Two- to four-person apartments from 350Lt, standard doubles ❹

Jūratė Pamario 3 ☎8-469/52300, ⓦwww .hotel-jurate.lt Plain but agreeable hotel in a central location; a good mid-range fall-back if other options don't work out. ❺

Miško namas Pamario 11–2 ☎8-469/52290 or 8-687/36902, ⓦwww.miskonamas.com. Charming B&B in a traditional-style house on the northern fringes of the centre. Rooms come in subdued colours; those on the top floor boast sloping ceilings and skylights, while most of those lower down have small balconies. ❹–❺

Naglis Naglių 12 ☎8-469/51124 or 8-699/33682, ⓦwww.naglis.lt. Waterfront cottage decked out in Nida's traditional maroon and blue colour scheme, with small but stylish en-suite doubles in the attic and a brace of bright, kitchenette-equipped apartments (from 350Lt), one of which boasts a fireplace and sauna. Breakfast available. ❺

Plunksna Taikos 32 ☎8-699/91585.Ten minutes' walk uphill from central Nida, this was once the holiday home of the Lithuanian Writers Union, and although now open to all it retains a pen-wielding clientele. The building is a partially renovated Soviet-era affair, so expect good-value but basic en-suites with tired, seen-it-all furnishings. Well-kept gardens, proximity to Nida's dunes, and the on-site *In Vino* wine bar (see p.341) are big pluses. ❸

Vandėja Naglių 17 ☎8-469/52742 or 8-614/67197, ⓦwww.kopos.lt/vandeja or www .forelle.lt. Central family house in a neat garden, offering bright and spacious en-suites with satellite TV. Breakfast available on request. ❺

Vila Elvyra Purvynės 2 ☎8-618/31449 or 8-620/64060, ⓔvilaelvyra@info.lt. B&B in an attractive two-storey lagoon-side house at the northern end of Nida, about 20min walk from the centre. Choose between compact en-suite doubles and roomy apartments (from 300Lt). May–Oct only. ❹–❺

The village

Some of Nida's prettiest houses are just south of the main square, along narrow streets like Lotmiškio and Naglių. Here you'll find neat lines of wooden fishermen's dwellings, painted in maroons, yellows and blues, their tidy, picket-fenced gardens crammed with flowers and fruit trees. One of the best examples, at Naglių 4, is now the **Fishermen's Ethnographic Homestead** (Žvejo etnografinė sodyba; June to mid-Sept daily 10am–6pm; mid-Sept to May Mon–Sat 10am–5pm; 6Lt), a plain, wooden structure set end-on to the road. The reconstructed interior provides a fascinating insight into the domestic life of Curonian fishermen in the nineteenth century. Oblong dwellings such as this were designed to accommodate two households, one at each end, each with their own kitchen, sitting room and bedroom. If the furnishings here are anything to go by Curonian families were very much into colour-coordinated interiors – wooden chests, wardrobes and bedsteads are painted the same bright blue as many of the house exteriors. Walls were left bare except for uplifting religious mottoes, neatly embroidered and framed.

East of the main square lies Lithuania's most fashionable yacht marina, the starting point of a seaside path that heads north past well-tended lawns and flowerbeds. Cutting inland and ascending Pamario gatvė takes you towards Nida's ruddy-coloured

parish church, its bell tower sprouting ten mini-pinnacles resembling pine cones. The nearby graveyard contains a fair number of traditional wood-carved crosses (*krikštai*) many fashioned into abstract, thistle-like forms, a symbol of rebirth that goes back to pre-Christian times.

Five minutes' walk further up Pamario, the **Neringa History Museum** at no. 53 (Neringos istorijos muziejus; June to mid-Sept daily 10am–6pm; mid-Sept to May Mon–Sat 10am–5pm; 6Lt) contains a colourful, well-labelled local history display. Scale models of traditional waterborne craft include the sail-powered sledges once used for crossing the lagoon in winter, and the *kurėnas*, a fishing boat particular to the region, characterized by a tall, oblong main sail and big lee boards like the gills of a fish. There's a large collection of the metal weather vanes that have decorated local fishing vessels ever since 1844, when new laws specified that each boat had to display a sign showing which of the Curonian fishing villages it belonged to. Originally these consisted of a simple two-colour design rather like a flag, but with time, fishermen began to add pictorial details – shapes representing buildings, trees, lighthouses, churches and horses – hence the highly stylized weather vanes still made today. Looking more like something out of a horror film are the interwar photographs of villagers laying nets to catch crows, swarms of which descended on the spit every autumn. Tasting a bit like wild pigeon, the crows were prized as a delicacy – and being given a crow as a gift was considered the highest honour. Once caught, they were killed by administering a swift bite to the neck. You might be relieved to know that crow no longer forms part of the local diet.

Diagonally opposite the history museum, the **Nidos Smiltė hotel** at Skruzdynės 2 has a small memorial room devoted to Friedrich Blode, who opened a B&B here in 1867 and went on to cultivate a clientele that included artists and intellectuals from all over the German-speaking world. A flourishing art colony developed around expressionist painters Max Pechstein and Karl Schmidt-Rottluf; facsimiles of their Nida-inspired paintings are on show here.

Thomas Mann's House

Carrying on up Pamario and bearing right into Skruzdynės brings you after ten minutes to the most famous of Nida's wooden houses, **Thomas Mann's House**, at no. 17 (Tomo Manno namelis; May–Sept Tues–Sun 10am–6pm; 64Lt), a thatched cottage of almost fairytale loveliness, where the writer spent his summers from 1930 to 1932. The rather disappointing museum within contains a few photos of Mann and family and various editions of his books, including *The Story of Jacob* (1933), and *Young Joseph* (1934), both of which were largely written here. Mann first visited Nida in 1929 on an excursion from the nearby summer resort of Rauschen (now Svetlogorsk in Kaliningrad Province), and was immediately enchanted by the landscape and its people – whom he described as "not exactly good-looking, but friendly". He engaged Klaipėda architect H. Reissmann to build a summer house ready for his return the following year. When he arrived in July 1930, the locals lined the streets to greet him, an event recorded by press cuttings in the museum.

The dunes

The highlight of any trip to Nida are the **dunes**, which begin just south of the village. From the southern end of Naglių a shore path runs to a flight of wooden steps that forges up past wild raspberry bushes onto the shoulder of the 50m-high **Parnidis Dune** (Parnidžio kopa), one of the biggest that Neringa has to offer. The summit is marked by a modern **sundial** in the form of an imposing obelisk decorated with rune-like inscriptions. Struck from its pedestal by lightning in 1999, it has been only partially reconstructed, and now looks like the mysterious remnant of some ancient civilization.

From the summit extends a rippling sandscape of semolina-coloured dunes, their flanks mottled with patches of grey-green moss and purplish thistle flowers. The eastern, lagoon-facing sides of the dunes are roped off in order to prevent subsidence, although you can strike out southwards for about 1.5km before coming up against the boundary of a strict nature reserve – a glorious pale-sand wilderness into which you are not permitted to venture, stretching as far as the Russian border 2km beyond.

You can walk west from the sundial – or take any of the paths leading westwards from Nida – to reach the **beach** on the spit's far shore, where you'll find a handful of food-and-drink shacks. It's a glorious place for a stroll even in bad weather, when gun-metal seas roll in under glowering skies. A north–south foot- and cycle-path, handy for exploring the woods just behind, runs parallel to the strand.

The Nida–Preila–Pervalka cycle route

One of the best ways to explore the Curonian Spit's tranquil woodland is to follow the **Nida–Preila–Pervalka cycle route** (dviračių takas Nida–Preila–Pervalka), a 16km-long asphalted path that leads through the mixed birch and pine forest on the eastern side of the spit. As popular with walkers as it is with cyclists, it provides access to a wonderfully serene landscape, with numerous opportunities for climbing up and down trail-side dunes.

Leaving Nida via the *Skalva* hotel at the northern end of the village, the path forges inland for the first few kilometres, running beneath the forest-blanketed western slopes of the spit's central ridge. After about 5km you'll see Vecekrugo kalnas – at 67m high, the park's highest point. The pine-covered dune gets its name ("Old Pub Hill") from an inn that used to stand at its foot, catering to a local population whose villages have long since vanished under the sands. After another 3km the trail rejoins the shores of the lagoon, running alongside the reedy Preila Bay before entering Preila itself, a single street of lush-lawned, seaside suburbia, harbouring a couple of simple snack bars. From here it's another 6km to Pervalka, passing another lofty dune, Karvaičių kalnas, en route. Somewhere under the dune's western slopes lies the village of Karvaičiai, abandoned in 1797 owing to shifting sands, but still very much remembered as the birthplace of Liudvikas Rėza (1776–1840), the Königsberg-educated poet and publisher who kick-started the process of cultural revival in Lithuania Minor.

Eating, drinking and entertainment

A handful of kiosks near the bus station and on the waterfront serve **smoked fish** (rūkyta žuvis), a local speciality that's usually served whole, complete with head and bones, and which you are supposed to eat with your fingers. An appealingly tangy snack, it makes the perfect accompaniment to a glass or two of beer. For fresh bread, pastries and cakes head for the *Gardumelis* **bakery** at Pamario 3, which also has a sit-down café section with free wi-fi.

The cultural centre on the main square hosts films and concerts in summer, and is the main venue for July's **Thomas Mann Cultural Festival** (Ⓦ www.mann.lt).

Restaurants and cafés

Ešerinė Naglių 2A. A modern pavilion with a thatched-roof makeover, *Ešerinė* offers a satisfying range of main courses and is a nice place for a beer. May–Sept; 10am–midnight.

In Vino Top floor of *Plunksna* hotel (see p.339). Popular wine bar with a good choice of wines by the glass, fancy Belgian beers, and a menu of tapas-style snacks and Mediterranean-influenced mains. Great views of sea and dunes from the rooftop terrace. June–Aug; 10am–midnight.

Seklyčia Lotmiškio 1. Nida's fanciest restaurant, a big wooden villa with lots of seating inside and out; they serve everything from local fish to rack of lamb. Mains around 30–40Lt. All year; 10am–11pm.

Sena sodyba Naglių 6. A wonderfully relaxing garden café serving omelettes, pancakes and Baltic Sea fish in a miniature orchard. Mains around 25–30Lt. May–Sept: 11am–11pm.

The Nemunas delta

Roughly opposite Nida, on the eastern side of the Curonian Lagoon, the River Nemunas divides into several branches before emptying into the sea. The lush green flatlands of the delta are prone to seasonal flooding, producing a distinctive landscape of water meadows (grazed by dairy herds when dry), bogs and riverside marsh. Rich in fish and insects, the delta supports a large population of white storks, cranes and cormorants, and is an important stopping-off point for migrating species in September and October – when millions of birds pass along the shores of the Curonian Lagoon. The **Nemunas Delta Regional Park** (Nemuno deltos regioninis parkas; Ⓦwww.nemunodelta.lt) operates a small visitors' centre near Rusné in the middle of the delta, while the ornithological station at **Ventés ragas** on the northern side of the delta provides great views of the Curonian Lagoon and its wildlife. The inland market town of **Šilutè** is the delta's main service centre, and there is plenty of B&B accommodation in local villages. Public transport is meagre, so you'll need a car or long-distance-cycling stamina to get around.

Šilutė, Ventės ragas and around

The pleasant one-street town of **ŠILUTĖ**, 55km south of Klaipėda, is home to the regional **tourist office**, Lietuvininkų 10 (Mon–Fri 8am–noon & 1–5pm; ℡8-441/77785, Ⓦwww.siluteinfo.lt), which sells maps of the region and can book you into B&B **accommodation** (❷) in local farmsteads.

Heading northwest from Šilutė via the village of Kintai brings you after 19km to **Ventés ragas** ("Venté Horn"), a stubby peninsula that protrudes over the northern side of the delta. Ventés ragas is the perfect place from which to observe the comings and goings of the Curonian Lagoon's birdlife, and has become a cult destination among birdwatchers as a result. An **ornithological research station** (ornitologijos stotis) has been operating here since 1901, employing huge funnel-shaped nets to capture migrating birds – which are then tagged by researchers and released. The station holds a small display of stuffed birds (daily 10am–5pm; 1Lt), and allows access to the neighbouring lighthouse for a sweeping panorama of the Lagoon. Whether you're interested in birds or not, fine views of the Curonian Spit to the west more than justify the trip.

The Ventés ragas area is a beautiful and restful place **to stay**, with the shore-side *Ventainé* tourist complex 3km to the north of the cape (℡8-441/68525 or 8-68670490, Ⓦwww.ventaine.lt) offering a fully equipped **campsite** and an attractive small **hotel** (❹) with comfortable en-suites and great lagoon views. The veranda of the *Ventainé*'s restaurant is the perfect place from which to watch the sun setting over the Spit. A further 2km northeast, the 🍴 *Sturmų švyturys* hotel (℡8-68797756 or 8-65029420, Ⓦwww.sturmusvyturys.lt; ❺) is one of the most romantic spots on the Lithuanian coast, offering rooms with pine furnishings and nautical blue-and-white colour schemes – the family-sized triples and quads include child beds in the shape of fishing boats. The **restaurant** (daily in summer, weekends in winter) serves up freshly caught fish baked on an open grill.

Some 5km inland from Ventés ragas and accessible via gravel roads from Kintai, the village of **MINGÈ** straddles both banks of the (so far bridge-less) Minija River – locals still get around by boat, earning the place the unlikely sobriquet of "Lithuanian Venice". While it doesn't live up to such comparisons it's an undeniably pretty spot, with some lovingly restored fishermen's houses and a busy little yacht marina.

Rusné

Some 7km southwest of Šilutè lies the island of **Rusné**, a croissant-shaped piece of lowland no more than 10km from north to south which is enclosed by the Curonian Lagoon on one side and the Atmata and Skilvutè branches of the Nemunas on the other. Made up of cow-grazed meadows and bird-infested marshes, Rusné has bags of wild, untouched-by-modernity charm. At the eastern edge of the island, the village of **RUSNÈ** boasts some lovely traditional timber houses, especially along either side of the Pakalné River, the banks of which are popular with local strollers. There's plenty of **farm accommodation** (❶–❷) in and around the village; book through the tourist office in Šilutè (see above). The tiny settlement of Pakalné, 5km beyond Rusné village, boasts a small **Nemunas Delta Regional Park Visitors' Centre** (Lankytojų centras; ☎8-441/58154; Mon–Thurs 8am–5pm, Fri 8am–3.45pm), where you can pick up maps of the island and ask directions to the birdwatching tower at the end of a track 4km to the north, the perfect vantage point from which to observe the coastal reed-beds. On the riverside just beyond the Visitors' Centre, there's a **tent-pitching site** (stovyklavietė) with simple earth toilets.

At the northern end of the island, the sleepy hamlet of **UOSTADVARIS** is the site of an attractively stumpy red-brick lighthouse, and a nineteenth-century pumping station built to serve Rusnė's irrigation channels. With bleak coastal marshes on either side, it's a fittingly atmospheric place at which to wind up your tour of the delta.

Palanga and around

A short drive up the coast from Klaipėda, **PALANGA** is Lithuania's favourite beach resort and summertime playground, a self-contained empire of ice cream and candy-floss visited by everyone from bucket-and-spade-wielding families to drink-fuelled party animals. On summer evenings you can see all of them parading up and down the bar-lined central strip, **Basanavičiaus**.

This erstwhile fishing village was developed as a resort by Polish-Lithuanian aris-tocrat Jozef Tyszkiewicz (1835–91), who invited the doyen of wooden architecture, Stanislaw Witkiewicz, to build a Kurhaus here. Though the building no longer stands,

PALANGA

BALTIC SEA

Liepāja

Kretinga

Genocide Memorial *Klaipėda*

ACCOMMODATION
Infohotel	C
Kerpė	B
Palanga	D
Palangos vėtra	G
Parko viešbutis	F
Vandenis	E
Vila Ramybė	H
Žalias namas	A

RESTAURANTS, CAFÉS & BARS
1925	4
Feliksas	1
Klubas Ramybė	5
Palanga	D
Vandenio muzikos klubas	E
Vila Ramybė	H
Žuvinė	2
Žvaigždė	3

Ferris Wheel

Bus Station

Antanas Močys Museum

Dr. Jonas Šliūpas Memorial House

Botanical Gardens

Orangery

Amber Museum

Birutė's Hill

0   200 m

Witkiewicz's trademark style – spindly balustrades, pointy gables and fanciful turrets – can still be seen in many of the town's older villas. Originally patronized by well-to-do Poles, Palanga became the resort of choice for Lithuanians after World War I; it was cheaper than Juodkrantė and Nida, which tended to be monopolized by the Klaipėda Germans.

Aside from the beach and the nightlife, ample reason to visit is provided by the lush and leafy **Botanical Gardens**, laid out by Jozef Tyskiewicz's son Felix, and an absorbing **Amber Museum** in the Tyskiewicz Palace. Tyskiewicz's **Winter Garden** at nearby **Kretinga** is an easy half-day excursion.

Arrival and information

Palanga is served by regular municipal **buses** from Klaipėda bus station, though these tend to stop at every minor halt en route; it's best to take one of the faster minibuses, also from Klaipėda bus station (7.30am–10.30pm), which depart when full. There's a handful of direct services from Vilnius and also four daily buses from and to Liepāja in Latvia (some of these are based in Kaliningrad, so destination boards will be in the Cyrillic script).

Palanga's **bus station** is just off Vytauto gatvė, the main street running north–south through town. The **tourist office** (Mon–Fri 9am–1pm & 2–6pm; June–Sept also Sat & Sun 9am–1pm & 2–4pm; ☎8-460/48822), at Kretingos 1, is right in the bus station forecourt. You'll find outdoor stalls hiring **bikes** along all of Palanga's main streets.

Accommodation

The tourist office can book you into a **private room** (❶). The Litinterp office in Klaipėda (see p.332) offers the same service, but charges slightly more (❷). If you're prepared to search yourself, you'll turn up rooms at even cheaper rates – there are plenty of *kambarių nuoma* ("rooms for rent") signs in the suburban streets northwest of the bus station; this can be a time-consuming business, however, and not all hosts speak English.

A few unrenovated, Soviet-era hulks aside, Palanga is well stocked with modern **hotels**. Owing to the resort's popularity, however, prices are high in peak season (June–Sept). At other times, rates may be thirty to fifty percent lower than those quoted below.

Infohotel Kretingos 52 ☎8-460/40011, ☻www .feliksas.lt. Functional but chic rooms in a contemporary, box-like building on the eastern approaches to town but only 15min walk from the seafront. Rooms feature cheerful, bright-orange carpets; the larger rooms have fold-down sofas and at a pinch can sleep four. ❺

Kerpė Vytauto 76 ☎8-460/52379, ☻www .kerpehotel.lt. Modern, mid-sized hotel offering contemporary rooms with big windows. The top-floor, split-level suites are perfect if you want to spread out. ❺–❻

Palanga Birutės alėja 60 ☎8-460/41414, ☻www.palangahotel.lt. Elegant, crescent-shaped contemporary building near the sea. Rooms have bold modern furnishings, ample desk space, swish bathrooms and balconies; the upper-floor apartments (from 1200Lt) have invigorating treetop views. Saunas (free in the mornings, 80–150Lt/hr afterwards), a small indoor pool and a heated outdoor pool complete the picture. One room is adapted for wheelchair-users. ❼–❽

Palangos Vėtra Daukanto 35 ☎8-460/53032, ☻www.palangosvetra.lt. Boasting a casino and beauty centre on the ground floor, and saunas in the basement, this hotel, handily located beside the Botanical Gardens, is perfect if you want a host of holiday-resort facilities under one roof. Standard rooms are bland but comfortable, and there are some spectacular top-floor suites with balconies or bay windows. ❺–❼

Parko viešbutis Dariaus ir Gireno 11 ☎8-460/51175, ☻www.smilciutulpe.lt. Modern mid-range choice at the quiet end of town, opposite the Botanical Gardens, offering doubles and self-catering 2- to 6-person apartments. ❺

Vandenis Birutės alėja 47 ☎8-460/53530, ☻www.vandenis.lt. The floorboards are a little creaky at this twenty-room hotel, but rooms are bright and comfortable. Near the seafront, and home to one of Palanga's most popular live music clubs. ❹

Vila Ramybė Vytauto 54 ☎8-460/54124, ☻www.vilaramybe.lt. Cute B&B in a traditional house offering en-suites with balcony, split-level suites, and cosy top-floor doubles with attic ceilings. The *Vila Ramybė* café (see p.346) is directly below. **④**

Žalias namas Vytauto 97 ☎8-460/51231, ⓦwww.zaliasnamas.lt. Cheerful B&B offering functional, neat en-suites with TV, minibar and plenty of wardrobe space. **④**

The Town

Palanga is made up of an easily navigable grid of broad avenues lined with lime trees and pines. Pedestrianized **Basanavičiaus** is the resort's premier promenading ground, lined with a garish succession of amusement arcades, cafés and bars. At its western end the simple, wooden **pier** (jūros tiltas) stretches out to sea for almost half a kilometre – a stroll to the end is considered an essential part of the Palanga experience, and does at least provide you with a wide-angle view of the dune-backed beach, which stretches as far as the eye can see in either direction.

Once you've cast an eye over the seascape, you need to make a beeline for Count Felix Tyszkiewicz's **Botanical Gardens**, a huge expanse of parkland that drapes itself across the southern end of town. Comprising clipped lawns, a myriad of different tree species and untamed forest, the park was laid out in 1897 by much-travelled Frenchman Edouard André, whose landscaped gardens can be seen in locations as diverse as Sefton Park in Liverpool and Evksinograd in Bulgaria. Over on the northeastern side, beyond a bow-shaped lake, the **Orangery** (Oranžerija; Tues–Sat 10am–6.30pm; 3Lt) houses a diverse collection of cacti, umpteen varieties of begonia and fig, and spectacular, exploding-firework bromelias. In the centre of the park, the Neoclassical **Tyszkiewicz Palace** hosts orchestral concerts on its colonnaded portico, and the interior harbours an enjoyable **Amber Museum** (Gintaro muziejus; Tues–Sun: June–Aug 10am–9pm; Sept–May 10am–5pm; ⓦwww.pgm.lt; 8Lt). It's a tour de force, presenting the natural history of the substance and bombarding with an array of examples, prehistoric insects trapped in pieces of amber, and roomfuls of amber jewellery.

Just southwest of the palace, a Christmas pudding-shaped mound known as **Birutė's Hill** (Birutės kalnas) is associated with the story of pagan princess Birutė,

Amber

According to Lithuanian folklore, **amber** came into being when king of the gods Perkūnas discovered that Jūrate, queen of the Baltic Sea, was having an affair with mortal fisherman Kastytis, despite being betrothed to water-god Patrimpas. Perkūnas showed his displeasure by zapping Jūrate's undersea palace with a thunderbolt, scattering numerous golden-coloured fragments across the Baltic.

The scientific version of events is rather different, maintaining that amber is essentially the fossilized resin of fifty-million-year-old pine trees, deposited on the Scandinavian side of the Baltic, and washed up on the shores of Lithuania, Latvia and Estonia. Taking the form of translucent, orange-brown nuggets, amber is usually clear, although it sometimes includes pine needles or insects caught in the resin before it solidified, allowing today's scientists the chance to study creepy-crawlies that may have died out millennia ago. Valued as an ornament since Neolithic times, amber provided the ancient Baltic tribes with an important means of exchange, putting them at the supply end of trade routes that extended south to Rome, Byzantium and beyond. Although amber can still be found all along the Baltic coast, the richest deposits are in the Russian province of Kaliningrad – as much as ninety percent of the world's amber is thought to lie underneath the town of Yantarny.

In all three Baltic states, amber jewellery is the main trade of souvenir stalls and gift shops. It can also be picked up in its raw form on the beaches – fragments may be washed up after storms, when you'll see lots of people, gimlet-eyed, earnestly searching the sands.

who was keeper of the hill's pagan shrine until forcibly abducted by her suitor, Grand Duke Kęstutis. It's said that Birutė's heart softened during the journey to Kęstutis's capital, Trakai (where they were married and Birutė gave birth to the future Grand Duke Vytautas the Great), but she returned to her hilltop shrine in Palanga after Kęstutis's death to keep pagan traditions alive in a country slowly turning to Christianity. Despite Birutė's status as a standard bearer for the old gods, both she and Kęstutis are pictured in the stained glass that adorns the octagonal nineteenth-century chapel at the hill's summit. Following paths south from here will bring you after ten minutes to a small and easily-missed **Jewish Genocide Memorial** (Žydų genocido vieta), marking the spot where the bulk of Palanga's Jews were murdered by German troops and Lithuanian auxiliaries in the summer of 1941. A simple granite block rears up out of the grass, bearing a Star of David and an inscription so worn that it's illegible – the figure of 105 (the number of victims) is all that can be made out.

Returning from the park towards central Palanga along Vytauto gatvė will take you past the **Dr Jonas Šliūpas Memorial House** at no. 23 (Dr Jono Šliūpo memorialinis namas; Tues–Sun: June–Aug noon–7pm; Sept–May 11am–5pm; 2Lt), a charming nineteenth-century dwelling that honours one of Palanga's former mayors. The Šiauliai-born Dr Šliūpas began his political career in the 1890s with the clandestine distribution of Lithuanian-language magazine *Aušra*, an epoch-defining publication that brought together all the leading intellectuals of the day. Escaping Tsarist persecution, he emigrated to the US, where he began to canvass international support for the Lithuanian national movement.

At Daukanto 16, the **Antanas Mončys Museum** (Antano Mončio muziejus; Tues–Sun: June–Aug 10am–9pm; Sept–May noon–5pm; 6Lt) celebrates the work of émigré sculptor Mončys (1921–93) with an impressive display of his anguished, skeletal creations. The gallery space downstairs is dedicated to seasonal exhibitions by contemporary Lithuanian artists.

Eating, drinking and entertainment

Pretty much everything you need is on or near the two main streets, **Vytauto** and **Basanavičiaus**; there are innumerable stalls selling hot dogs and *čeburekai*, and probably more pizzerias than in the rest of Lithuania put together. Many places feature live music in summer – if you're lucky you'll be treated to classy jazz or pop-rock covers, although more often than not be prepared for Lithuanian techno or medallion-man balladeering.

1925 Basanavičiaus 4. One of the classier places on the main strip: a little yellow wooden house with an intimate, if slightly ersatz, rustic-style interior. The well-presented Lithuanian food (with the accent more on meat than fish) includes plenty of tasty salads; a good place for a civilized meal or drink. Daily 10am–midnight.

Feliksas Vytauto 116. Smart café-bar with dark-wood interior and streetside seating. There's a full menu of main meals and plenty of desserts, making it a popular stop-off for coffee-and-cake addicts in the afternoon. Plus frequent live jazz, easy-listening crooners or piano-tinklers on summer evenings. Sun–Thurs 8am–midnight, Fri & Sat 8am–2am.

Klubas Ramybė Vytauto 35 ⓦ www.klubasramybe .lt. A cosy bar which also functions as a mildly wacky cultural centre, this is a fantastic alternative to the mainstream café-restaurants lining

Basanavičiaus. Year-round programme of live gigs, literary readings, film evenings and other events. Daily 7pm–2am or later.

Palanga Birutės alėja 60. Upscale restaurant in the hotel of the same name, with floor-to-ceiling windows allowing you to commune with the surrounding pine trees. The international cuisine is first-rate (this is one place where you can order a Caesar Salad and not be disappointed), with exotic seafood and exquisite desserts standing out. Expensive but well worth it. Daily 11am–midnight.

Vandenio muzikos klubas Birutės alėja 47. Café-bar occupying one wing of the *Vandenis* hotel, specializing in jazz and the classier end of the pop-rock spectrum. Gigs almost daily in summer and at weekends during the rest of the year. 9am–2am or later.

Vila Ramybė Vytauto 54. On the ground floor of the eponymous B&B, this café is more laid-back

than some along Basanavičiaus, with jazzy sounds on the stereo and jazzy clientele laying into the scrumptious pancakes. Mon–Sat 9am–midnight, Sun 11am–11pm.
Žuvinė Basanavičiaus 37A. A contemporary structure built in traditional Palanga style – with the exception that one side of the building is entirely glass, giving it the look of a huge dolls' house. Fish is the speciality: choose from delicious marinated-

herring starters, baked halibut or cod, and grilled trout. Mains 35–40Lt. Daily noon–midnight.
Žvaigždė Daukanto 6. Ukrainian-themed restaurant just off Basanavičiaus, with folksy textiles and equally folksy dishes – the borscht is a local lunchtime favourite. Also good are the Ukrainian *pelmeni* (pastry parcels) stuffed with potato, and the inevitable Chicken Kiev – accompanied by several varieties of *horilka* (Ukrainian vodka). Daily 10am–10pm.

Kretinga

Occupying hilly ground 12km east of Palanga, **KRETINGA** is visited both for its Winter Garden and its monastic heritage. It has been one of the most important monastic centres in the country since 1602, when a community of Bernardines established themselves here under the patronage of the Grand Hetman (supreme military commander) of Lithuania, Jan Karol Chodkiewicz (Katkevičius in Lithuanian). Closed down by the communists in 1945, the monastery was refounded by the Franciscans in 1993 and is flourishing once more. The lean-spired **monastery church of the Annunciation** still dominates the spacious town square, Rotušės aikštė. The interior is dominated by the Baroque high altar, a complex composition comprising Corinthian columns and crowned statuettes of saints. To the right, a miracle-working image of St Anthony of Padua is a popular destination for pilgrims.

Heading north past the church brings you after ten minutes to **Tyszkiewicz Palace** (June–Aug: museum Wed–Sun 10am–6pm; winter garden also Mon & Tues; Sept–May: Wed–Sun 10am–4pm, winter garden also Tues; 5Lt), an outwardly undistinguished mansion built by Jozef Tyszkiewicz in the 1890s and now occupied by the Kretinga museum. The modest collection of furnishings and paintings is totally upstaged by Jozef Tyszkiewicz's **Winter Garden**, a narrow, glass-enclosed chamber packed with palms, ferns, cacti and climbing plants, and overlooked by three elegant tiers of cast-iron balcony. The centrepiece at ground level is a fountain, surrounded by Greco-Roman pillars that have been encrusted with pebbles to provide a grotto effect. Stretching eastwards is a sizeable stretch of park, with swan-patrolled lily pond and a bathing lake (once a fish reservoir) with tiny beach.

Minibuses from Palanga and Klaipėda terminate on Kretinga's main square. *Pas Grafą*, the **café-restaurant** inside the Winter Gardens (open until 10pm), is a wonderful place to indulge in coffee, cakes or meat or chicken dishes among the palms. *Arbatinė Špitolė*, opposite the monastery church at Vilniaus 3, has a huge collection of leaf teas and some fetching cakes.

Žemaitija National Park and around

Lying in a gently rolling landscape of glacier-smoothed uplands 50km east of Palanga, **Žemaitija National Park** is one of the country's most compact conservation areas, comprising the placid waters of Lake Plateliai and the belt of pastureland, forest and bog that surrounds it. Barely 5km from north to south and 2km across, Lake Plateliai is one of the more attractive bodies of water in this part of Lithuania – its eastern shore is smooth and sandy, while the western shore is broken up by a confusion of tree-smothered promontories. Around 30 percent of the territory is made up of agricultural land and 45 percent woodland – largely spruce and pine, although there are enough deciduous trees (mostly birch, ash, alder and oak) to produce a more varied range of greens than you might find elsewhere in Lithuania. Although there are only a few signed paths, the country lanes and dirt roads are wonderful for woodland walks and bike rides, while the lake is perfect for messing about in rowing boats or pedaloes. There's also a strong tradition of **folk art** in the area.

The village of **Plateliai** on the lake's western shore is the park's main service and information centre; most of the park's accommodation is here or nearby. You can

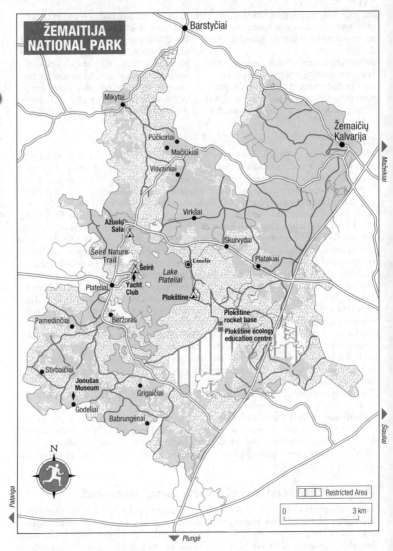

▲ Mažeikiai

▲ Šiauliai

◀ Palanga

▼ Plungė

access nearly all of Lake Plateliai's western side on foot or by bike from Plateliai, although to explore in any greater depth you'll probably need your own transport. Day-trip destinations include **Žemaičių Kalvarija**, a blissfully bucolic village and one of Lithuania's most popular Catholic pilgrimage centres; the disused Soviet-era rocket base at **Plokštinė**; and the eccentric **Orvydas Garden**, near the town of Salantai.

Plungė, just south of the park border, is the main access point to the park. It's linked by **bus** to Žemaičių Kalvarija and is served by numerous inter-city buses, as well as the Vilnius–Klaipėda **train**. If you're driving, note that the majority of roads in the park are unsurfaced once you get away from the main routes.

Plungė

Lying astride the main Klaipėda–Šiauliai rail and road routes, the market town of **PLUNGĖ** is the main jumping-off point for Žemaitija National Park. The town itself isn't up to much, but it's worth visiting the **Žemaitija Art Museum** (Žemaičių dailės muziejus; Wed–Sun 10am–5pm; 2Lt), housed in **Ogiński Palace** (Oginskių dvaras) on Dariaus ir Girėno, a short walk southwest from the train and bus stations. This creamy-coloured neo-Renaissance pile, complete with Greco-Roman-style statues perched along the roofline, was built for Polish-Lithuanian aristocrat Count Michał Ogiński in the late nineteenth century. Inside are some superb examples of local folk art, with tree trunks carved, totem pole-like, into likenesses of Christian saints and pagan deities. Behind the palace, and beyond a lily-filled pond, the grandiose red-brick stable block (žirgynas) stands in eloquent testimony to the count's enthusiasm for all things equine. Once you've strolled through the overgrown, tree-shaded palace park, there's not a great deal to get excited about in Plungė. A couple of basic **cafés** on the modern main square, **Senamesčio aikštė**, can provide refreshments; otherwise it's best to move on.

Plateliai and around

The lakeside village of **PLATELIAI**, 20km north of Plungė, revolves around a sleepy main square. Just to the south is the wooden parish church dating from 1744, its free-standing bell tower resembling a fortress or a fire-station lookout. Behind the church, a small park surrounds a venerable tree known as **Witch's Ash** (Raganos uosis) – with a girth of 7m, it's thought to be Lithuania's stoutest example of the species. Across the road stands a beautifully restored **Granary** (Dvaro svirnas; usually Mon–Fri; otherwise ask at the National Park Information Centre), now used for seasonal art exhibitions and a permanent display of local crafts, including a veritable crowd of wood-carved saints and devilish masks worn by Shrovetide revellers.

North of the main square, a surfaced road veers down towards the lakeside, where the Yacht Club (Jachtklubas) rents out **rowing boats** and pedalos (10Lt/hr); it's worth venturing out onto the water to savour the superb landward views of the wooded bays and peninsulas along the western shore. North of the Yacht Club lies an enchanting area of virgin forest traversed by the **Šeirė Nature Trail** (Šeirės gamtos takas), a 5km-long, figure-of-eight circuit whose starting point is marked by a national park information board on the Yacht Club access road, about 500m back from the lake. The trail passes through dark, dense forest before bridging a section of Gaudupis Bog (Gaudupio pelkė), a squelchy expanse of mosses punctuated by the odd stunted pine, and culminating at Piktežeris, a beautiful, spruce-encircled lake.

From the southern end of Plateliai, it's an easy 2km walk to the next village, **BERŽORAS**, site of another eighteenth-century wooden **church**, resembling an enormous stable with wonky crosses perched on its roof. Just east of the village lies a small **beach**, picturesquely situated in a bay between the densely wooded Kreiviškių and Auksalės peninsulas. Southwest from Beržoras a dirt road leads across undulating pastures to the hamlet of **GODELIAI**, 5km distant, where local couple Regina and Justinas Jonušas have established a **Museum of Folklore and Ethnography** (Tautodailės ir etnografijos muziejus; ask at National Park Information Centre about opening times; donation requested) in their farmstead. The main house holds Justinas's own wood sculptures, as well as pieces he's salvaged from decaying wayside shrines, while a barn across the way is packed with agricultural tools, wardrobes, hatboxes and bags salvaged from local households.

Practicalities

The **National Park Information Centre**, on Plateliai's main square at Didžioji 8 (Mon 8am–noon & 1–5pm, Tues–Fri 8am–6pm, Sat 10am–5pm; ☎8-448/49231, ⓦ www.zemaitijosnp.lt), sells maps, dishes out advice on what to see in the park and rents bikes (4Lt/hr). In addition, it can book **rooms** in local farmhouses (❶), most of which are in Plateliai or in the nearby village of Beržoras, and also runs the **hostel**-style *Dvaro svetainė* (35Lt), 200m south of the square at Didžioji 19. *Šaltinelis* (T 8-448/49315; ❷), just north of the village on the way to the Yacht Club, is a **B&B** with plain but comfortable rooms. A step up in terms of comfort, 2km south of Plateliai in Beržoras, 🅰 *Pas Tevukus* (T 8-448/49152, or 8-61529603, Ⓦ www .pastevukus.lt) has a lakeside ensemble of reed-thatched **holiday houses** with ultra-swish, hard-floored interiors – you can opt for a double room (❷) or an entire house (❹) – and guests can rent bikes. Further afield (a good 10km from Plateliai by road), the *Hotel Linelis*, on the opposite shore of the lake (T 8-448/49422 or 8-65577666, Ⓦ www.linelis.lt; ❷), offers small but comfortable en-suites, with a restaurant and a sandy beach on site – take the road to Žemaičių Kalvarija and turn right at the northeastern shoulder of the lake when you see the sign for "Poilsiavietė".

There's a handful of designated rough **camping** sites around Lake Plateliai – a warden calls every day or so to empty bins and collect fees (5Lt for tent and vehicle). The nearest site to Plateliai is the *Šeirė stovyklavietė*, just north of the Yacht Club; also within striking distance is *Ąžuolų sala*, 3km north –an idyllic lakeside spot signed off the road. On the opposite side of the lake, the *Plokštinė* site occupies a part-sandy, part-forested spot, 2km south of *Hotel Linelis*. For **eating**, the *Šašlykinė*, a pavilion in the forest just off the Yacht Club access road, does a reasonable line in Caucasian-style, skewer-grilled kebabs.

Plokštinė rocket base

It's perhaps not surprising that the Soviet authorities should consider the sparsely populated wilderness of forests and bogs in the **Plokštinė** area, southeast of Lake Plateliai, to be the perfect place to hide a rocket base. Built in 1962, the facility at Plokštinė was one of the first such silo sites in the Soviet Union, housing four nuclear missiles capable of hitting targets throughout western and southern Europe. Closed in 1978 and left to rot for decades, the base was reopened to the public in the early 2000s, and is being renovated to provide a home for a planned **Cold War Museum** (due in 2012–13). Contact the National Park Information Centre in Plateliai for details.

Žemaičių Kalvarija

Marking the northeastern corner of the park, about 20km from Plateliai, the village of **ŽEMAIČIŲ KALVARIJA** consists of a twin-towered hilltop church surveying a greeny-yellow collage of wooden houses, haystacks and fields of horses. It's one of the most important Catholic pilgrimage sites in the country, thanks to a three-and-a-half-centuries-old tradition of calvary processions, which draw thousands of celebrants every year between July 2 and July 12.

The village owes its prominence to Jerzy Tyszkiewicz, Bishop of Žemaitija, who in 1644 invited the Dominicans to establish a monastery and a school here. They brought with them an image of the Madonna, whose supposed prayer-answering powers soon transformed the settlement into the most popular shrine in Žemaitija. They also started the construction of nineteen calvary chapels around the village, forming a 5km-long processional route that has been the focus of religious ritual ever since. During the communist period local party bosses organized free folk festivals during the procession season in the hope that they would divert popular attention away from Žemaičių Kalvarija – a strategy that met with limited success. Nowadays, people from all over the country swarm to the village to take part in formal processions led by banner-wielding ecclesiastics, or to embark on a private circuit of the chapels, often approaching each chapel on their knees as a sign of devotion and sacrifice.

Scattered throughout the village, many of the chapels look like barns or outhouses and some are only recognizable from the wrought-iron crosses on their roofs. The chapel interiors, decorated with scenes from the Passion, are almost invariably closed outside the procession season, but the padlocked structures still provide an excellent excuse for a round-the-village stroll. Most of the chapels are concentrated on the hillocks around the church – there's an especially attractive cluster near the town grave-yard due west, and an outer loop of chapels dotting the cornfields just off the road to Barstyčiai to the northwest. Žemaičių Kalvarija's gleaming-white, nineteenth-century church is closed outside prayer times, but the local priest might open it to show you the much-revered image of the Virgin on the high altar.

Žemaičių Kalvarija is 2km off the main Plungė–Mažeikiai road. Just two **buses** a day run from Plateliai, but about seven daily Plungė–Mažeikiai services trundle past the turn-off – some stop in the village. There's a rudimentary **café** in the cultural centre opposite the church, and a couple of food shops on the main street nearby.

The Orvydas Garden

Well outside the territory of the national park, 25km northwest of Plungė on the Skuodas road, the undistinguished country town of Salantai would be a mere dot on the map were it not for its proximity to the **Orvydas Garden** (Orvydų sodyba; daily dawn till dusk; donation requested), an open-air sculpture park that ranks among the most offbeat and eccentric art collections in the Baltic region. It's 2km southwest of Salantai on the Plungė road, and served by the four daily Plungė–Salantai–Skuodas buses. The garden is on the farm of **Vilius Orvydas** (1952–92), a self-taught sculptor who specialized in the larger-than-life, tree-trunk-sized statues of religious and mythical subjects typical of Lithuanian folk art. He also collected graveyard crosses, religious sculptures from wayside shrines and Catholic-related folk art in order to save them from an atheistic Soviet regime that either had them destroyed or left them to decay. Orvydas arranged these objects in his own garden, adding features such as ponds, pathways and rocks carved with strange, rune-style signs. During the last years of the Soviet Union, the garden became a cult site among Lithuanian intellectuals who saw Orvydas's magpie activities as a sign of defiance; since independence, Orvydas has been acclaimed as an outstanding practitioner of naive, non-academic sculpture and landscape art – you'll see coffee-table books devoted to the man and his garden in Vilnius bookshops.

Still a private garden owned by Orvydas's descendants, the site has none of the touches, such as labelling or logical ordering, that you might expect to find in a state-run collection. Strolling around the garden is certainly a strange experience: like the Hill of Crosses (see p.325), its power rests in its seemingly unplanned, cluttered nature, with the presence of a Soviet-era rocket and a World War II tank adding to the junkyard feel.

Travel details

Buses

Klaipėda to: Kaunas (9 daily; 2hr 30min–3hr); Palanga (minibuses; every 30min–1hr; 30min); Šiauliai (3 daily; 3hr); Šilutė (5 daily; 1hr 20min); Vilnius (12 daily; 4–5hr).
Nida to: Juodkrantė (8 daily; 30min); Kaunas (1 daily; 4hr); Smiltynė (8 daily; 45min); Vilnius (1 daily; 6hr).
Palanga to: Kaunas (5 daily; 3hr 45min); Klaipėda (minibuses; every 30min–1hr; 30min); Kretinga (minibuses; every 30min–1hr; 20min); Šiauliai (3 daily; 3hr); Vilnius (7 daily; 5hr).

Plateliai to: Plungė (Mon–Sat 6 daily, Sun 3 daily; 25min); Žemaičių Kalvarija (2 daily; 40min).
Plungė to: Klaipėda (5 daily; 1hr 40min); Kretinga (9 daily; 1hr); Palanga (4 daily; 1hr 25min); Plateliai (Mon–Sat 6 daily, Sun 3 daily; 25min); Salantai (4 daily; 40min); Šiauliai (3 daily; 1hr 40min).
Smiltynė to: Juodkrantė (8 daily; 15min); Nida (8 daily; 45min).

Trains

Klaipėda to: Kaunas (1 daily; 6hr 30min); Plungė (5 daily; 2hr); Šilutė (2 daily; 1hr 30min); Vilnius (2 daily; 5hr).

Plungė to: Klaipėda (5 daily; 2hr); Šiauliai (4 daily; 1hr); Vilnius (2 daily; 3hr).

Flights

Palanga to: Vilnius (1weekly; 45min).

International buses

Klaipėda to: Kaliningrad (3 daily; 5hr); Liepāja (4 daily; 2hr); Rīga (2 daily; 5hr).
Palanga to: Kaliningrad (1 daily; 5hr 30min); Liepāja (4 daily; 1hr 30min); Rīga (2 daily; 4hr 30min).

International ferries

Klaipėda to: Åhus (1 weekly; 45hr); Gdańsk (1 weekly; 10hr); Karlshamn (6 weekly; 16hr); Kiel (3 weekly; 21hr); Sassnitz (3 weekly; 20hr).

International flights

Palanga to: Billund (5 weekly; 2hr 25min); Copenhagen (2 daily; 1hr 10min); Dublin (1 weekly; 3hr); Hamburg (1 daily; 2hr 20min); Oslo (3 weekly; 2hr 25min); St Petersburg (3 weekly; 1hr 40min).

Contexts

Contexts

History

W hile there is much that all three Baltic States have in common – most notably the shared experience of Tsarist rule in the nineteenth century and Soviet occupation in the twentieth – there are equally long periods when Estonians, Latvians and Lithuanians have pursued widely diverging destinies. The very expression "Baltic States" is itself merely a convenient geographical label of twentieth-century invention – under the surface of which lie three emphatically different cultures.

Estonia

The history of Estonia begins in the tenth millennium BC at the close of the last Ice Age, when the retreat of the glaciers finally made the region fit for human habitation. It's not known who first settled the area, but by 3000 BC they had been either assimilated or displaced by the ancestors of today's Estonians, a **Finno-Ugric** people closely related to the Finns – and more distantly, the Hungarians. The Estonians originally occupied a much larger territory than they do today, but were pushed back by the arrival of the Baltic peoples (forerunners of today's Lithuanians and Latvians) after 2000 BC – and Estonia has been a more-or-less stable ethnic unit ever since.

The early Estonians were farmers and fishermen, practising an animist religion of which little is known. There weren't really any villages or towns until the tenth century, when a tribal society emerged, presided over by chieftains ruling from stockade forts.

The Christian conquest of Estonia

Contacts with the outside world were limited until the tenth century, when the Vikings established trading posts on the northern coast and the emerging Russian towns of Pskov and Novgorod began sending mercantile missions to the southeast. In the early thirteenth century, land-hungry Western rulers persuaded the pope to authorize a crusade against the pagan peoples of the Baltic region, and with the German-based **Brotherhood of the Sword** (subsequently the Livonian Order) given free reign to invade what is now Latvia, rights to northern Estonia were granted to **King Valdemar II of Denmark**. Valdemar sent an army in 1219, founded the fortress town of Tallinn and went on to build castles at Rakvere and Narva. Meanwhile, the Brotherhood of the Sword, well established in Rīga since 1201, expanded into Estonia from the south.

Although the Estonians put up fierce resistance, they were no match for their heavily armed adversaries, and by the 1230s the Danes and the Brotherhood had succesfully carved up the country between them. The locals were forcibly **converted to Christianity** and their land divided up among a new ruling class of knights and bishops. While towns like Tallinn and Tartu filled up with German-speaking immigrants drawn by the region's mercantile potential, the Estonians themselves remained on the land, obliged as serfs to work on the feudal estates carved out by their conquerors – a situation which was to remain largely unchanged until the nineteenth century.

Feudal exactions in the Danish-controlled north provoked the so-called **St George's Night Uprising** of 1343, when Estonian peasants went on a rampage of violence, massacring landowners and burning monks in their monasteries. Worried by the cost of pacifying the countryside, the Danes sold all their possessions in northern Estonia to the Brotherhood of the Sword's successor organization, the **Livonian Order**. A geographical distinction between the southern and northern halves of the country remained: the south, together with northwestern Latvia, was known as Livland ("Livonia") and tended to look towards Rīga as its principal city; while the north, centred on Tallinn, was termed Estland ("Estonia") – a name which, centuries later, was to be applied to the whole country.

Under the Order, the gulf separating Estonian peasants from German-speaking landowners and townsfolk grew wider. Tallinn attracted a growing Estonian community of domestic servants and artisans from the fifteenth century onwards, but adoption of the **German language** was the prerequisite for social advancement.

Swedes and Russians

Estonian society under the Livonian Order was characterized by a slow-burning power struggle between the landed gentry, townsfolk and the Church. In the early sixteenth century, the cause of the **Reformation** (and especially its attack on ecclesiastical privilege and corruption) was enthusiastically taken up by aristocrats and burghers alike, transforming Estonia from a Catholic country into a bastion of Lutheranism almost overnight. Founded on medieval crusading ideals, the Order itself lost its *raison d'être*, producing a power vacuum eagerly exploited by neighbouring powers. In 1556, the **Swedes** captured Tallinn, using it as a base from which to expand across the whole of Estonia and northern Latvia. When the Russians invaded Estonia in 1558, the locals were glad of Swedish protection. The Swedes enlisted Polish support to throw the Russians back, beating them outside the Latvian town of Cēsis in 1578 and forcing them eastwards, and capturing Narva later the same year. In 1595, the Treaty of Tensina confirmed Swedish control over the whole of Estonia.

Estonians still refer to the seventeenth century as the **"Good Swedish Times"**. Although the power of the German magnates remained largely intact, Swedish rule brought a degree of justice to rural courts (torture was outlawed in 1686) and extended primary education to an increasing number of rural towns. Local government was placed in the hands of a new breed of competent, enlightened administrators – most of whom were graduates of the newly established Tartu University, founded by Swedish King Gustav Adolphus in 1632.

This comparative golden age came to an end with the **Great Northern War** (1700–21), a titanic struggle between Swedes and Russians which laid waste to large parts of Estonia and made Russian Tsar Peter the Great the undisputed master of the Baltic. Having incorporated Estonia into his empire, Peter won the support of the German magnates by reconfirming their privileges and offering them top jobs in the imperial administration. Manorial estates flourished, encouraging their owners to build ever grander manor houses (such as those at Palmse and Sagadi; see pp.119 & 122), although conditions failed to improve for the Estonian peasants, for whom eighteenth-century feudalism increasingly came to resemble a system of forced labour. The abolition of serfdom (in Estonia in 1816, Livonia in 1819) actually led to impoverishment for many peasants, who, cut loose by the big manorial estates that once supported them, ended up working as seasonal labourers for meagre wages.

The Estonian National Awakening

At the start of the nineteenth century, there was little in the way of an Estonian national consciousness. Even those Estonians who had escaped from the countryside to make a career in the towns had thoroughly Germanized themselves in order to do so. However, an increasing number of people were becoming interested in Estonian language and folklore. The **Estonian Learned Society**, founded by Germans attached to Tartu University in 1838, promoted the study of local culture and soon welcomed educated Estonians into its ranks. One of these, **Friedrich Reinhold Kreutzwald**, used traditional folk-tale fragments as the inspiration behind his epic poem *Kalevipoeg* ("Son of Kalev"; 1857), the first large-scale piece of narrative fiction to be written in the Estonian language. Estonian journalism was taking off too, with **Johann Voldemar Jannsen** publishing the weekly *Pärnu Postimees* ("Pärnu Courier") from 1857, then moving to Tartu in 1863 to found the (still-flourishing) daily *Eesti Postimees*. It was Jannsen who organized the first-ever **All-Estonian Song Festival** in Tartu in 1869.

The Russian authorities increasingly came to see Estonian–German struggles as an inconvenience and by the 1890s had begun a programme of **Russification** in a belated attempt to build a pan-national sense of Tsarist patriotism. Use of Russian was imposed on the (previously German-speaking) University of Tartu and the ensuing disruption led to a fall in academic standards. The chief result of the Russification campaign was to radicalize the Estonian national movement. Local intellectuals who had previously seen the Tsarist bureaucracy as a potential ally against the Baltic Germans now realized that they had to challenge both at the same time.

In 1904, Estonian parties won a majority of the seats on Tallinn City Council, with Tartu-educated lawyer **Konstantin Päts** (1874–1956) becoming vice-mayor – form dictated that the post of mayor itself go to a Russian. Estonians enthusiastically supported the anti-Tsarist **Revolution of 1905** in the hope that it would result in further constitutional reforms; its failure was a serious setback – most national leaders were forced into exile (including Päts, who was condemned to death *in absentia*) before an amnesty in 1910 allowed them to return.

The Estonian War of Independence

With the outbreak of **World War I** in 1914, the outlook for the Estonian national movement was pretty bleak. Hopes were revived, however, when the **Russian Revolution** of February 1917 delivered the sudden collapse of the Tsarist system. November 1917 saw the Bolsheviks win power in Russia; they won control of Tallinn, too, in early 1918, but soon evacuated the city, leaving the coast clear for a newly constituted Estonian government under the leadership of Päts to declare **Estonian independence** on February 24. Encouraged by the Bolshevik withdrawal, however, the German army marched into town the next day and had Päts arrested. When Germany surrendered to the Western allies on November 11, 1918, Päts quickly reassumed control, declaring Estonian independence again on November 18. Resurgent Bolsheviks occupied Narva and Tartu, but were prevented from capturing Tallinn by a swiftly assembled defence force that included teenage schoolboys. With former Tsarist officer **General Laidoner** at the helm, Estonia's nascent army soon developed into an efficient, highly motivated unit. Supplied with arms by the British and supported by volunteers from Finland (drawn to Estonia by the close ethnic ties between the two nations), Laidoner swiftly rolled back the Bolsheviks, forcing them to accept peace terms by autumn 1919.

At the same time, the Estonians had to counter the threat of a Baltic-German army under General von der Goltz advancing towards their southern borders from Rīga. In June 1919, Estonian troops, accompanied by Latvian volunteers, marched into northern Latvia, defeated the Germans at the **Battle of Cēsis** and chased them all the way back to Rīga before signing an armistice and returning home.

The interwar years

The Constituent Assembly elected in April 1919 opted for an idealistic constitutional model, establishing a single-chamber parliament (Riigikogu) to be presided over by a head of state (Riigivanem, or "State Elder") who combined the duties of prime minster and president. Estonian democracy never functioned as perfectly as had been intended, however, and left-wing coup attempts in 1924 led to outlawing of the Communist Party and the execution of its leaders. The 1920s were good years for agriculture (Estonian tinned pork was a big hit in the UK), but post-independence prosperity was brought to an end by the Great Depression after 1929. Many of those who had fought in the 1918–19 War of Independence were now disillusioned with an Estonian state unable to provide them with the rising living standards they'd expected and voiced their discontent by joining the **VAPS** – a fascistic pressure group which called for the imposition of authoritarian rule. Konstantin Päts sidestepped the appeal of VAPS by carrying out an authoritarian coup of his own: parliamentary parties were banned in 1934 and the Fatherland Front (Isamaaliit) was created to provide the country with a single, guiding ideological force. Päts appointed himself president and set about transforming Estonia into a corporatist state similar to Mussolini's Italy, although World War II intervened before his reforms bore fruit.

World War II

As a small state lying between powerful neighbours, Estonia never had much room for manoeuvre in international affairs, and its fate was sealed by the **Molotov-Ribbentrop Pact** of August 1939, a secret agreement between Germany and the USSR which placed the Baltic States firmly within the Soviet sphere of influence. The Soviets established military bases in Estonia in October 1939, going on to occupy the country outright in **June 1940**. Fixed elections produced a pro-Soviet parliament, which obediently declared Estonia's accession to the USSR. Hostility to the new order was widespread; the Soviet authorities tried to break the back of Estonian opposition by organizing mass **deportations** – on June 14, 1941, as many as ten thousand Estonians of all social classes were bundled into cattle trucks bound for the east.

Many young Estonians took to the forests at this time, fearing that further round-ups were on the cards. They formed partisan groups that helped kick the Red Army out when **Nazi Germany** declared war on the Soviet Union on June 22. Any hopes that the Germans would behave like liberators were soon disappointed, however, with the country being incorporated into the new protectorate of Ostland – which, ironically, fell under the aegis of the Tallinn-born Nazi Alfred Rosenberg, leading ideologue of Aryan superiority and no great friend of the Estonians.

The second Soviet occupation

By September 1944, the Germans had been thrown out of Estonia by the advancing Red Army and the country once more became part of the USSR. If anything, the **second Soviet occupation** was even harsher than the first: a hard core of Moscow-trained activists was brought in to run the country and a second wave of **deportations** in March 1949 removed as many as twenty thousand Estonians (2.5 percent of the total Estonian population) to camps in the east. Women, children and the elderly made up ninety percent of the total – suggesting that deportees were arbitrarily chosen to fulfil a pre-determined quota. The bulk of deportees came from the countryside, leading to a collapse in agricultural production, only made worse by forced collectivization.

Thousands of young Estonians joined the anti-Soviet partisan movement known as the **Forest Brothers**, believing that the Western powers were bound to declare war on the USSR sooner or later. The British secret services trained Estonian exiles in London before shipping them across the Baltic Sea to join the Brothers, unaware that their movements had already been betrayed to the KGB by London-based moles. The movement had petered out by the early 1950s, by which time it was clear that no further help from the West was forthcoming. Amnesties in 1956–57 encouraged most surviving partisans to give themselves up, although the last known Forest Brother, August Stubbe, survived until September 1978, when he committed suicide to avoid capture by the KGB.

Towards the "Singing Revolution"

Communist discipline was relaxed during the post-Stalin thaw of the late 1950s, but expressions of Estonian patriotism were still discouraged by the party hierarchy. Things didn't really change much until the mid-1980s, when the policy of **Glasnost** ("Openness") initiated by Kremlin leader Mikhail Gorbachev gradually released long-repressed feelings of national resentment and outrage.

The first signs of change in Estonia came on August 23, 1987, when two thousand protesters met in Tallinn's Hirvepark to mark the anniversary of the Molotov-Ribbentrop Pact, followed by a three-thousand-strong demonstration in February 1988, to commemorate the anniversary of Estonia's 1918 declaration of independence. In April 1988, Tartu University history professor Edgar Savisaar called for the formation of a **Popular Front** during a TV phone-in, launching a mass popular movement at a single stroke. In September of the same year, over 250,000 Estonians converged on Tallinn's Song Grounds in a mass gesture of support for independence. TV pictures of singing, flag-waving crowds were beamed around the world, and the Baltic push for independence has been known as the "**Singing Revolution**" ever since. On August 23, 1989, the fiftieth anniversary of the Molotov-Ribbentrop Pact was marked in all three Baltic nations with over 200,000 people joining hands to form a **human chain** from Tallinn to Vilnius.

Filled with pro-independence delegates, the Estonian Supreme Soviet initially adopted a cautious approach, pressing for increased autonomy rather than outright secession from the union. Despite abortive attempts to crush the independence movements in Lithuania and Latvia in January 1991, the Soviet regime held back from launching a similar crackdown in Estonia. In March 1991, the Estonians felt confident enough to hold a **referendum** on full independence from the USSR, with 65 percent voting in favour. With the **Moscow Coup** of August 1991 threatening a return to the bad old days of hardline rule, the Estonian Supreme Soviet swiftly convened to make a full **declaration of independence**. On the collapse of the coup, international recognition of Estonian independence quickly followed.

From independence to the present

In September 1992, Estonia's first fully free elections in over sixty years were won by the right-of-centre Fatherland Party, whose youthful leader **Mart Laar** became prime minister. Despite numerous political realignments in the years that followed, the tone of post-independence politics has remained essentially the same, with a succession of cabinets – usually staffed by young technocrats untainted by involvement in Soviet politics – pursuing unabashedly free-market policies.

The speed of Estonia's transformation into a modern capitalist state made it an obvious candidate for membership of the EU. A referendum on accession in September 2003 received overwhelming support, paving the way for full membership in May 2004. Estonia joined NATO in the same year, confirming the country's position as a fully integrated member of the Western community.

One enduring aspect of the country's Soviet heritage is the continuing presence of a large Russian community on Estonian territory. Before the Soviet occupation, Estonia had been one of the most ethnically homogenous nations in Europe. After 1945, however, **Russian-speaking immigrants** from all over the USSR had been encouraged to move to Estonia – both to provide an industrial workforce and to engineer a new, less wholly Estonian, demographic profile. By 1990, Russian-speakers constituted about thirty percent of the population, concentrated especially in Tallinn, Narva and the oil-shale mining towns of the northeast. The introduction of a **citizenship law** that required non-Estonians to take a language test resulted in the exclusion of almost all of the non-Estonian population. Over a period of years, most Russian-speakers passed the test and became Estonian citizens – although an estimated 100,000 so-called "non-citizens" still remain. Whether citizens or not, many Russians are not fully integrated into Estonian national life, and their social and economic problems are often treated with indifference by the Estonian majority.

Bad feeling between the two communities came into the open in 2007, when the so-called Bronze Soldier, a monument to the Red Army war dead situated on Tõnismägi hill in the centre of Tallinn, became the focus of ad hoc demonstrations by both Russian nationalists and their Estonian opponents. Prime Minister Andrus Ansip of the right-of-centre Reform Party suggested moving the statue to an out-of-town location, ostensibly to take the heat out of the situation – although analysts were quick to point out that with general elections looming, Ansip stood to gain from an upsurge in Estonian national sentiment. On April 25, government workmen moved in to exhume the bones of thirteen Soviet soldiers buried beneath the monument, sparking Russian fears that the Bronze Soldier itself was about to be dismantled. Two nights of rioting followed, with ethnic Russian youths smashing city-centre windows and looting shops. The statue itself was spirited away to the Siselinna military cemetery south of the centre (where it has taken on a new life as an offbeat tourist attraction), provoking a storm of protest from the Russian government in Moscow. Most Estonian Russians distanced themselves from the rioters and the violence in Tallinn soon subsided. The dispute took on new shape, however, when Russian computer hackers successfully disabled commercial and banking websites on which an increasing number of Estonians relied to do their daily business.

Almost two decades of economic progress were brought to an end by the financial crisis of 2008, although the right-of-centre Estonian government was able to introduce an austerity programme while avoiding major social unrest. Proof of Estonia's relative economic stability was provided by its adoption of the **euro** in January 2011.

Latvia

It's far from certain who the original inhabitants of Latvia were, and the history of the region doesn't really begin until around 2000 BC, when the **Baltic tribes** – the ancestors of today's Latvians and Lithuanians – migrated to the Baltic seaboard from their original home somewhere in west-central Russia. They soon coalesced into a handful of regionally based tribal units, with the Curonians (Kurši) in the west, the Zemgalians (Zemgaļi) in central Latvia and the Selonians (Sēļi) and Latgalians (Latgaļi) further east. Initially they had to share northern and central Latvia with remaining pockets of Livs, a Finno-Ugric people closely related to the Estonians, who lived around the Gulf of Rīga. None of these tribes had unified state structures based on capital cities, living instead in a network of loosely allied rural communities defended by stockade forts.

The Baltic crusades

The pagan Latvians remained wholly outside the orbit of Western Europe until the twelfth century, when ambitious German clerics conceived the idea of converting the Baltic peoples to Christianity. First to make the arduous trip to Latvia's shores was Father Meinhard of Holstein, who built a church at Uexküll (Ikšķile) on the banks of the Daugava, east of present-day Rīga, and persuaded the pope to declare him Bishop of Uexküll in 1188.

Although Meinhard died soon afterwards and his followers were chased off by hostile locals, the publicity generated by his enterprise encouraged Pope Innocent III to declare a full-scale **crusade** against the Baltic pagans in 1198. Three years later the Bremen-based ecclesiastic, Albert of Buxhoeveden, led a fleet of ships to the mouth of the Daugava River and chose Rīga (formerly a Liv fishing village) as the site of his projected crusader capital. Albert's retinue of idealistic Christian knights and plunder-hungry freebooters formed themselves into the **Brotherhood of the Sword**, a military-religious organization, that (initially at least) enforced a strict, almost monastic code of behaviour on its members. The Brotherhood advanced from Rīga, conquering the Latvian communities one by one and confiscating their land – subsequently divided up between the Brotherhood's members. The social order established by the Brotherhood, in which a German feudal aristocracy ruled over a Latvian-speaking peasant majority, was to remain in place for the next seven centuries.

The Brotherhood didn't have things all their own way, encountering stiff resistance from the Zemgaļi and failing to extend their crusade south towards Lithuania as planned. Defeated by a combined Zemgalian-Lithuanian army near Šiauliai in 1236, the Brotherhood lost so many knights that it was forced to merge with the Prussian-based German Order to form a new grouping, the **Livonian Order**. The Order consolidated its rule over the Latvian lands, expanded northwards into Estonia and established the Livonian Confederation – to remain the dominant political force in the region for over three hundred years.

The archbishop of Rīga served as the Confederation's titular head, although he presided over a far from unified body politic: the Livonian Order and the Church were both major landowners and tended to be competitors for temporal power rather than spiritual partners, while the mercantile city of Rīga enjoyed privileges that increasingly made it hostile to both.

The end of the Livonian Order

It was the townsfolk of Rīga who spearheaded support for the **Reformation** in the early sixteenth century, seeing the new creed as a useful way of avoiding the financial demands made on them by the Catholic Church authorities. The Reformation also had unforeseen benefits for Latvian culture, with rural aristocrats funding vernacular translations of the gospels in order to popularize the new faith among their serfs.

Riven by religious dissent, the Livonian Order was incapable of defending its territories against ambitious neighbours. The region was devastated by the **Livonian Wars** of 1558–83, a three-way struggle involving Sweden, Russia and the Polish-Lithuanian Commonwealth. The Livonian Order was dissolved in 1562 by its last grand master, Gottfried Kettler, who appointed himself secular duke of Courland (see p.194) and placed himself under the protection of the Polish-Lithuanian crown – which also gained control of Latgale in the southeast. With Rīga and the northeast falling to the Swedes in 1621, the Latvian lands were effectively divided between two rival empires.

Latvia remained a target for Russian territorial ambitions, too, however, and in the **Great Northern War** (1700–21), Peter the Great kicked the Swedes out of the east and dragged the Polish-controlled west into the Russian sphere of influence. Full Russian control of Latvia was confirmed in 1795, when the so-called Third Partition finished off what was left of the Polish-Lithuanian state.

The Latvian National Revival

Despite these changes in sovereignty, little changed for the Latvians themselves, the vast majority of whom continued to work on agricultural estates owned by a German-speaking aristocracy. It was only in the mid-nineteenth century that a Latvian middle class began to emerge in Rīga and other towns, eager to develop indigenous language and culture. The Baltic Germans continued to regard the Latvians as second-class citizens who had to either abandon their culture or stay on the farm – an attitude best summed up by Rīga newspaper editor Gustav Keuchel, who declared that "to be both Latvian and educated is an impossibility".

Unsurprisingly, a rising generation of Latvian patriots increasingly saw German-language culture as an instrument of oppression. The leader of these so-called **New Latvians** (Jaunlatvieši) was **Krišjānis Valdemars** (1825–91), who founded the first Latvian newspaper, *Pēterburgas avīzes* ("St Petersburg News"), in 1862, and helped set up a series of Latvian naval colleges that, it was hoped, would create an indigenous technocratic elite. Encouraged by Valdemars, **Krišjānis Barons** (1835–1923) embarked on the collection of *dainas* or traditional folk songs, helping to provide Latvians with a sense of their own cultural history.

The New Latvians had always assumed that the Tsarist bureaucracy was their most likely ally in the struggle against the Baltic Germans – a delusion that it took the turmoil of the **1905 Revolution** to dispel. A pro-democracy uprising that spread from St Petersburg across the Russian Empire, the revolution was followed by a mercilessly authoritarian crackdown, and in Latvia a whole generation of nationalist activists were exiled or imprisoned.

War and independence

The outbreak of **World War I** in 1914 pushed national aspirations further into the background. The Russian Revolution in 1917 led to the eastern front's wholesale collapse, and Latvia fell to the Germans. With Germany surrendered to the Western allies, however, a hastily convened Latvian National Council rushed to seize the initiative, declaring Latvia's independence on November 18, 1918. Farmers' Union leader Karlis Ulmanis became head of government and was to remain at the apex of Latvian politics for the next twenty years. Ulmanis's freedom of manoeuvre was limited by the fact that German troops were still in control of Latvia and had no intention of withdrawing. Indeed the British and French – neither of whom could spare the troops to garrison Latvia themselves – wanted the Germans to stay put in order to defend the region from Bolshevik Russia. In the event, both the Latvians and the Germans ended up fleeing Rīga in the face of the Bolsheviks, who captured the city on January 3, 1919, and established a Latvian Soviet Republic.

Ulmanis and his government took refuge in the port city of Liepāja, where they remained virtual pawns of a more powerful German force led by the charismatic General Rudiger von der Goltz. Supported by the local aristocracy, von der Goltz dreamed of turning Latvia into a German-dominated statelet that would both stem the tide of Bolshevism and put the indigenous population in their place. Ulmanis formed a fledgling Latvian army as a counterweight to von der Goltz's Germans, but this didn't prevent the latter from trying to depose Ulmanis in favour of a more malleable puppet in April 1919. Ulmanis was saved by the British, who installed him on a ship in Liepāja harbour and began delivering arms and supplies to his men. The Germans threw the Bolsheviks out of Rīga in May, but were themselves compelled to leave by a combined force of Estonians and Latvians – backed up by British and French warships. The British arranged for Ulmanis's return to Rīga in July, and after the failure of another German attack on the capital in October, the independent state of Latvia looked secure. The Bolsheviks, who still occupied parts of southeastern Latvia, were beaten off in the winter war of 1919–20 and the Latvian–Soviet treaty, signed on August 11, 1920, officially ended hostilities.

The interwar period

Interwar Latvian politics were characterized by the proliferation of small parties and a succession of short-lived coalition governments – although the presence of the Farmers' Union (and their leader Karlis Ulmanis) in all cabinets ensured a degree of continuity. During the 1920s, Latvia won export markets both for its dairy products and the consumer goods made by Rīga's VEF electronics factory, but a period of steadily rising living standards was cut short by the onset of the **Great Depression** after 1929. The ensuing economic slowdown led to widespread disillusionment with parliamentary politics, and the emergence of anti-democratic (and often anti-Semitic) right-wing groups, such as **Perkonkrusts** (Thunder Cross), persuaded Prime Minister Ulmanis to declare a **state of emergency** on March 16, 1934. Fearing that a return to democracy would render the country ungovernable, Ulmanis appointed himself president in 1936 and proceeded to dismantle Latvia's liberal institutions, presiding over the construction of a corporatist state based on Mussolini's Italian model.

World War II

With the rise of Nazi Germany and consolidation of communist rule in Russia, the fragility of Latvian independence became increasingly apparent as the 1930s wore on. With the signing of the **Molotov–Ribbentrop Pact** on August 23, 1939, Germany and the USSR agreed to the establishment of spheres of influence in north-central Europe. Along with the other Baltic States, Latvia was designated part of the Soviet sphere. Latvia was forced to sign a mutual assistance pact with the USSR in October 1939, a prelude to the wholesale military occupation of the country on **June 17, 1940**. Deciding that armed resistance would be futile, President Ulmanis advised the nation to stay calm and adopt a wait-and-see approach, famously announcing in a live radio broadcast, "I'm staying where I am, and I want you to stay where you are." In the event, the Soviet invaders simply sidestepped Latvia's timorous political elite and did as they pleased. Stage-managed elections were held in July, and the resulting parliament, packed with Soviet puppets, voted to join the USSR. Ulmanis himself was exiled to Siberia, where he died in September 1942.

As the likelihood of war between the Soviet Union and Germany drew near, Stalin decided to tighten his grip on Latvia by **deporting** a large part of the country's intelligentsia to Siberia, and an estimated 16,000 people were rounded up and shipped east on the night of June 13–14, 1941. The **German army** began its invasion of the Soviet Union on June 22, 1941, and were in total control of Latvia two weeks later. Although most Latvians initially greeted the Germans as liberators, they were soon disappointed by the realities of occupation, with Latvia becoming a marginal province in the new Nazi protectorate of Ostland. Special units arrived almost immediately to deal with Latvia's Jewish population, murdering an estimated 30,000 in the first six months of the war and a further 40,000 by 1945.

Fears that Germany might lose the war and leave Latvia to the mercies of the Soviet Union encouraged more Latvians to sign up to the Nazi cause. A **Latvian Legion** was formed as an auxiliary to the SS in 1943 and led Latvia's defence against the advancing Red Army a year later. Rīga itself fell to the Soviets in October 1944 – thousands of Latvians were immediately conscripted into the Red Army and sent to fight their own countrymen in the Legion, who were still holding out in the northwest. As the war neared its end, as many as 200,000 Latvians **fled the country**, preferring life in West European refugee camps to the future offered by the Soviet Union.

Latvia under the Soviets

Resistance to the reimposition of communist rule was initially encouraged by the erroneous belief that the Western powers would sooner or later come to Latvia's aid. In the immediate postwar years, as many as 20,000 Latvians took to the countryside to join the anti-Soviet partisan movement known as the **Forest Brothers**. The Soviet security services responded by creating bogus partisan units of their own and using them to lure the real Forest Brothers into the open. The Soviet grip on the country was confirmed by a new wave of **deportations**, which saw the transport of over 43,000 Latvians to work camps in Siberia and beyond in March 1949.

Loyal Moscow-trained communists were imported to run the local party, and tens of thousands of workers were encouraged to emigrate to Latvia from other parts of the USSR in order to render the republic less ethnically homogenous. The death of Stalin in 1953 led to a gradual relaxation of ideological controls, but outright opposition to official Kremlin policy remained off the agenda. When leading Latvian communists **Berklavs** and **Krūmiņš** began openly to voice misgivings about the ongoing Russian emigration into Latvia, they were thrown out of the party in 1959 – Berklavs himself was exiled to Russia.

Denied political expression, patriotic Latvians threw their energies into the **cultural sphere**. In the 1970s and 1980s, folklore groups and choral societies blossomed: music was one of the few areas of Latvian life in which national sentiment could be expressed without provoking a clampdown by the Soviet state.

Latvians also prided themselves on being more culturally liberated than their conservative Soviet counterparts, and it's no surprise that the Soviet Union's first (and last) sex manual – psychotherapist Jānis Zālītis's *In the Name of Love* – was published here in 1981. After selling 100,000 copies, it was banned by party officials, scandalized by the explicit illustrations – a picture-free second edition went on to shift another 75,000 units.

The road to independence

The appointment of the reformist **Mikhail Gorbachev** as General Secretary of the Soviet Communist Party in 1985 began a gradual erosion of ideological certainties throughout the USSR. Latvian intellectuals were suddenly able to discuss subjects that had been taboo for years – notably the highly illegal nature of the Soviet Union's initial occupation of Latvia in 1940. In autumn 1988, Latvian communists tried to take control of the growing tide of anti-Soviet feeling by forming a **Popular Front** with themselves at the helm – they were soon outmanoeuvred by more genuine patriots. Swiftly growing into a broad-based mass organization, the increasingly confident Front called for the full restoration of Latvian independence in October 1989. Relatively **free elections** to the Latvian Supreme Soviet in March 1990 produced a pro-independence majority which immediately issued a Declaration of Restored Independence and announced the restoration of the 1922 Latvian Constitution.

Although many of Latvia's communists swung behind the independence drive, a pro-Moscow faction under Alfrēds Rubiks took control of the party in May 1990, and kicked pro-independence members out. Exploiting the fears of a sizeable ethnic Russian population made anxious by the implications of Latvian independence, the pro-Moscow lobby also launched a mass organization called **Interfront**, which attempted to storm Latvia's Supreme Soviet on May 14.

For the next nine months Latvia drifted in a strange limbo between independence and Soviet rule, with most people waiting on the outcome of the power struggle between Gorbachev, reformists and hardliners then unfolding in Moscow. In **January 1991,** Gorbachev sided with the hardliners, launching a military operation to seize key installations in the Lithuanian capital Vilnius. Fearing that the same would happen in Rīga, Latvians converged on the capital to mount a 700,000-strong pro-independence demonstration on January 13. Many of the participants stayed on to man barricades hastily erected around the Supreme Soviet, Telephone Exchange and TV Tower. On January 20, Soviet special forces attempted to gain control of the Latvian Interior Ministry, gunning down five innocents in the process. Stung by criticism from the international community, Gorbachev abandoned plans for a further Baltic crackdown and another period of uneasy stand-off ensued. When conservative communists tried to unseat Gorbachev in the **Moscow Coup** of August 1991, only to surrender power several days later, the Soviet Union entered its death throes. Latvia reiterated its independence declaration later the same month and international recognition soon followed.

Independent Latvia

The main issue facing Latvia's post-independence rulers was the question of how best to deal with the country's sizeable **non-Latvian population**. Of a population of 2.5 million, as many as forty percent were Russian-speaking – a direct result of the resettlement policies pursued by the Soviet regime. Latvian demographic angst was compounded by the fact that the country had one of the lowest birth rates in Europe and was therefore most unlikely to breed its way out of a population crisis. In the end, the Latvian government opted to bestow citizenship on post-1945 immigrants who had a "basic proficiency" in the Latvian language, while the European Union helped to fund language-study opportunities for those who wanted to qualify. Those who remained non-citizens retained the right to reside in Latvia, but couldn't vote and were barred from civil service jobs. In the early 1990s, there were an estimated 750,000 non-citizens in Latvia, a number that has now fallen to just under 250,000 – although this is due as much to outward migration and natural death as to any real improvement in language learning.

The other main theme of post-independence domestic politics was the transformation of a dysfunctional state-run economy into a free, consumer-driven market. This was achieved at miraculous speed, but at great social cost, with a minority making big bucks from the transition to pure and unfettered **capitalism**, while the majority eked out a living on meagre wages. The failure of successive governments to battle corruption and raise living standards for all produced a fluid political landscape in which few parties could count on consistent mass support. A succession of coalition governments, each made up of broadly right-of-centre parties, has come and gone without producing any leaders of real charisma or authority.

Joining the **EU** in 2004, Latvia underwent a spectacular economic boom, accompanied by a dizzying rise in real estate prices. The financial crisis of 2008 brought this to a sudden halt, and the imposition of austerity measures caused **riots** and the collapse of the government in March 2009. The incoming right-of-centre coalition government led by Valdis Dombrovskis had little option but to continue with cuts in public spending and stringent financial controls. The national currency was protected from collapse, and Latvia's entry into the eurozone in 2014–15 remains a possibility.

Lithuania

Along with the ancestors of the Latvians, the forebears of today's Lithuanians moved into the Baltic seaboard from western Russia from around 2000 BC onwards. These tribes originally lived in loose, clan-based units closely related by language, speaking a unique and ancient group of Indo-European dialects distinct from the Slav tongues of their near neighbours – indeed contemporary Lithuanian is said to be the closest of all living languages to Sanskrit. They also had a common religion, involving a pantheon of gods, of which Perkūnas (the thunder god) and Laima (Fortune) were among the most prominent. There was also much nature-worship, with trees, lakes and glades accorded a sacred importance.

Protected by belts of forest and swamp, the early Lithuanians lived largely undisturbed by events elsewhere in Europe, preserving a village-based, Iron Age lifestyle until well into the Middle Ages. In the twelfth century, eastern Lithuanian tribes began to unite into something resembling a centralized state, with the fortresses of Kernavė, Trakai and **Vilnius** serving as its main strongholds. The absence of defendable frontiers meant that the nascent Lithuanian state could only ensure security by expanding, leading to the emergence of a highly mobile military machine which soon imposed its rule on Slav lands to the south and east.

The western Lithuanians (known as **Žemaitijans** and speaking a slightly different dialect) were still divided into small tribes at this time, although they managed to come together in inflicting a crushing defeat on Rīga-based crusaders the Brotherhood of the Sword at the **Battle of Saulė** in 1236. Other tribes closely related to the Lithuanians fared less well: the **Yotvingians** to the southwest and the **Prussians** to the west either died out or were assimilated by more powerful neighbours, although the name of Prussia was subsequently adopted by that region's German conquerors.

The rise of the medieval state

Little is known of Lithuania's rulers until the emergence of **Mindaugas** in the mid-thirteenth century, a powerful chieftain who had become master of the state by the 1240s and accepted Christianity in the hope of winning recognition from Western rulers. He was crowned King of Lithuania by a papal representative in 1253, only to be murdered ten years later by nobles eager to preserve Lithuania's pagan culture.

Lithuania's status as the last pagan state in Europe increasingly attracted the attention of Germany's crusading orders, with the Teutonic Knights raiding the country from the west and the Livonian Order mounting frequent attacks from the north.

The experience of constant warfare against the crusaders helped forge Lithuania into a major military power. Fourteenth-century ruler **Gediminas** (1271–1341) extended Lithuanian rule eastwards into Russia and Ukraine. Slav chieftains from the conquered territories were co-opted into the Lithuanian ruling elite, and a Slav dialect close to modern Belarusian became the language used in court documents – the Lithuanians themselves still didn't have a written form of their own tongue.

Jogaila and Vytautas

By the late fourteenth century, Lithuania was a vast multinational empire, which, despite being demonized by Western propagandists for its continuing pagan sympathies, was an increasingly important player in Central European affairs. When King of Poland Louis of Anjou died without a male heir in September 1382, Polish nobles offered the hand of his daughter **Jadwiga** to Gediminas's grandson and current Lithuanian ruler **Jogaila** – henceforth known to history by the Polonized form of his name, Jagiełło. The Poles hoped that the marriage would provide them with a key ally in their struggles against the crusaders and facilitate joint Lithuanian-Polish expansion into Eastern Europe. Jogaila jumped at the chance to internationalize his power base, forging a dynastic link between Lithuania and Poland that would endure for the next four centuries. Jogaila's part of the deal was to promise the **Christian conversion** of his country, bringing down the curtain on Europe's longest-enduring pagan culture.

The marriage took place in 1389, after which Jogaila was crowned King of Poland and went on to spend most of his time in Kraków. A large part of the Lithuanian nobility saw Jogaila as a traitor who had sold out to the Poles, and supported a rebellion by his cousin Vytautas in 1392. Jogaila offered Vytautas the position of Grand Duke of Lithuania, on condition that Lithuania would pass to Jogaila or his heirs after Vytautas's death. On July 15, 1410, Jogaila and Vytautas together led Polish-Lithuanian forces to victory at **Žalgiris** (called Grünwald in Poland; Tannenberg in Germany), a battle which destroyed the Teutonic Order as an effective military power. Vytautas went on to rule Lithuania as a virtually autonomous sovereign – a situation which suited Jogaila, because it demonstrated to the Polish nobles that Lithuania was still a powerful state with a will of its own. It was under Vytautas that Lithuania achieved its greatest territorial extent, stretching from the Baltic in the north to the Black Sea in the south – not surprisingly, Grand Duke Vytautas "the Great" has always been a bigger national hero in Lithuania than Jogaila.

The sixteenth and seventeenth centuries

After Jogaila's death, his descendants continued to rule in Poland while Lithuania remained an autonomous Grand Duchy. Sometimes the King of Poland appointed himself Grand Duke of Lithuania; at others he would award the title to a trusted son or cousin. Although technically separate from Poland, Lithuania was soon drawn into the Polish cultural orbit. The Polish language was the main vehicle by which Catholic ritual and Renaissance culture arrived in Lithuania, and by the sixteenth century almost all of the Lithuanian nobility was **Polish-speaking**. Leading magnates retained a sense of regional patriotism, however, and the defence of Lithuania's special status vis-à-vis the Polish crown remained a popular rallying cry.

By the mid-sixteenth century, Lithuania's eastern borders were increasingly threatened by an aggressively expansionist Russia. Fearful that their Polish counterparts would abandon Lithuania rather than assist in its defence, the Lithuanian nobles allowed themselves to be rushed into a more formal union between the two states. In 1569, the agreement known as the **Union of Lublin** created the **Polish-Lithuanian Commonwealth**, in which the Grand Duchy retained certain self-governing rights but lost its wholly autonomous status.

The Grand Duchy's position on the eastern fringes of a large state centred on Warsaw didn't leave it immune to intellectual currents coming from the rest of Europe. Although the **Reformation** arrived here somewhat later then elsewhere, an estimated sixty percent of the aristocracy had turned Protestant by the late 1500s. The atmosphere of religious debate occasioned the first attempts at Lithuanian publishing, with Protestant nobles sponsoring the production of native-language prayer books and Counter-Reformers responding with texts of their own. The gradual re-Catholicization of the country was carried out without recourse to violence.

Among the beneficiaries of the Grand Duchy's reputation for religious tolerance were the **Jews**. Present in Lithuania ever since the Middle Ages, their numbers increased massively in the sixteenth century owing to an influx of Yiddish-speaking Jews from Germany. They soon became the dominant ethnic group in many provincial towns, with Vilnius serving as their spiritual capital.

Lithuania under the Tsars

Having taken control of most of Estonia and Latvia in the **Great Northern War** of 1700–21, Russia exerted an increasing amount of influence in the affairs of the Commonwealth and installed a succession of weak kings on the Polish throne. Russia, Austria and Prussia progressively helped themselves to more and more of the Commonwealth until wiping it off the map once and for all in the so-called **Third Partition of Poland** in 1795. The Grand Duchy of Lithuania was formally absorbed into Tsarist Russia and, carved up into lesser administrative units, ceased to exist as a territorial entity.

With Lithuania's aristocracy and intelligentsia thoroughly Polonized, any aspirations to independence were invariably tied to the idea of a resurrection of the Polish-Lithuanian Commonwealth. Lithuanian landowners, priests and peasants took an enthusiastic part in the **Polish Uprising of 1830**, liberating much of the countryside, until Tsarist troops arrived to restore order. Lithuanian participation in the **Polish Uprising of 1863** was even more widespread, provoking a brutal crackdown engineered by new governor-general Mikhail "the hangman" Muravyev. Muravyev's response to the threat of Polish-Lithuanian patriotism was to embark on a wholesale programme of **Russification**. Russian became the language of instruction in all but a handful of schools, and a ban on the printing of books in any script other than Cyrillic effectively put paid to any Lithuanian-language publishing.

The 1863 Uprising was the last occasion on which Lithuanians and Poles fought side by side for the restitution of a common state. A new generation of educated Lithuanians increasingly saw Polish culture as a barrier to national self-realization. The main ideologue behind this new course was **Jonas Basanavičius** (1851–1927), who encouraged research into traditional folk culture and promoted fresh study of Lithuania's period of medieval greatness. From 1883 onwards many of these ideas found expression in the magazine *Aušra* (Dawn), printed over the border in Germany and smuggled into Tsarist Russia by a dedicated underground team of *knygnešiai*, or "**book-bearers**". In 1904, the forty-year ban on printing Lithuanian in the Latin alphabet was rescinded, leading to a flowering of indigenous-language culture.

World War I

Lithuania represented a key line of defence for Tsarist armies on the outbreak of **World War I** in 1914, but within a year the whole country had been overrun by the Germans. The collapse of the Tsarist regime in 1917 persuaded Lithuanian national leaders that the time had come to make some kind of pro-independence statement, although they were extremely wary of upsetting either their German occupiers or the Western powers. In December 1917, the recently formed Lithuanian **Taryba**, or Council, declared Lithuania an independent state under the protection of Germany. On February 16, 1918, they reissued the declaration, this time cutting any explicit reference to the Germans. The Germans quietly ignored both declarations and the Taryba was left in limbo until November 1918, when Germany's unexpected collapse left surprised Lithuanian leaders in command of a newly independent country.

The interwar years

It had always been assumed that the Lithuanian state would be centred on the old ducal capital **Vilnius**, an ethnically mixed city that was also claimed by Lithuania's neighbours. After an inconclusive three-way tug of war between Poles, Lithuanians and Bolsheviks, the city was finally seized by Polish General Żeligowski in 1920. The Lithuanian government took up residence in **Kaunas** instead, but refused to recognize the loss of Vilnius, declaring Kaunas to be only the "provisional capital" and freezing relations with Poland as a sign of their displeasure. Having failed to prevent the Polish seizure of Vilnius, the international community turned a blind eye when the Lithuanians themselves grabbed the German-speaking port city of **Memel** (**Klaipėda** in Lithuanian) in 1923.

The emerging nation's attempts to build a viable democracy were short-lived. In 1926, a left-of-centre government signed a treaty of friendship with the Soviet Union, enraging right-wing nationalists and encouraging the authoritarian-minded President **Antanas Smetona** to suspend parliament. A decade and a half of benign dictatorship followed, with the main opposition coming from radical right-wing groups such as Iron Wolf (Geležinis Vilkas), which peddled a modish mixture of anti-liberal, anti-Semitic ideas. On the international stage, Lithuania was the most isolated of all the Baltic States, distrustful of neighbours like Poland and Soviet Russia and in dispute with Germany over the status of Klaipėda – when Hitler reoccupied the city in March 1939, the Lithuanians had no choice but to meekly stand aside.

World War II

Lithuania was in no position to offer resistance when the **Soviet Union**, having grabbed the eastern half of Poland in autumn 1939, moved to occupy all three Baltic States in June 1940. Stage-managed elections produced a pro-Soviet Lithuanian parliament which voted for immediate incorporation into the USSR. With the threat of war with Nazi Germany looming, the Soviet Union tightened its grip on Lithuania with the **deportation** of a randomly chosen cross-section of its citizens to Siberia in June 1941.

The Germans launched **Operation Barbarossa** against the Soviet Union on June 22, 1941, overrunning Lithuania within days. Almost immediately, a murderous campaign of terror was launched against the country's 240,000-strong Jewish population. Special units known as Einsatzgruppen were sent to the Baltic to "deal" with the "Jewish problem" – thousands of Lithuania's Jews were taken to forest clearings and shot within weeks of the Nazi occupation. Many Lithuanians participated enthusiastically in round-ups and killings – it was widely believed that Jews were more likely than Lithuanians to harbour communist sympathies and therefore had to pay for the Soviet occupation of 1940–41. **Ghettos** were established in the cities of Vilnius, Kaunas and Šiauliai, where a semblance of Jewish life continued until summer 1943, when SS leader Heinrich Himmler ordered the deportation of their inhabitants to concentration camps, where the majority were murdered. About ninety percent of Lithuania's Jewish population was wiped out during the Holocaust, and many of the survivors emigrated to Israel or the US after the war. There are currently around four thousand Jews left in the country, most of whom live in Vilnius.

From occupation to independence

With the Red Army's advance into Lithuania in 1944, resistance to Soviet rule started up almost immediately, with various partisan groups joining forces to form the movement subsequently known as the **Forest Brothers**. Despite the KGB's success in infiltrating the organization, armed resistance continued for almost a decade, finally petering out after the arrest and execution of the Brothers' most senior leader, Jonas Žemaitis, in 1953. Meanwhile, in March 1949, another round of **mass deportations** had deprived Lithuania of much of its intelligentsia. The **Church** continued to provide a limited outlet for anti-Soviet sentiment, most notably in the person of Bishop Sladkievičius, who, despite being exiled to a rural village in 1959, organized the production and distribution of the underground dissident journal *Chronicle of the Lithuanian Catholic Church*. Sladkievičius later became archbishop of Kaunas and was made a cardinal by the pope in 1988.

The postwar political scene was dominated by **Antanas Sniečkus**, a trusted servant of Moscow who presided over a purge of "national communists" in 1959. A political thaw in the mid- to late 1960s led to a modest cultural revival, although Lithuanians had to wait until the Glasnost era of the 1980s before outright political dissent was allowed into the open. The first **anti-Soviet demonstration** in Lithuania, held on August 23, 1987, to demand the publication of the Molotov-Ribbentrop Pact (the secret Nazi-Soviet agreement which sealed the fate of the Baltic States in 1939), only attracted a crowd of a few hundred. Within a year, however, the opposition had mushroomed into a mass movement, with the openly pro-independence **Sąjūdis** ("Movement") organization holding its first congress in October 1988. The same year saw the Lithuanian Communist Party elect a new leader, Algirdas Brazauskas, who began to offer cautious support to the independence movement.

Elections to the Lithuanian Supreme Soviet in February 1990 produced a majority for the Sąjūdis camp, with professor of music **Vytautas Landsbergis** becoming its chairman. Landsbergis declared Lithuania's independence from the Soviet Union on March 11, 1990, the first Soviet republic to do so. The Kremlin responded with an economic blockade of Lithuania that led to severe shortages of food and fuel. Egged on by hardliners in Moscow, Mikhail Gorbachev authorized a military **clampdown** in January, 1991, which began with an attack on the Vilnius TV Tower by Soviet tanks. After the deaths of thirteen unarmed demonstrators (a further five hundred were injured), the operation was called off by a Soviet leadership fearful of causing a bloodbath. Kremlin hardliners remained eager to teach Lithuania a lesson, and on July 31, 1991, a special forces' detachment attacked a frontier post at Medininkai on the Lithuanian–Belarusian border, killing seven Lithuanian border guards in the process. With the failure of the anti-Gorbachev Moscow coup of August the same year, however, Soviet power quickly evaporated, leaving Lithuania suddenly, and joyously, independent.

The political present

Although the nationalist-conservative Landsbergis remained the dominant figure in parliament during the first ten years of independence, he surprisingly lost the first presidential elections of 1992 to former communist and born-again Social

Democrat **Algirdas Brazauskas**. Brazauskas was on hand to welcome Pope John Paul II to Lithuania in September 1993, the pontiff's visit serving as a powerful symbol of the country's break with the communist past.

The Conservative Party of Landsbergis provided much of the ideological impetus behind the wholesale switch to **free-market economics** that transformed Lithuania in the 1990s. The change was not without negative consequences, however, with the collapse of loss-making industries, rising unemployment and declining living standards for the majority. The Social Democrats of Brazauskas frequently emerged from elections as the largest group in parliament, although the balance of power was often held by a shifting constellation of pragmatic, centre-right parties whose popularity was often based on the personal charisma of their leaders rather than any coherent ideology.

One notable feature of post-independence politics has been the pro-Western orientation of the country's foreign policy, with successive administrations championing the cause of Lithuanian entry into NATO and the EU. A referendum on **EU membership** in May 2003 produced a huge majority in favour, signalling genuine popular excitement – a result that symbolized for many Lithuanians their extraordinary voyage from Soviet satellite to modern European state.

Books

P lenty was written about the Baltic States during the collapse of the Soviet
Union and its aftermath, and if a brief grounding in the region's history
and politics is what you're after, there's a good deal to choose from. Books
on other aspects of Baltic culture, however, are far less available; many of
the most perceptive accounts of travel in the area were produced by nineteenth-
and early twentieth-century writers whose works are nowadays hard to find. A
number of non-Baltic writers have used the Baltic States as a background for their
fiction, but – curiously, and sadly – the rich traditions of Lithuanian, Latvian and
Estonian literature are almost invisible in English-speaking countries, with far too
few novelists getting translated. Titles marked with the ⚡ symbol are particularly
recommended.

General Baltics

History and politics

Eric Christiansen *The Northern
Crusades*. Definitive account of the
thirteenth-century conquest of Estonia
and Latvia by German-speaking
knights and priests. The mixture of
missionary zeal and near-genocidal
savagery that characterized the times
comes in for thought-provoking scru-
tiny.

John Hiden and Patrick Salmon
The Baltic States and Europe. Excellent
introduction to the main themes of
Baltic history, concentrating on the
twentieth century.

David Kirby *The Baltic World. Vol. I
1492–1772; vol II 1772–1993*. General,

broad history examining long-term
German, Swedish and Russian interests
in the region, as well as the fates of the
Baltic peoples themselves.

⚡ **Anatol Lieven** *Baltic Revolution*.
Witty, erudite and endlessly
stimulating book which successfully
mixes history, reportage and where-
do-the-Baltics-go-from-here analysis,
written by the journalist descendant of
a long line of Latvian aristocrats.

Clare Thomson *The Singing Revolution*.
The main events of the late 1980s and
early 1990s, presented with involving
immediacy by a journalist who was
there at the time.

Literature about the Baltic States

Johannes Bobrowski *Shadow Lands*.
One of Germany's greatest twentieth-
century poets, Bobrowski grew up
in an East Prussian town shaped
by German, Lithuanian, Polish and
Jewish influences, only to see this
cosmopolitan world destroyed during
World War II. Feelings of cultural loss
(and German guilt) fill his poems.

Ed Carey *Alva & Irva*. Fantasmagorical
modern fable focusing on the
adventures of two girls in the mythical
city of Entralla, loosely based on the
Lithuanian capital Vilnius. Dark,
quirky, mesmeric stuff.

Stephan Collishaw *The Last Girl*.
Eminently readable offering in which

an elderly Lithuanian poet stalks the streets of post-Soviet Vilnius, haunted by memories of wartime betrayal. The atmosphere of Lithuania in the 1990s is authentically rendered.

Jonathan Franzen *The Corrections*. Award-winning novel about contemporary America and its discontents, centring on a Midwestern couple and their far-flung offspring – one of whom ends up in the Lithuanian capital in the early 1990s. The Vilnius portrayed by Franzen – a post-communist wild east characterized by organized crime and pollution – is rather different from the one that exists today.

Tadeusz Konwicki *Bohin Manor*. Elegiac novel set among the Polish-Lithuanian gentry in the wake of the 1863 anti-Tsarist uprising, written by one of Poland's leading twentieth-century novelists – himself a native of the Vilnius region. Capturing wonderfully the tone of manor-house life in the Lithuanian backwoods, this is an attempt to update *Pan Tadeusz* (see below) for a modern audience.

Henning Mankell *The Dogs of Rīga*. World-weary Swedish cop Kurt Wallender heads for Rīga looking for help in solving a murder case. Set in 1990, with Latvia in an uneasy limbo between communism and independence, this book paints a convincing picture of the paranoia and uncertainty of the times.

Adam Mickiewicz *Pan Tadeusz*. Poland's national epic, a poem of Homeric proportions describing the ructions and reconciliations of a Polish-Lithuanian gentry family on the eve of Napoleon's invasion of the Tsarist Empire.

Czeslaw Miłosz *The Issa Valley*. Wonderfully lyrical, semi-autobiographical account of a post-World War I boyhood spent in the Lithuanian countryside by Nobel Prize-winning Miłosz. The Issa of the title is based on the real-life River Nevėžis, north of Kaunas.

Denise Neuhaus *The Christening*. Spellbinding novel about the fates of three Estonian women split between Stockholm and Tallinn in the 1970s and 80s. Combining elements of family saga and political thriller, its depiction of life in the last decades of Soviet Estonia is totally believable.

William Palmer *The Good Republic*. Well-written, intelligent and thought-provoking novel about a London-based émigré returning to the unnamed Baltic state of his birth (an artistic amalgam of Estonia and Latvia), to be confronted by the ghosts of his politically ambiguous past.

Anthony Powell *Venusberg*. An interwar novel involving a junior English diplomat who is posted to an East European capital – clearly based on a mixture of Tallinn and Rīga – where he falls in with a bunch of tedious expats and ridiculously Ruritanian locals. A whimsically intriguing period piece, but hardly Powell's best.

Estonia

History, politics and culture

Madli Puhvel *Symbol of Dawn*. A well-researched biography of Estonia's leading nineteenth-century poetess, Lydia Koidula, written in accessible style by an American-Estonian academic, and providing background on the formation of nineteenth-century society and culture. Available in big bookshops in Tallinn and Tartu.

Toivo U. Raun *Estonia and the Estonians*. Best of the general histories, covering the main themes of Estonian society and politics from the earliest times up to 1991, in readable style.

Rein Taagepera *Estonia: Return to Independence*. A useful addition to the above titles, this provides plenty of detailed analysis on the fall of the Soviet Union and the political landscape of the 1990s.

Travel and memoirs

Tania Alexander *A Little of All of These*. Memories of a childhood spent on an Estonian country estate during the interwar years, among a cosmopolitan bunch of Russo-German aristocrats.

Arthur Ransome *Racundra's First Cruise*. The author of children's classic *Swallows and Amazons* spent the summer of 1922 sailing from Rīga to Tallinn, stopping off at sundry Estonian ports and islands on the way.

If you know your sextant from your spinnaker, this is an absorbing read.

Ronald Seth *Baltic Corner: Travels in Estonia*. Engaging, if low-key, memoirs of an English teacher in interwar Estonia. Some good stuff on daily life in the Tallinn of the 1930s, and lively descriptions of trips to Narva and Petseri monastery – the latter a Setu shrine which was then part of Estonia, but subsequently awarded to Russia by post-World War II border changes.

Literature

ELM (*Estonian Literary Magazine*). Biannual magazine published by the Estonian Institute and available from Tallinn bookstores, featuring contemporary poetry and prose in English translation, and a round-up of literary news. Content is posted on the Institute's website: ⓦ www.einst.ee.

Jaan Kaplinski *The Same Sea in Us All* and *The Wandering Border*. Two collections from Estonia's leading contemporary poet, whose verse is imbued with an almost spiritual appreciation of nature. You can read more of his poems on ⓦ jaan. kaplinski.com.

Jaan Kross *The Czar's Madman*. First published in Estonia in 1978, the best-known work from the country's greatest twentieth-century prose writer functions both as a rich historical novel and subtle allegory of

life in Brezhnev's USSR – which makes it all the more remarkable that it ever got past the censor. The kernel of the story involves a nineteenth-century Baltic German aristocrat who is locked up in the madhouse for daring to criticize the Tsar, with the stoical, self-denying lives of rural Estonians providing the intricate background weave. Kross's most recent work to be translated into English, *Treading Air*, is a richly textured guide to twentieth-century Estonia in the form of a civil servant's life story, and comes with an invaluable introduction to Kross's life and times by translator Eric Dickens. *Professor Martens' Departure*, in which a nineteenth-century Estonian adviser to the Tsar looks back on his life, is an altogether less penetrable meditation on the Estonian-Russian relationship.

Mati Unt *Diary of a Blood Donor, Brecht at Night, Things in the Night*. Vampires in

St Petersburg, werewolves in Glasnost-era Tallinn and exiled German playwrights in Helsinki people this trio of novels, presenting a phantasmagorical voyage through Estonian history and the break-up of the Soviet system, as seen through the eyes of the incorrigibly individualist Unt (1944–2005).

Various *The Dedalus Book of Estonian Literature*. Highly useful sampler of 17 short stories. Authors range from early twentieth-century classic names like Vilde and Tammsaare to contemporary voices like Peeter Sauter.

Latvia

History, travel and memoirs

Lucy Addison *Letters from Latvia*. Addison was an Anglo-Latvian who chose to stay in Latvia throughout World War II and the Soviet occupation, recording the madness of war and political repression from the sanctuary of a wooden cottage in Jūrmala. These letters are both gripping historical narrative and a touching read.

Peggie Benton *Baltic Countdown*. Recollections of Rīga in the late 1930s, written by the wife of a British diplomat. From beach holidays in Jūrmala to the arrival of Soviet tanks in 1940, this is an enjoyable slice of Englishwoman-abroad writing.

Modris Eksteins *Walking Since Daybreak*. Mixing family memoir with a general history of Latvia's tragic twentieth century, this is beautifully written, totally engrossing stuff. If you buy just one book about Latvia, let it be this.

Sandra Kalniete *With Dance Shoes in Siberian Snows*. Born into a family of Latvians exiled to Siberia, Kalniete grew up to become a leading art historian, Latvian foreign minister, then EU commissioner. This touching autobiography is also a thought-provoking meditation on exile, return and commitment to the national cause.

Literature

Alberts Bels *The Cage*. Beginning like a hard-boiled detective story and ending as a disturbingly surreal fable, this is an outstanding piece of contemporary fiction – and subtle critique of the Soviet system (it first appeared in 1971). It's also one of the few morsels of Latvian literature that's available in English.

Various *All Birds Know This*. Well-translated and representative anthology of contemporary Latvian poets, including formidable national literary figures like Vesma Belševica and Imants Ziedonis. Available from the bigger Rīga bookshops.

Lithuania

History, politics and travel

Laimonas Briedis *Vilnius City of Strangers*. Vilnius is one of Europe's most multilayered, multicultural cities – something that is often best observed by visitors rather than locals. Briedis examines the writings of perceptive outsiders to arrive at a fascinating portrait of the city that also serves as a revealing slice of cultural history.

Czesław Miłosz *Native Realm*. Born in Lithuania to Polish parents, Miłosz is especially illuminating on the Polish–Lithuanian relationship in particular, and East European culture in general, in this meditative autobiography. The same author's *Beginning with My Streets* is a collection of essays, including some invigorating pieces about Vilnius.

S.C. Rowell *Lithuania Ascending*. Few sources reveal the exact processes by which Lithuania rose from being a tribal statelet to a huge empire stretching from the Baltic to the Black Sea, but Rowell has done a remarkable job in sifting the evidence; this groundbreaking analysis of thirteenth-century power politics is the result. One for medievalists rather than general readers.

Alfred Eric Senn *Lithuania Awakening*. Account of the rise of Sąjūdis and the push towards freedom, written with eyewitness freshness by an American academic who was there for most of the events described.

V. Stanley Vardys and Judith B. Sedaitis *Lithuania the Rebel Nation*. Good overview of twentieth-century history and a blow-by-blow account of the drive to independence. Eager to nail Western darling Gorbachev for his part in the anti-democratic crackdown of January 1991.

Various *Lithuania: Past, Culture, Present*. Published in Lithuania by Baltos Lankos and sold in most bookshops in central Vilnius, this coffee-table book contains intelligent, readable essays on key aspects of Lithuanian identity, accompanied by a wonderful selection of photographs.

Literature

Ričardas Gavelis *Vilnius Poker*. Vodka, paranoia, bad sex and body parts fill this Joycean voyage through the Vilnius of the pre-perestroika era. Gavelis began writing this modern Lithuanian classic at a time when there was no realistic chance of it being published – and pure, written-for-posterity literature is the result.

Sigitas Geda *Biopsy of Winter*. Arrow-sharp shards of verse from one of the country's leading literati, deftly translated by American poet Kerry Shawn Keys. Published by Vaga and available from their bookshop in Vilnius (see p.282).

Jonas Mekas *There Is No Ithaca*. Collection of poems by the Lithuanian-born, New-York-based writer and avant-garde filmmaker. Contains *Idylls of Semeniskiai*, a lyrical evocation of Lithuanian village life. Parallel English/Lithuanian texts.

Kornelijus Platelis *Snare for the Wind*. Varied, career-spanning selection from one of Lithuania's most

respected contemporary poets.
Available from Vaga and other big
bookshops in Vilnius.

Balys Sruoga *Forest of the Gods*.
Powerful, concentration-camp

memoirs from a poet and playwright
who was imprisoned in Stutthof
towards the end of World War II.
Available in Vilnius bookshops.

Lithuanian-Jewish history and memoirs

Lucy S. Dawidowicz *From That
Place and Time*. American academic
Dawidowicz went to study at Vilnius's
YIVO (Yiddish Institute) as a young
graduate in 1938 and wrote this
memoir as a nostalgic tribute to the
city. The same author's *The War
Against the European Jews* is one of the
best overall histories of the Holocaust.

Waldemar Ginsburg *And Kovno Wept*.
Gripping, unforgettable account
of ghetto life in Kaunas (Kovno to
its Jewish inhabitants), written by a
survivor.

Dan Jacobson *Heshel's Kingdom*.
Involving account of a voyage through
Lithuania inspired by memories of
Jacobson's grandfather Heshel, who
was a rabbi in the western Lithuanian
town of Varniai. This is a wistful,
elegiac book with insights into
contemporary Lithuania's ambiguous
relationship with its multicultural past.

Howard Jacobson *Roots Schmoots*. Both
humorous travelogue and identity-
seeking enquiry, this book ends up
in the southern Lithuanian town of
Lazdijai – home town of Jacobson's
great-grandparents. Lithuania sounds
pretty grim the way Jacobson describes
it, but then he was travelling in the
post-Soviet early 1990s.

Dovid Katz *Lithuanian Jewish
Culture*. Excellent introduction to
the all-but-vanished world of the
Litvaks. Handsomely illustrated, and
written with enthusiasm and verve,

this is one that will satisfy specialists
and general readers alike. Published by
Baltos Lankos and available from
Vilnius bookshops.

Herman Kruk *The Last Days of the
Jerusalem of Lithuania*. Chronicle of
Vilnius's wartime ghetto, scribbled
down nightly by Kruk, who dedicated
himself to documenting a culture
he knew was being snuffed out.
Enormously valuable as a social
document, this also makes for gut-
wrenching reading.

Hillel Levine *In Search of Sugihara*.
Well-researched and engagingly
written biography of the diplomat
frequently dubbed the "Japanese
Schindler". Levine clearly likes his
subject, and yet his determination
to portray him as a complex, often
flawed human being has earned the
enmity of the Sugihara family.

William W. Mishell *Kaddish for
Kovno*. The story of Kaunas's Jewish
community, with a sensitive overview
of Lithuanian–Jewish relations over
the centuries, and an unflinching
narrative of the Nazi occupation.

Avraham Tory *Surviving the Holocaust:
Kovno Ghetto Diary*. Harrowing tale
of survival in World War II Kaunas,
written by the deputy secretary of the
ghetto council. Retained as a personal
memoir by Tory, the manuscript was
dusted off in 1982, when the author
was called to testify against Kazys
Palciauskas, the city's wartime mayor.

Lithuanian-Jewish literature

Chaim Grade *My Mother's Sabbath Days*. Outstanding prose from one of Vilnius's best Yiddish-language writers. The first half of this book consists of quirky short-story snapshots of life in Jewish Vilnius on the eve of World War II; the second is harrowing autobiography, with Grade escaping the Nazi invasion while his wife chooses to stay in the Vilnius ghetto.

Menke Katz *Burning Village*. Powerful cycle of poems set on the eve of World War II in the author's native Michalishek, a Jewish village in the Lithuanian–Belarusian borderlands.

Avram Sutzkever *Selected Poetry and Prose*. Leading light of the Yung Vilne movement, who escaped from the Vilnius ghetto and lived as a partisan in the forest before emigrating to Israel after the war. Electrifying verse and experimental prose poems about Vilnius and the war, highly charged with imagery and nostalgia.

Baltic folk music

The characteristic Baltic song festivals – hugely popular events – played a signifi-cant role in the emergence to independence of Estonia, Latvia and Lithuania, and have long been a focus for national consciousness.

Despite the considerable national and regional differences between (and within) the three countries, they have certain important features in common. All have archaic folk song-poetry dating back to the pre-Christian era and they have in common several traditional instruments, notably **Baltic zithers** variously called *kantele, kannel, kokles* or *kanklės*.

Though changes in village life throughout the twentieth century have meant that the social contexts of much traditional song and dance have all but disappeared, there's still a great deal to be found in living memory. The **folklore movements** that sprung up in the 1960s and 70s saw urban enthusiasts making trips to the vil-lages, and performing the material they found there. These attempts to celebrate still-living musical traditions paved the way for today's musicians: in all three countries bands are seeking to create music that uses traditional musical forms, but connects with the present day.

Estonia

Estonia's traditional culture, while distinct, has strong links with that of the linguistically and geographically close Finland, with **runo-songs** and its own variants of **Baltic zither**.

Runo-song

Estonian runo-song, *regilaul*, has the same basic form as the Finnish variety to which it is related. A large number of runo-song texts have been collected, largely from women, thus offering a female point of view. Typical subjects include work, rituals, spells, ballads and mythical stories, and the songs tend to a stoic sadness, or wry observation of life's realities, rather than extreme expressions of joy or love. The more ornamented **swing-songs** were sung while sitting on the big communal village swing whose movement made its own rhythmic demands.

Estonia's national epic **Kalevipoeg**, by folklorist **F. Reinhold Kreutzwald** (1803–82), was published in the 1860s, paralleling folklorist Elias Lonnröt's creation from runo-song sources of Finland's *Kalevala*, first published in 1835. By the early twentieth century runo-song was largely overtaken by more European forms of rhyming folk song with wider-spanning tunes and occa-sional instrumental accompaniment. Nevertheless it survived in a few areas – notably in **Setumaa**, which straddles Estonia's Russian border, and also on the island of **Kihnu**.

Setu song

The songs of the **Setu people** have considerably influenced contemporary roots singers, both in Estonia and in Finland. There's been a recent revival in Setu culture and the speaking of its dialect. Several villages, such as Värska, Kosselka, Helbi, Obinitsa and Uusvada, have established women's vocal groups that perform songs traditionally sung and danced while working or at social events, particularly the three-day wedding celebration. The eight-syllable runo pattern of these songs is often interrupted by extra syllables and refrains, and unlike other Estonian vocal traditions, they are sung polyphonically.

Festivals

During the 1960s, instructions were sent by Moscow to cultural organizers throughout the Soviet Union that supervised manifestations of genuine, living folk culture were to be encouraged, to demonstrate the government's support for the needs and expressions of the masses. In the Baltics, reluctant members of these "masses" were researching these same living cultures, not in response to Moscow's wishes but in order to explore the distinctiveness of their own culture.

Performing ensembles fell into two groups: "ethnographic" – which came from a particular area and specialized in local forms – and "folkloric" – which drew on the whole country's traditions. The first of the "ethnographic" type to appear in the more liberal climate of the 1960s was the Setu choir **Leiko** from Värska, formed in 1964. Of the "folkloric" type, **Leigarid** (formed in 1969 to entertain tourists at Tallinn Open-air museum) soon turned away from the colourful folkloric-spectacle approach towards a more authentic style rooted in village traditions. Regional ethnographic performance groups were formed, too, as were young city-based ensembles such as **Leegajus** (led by **Igor Tõnurist**) and **Hellero**.

The mass singing festivals continue: the All Estonian Song Festival, **Laulupidu**, which started in Tartu in 1869, is held every five years in Tallinn. It's still a huge event: there can be over 20,000 choir members and 100,000 in the audience. The Setu people have their own song festival, **Leelopäev**, a gathering of singing groups for performance and celebration with traditional food and costume, held every three years in the village of Värska. **Viljandi Folk Music Festival**, which concentrates on young Estonian folk bands, plus foreign guests mainly from neighbouring Baltic countries, began in 1993. The **Baltica** festival, which moves each year to a different Baltic state, began in 1987, and Tallinn first hosted it in 1989.

Latvia

The land of amber has more Baltic zithers, as well as drone-based singing and a large body of traditional song-poetry – **dainas** – with strong pre-Christian symbolism and a lack of heroes.

The daina

The Latvian **daina** is a short song of just one or two stanzas, one or two lines in length, without rhyme, and largely in the same four-footed trochaic metre as runo-songs. *Dainas* feature mythological subjects and reflect most aspects of village life, but the stories and heroic exploits described in many countries' folk songs are notably absent.

The sun is a dominant image, often personified as **Saule**, and her daily course across the sky and through the year is linked metaphorically with human life. While the sun is female, **Mēness**, the moon, is male, and a frequent song theme is courtship between them or other celestial figures such as the twin sons of Dievs (God) and the daughter of the sun. The solstices were traditional occasions for celebration – in particular Jāņi (midsummer), whose central figure was Jānis, the archetypal vigorous, potent male with strong phallic associations. As the *ligotne* (midsummer song) *Jāņa Daudzinajums* describes him:

Oh Jānis, the son of Dievs,
what an erect steed you have
The spurs are glittering through forests
the hat above trees
Jānis was riding all the year
and has arrived on the Jāņi eve;
Sister, go and open the gate, and let Jānis in.

Translation by Valdis Muktupāvels

The major collection of **dainas** was made by **Krišjānis Barons** (1835–1923); the six volumes of his *Latvju Dainas* were published between 1894 and 1915, and contain about 300,000 texts.

In keeping with other regions of the Baltics, newer song-forms spread during the nineteenth century, when chordal, fixed-scale instruments – such as the accordion – arrived. Thus **zinge** is a singing style with a strong German influence. The older forms remained, however: **dziesma** means a song with a definite melody, while **balss** means "voice" or "speech" and has no clearly defined melody, changing with the rhythm of the words. *Balss* was the style used in calendar celebrations, as well as during work. It usually follows a three-voice form: the leader sings a couple of stanzas of a *daina*, then the others repeat them. In some regions these repetitions are sung over a vocal drone – a distinctive feature not found elsewhere in the Baltics.

Festivals and performers

Latvia's national song festival has been taking place, usually at five-year intervals, since 1888. In 1990, the first after the country's return to independence, it reached its largest size with over 35,000 singers, dancers and instrumentalists. Latvia also takes its turn as host of the **Baltica** festival, and has a range of other folk-music-related festivals of varying regularity.

Like the other Baltic States, Latvia still has a large number of local and regional **folklore groups** and **ethnographic ensembles**, most of them largely vocal rather than instrumental; the website ⓦfolklora.lv has a list of many of them. While what they do is a preservation, both of songs and of costume, it is nevertheless a community activity – they meet to rehearse, make costumes and so on – and these groups, often established many decades ago and with members of all ages, are in themselves a folk culture, and a living source of much traditional music.

Then there are the folk bands going deep into traditional music and its instrumentation, but using it in new configurations. Since they don't feel themselves to be folk musicians in the old sense of village culture, they dub their music 'post-folklore'. There have been a number of formative bands in this development but most influential have been those of ethnomusicologist, *kokles* player and bagpiper **Valdis Muktupāvels**, and of the band **Iļgi**, which since its formation in 1981 by singer and fiddler **Ilga Reizniece**, has developed from a quiet acoustic group to a strong performing and recording unit.

Iļgi's and Muktupāvels' albums, and most of today's other Latvian tradition-rooted music as well as some pop and jazz, are on the **UPE** label, owned and run by **Ainars Mielavs**. Mielavs had considerable pop success in Latvia as leader of the band Jauns Mēness, and is now a singer-songwriter in his own right. At a time when there were almost no recordings of Latvian traditional or post-folklore music available, and little money around to finance them, Mielavs gathered leading musicians on the post-folklore scene and began a series of elegantly recorded and well-packaged CD projects on UPE including the ongoing *Latvian Folk Music Collection*.

Lithuania

The largest Baltic state has a rich variety of folk forms, including layered **poly-phonic music**, sung or played on reed instruments, flutes and – in common with its neighbours to the north – Baltic zithers.

Song

Thousands of Lithuanian traditional songs – **dainos** – have been collected. They deal with every aspect of life, and wedding and love songs feature particularly prominently. Some would be passed on as well-known songs, but others, such as lullabies, would be varied or improvised to suit the occasion. In the early twentieth century many women, who were predominantly the creators and carriers of songs, had repertoires of a hundred or more songs.

Singing can be solo or in a group, in unison or in parallel chords of thirds, fourths or fifths. Aukštaitija, Lithuania's northeastern region, has a distinctive and well-known tradition of polyphonic songs, **sutartinės**, whose melody and form are also transferred to instrumental music. They are duophonic – two voices, or groups of voices in harmony. In the case of **dvejinės** (by twos) and **keturinės** (by fours), two harmonizing lines are sung together, then they stop and are replaced by a second group of singers and two different harmonizations, while in **trejinės** three parts overlap, two at a time, as in a canon. The word stresses create a syncopating internal rhythm.

Instruments

There is a relatively large range of Lithuanian traditional instruments. The basic form of the Lithuanian version of the Baltic zither, the **kanklės**, differs regionally in playing style and in the number of strings, which can be anywhere between five and twelve. The repertoire of the traditional *kanklės* consisted of old-style material such as *sutartinės* and more modern dance tunes such as polkas, waltzes and quadrilles. A "concert series" of large, many-stringed box *kanklės* was devised for the Soviet-style ensembles.

Whereas the old round dances (*rateliai*) were traditionally accompanied by singing only, during the nineteenth and twentieth centuries instrumental ensembles commonly played the newer dance forms. Instrumental groups playing *kanklės* and *lamzdeliai* (wooden or bark whistles) existed as far back as the sixteenth century. Later the fiddle and three-stringed bass *basetle* joined them, followed in the nineteenth and early twentieth centuries by accordions, bandoneons, concertinas, Petersburg accordions and harmonicas, mandolins, balalaikas, guitars, modern clarinets and cornets. During the Soviet era, dressed-up ensembles emerged using box *kanklės* and *birbynės* (folk clarinets – they used the developed form which is a mellow-sounding thick tube with a cowhorn bell). These groups actually made quite a pleasant sound, not so different from a disciplined village band, but they were often used, to the annoyance of those searching out the "real thing", in classically influenced arrangements to accompany choral singing of harmonized and denatured so-called *sutartinės* with all their dissonances smoothed out.

Svjata Vatra (EST)

One of the most popular live acts in Estonia, Svjata Vatra are an Estonian-Ukrainian crossover band whose gigs contain a healthy dose of ska-punk attitude. The 2010 album *Zillja Zelenen'ke* is an apt summation of Svjata Vatra's career to date.

Veljo Tormis (EST)

An influential composer celebrated for his choral works, Tormis has spent a lifetime exploring the archaic roots of Estonian song. His *Curse Upon Iron* (1972) was banned by the Soviet authorities unused to such earthy statements of ethnic belonging. Tormis's more recent *Songs of Estonian Men* was turned into a spectacular stage show by Tallinn's Von Krahl theatre in 2008.

Iļģi (LAT)

Formed in 1981 by singer and fiddler Ilga Reizniece, Iļģi have continued to develop and inspire throughout all Latvia's changes. Their album of traditional Latvian wedding songs *Ne uz vienu dienu* (2006) is one of the most spirited folk-rock recordings of recent years. 2009's *Isākāas nakts dziesmas* ("Songs of the Shortest Night") injects similar energy into the traditional repertoire of Midsummer's Eve songs.

Skyforger (LAT)

Active since 1995, Latvian band Skyforger are the Baltics' prime practitioners of pagan metal. Their 2003 album *Zobena dziesma* ("Swordsong") was made up of traditional folk material and came as a bit of a shock to the head-banging contingent; 2010's *Kurbads* (released internationally on the Metal Blade label) is a return to hard-riffing territory.

Atalyja (LITH)

A large band with five singers and a huge number of instruments ranging from Lithuanian *kanklės* to rock guitars and Indian tabla drums, Atalyja bring a modern multicultural approach to the traditional folk repertoire. 2009's *Saula riduolēla* (on Dangus records) is their most accomplished album to date.

Donis (LITH)

The electronic music project of Klaipėda-based musician Donatas Beliauskas, Donis's output ranges from dark ambient soundscapes with only the vaguest folk underpinning to multi-layered synth-swathed arrangements of traditional songs. Featuring the stirring vocals of Rasa Serra, Donis's 2010 album *Kas tave šaukia* is a great example of what electro-folk crossover can achieve.

In the northeast, tunes of the *sutartinė* type were played on *skudučiai* – rather like dismantled pan-pipes, played by a group of men. The same type of tune was played by five-piece sets of birchbark-bound wooden trumpets (*ragai*).

Festivals and performers

Lithuania's first Song Festival or **Dainų Šventė** took place in Kaunas in 1924. After 1945 these festivals remained acceptable to the Soviet regime, although the back-to-the-villages folklore movement that began in the 1960s was considerably more suspicious. Rasa (the summer solstice) and other Baltic pagan events were publicly celebrated despite persecution by the KGB. **Folklore ensembles** sprang up in towns and cities, and the village musicians from whom they collected formed performing units themselves, usually known as "ethnographic ensembles".

The annual **Skamba Skamba Kankliai** festival in Vilnius's old town began in 1975, while the first **Baltica** International Folklore Festival, which moves between the Baltic States each year, took place in 1987 in Vilnius.

The current undisputed doyenne of Lithuanian folk singing is **Veronika Povilionienė**, a native of the Dzūkija region who has been the nation's outstanding performer of unaccompanied female narrative songs ever since her student days in the late 1960s. Her repertoire consists of traditional material from all over the country, although she has also made several excursions into crossover territory – the 1993 album *Povilionienė/Vyšniauskas* (recorded with jazz saxophonist Petras Vyšniauskas) is one of the most startling exercises in fusion to come out of the Baltics, and can still be picked up from Vilnius record shops.

The next generation of tradition-rooted progressive bands, such as folk-rock band **Atalyja**, combines *kanklės*, bagpipes and other traditional instruments with those of rock for an emphatic, wild expression of *sutartinės* and other traditional material. Beyond folk-rock stretches a spectrum of post-Soviet, pan-Baltic, neo-pagan bands, from "ritual folk" such as that of **Kulgrinda**, through "folk-metal", "dark-metal" and "dark-ambient" – and it's the neo-pagan Dangus label (Ⓦ www .dangus.net) that is home to many of the most exciting Lithuanian acts today. The Dangus-organized festival Menuo Juodaragis, held at the end of August (see p.36), is the best opportunity to catch these acts playing live.

Adapted from a piece originally written and researched by Andrew Cronshaw

A history of the Baltic States in seven musical incidents

I t was Estonian illustrator and cartoonist Heinz Valk who first used the term "Singing Revolution" to describe the spontaneous musical gatherings that swept Estonia in the summer of 1988. Far from being a piece of hyperbole, Valk's memorable turn of phrase was an accurate description of what was happening in the Baltic States at the time. It also shed profound light on the role of **music** in Baltic history, and its importance as a herald of social convulsions.

1869: The first Estonian Song Festival, Tartu

Nineteenth-century newspaper editor Johann Voldemar Jannsen was concerned about the declining role of authentic folk culture in Estonian life and thought that the encouragement of choral music would not only reverse this trend but also promote Estonian patriotism at the same time. The result was the all-Estonian Song Festival of 1869, a huge undertaking that brought together 46 choirs, five brass bands, 800 singers and an audience of 15,000. Jannsen's daughter Lydia Koidula (see p.109) wrote the patriotic hymn *Mu Isamaa* ("My Fatherland") especially for the festival – it went on to serve as an unofficial national anthem during consecutive periods of foreign occupation.

1967: Four White Shirts

Maverick Latvian filmmaker Rolands Kaniņš was one of the first Soviet directors to try and make a "youth" film complete with a modish pop-music soundtrack provided by Imants Kalniņš. The result was *Four White Shirts* (*Četri Balti Krekli*), in which a local beat group face problems from the public censor – who fears that their (nowadays harmless-sounding) songs are examples of western decadence. The real-life film censors in Moscow felt that they were being ridiculed by

Kalniņš, and the film was shelved for twenty years. Despite the ban, the film's songs were adopted immediately by the Latvian public, with the "white shirts" of the title track widely perceived to be a metaphor for Latvian cultural purity. Imants Kalniņš's lyrical songwriting style became a patriotic musical trademark, serving as a template for the Latvian-language pop groups of the 1970s and 80s. Imants Kalniņš himself remained much in demand as a writer of intelligent pop songs, creating a huge and much-loved body of work that is today celebrated at the annual Imantdienas (Days of Imants) festival.

1976: *Con Anima* released by the Ganelin-Chekasin-Tarasov Trio

Initiated in 1967, the Tallinn Jazz Festival demonstrated that the Baltic States were far enough away from Moscow to allow a certain degree of musical freedom. However it was the emergence of the Ganelin-Chekasin-Tarasov Trio in Vilnius that showed just how far the boundaries could be pushed. Comprising pianist Vyacheslav Ganelin, saxophonist Andrei Chekasin and percussionist Vladimir Tarasov, the Trio gave birth to a howling mongrel of free jazz and contemporary classical music, creating something far more cacophonous than anything yet experienced in the Soviet Union. Protected from official censorship by

Vilnius's clannish small-town nature, the trio were accorded professional status by becoming the "Contemporary Chamber Music Ensemble" of the Vilnus Philharmonia. Despite being released on the state record label Melodiya, their first album *Con Anima* was largely ignored by the Soviet press, and it was left to Polish magazine *Jazz Forum* to claim it as a modern classic. The Trio quickly became a cult in the USSR, drawing vast crowds wherever they played. At a time when avant-garde visual artists were prevented from displaying their work anywhere except in their own flats, the Trio's musical version of the same thing had an electrifying effect.

1988: The Tartu Popular Music Days

The famous "Singing Revolution" began in Tartu on May 14, 1988, when a routine pop-music festival attracted crowds of students brandishing Estonian flags. Similar flag-waving had been witnessed at the same city's Heritage Preservation Festival a month previously, and Tartu's students saw the Popular Music Days as the next opportunity to demonstrate their newfound sense of patriotic confidence. Providing the emotional catalyst was prog-rock performer Alo Mattiisen, whose song *No Land Is Alone* (*Ei ole üksi üksi maa*) – specially penned for the festival – became the patriotic anthem of the summer. Tallinn soon took up the baton: during the Old Town Festival of June 1988, thousands flocked spontaneously to the Tallinn Song Grounds to sing patriotic songs. By the time the Estonian Song Festival took place in September 1988, the Song Grounds had become the focus of an anti-Soviet revolution.

1989: JMKE release *Külmale Maale* ("To the Cold Country")

Its no surprise that an exhibit labelled "jacket worn by an Estonian punk" occupies pride of place in the ethnographic collection of the Estonian National Museum. There was a small but visible community of punks in Tallinn in the early 1980s, and fear of youth culture prompted the authorities to ban a concert by proto-punk band Propellor in 1980. Riots and police beatings ensued, causing forty Estonian intellectuals to sign a letter of protest to the authorities. Genuine punk bands didn't emerge until a few years later, with JMKE – led by mohawk-crested singer Villu Tamm – leading the way. It wasn't until 1989 that JMKE succeeded in releasing an album, taking advantage of the new freedom of travel and recording it in Helsinki for Finnish label Stupido Twins. Standout track *Tere Perestroika* ("Hello Perestroika") caught the spirit of the times, and was the first Estonian song to become a top-five hit in Finland.

1991: BIX release *Aki kariai*

Throughout the 1980s Šiauliai art college in Lithuania had a reputation for unleashing the unconventional, serving as the incubator for a succession of Lithuanian conceptual-art pranksters. In 1987 it gave birth to BIX, a post-punk outfit whose jagged, confrontationist style seemed to capture the anti-Soviet, anti-mainstream spirit of the times. As well as playing at outdoor gatherings in pre-indepenence Lithuania, BIX also toured the alternative rock clubs of western Europe, where they were greeted as emissaries of the unfolding Baltic revolution. BIX's first album *Aki kariai* ("Blind Soldiers") wasn't released until 1991, its spiky riffs offering aural commentary on a turbulent social scene. Its best-known track *Neverk Mama (Sex Revolution)* was an acidic satire of the individualism that so often went hand-in-hand with new, post-independence social freedoms.

2010: Alina Orlova releases second album *Mutabor*

The Eurovision Song Contest triumphs of Estonia (2001) and Latvia (2002) were cultural catastrophes for the Baltic States, unleashing an avalanche of mediocre music and trivial cultural aspirations. Given the small size of the Baltic musical markets, talented pop performers were forced to make compromises with mainstream media (whether taking part in Eurovision competitions or appearing as judges on reality TV shows) in order to make money – and the career trajectories of genuine talents were severely limited as a result. One of the few to buck this trend with any real conviction is Alina Orlova, the young singer-songwriter (born 1988) who came from nowhere to become Lithuania's most promising musical export. Featuring brittle vocals, delicate piano and string arrangements, and the kind of introspective lyrics that local critics refer to as "sung poetry", the two albums *Laukinis šuo dingo* (2008) and *Mutabor* (2010) have won her acclaim at home and cult status elsewhere. If Orlova is anything to go by, the Baltic tradition of rousing song, underground pop and musical avant-garde still enjoys some kind of future.

Language

Language

Estonian

E stonian belongs to the Finno-Ugric family of languages; it's closely related to Finnish and somewhat more distantly to Hungarian. Despite the importance of Germans, Swedes and Slavs in Estonia's history, the language itself has remained remarkably free of foreign-influenced words, and its relative purity is regarded by the locals as a powerful symbol of their own ability to survive hundreds of years of foreign domination with their culture unscathed. Bearing little relation to any Indo-European language, Estonian is a difficult language for outsiders to master. Although it has no masculine or feminine gender, the situation is complicated by the existence of fourteen noun cases, which take the form of a fiendishly difficult-to-learn set of suffixes. "Tallinna" ("Tallinn's"), "Tallinas" ("in Tallinn"), "Tallinast" ("from Tallinn") are just three examples of the way the system works.

If you wish to investigate further, *Colloquial Estonian* (Routledge) makes an admirable attempt to render this notoriously impenetrable language both fun and accessible.

Pronunciation

In Estonian, words are pronounced exactly as they're written, with the stress almost always falling on the first syllable. Estonian consonants are pronounced pretty much as they are in English, and it's only really the vowels, listed below that require particular attention. If you're leafing through an Estonian dictionary, bear in mind that the vowels õ, ä, ö and ü usually come at the end of the alphabet, just after z.

a "a" as in att**i**tude
aa "a" as in c**a**rt
ä midway between the "a" in hat and "e" in met
e "e" as in m**e**t
ee "é" as in caf**é**
j "y" as in **y**ellow
o "o" as in d**o**g
oo "o" as in p**o**rt

ö the same as German ö; a combination of o and e that sounds like the "u" in fur
õ no equivalent in English; midway between the "ur" in fur and the "i" in sit
š "sh" as in **sh**iny
u "oo" as in f**oo**l
ü the same as German "ü"; a combination of u and e that sounds like the French "u" in "sur"

Estonian words and phrases

Basics

Yes	Jah
No	Ei
I don't understand	Ma ei saa aru
Please	Palun
Thank you	Tänan/aitäh
Excuse me	Vabandage

Hello	Tere
Good morning	Tere hommikust
Good evening	Head õhtust
Goodnight	Head ööd
Goodbye	Nägemiseni/nägemist
Bye!	Hüvasti!
How are you?	Kuidas sa elad?
Fine, thanks	Tänan, hästi

391

What is your name?	Kuidas sinu nimi on?
My name is...	Minu nimi on...
Yesterday	Eile
Today	Täna
Tomorrow	Homme
In the morning	Hommikul
In the afternoon	Pärastlõunat
In the evening	Õhtul
I'd like...	Ma soovin...
Cheap	Odav
Expensive	Kulukas
Good	Hea
Bad	Halb/paha

Questions

Do you speak English?	Kas te räägite inglise keelt?
Where is..?	Kus on..?
When?	Millal?
What?	Mis?
Why?	Miks?
How much?	Kui palju?
How much does this cost?	Kui palju see maksab?

Some signs

Entrance	Sissepääs
Exit	Väljapääs
Arrival	Saabumine
Departure	Väljumine
Open	Avatud
Closed	Suletud
Toilet	Tualett
No smoking!	Mitte suitsetada!

Directions and travel

Left	Vasak
Right	Parem
Straight on	Otse
Ticket/ticket office	Pilet/piletikassa
Train station	Jaam, vaksal
Bus station/bus stop	Bussijaam/peatus
Here	Siin
There	Seal
Train/bus/ferry/ bicycle	Rong/buss/laev/ jalgratas

Days

Monday	Esmaspäev
Tuesday	Teisipäev
Wednesday	Kolmapäev
Thursday	Neljapäev
Friday	Reede

Saturday	Laupäev
Sunday	Pühapäev

Months

January	Jaanuar
February	Veebruar
March	Märts
April	Aprill
May	Mai
June	Juuni
July	Juuli
August	August
September	September
October	Oktoober
November	November
December	Detsember

Numbers

1	üks
2	kaks
3	kolm
4	neli
5	viis
6	kuus
7	seitse
8	kaheksa
9	üheksa
10	kümme
11	üksteist
12	kaksteist
13	kolmteist
14	neliteist
15	viisteist
16	kuusteist
17	seitseteist
18	kaheksateist
19	üheksateist
20	kakskümmend
30	kolmkümmend
40	nelikümmend
50	viiskümmend
60	kuustkümmend
70	seitsekümmend
80	kaheksakümmend
90	üheksakümmend
100	sada
200	kaksada
1000	tuhat

Some countries

Estonia	Eesti
Latvia	Läti
Lithuania	Leedu

Poland	Poola	Finland	Soome
Sweden	Rootsi	Belarus	Valgevene
Germany	Saksamaa	Russia	Venemaa

Food and drink

Basic words and phrases

Menüü/toidukaart	Menu
Hommikueine	Breakfast
Lõuna	Lunch
Head isu!	Bon appetit!
Terviseks!	Cheers!
Arve	Bill

Essentials

Eelroad	Starters
Juust	Cheese
...kastmes	In...sauce
Kaste	Sauce
Leib	(Brown) bread
Päevapraad	Dish of the day
Pipar	Pepper
Roog	Dish, course
Sai	(White) bread
Sool	Salt
Suhkur	Sugar
Või	Butter
Vorm	Stew

Snacks and starters

Kartulisalat	Potato salad
Pannkook	Pancake
Pelmeenid	Dough parcels with meat stuffing
Pirukas	Dough parcel stuffed with cabbage and bacon
Salat	Salad
Sült	Cold meat in jelly
Supp	Soup

Meat (*liha*)

Kana	Chicken
Kanapraad	Roast chicken
Karbonaad	Pork chop in batter
Lammas	Lamb
Peekon	Bacon
Šašlõkk	Shish kebab

Sealiha	Pork
Seapraad	Roast pork
Sink	Ham
Šnitsel	Schnitzel (usually veal, but can be pork or chicken)
Verivorst	Blood sausage, black pudding

Fish (*kala*) and seafood (*mereannid*)

Haug	Pike
Krevet	Shrimp
Makra	Crab
Räim	Baltic herring
Sprott	Sprat
Tuunikala	Tuna

Vegetables (*köögivili*)

Ahjukartulid	Roast potatoes
Hapukapsas	Sauerkraut
Hapukurk	Pickled gherkin
Hernes	Pea
Kartulid	Potatoes
Küüslauk	Garlic
Mädarõigas	Horseradish
Porgand	Carrot
Sibul	Onion
Tomat	Tomato

Desserts (*desserdid*)

Jäätis	Ice cream
Juustukook	Cheesecake
Kook	Cake
Piparkook	Gingerbread
Saiake	Bun
Sokolaadikook	Chocolate cake

Fruit (*puuvili*)

Apelsin	Orange
Õun	Apple
Pirn	Pear
Ploom	Plum
Vaarikas	Raspberry

Drinks (*joogid*)

Hõõgvein	Mulled wine
Kohv	Coffee
Mahl	Juice
Õlu	Beer
Piim	Milk
Vesi	Water
Vein	Wine
Viin	Vodka

Glossary

Aed	Garden
Apteek	Pharmacy
Järv	Lake
Jõgi	River
Kauplus	Shop
Kesklinn	Town centre
Kirik	Church
Laht	Gulf
Linn	Town
Linnus	Castle
Loss	Castle
Maantee	Road
Mägi	Hill
Mõis	Manor house
Muuseum	Museum
Pakihoid	Left-luggage office
Pank	Bank
Pood	Shop
Postkontor	Post office
Raba	Bog
Saar	Island
Saatkond	Embassy
Sild	Bridge
Soo	Bog
Supelrand	Beach
Tänav	Street
Toidupood	Food shop
Toomkirik	Cathedral
Turg	Market
Tuulik	Windmill
Väljak	Square

Latvian

A long with Lithuanian, Latvian is a member of the Baltic family of languages and in terms of grammar and basic vocabulary is very close to its southerly neighbour. There, however, the similarity ends: unlike the staccato, almost Mediterranean-sounding delivery of Lithuanian, Latvian has a melodic, rolling quality that sounds closer to Scandinavia than the European mainland. The stress always falls on the first syllable of the word (the only exception to this rule being "*paldies*", meaning "thank you"); accented vowels are pronounced in a long, drawled-out way; and unaccented vowels are clipped back in everyday speech to the extent that you can't always hear that they're there at all.

Colloquial Latvian (Routledge) is a good place to start if you're learning, although it's less fun than the excellent *Paliga!* series of textbooks published by Latvian television (and available from the Zvaigzne bookshop at Valdemāra 6, Rīga) – although they're intended for Russian-speakers and don't have any instructions in English.

Pronunciation

Aside from a few tricky consonants not found in English, Latvian pronunciation is pretty straightforward, providing you pay attention to the vowel sounds below.

a "a" as in clap
ā "a" as in hard
c "ts" as in cats
č "ch" as in church
e usually pronounced like "e" as in bet, but in some words resembles the "aa" in aah
ē like French "é" in café, but in some words resembles the "aa" in aah
ģ somewhere between the "d" in endure and the "j" in jeep
i "i" as in hit
ī "ee" as in green

j "y" as in yesterday
ķ "t" as in future
ļ rolled combination of "l" and "y"; like the final "l" and initial "y" of "cool yule" pronounced together
ņ "n" as in new
o "wo" as in water
š "sh" as in shut
u "u" as in put
ū "oo" as in fool
ž "s" as in pleasure

Latvian words and phrases

Basics	
Yes	Jā
No	Nē
I don't understand	Es nesaprotu
Please	Lūdzu
Thank you	Paldies
OK	Labi
Excuse me/Sorry	Atvainojiet/Piedodiet

Hi!	Sveiks! (sing); sveiki! (pl); čau!
Hello/Good day	Labdien
Welcome	Esiet sveicināti
Good morning	Labrīt
Good evening	Labvakar
Good night	Ar labu nakti
Goodbye	Uz redzēšanos
Bye!	Atā!

395

What is your name?	Kā Jūs sauc? (formal); kā tevi sauc? (informal)
My name is...	Mani sauc...
Today	Šodien
Yesterday	Vakar
Tomorrow	Rīt
In the morning	Rītā
In the afternoon	Pēcpusdienā
In the evening	Vakarā
I'd like	...Es vēlos...
Cheap	Lēts
Expensive	Dārgs
Good	Labs
Bad	Slikts
Hot	Karsts
Cold	Auksts

Questions

Do you speak English?	Vai Jūs runājat angliski?
Where?	Kur?
Where is...?	Kur atrodas...?
When?	Kad?
What?	Kas?
Why?	Kāpēc?
How much?	Cik?
How much does it cost?	Cik tas maksā?
What time is it?	Cik ir pulkstenis?

Some signs

Entrance	Ieeja
Exit	Izeja
Arrival	Pienākšana, pienāk
Departure	Atiešana, atiet
Open	Atvērts
Closed	Slegts
Toilet	Tualete
No smoking!	Smēķēt aizliegts!

Directions and travel

Left	Pa kreisi
Right	Pa labi
Straight on	Taisni
Ticket/ticket office	Bilete/bilesu kase
Train/bus station/ bus stop	Štacija/autoosta/ pietura
Here	Šeit
There	Tur
Where is the railway station?	Kur ir dzelceļa stacija?
Train/bus/bicycle	Vilciens/autobuss/ velosipēds

Near/far	Tuvu/tālu
To Rīga	Uz Rīgu
To Ventspils	Uz Ventspili
Now	Tagad
Early, earlier	Agri, agrāk
Late, later	Vēlu, vēlāk

Days

Monday	Pirmdiena
Tuesday	Otrdiena
Wednesday	Tresdiena
Thursday	Ceturtdiena
Friday	Piektdiena
Saturday	Sestdiena
Sunday	Svetdiena

Months

January	Janvaris
February	Februaris
March	Marts
April	Aprilis
May	Maijs
June	Junijs
July	Julijs
August	Augusts
September	Septembris
October	Oktobris
November	Novembris
December	Decembris

Numbers

1	viens (m); viena (f)
2	divi (m); divas (f)
3	trīs
4	četri
5	pieci
6	seši
7	septiņi
8	astoņi
9	deviņi
10	desmit
11	vienpadsmit
12	divpadsmit
13	trīspadsmit
14	četrpadsmit
15	piecpadsmit
16	sešpadsmit
17	septiņpadsmit
18	astoņpadsmit
19	deviņpadsmit
20	divdesmit
30	trīsdesmit
40	četrdesmit
50	piecdesmit

60	sešdesmit
70	septiņdesmit
80	astoņdesmit
90	deviņdesmit
100	simts
200	divi simti
1000	tūkstotis

Some countries

Belarus	Baltakrievija
Estonia	Igaunija
Finland	Somija
Germany	Vācija
Latvia	Latvija
Lithuania	Lietuva
Poland	Polija
Russia	Krievija
Sweden	Zviedrijan

Food and drink

Essentials

Cukurs	Sugar
Krējums	Sour cream
Maize	Bread
Merce	Sauce
Olas	Eggs
Pipari	Pepper
Rupjmaize	Rye bread
Sāls	Salt
Siers	Cheese
Soļanka	Meat-and-vegetable broth
Sviests	Butter
Zupa	Soup

Latvian staples

Cūkas galerts	Pork in aspic
Pelēkie zirņi	Peas with bacon
Pelmeņi	Dough parcels with meat stuffing
Pīrāgs/pīrādziņš	Doughy pasty stuffed with bacon and/or cabbage
Rasols	Salad consisting of chopped meat and vegetables dressed in sour cream
Zirņu pikas	Mashed peas with bacon

Meat (*gala*)

Cālīšu gaļa	Chicken
Cūkas gaļa	Pork
Desa	Sausage
Karbonāde	Pork chop
Liellopu gaļa	Beef
Teļu gaļa	Veal
Žāvēta desa	Smoked sausage

Fish (*zivs*)

Forele	Trout
Lasis	Salmon
Siļķe	Herring
Šprotes	Sprats
Tuncis	Tuna
Zandarts	Pike-perch
Zutis	Eel

Vegetables (*dārzeņi*)

Burkāni	Carrots
Gurķi	Cucumbers
Kartupeļi	Potatoes
Kāposti	Cabbage
Ķiploks	Garlic
Loki	Spring onions
Salāti	Lettuce
Sēnes	Mushrooms
Sīpoli	Onions
Skābie kaposti	Sauerkraut
Skābie gurķi	Pickled gherkins
Tomāti	Tomatoes

Desserts (*deserts*)

Biezpiens	Curd cheese
Kūka	Cake
Ķīselis	Sweet porridge with fruit
Pankūkas	Pancake
Pudiņš	Pudding
Rieksti	Nuts
Saldējums	Ice cream
Torte	Gateau

Fruit (*auglis*)

Ābols	Apple
Apelsīns	Orange

Drinks (*dzerieni*)	
Alus	Beer
Balzāms	Balsam – gloppy black liqueur
Degvīns	Vodka
Kafija	Coffee
Karstvīns	Mulled wine
Piens	Milk
Sula	Juice
Šņabis	Vodka
Teja	Tea
Ūdens	Water
Vīns	Wine

Glossary

Aptieka	Pharmacy	Parks	Park
Banka	Bank	Pasts	Post office
Baznīca	Church	Pils	Castle
Darzs	Garden	Pilskalns	(Iron Age) castle mound
Dome	Cathedral		
Ezers	Lake	Purvs	Bog
Iela	Street	Sala	Island
Laukums	Square	Slimnīca	Hospital
Mežs	Forest	Tilts	Bridge
Muiža	Manor house	Tirgus	Market
Muzejs	Museum	Upe	River

Lithuanian

L ithuanian is an Indo-European language belonging to the Baltic family, of which Latvian is the only other surviving member – other Baltic peoples such as the Prussians and the Yotvingians having died out in the Middle Ages. It's thought that the vocabulary and grammar of Lithuanian have changed little over the centuries, leading some linguists to argue that it is closer to ancient Sanskrit than any other living language. Few Lithuanian words bear much resemblance to those you may have encountered elsewhere in Europe, lending the language an exotic aura – and although it's a difficult language to pick up at first, it soon becomes addictive. If you are interested in learning, then *Colloquial Lithuanian* published by Routledge is the best of the available self-study courses. Once you get to Vilnius, a range of Lithuanian-produced textbooks aimed at foreign students is available from bigger bookshops.

There are two **genders** in Lithuanian – masculine and feminine. Masculine nouns almost always end with -s, feminine nouns usually with -a or -e. Even foreign names are made to fit in with Lithuanian rules, as you will see from local newspaper references to figures such as Elvis Preslis and Mickas Jaggeris. Plurals are formed by adding -ai or -iai to masculine nouns; -s to feminine ones. It's also worth bearing in mind that there are six noun **cases** in Lithuanian, ensuring that each noun changes its ending according to which part of the sentence it occupies: thus "*į Vilnių*" means "to Vilnius", "*is Vilniaus*" "from Vilnius", and "*Vilniuje*" "in Vilnius".

Pronunciation

Pronunciation is not as difficult as it first appears. Every word is spoken exactly as it's written, and each letter represents an individual sound. Most letters are pronounced as they are in English, with the following exceptions:

a	"a" as in cl**a**p	i	"i" as in h**i**t
ą	originally a nasal vowel; nowadays pronounced in much the same way as "**a**"	į	"i" as in h**i**t
		j	"y" as in **y**esterday
c	"ts" as in ca**ts**	š	"sh" as in **sh**ut
č	"ch" as in chur**ch**	u	"u" as in p**u**t
e	usually pronounced like "e" as in bet, but in some words resembles the "ai" in fair	ū	"oo" as in f**oo**l
		ų	"u" as in p**u**t
ė	like French "é" in caf**é**	y	"i" as in h**i**t
ę	"e" as in b**e**t	ž	"s" as in plea**s**ure

Lithuanian words and phrases

Basics			
		No	Ne
		Please	Prašau, prašom
I don't understand	Nesuprantu	Thank you	Ačiū
Yes	Taip	OK	Gerai

Excuse me/sorry	Atsiprašau
Hi!	Labas!, Sveikas (m)/ sveika (f)!
Hello/Good day	Laba diena
Good morning	Labas rytas
Good evening	Labas vakaras
Goodnight	Labanakt
Goodbye	Viso gero
Bye!	Ate!
See you!	Iki!
How are you?	Kaip gyveni?/Kaip sekasi?
Fine, thanks	Ačiū, gerai
What is your name?	Koks tavo vardas?/ Kuo tu vardu?
My name is…	Mano vardas…
Today	Šiandien
Yesterday	Vakar
Tomorrow	Rytoj
In the morning	Rytą
In the afternoon	Popiet
In the evening	Vakare
Good	Geras
Bad	Blogas
More	Daugiau
Less	Mažiau
Big	Didelis
Small	Mažas
Cheap	Pigus
Expensive	Brangus
Hot	Karštas
Cold	Šaltas

Questions

Do you speak English?	Ar Jūs kalbate angliškai?
Where is…?	Kur yra…?
When?	Kada?
What?	Kas?
What time is it?	Kiek valandų/Kelinta valanda?
How much is it?	Kiek kainuoja?
Do you have anything cheaper?	Ar tūrite ką nors pigiau?

Some signs

Entrance	Įejimas
Exit	Išejimas
Arrival	Atvykimas
Departure	Išvykimas
Open	Atidaryta
Closed	Uždaryta
Market	Turgus
Hospital	Ligoninė

Pharmacy	Vaistinė
Toilet	Tualetas
No smoking!	Nerūkyti/Nerūkoma!

Directions and travel

Left	Kairė
Right	Dešinė
Straight on	Tiesiai
Ticket/ticket office	Bilietas/bilietų kasa
Bus stop	Autobusų stotelė
Bus station	Autobusų stotis
Train/bus/boat/ ferry/bicycle	Traukinys/autobusas/ laivas/keltas/dviratis
Now	Dabar
Early, earlier	Anksti, anksčiau
Late, later	Vėlu, vėliau
Near/far	Arti/toli
A ticket to… please	Prašom, vieną bilietą į…
Single	Į viena puse
Return/round-trip	Pirmyn ir atgal
Single room	Vienutė
Double room	Kambarys dviems
I'd like…	Norečiau

Days

Monday	Pirmadienis
Tuesday	Antradienis
Wednesday	Trečiadienis
Thursday	Ketvirtadienis
Friday	Penktadienis
Saturday	Šestadienis
Sunday	Sekmadienis

Months

January	Sausis
February	Vasaris
March	Kovas
April	Balandis
May	Gegužė
June	Birželis
July	Liepa
August	Rugpjūtis
September	Rugsėjis
October	Spalis
November	Lapkritis
December	Gruodis

Numbers

1	vienas (m), viena (f)
2	du (m), dvi (f)
3	trys
4	keturi (m), keturios (f)
5	penki (m), penkios (f)

6	šeši (m), šešios (f)	60	šešiasdešimt
7	septyni (m), septynios (f)	70	septyniasdešimt
8	aštuoni (m), aštuonios (f)	80	aštuoniasdešimt
9	devyni (m), devynios (f)	90	devyniasdešimt
10	dešimt	100	šimtas
11	vienuolika	200	du šimtai
12	dvylika	1000	tūkstantis
13	trylika		
14	keturiolika		

Some countries

Belarus	Baltarusija
Estonia	Estija
Finland	Suomija
Germany	Vokietija
Latvia	Latvija
Lithuania	Lietuva
Poland	Lenkija
Russia	Rusija
Sweden	Švedija

15	penkiolika
16	šešiolika
17	septyniolika
18	aštuoniolika
19	devyniolika
20	dvidešimt
30	trisdešimt
40	keturiasdešimt
50	penkiasdešimt

Food and drink terms

Basic words and phrases

Prašom, meniu	The menu, please
Prašom, kavos	A coffee, please
Prašom, du alaus	Two beers please
Aš vegetaras (m), vegetarė (f)	I am a vegetarian
Ar yra kas nors be mėsos?	Do you have anything without meat?
Į sveikatą!	Cheers!
Skanaus!	Bon appetit!
Prašom, sąskaitą	The bill, please

Essentials

Cukrus	Sugar
Druska	Salt
Duona	Bread
Grietinė	Sour cream
Kiaušiniai	Eggs
Medus	Honey
Padažas	Sauce
Pienas	Milk
Pipirai	Pepper
Sriuba	Soup
Sūris	Cheese
Sviestas	Butter

Lithuanian staples

Blynai	Pancakes
Bulvių blynai	Potato pancakes
Bulvių plokštainis	Baked slab of potato
Cepelinai	Zeppelin-shaped potato parcels stuffed with meat
Didžkukuliai	see "cepelinai"
Kibinas	Meat pasty
Koldūnai	Ravioli-like parcels with meat stuffing
Kugelis	see "bulvių plokštainis"
Šaltibarščiai	Cold beetroot soup
Vedarai	Pig intestine stuffed with potato

Meat (*mėsa*)

Dešra	Thick, salami-like sausage
Dešrelė	Frankfurter-like sausage
Jautiena	Beef
Kalakutiena	Turkey
Karbonadas	Pork chop
Kepsnys	Fried or roast cut of meat
Kumpis	Ham
Kiauliena	Pork
Vištiena	Chicken

Fish (*žuvis*)

Lašiša	Salmon
Menkė	Cod
Rukyta žuvis	Smoked fish

Unguris	Eel
Upėtakis	Trout

Vegetables (*daržovės*)

Agurkas	Cucumber
Bulvės	Potato
Česnakas	Garlic
Grybai	Mushrooms
Kopūstas	Cabbage
Moliūgas	Pumpkin
Morkos	Carrots
Pomidoras	Tomato
Pupelės	Beans
Svogūnas	Onion
Žirniai	Peas

Fruit (*vaisiai*)

Apelsinas	Orange
Avietės	Raspberries
Braškės	Strawberries
Citrina	Lemon

Kriaušė	Pear
Obuolys	Apple
Slyva	Plum
Vyšnia	Cherry

Desserts (*desertai*)

Ledai	Ice cream
Pyragaitis	Small cake
Pyragas	Cake or pudding
Riešutai	Nuts
Tortas	Cake
Uogienė	Jam

Drinks (*gerimai*)

Alus	Beer
Arbata	Tea
Degtinė	Vodka
Kava	Coffee
Sultys	Juice
Vanduo	Water
Vynas	Wine

Glossary

Aikštė	Square
Bankas	Bank
Bažnyčia	Church
Dviračių takas	Cycle path
Ežeras	Lake
Gatvė	Street
Giria	Forest
Kaimas	Village
Kalnas	Hill
Katedra	Cathedral
Kopa	Dune
Ligoninė	Hospital
Miestas	Town
Miškas	Forest
Muziejus	Museum
Naujamiestis	New Town

Parkas	Park
Paštas	Post office
Piliakalnis	(Iron Age) castle mound
Pilis	Castle
Rotušė	Town hall
Sodas	Garden
Senamiestis	Old Town
Stotis	Station
Takas	Path
Tiltas	Bridge
Turgus	Market
Upė	River
Vaistinė	Pharmacy
Vienuolynas	Abbey

Small print and
Index

A Rough Guide to Rough Guides

Published in 1982, the first Rough Guide – to Greece – was a student scheme that became a publishing phenomenon. Mark Ellingham, a recent graduate in English from Bristol University, had been travelling in Greece the previous summer and couldn't find the right guidebook. With a small group of friends he wrote his own guide, combining a highly contemporary, journalistic style with a thoroughly practical approach to travellers' needs.

The immediate success of the book spawned a series that rapidly covered dozens of destinations. And, in addition to impecunious backpackers, Rough Guides soon acquired a much broader and older readership that relished the guides' wit and inquisitiveness as much as their enthusiastic, critical approach and value-for-money ethos.

These days, Rough Guides include recommendations from shoestring to luxury and cover more than 200 destinations around the globe, including almost every country in the Americas and Europe, more than half of Africa and most of Asia and Australasia. Our ever-growing team of authors and photographers is spread all over the world, particularly in Europe, the US and Australia.

In the early 1990s, Rough Guides branched out of travel, with the publication of Rough Guides to World Music, Classical Music and the Internet. All three have become benchmark titles in their fields, spearheading the publication of a wide range of books under the Rough Guide name.

Including the travel series, Rough Guides now number more than 350 titles, covering: phrasebooks, waterproof maps, music guides from Opera to Heavy Metal, reference works as diverse as Conspiracy Theories and Shakespeare, and popular culture books from iPods to Poker. Rough Guides also produce a series of more than 120 World Music CDs in partnership with World Music Network.

Visit www.roughguides.com to see our latest publications.

Rough Guide credits

Text editor: Samantha Cook
Layout: Ajay Verma
Cartography: Jasbir Sandhu
Picture editor: Michelle Bhatia
Production: Rebecca Short
Proofreader: Stewart Wild
Cover design: Nicole Newman, Dan May
Photographer: Kerry Dean
Editorial: **London** Andy Turner, Keith Drew,
Edward Aves, Alice Park, Lucy White, Jo Kirby,
James Smart, Natasha Foges, Róisín Cameron,
James Rice, Emma Beatson, Emma Gibbs,
Kathryn Lane, Monica Woods, Mani Ramaswamy,
Harry Wilson, Lucy Cowie, Alison Roberts,
Lara Kavanagh, Eleanor Aldridge, Ian Blenkinsop,
Joe Staines, Matthew Milton, Tracy Hopkins;
Delhi Madhavi Singh, Jalpreen Kaur Chhatwal,
Jubbi Francis
Design & Pictures: **London** Scott Stickland, Dan
May, Diana Jarvis, Mark Thomas, Nicole Newman,

Sarah Cummins, Emily Taylor; **Delhi** Umesh
Aggarwal, Jessica Subramanian, Ankur Guha,
Pradeep Thapliyal, Sachin Tanwar, Anita Singh,
Nikhil Agarwal, Sachin Gupta
Production: Liz Cherry, Louise Daly, Erika Pepe
Cartography: **London** Ed Wright, Katie Lloyd-
Jones; **Delhi** Rajesh Chhibber, Ashutosh Bharti,
Rajesh Mishra, Animesh Pathak, Swati Handoo,
Deshpal Dabas, Lokamata Sahu
Marketing, Publicity & roughguides.com:
Liz Statham
Digital Travel Publisher: Peter Buckley
Reference Director: Andrew Lockett
Operations Coordinator: Becky Doyle
Publishing Director (Travel): Clare Currie
Commercial Manager: Gino Magnotta
Managing Director: John Duhigg

SMALL PRINT

Publishing information

This third edition published April 2011 by
Rough Guides Ltd,
80 Strand, London WC2R 0RL
11, Community Centre, Panchsheel Park,
New Delhi 110017, India

Distributed by the Penguin Group

Penguin Books Ltd,
80 Strand, London WC2R 0RL

Penguin Group (USA)
375 Hudson Street, NY 10014, USA

Penguin Group (Australia)
250 Camberwell Road, Camberwell,
Victoria 3124, Australia

Penguin Group (NZ)
67 Apollo Drive, Mairangi Bay, Auckland 1310,
New Zealand

Rough Guides is represented in Canada by
Tourmaline Editions Inc. 662 King Street West,
Suite 304, Toronto, Ontario M5V 1M7

Cover concept by Peter Dyer.

Typeset in Bembo and Helvetica to an original
design by Henry Iles.

Printed in Singapore
© Jonathan Bousfield, 2011
Maps © Rough Guides
No part of this book may be reproduced in any
form without permission from the publisher except
for the quotation of brief passages in reviews.
416pp includes index
A catalogue record for this book is available from
the British Library
ISBN: 978-1-84836-888-0

The publishers and authors have done their
best to ensure the accuracy and currency of
all the information in **The Rough Guide to
Estonia, Latvia & Lithuania**, however, they can
accept no responsibility for any loss, injury, or
inconvenience sustained by any traveller as a
result of information or advice contained in the
guide.

1 3 5 7 9 8 6 4 2

MIX
Paper from
responsible sources
FSC
www.fsc.org   FSC™ C018179

Help us update

We've gone to a lot of effort to ensure that the
third edition of **The Rough Guide to Estonia,
Latvia & Lithuania** is accurate and up-to-
date. However, things change – places get
"discovered", opening hours are notoriously
fickle, restaurants and rooms raise prices or lower
standards. If you feel we've got it wrong or left
something out, we'd like to know, and if you can
remember the address, the price, the hours, the
phone number, so much the better.

Please send your comments with the subject
line "**Rough Guide Estonia, Latvia & Lithuania
Update**" to © mail@uk.roughguides
.com. We'll credit all contributions and send a
copy of the next edition (or any other Rough
Guide if you prefer) for the very best emails.

Find more travel information, connect with
fellow travellers and book your trip on ℗ www
.roughguides.com

Acknowledgements

Jonathan Bousfield would like to thank Kerry, Sonata and the terror twins, Maia and Alex Naveriani, Martiņš Zaprauskis, Maris Hellrand & Liina Guiter at the Tallinn 2011 Foundation, Mai-Liis Mägi of Tallinn Tourist Office, Andre Help at the Estonian Institute, Urmas Dresen of the Estonian Maritime Museum, Oksana Skorobatjuk at the Estonian Tourist Board, Tõiv Jõul at the Pärnu City Tourist Office, Silvia Varik in Tartu County Tourist Board, Kadri Kusterpalu at Eesti Teatri Festival, Augusta Jaudegytė of the Lithuanian National Tourist Office London, Edita Mongirdaiteė at Kedainiai Tourist Board, Jurga Počiūtė and Nijolė Beliukevičienė in Vilnius City Tourist Department, Jūratė Besigirskienė in Vilnius, and Lolita Jablonskienė in the Lithuanian National At Gallery. Thanks also go to Sam(antha) Cook for patience and encouragement on the editing front, Monica Woods for getting the project under way, Stewart Wild for proofreading, Michelle Bhatia for picture research, Ajay Verma for his layout skills, and Jasbir Sandhu for meticulous maps.

SMALL PRINT

Readers' letters

Thanks to all the readers who have taken the time to write in with comments and suggestions (and apologies if we've inadvertently omitted or misspelt anyone's name):

David Allen, Mrs DJ Coode, Liz Hatherley, Loretta Lubinskas, Quinn Okamoto, Visnja Pentic, Christopher Polkinghorne, James Tartaglia & Zoe Hoida, and Alan Weiley.

Photo credits

All photos © Kerry Dean/Rough Guides except the following:

SMALL PRINT

Index

Map entries are in colour.

O

INDEX

411

I

INDEX

Map symbols

maps are listed in the full index using coloured text

– – –	Chapter boundary	✳	Ferry wheel
▪–▪–▪	International border	✈	Airport
▪▪–▪▪	Provincial boundary	★	Bus stop
▬▬▬	Motorway	⚓	Boat
═══	Road	◆	Point of interest
───	Unpaved/gravel road	@	Internet access
··········	Track	ⓘ	Information office
▬▬▬	Pedestrianized street	⊠	Post office
⊞⊞⊞⊞	Steps	⊞	Hospital
●▬●▬●	Railway	⊤	Public gardens
··············	Funicular railway	⚠	Campsite
- - - - -	Footpath	⊛	Swimming pool
────	Waterway	◉	Accommodation
— —	Ferry route	♜	Castle
•–-–•	Cable car and station	♦	Museum
────	Wall	🏛	Monument
⊠	Gate	⊙	Statue/memorial
⤫	Bridge/tunnel	⚰	Concentration camp
▲	Mountain peak	⚑	Mosque
ᴨᴧᴨ	Rocks	✡	Synagogue
◒	Cave	♦	Church (regional maps)
⯆	Viewpoint	⊟	Church/cathedral
⫘⫘	Cliff	▦	Building
/∥\\	Hill	▢	Market
⁂	Crater	◯	Stadium
⁂	Dune	▭	Jewish cemetery
⩗	Spring	✝▦	Christian cemetery
⚘	Waterfall	▦	Park/national park
⯗	Lighthouse	▦	Marshland/bog
⯗	Border post	▦	Beach

So now we've told you about the things not to miss, the best places to stay, the top restaurants, the liveliest bars and the most spectacular sights, it only seems fair to tell you about the best travel insurance around

WorldNomads.com

keep travelling safely

Recommended by Rough Guides